Strategic Marketing

Strategic Marketing

Creating Competitive Advantage

THIRD EDITION

Douglas West,
John Ford, and
Essam Ibrahim

OXFORD
UNIVERSITY PRESS

OXFORD
UNIVERSITY PRESS

Great Clarendon Street, Oxford, OX2 6DP,
United Kingdom

Oxford University Press is a department of the University of Oxford.
It furthers the University's objective of excellence in research, scholarship,
and education by publishing worldwide. Oxford is a registered trade mark of
Oxford University Press in the UK and in certain other countries

Second Edition 2010
First Edition 2006
Impression: 1

Published in the United States of America by Oxford University Press,
198 Madison Avenue, New York, NY 10016, United States of America

British Library Cataloguing in Publication Data
Data available

Library of Congress Control Number: 2014959482

ISBN 978-0-19-968409-0

Printed in Italy by L.E.G.O. S.p.A.

Dedicated to Lynda, Alexandra, and Olivia, and the memory of my parents.

DCW

This book is dedicated to my wife, Sarah, and my children, Lisa, Kimberly, John, and Jamie.

JBF

I dedicate this book to my small family, Abeer, Wasyla, and Sondos, and the memory of my father.

EI

Acknowledgements

A wider team supports the production of a book like this and there is always a risk, in attempting to acknowledge the contributions of others, that some people will be missed. Nonetheless the attempt to acknowledge must be made. We would like to give our thanks to the staff at Oxford University Press who have had a significant effect on the shape of the book and its evolution. In particular, thanks to Lucy Hyde and Melanie Smith for their encouragement, advice, and professional management of the process of this third edition. Also, our thanks to Sacha Cook for helping us see it into print in the first place with the first and second editions. As well, there has been a small group of anonymous reviewers who have provided guidance on the book's structure and updating of the content. There are also many people we would like to thank who have helped us with specialist content. In particular we would like to mention: Sean Adams, Head of Insight, News UK, London, UK; Julian Stubbs of Up there, everywhere: the cloud based agency; Graham Thomas of Radical; Chris Macleod of TfL (Transport for London); Tim Pile and Claire Wright of Cogent Elliott; and Melody Bartlett (the Editor) and Muireann Bolger (the Features Editor) of the CIM Marketer Magazine.

Thanks to Drs Ramendra Singh and Anurag Beniwal from IIM Calcutta, India, Drs Selcen Ozturkcan and Burcu Gumus from Istanbul Bilgi University, Turkey, Drs Balan Sundarakani and Sushmera Manikanadan from University of Wollongong in Dubai, UAE, and Dr Nnamdi O. Madichie from Canadian University of Dubai, UAE, for their outstanding work in developing new end of book cases.

We also utilized completely new end of chapter cases, which were developed by graduate students who worked separately under the supervision of Professor Hope Corrigan at Loyola College of Maryland and Dr Georgiana Craciun, Katz Graduate School of Business, University of Pittsburgh. They are listed in alphabetic order: Scott Cruff, Brian DeSena, Tara Daly, Allison Davis, Jeff Fromer, Lauren Geier, Patrick Glaessner, Evan Goldstein, Andrew Hoon, Courtney Jason, Lauren Kanick, Stephen King, Jeff Long, Stacey Maniscalco, Becca Martin, Kyle McGovern, Joe Morelli, Morgan Munnelly, Rich Palm, Matthew Protulipac, Alyssa Roffol, Ashley Rudy, Ozzy Torres, Abby Trainer, Dominic Trozzi, Sharon Van Het Hof, Mike Verrier, Megan Ward, Jani Willis, and Stephanie Zanin. Many thanks for their first-rate work on these cases and for Hope's and Georgiana's supervisions.

Thanks also to faculty members George Nakos and David Furman of the School of Business, Clayton State University, and Robert Moussetis, North Central College, Naperville, in the USA and Roy Larke of the University of Waikato, New Zealand, for their end of case contributions. We would like to thank our research and business colleagues and students over the years who have helped shape our thinking.

Finally, we each owe a special debt to our wives and children who have been constant sources of encouragement and support throughout.

Preface

This third edition of the book has been completely overhauled and updated. Nevertheless, its strategic approach remains with Porter's tried-and-tested cost-differentiation framework. As an approach, it remains second to none in capturing the essence of marketing strategy.

The book continues to utilize the popular 'WWHD' framework consisting of the four questions:

1. Where are you now?
2. Where do you want to be?
3. How will you get there?
4. Did you get there?

As with the first and second editions, we concluded that choosing a different framework would only be counterproductive. It works, and in our view it does not need a 'fix'. The application of strategy to the marketing mix at the 'how will you get there' stage continues to be a feature of the book.

As before, each chapter contains mini cases and one longer end of chapter case with questions for class discussion or assignment work. There are also four longer end of book cases with questions that integrate the central themes placed within the context of marketing strategy 'blueprint' offered by the book. Please note though that the examples and cases cited are for illustrative purposes only and are not in any way tied to any judgements about marketing strategy.

A feature new to each chapter is a short introduction to the topic either in the form of a news item or viewpoint from a well-respected and experienced practitioner. Each chapter has been revised to incorporate advances in the field, to reflect changes in technology as well as plug some gaps identified by readers and reviewers of the first and second editions.

The changes are too numerous to mention in their entirety, but the main one I would point out is that the international perspective has been extended to include more insights from developing economies. Furthermore, whereas we had previously decided against having an 'international marketing strategy' chapter, we listened to the feedback and were persuaded that a dedicated chapter would be a great addition. This coincided neatly with a debate that we had been having over whether a dedicated 'e-marketing strategies' chapter made any sense. Let's face it, e-marketing is an integral part of pretty much every aspect of marketing strategy and marketing today, so a stand-alone chapter made increasingly less sense. Thus the e-marketing chapter has been removed and replaced by a new chapter on 'international marketing strategy', which explores theory and practice within Porter's framework with numerous examples.

In addition, all the mini cases and end of chapter cases are new. A couple of the end of book cases have been extensively revised and one new one added. Each of these changes, and many others, will hopefully assist in gaining a thorough understanding of the theory and application of marketing strategy and the underlying issues involved. The online resource centre continues to provide a wealth of additional materials for anyone interested in marketing strategy and provides links to additional resources.

Turning to our readers, this third edition is not intended as an introduction to marketing; the book is designed for postgraduate students and undergraduates in their final years of studies.

This is the third updated edition of our account of strategic marketing. We recognize that there are many great books on marketing strategy to choose from; we hope that you—along with learning from it—will enjoy reading it. From our side of things we too have learnt much from the update and enjoyed writing it (and of course seeing it finally off to print!).

DCW

Outline contents

PART V: **Did we get there?**

Detailed contents

Part I

Introduction

I. Introduction

1 Overview and strategy blueprint
2 Marketing strategy: analysis and perspectives

II. Where are we now?

3 Environmental and internal analysis: market information and intelligence

III. Where do we want to be?

4 Strategic marketing decisions, choices, and mistakes
5 Segmentation, targeting, and positioning strategies
6 Branding strategies
7 Relational and sustainability strategies

V. Did we get there?

14 Strategy implementation, control, and metrics

IV. How will we get there?

8 Product innovation and development strategies
9 Service marketing strategies
10 Pricing and distribution strategies
11 Marketing communications strategies
12 International marketing strategy
13 Social and ethical strategies

Overview and strategy blueprint

Learning Objectives

1. Be able to define marketing strategy.
2. Understand the essential differences between the main approaches towards marketing strategy.
3. Be familiarized with the structure of the book.
4. Understand the importance of marketing strategy to a business and identify the kinds of things that can go wrong.

Chapter at a Glance

I. Introduction
1 Overview and strategy blueprint
2 Marketing strategy: analysis and perspectives

II. Where are we now?
3 Environmental and internal analysis: market information and intelligence

III. Where do we want to be?
4 Strategic marketing decisions, choices, and mistakes
5 Segmentation, targeting, and positioning strategies
6 Branding strategies
7 Relational and sustainability strategies

V. Did we get there?
14 Strategy implementation, control, and metrics

IV. How will we get there?
8 Product innovation and development strategies
9 Service marketing strategies
10 Pricing and distribution strategies
11 Marketing communications strategies
12 International marketing strategy
13 Social and ethical strategies

 Case study: My life as a strategy planner

I've been lucky. My career path to date has been extremely varied and stimulating. I've worked in the UK and Australia in a variety of jobs across advertising, media and research. But despite the diversity of roles, there has been one common strand across everything—I've always placed strategic thinking and planning at the heart of what I do.

I am now working for News UK—the country's largest newspaper publisher and owner of titles like *The Times*, the *Sunday Times*, and the *Sun*. My role is to manage the company's extensive research output and gather audience insight to help support the advertising sales teams in their pitches to advertisers and their agencies.

I feel there are two main benefits to a career in strategy planning, regardless of what type of organization it is based in. Firstly, it is hugely varied, requiring you to apply your mind continually to solving new problems and developing new solutions. Secondly, it plays an increasingly influential role in many organizations who recognize that to gain an advantage over their competitors, they need deeper insights into their brands, their customers, their category, or their broader environment.

So what makes for a successful strategy planner? I would say the key ingredients could be summarized as being the 4 C's: curiosity, completeness, courage and clarity. Let me explain:

1. You have to be **curious** because the answers are rarely obvious. You have to be interested in people and what makes them tick. You have to enjoy digging beneath the surface to find out what new insights you can discover.

2. You have to be **complete** in what you do. Often your recommendations will have far-reaching consequences so you must be rigorous in your analysis and be sure you have left no stone unturned.

3. You have to be **courageous**. Great strategic ideas that can change a business will challenge existing thinking and are uncomfortable for many. You have to be confident in your ability and be willing to stick your neck out if you want to make a difference.

4. And you have to be a **clear** communicator. Good planning means being able to express your ideas in a clear, simple and motivating way. Without that ability, even the best ideas can remain hidden.

I'd like to illustrate what I mean by looking back to a previous role where I spent ten years running a strategic research company in Australia. In this role, I would be approached by a wide range of different clients to help them solve often quite complex marketing problems.

Indeed, over this ten year period, I would estimate I ran upwards of 500 projects for clients selling products ranging from Alcohol to a Zoo and just about everything in between.

Often these projects would be for a product I was unfamiliar with in a category where I had no prior knowledge. I would begin with no ideas, but knew I would have to report back to my clients in a relatively short period of time and tell them something they didn't already know about their business that would in turn help them solve their strategic problem. A tough challenge, but an exciting one too.

To highlight the diversity of clients and the types of work I was involved with, here is just a small sample of the strategic insights that emerged from some of my projects. Hopefully this will underline the variety and influence that a strategic role can involve:

- **Scotch whisky**—research explored male reactions to a potential ad campaign for a Scotch whisky brand based on the concept of 'chivalry'. It discovered the insight that, far from being an outdated idea, the values behind chivalry were more relevant than ever today. Values such as honesty, commitment, manners, loyalty, honour, respect and courtesy were seen as a call to arms for Aussie men, and were often perceived as a welcome antidote to much of society's greed and selfishness.

- **Homemaker magazines**—research for a magazine publisher into the relationship between Australians and their homes showed the appeal of 'mix 'n' matching'. This may involve pairing expensive antiques with an Ikea table or incorporating a family heirloom into an otherwise modern interior. This insight illustrated the importance of one's home reflecting a sense of individual personal style.

- **Printing franchise**—research into one of Australia's largest chain of printers revealed that much of their small business client base, which had been classed as 'lapsed', still regarded themselves as being current customers, albeit with more occasional requirements. This insight helped to drive future Customer Relationship Management (CRM) programmes to encourage more frequent purchases.

- **Multivitamin tablets**—research into a new multivitamin targeting the over 50s provided rich insight into how that age group perceive themselves. It showed they still felt young and aspired to maintain a fit and healthy lifestyle. The proposed advertising campaign had missed the mark by presenting a far older lifestyle than the audience's self-perception and could therefore be reworked to create far greater resonance amongst its proposed target audience.

- **Computer magazine**—a 20 year old magazine had built its business around the PC, but had seen circulation steadily erode. Research helped reveal what people are looking for nowadays from a computer/tech- based publication, leading to a name change, a shift to a digital-first strategy and a complete overhaul of both content and design.

- **Indigenous dance theatre**—research into a leading Australian dance troupe revealed a lack of understanding of the narrative behind their different shows, meaning many people felt they only needed to see it once. This insight revealed the importance of differentiating the shows better and focusing on the unique storytelling underlying them, thus encouraging repeat visitation.

- **Education institution**—research into a leading education group offering a range of different types of institutions (English language, Information Technology, Design, etc.) helped provide insight into both how each individual college should be positioned to maximize appeal, but also how the overall group should start to position itself as a provider of quality education brands.

- **Insurance company**—research into a leading insurance company, primarily servicing the corporate sector and considering changing their name, revealed that whilst brand wasn't necessarily a key discriminator in this category, the latent reassurance was surprisingly powerful, thus making the proposed name change a far riskier proposition than first considered.

Eight random stories from eight different categories, but each in its own way required a combination of curiosity, completeness, courage and clarity to deliver the insights to clients in a way they could understand, trust, and use.

As a final thought to leave you with, if I had to summarize strategy planning in a few words, I'd say it is the art of making complicated things simple. And I reckon that's a pretty good career goal to have.

Sean Adams, Head of Insight, News UK, London, UK

Introduction

Have you ever heard of Tencent, Sinopec, or Baidu? While not household names in the West, they are amongst the top brands in the 1.5bn people Chinese market. Tencent is China's biggest Internet service provider with over 400m customers and is valued at around $34bn. Its first major mobile app was downloaded by some 20m people in just three days. Sinopec is China's largest integrated oil and gas company, and it operates the largest network of service stations (it's valued at about $13bn). How about Baidu? Well, Baidu, a $20bn company, is China's top Internet search engine. The company is currently rapidly expanding its operations into mobile. Unless you know the market well, you are unlikely to know much about these companies because local Chinese firms are mainly focused on their domestic markets. Furthermore, Chinese brands still tend to be sold at lower price points against international brands despite being better known and having greater distribution, because the perception amongst most Chinese consumers is that they cannot (yet) match foreign brands. How long before Chinese brands arrive at a place closer to you? Beijing will need to relax capital controls before people start taking out loans with the Bank of China, but there is little doubt that the bank, worth nearly $14bn, has ambitions to become a premium international banking brand. Much depends on what these and other top brands in China do in terms of their marketing strategies. OK, so marketing matters. Let's take a brief review of marketing's role and capabilities.

Marketing operates at both a functional and philosophical level. At the functional level it is someone's job (see 'My life as a strategy planner' above). These generally involve developing the Product (good or service), Pricing it, Placing it in the market, Promotion, and dealing with People who influence the buying of it (the famous 5Ps). Organizations of all kinds (profit and not-for-profit) employ people to undertake marketing activities. On the other hand, marketing may also be seen as a 'philosophy': a way of doing business where the view is often held that everyone in the organization, from the front to the back end, is involved in marketing and it is not the sole domain of the marketers.

The aim of the book is to develop 'marketing strategy acumen'; that is, the keenness and speed in understanding when deciding how to tackle a marketing problem. It's about having the 'marketing smarts' or 'marketing sense'. The essential elements are to:

1. Obtain the key information about a marketing problem.
2. Concentrate on suitable marketing objectives.
3. Identify the relevant options available.
4. Select the appropriate course of action.
5. Establish a marketing plan to get the job done.

People who have marketing strategy acumen don't always make the right decisions, but when things go wrong they are willing to adapt to unforeseen circumstances and make necessary adjustments to keep the marketing strategy on course.

Marketing strategy acumen involves identifying, anticipating, and satisfying customer needs and wants, while making a profit. Given sufficient resources any one of us could likely set up a new hotel that would satisfy customers. It might have staff to greet people at the entrance as well as take care of luggage, a beautiful reception area, courteous reception staff, fabulous rooms with added touches like choice of soft, medium, or firm mattresses and pillows, fresh flowers, free Wi-Fi, the use of an iPad, wonderful room service, and so on. We could all draw up a nice list in ten minutes. But could we offer all this and make a profit? Would it be possible to charge enough to cover the cost of running such a hotel and leave money over to pay the bills, invest in the future, repay loans, and have something to spare? Without this no organization is viable and a business goes bankrupt.

Thus marketing is not solely about consistently anticipating and satisfying customer needs and wants. It's also about making a profit in a competitive environment while doing this. Marketing strategy is the thinking that underpins the viability of any market position.

To a large extent, marketing strategy involves analysing a gap. The gap is between what you want to achieve, the competitive forces you face in the market, and the resources at your organization's disposal. Should Samsung develop smart watches? That's a strategic decision. Should Samsung invest in smart watches aimed at the cheap end of the market? That's also a strategic decision. Should Samsung invest in developing a cheap smart watch to compete with a rival's offering? Again, that's a strategic decision. However, should that same smart watch have hands-free voice commands, messages and alerts display, and smartphone camera controls? Well that's a strategic decision as well, in terms of whether a number of features should be offered. But precisely what features, at what price, and so on; those are tactical decisions that should comply with the strategy (e.g. a cheap or upmarket smart watch should have the requisite features and pricing). Marketing strategy is about the big picture. It's about

Mini Case 1.1   Sustainable competitive advantage and emerging market multinationals

When *Forbes* first published its Global 2000 list of the world's largest public companies, the top ten entries were all from developed economies. By 2012 two Chinese firms and a Brazilian company had broken into the top ten, and dozens of emerging-market companies were edging toward the top of their industry sectors (Guillén and García-Canal, 2012). For example: Gazprom (Russia) is the largest energy group, excluding oil companies; Arcor (Argentina) is the world's largest sweets manufacturer; DP World of Dubai is the fourth-largest port operator; and Tata Communications (India) is the world's leading wholesale voice carrier. What is their sustainable competitive advantage (SCA) over companies in developed markets? The indications are that:

1. Their home markets are 'uncomfortable' so rather than cautiously expand abroad they use their hard-won knowledge to do more with less and dive in with abandon.

2. Whereas developed multinationals tend to shy away from chaos and turbulence in markets where legal, financial, communications, and transport support is weak, emerging market multinationals have experience of such markets and remain unfazed by such difficulties. Consider the Mahindra Group, an $11 billion multi-business company based in Mumbai that employs 117,000 people in 100 countries operating in many industries, including automobiles, finance, and IT. It invests in creating a culture based on a common purpose to provide coherence amidst diversity (Kanter, 2011).

One consequence of this is that as emerging markets become more unpredictable and complicated, emerging market multinationals have an advantage.

asking the underlying questions: Should we be in this market? Are we offering the right things to this market? Do we have the resources to support our offerings in this market?

To be viable (survive in the longer term) firms need a sustainable competitive advantage (SCA). An SCA is something that attracts customers to their offerings (see Mini Case 1.1). In the broadest sense there are two kinds of sustainable advantage. One is based on satisfying the market; the other on capitalizing on resources—both are intertwined.

The resource-based view (RBV) concentrates upon the available tangible and intangible resources of the organization and how best to leverage them; note it is often the intangible assets such as brand name and reputation that are most linked to marketing. These resources need to be identifiable, of value, difficult to copy, hard to substitute, and rare (for a full discussion of RBV see: Hooley et al., 1998). This is not easy to do. Organizations need to be capable in their deployment of resources and the better they can deploy, the more likely a competitive advantage will be developed over rivals.

Alternatively the market-based view (MBV) suggests that an organization's resources should be managed in response to market requirements. Organizations need to scan their markets, analyse and identify trends, and then re-invest or modify their resource base in response. Fashion is one example. Recently there has been a trend towards a minimalist 1960s clean-cut look in women's clothing, which has superseded a previous floral (e.g. cabbage roses) look. Your clothing or accessories simply won't sell as well if you ignore the trends in the market. Having said that, it must be recognized that fashions are more widespread these days and don't just constitute one trend. Also the global market for fashion means differences in diverse parts of the world as to what is 'fashionable'.

The basic point is that the RBV is focused on the organization's resources to match the market's needs and wants whereas the MBV is about matching the market's needs and wants first by adjusting the requisite resources. It would be a mistake, however, to think it was all about competition. A lot of organizations choose to cooperate; known as 'coopetition'— dividing up the value created in markets. Coopetition occurs when firms in the same industries act in ways that recognize congruence of interests. For example, PSA Peugeot Citroen supplies Toyota Motors medium-sized commercial vans to sell under the Toyota brand in Europe. Toyota, having discontinued its own European medium van distribution, still has an offering for its customers while Peugeot Citroen gains an additional route to the market. Another consideration is that a resource is only valuable in relation to a market. For example, Marks & Spencer have a fantastic resource with the long-term ownership and long leases on their high street shops. However, this advantage was eroded by out-of-town shopping.

When it comes to the nature of strategies, Michael Porter (2001) has forcefully argued that the fundamentals of strategy remain unaltered. He argued organizations can only create value if they focus on industry structure, which determines profitability, and find a sustainable competitive advantage (SCA), which will allow a company to outperform the average.[1] His two strategic tenets are, and remain, 'cost' or 'differentiation'.

Porter argued that to find an SCA, organizations need to consider costs (not to be confused with price). By focusing on driving down costs, organizations can maintain a higher margin between those costs and what a good or service is sold for. Alternatively, he suggested organizations can focus on differentiation. For example, a pen manufacturer might make a basic pen and, having driven down its costs, sell it for the same price and specification as a competitor, but by so doing, enjoy a wider margin. Another pen manufacturer might go the differentiation route. Their pen might include a calculator, a digital radio to be hooked to headphones, an eraser, and many other 'must-have' features. The result will be higher costs of manufacture, but the offering might be much more attractive to many customers than a basic pen and they may well be prepared to pay more for it.

I can hear you say, 'if you are talking about competitive advantage: what about the Internet?' Well the Internet offers considerable scope for operating at a lower cost, commanding a premium price, or doing both. Thus, for example, Oxfam introduced an online newsletter to cut the costs of postal services. Furthermore, their monthly newsletter, which is sent to several hundred thousand donors, can be personalized to closely match the interests of individual supporters.

One of the key characteristics of the e-marketing competitive environment is the use of so-called 'judo strategy.' The analogy to the art of judo is because players attempt to use the strength and weight of their opponents to gain advantage, rather than to exchange blows directly (see Chapter 8 and Yoffie and Cusumano (1999)). Sumo matches, i.e. wrestling each other face-to-face to force the opponent to the ground or out of the ring, are what Internet companies try to avoid, as relatively small players tend to lose in sumo. Judo strategy is where e-marketers set out to turn their rival's size, strength, and resources against them using three key principles. Consider Google's open Android operating system along with its various closed system products— think Google Search and Google Earth. Something that Apple would be unlikely to contemplate.

---

[1] Industry structure is determined by the five underlying forces of competition: rivalry, the bargaining power of suppliers and buyers, barriers to entry for new competitors, and the threat of substitutes (see Chapter 2).

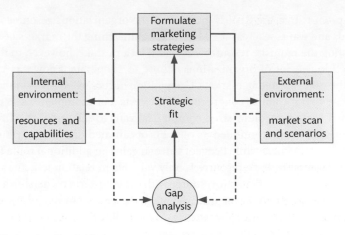

1.1 Marketing Strategy is a Gap Analysis

To a large extent, marketing strategy starts with the mission purpose of the organization. For example, the guiding vision of the Estée Lauder Companies (and their motto) is 'Bringing the best to everyone we touch'. By 'the best' Estée Lauder mean the best products, the best people, and the best ideas. These three pillars have been the hallmarks of the company since it was founded in 1946. Aside from Estée Lauder, its brands also include Clinique and Bobbi Brown. This focus on quality helps formulate their corporate, competitive, and functional marketing strategies. These must be set in line with their external environment (MBV) and their internal environment (RBV). There may be a gap between the marketing strategies and the strategic fit with the internal environment (see Figure 1.1). There has to be a fit between their marketing strategies and the external and internal environment. For example, social pressure and government regulation may well have a bearing on the testing regime and use of animals by cosmetics companies, which may have to formulate marketing strategies to accommodate them, for example in testing and labelling.

Approaches to competitive marketing strategy

Thinking First

The book takes rational 'Thinking First' as the basis for marketing strategy, which is an approach that is primarily logical, sequential, and linear. Thinking First is one of four approaches (see Figure 1.2) and is about analysing a strategic marketing problem and developing the solution and the strategy through a carefully thought through and largely sequential process. Instant views and decisions are not made, though it can help to occasionally see the 'big picture'. It can involve some inspiration and insight, but largely the process is one of painstakingly doing your homework to arrive at a solution. For example, Procter & Gamble uses a bicycle distribution network for its brands in Ghana, given the inaccessibility of many of the towns and villages outside of the capital, Accra.

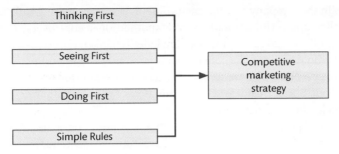

1.2 Four Ways of Approaching Marketing Strategy

Thinking First is closely connected to a **market-driven approach**. Examples would include organizations such as Samsung, John Lewis, and BMW which stand apart by their devotion to customer value and their culture, process, and abilities.

'Market Driven Marketing Strategy' has its weaknesses, but remains the primary approach for most organizations. Marketing is an activity that continues to largely rely upon the successful generation, dissemination, and response to market intelligence (see, for example, Matsuno and Mentzer, 2000). Marketing strategy is part-and-parcel of a market driven approach. However, business, as in life for that matter, is rarely quite so rational. Decisions can be taken from a variety of perspectives and logic and rationality may provide only one perspective. The main alternatives (see Figure 1.2) are:

- Seeing First
- Doing First
- Simple Rules

Each of these will now be considered in turn.

Seeing First

Seeing First reminds us that the importance of seeing the overall decision is sometimes greater than thinking about individual elements. As Mozart noted—the best part of creating a symphony was to 'see the whole of it at a single glance in my mind' (Mintzberg and Westley, 2001). Seeing First is basically insight, and insight often only comes after a period of preparation, incubation, illumination, and verification in the cold light of day (Wallas, 1926), so the best way of Seeing First might, arguably, be after a process of rational analysis! The 'eureka' moment has been often known to come after sleep, as rational thought is generally switched off during sleep. Thus, Seeing First is cognitive process, but it relates to the whole picture rather than a sequential analysis.

Some inspirational leaders can scan the signals in the environment, sense what is going on before it is articulated, and rely upon their intuition (Gofee and Jones, 2000). For example, Franz Humer, the former CEO of Roche, was someone who easily detected changes in climate and ambience and sensed underlying currents of opinion. Humer, who led Roche for more than a decade, is credited with integrating its diagnostics and drugs units to create medicines targeted at individual patients. Such leaders are skilful at sensing and keeping on top of changes in the company and the environment. However, sensing skills can be danger-ous if overly relied upon. Muhammad Yunus is another, albeit controversial, person to men-tion (Achrol and Kotler, 2012). Yanus is a Bangladeshi banker, economist, and Nobel Peace Prize recipient who developed the concepts of microcredit and microfinance whereby loans are given to entrepreneurs who are too poor to qualify for traditional bank loans. In 2011 he co-founded Yunus Social Business–Global Initiatives (YSB) to empower socially oriented businesses to help alleviate social problems.

Overall, 'Seeing First' has most relevance with new ventures or dramatic changes of direc-tion. For the most part, however, marketers need to examine the trends and the evidence and be able to develop some sense of what is important within the mass of actions and events. As such, Seeing First is rarely of much relevance to day-to-day marketing.

Doing First

When you cannot think it through and you do not see it, what do you do? '**Doing First**' is when marketing managers experiment and learn from the mistakes and successes. The process is: (1) do something, (2) make sense of it, and (3) repeat the successful parts and discard the rest (see Figure 1.3). Instead of marketing strategy, the reality is often that 'doing' drives. For example, many companies that have successfully diversified their businesses have done so by a process of figuring out what worked and what did not (see Mini Case 1.2). It's a process of trial and error. Danone bought into the Hungarian biscuit and chocolate market and took over one of the most famous local brands of biscuit. It decided to eliminate Pilota Keksz from its portfolio, which led to Hungarians taking to the streets with many wearing T-shirts with 'DaNOne' in large black letters. Pilota Keksz sur-vived and is still there today. A lesson was learnt, and Danone's management and marketers reflected on their mistake and brought the biscuit back. A final point to make is that Doing First should not be confused with first entrance into a market. It is often the case with market entrance that being a follower is not such a bad thing. Tesco were by no means first

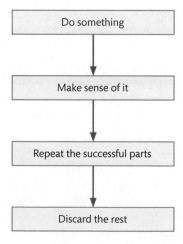

1.3 Doing First

Mini Case 1.2   Doing First with Skype

In the second half of 2005 eBay Inc. acquired Luxembourg-based Skype Technologies SA for around $2.6 billion in cash and eBay stock. The aim was to provide people across the world with an e-commerce platform embracing Skype, eBay, and PayPal. The core of the original idea was for eBay to employ Skype to further generate trade on the auction site. Skype would enable sellers to talk directly to buyers on-line which would be particularly useful for high value items such as cars and antiques where a basic listing failed to scratch the surface deep enough and the lack of discussion between buyer and seller presented a barrier.

Skype provides voice communication to anyone with an Internet connection and subscription anywhere in the world and video if they have a web cam. This is known as VOIP (Voice over Internet Protocol); the software is straightforward to install and calls are free between fellow Skype users. Additional relatively low-cost calls to land lines and mobiles can be bolted on along with voicemail, call forwarding, instant messaging, and video conferencing. When eBay purchased Skype it had about 54 million registered users across the world; this has grown to over 405 million, largely by word-of-mouth' and it's essentially the market leader in nearly every country where it operates.

However, the idea of changing the way people communicate, shop, and do business online failed to come to fruition. Skype has revolutionized how many people communicate, but the revolution to shopping on eBay failed to materialize. The intention had been that buyers would be able to talk to sellers seamlessly and get the deeper information that they need to buy. On the other side sellers could more easily build relationships with customers and close sales for such things as antiques, used cars, and business and industrial equipment. It might also provide a way of increasing market penetration and dominance in the BRIC economies of Brazil, Russia, India, and China, where vast distances presented barriers to a lot of commerce where bargaining was a powerful driver in transaction. Factoring in fees for Skype communications combined with PayPal would also make for a powerful combination. Creating a PayPal account for each Skype account would make it much easier for users to pay for Skype fee-based services and in turn have synergies with PayPal by adding to the number of accounts and increasing payment volume.

Overall combining the different Internet platforms of eBay, PayPal, and Skype with their obvious synergies and complementary elements appeared to make a great deal of sense.

Fast forward to the news that eBay had decided to float Skype as a stand-alone company in 2010. Microsoft purchased Skype and all its technologies for $8.5billion seeing a fit with its development of communications technology strategy.

What did investors make of this decision? Shares in eBay immediately rose in price. Why? There was certainly considerable logic to the original acquisition of Skype in 2005, and the brand has proved to be a very successful Internet business and has quickly moved beyond the early adopter phase to become a mainstream consumer and business technology. The problem was that the synergies envisaged with eBay failed to materialize. Buyers and sellers didn't use it in the volumes anticipated. The basics of the auction process involving the hands-off relationship between buyers and sellers and the anonymous competition between the bidders prevailed. To most eBay investors Skype was a distraction to the core of the business and had tied up too much capital.

Had eBay made a mistake? Hindsight is a wonderful thing. It was only by undertaking the acquisition and observing buyers' behaviours that the lack of synergy with Skype was revealed. Did it makes sense in the first place? Undoubtedly the answer is 'yes'. What is more, Skype has proved to be an Internet phenomenon with a bright future; it's just that for the foreseeable it won't pivot around eBay—it will be Microsoft.

at computerized integrated home order and delivery systems, but the company managed to capture value in the market and become global leaders. Doing First in the context here is about making marketing decisions that you are uncertain of, being willing to take risks, and being ready to evaluate the results and make necessary changes.

'Doing First' is a credible and viable strategic approach. There are often circumstances and issues where it is virtually impossible to disentangle the best course of action or outcome. Doing First enables organizations to try out marketing strategies and, with careful monitoring, assess the results (Edmondson, 2011). This is the way to test the boundaries of stretching a brand, the viability of new kinds of distribution channel, and so on. However, Thinking First is still a necessity in establishing how you will define and measure the success of any Doing First strategy.

Simple Rules

Marketing strategy as Simple Rules is about selecting a few key marketing strategic processes, crafting a handful of simple rules, and 'jumping in' rather than avoiding uncertainty (see Figure 1.4). In many respects the approach is related to 'Doing First' aside from the main difference in that the rules are predefined. Companies like Vodafone and Yahoo! have excelled without the traditional advantages of superior resources or strategic positions. According to Eisenhardt and Sull (2001) the key to their success has been the use of Simple Rules.

- **How-to** rules are about keeping managers organized enough to be able to seize opportunities. For example, Dell applies a rule that when any customer segment's revenue reaches $1 billion, the segment must be split into two halves.

- **Boundary** rules help managers to pick the best opportunities based on geography, customers, or technology. When Miramax decides on a film project it has to satisfy four boundaries: (1) the film must revolve around the human condition, such as love; (2) the main hero must be flawed in some way; (3) there must be a clear beginning, middle, and end; (4) a firm cap on production cost must be established. Just look at Miramax's top ten grossing films: *The English Patient*, gross $79m; *Cold Mountain*, gross $96m; *The Others*, gross $97m; *Shakespeare in Love*, gross $100m; *The Aviator*, gross $103m; *Pulp Fiction*, gross $108m; *Spy Kids*, gross $113m; *Good Will Hunting*, gross $138m; *Scary Movie*, gross$157m; *Chicago*, gross $171m.

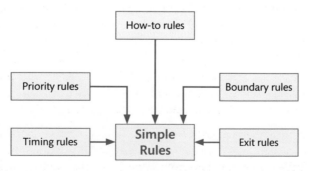

1.4 Simple Rules

- **Priority** rules are about allocating resources amongst competing opportunities. For example, Intel allocates manufacturing capacity based on a product's gross margin.

- **Timing** rules relate to the rhythm of key strategic processes. For example many Silicon Valley companies set timing rules for NPD. When developers approach a deadline they are often forced to drop features in order to meet the schedule.

- **Exit** rules are about pulling out from past opportunities. New initiatives might be dropped if set sales and profit goals are not being met. Some rules can be specific. At the Dutch hearing aid company, Oticon, product development is halted if any key team member decides to leave for another project.

How many rules are optimum? Ideally companies should develop from two to seven rules and nothing complex: marketing strategic rules should be easy-to-follow directives. It is better to have fewer rules when the market is unpredictable and you need flexibility. Also, when the rules go stale, they need to be changed. The basic tenet is that when business is complicated, marketing strategy should be simple.

Postmodern

A completely different view of strategy is provided by the **postmodern** school. Underpinning the approach of postmodern marketing strategy is the proposition that buyers are increasingly sophisticated and cynical about 'regular' marketing.

The diffusion of psychological concepts and language into our culture also plays a role, as does formal education in schools about marketing issues. Developing over time, consumers' persuasion knowledge is an important factor shaping their response to attempts to persuade (O'Donohoe, 2001). Individuals develop context-specific persuasion knowledge in situations that they frequently encounter. Marketing persuasion knowledge has migrated widely. Thus, when commercial television first appeared in 1955, its persuasive attempts were novel and powerful. Moving black and white commercials inside people's homes had never been experienced before. However, since then cultural knowledge about television advertising and other marketing techniques has developed in greater depth.

One of the leading proponents of the postmodern view, Stephen Brown (2001), argues that customer-centric marketing has gone too far and now places many companies in the position of Uriah Heep: 'unctuous, ubiquitous and unbearable.' His view is that people do not want the truth, the whole truth, and nothing but the truth. They certainly do not expect truth from marketers. People want marketing to be about glitz and glamour and to be mischievous and mysterious. Marketing should be fun, but any nastiness is forbidden. Contemporary consumers find marketing's obsession with love, honour, and obey embarrassing. They would prefer a lovable rogue to the Disneyfied version that is the norm of today. Retromarketing harks back to the 'good old bad days' when marketers were pranksters and proud of it. To undertake a retro strategy, marketers need to practice TEASE: 'tricksterism', entertainment, amplification, secrecy, and exclusivity (see Figure 1.5).

- **Tricksterism** has to be played as a postmodern joke. Tango's numerous attempts to trick its customers, leaving them 'Tango'd,' qualifies, especially its bogus hotline for customers to notify the company of knockoffs of the brand that were not fizzy. It turned out to be a new non-carbonated version of the drink.

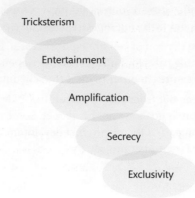

1.5 Postmodern View

- **Entertainment** is one of the major elements in retro's armoury according to Brown. The idea here is that marketing has forgotten how to 'flirt'. The surreptitious and ambitious Web-based promotions of Spielberg's *AI* were highly entertaining. They involved using a Web-search discovery of a murder and a 'body' of clues, providing a perfect example of entertaining consumers rather than boring them.
- **Amplification** is about ensuring that the hot ticket or cool item is talked about and especially that the talking about is talked about. The idea is to turn a tiny advertising spend into a mega-budget monster. Examples include Benetton, the Citroën Picasso, Calvin Klein, and, in perhaps the most extreme example, when Pizza Hut paid to place its logo on the side of a Russian rocket.
- **Secrecy** in retro is the opposite of upfront and above board. It is best seen in 'secret' recipes for Coca Cola, Heinz Ketchup, Kentucky Fried Chicken, and Mrs. Fields Cookies, but can also be found in cosmetics and hideaway holiday packages.
- **Exclusivity** is central to retro. 'Get it now while supplies last' replaces 'There's plenty for everyone.' It is practised for example by Beanie Babies, De Beers diamonds, Disney's videos, Harley, Harry Potter, the Honda Odyssey, and the Mazda Miata. The end result is less inventory and consumers who luxuriate in feeling that they are the lucky few.

All sorts of definitions and interpretations of postmodern marketing have been suggested: it's about the 'co-creation of meaning' (Cova, 1996); it's about 'reflexivity' (O'Donohoe, 1997); it's about 'intertextuality' (Thompson, 2000); or being 'critical' (Brownlie, 2006). The important point, as noted by Brown (2006), is that postmodern marketing is capable of a multitude of interpretations.

Perhaps the best attempt to make sense of the postmodern phenomenon was provided by Firat and Venkatesh (1995). They argue that postmodern marketing is characterized by five themes.

1. **Hyperreality:** Relates to the creation of marketing environments that are sanitized, but in a sense more real than real. Fake becomes superior to the nature of everyday life as with Disneyland and the Warner Brothers tour.

2. **Fragmentation:** Consumption in postmodern terms often lacks an overarching narrative. Rather than being thoughtful and enduring consumption is frenzied, and fleeting, and hyperactive.

3. **Reversed Production and Consumption:** Postmodern consumers are not transfixed rabbit-like in the headlights of marketing. Instead they often partake of production and consumption (YouTube is awash with user generated videos discussing products of all kinds).

4. **Decentred Subject:** It has become increasing accepted that traditional segmentation and targeting techniques are harder to implement as consumers are becoming 'marketing literate' (e.g. understanding product life cycles and accurately predicting when sale prices are likely).

5. **Juxtaposition of Opposites:** It is still possible to engage with and appeal to postmodern consumers. Generally the more ironic and knowing the marketing strategy, the more likely it will meet with a positive reaction from the postmodern consumer (Do you like Marmite?).

In short, 'Postmodern Marketing Strategy' can provide considerable insight into markets. Most markets, be they business-to-consumer or business-to-business, have enormous levels of 'savvy'. Buyers are smart and have a good appreciation of the motives and methods of marketing strategies. The vast majority of marketers set out to create genuine value for their customers, but strategies, faced with increased suspicion and cynicism, need to increasingly take into account the postmodern perspective. The end point of the strategy needs to engage, be interactive and take into account the buyer's perspective. A significant minority of creative customers or groups continually adapt, modify, or transform goods and services as with people who 'pimp' their cars or work with open code software (Berthon et al., 2006).

Which one to choose?

Considering marketing strategy overall, the key issue is to recognize what method is appropriate. The interrelationship between the four main approaches towards competitive marketing strategy is summarized in Figure 1.6. Both Thinking First and Seeing First are largely cognitive, whereas Doing First and Simple Rules are largely experiential in nature. On the other hand, both Doing First and Thinking First are largely long-term and formative, whereas Simple Rules and Seeing First are largely short-term in their application. 'Largely' is the key word here as there are elements of experience, cognition, immediacy, and longer time scales in all four approaches. Thus, the figure illustrates tendencies rather than any absolute points.

Thinking First works best when the issues are clear, the data are reliable, the context is structured, thoughts can be pinned down, and discipline can be applied. On the other hand, Seeing First works best when many elements have to be creatively integrated (e.g. in NPD). Doing First and Simple Rules work best when the situation is novel and confusing, complicated specifications would get in the way, and a few simple steps can help make an effective decision.

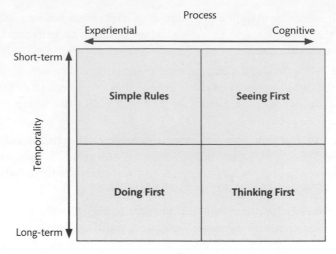

1.6 Process and Temporality and the Four Main Approaches to Competitive Marketing Strategy

The Postmodern orientation needs to be continually borne in mind to provide a check on how, in reality, buyers will interpret the final offering, but the book essentially takes a 'Thinking First' view of competitive marketing strategy from a market-driven perspective. Thus, it nods more towards the Igor Ansoff (1991) synoptic and deliberate approach to strategy than the more incremental and emergent approach advocated by Henry Mintzberg (1990).

The book's framework

In reality, marketing strategy is neither completely deliberate/cognitive—nor completely emergent. As such, the book's thesis is that marketing strategy is endemic. The central structure of the book is thus unashamedly on the 'deliberate side' and rests on four central questions:

1. Where are we now?
2. Where do we want to be?
3. How will we get there?
4. Did we get there?

This is the most widely used competitive marketing strategy frameworks. See Figure 1.7, which identifies how the chapters fit the framework. The particular value of the framework is that the four stages neatly define the necessary mindsets and place the associated key tools to develop the marketing strategy. However, there is always a danger of 'BloatText' with new editions, where each succeeding update gets bigger than the last. We wanted to avoid that and came to a conclusion based on a pedagogical reality. E-marketing is everywhere and part of everything. There is hardly a marketing strategy untouched by it. Each chapter of this edition includes e-marketing issues and practice, so could we justify a separate

I. Introduction

1. Overview and Strategy Blueprint
2. Marketing Strategy: Analysis and Perspectives

II. Where are we now?

3. Environmental and Internal Analysis: Market Information and Intelligence

III. Where do we want to be?

4. Strategic Marketing Decisions, Choices, and Mistakes
5. Segmentation, Targeting, and Positioning Strategies
6. Branding Strategies
7. Relational and Sustainability Strategies

V. Did we get there?

14. Strategy Implementation, Control, and Metrics

IV. How will we get there?

8. Product Innovation and Development Strategies
9. Service Marketing Strategies
10. Pricing and Distribution Strategies
11. Marketing Communications Strategies
12. International Marketing Strategies
13. Social and Ethical Strategies

1.7 The Book's Structure

chapter on the topic? We concluded that we could not. As a consequence, we have removed the e-marketing chapter that appeared in the first and second editions and replaced it with something we think will be more valuable: New to this edition is a chapter on international marketing strategies, something both students and teachers have been asking us to add for some time. We've previously argued that the book is imbued with international theories and examples, but we have concluded that this does not negate the value of a separate chapter on the topic completely devoted to international competitive strategies and practices.

Marketing strategy blueprint

Another way of looking at the book's structure is provided in Figure 1.8 which offers a strategy 'blueprint'.

- You can see that the key tools in **phase one** provide an **audit,** essentially a starting point with an environmental scan. These tools can be applied in conjunction with an internal

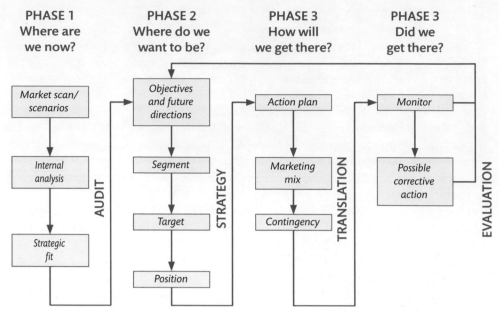

1.8 Marketing Strategy Blueprint

analysis and finally placed within the context of a SWOT (Strengths-Weaknesses-Opportunities-Threats) analysis.

- **Phase two** sees the narrowing of the marketing **strategy** in terms of objectives and future directions, segmentation, targeting, and positioning. For example, if the audit identifies that the market is largely unattractive, then the objectives and future direction may focus upon seeking new segments, distributive channels, or geographic markets, and this will affect subsequent targeting and positioning.

- **Phase three** is concerned with how will we get there? This involves the translation of the strategy to the marketing mix or five Ps (product, price, promotion, place, and people). The focus here is on product innovation and development, branding, services, pricing and distribution, marketing communications, social and ethical strategies, and international.

- In **phase four** the organization needs to undertake an evaluation based upon a variety of metrics, which may cover such elements as 'share of hearts and minds and markets', 'margins and profits', 'customer profitability', 'channel management', 'pricing strategy', and 'advertising and promotion'.

The book's focus is very much upon the actions of the firm. But let's not forget that marketing strategy also has a wider societal role to play. As noted by Webster and Lusch (2013), marketing is undergoing broader macro changes and replacing the old concept of manufacture controlled production with a responsibility for educating, rather than just informing, potential customers.

Things that can go wrong

Whatever the approach towards strategy, it does not always work. Managers often have to work within a variety of constraints (Bauer et al., 2013) such as time and resources. IBM's decision to open up and outsource to Microsoft and Intel as it developed the PC has been called the 'outsourcing blunder of the century' by Jacobides and MacDuffie (2013) with admitted 20/20 hindsight. And Steve Bulmer, the former CEO of Microsoft, noted his regret at focusing on the Windows operating system for PCs and taking his eye off the opportunities for mobile. Sometimes the problem is the strategy and sometimes the implementation, which begs an interesting question as to whether it would be best to have a great strategy with a weak implementation or a weak strategy with great implementation?

Beer and Eisenstat (2000) have identified what they call 'six silent killers' of great strategy related to management style, unclear strategy, ineffective management, vertical communications, cross-functional coordination, and down-the-line leadership.

Many firms attempt to adopt a market-oriented strategy, but according to Day (1998) many adopt one of three less successful orientations: the 'self-centred,' the 'customer compelled' and the 'sceptical'. Each orientation is a form of myopia that inhibits organizations from realizing the potential from their marketing strategy.

1. The **self-centred trap** is when an organization takes its place for granted. IBM's orientation of the 1980s is a classic example: its strong profitability masked a total loss of focus as the company became distant, arrogant, and unresponsive. By 1990 it had squandered its trust with customers, with IBM compatible competitors educating them on the alternatives.

2. **Customer compelled** organizations try to be all things to their markets. Thus, IBM attempted to satisfy large and medium-sized customers in every industry in the early 1990s with a total offering that was incoherent.

3. The **scepticism trap** is a curious backlash to the customer focus. The assertion is that customer research leads to bland offerings and is a distraction to the real work. For example, Apple has failed to penetrate the Indian market with the iPhone; it's incompatible with India's CDMA technology, Indians prefer unlocked phones, and, being sold at the same price as it is in the USA, it is too expensive.

Conclusion

Developing a marketing strategy is a largely subjective activity.

- *Thinking First* is the best model to adopt given a rational and linear thinking perspective. Nevertheless, while Thinking First dominates our view of marketing strategy, there are alternative approaches.
- *Seeing First* suggests a single glance at the organization and its market to produce the key flash of insight of the central strategy such as the flash of insight from Sir Stelios Haji-Ioannou and the easyGroup that the market wanted 'simple'.

- On the other hand, *Doing First* recognizes that Seeing First is rarely straightforward. Quite often in strategy there is no clear way forward and so the best solution is to make a decision and to try and make sense of it—then repeat the successful bits, and leave out the rest. A number of companies have undertaken acquisition and mergers (A&M) on the basis of Doing First. Sometimes they work (e.g. Vodafone and AirTouch Communications) and sometimes they do not (e.g. Daimler Benz and Chrysler), and it is not always clear what makes the difference. Often it is culture, but it can be resources or market issues and it is only by trying out the A&M that such aspects are revealed, such is the complexity of the activity. There is a difference between acquiring a company where the acquirer takes charge (sometimes called a takeover and may be friendly or hostile) and merging, where both companies integrate on a largely equal basis.

- *Simple Rules* are especially relevant to complex markets where triggers can be established to set strategies in motion. Thus, a tea manufacturer might decide to introduce a herbal tea range if the market reaches a certain size or a rival does something similar. Once established, such rules are not matters for debate but should be followed to the letter.

- *Postmodern* strategy offers a completely different view. The postmodern view of marketing is that the scientific twentieth century of marketing is waning in impact as buyers know many of the 'tricks of the trade.' Faced with cynical and suspicious buyers, the argument is that the tried and trusted tools of marketing no longer have such saliency. Postmodernism reminds us that marketing strategies can neglect the all-important question of how the intended audience will respond to the strategy. For example, a claim that a smartphone is 'new and improved' may be greeted with derision, even if true.

Marketers appreciate that there are constraints on our ability to make optimal choices. All decision-making is in a state of 'bounded rationality' owing to complexity, limited time, and inadequate mental computational power (Buchanan and O'Connell, 2006). Strategy has been shown to be a fundamental component of business success along with execution, culture, and structure. Things can go badly wrong, such as with poor vertical communications or conflicting priorities, and, unfortunately, they often do.

Summary

This chapter has taken a somewhat 'left field' and alternative view of strategy. The book is devoted to a Thinking First and rational view of marketing strategy; this opening chapter has taken the opportunity to review and discuss alternative approaches that are less mainstream. A bit like learning to walk before you can run, Seeing First or Doing First are approaches to decision-making that normally need a prior understanding of Thinking First. You need to know the rules before you should break them. You can then break all the rules once you know what they are!

Key terms

- **Doing First:** making experimental strategic marketing decisions and learning from mistakes and successes.
- **Postmodern:** a reaction to the 'modern' marketing practices of the twentieth century favouring a more ironic, cynical, and less scientific view of marketing.
- **Scenarios:** plausible written narratives based upon problems that exist in some small form today that may become unexpectedly important marketing problems in the future.
- **Seeing First:** appreciating the wider strategic picture with one glance based upon insight.
- **Simple Rules:** identifying market triggers that set in motion key changes in strategy.
- **Thinking First:** rationally addressing marketing strategy problems with a view to finding a solution.

Discussion questions

1. Examine the pros and cons of the Seeing First approach to strategy.

2. Imagine a chocolate manufacturer is going to launch an ice-cream based on its leading brand. It has decided there are too many uncertainties to be sure of the outcome and so is just going to 'do it' and see what happens. What kinds of things might it measure to see what did and did not work?

3. Would it be fair to say that there are more examples of Postmodern approaches to strategy in consumer rather than business markets? If so, why?

4. Write a short (single) scenario on one of the following markets with implications for marketing strategy:

   a. The personal digital audio player.

   b. The hybrid (part petrol engine/electric battery) car.

   c. Convenience food.

Online resource centre

 Visit the Online Resource Centre for this book for lots of interesting additional material at: **<www.oxfordtextbooks.co.uk/orc/west3e/>**

References and further reading

Achrol, Ravi S. and Philip Kotler (2012), 'Frontiers of the Marketing Paradigm in the Third Millennium', *Journal of the Academy of Marketing Science*, 40, pp. 35–52.

Bauer, Johannes C., Philipp Schmitt, Vicki G. Morwitz and Russell S. Winer (2013), 'Managerial Decision Making in Customer Management: Adaptive, Fast and Frugal?' *Journal of the Academy of Marketing Science*, 41, pp. 436–55.

Beer, Michael and Russell A. Eisenstat (2000), 'The Silent Killers Of Strategy Implementation and Learning', *Sloan Management Review*, Summer 41(4), pp. 29–40.

Brown, Stephen (2001), 'Torment Your Customers (They'll Love It)', *Harvard Business Review*, October, pp. 83–8.

Brown, Stephen (2006), 'Recycling Postmodern Marketing', *The Marketing Review*, 6, pp. 211–30.

Brownlie, D. (2006), 'Emancipation, Epiphany and Resistance: On the Underimagined and Overdetermined in Critical Marketing', *Journal of Marketing Management*, 22(5-6), pp. 505–28.

Buchanan, Leigh and Andrew O'Connell (2006), 'A Brief History of Decision Making', *Harvard Business Review*, January, pp. 33–41.

Cova, B. (1996), 'What Postmodernism Means to Marketing Managers' *European Management Journal*, 14(5), pp. 494–9.

Day, George S. (1998), 'What Does It Mean To Be Market-Driven?', *Business Strategy Review*, Spring, pp. 1–14.

Edmondson, Amy C. (2011), 'Strategies for Learning from Failure', *Harvard Business Review*, April, pp. 48–55.

Eisenhardt, Kathleen M. and Donald N. Sull (2001), 'Strategy as Simple Rules', *Harvard Business Review*, January, pp. 107–16.

Firat, A. F. and Venkatesh, A. (1995), 'Liberatory Postmodernism and the Reenchantment of Consumption', *Journal of Consumer Research*, 22 December, pp. 239–67.

Gofee, Robert and Gareth Jones (2000), 'Why Should Anyone Be Led By You?', *Harvard Business Review*, Sept-Oct, pp. 63–70.

Hooley, Graham, Amanda Broderick, and Kristian Möller (1998), 'Competitive Positioning and the Resource-Based View of the Firm', *Journal of Strategic Marketing*, 6, pp. 97–115.

Kanter, Rosabeth Moss (2011), 'How Great Companies Think Differently'. *Harvard Business Review*, November, pp. 66–78.

Matsuno, Ken and John T. Mentzer (2000), 'The Effects of Strategy Type on the Market Orientation-Performance Relationship', *Journal of Marketing*, 64(4), pp. 1–16.

Mintzberg, Henry and Frances Westley (2001), 'Decision Making: It's Not What You Think', *MIT Sloan Management Review*, 42, Spring, pp. 89–93.

O'Donohoe, Stephanie (1997), 'Raiding the Pantry: Advertising Intertextuality and the Young Adult Audience', *European Journal of Marketing*, 31(3/4), pp. 234–53.

O'Donohoe, Stephanie (2001), 'Living With Ambivalence: Attitudes to Advertising in Postmodern Times', *Marketing Theory*, 1(1), pp. 91–108.

Porter, Michael (2001) 'Strategy and the Internet', *Harvard Business Review*, March, pp. 63–78.

Thompson, C.J. (2000), 'Postmodern Consumer Goals Made Easy!!!', in Ratneshwar, S., Mick, D. G., and Huffman, C. (eds), *The Why of Consumption: Contemporary Perspectives on Consumer Motives, Goals and Desires*, London: Routledge, pp. 120–39.

Wallas, G. (1926), *The Art of Thought* (New York: Harcourt Brace).

Webster, Frederick E., Jr., and Robert F. Lusch (2013), 'Elevating Marketing: Marketing Is Dead! Long Live Marketing!' *Journal of Academy of Marketing Science*, 41, pp. 389–99.

Yoffie, David B. and Michael A. Cusumano (1999) 'Judo Strategy: The Competitive Dynamics of Internet Time', *Harvard Business Review*, January-February, pp. 70–81.

Zenger, Todd (2013), 'What is the Theory of Your Firm?', *Harvard Business Review*, June, pp. 72–8.

 End of Chapter 1 case study   To eat or not to eat

Supermarket dietitians

One third of all US adults were obese in 2009–2010. It is no surprise, then, that according to the recent study *Shopping for Health* 2012, just over 30 per cent of grocery shoppers surveyed reported that they are now buying more foods based on nutritional components versus last year (*Prevention Magazine*, 2012).

As this consumer interest in health and wellness continues to grow, food retailers must market their ability to deliver a holistic offering that meets these needs. Many retailers are moving to offer customers more health and wellness-focused foods and services, and using in-store dietitians as the centrepiece for these efforts. Supermarkets across the country are benefiting from the expertise of their dietitians, and are maximizing this benefit by utilizing marketing's 4Ps: product, price, placement, and promotion.

Regional Grocer

Total supermarket sales in 2011 surpassed $584 billion. While this may pique the interest of entrepreneurs, the realization that there are more than 36,000 potential competitors nationwide may quickly hamper that interest (Supermarket Facts, 2012).

Regional Grocer, Inc. owns and operates more than 230 of these 36,000 US supermarkets. With locations in western Pennsylvania, Ohio, Maryland, and West Virginia, Regional Grocer's supermarkets offer fresh produce, meat, and seafood. They offer deli services, bakeries, and prepared food sections. Health and wellness services, such as in-store pharmacies and health care clinics, are available in addition to convenience offerings such as wine and spirits and other-retailer gift cards. Regional Grocer now offers counselling to help consumers maintain a healthy lifestyle through nutritional analysis to determine ideal nutritional intake and dietary advice based on individual needs. The company also offers a variety of weight management, diet and nutrition, and health and wellness products to help consumers achieve their goals and stay fit. Building on its dietitian services, the supermarket is embracing the health and wellness trend by engaging in gluten-free resources, wellness newsletters, and diabetes care programmes (Regional Grocer.com).

Regional Grocer uses brand equity built over its 80-year history to successfully capitalize on consumer trends by introducing new store concepts, customer loyalty programmes, and in-store services that allow the organization to differentiate from the competition. With 21 dietitians now servicing stores across its marketing areas, Regional Grocer has decided to use these nutrition experts as ambassadors for the company's health and wellness initiatives.

In-store dietitians

The challenge of expanding upon this health and wellness trend is also its greatest opportunity, namely that each consumer manages it differently. For instance, most Americans believe that organic foods are healthier than conventional foods, making these foods an important part of a healthy diet for them. Many other consumers are battling with food-related medical issues such as colitis, diabetes, and heart disease, which drive how they eat. And some others simply want help with understanding how to read nutrition labels. The ability to effectively address unique motivators such as these is vital to any organization looking to succeed in marketing health and wellness.

In-store dietitians offer retailers the opportunity to engage with customers on a one-on-one basis, allowing them to effectively respond to these unique needs. Regional Grocer's dietitians employ numerous tactics to meet such needs.

The offering

- In-store dietitians as the **product**: Regional Grocer's stores offer a wide selection of fresh produce, high quality meats and seafood, and Nature's Basket organic products. The supermarket is currently offering dietitian and wellness services in addition to their variety of food products. The dietitians are in many ways products themselves, with the knowledge they possess being their main product benefit. This knowledge is shared with consumers in numerous ways, both online and in-store. Online dietitians provide several health-related articles, nutritional and gluten-free recipes, health tips, and a complete list of available in-store services. Consumers can use these tools to create a meal plan or grocery list before heading to the supermarket, often being able to convert the ingredients of a recipe into an online shopping list with the click of a button. These tools are a great complement to the in-store offerings. In-store dietitian services are geared towards helping customers eat healthier and range from both individual and group consultations, to group store tours and food demonstrations. Consumers highly involved in their personal wellness will likely take advantage of meeting with a dietitian, while consumers less involved may take advantage of the in-store food demonstrations as they shop.

- Regional Grocer already has in place a strong **pricing** strategy. As previously mentioned in the product section, information on the various dietitian services can be found on Regional Grocer's website, with five dietitian programmes offered at various fees. Regional Grocer pricing takes into account the consumer's level of involvement. Introductory meetings are free for those less involved, simply looking to learn more about what is available. For those more involved in health and wellness, services such as 10-week group weight loss classes and ongoing personal nutrition coaching come with a cost.

- Regional Grocer has expanded its health and wellness service departments in many **locations**. The company's larger Market District stores are geared toward customers who want more than the traditional grocery shopping experience and have become an ideal setting for these departments. Launched in Pittsburgh in 2006, Regional Grocer Market District locations offer an open market-style floor plan and expanded departments. The produce section includes a wide assortment of high quality, fresh fruits and vegetables. The meat and seafood department features an array of top quality meats including organic, natural antibiotic, and hormone-free. Some stores also include the expansion of a sit-down café featuring diverse, high quality prepared dishes in addition to a fresh salad bar and grab-n-go meal solutions. Whether located in a Market District or a Regional Grocer location, the company's health and wellness departments are founded on offering quality and variety. They are filled with natural and organic cosmetics, vitamins, supplements, and personal care products.

- The product, pricing, and placement related to offerings and services are of little value if they are not **promoted** in a manner that grabs the attention and interest of the consumer. Regional Grocer is currently piloting unique item-specific shelf tags that call out healthy attributes of the products (heart healthy, gluten-free, etc.). The unique tags make it much easier for low-involvement consumers to increase their nutritional knowledge regarding the foods they purchase, making them more likely to reference the tags in the future and as a result building brand loyalty with Regional Grocer. The tags act as a driver for the dietitians, as the dietitians become a resource to learn more about the information introduced by the tags. To build awareness and source credibility for the dietitians, Regional Grocer offers a brochure at each participating store that provides biographical background on the dietitians and outlines the specific services available, making it easier for the less-engaged customer to become more familiar with the offering. Also, customers can find health and wellness services both in-store and online. Regional Grocer's website offers information regarding dietitian services, in-store clinics, and healthy living. This information is also available to customers via electronic newsletters and weekly circulars that are mailed to customers' homes. Regional Grocer also utilizes television commercials and radio advertisements to reach customers and encourage their involvement in the many different programmes and services they offer to ultimately increase customer loyalty to the Regional Grocer brand.

- **Services** play a key role too (see Table C1.1). Regional Grocer's dietitians activate many of the organization's cause-related marketing efforts, expanding upon awareness and source credibility (Cooking for Wellness). The company is affiliated with numerous non-profit organizations including the American Diabetes Association, the Greater Pittsburgh Community Food Bank, and Susan G Komen for the Cure. By joining the numerous other Regional Grocer team members participating in charity-related events, the company's dietitians build credibility and loyalty in a meaningful way. Furthermore, its stores are staffed with a licensed skin care professional and a licensed dietitian conducting ongoing wellness events and activities.

Table C1.1 Dietitian Services and Classes

Dietitian Services and Classes	Description	Highmark Members	Non-members
Weight Loss Classes	60-minute classes per week for 10 weeks	$20 for materials	$105 including materials fee
Nutrition for Life Classes	Eat Well for Life I and II: both 90-minute classes per week for four weeks	No fee	$65 per four-week session
	Nutrition for Life I and II: both 90-minute classes per week for four weeks	$65 per four-week session	$65 per four-week session
Diabetes Classes	Intro to Diabetes: 60-minute class per week for four weeks	$20 per four-week session	$20 per four-week session
	Diabetes Management: 60-minute classes per week for four weeks	$20 per four-week session	$20 per four-week session
Personal Counselling	Initial Personal Nutrition Coaching: one 60-minute visit	No fee for one 60-minute visit per year	$60 per 60-minute visit
	Initial Personal Nutrition Counselling: one 60-minute session	$60 per one 60-minute session	$60 per 60-minute visit
	Follow-Up Personal Nutritional Coaching: 30-minute visits	No fee for 30-minute visits (limit of six per year)	$30 per 30-minute follow-up session
	Follow-Up Personal Nutritional Counselling: 30-minute sessions	$30 per 30-minute follow-up session	$30 per 30-minute follow-up session
Aisle Excursions	Various 60-minute tours	No fee	No fee

Discussion questions

Place yourself in the role of a marketing consultant advising Regional Grocer.

1. Assuming that Regional Grocer is developing its strategy for the next three years, critically evaluate the potential role of the Thinking First, Seeing First, or Doing First strategies.

2. Suggest two or three Simple Rules to help guide their competitive marketing strategy over the period.

3. Given that the company's consumers have a lot of market 'savvy' and are often cynical about health products, what role might postmodern approaches play in developing competitive marketing strategy?

This case was prepared by Lauren Geier, Ashley Rudy, and Abby Trainer under the supervision of Dr Georgiana Craciun, Katz Graduate School of Business, University of Pittsburgh (gcraciun@pitt.edu). The case is solely for the basis of class discussion and is not intended to illustrate effective or ineffective management or administrative situations or any form of endorsement.

Marketing strategy: analysis and perspectives

Learning Objectives

1. Appreciate the historical background of strategy concept and how this concept has migrated from military planning to the business field.
2. Understand the definitions of corporate strategy, business strategy, and functional strategies.
3. Be able to compare the different definitions of marketing strategy, and its importance for corporate success.
4. Be able to discuss the possible orientations of marketing strategy and define competitive marketing strategy.
5. Understand the strategic models for strategy development.

Chapter at a Glance

I. Introduction

1 Overview and strategy blueprint

2 Marketing strategy: analysis and perspectives

II. Where are we now?

3 Environmental and internal analysis: market information and intelligence

III. Where do we want to be?

4 Strategic marketing decisions, choices, and mistakes

5 Segmentation, targeting, and positioning strategies

6 Branding strategies

7 Relational and sustainability strategies

V. Did we get there?

14 Strategy implementation, control, and metrics

IV. How will we get there?

8 Product innovation and development strategies

9 Service marketing strategies

10 Pricing and distribution strategies

11 Marketing communications strategies

12 International marketing strategy

13 Social and ethical strategies

 Case study: Plymouth Citybus—another one rides the bus

The brief

A smartphone is the modern equivalent of a Swiss army knife—a small pocket device that can make a big difference to a stressful day. The wide assortment of apps that can be added to smartphones has made daily lives more convenient than ever before—as at 2013 the number of apps available from Apple's App Store had soared to 775,000.

Plymouth based company, Citybus, launched a campaign, 'Plymouth in your pocket', to promote its new app and sought to play on this simple concept of handiness. It also wanted a campaign that would provide cut through to its target audience of younger passengers aged 18 to 34. The Citybus customer database suggested a significant proportion of bus users were younger people and students. Citybus was confident that a large proportion of its customers were smartphone users because records showed that 50 per cent of visitors to its website log on using mobile devices, a leap of 23 per cent compared to two years ago.

Plymouth Citybus marketing manager Mark Collins says:

We created the app as an additional channel to market our service and improve efficiency levels, for both our passengers and own business. The idea is to reduce queues for tickets and the time spent by bus drivers fiddling with change. The Citybus mobile app allows customers to buy tickets, see prices, link to Google Maps and view a Twitter feed of traffic updates. Passengers scan their smartphone when they board a bus instead of using a paper ticket.

The strategy

The campaign focused on younger people. This was based on widespread evidence that smartphones are used more by young people than other demographic groups. Telecoms regulator Ofcom, for example, has found that while 39 per cent of adults owned a smartphone in 2012, this figure rose to 66 per cent among 16 to 24 year olds and 60 per cent among 25 to 34 year olds. Citybus estimated the app could appeal to at least 7,000 who already engage with its brand online. The company has just over 6,500 'likes' on Facebook and 3,185 followers on Twitter.

Agency Bluestone360 was commissioned to deliver the campaign, which launched on 1 September 2012 and is ongoing. 'We asked Bluestone360 for creative that matched the innovative nature of the product and reflected how it would conveniently help people get the best out of the city,' says Collins.

Bluestone created a campaign that emphasised how the app would allow people to access activities in Plymouth, make life easier and save time. The slogan of the £20,000 campaign was 'Plymouth in your pocket'. The creative shows the glinting screen of an iPhone with various images leaping off it towards the viewer. Each image represents an activity, including a shark for the city's aquarium, a carton of popcorn for the cinema, a bowling ball for the bowling alley. 'We wanted artwork that jumped off the page to give the campaign energy and appeal to younger people, who we knew would be more likely to use apps', says Collins.

The execution

The campaign was multi-channel. Citybus wrapped an advert around one of its buses, e-mailed its database, and alerted online followers and friends. Posters were placed at its bus stops and bus shelters, and sent to shops that sell bus tickets. Two full-page adverts were placed in the most widely read local paper in the area, the *Plymouth Herald*. 'We also took all the advertising space on the *Plymouth Herald*'s homepage for five days', says Bluestone 360's account manager, Daniel Porter.

The adverts included a QR code to encourage people to download the app. 'This allows people to scan the code with their phone and get onto it immediately. 'Once they've put their card details in, they are ready to start buying tickets,' says Porter. The campaign featured a promotional incentive, entering people who downloaded the app within the first six weeks of the campaign into a draw to win an iPhone. A large proportion of the advertising space was secured at no cost because adverts featured on buses owned by the client. As a result the campaign cost £10,000, 50 per cent below budget. Collins says: 'Effectively free advertising space allowed us to punch much higher than our weight. Just to have the bus alone for advertising would normally cost around £12,000 a year.'

The outcome

The target for the campaign was 1,000 downloads in the first three months. In fact the app was downloaded 1,000 times in the campaign's first week. Since the app went live in August, it has had 4,563 downloads. Less impressively, perhaps, the conversion rate—the number of people who actually buy tickets after downloading the app—is 25.6 per cent. The number of tickets sold through the app so far stands at 3,446, while Citybus sees some 22,000 tickets bought every day.

Analysis

Porter insists, however, he is pleased with the conversion rate. 'We don't have anything to compare it to, so it's hard to gauge, but we are happy with it because it does clearly show the changing behaviour of an audience'; he explains the app was free to download, so Citybus did not have financial targets for the campaign.

Collins believes though that increasing use of the app will save money in terms of the reduced manpower that will be needed to sell tickets. 'We'll be able to reinvest those savings in further innovation', he says. Collins says Citybus would not change anything about the campaign but admits the challenge will now be to maintain the momentum. Regular updates are standard practice for apps and Citybus plans to update Plymouthbus Mobile by adding a journey planner function. 'We will want to promote the updated app but we would have to justify the extra marketing spend and it's clear that each new update will bring that challenge,' he says.

Roxane McMeeken, The Marketer, 25 March 2013

Introduction

Marketing strategy has been the subject of considerable research in both the business and marketing literature in the last four decades. It has become an area of primary concern to all organizations, depending critically on a subtle understanding and analysis of the market. Its importance becomes even greater in today's ever-challenging and fast-changing business environment. Marketers worldwide face an external environment characterized by rapid change, and it is imperative that marketers understand today's flat, boundaryless market-place—a world in which companies still continue to make strategic and tactical decisions, yet do so with an understanding that the global marketplace can turn on a dime (Crittenden and Crittenden, 2012). It has been suggested though that the development of marketing strategy in such a complex and challenging business environment requires forming a strategic vision and selecting the market targeting and positioning strategy for each market target (Cravens et al., 2009). At the centre of the process is the understanding of the marketing environment and competitive space.

The development of marketing strategy is essential for success not only in developed markets, where the competition can be intense and with every player attempting to gain market share, but also in emerging markets where the elements of product, price, communications, and distribution are recognized as valuable sources for competitive advantage. This importance becomes even more vital in the case of developing markets where local producers are coming under increasing pressure to become more competitive in order to face the intense competition from their foreign counterparts. In fact increasing competition from abroad, coupled with environmental uncertainties, presents a formidable challenge to the business community in these markets to formulate and implement their marketing strategy more effectively. No doubt the presence of many global companies such as Carrefour, Burger King, HSBC, and Vodafone in several emerging markets has forced local competitors to search for new competitive advantages through the effective use of their marketing resources.

Organizations that aim to encounter the difficulties of the fast-changing marketing environment need their strategic decisions to be founded on well-conceived strategies. Clearly defined and well-developed marketing strategies are a must if the organization is to fulfil its objectives in the markets in which it competes (Ward and Lewandowska, 2008).

Marketing strategy in a changing environment

In their perspective on 'strategic marketing in a changing world', Crittenden and Crittenden (2012) note that while marketers have historically relied on trends for making sound decisions, strategic marketing in today's rapidly changing world is made more treacherous than before since trends are not what they used to be. For example, demographics have long been a foundation of market planning, and population growth has been a key macro component of demographics. But future demographic trends are unlikely to follow the historical path. With lower fertility rates in many developed countries, there may be a decline in population. A change in that trend will leave national and international economies with less accurate planning models for growth. The same applies for trends in consumer spending. The global recession has created a consumer who focuses largely on finding the best value for money.

The continuous changes in business environment urge marketers to re-think the sources of competitive advantages (Dewar, 2013). The strategic question that should drive businesses in today's environment is not 'What else can we make?' but 'What else can we do for our customers?' Upstream activities such as sourcing, production, and logistics are being commoditized or outsourced, while downstream activities aimed at shaping customers' perception and reducing their costs and risks are emerging now as the main sources of competitive advantage.

One of the greatest challenges facing marketing managers in the changing business environment is the development of the critical strategic thinking and analytical skills required to adapt quickly and effectively to the environmental and market changes. Selecting strategies for fast-changing markets begin with the identification and evaluation of potential market changes and the strategy implications (Cravens et al., 2009). From this process a strategic vision for the future should emerge. This vision provides the basis for developing strategic targeting and positioning changes based on the implications of the vision (e.g. changes in market boundaries and structure). There are many examples of strategic marketing initiatives by companies in response to environmental and market changes. Hewlett Packard extended beyond their traditional industry boundaries to open up new markets and to deliver new value to customers with HP PhotoSmart. Samsung utilized its vast knowledge of consumer electronics to create a cohesive strategy for designing digital devices, many of which are leading the market today.

The success of an organization depends primarily on its management's ability to understand the marketing environment, and on their ability to think critically and react strategically to any market changes. The strategic marketing concept should be viewed as all-embracing, flexible, and adoptable (Trim and Lee, 2008). It requires that marketing managers ensure that the organization achieves a sustainable competitive advantage through a structured approach to planning and strategy development.

Strategy concept and definitions

Originally, the word *strategy* comes from the Greek word *strategos*, strictly meaning a general in command of an army; it is formed from 'stratos', meaning army and 'ag', meaning to lead. Therefore, the concept of 'strategy' was first introduced and defined in the ancient military dictionaries. Strategy is defined in the military literature as '*a plan of attack for winning the battle*' or '*a plan for beating the opposition*'. Similar definitions are used today in the field of business. In reflecting upon the link between military and business usage of the strategy concept, Horton (2003) claimed that the discourse and practice of strategy is distinctively a mechanism of power whether seen from a military or business angle.

The word 'strategy' appeared for first time in the business literature in 1952 in a book by William Newman. At that time strategy was implicitly regarded as a plan for achieving organizational goals. Since then there have been several attempts to present the concept of strategy in the business literature; most notable, the pioneering work by Ansoff (1965) and Hofer and Schendel (1978). The contributions of those writers and others can be classified into three categories. In the first, writers who produced analytical or rationalistic models, which while precise, are neither sufficiently comprehensive nor useful enough for practice. In the second, other writers who were more eclectic and introduced many frameworks that collectively define the underlying notion of strategy in business management. Finally, some writers have been primarily 'verbal' in presenting their understanding of strategy.

Academic interest in strategy has grown rapidly in the business literature in the last four decades. Cummings and Daellenbach (2009) reviewed some of the ongoing debate in the literature about 'what strategy really is', and 'whether one view of what it is' is better than another. It is not surprising today to find a profusion of books and articles on strategic planning, **corporate strategy**, **business strategy**, and marketing strategy—a fashionable word in business language.

Strategy has been defined in a very short sentence as 'the means an organization uses to achieve its goals'. Whilst this definition describes strategy as a means to achieving a company's objectives, it does not establish a distinct boundary between strategy and tactics. It is not clear in this definition what type of organizational decisions could be regarded as strategic and what distinguishes these from operational decisions? This question is central in any discussion of strategy. Is strategy only plans made by senior strategists; or can even the smallest micro-activity be strategic; and if so, how do we know which are strategic and which are not (Cummings and Daellenbach, 2009)? For example, how could we describe Apple's decision to adopt a business model of selling directly to consumers? Should this be seen as a strategic decision or something else?

Taking the two together, strategy can be defined as 'the overall plan for deploying an organization's resources to establish a favourable position in the market', while a tactic is 'a scheme for a specific action'. It appears from this definition that one of the core tasks of strategy is identifying how a firm can deploy its resources in a market to achieve its long-term goals and how it will organize its activities to execute this strategy. Honda, the Japanese car producer, announced a shutdown of its UK plant in Swindon for four months during 2009. This move was viewed by some experts as an operational decision in response to the downturn in the UK car market. Others have seen this move as more of a strategic decision that aims to re-deploy the company's resources from a less profitable market (at that time) to more attractive areas.

From a multi-angular view, Mintzberg and Quinn (1996) proposed in their seminal text five definitions of strategy (5Ps)—strategy as plan, ploy, pattern, position, and perspective—and looked at the interrelationships between these five definitions. These definitions reflect that successful strategies typically are characterized by four key ingredients:

- they are directed toward unambiguous long-term goals;
- they are based on insightful understanding of the external environment;
- they are based on intimate self-knowledge by the organization or by individuals of internal capabilities; and
- they are implemented with coordination and effective harnessing of the capabilities to achieve the targeted competitive position.

Within the boundary of the above definitions, three types of strategy can be specifically defined in relation to organizational structure. Strategy exists at multiple levels in an organization: *corporate*, *business unit*, and *functional* (Varadarajan and Jayachandran, 2000). Figure 2.1 shows this hierarchical relationship.

Corporate strategy: describes a company's overall direction in terms of its general attitude toward growth and the management of its various businesses and product lines to achieve a balanced portfolio of products and services. Additionally, it is (a) the pattern of decisions regarding the types of business in which a firm should be involved, (b) the flow of financial and other resources to and from its divisions, and (c) the relationship of the corporation to key groups in its environment. In a drastic change to the company corporate strategy, AT&T decided to obtain local access for its long-distance customers and chose to acquire the country's biggest cable operators, TCI and Media One, for $110 billion. This was a significant advantage of the company's corporate strategy.

Business strategy: sometimes called competitive strategy, is usually developed at divisional level and emphasizes improvement of the competitive position of a corporation's products or services in the specific industry or market segment served by that division. Business strategy asks how the company or its strategic business units (SBUs) should compete or cooperate in each industry. In order for AT&T to achieve its corporate objective described above, should the company purchase more cable companies (expensive option), form strategic alliances

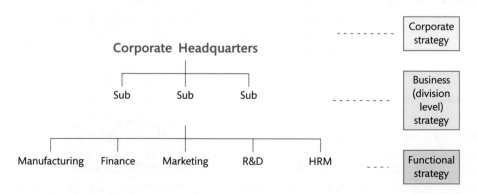

2.1 Hierarchy of Strategy*

* Strategic management may be initiated at any or all of these hierarchical levels of an organization.

Source: Thomas L. Wheelen and David J. Hunger (2012), Strategic Management and Business Policy, 13/e, Pearson Education, Inc.

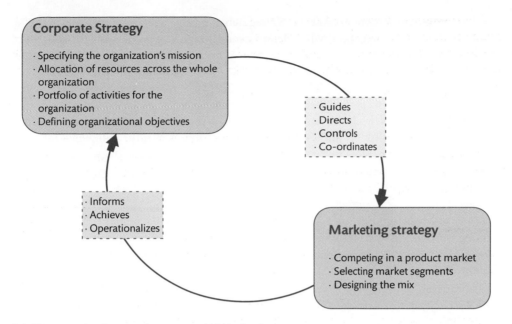

2.2 The Interaction Between Corporate and Marketing Strategy

Source: Frances Brassington and Stephen Pettitt (2006), Principles of Marketing, 4th edition, p.938, Pearson Education, Inc., Upper Saddle River, NJ.

with cable companies (who might be not interested), or try something else? Business strategies should also integrate various functional activities to achieve divisional objectives.

Functional strategy: within the constraints of the corporate and business strategies around them, functional departments, such as marketing, finance, R&D, and production, develop strategies to pull together their various activities and competencies to improve performance. But where should a function be housed? Should it be integrated within the organization or purchased from an outside contractor? Some voices suggest that organizations should only purchase from outside those activities that are not critical factors in the company's distinctive competencies. Otherwise the company may give up the capabilities that made it successful in the first place.

The three levels of strategy interact closely and must be well integrated for corporate success. Figure 2.2 illustrates how corporate and marketing strategy interact to achieve the overall objectives of an organization.

Marketing strategy: nature and definitions

In the early 1970s, marketing strategy was seen as being an indication of how each element of the marketing mix will be utilized to achieve the marketing objectives. With this view, marketing strategy was looked at as the broad conception of how product, price, promotion, and distribution are to function in a coordinated way to overcome resistance to meeting marketing goals. Such a view was completely reliant on the marketing mix and, therefore, the utilization of the mix elements is the marketing strategy. This view was later broadened to incorporate other marketing concepts (e.g. segmentation and positioning, product life cycle, market share, and competition) when defining marketing strategy. Utilizing the concept of segmentation and positioning, marketing strategy was seen as a means to identify target markets at which to direct activities and the types of competitive advantages to develop and exploit in each target market (Dibb et al., 2012). This view advocates the use of segmentation and targeting concepts and, hence, the competitive advantages are directed toward specific market segments, while the positioning strategy is the employment of the organization's product, distribution, price, and promotion activities to position the company's offerings against those of competitors in the target markets. The positioning strategy should provide the unifying concept for deciding the role of each element of the marketing mix.

Ries and Trout (1981: 219) had earlier stated that '*positioning strategy is thinking in reverse. Instead of starting with yourself, you start with the mind of the prospect. Instead of asking what you are, you ask what position you already own in the mind of the prospect*'. Thus the positioning concept goes beyond image creation, which merely identifies the attributes that are strengths, to provide guidance on which attributes should be used in the positioning/repositioning strategy.

These definitions belong to the school of thought that sees marketing strategy as a functional strategy that is developed in the marketing department and aims to achieve marketing goals only.

Other marketing scholars, at a simple level, defined three principal marketing strategies: differentiated, undifferentiated, and concentrated, which sound similar to those of Porter's generic strategies (i.e. low-cost, differentiation, and focus) which normally develop outside the marketing department and aim to achieve the SBU objectives.

Another approach to defining marketing strategy is the use of Ansoff's classical matrix that combines two dimensions, 'products to offer' and 'market to target', to suggest four strategies: *market-penetration strategy*, *market-development strategy*, *product-development strategy*, and *diversification strategy*. Producers of consumer products, such as P&G, Unilever, and Colgate-Palmolive, are very experienced in using advertising and other communication tools to implement a market penetration strategy to gain the dominant share in a market. By means of a *product-development strategy* a company can develop new products for existing markets or develop new products for new markets. The Sara Lee Corporation uses its successful brand name 'Sara Lee' to promote other products such as premium meats and fresh-baked food products. Adopting a similar approach, it is possible to suggest several marketing strategies using the categories of product line, pricing, distribution, advertising, and promotion. For example, combining promotion and distribution, a company can choose between *push* and *pull* marketing strategies. Most of the large fast-moving consumer goods (FMCG) companies follow a push strategy by spending a great amount of money on a particular trade sector to gain/hold shelf space in major retail outlets. With pricing and distribution also, a firm can adopt either a *skim pricing strategy* or a *penetration pricing strategy*. Skim pricing strategy is typically designed for the upmarket segment where customers are willing and can afford to pay a premium price for quality products/services. Virgin Atlantic tends to focus on particular upmarket segments and charges them premium prices. Penetration pricing strategy targets several market segments with much lower prices to gain market share. Air France-KLM serves many segments and offers a range of prices that suit a large number of travellers.

Marketing strategy development

Based on the previous definitions, one could argue that the development of marketing strategy can occur at three main levels of a firm. At the top level, the company's core strategy is selected, and marketing objectives and the broad focus for achieving them are identified. At the next level, market segments and targets are chosen and the company's differential advantage in serving the target markets better than the competition is identified. At the functional level, a marketing department capable of putting the strategy into practice must be created. The marketing department, at this stage, is responsible for designing the marketing mix programmes that can convey the positioning and the products/services to the target market (Hooley et al., 2011). Applying this structural concept of marketing strategy development to British Airways (BA), it is possible to see at the first level that the company's core strategy and marketing objectives have been set to ensure that BA is the customer's first choice through the delivery of an unbeatable travel experience. At the next level, BA has elected to provide superior service quality in all market segments it competes in. At the third level, BA's marketing mix programmes should be designed to support its product/service positioning in the forefront of the globalization of the airline industry.

Cravens (1994) suggested a step-wise approach to marketing strategy development. This approach is shown in Table 2.1, which presents a summary of the important issues to be considered at each step, and the major actions/decisions that are required.

Table 2.1 Selecting and Developing Marketing Strategies for Different Market and Competitive Situations

	Important Issues	Major Actions/Decisions
Product-market definition and analysis ▽	• Evaluating the complexity of the product-market structure. • Establishing product-market boundaries	• Defining product-market structure • Customer profiles • Industry/distribution/competitor analysis • Market size estimation
Market segmentation ▽	• Deciding which level of the product-market to segment. • Determining how to segment the market.	• Select the basis of segmentation • Form segments • Analyse segments
Define and analyse industry structure ▽	• Defining the competitive area • Understanding competitive structure • Anticipating changes in industry structure	• Sources of competition • Industry structure • Strategic group analysis
Competitive advantage ▽	• Deciding when, where, and how to compete	• Finding opportunity gaps • Cost/differentiation strategy/focus • Good/better/best brand positioning strategy
Market targeting and positioning strategies ▽	• Deciding market scope • Good/better/best brand positioning strategy	• Selecting targets • Positioning for each target • Positioning concept • Marketing mix integration

Source: David W. Cravens (1994), Strategic Marketing, McGraw-Hill Education, Inc.

Marketing strategy orientation

This part of the chapter sheds some light on the different orientations of marketing strategy. Should the development of marketing strategy be oriented by consideration of customers, competitors, or both?

In the 1960s and 1970s, academics and practitioners gave much attention to customers and emphasized the importance of understanding and satisfying customers' needs and wants. In the late 1970s, orientation towards competitors was seen as preferable. In the early 1990s it was argued that organizations need to pay equal attention to both customers and competitors, that is, to adopt a *marketing orientation*.[1] One study examined what orientation of marketing strategy (customer or competitor) will be most effective in which particular business environment, and suggested that a firm's emphasis on a particular orientation may yield different results in different business environments (Ward and Lewandowska, 2008). The study found that customer-oriented marketing strategy seems to be most effective in turbulent environments, while competitor-oriented strategy will be best suited to placid-clustered environments, which are seen by firms as favourable and thus attract greater competition. They suggest that the focus on the marketing orientation must be based on the environmental conditions in which these aspects will work best.

Value co-creation as a strategy orientation

Recently the concept of **value co-creation** has emerged as a marketing orientation that emphasizes the generation and realization of mutual company–customer value. It views markets as forums for organizations, and active customers may share, combine, and renew each other's resources and capabilities to create value through new forms of interaction, service, and learning mechanisms. It differs from the traditional market construct of active company–passive consumer. The emergence of the co-creation of value concept begins by recognizing that the role of customer in the market has changed from isolated to connected, from unaware to informed, from passive to active (Prahalad and Ramaswamy, 2004). The authors believe that the impact of the connected, informed, and active consumer is manifest in many ways.

Value is co-created with customers if and when a customer is able to personalize their experience using a firm's product-service proposition to a level that is best suited to get their job/s or tasks done and which allows the firm to derive greater value from its product-service investment in the form of new knowledge, higher revenues, and/or superior brand value. The net result of the changing role of consumers is that companies can no longer act autonomously, designing products, developing production processes, crafting marketing messages, and monitoring sales channels with little or no interference from customers (Prahalad and Ramaswamy, 2004). Customers seek to exercise their influence in every part of the business. Because the co-creation experience depends highly on individuals, each

---

[1] The contributions of marketing orientation to corporate success have been the subject of several research studies that are discussed later in this chapter (e.g. Kohli and Jaworski, 1990, 1993; Narver and Slater, 1990; Slater and Narver, 1994, 2000, 2004).

person's uniqueness affects the co-creation process as well as the co-creation experience. Co-creation is neither the transfer nor the outsourcing of activities to customers nor a marginal customization of products and services. Nor it is a scripting or staging of customer events around the company's offerings.

Many manufacturers have deployed co-creation as a tool for engaging customers in product design. For example, Nike gives consumers online tools to design their own trainers. At a MacWorld conference in 2007, Sam Lucente, the legendary designer at Hewlett Packard described his epiphany that designers can no longer design products alone using their brilliance and magic. They are no longer in the business of product and service design; instead they are in the business of customer co-creation.

Value co-creation has played an even bigger role at companies such as Cisco and Goldcorp where executives have involved outside resources, such as researchers, academics, and customers, to actually change and redesign the ways things are done inside the firm. Customer-facing functions such as sales or customer service were also opened up to co-creation at companies like Starbucks and Dell Computer. Co-creation became global, as practices reached senior managers at companies in Europe and Asia including Linux (open software), Procter & Gamble's Connect & Develop (dramatically improved research productivity through reliance on a global collaboration platform with people outside P&G), and InnoCentive (a research collective in the pharmaceutical industry).

In relation to services, Adrian et al. (2008) developed a process-based framework for managing/improving value co-creation. The value co-creation process involves the supplier creating superior value propositions, with customers determining value when a service is consumed. Superior value propositions should result in greater opportunities for co-creation and result in benefits (or 'value') being received by the supplier by way of revenues, profits, referrals, etc. By successfully managing value co-creation and exchange, companies can seek to maximize the lifetime value of desirable customer segments. In the same vein, Kristensson et al. (2008) suggested seven key strategies required for the successful involvement of customers in the co-creation of new technology-based services. These are *derivation from user situation, derivation from various roles, analytical tools, apparent benefits, non-use of brainstorming, limited expertise*, and *ensuring heterogeneity*.

An examination of value creation in the context of a service perspective on business and marketing (service logic) specifically analysed the co-creation aspect of value creation and, respectively, the roles of the customer and the firm (Christian, 2011). The research found that it is not that customers are always co-creators of value, but rather that under certain circumstances the service provider gets opportunities to co-create value together with customers.

While value co-creation has been viewed as a customer-based approach, social media could be regarded as both: competitive- and customer-based orientation that contributes to the marketing strategy development.

Social media and intelligence gathering

Social media enables the creation, sharing, and/or exchange of information and ideas via networks and virtual communities. One of the main purposes of social media marketing involves the use of networks such as Facebook and Twitter, COBRAs (consumers' online

		Social presence/media richness		
		Low	**Medium**	**High**
Self-presentation/ self-disclosure	**High**	Blogs	Social networking sites (e.g. Facebook)	Virtual social worlds (e.g. Second Life)
	Low	Collaborative projects (e.g. Wikipedia)	Content communities (e.g. YouTube)	Virtual game worlds (e.g. World of Warcraft)

2.3 Classification of Social Media by Social Presence/Media Richness and Self-Presentation/Self-Disclosure
Source: Andreas Kaplan and Michael Haenlein (2010), 'Users of the world, unite! The challenges and opportunities of social media', Business Horizons, 53, 59–68.

brand-related activities) and eWOM (electronic word of mouth) to successfully advertise to and interact with clients online. Kaplan and Haenlein (2010) grouped the various forms of social media under two dimensions: self-presentation/self-disclosure and social presence/ media richness. The combination of these dimensions is shown in Figure 2.3.

Through establishing their own presence on social network sites, brands can interact with individuals, and this personal interaction can instil a feeling of loyalty into followers and potential customers. Procter & Gamble was an early adopter of social media; now all its businesses have sites aimed at specific markets and communities with the main value that they drive product sales, rather than 'illuminate' the consumers world'.

The strategic implications of social media have yet to be fully appreciated and many businesses are wrestling with how to work with social media from a marketing perspective. Most tend to use them to highlight their brands, monitor consumer conversations about their brands and rival brands (known as 'sentiment'), and target advertising. Issues of privacy mean brands cannot directly target individuals via social media or directly monitor their conversations. Instead social media owners, most noticeably Facebook, allow advertisers to target related ads to conversations without the advertiser knowing directly who they are.

Social networking platforms may also include a great amount of information on what products/services prospective clients might be interested in. For example, Nike introduced its 'MakeItCount' social media campaign in 2012 by launching a YouTube video about two 'YouTubers' travelling 34,000 miles to visit 16 cities in 13 countries.

The primary point, in the context of this chapter, is that the customer-based benefits of social media have a flip side; they have been utilized by many companies for intelligence gathering. Competitors join other companies' Twitter, Facebook, or LinkedIn listings to monitor their activities, gauge strategic directions, and track 'sentiment'. They classify it in this regard as a primary competitive tool and sometimes they employ agencies such as Dunnhumby, Cardlytics, Weve, and AIMIA to do this for them—to 'data monetize' as part of strategy. Coosto, for example, is a European company that specializes in competitor monitoring and competitive intelligence from social media to enable organizations to adapt to their competitor news from different sources and allow them to take advantage of what consumers specifically like or dislike about a competitor's brands.

There are several reasons why organizations should monitor the online output of their competitors. Social media monitoring tools look at a vast amount of information so they can create some interesting information that will help organizations to target areas for development (Windels, 2013). For example, by evaluating the sentiment of the comments surrounding a competitor's brands through social media, companies can focus on negative points brought forward by consumers. Social media monitoring can also bring to light influential authors (bloggers) who frequently discuss a competitor, marketplace, or the company's own brand. This creates opportunities for brands to make contact with key influencers and demonstrate why their product is superior to those offered by competitors. Similarly, by analysing the followers who are discussing the company's own brand compared with a competitor's brands, a company will have a better understanding of their potential target audience. This information can change a current marketing strategy and influence future ones.

With these multiple benefits and activities of social media, one can argue that the use of social media in business could be viewed as a marketing orientation that is driven by consideration of both customers and competitors. This strategic view is to highlight the valuable contributions social media can make to the marketing strategy development.

 Mini Case 2.1   Five steps to social sales success[2]

Social media can help marketers cosy up to potential customers and deliver soaring results

1. Social selling

No marketer would ever dare to deny the importance of social media. But ask them what the purpose of their brand's social media activity is and they will most likely say raising brand awareness, or engaging with a target audience, or perhaps customer service and support. It is very unlikely they will state that the primary function of their social media strategy is sales.

While it is clear that the ultimate goal of most marketing activity is to increase sales, much like PR, the role social media campaigns play in generating leads and boosting the top line is often viewed as indirect. But The Whiteoaks Consultancy managing director James Kelliher says this does not need to be the case. 'Unlike traditional media relations, where the majority of our industry has always argued that a tangible link between PR and sales can never—and should never—be established, with digital communications it is completely possible to not only establish this link, but to make it the primary objective of any campaign', he says.

A brand's social media presence can directly influence sales when used for content creation and distribution, monitoring, mining data and engaging in conversations with the aim of encouraging target audiences to take the actions that engage and qualify them as real sales leads. 'Once engaged and qualified, via information provided by the prospect during the process, the intelligence can be passed on to the organization's sales function to contact and convert these prospects into real revenue opportunities', says Kelliher.

[2] John Manning, *The Marketer Magazine*, July/August (2013), pp.44–5.

2. Meaningful conversations

Some within the industry remain dubious about whether social media is a useful tool in a B2B environment, and this is generally because B2B sales cycles are often longer, more complex, and of higher value—in this context a tweet or a status update just won't do. 'Complex products require actual human service, and a trusted adviser to guide prospective customers through the buying cycle', says Hearsay Social European director Peter Caryotis.

Artesian Solutions chief executive Andrew Yates says that in instances such as these it is vital that organizations build a strong affinity with buyers. 'The only way to build strong customer relationships that ultimately translate into revenue is to shape conversations around the customer, review the brand experience and enhance services. The way to successfully achieve this is by obtaining intelligence about customers' and prospects' opinions', says Yates.

Social media might not be the primary platform for developing such relationships, but the wealth of information smart marketers can derive from it can provide the basis for getting closer to prospective clients. 'People share some of the most meaningful moments of their lives on social media, providing an unprecedented opportunity for salespeople to get to know and communicate with their customers and prospects', says Caryotis. 'Social media monitoring alerts brands to the important events in the lives of people in their network, so they know when to reach out to the right people and have the context they need to have more meaningful conversations'.

3. Sales signals

Research by member-based advisory service CEB (Corporate Executive Board Company) shows that using social media to strengthen relationships has the potential to increase sales by more than 13 per cent. Integrating social media intelligence into the sales cycle does not need to be a complex process. Omarketing managing director Rose Ross explains how Twitter can be used to this purpose. 'By listening, you get to know your prospects on a personal level, identifying opportunities to connect and establish rapport', she says. 'If your prospect tweets that she is an Arsenal fan, for example, and you have a spare ticket you can invite her to the game. If she tweets that she loves a certain kind of biscuit you might send her a pack with your business card. If she has the flu, you can reply that you hope she feels better', she adds. 'The list goes on. Twitter savvy sales professionals can and do use Twitter to create a multitude of opportunities to strengthen relationships with existing and potential customers.'

As well as providing an 'in' with an existing prospect, information posted on social media can immediately identify a new potential customer. 'In the social era the same type of updates people love to share on Facebook and LinkedIn happen to be buying signals for many B2C relationship-based sellers and offer opportunities for B2B sales reps to build rapport', says Caryotis.

4. Don't sell

While Ross is enthusiastic about the potential of Twitter to strengthen relationships with prospects, she insists brands must not overtly use the platform to sell to them. 'Prolific tweeter Stephen Fry and many others have pointed out that the purpose of Twitter is to be social', she says. 'And companies that use Twitter only to broadcast their own sales and marketing messages are in fact being antisocial.' The same principle applies to other social platforms. 'Any form of selling to people on social networks is frowned upon', says Return On Digital chief executive Guy Levine. 'Campaigns have to be well thought out; get it wrong and it could go "anti-viral", creating a reputation management nightmare.'

Zoodikers Consulting managing director Katie King echoes the sentiment. 'If you are using social media for new business, brands must avoid tweets and posts that are too commercial', she says. 'Instead, get to know your audience and find out what they are interested in, what's worrying them' and who they partner with.'

---

5. Platform hopping

The range of social networks seems to be ever expanding, each one attracting a different demographic and being used by its members for different purposes. This can make it tempting for marketers to stick to a particular network in an attempt to reach an audience appropriate to them. This is most clearly the case when distinguishing between B2B and B2C leads. 'There are specific social networks targeted for business use, such as LinkedIn, which will always yield more targeted B2B leads, and similarly Facebook for B2C, but Twitter tends to be a mix', says Levine.

While on the face of it targeting an individual on a business network with B2B sales in mind makes perfect sense, King says that an understanding of the dynamic of different networks and communicating with prospects across the range can be more beneficial. 'The more astute social media managers will interconnect and cross-reference their social media platforms', says King. 'For example, LinkedIn can be used to find connections, grow relationships, and showcase expertise in open and closed groups, while Twitter is more personable and interactive. By data mining to find the right decision makers on LinkedIn you are then able to follow and interact with them on Twitter.'

Examples of successful social media marketing campaigns are numerous (Cassinelli, 2013). And it has been reported that of the top ten factors that correlate with a strong Google organic search, seven are social media dependent (Mahapatra, 2013). This means that if brands are less or non-active on social media, they tend to show up less on Google searches.

There is little doubt that social media has introduced substantial and pervasive changes to communication between organizations, communities, and individuals and, as a consequence, has influenced marketing strategies. Customers no longer want to be talked at; instead, they want firms to listen, appropriately engage, and respond. A useful typology has been introduced— the 'honeycomb framework'—which defines social media by using seven functional building 'blocks' (Kietzmann et al., 2011): identity, conversations, sharing, presence, relationships, reputation, and groups. By analysing these seven blocks, firms can monitor and understand how their social media activities vary in terms of function and impact, so as to develop a consistent social media strategy based on the appropriate balance of building blocks for their community.

Marketing orientation and corporate success

Marketing has traditionally been defined as a social process by which individuals and groups obtain what they want through creating, offering, and exchanging products and services of value with others.[3] Another view has seen marketing as organizational activities that facilitate and expedite satisfying exchange relationships in a dynamic environment through the creation, distribution, promotion, and pricing of goods, services, and ideas (Dibb et al., 2012). A different view suggests that the 'marketing' function in organizations, besides being responsible for the content, process, and implementation of marketing strategy at the product-market level, plays a significant role in the strategy development process and the determination of strategy content at the business and corporate levels (Varadarajan and

---

[3] For more information about marketing as exchange process you can consult the classical article by Bagozzi (1975) who argues that the core of marketing is 'exchange'.

Jayachandran, 2000). The strategic role of marketing arises from the boundary-spanning nature of the marketing function (i.e. its interactions with consumers and competitors). This view emphasizes that marketing has an important role to play in strategy development and corporate success not only at the functional level, but also at the business and corporate levels. Marketing, therefore, can be categorized into **operational marketing**, the classical commercial process of achieving a target market share through the use of tactical means related to the 4Ps, and **strategic marketing,** to specify the firm's mission, define objectives, elaborate a development strategy, and ensure a balanced structure of the product portfolio (Lambin 2000). The specific roles of operational and strategic marketing are shown in Table 2.2.

It must be emphasized here that the marketing 'concept' or 'orientation' is not a second definition of marketing. The marketing concept is a way of thinking: a management philosophy guiding an organization's overall activities. This philosophy which holds the key to achieving organizational goals consists of the company being more effective than competitors in creating, delivering, and communicating customer value to its chosen target (Kotler and Keller, 2011). The marketing concept defines the set of activities developed by organizations to permanently monitor, analyse, and respond to market changes such as consumer preference, faster technological growth, and growing competitive rivalry (Nwokah, 2008).

Foley and Fahy (2009) argue that in response to the operationalization problem of the marketing concept, the seminal work of Kohli and Jaworski (1990) developed the three pillars of the marketing concept into precise aspects (manifestation) of what they call a 'market orientation', and for the first time organizations were given a useful template for assessing how market-oriented they are. A company is market-oriented (Dawar, 2013) if it has mastered the art of listening to customers, understanding their needs, and developing products and services that meet those needs. Believing that this process yields competitive advantage, companies spend billions of dollars on focus groups, surveys, and social media. But the reality is that companies are increasingly finding success not by being responsive to customers' stated preferences but by defining what customers are looking for and shaping their 'criteria of purchase'. Zara, the fast-fashion retailer, places only a small number of products on the shelf for relatively short periods of time—hundreds of units per month compared with a typical retailer's thousands per season. The company is set up to respond to actual customer purchase behaviour, rapidly making thousands more of those products that fly off the shelf and culling those that don't.

Table 2.2 Contrasting Operational and Strategic Marketing

Operational Marketing	Strategic Marketing
Action-oriented	Analysis-oriented
Existing opportunities	New opportunities
Non-product variables	Product market variables
Stable environment	Dynamic environment
Reactive behaviour	Proactive behaviour
Day-to-day management	Longer-range management
Marketing department	Cross-functional organization

Source: Jean-Jacques Lambin (2000), Market-driven Management: Strategic and Operational, MacMillan Business.

How significant is the adoption of a *market orientation* on the firm's strategy and business performance? While this question has been extensively examined in the marketing literature, the results of empirical research vary. The pioneering work by Kohli and Jaworski (1990, 1993) found that a market orientation provides a unifying focus for the efforts and projects of individuals, thereby leading to superior performance. Similar results were found by Narver and Slater (1990). They concluded that a market orientation has, in some cases, a substantial positive effect on profitability. Further research by Slater and Narver (1994, 2000, 2004) found that a market-oriented culture provides the foundation for value-creating capabilities which enables businesses to consistently deliver superior value (that is, competitive advantage which leads to the achievement of superior performance) to customers. Other studies produced inconsistent results. Ward and Lewandowska (2008) conducted a comprehensive review of research that examined the relationship between marketing orientation and corporate success. Indeed, many companies today are eager to create superior value to consumers (Ward and Lewandowska, 2008); Volvo sets the bar up high on safety, shaping customers' expectations for features from seatbelts to airbags to side-impact protection systems and active pedestrian detection; Febreze redefined the way customers perceive a clean house; and Nike made customers believe in themselves.

Despite the credibility and importance of market orientation, it is still not being fully realized by practitioners (Mason and Harris, 2005). While many perceive their companies to be customer-orientated, the evidence is to the contrary and the development of a genuine market orientation remains elusive. The study found that executives often develop skewed, inaccurate, or incomplete assessments of the market orientation of their company. It has been suggested too that the proof of a positive relationship between market orientation and performance is not manifest (Foley and Fahy, 2009).

Competitive marketing strategy: various perspectives

What is competitive marketing strategy? Should it be viewed as a typical marketing strategy which is oriented by the consideration of competition in the marketplace? Or should it be defined as a 'business' strategy that is driven by the market orientation. To answer this question we critically analyse the definitions of 'competitive strategy' and 'marketing strategy';[4] then we can establish what 'competitive marketing strategy' is.

While corporate strategy sets the broad direction for the company, the business 'competitive' strategy details how a sustainable competitive advantage can be achieved, allowing the strategic business unit (SBU) to contribute to the overall corporate objectives (Doyle and Stern, 2006). Aaker and McLoughlin (2010) noted that business strategy, which is sometimes termed competitive strategy, can be defined in terms of six elements or dimensions: (1) the product market in which the business is to compete, (2) the level of investment, (3) the functional area strategies needed to compete in the selected market, (4) the strategic assets or skills that underlie the strategy and provide the SCA, (5) the allocation of resources to the business units, and (6) the development of the synergistic effects across the businesses (see Mini Case 2.2).

---

[4] Refer to the definitions of marketing strategy discussed earlier in this chapter.

Mini Case 2.2 How to align marketing with business strategy[5]

Marketing is increasingly woven into the fabric of every part of the business. Muireann Bolger looks at how marketing can strengthen ties across departments to achieve wider strategic goals.

Many marketers have an instinctive urge to stand apart from the rest of the pack in their drive to deliver unique and creative work. But when it comes to business strategy, this lone wolf approach can backfire. Marketing can come to be seen as a distant, troublesome relative rather than an integral part of a close-knit team.

Millward Brown chief global analyst, Nigel Hollis, explains that a classic mistake of marketers is to assume their sole responsibility is to create brand awareness. 'There is a trend in the industry to say that marketing is about making a brand salient. That is true on one hand, but the goal is not just about name recognition or buzz. You can't have a strong brand unless you have a strong business', he warns.

The number one priority of a chief marketing officer (CMO) is to ensure marketing is aligned to the business strategy, says Sage chief marketing officer Amanda Jobbins. 'Marketing is, by definition, strategic. No strategy conversation should take place without marketing at the table'. Marketers who fail to work across all parts of the business and take the lead in shaping strategic direction will quickly be perceived as out of step with other departments.

Business discord

In-house perceptions of marketing generally seem to reflect this view. In a 2011 study of 600 chief executives and 'decision makers' by the Fournaise Marketing Group, 73 per cent said that CMOs lack business credibility and the ability to generate sufficient business growth.

So how can marketers ensure their activities are better aligned with wider business objectives? The first step is to collaborate with other departments and to cultivate a common understanding, explains APS business services director Ann McLaughlin, 'You have got to develop a high profile within the organization and you have to understand your counterparts in other departments–what they are doing and what their goals are. In this way, marketers can work with other departments in a more strategic way', she explains.

The sales department is the function most closely linked with marketing, but like many close relationships, this bond can quickly descend into rivalry. Martin Moll, Honda Europe marketing director, explains that marketers need to be clear about their fundamental connection to sales. 'Marketing's sole function and purpose is as a service provision to the business—it needs to end up helping sales. In terms of the overall direction and strategy, every business seeks to sell'.

'Problems tend to arise when the sales team concentrates on short to medium-term targets while the marketing department is more focused on the creation of long-term brand awareness', explains Cognosis senior manager, Amandeep Deol. This can create a misalignment between the goals of the two departments. Deol points out that often the sales team only engages with marketing at the execution stage of a campaign, but better results can be gained if it is included at an earlier stage of the strategy process. Presentations and feedback can help both teams understand the objectives of both departments and how they can collaborate more effectively, says Deol. In some cases, she adds, it may be useful if the marketing and sales directors share KPIs in order to cultivate a better mutual understanding of their roles.

[5] *Muireann Bolger,* **The Marketer***, November/December (2013), p.35.*

This view seems to see the competitive dimension of business strategy rather implicitly, but others have explicitly defined business strategy as a competitive strategy. Business strategy, which is often called competitive strategy, focuses on improving the competitive position of a company's products or services within the industry or market segment that the company or business unit serves (Wheelen and Hunger, 2012). Two alternative competitive strategy orientations will now be reviewed.

Marketing-oriented competitive strategy: allows marketing to decide the direction pursued by a business, as well as adopting a supporting role in relation to strategy. Marketing can help to find a match between firms and their environment by deciding (1) what kinds of business firms may enter in the future, and (2) how the chosen field of endeavour may be successfully conducted in a competitive environment, by pursuing product, price, promotion, and distribution perspectives to position the company's offerings competitively in the target market/s. IKEA has been transformed from a local mail-order furniture business into one of the key retail furnishing businesses in the world by having a clear differential advantage over competitors and providing value-for-money products.

Technology-oriented competitive strategy: involves serving high-income markets with a flow of new, preferably unique, high-performance and high-technology products. Apple and Samsung are typical examples of the large corporations that pursue technology leadership in their industry. Competitive strategies adopted by those companies have been developed to flag up their substantial investment in technology and R&D activities. In fact, technology and competitive strategy are inseparable and technological decisions are of fundamental importance to businesses as a valuable source of competitive advantage.

These definitions of competitive strategy and the previously presented definitions of marketing strategy should support the view that **competitive strategy** is a business strategy that exists at the SBU level and deals primarily with the question of competitive position, while **marketing strategy** is arguably seen as a functional strategy that is limited to a specific set of actions/functions within an organization. A comparison of competitive and marketing strategies is shown in Table 2.3.

From these points, it could be argued that an organization's development of a functional strategy is dictated by the SBU strategy of its parent. For example, an SBU following differentiation strategy requires a manufacturing functional strategy that emphasizes a sophisticated quality assurance process, a human resource functional strategy that emphasizes the hiring of a highly skilled workforce, and a marketing functional strategy that emphasizes distribution channel 'pull' using advertising to increase consumer demand, rather than 'push' using promotional allowances to retailers. If an SBU, however, is to follow a low-cost strategy, a different set of functional strategies will be required to support the business strategy. If a company choose to adopt different competitive strategies in different markets, then functional strategies have to vary accordingly. Ford, for example, has a different set of functional strategies in the Middle East than those adopted in the UK. Ford is seen as a differentiated car producer in the Middle East, while this is not the case in Britain.

Based on this critical analysis of the various definitions of 'competitive strategy' and 'marketing strategy', our view, which recognizes marketing as a business philosophy, is that competitive marketing strategy cannot be seen as a functional strategy developed to serve the

Table 2.3 Illustrative Comparison of Business and Marketing Strategies

	Corporate and Business Units Strategy	Marketing Strategy
Perspective	Organizational and/or competitive focus, often with a heavy industry orientation	Customer and/or product focus, often with a heavy end-user orientation
Decisions	• Mission determination • Allocation of business resources to business units • Acquisition/diversification • Elimination of business units • Product development and management • Selection and implementation of SBU strategies	• Identification of market opportunities • Choice of target market(s) • Marketing programme positioning strategy • Product, distribution, price, and promotion strategies
Strategic focus	• How to gain and keep strategic advantage • How to determine business strategies • How to organize the business for planning/control	• How to divide product/markets into segments • What segment(s) to serve • How to position for each segment
Information needs	• Financial performance • Business opportunity assessment • Market performance and forecasts • Competitors' strategies and performance	• Financial performance by market target and product type • Customer/prospect description and requirements • Market position and forecasts • Competitors' marketing strategies and performance

Source: David W. Cravens (1994), Strategic Marketing, McGraw-Hill Education, Inc.

4Ps only. It should rather be seen as a marketing-oriented business strategy. We suggest the following definition of competitive marketing strategy:

> Competitive marketing strategy is '*a market-oriented approach that establishes a profitable competitive position for the firm against all forces that determine industry competition by continuously creating and developing a sustainable competitive advantage (SCA) from the potential sources that exist in a firm's value chain*'.

Planning frameworks for making strategy

Strategy is the outcome of an organization's planning activities through a process in which strategy is developed, approved, implemented, and evaluated. This process of strategy making has been described over the years in different terms such as: 'budgeting,' 'long-range planning,' 'strategic planning,' '**strategic market planning**,' 'strategic management', and 'strategic market management'. These terms are often used interchangeably in the literature. They can, however, be put in a historical context as four key phases in the evolution of the management planning discipline (Wheelen and Hunger, 2012). The focus of our discussion here is on the third and fourth phases only.

Strategic planning

Strategic planning and associated concepts were born amid a flurry of optimism and industrial growth in the 1960s and early 1970s. There are several reasons for this, perhaps the most notable of which is that, largely because of the growing and continuously buoyant markets of the 1950s and 1960s and the turbulence of the early 1970s, many managers needed to find a radically different approach to the running of their business.

Ansoff (1965) was one of the first scholars in the strategy field to define strategic planning (which he referred to then as strategic decisions). Strategic planning was later defined as the process which defines the long-term objectives of a company and the means by which these objectives are to be achieved. Planning horizons may, however, vary from one company to another and from industry to industry. For example, in a retail company, a 3-year plan may be appropriate. In companies operating in the oil industry, planning horizons may be as long as 10–15 years. The above definition may also give the impression that strategic planning and strategic thinking are similar. They are not. Whereas strategic thinking involves creative and entrepreneurial insights into a company and its environment, strategic planning has often degenerated into frameworks for the systematic and comprehensive analysis of known options. Strategic thinking is a shaping process in which a reflective conversation with a situation takes place in order to reduce the complexity of such a situation, while strategy making is a process of continuous adaptation between the industry environment and the organization's capabilities. For example, the management of Hewlett Packard (HP), after a careful study of trends in its market, found that the company needed to stop thinking of itself as a collection of stand-alone products with a primary focus on instrumentation and PC hardware. Instead, the top management felt that the company needed to become a customer-focused and integrated provider of information appliances, highly reliable information technology infrastructure, and e-commerce services. A comprehensive framework of strategic planning, which illustrates the firm's internal and external appraisal of its environment, is shown in Figure 2.4.

2.4 Strategic Planning Process

Source: Henry Mintzberg (1994a), The Rise and Fall of Strategic Planning, Pearson Education, Inc., Upper Saddle River, NJ.

Strategic planning as a model of strategy making has its supporters. For example, it has been pointed out that strategic planning is strongly related to improved financial performance of businesses, evidenced by several research studies and practical surveys of firms (Wheelen and Hunger, 2012). The validity of this model, however, was subject to many criticisms (see: Mintzberg 1990, 1994a, 1994b). Ocasio and Joseph (2008) claim that the role and importance of strategic planning in corporate practice remains a subject of controversy for both academics and practitioners. The contribution of strategic planning to firm innovation and competitiveness was often questioned, and the critiques culminated with Mintzberg's writings on the subject. Also the debate in this area, which focused on whether strategic plans are effective in setting strategic directions and whether firms that undertook strategic planning out-performed no-planning companies, was mixed (Whittington and Cailluet, 2008).

Despite this controversial debate, strategic planning processes are still among the most demanding tasks that managers need in today's complex marketplace (Eppler and Platts, 2009). Since 1996, Bain & Co's survey of management tools has regularly reported strategic planning being used by around 80 per cent of its responding firms, and in 2007 found it the most popular tool for all, with an 11-year record of 88 per cent of companies using it (Whittington and Cailluet, 2008). Strategic planning can be an overwhelming challenge: to take into account, simultaneously, the developments of technologies and societal trends, the behaviour of competitors, customers, and regulators, all within a changing legal, environmental, and financial framework. When this is compounded with time pressure, environmental uncertainty, and internal tensions, making sound and effective strategic decisions becomes essential and requires these decisions to be made in a systematic manner.

Strategic market planning was added to the lexicon of strategic concepts by Abell and Hammond (1979). The inclusion of the word 'market' serves to emphasize that strategy development should be driven by the forces of market environment rather than by internal factors. Strategic market planning could be defined as the managerial process that entails analysis, formulation, and evaluation of strategy, and that enables an organization to achieve its objectives by finding a strategic fit between its capabilities and the environmental opportunities.

The planning side of strategy is concerned with functional decisions related to the marketing mix elements but there is still a significant role to be played by marketing in the strategic planning process. While strategic market planning should always look outward and keep the business in tune with its environment, the lead role in achieving this is played by marketing. As a general management responsibility, marketing embraces the interpretations of the environment and the crucial choices of which customers to serve, which competitors to challenge, and with which product characteristics the business will compete. Marketing, in fact, has a presence at the corporation's three organizational levels. At the corporate level, marketing can influence organizational culture, while at the SBU level marketing guides the company's competitive positioning, and at the operational level marketing takes care of the 4Ps planning.

Strategic management

Strategic management was introduced in the late 1970s in response to the criticisms of strategic planning. Strategic management stems from an assumption that the planning cycle is inadequate to deal with the rapid rate of change that can occur in the environment facing the firm. Strategic management was defined as a set of managerial decisions and actions that determines the long-run performance of a corporation (Wheelen and Hunger, 2012). To cope with fast-developing threats and opportunities, firms' strategic decisions need to be made outside the planning cycle (Aaker and McLoughlin, 2010).

In the business literature, Ansoff et al. (1976) were the first academics to transform the concept of strategic planning into strategic management. In the world of business, General Electric Corporation (GEC), one of the pioneers of strategic planning, led the transition from strategic planning to strategic management during the 1980s. Because strategy formulation and implementation are of equal importance, and interdependent, it has been suggested that the largest companies in the world all have to take strategic management seriously. The strategic management process and its four elements—environmental scanning, strategy formulation, strategy implementation, and evaluation and control—are shown in Figure 2.5.

Research on the validity and credibility of the strategic management model has produced conflicting views. While many studies revealed that strategic management, in general, leads to improved performance, others have criticized the concept and its benefits to business organizations. An assessment of the development and evolution of strategic management in the past forty years reported that, while strategic management should have grown up years ago to overcome its theoretical and application problems, it still has distinctive contributions to make to business thinking and practice (Cummings and Daellenbach, 2009).

Strategic market management emerged as an extension of the term strategic management to emphasize that strategy development should be informed by the market environment rather than being internally oriented. Aaker and McLoughlin (2010) defined strategic market management as a system designed to help organizations in developing,

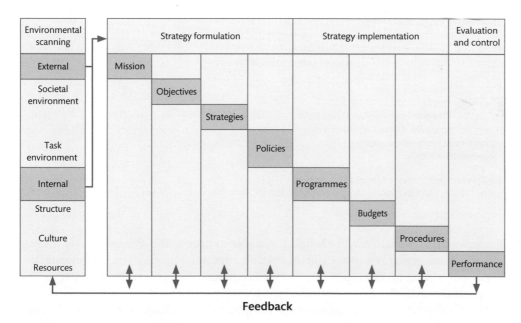

2.5 Strategic Management Framework

Source: Thomas L. Wheelen and David J. Hunger (2012), *Strategic Management and Business Policy*, 13/e, Pearson Education, Inc.

EXTERNAL ANALYSIS	SELF-ANALYSIS
• **Customer analysis** Segments, motivations, unmet needs • **Competitive analysis** Identity, strategic groups, performance, objectives, strategies, culture, cost structure, strengths, weaknesses • **Industry analysis** Size, projected growth, industry structure, entry barriers, cost structure, distribution system, trends, key success factors • **Environmental analysis** Technological, governmental, economic, cultural, demographic, scenarios, information need areas ↓	• **Performance analysis** Return on assets, market share, product value and performance, relative cost, new product activity, manager development and performance, employee attitude and performance, product portfolio analysis • **Determinants of strategic options** Past and current strategy, strategic problems, organizational capabilities and constraints, financial resources and constraints, flexibility, strengths, weaknesses ↓
Opportunities, threats, and strategic questions	Strategic strengths, weaknesses, problems, constraints, and questions
↓	↓
STRATEGY IDENTIFICATION AND SELECTION	

• **Specify the mission**
• **Identify strategic alternatives**
      • Investment strategies by product market
        Withdraw, milk, hold, or enter/grow
      • Strategies to gain sustainable competitive advantage
        Functional area strategies
        Assets and skills
• **Select strategy**
      • Consider strategic questions
      • Evaluate strategic alternatives
• **Implementation—the operating plan**
• **Review of strategies**

2.6 Overview of Strategic Market Management
Source: David A. Aaker and Damien McLoughlin (2010), Strategic Market Management, John Wiley & Sons, Inc.

implementing, evaluating, and changing business strategies. This system will (1) provide vision to businesses, (2) monitor and understand a dynamic environment, (3) generate strategic options, and (4) develop strategies based on sustainable competitive advantages. This system is shown in Figure 2.6.

Strategic marketing management was originated to highlight the lead role of marketing as the primary link between the organization and its environment, and also to appreciate the pivotal importance of marketing in formulating and directing the implementation of the overall organization strategies. Marketing is likely to play an analytical and diagnostic role in the search for competitive advantages where the business's unique capabilities match the key success factors of one or more product markets. And since strategic marketing activity generates imperatives for organizational transformation, marketing considerations are also the starting point for the strategic management process.

The latest thinking: the uncomfortable zone of strategy

'A detailed plan may be comforting, but it's not a strategy', Martin (2014) says. He believes that strategic planning attempts to make strategy feel comfortable, when in reality fear, discomfort, and uncertainty are intrinsic to good strategy making. If managers are entirely comfortable with their strategy, there's a strong chance it is not very good. In fact, managers have to be *uncomfortable* and *apprehensive*: True strategy is about placing bets and making hard choices. Managers need to accept that good strategy is not the product of hours of careful research and modelling leading to an inevitable and perfect conclusion. Instead, it's the result of a simple and quite rough-and-ready process of thinking through what it would take to achieve what you want and then assessing whether it's realistic to try. If managers just accept that, then maybe they can keep strategy where it should be: '*outside the comfort zone*'.

The whole idea is that strategy making is uncomfortable; it's about taking risks and facing the unknown. Unsurprisingly, managers try to turn it into a comfortable set of planning and modelling activities. These sets of activities are seen by Martin (2014) as comfort traps. He identified three comfort traps:

(1) that of strategic planning,

(2) that of cost-based thinking, and

(3) that of self-referential strategy framework

To escape these traps, Martin (2014) suggests that executives should reconcile themselves to feeling uncomfortable, and follow three rules.

1. *Keep it simple. Capture your strategy in a one-pager that addresses where you will play and how you will win.*

2. *Don't look for perfection. Strategy isn't about finding answers. It's about placing bets and shortening odds.*

3. *Make the logic explicit. Be clear about what must change for you to achieve your strategic goal.*

For an open debate, HBR published an interaction section in April (2014: p.20) '*Strategy Should Be Uncomfortable*'? Three practitioners/consultants commented on the issue, and there was common agreement as they suggested:

> This article helps explain why I feel it may make more sense for the strategic planning function to report through marketing than through finance. Marketing is more concerned with the

consumer and less prone to falling into some of those traps. That being said, I still think strategic planning should report directly to the CEO.

Gerald C. Nanninga, principal consultant, Planninga from Nanninga.

I appreciate Rule 3 (make the logic explicit). As a consultant I see so much wishful thinking masquerading as plausible strategy. The logical framework approach is an emerging best practice for strategy design, because it incorporates causal thinking in a simple way that gets everyone on the same page, and exposes flaky thinking.

Terry Schmidt, founder of Strategic Planning Academy.

Strategy should not be seen as a straitjacket but rather as a road map clearly pointing out the goal and describing the terrain and the chosen route under the known or assumed conditions.

Peter Sørensen, owner, PSB-Management.

Strategy is a unique challenge, and although it might be expected that strategists opt for a unique approach to strategy development and evaluation, incentives lead most of them in the opposite direction (Zenger, 2013). The author refers to the financial markets which undervalue companies with unique and complex strategies—even though these strategies are often the most valuable. This is because unique or complex strategies take longer to evaluate, so analysts often avoid assessing them. Simple strategies, though, are the most easily copied and, therefore, the least sustainable.

The quality of a strategy is extremely difficult to develop and assess—even for the manager doing it. To ease the challenge, strategies may be categorized into two dimensions (Zenger, 2013): quality (*measured by a strategy's ability to generate cash over the long run*), and ease of evaluation (*measured by the effort required to estimate the future performance*). These two dimensions generate four potential strategy categories (shown in Figure 2.7).

Quality of strategy

2.7 Corporate Strategies Along Two Dimensions of the Challenge: Quality of Strategy and Ease of Evaluation.

Source: Todd Zenger (2013), 'Strategy: The Uniqueness Challenge', **Harvard Business Review**, 91(November), pp.52–8.

Two of these categories are likely to be poorly populated and therefore of limited interest. *Type 1* strategies are high in quality and easy to assess and are rare because a strategy which is easily evaluated is typically easy to replicate. *Type 4* strategies are low in quality and difficult to assess making them universally unattractive. That leaves strategy makers with a choice between low-quality strategies that are easier to assess (*Type 2*) and high-quality strategies that are difficult to assess (*Type 3*). That is the nature of strategy and there is no easy algorithm to apply for a solution of which one to choose.

Conclusion

The current view of the development of marketing strategy is consistent with the early literature about the marketing concept, which is recognized as not only a set of functions but also a guiding philosophy for all of an organization's activities. At the functional level, the marketing manager is to influence the level, timing, and character of demand in a way that will help achieve the organization's marketing objectives. The marketing manager must focus on the development of the organization's positioning strategy and marketing mix programmes. At the strategic (SBU) level, marketing as a business philosophy can play a significant role in guiding all of an organization's activities. Therefore, we defined competitive marketing strategy in this book as 'a market-oriented approach that establishes a profitable competitive position for the firm against all forces that determine industry competition by continuously creating and developing a sustainable competitive advantage (SCA) from the potential sources that exist in a firm's value chain'.

Summary

This chapter has reviewed the nature, concept, and definitions of marketing strategy. The chapter has also discussed the various marketing orientations, and the contributions of value co-creation and social media to the development of marketing strategy. Marketing strategy is typically seen as having developed through three sequential phases. First, the core company strategy will be selected and the marketing objectives and the broad focus for achieving them will be identified. Secondly, market segments and target consumers are chosen, and the company's differential advantage in serving the customer targets better than the competition is identified. The identification of targets and the differential advantage constitute the creation of the competitive positioning of the company and its offerings. Finally, the marketing department is concerned with establishing the marketing mix programmes that can convey both the positioning and the products/services themselves to the target market.

Key terms

- **Business strategy:** is usually developed at the strategic business unit (SBU) level and emphasizes improvement of the competitive position of a corporation's products or services in the specific industry or market segment served by that SBU.

- **Corporate strategy:** describes a company's overall direction in terms of its general attitude toward growth and the management of its various businesses and product lines to achieve a balanced portfolio of products and services.

- **Functional strategy:** is concerned with maximizing resource productivity. Within the constraints of the corporate and business strategies around them, functional departments, such as marketing, finance, and production, develop strategies to pull together their various activities and competencies to improve performance.

- **Market positioning strategy:** is the employment of the organization's product, distribution, price, and promotion activities to position the company's offerings against the competitor's offerings in meeting the needs and wants of the target market. The positioning strategy provides the unifying concept for deciding the role of each component of the marketing mix.

- **Marketing concept:** is 'a way of thinking—a management philosophy guiding an organization's overall activities. This philosophy which holds the key to achieving organizational goals consists of the company being more effective than competitors in creating, delivering, and communicating customer value to its chosen target' (Kotler, 2000).

- **Marketing targeting strategy:** is a strategy that aims to select groups of consumers (or organizations) the management wishes to serve in the product market.

- **Strategic market planning:** is defined as the managerial process that entails analysis, formulation, and evaluation of strategy and that enables an organization to achieve its objectives by developing and maintaining a strategic fit between the organization's capabilities and the threats and opportunities arising from its changing environment.

- **Strategic marketing:** is an intelligence focused and led process that has both an internal and an external dimension, which utilizes the skills of competitive intelligence officers who work with marketing managers and strategists to establish trust-based relationships throughout the partnership arrangement, which . . . ultimately results in the organization fulfilling its mission statement (Trim and Lee, 2008).

- **Strategic thinking:** strategic thinking involves creative and entrepreneurial insights into a company and its environment. It is a shaping process in which a reflective conversation with a situation takes place in order to reduce the complexity of this situation.

Discussion questions

1. It has been argued that the value co-creation concept will change the way organizations develop their marketing strategy. To what extent do you agree or disagree with this argument and how you would assess the contribution of value co-creation to marketing strategy.

2. Discuss the relationship between corporate, business, and marketing strategies in relation to a market of your choice. Provide illustrative examples to support your discussion.

3. Marketing has always been seen as the function responsible for the management of the 4Ps, but in the last two decades it was also viewed as a business philosophy that guides the organization's overall activities. Write a report debating these two views.

4. Social media has been used by many companies as a communications tool that connects the organization to its target consumers. How do you see the contribution of social media to the marketing strategy development?

5. Discuss the strategic marketing management process and assess the extent to which you agree/disagree that this process is of real value to large organizations.

Online resource centre

 Visit the Online Resource Centre for this book for lots of interesting additional material at: <www.oxfordtextbooks.co.uk/orc/west3e/>

References and further reading

Aaker, David A. and Damien McLoughlin (2010), *Strategic Market Management* (New York: John Wiley.).

Abell, Derek F. and John S. Hammond (1979), *Strategic Market Planning: Problems and Analytical Approaches* (Englewood Cliffs, NJ: Prentice-Hall).

Ansoff, Igor H. (1965), *Corporate Strategy*, (New York: McGraw-Hill).

Ansoff, Igor H. (1991), 'Critique of Henry Mintzberg's The Design School: Reconsidering the Basic Premises of Strategic Management', *Strategic Management Journal*, 12 (6), pp. 449–61.

Ansoff, Igor H. (1994), 'Comment on Henry Mintzberg's Rethinking Strategic Planning', *Long Range Planning*, 27 (3), pp. 31–2.

Ansoff, Igor H., Roger P. Declerck, and Robert L. Hayes (1976), *From Strategic Planning to Strategic Management* (New York: John Wiley).

Bagozzi, R. (1975), 'Marketing as Exchange', *Journal of Marketing*, 39 (4), pp. 32–9.

Barwise, Patrick and Sean Meehan (2010), 'The One Thing You Must Get Right When Building a Brand', *Harvard Business Review*, 88, December, pp. 80–4.

Cassinelli, Alan (2013), '13 Best Social Media Campaigns of 2013', POSTANO, December 31, 2013. <http://www.postano.com/blog/13-best-social-media-campaigns-of-2013>

Cravens, David W., Nigel F. Piercy, and Artur Baldauf (2009), 'Management Framework Guiding Strategic Thinking in Rapidly Changing Markets', *Journal of Marketing Management*, 25 (1/2), pp. 31–49.

Cravens, David W. (1994), *Strategic Marketing* (US: Richard D. Irwin).

Crittenden, Victoria L. and William F. Crittenden (2012), 'Strategic Marketing in a Changing World', *Business Horizons*, 55, pp. 215–17.

Cummings, Stephen and Urs Daellenbach (2009), 'A Guide to the Future of Strategy?', *Long Range Planning*, 42 (1), pp. 234–63.

Dawar, Niraj (2013), 'When Marketing is Strategy', *Harvard Business Review*, 91, December, pp. 101–8.

Dibb, Sally, Lyndon Simkin, William M. Pride, and O.C. Ferrell (2012), *Marketing: Concepts and Strategies*, 6th edn, Cengage Learning.

Doyle, Peter and Philip Stern (2006), *Marketing Management and Strategy*, (UK: Prentice-Hall).

Eppler, Martin J. and Ken W. Platts (2009), 'Visual Strategizing: the Systematic Use of Visualization in the Strategic-Planning Process', *Long Range Planning*, 42 (2), pp. 42–74.

Foley, Anthony and John Fahy (2009), 'Seeing Market Orientation through a Capabilities Lens', *European Journal of Marketing*, 43 (1), pp. 13–20.

Frentzel, Y. William, John M. Bryson, and Barbara C. Crosby (2000), 'Strategic Planning in the Military', *Long Range Planning*, 33, pp. 402–29.

Grönroos, Christian, (2011), 'Value Co-creation in Service Logic: A critical Analysis', *Marketing Theory*, 11 (3), pp. 279–301.

Hooley, G., J. Fahy, G. Greenly, J. Beracs, K. Fonfara, and B. Snoj (2003), 'Market Orientation in the Service Sector of the Transition Economies of Central Europe', *European Journal of Marketing*, 37 (1/2), pp. 86–106.

Hooley, Graham, Nigel Piercy, and Brigitte Nicolaud (2011), *Marketing Strategy and Competitive Positioning*, (UK: Pearson Education).

Kaplan, Andreas and Michael Haenlein (2011), 'Two Hearts in Three-quarter Time: How to Waltz the Social Media/Viral Marketing Dance', *Business Horizons*, 54, pp. 252–64.

Kaplan, Andreas and Michael Haenlein (2010), 'Users of the World, Unite! The Challenges and Opportunities of Social Media', *Business Horizons*, 53, pp. 59–68.

Kietzmann, Jan H., Kristopher Hermkens, Ian P. McCarthy, and Bruno S. Silvestre (2011), 'Social Media? Get Serious! Understanding the Functional Building Blocks of Social Media', *Business Horizons*, 54, pp. 241–51.

Kohli, A.K. and B.J. Jaworski (1993), 'MARKOR: A Measure of Market Orientation', *Journal of Marketing Research*, 57, November, pp. 467–77.

Kohli ,Ajay K. and Bernard J. Jaworski (1990), 'Market Orientation: The Construct, Research Propositions, and Managerial Implications', *Journal of Marketing*, 54, April, pp. 1–18.

Kotler, Philip and Kevin Keller (2012), *Marketing Management*, 14th edn, (UK: Pearson Education)

Kristensson, Per, Jonas Matthing, and Niklas Johansson (2008), 'Key Strategies for the Successful Involvement of Customers in the Co-creation of New Technology-based Services', *International Journal of Service Industry Management*, 19 (4), pp. 474–91.

Lambin, Jean-Jacques (2000), *Market-driven Management: Strategic and Operational Marketing*, (Basingstoke: Macmillan Business).

Mahapatra, Lisa (2013), 'Social Media Marketing: How Do Top Brands Use Social Platforms?', **International Business Times**. *IBTimes.com* (9 August 2013). <http://www.ibtimes.com/social-media-marketing-how-do-top-brands-use-social-platforms-charts-1379457>

Martin, Roger L. (2014), 'Strategy Should be Uncomfortable', *Harvard Business Review*, 92, April, p. 20.

Martin, Roger L. (2014), 'The Big Lie of Strategic Planning', *Harvard Business Review*, 92, January-February, pp. 79–84.

Mason, Katy and C. Lloyd Harris (2005), 'Pitfalls in Evaluating Market Orientation: An Exploration of Executives', *Long Range Planning*, 38 (4), pp. 373–91.

Mavondo, F.T. and M.A. Farrell (2000), 'Measuring Market Orientation: Are there Differences between Business Marketers and Consumer Marketers?', *Australian Journal of Marketing*, 54 (4), pp. 223–44.

Mintzberg, Henry (1990), 'The Design School: Reconsidering the Basic Premises of Strategic Management', *Strategic Management Journal*, 11 (3), pp. 171–95.

Mintzberg, Henry (1994a), *The Rise and Fall of Strategic Planning* (Upper Saddle River, NJ: Prentice-Hall).

Mintzberg, Henry (1994b), 'Rethinking Strategic Planning Part I: Pitfalls and Fallacies', *Long Range Planning*, 27 (3), pp. 12–21.

Mintzberg, H. and J. Lampel (1999), 'Reflecting on the Strategy Process', *Sloan Management Review*, 40, Spring, pp. 21–30.

Mintzberg, Henry and J.B. Quinn (1996), *The Strategy Process: Concepts, Contexts, Cases* (UK: Prentice Hall International).

Muntinga, Daniel, M. Moorman, and E. Smit (2011), 'Introducing COBRAs Exploring Motivations for Brand-related Social Media Use'. *International Journal of Advertising*, 30 (1), pp. 13–46.

Narver, John C. and Stanley F. Slater (1990), 'The Effect of a Market Orientation on Business Profitability', *Journal of Marketing*, 54, October, pp. 20–35.

Neti, Sisira (2011), 'Social Media and its Role in Marketing', *International Journal of Enterprise Computing and Business Systems*, 1 (2), pp. 1–16.

Nwokah, Gladson N. (2008), 'Strategic Market Orientation and Business Performance: The Study of Food and Beverages Organizations in Nigeria', *European Journal of Marketing*, 42 (3/4), pp. 279–86.

Ocasio, William and John Joseph (2008), 'Rise and Fall -or Transformation? The Evolution of Strategic Planning at the General Electric Company 1940–2006', *Long Range Planning*, 41 (3), pp. 248–72.

Payne, Adrian F., Kaj Storbacka, and Pennie Frow (2008), 'Managing the Co-creation of Value', *Journal of the Academy of Marketing Science*, 36, pp. 83–96.

Prahalad, C.K. and V. Ramaswamy (2004), 'Co-creating Unique Value with Customers', *Strategy & Leadership*, 32 (3), pp. 4–9.

Ries, A. and J. Trout (1981), *Positioning: The Battle for Your Mind* (New York: McGraw-Hill).

Slater, Stanley F. and John C. Narver (1994), 'Market Orientation, Customer Value, and Superior Performance', *Business Horizons*, 37 (2), pp. 22–8.

Slater, Stanley F. and John C. Narver, (2000), 'The Positive Effect of a Market Orientation on Business Profitability: A Balanced Replication', *Journal of Business Research*, 48, pp. 69–73.

Slater, Stanley F., John C. Narver, and D.L. MacLachlan (2004), 'Market Orientation, Innovativeness, and New Product Success', *Journal of Product Innovation Management*, 21, pp. 334–47.

Trim, Peter R. J. and Lee Yang-Im (2008), 'A Strategic Marketing Intelligence and Multi-organizational Resilience Framework', *European Journal of Marketing*, 42 (7/8), pp. 731–45.

Varadarajan, Rajan P. and Jayachandran Satish (2000), 'Marketing Strategy: An Assessment of the State of the Field and Outlook', *Journal of the Academy of Marketing Science*, 27 (2), pp. 120–43.

Wheelen, Thomas L. and David J. (2012), *Strategic Management and Business Policy: Toward Global Sustainability* (US: Pearson Education).

Ward, Steven and Aleksandra Lewandowska (2008), 'Is the Marketing Concept always Necessary? The Effectiveness of Customer, Competitors and Societal Strategies in Business Environment Types', *European Journal of Marketing*, 42 (1/2), pp. 222–37.

Whittington, Richard and Ludovic Cailluet (2008), 'The Craft of Strategy', *Long Range Planning*, 41 (3), pp. 241–47.

Zenger, Todd (2013), 'Strategy: The Uniqueness Challenge', *Harvard Business Review*, 91, November, pp. 52–8.

 End of Chapter 2 case study   British Petroleum: can a tarnished brand recover following an ecological disaster?

Brand strategy: student-centred case study

In the summer of 2009 British Petroleum (BP) made world headlines with the Deepwater Horizon oil spill, the largest oil spill in United States history. There was immediate and immense outrage from ecological activists as well as consumers that BP could allow this to happen. The damage to the Gulf of Mexico's ecology and wildlife was substantial, putting BP's clean-up costs near almost $1 billion. But the damage to BP was more than economic; this disaster had a huge impact on BP's brand image. BP had branded themselves as 'beyond petroleum'; they were known as the oil company that cared about more than profits, the company that paid attention to and cared about the environment, looking for new ways to make sustainable energy. This case study will require you to search the Online Resource Centre and other sources of information to examine the current state of BP brand strategy and provide an in-depth analysis of different approaches that BP can adopt to recover from this disaster.

You will need to examine and evaluate how BP handled the Deepwater Horizon oil spill, learning the facts from the disaster and explaining BP's response to consumer outrage. You will also weigh the pros and cons of BP changing their name back to Amoco to determine if this would be a beneficial move to help BP's brand equity and identity. Furthermore you will need to compare and contrast how BP and Exxon handled their respective oil spills, showing how BP and Exxon acted similarly and which one handled the situation better. Finally, you will need to provide examples of companies that have successfully and unsuccessfully handled a crisis and explain how the company's response helped or hurt the brand names. This analysis will allow you to determine the best marketing strategies for BP to restore their brand name and corporate image.

Discussion questions

● Critically evaluate BP's marketing strategy in response to the oil spill. Your evaluation of marketing strategy should include a situation analysis of their marketing activities along with a detailed analysis of competitors' actions.

● Compare BP's marketing strategy with those of Exxon. Provide a detailed and justified set of strategic initiatives based upon your understanding of how any company can rebuild their brand strategy when confronted by such cataclysmic events.

Please note that this case study should be used as a student-centred learning activity. Students can log in to the Online Resource Centre and use other sources, plus their own readings, to explore the above questions

Part II

Where are we now?

I. Introduction

1 Overview and strategy blueprint

2 Marketing strategy: analysis and perspectives

II. Where are we now?

3 Environmental and internal analysis: market information and intelligence

III. Where do we want to be?

4 Strategic marketing decisions, choices, and mistakes

5 Segmentation, targeting, and positioning strategies

6 Branding strategies

7 Relational and sustainability strategies

IV. How will we get there?

8 Product innovation and development strategies

9 Service marketing strategies

10 Pricing and distribution strategies

11 Marketing communications strategies

12 International marketing strategy

13 Social and ethical strategies

V. Did we get there?

14 Strategy implementation, control, and metrics

3

Environmental and internal analysis: market information and intelligence

Learning Objectives

1. Understand the three areas of the strategic marketing management (SMM) process.

2. Appreciate the marketing environment and comprehend how organizations can undertake environmental and internal analysis.

3. Be able to understand the strategic use of market research, and the role of big data in environmental analysis.

4. Grasp the analytical models/frameworks that can be used to undertake strategic marketing analysis.

5. Be able to summarize the potential outcome of the strategic marketing analysis and the possible implications for the future strategic choices.

Chapter at a Glance

I. Introduction

1 Overview and strategy blueprint

2 Marketing strategy: analysis and perspectives

II. Where are we now?

3 **Environmental and internal analysis: market information and intelligence**

III. Where do we want to be?

4 Strategic marketing decisions, choices, and mistakes

5 Segmentation, targeting, and positioning strategies

6 Branding strategies

7 Relational and sustainability strategies

V. Did we get there?

14 Strategy implementation, control, and metrics

IV. How will we get there?

8 Product innovation and development strategies

9 Service marketing strategies

10 Pricing and distribution strategies

11 Marketing communications strategies

12 International marketing strategy

13 Social and ethical strategies

 Case study: Exodus's digital strategy

Travel operator Exodus explored real time chat options on its website to engage users in search of a great escape.

The brief

An adventure packed trip to a dream destination is on the bucket list of many. But the cost and commitment of booking a once-in-a-lifetime experience can deter many would-be thrill seekers from embarking on their journey of discovery. Travel company Exodus wanted to engage website visitors, provide guidance, and increase online bookings.

The 40-year-old tour operator offers more than 500 adventure and alternative holidays in more than 100 countries. Expeditions range from trekking and cycling trips to wildlife adventures and polar expeditions led by local experts. But due to the high-end nature of the product and the equally high level of commitment involved in booking such an adventure, conversion rates on the website are low, says Exodus digital performance manager Imran Arshad. 'Exodus products are above the typical package holiday with expensive quality hotels and quality transportation', he says.

The average age of an Exodus customer is 40, and typically includes city dwellers with disposable incomes, empty-nesters and adrenalin junkies in search of adventure. Half are single and the rest are couples, says Arshad. While this target market appreciates the ease of online bookings, they often require advice before they commit to a considerable investment of their time, energy and money. The Exodus team needed to find a way to attract and engage its target customer on its website to boost bookings.

The strategy

Exodus hired digital marketing agency 'LivePerson' to implement a website tool, 'Live Chat', to engage customers as they browsed the online catalogue of expeditions available. Exodus spends about £1,000 a month on the package, which includes content targeting and web analytics-based targeting. On the bottom of the website pages, a link to the 'Live Chat' tool invites users to send a message to an expert and discuss their questions about a particular trip. 'The objective of Live Chat is to guide customers with any problems or enquiries, and engage them with help and information to drive sales and improve customer service, while also collecting valuable data for future promotional activity', explains Arshad.

The execution

The Live Chat team is stationed across different time zones in London, Melbourne and Toronto to ensure the service is available 24 hours a day. In addition to ensuring that people who need assistance get the right advice, it also allows Exodus to focus on travellers who are genuinely interested in booking, says Arshad. 'Our trained experts are a well-travelled team who can easily filter out lookers from bookers—people who are genuinely interested in buying a holiday—and establish a dialogue with them', says Arshad.

But the team discovered that the brand needed to promote the Live Chat tool more to attract the attention of visitors. 'The link was just sitting at the bottom of the page so we needed a more aggressive approach to engage people and drive better results', he explains. It was decided that a pop-up would be an effective way to grab the attention of users. LivePerson devised an algorithm to target people using the average length of the user journey on the site. This information was used by Exodus to trigger a pop-up that offered a chat invitation or a call back request.

The data showed that a person will spend an average of one minute on the home page, so within a minute of the user's duration on the page, a pop-up would be triggered, says Arshad. The frequency and timing of that pop-up varies from one page to another depending on the average time spent on the page. The team customised the chat and call back request buttons to complement the look and feel of the overall website.

Exodus used LivePerson's content targeting tool to target promotions and channel traffic to appropriate areas of the website. Campaigns were segmented by customer type, grabbing new visitors' attention with targeted offers, while encouraging returning traffic to book a trip. It also allowed the operator to tailor offers to customers according to their geographical location. During months when bookings at ticket price were typically high, Exodus used the content targeting tool to tailor non sales-based messaging that encouraged people to engage with its online community. Promotional offers to drive conversions are often the primary objective of online campaigns, but the travel sector isn't continually discount driven, explains Arshad. This helped Exodus to develop user-generated content and invite useful feedback from customers.

The outcome

Exodus receives an average of two million visitors per year. Around 1,500 visitors per month will engage with an Exodus member via Live Chat, explains Arshad. Not all are interested in making a new booking, however. Users may contact a Live Chat member for a number of reasons, including enquiries about their trip after they have booked, or to request details about the injections that are required for their destination of choice.

Approximately half of the visitors who engage with Live Chat per month are known by the team as 'hot leads' and are genuinely interested in booking a trip. Following guidance from a Live Chat member, three out of four of these leads will go on to make a booking, explains Arshad. The Live Chat tool has increased conversion rates on the site—a quarter of online sales are now generated through Live Chat and it has boosted total online sales by 14 per cent.

The analysis

Arshad believes the LivePerson technology generated good results for Exodus. 'There is a lot more engagement with website users as a result of this interaction', he says. But the team has identified a number of ways to further exploit the potential of Live Chat and improve the user experience on the website. Exodus will start to offer a questionnaire to site visitors to divide sales and customer service queries so Exodus can respond more efficiently to these requests. The company has also recognized the need to update Live Chat for mobile, incorporating the chat option into its updated app as it moves from 3G to 4G in 2014. Exodus also decided to update its website to improve the user experience and tailor the home page to specific geographical locations. 'We were using quite old code and we wanted to improve security and provide a better mobile experience', says Arshad. But Live Chat will continue to play a major role in the user journey on the website. 'The results speak for themselves and LivePerson tools will definitely be part of the DNA of our new site', he says.

Muireann Bolger, **The Marketer***, March/April 2014, pp.20–2.*

Introduction

Building on the discussion in Chapter 2, this chapter and Chapter 4 discuss in great detail the first two stages of the strategic marketing management (SMM) process, namely strategic analysis and **strategic choices**, while the remaining chapters of the book are devoted to the third stage of the SMM process, namely **strategy implementation**. Porter's generic strategy (low-cost, differentiation, and focus) forms the backdrop to the discussion in this book.[1] The book will also benefit from the link between marketing and strategic management. In the past two decades, strategy and marketing researchers have improved the conceptual and practical understanding of the role of marketing in enabling organizations to create and sustain competitive advantage (Morgan, 2012).

The SMM process involves three subsequent stages: *strategic analysis*, *strategic choices*, and *strategy implementation* (Figure 3.1).[2]

---

[1] Porter's generic strategy is not the only typology available (see: Miles and Snow, 1978; Utterback and Abernathy, 1975), but it is the one that has received wide appreciation from both academicians and practitioners.

[2] There has been a typical academic debate between two key scholars in the area of strategy, namely Ansoff and Mintzberg, in support of and against the validity of the SMM model (see: Ansoff, 1991, 1994; Mintzberg, 1990, 1994a; Mintzberg and Lampel, 1999).

3.1 The Strategic Marketing Management Process

Source: Gerry Johnson, Kevan Scholes, and Richard Whittington (2008), *Exploring Corporate Strategy*, FT: Prentice-Hall Education, Ltd.

The three stages of the SMM have been described by Johnson et al. (2008) as follows. **Strategic (position) analysis** is concerned with identifying the impact on strategy of the external environment, an organization's strategic capability, and the expectations and influence of stakeholders. **Strategic choices** involve the options for strategy in terms of both the directions in which strategy might move and the methods by which strategy might be pursued. **Strategy implementation** is concerned with ensuring that chosen strategies are actually put into action. It is the translation of strategy into organizational action through organizational structure and design, resource planning, and the management of strategic change.

The marketing environment and its components

Any organization is a creature of its environment. Success in today's business environment is dependent upon leveraging a firm's scarce resources and limited capabilities (Crittenden and Crittenden, 2012). Success is not only affected by factors in the external environment but also by many internal factors including the organizational culture, which is seen by some researchers as a pivotal strategic resource that influences the firm's competitive advantage and business performance (Wei et al., 2014). The strategic marketing concept requires that marketing managers ensure that the organization achieves a sustainable competitive advantage in its environment through a structured approach to planning and strategy formulation (Trim and Lee, 2008). Strategy formulation is, therefore, seen as the development

3.2 The Marketing Environment

Source: Drawn by the authors.

of long-range plans for the effective management of the environmental opportunities and threats while taking into account the organization's strengths and weaknesses.

The firm's marketing environment involves two distinct levels: the internal environment, consisting of variables within the organization but not usually within the long-run control of top management, and the external environment consisting of variables outside the organization and not typically within the short-run control of top management. The external environment is further divided into two sub-environments: (a) the 'macro' or remote environment, and (b) the 'micro' or competitive environment. The potential output of analysing the external environment is the detection of opportunities and threats, both present and potential, which face the organization, while the key output of analysing the internal environment is the identification of strengths and weaknesses that exist within the organization's culture and structure. See Figure 3.2 for the marketing environment and its components.

Strategic analysis of the external environment

To be successful over time an organization must be in tune with its external environment. Success is no longer a matter of absolute performance but depends on how well a company does relative to others. This is the essence of strategic analysis, which entails a company anticipating the moves of other rivals (Rosenzweig, 2013). Viagra, once at the top of the market for erectile dysfunction, had reached annual sales of $1.5 billion in 2001, but in 2003 Bayer introduced Levitra, the first competitor to Viagra, with a profile similar to Viagra's but a slightly lower price (a classic 'me too' positioning). Very recently, in 2012, Cialis passed Viagra's $1.9 billion in annual sales, with duration supplanting efficacy as the key criterion of purchase in the erectile dysfunction market.

Marketers have to realize that the forces at work in the external environment can turn on a dime; nothing is stable and nothing is sacred. Successful marketing practice mandates regular scanning for opportunities in the external environment (Crittenden and Crittenden, 2012). There also must be a 'strategic fit' between what the environment wants and what the organization has to offer, as well as between what the organization needs and what the environment can provide. While most airline companies saw the horrific event of 9/11 as a major threat affecting the whole industry and therefore slowed down their businesses, the low-cost airline Easyjet responded differently. Two months after 9/11 it was reported that the market share of Easyjet was not only in good shape but actually increasing. Similarly, while the financial crisis of 2008/09 has left many organizations in shaky positions, some companies turned this into an opportunity and increased their investment for the future.

Strategic analysis of the macro (remote) environment

The 'macro' or remote environment includes general forces that do not directly touch on the short-run activities of the organization but can influence its long-run strategic decisions. These variables generally affect, but in different ways, every single organization in the marketing environment regardless of the market in which it operates. The number of strategic variables in the macro environment is enormous, given the fact that each country has its own unique set of macro variables. For example, although countries such as China, Thailand, Hong Kong, and Japan are parts of Asia's Pacific Rim, they have different views on the role of businesses in society. It is generally believed in China, for example, that the role of businesses is primarily to contribute to national development, whereas in Hong Kong and Thailand the role of business is primarily to make profits for the shareholders. Such differences may translate into different trade regulations and varying degrees of opposition to foreign competitors.

The variables in the macro environment are enormous and can be clustered in various ways, the most notable being the PESTLE model (political, economic, socio-cultural, technological, legal, and environment). See Table 3.1 for the detailed variables of the macro environment.

To remain competitive, organizations are required to continuously analyse the external environment and identify any possible impact on the firm's activities. Most organizations are required to anticipate changes in their external marketing environments and be prepared to adapt their marketing/business activities accordingly (Johnston et al., 2008). Every organization has to anticipate how its environment might change in the short, medium, and long term. Such anticipated changes will have a direct impact on strategic marketing decision-making. Table 3.2 is a simple framework organizations can use to measure the possible impact of the variables in the organization's macro environment.

In a dynamic environment where changes occur in unpredictable ways, the challenge for an organization is to collect relevant information on which to base its decisions. Recently, a great deal of attention has focused on warning marketing managers to be aware of common biases of available information and to avoid their ill-effects (Rosenzweig, 2013). This means that, within the context of the strategy formulation process, a firm needs to find ways of collecting and analysing relevant information about its external environment, as well as dealing with the unpredictability of this environment. This would mean that an organization should systematically scan and analyse its external environment.

Environmental scanning and analysis can be defined as follows. **Environmental scanning** is the process of collecting information about the forces and trends in the environment. Scanning involves observation and perusal of secondary sources, such as business, trade,

Table 3.1 PESTLE Framework for Environmental Analysis

POLITICAL FACTORS

- Political stability
- Regime orientations
- Government stability
- Pressure groups
- Trade union power

ECONOMIC FACTORS

- Business cycles
- Interest rates
- Inflation rates
- Investment levels
- Unemployment
- GNP trends
- Patterns of ownership

SOCIAL-CULTURAL FACTORS

- Demographics
- Lifestyles
- Social mobility
- Educational levels
- Attitudes
- Consumerism

TECHNOLOGICAL FACTORS

- Levels and focuses of government and industrial R & D expenditure
- Speed of technology transfer
- Product life cycles

LEGAL FACTORS

- Legislative structures
- Anti-trust laws
- Trade policies
- Employment legislation
- Foreign trade regulation

ENVIRONMENT FACTORS

- Sustainability legislation
- Green issues
- Energy supply

Source: Drawn by the authors.

Table 3.2 PESTLE for Environmental Scanning and Analysis

SOURCE	DESCRIPTION	IMPLICATION	CERTAIN 1-5	IMPACT 1-5
POLITICAL				
ECONOMIC				
SOCIAL				
TECHNOLOGICAL				
LEGAL				
ENVIRONMENT (GREEN)				

Source: Drawn by the authors.

government, and general interest publications (Dibb et al., 2012). Motorola, the mobile handset producer, has its intelligence department to monitor the latest technology developments introduced at scientific conferences, in academic journals, and in trade gossip. This information helps it build 'technology roadmaps' that assess where breakthroughs are likely to occur, when they can be incorporated into new products, how much money their development will cost, and which of the developments is being worked on by competition. **Environmental analysis** is the process of assessing and interpreting the information gathered through market intelligence and environmental scanning.

Despite the difficulties of environmental scan and analysis that act as deterrents to the formulation and implementation of an effective scanning system, there are several principal benefits. The essence of strategy formulation is relating a company to its environment. The competitive dimension of the environment is strongly influential in determining the competitive rules of the game as well as the competitive strategy that is to be pursued. For example, it has been claimed that businesses following a differentiation strategy tend to scan the environment primarily for opportunities and closely monitor customer attitudes, while firms following a cost leadership strategy tend to scan the environment primarily for threats and closely monitor competitors' activities. Organizations usually develop their strategies on the bases of environmental analysis and scanning to find the 'strategic fit' between external opportunities and threats, on the one hand, and internal strengths and weaknesses, on the other. IKEA's experiment with housing trends in Europe in the late 1990s was presumably the result of its ability to identify a possible market opportunity and also its attempt to capitalize on its skills in developing kit-form products at reasonable prices to customers.

In responding to the macro environmental forces, some companies may accept these forces as uncontrollable and remain passive or reactive. Others may believe that environmental forces can be shaped, and they may adopt a more proactive direction. See Mini Case 3.1 which discusses how businesses in the UK are taking advantage of the economic recovery in 2014, and how some sectors benefit from this more than others.

Environmental uncertainty and scenario analysis

The quality of a strategy is extremely difficult to evaluate. Managers can temporarily disguise a low-quality strategy as one of high quality. And those that actually have high-quality

Mini Case 3.1 Digital economy[3]

The recession has driven a fast pace of change and digital has put the spring back in the step of the UK economy

As the spring of 2014 blossoms, the news has continued to be bright for the UK economy. Chancellor George Osborne was able to announce the biggest upgrade to growth forecasts between budgets in 30 years. The UK economy is growing at its fastest pace since before the financial crisis in 2007. And as employment continues to grow and the pace of pay rises start to quicken, it looks like households will finally start to feel the positive effects of economic recovery this year. How are businesses taking advantage of this? Have some sectors benefited more than others? Looking back over the past year, it's clear that the consumer has been buoyed by the resurgent housing market, but that the wider economic recovery has translated into job growth that has bolstered confidence across the economy. The Asda Income Tracker measure of household spending power has shown a consistent run of year-on-year gains in recent months. These initially modest improvements are now starting to translate into more meaningful gains. This has been driven by the improvement in the labour market—unemployment has fallen far faster than expected towards seven per cent from closer to eight per cent only a year or so ago. But also important has been more modest inflation. The annual increase in consumer prices has fallen beneath the Bank of England two per cent target to its lowest level in four years. With prices going up more slowly and pay growth now starting to pick up, UK consumers will finally see modest real-income growth this year.

Against this background, we have seen retail sales pick up. But traditional retailers are finding it harder going. While the past six years have been traumatic in many ways, with after-effects of the financial crisis persisting, technological change has been dramatic. This has been transforming the economy, and the creative destruction that a recession creates has driven a fast pace of change across the economy. Interestingly, the retail sector has seen this trend play out with particular significance. We have seen internet retail sales explode and the ways in which consumers make buying decisions has changed forever. Customer research prior to purchases and indeed purchase decisions themselves are increasingly made via smartphone and tablet, while social media plays an ever more important role in product reviews and decision making.

This has been a major challenge for traditional retail business models that face considerable fixed costs from the challenges of operating premises. The major retail players have had to innovate or risk losing out to stellar upstarts such as Asos and Cult Beauty. Those that have found ways to take advantage of the digital revolution have thrived—and this is fundamentally changing the economy.

Indeed, research undertaken by Cebr for Royal Mail showed how, despite the recession, e-tail has exploded over the past five years. The number of e-tail-only businesses in the UK more than doubled from 6,700 in 2008 to 14,400 in 2012. This created around 15,000 jobs, taking total employment to 72,000. This remarkable growth story in a period of very weak macroeconomic performance shows the incredible rise of the digital economy. The information and communication sector has also been boosted by the rapid pace of technological change. Cebr's regular analysis of business sentiment and performance in the Federation of Small Business's Small Business Index has shown that the 'computer and related activities' sector has the highest confidence across all sectors of the economy as small businesses latch onto the digital revolution.

Taking a step back, there is some concern that investors have got too excited about the digital revolution as tech sector company valuations come in at eye-watering levels. Some have even talked about another dot.com bubble. While it's easy to have some sympathy with this as we live in a world where money is very cheap—the Bank of England, US Federal Reserve and European Central Bank still have interest rates at rock-bottom levels seven years post-crisis—there has been major structural change

[3] Charles Davis, *The Marketer*, May–June 2014, p.13

across the economy over the past few years and this process creates big winners. But there will also be businesses that bite off more than they can chew and fall by the wayside.

Businesses have to plan for growth to slow in the UK as the Bank of England starts to raise interest rates and the government attempts to reduce the still £100bn-plus borrowing requirement. This will mean more spending cuts and tax rises, whichever government comes in next year. So while Chancellor Osborne may have a spring in his step for now, marketers and their businesses must make sure they haven't overstretched themselves.

strategies have difficulty convincing the markets of this (Zenger, 2013). Managers have to make strategic decisions with varying degrees of incompleteness of information about the future of the organization. One option for dealing with the future is anticipatory action based on the awareness of possible futures. This is the essence of **scenario analysis** which enables a firm to evaluate the effect of change in multiple variables, and the uncertainties that each holds, thereby allowing the firm to consider strategic actions (Johnston et al., 2008). Scenario analysis provides a conceptual framework by which organizations can understand the external environment as it unfolds, accept the uncertainty as given, and use it to provide a description of two or more future scenarios. By writing a few market scenarios and evaluating their likelihood and impact, scenario analysis can be a powerful strategic tool that deals with complex environments.

Scenarios are normally written as narratives, like Hollywood scripts, that provide an image of some kind of future end-state. Such scenarios are based on plots with beginnings, middles, and ends. Another characteristic is that scenarios are usually written in sets of three or four. The final element is that most scenarios provide a progression from the present to the future rather than a single-point forecast. They weave a plot that connects as a series of inter-related events. While there is a great deal of variety in the nature of scenario writing, when viewed as an aggregate, four steps can be observed. The starting point for most scenarios is normally to identify the key drivers that will affect the issue at hand and, thereby, generate a list of trends or factors. The next stage is normally to rank or combine all the identified drivers into a smaller, more meaningful set that can be used for structure. A PESTLE analysis can be used to identify the kinds of issues facing an organization over a defined period (say five years). These issues can be scored on two scales, certainty and importance, from 1 (low) to 5 (high). See Figure 3.3.

Issues that score 1–3 on both scales can be abandoned, as can issues scoring 1–3 on importance even if they score 3–5 on certainty. They clearly are not worth devoting too much time and effort to. On the other hand, issues scoring 3–5 on both certainty and importance are issues central to the marketing strategy. However, issues scoring 3–5 on importance, but 1–3 on certainty, can be placed in the scenario quadrant. These are issues that could have a significant impact on the organization, but it is not clear whether or not they will occur in the time-frame being considered. The issues in the scenario quadrant need to be carefully considered from the point of view of what kind of future environment might develop.

The third part is to write the scenarios. Three scenarios remain the most popular ('best guess', 'base case', and 'middle ground'). However, drilling down to just two scenarios overcomes the problem of focusing on middle ground. Good practice is to identify the most likely scenario. Finally, a single marketing strategy has to be created to cope with the identified

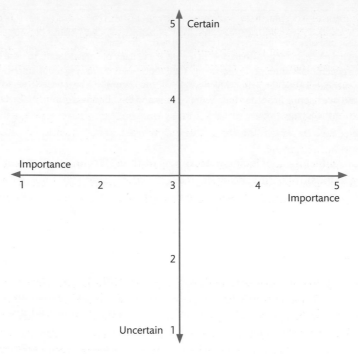

3.3 PESTLE Factors and Scenario Analysis

Source: Drawn by the authors.

scenarios. One of the key problems in scenario writing is the 'reduction problem' of reducing the multitude of plausible scenarios to just 2–5. The best way of doing this is to keep the initial analysis simple and to combine trends into logical themes. It is not as easy as it sounds.

Scenario analysis and planning enable staff to find unique solutions to complex, ongoing problems and, if coupled with simulation exercises, i.e. used to develop individual's decision-making skills, can reinforce the organization's resilience value system by making key decision-makers aware of the changes occurring in the environment and what the likely impact will be should a certain impact materialize (Trim and Lee, 2008). Shell was among the first to practice scenario planning in the late 1960s and was one of the few companies ready when the oil crisis hit in 1973 (Kachaner and Deimler, 2009).

There are two types of scenario analysis. The first is strategy-developing scenarios—its key objective is to provide insights into future competitive context, and then use these insights to assess existing business strategies and stimulate the creation of new ones. This type of scenario analysis can help create contingency plans to protect organizations against unexpected events or disasters. It can also suggest investment strategies that allow organizations to capitalize on future opportunities caused by new trends in the market or technological breakthrough. In the second type of scenario analysis, which is 'decision-driven scenarios', a strategy is proposed and evaluated against several scenarios. The key objective is to challenge the strategies, thereby helping to make decisions and suggesting ways to make the strategy more robust in withstanding competitive forces. If the decision, for example, is to enter a new market with new technology, alternative scenarios could be developed about product acceptability in the marketplace, competitor response, and the stimulation of customer applications.

In either type, scenario planning will involve three sequential stages (Aaker and McLoughlin, 2010). These are: the creation of scenarios; relating these scenarios to existing or potential strategies; and assessing the probability of each scenario. When developing scenarios, it is useful to create them based on probable outcomes: for example, pessimistic scenario, optimistic scenario, and the most likely scenario. It is important for organizations to reduce the number of scenarios created by identifying a small set that ideally includes those scenarios that are credible and those that are substantial enough to affect strategy development. Having developed a fewer number of credible scenarios, an organization has to relate them to existing and new strategies.

Scenario analysis has not been without criticism. It is not widely used because its methodological applications are confusing to infrequent users, matching the methodology and the analysis level to business issues is difficult, and a large amount of resource is required (Verity, 2003).

Strategic analysis of the micro (competitive) environment

The 'micro' environment includes those forces or groups that directly affect, and are affected by, an organization's major operations. An organization's competitive environment is often referred to as the industry in which the organization competes. A fundamental stage in strategy development is the anticipation and analysis of the major structural elements of the industry. Such structural elements of any industry are identified as industry size, growth, competitive structure, cost structure, channels, trends, and key success factors (Aaker and McLoughlin, 2010). The analysis of the industry's environment, however, should not only include the characteristics and trends of the industry but also the forces that influence such characteristics and trends.

Industry can simply be defined as a group of firms producing similar products or services. From a competitive perspective, industry can also be defined as a group of competitors producing products or services that compete directly with each other. However, one of the most difficult problems in industry analysis is defining the specific industry to which the company's product belongs. This might be because no clear boundaries exist between industries in terms of either products or geographical area. In practice, many organizations compete for customer's money, e.g. Coke versus Pepsi versus Crisps versus a lottery ticket versus a hamburger versus whatever consumers can spend their money on at the same price. Instead of looking at industry as an aggregate group of companies that produce similar products, Kotler and Keller (2012) looked at it as different sets of companies that satisfy the customers' needs. Hence, industry could be defined in terms of four levels of competition.

- **Industry definition based on brand competition:** here Ford might compete against Fiat, Toyota, and Honda but not against Mercedes.
- **Industry definition based on product competition:** here Ford might compete against all automobile manufacturers.
- **Industry definition based on form competition:** here Ford might compete against not only other automobile manufacturers but also manufacturers of motorcycles, bicycles, and trucks.
- **Industry definition based on generic competition:** here Ford might compete against companies that sell major consumer durables, foreign holidays, and new homes.

Industry analysis should include not only existing players but also the potential companies (new entrants) that may come on to the scene. A few years ago no one would have imagined that Asda might compete in other product lines than food, beverages, and grocery goods. Today Asda is displaying under one roof a variety of clothing products, appliances, and financial products alongside its conventional grocery goods. Although identifying the new entrants to an industry is not an easy task, they can often be expected to come from the following groups:

- firms not in the industry but which could overcome entry barriers
- firms for which there is obvious synergy from being in the industry
- firms for which competing in the industry is an obvious extension of the strategy
- customers or suppliers who may integrate backwards or forwards.

Another way of analysing the micro environment, which takes full account of the competitive forces that shape the industry structure, is Porter's five forces model (1979). According to Porter's view, the state of competition in an industry depends on five basic competitive forces, the collective strength of these forces determining the ultimate profit potential of the industry and the ability of firms in an industry to earn rates of return on investment in excess of the cost of capital (Porter, 1985). Porter's five forces are shown in Figure 3.4.

Understanding the competitive forces and their underlying causes reveals the roots of an industry's current profitability while providing a framework for anticipating and influencing competition and profitability over time. If the forces are intense, as they are in such industries as airlines, hotels, and banking, almost no company earns more than above average return on investment. If the forces are benign, as they are in industries such as software, soft drinks, and toiletries, many companies earn high levels of profit (Porter, 2008).

Porter (1980) discussed the link between the five forces and strategy development. The goal of competitive strategy for a business is to find a position in the industry where the company can best defend itself against these competitive forces or can influence them in its favour. A strategist can analyse any market by rating each competitive force as high, medium, or low in strength. Looking at the sportswear industry in the UK, for example, the five forces could be rated as follows. Competition among existing rivals is high as key players such as Adidas, Reebok, Nike, and Puma compete closely and strongly in the market. The threat of new entrants might be seen as low since the UK market has reached the maturity stage and sales growth is not as high as it used to be. Threat of substitutes could also be seen as low because other available products do not appeal to customers and do not sponsor sports activities. The bargaining power of buyers could be rated medium in strength as buyers are interested in buying trendy sports products (well-known brands) but they cannot influence the price in their favour.

The configuration of the five forces differs by industry. For example, in the market for commercial aircraft, fierce rivalry between dominant manufacturers Boeing and Airbus and the bargaining power of the airlines that place large orders for aircraft are strong, while the threat of new entries, the threat of substitutes, and the bargaining power of suppliers are more benign. In the movie industry, the proliferation of substitute forms of entertainment and the power of the movie producers and distributors who supply movies, the critical input, are very important.

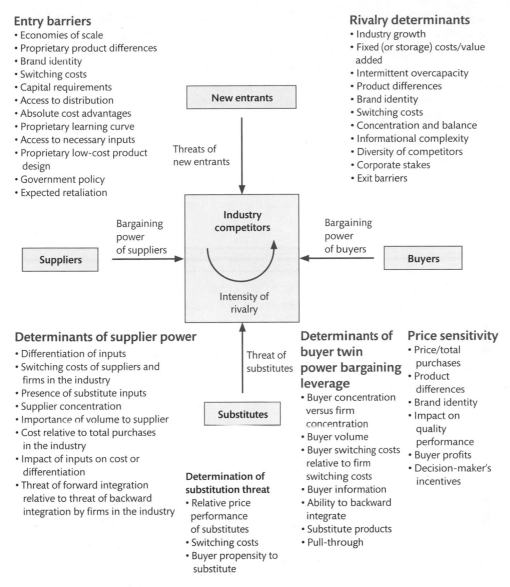

Entry barriers
- Economies of scale
- Proprietary product differences
- Brand identity
- Switching costs
- Capital requirements
- Access to distribution
- Absolute cost advantages
- Proprietary learning curve
- Access to necessary inputs
- Proprietary low-cost product design
- Government policy
- Expected retaliation

Rivalry determinants
- Industry growth
- Fixed (or storage) costs/value added
- Intermittent overcapacity
- Product differences
- Brand identity
- Switching costs
- Concentration and balance
- Informational complexity
- Diversity of competitors
- Corporate stakes
- Exit barriers

New entrants

Threats of new entrants

Bargaining power of suppliers

Industry competitors

Intensity of rivalry

Suppliers

Bargaining power of buyers

Buyers

Determinants of supplier power
- Differentiation of inputs
- Switching costs of suppliers and firms in the industry
- Presence of substitute inputs
- Supplier concentration
- Importance of volume to supplier
- Cost relative to total purchases in the industry
- Impact of inputs on cost or differentiation
- Threat of forward integration relative to threat of backward integration by firms in the industry

Threat of substitutes

Substitutes

Determination of substitution threat
- Relative price performance of substitutes
- Switching costs
- Buyer propensity to substitute

Determinants of buyer twin power bargaining leverage
- Buyer concentration versus firm concentration
- Buyer volume
- Buyer switching costs relative to firm switching costs
- Buyer information
- Ability to backward integrate
- Substitute products
- Pull-through

Price sensitivity
- Price/total purchases
- Product differences
- Brand identity
- Impact on quality performance
- Buyer profits
- Decision-maker's incentives

3.4 Porter's Five Forces Model

Source: Michael E. Porter (1985), *Competitive Advantage: Creating and Sustaining Superior Performance,* Redrawn with the permission of the Free Press, a division of Simon & Schuster Adult Publishing Group.

The five forces model suggests that competition extends beyond the companies within the industry to include new entries, substitutes, suppliers, and buyers. The stronger the force is, the greater the restrictions on companies to raise prices and earn greater profits. In other words, a strong force may be regarded as a threat because it is likely to reduce profits, whereas a weak force may be viewed as an opportunity because it may allow the company to earn higher profits.

Although widely used, Porter's five forces model has been subject to several criticisms, the principal one being of Porter's methodology in that many of his points do not appear to be justified. There is also no indication of how to assess the relative power of the forces, or how to determine what reactions to take.

Another approach for analysing the competitive 'micro' environment is to categorize the various competitors within the industry into strategic groups. Strategic group analysis is essential for identifying the group of companies with which the organization will compete. A strategic group can be defined as a group of firms pursuing the same or a similar strategy with similar resources. For example, although McDonald's and Subway are in the fast food market, they may have different objectives and strategies, and thus may belong to different strategic groups. They generally have very little in common and pay little attention to each other when planning competitive actions. Burger King, however, has a great deal in common with McDonald's in that both have a similar strategy of servicing low-priced fast food targeted for sale to the average family.

Two approaches can be used for forming strategic groups. The first is a two-dimensional analysis by which a firm selects two strategic variables that differentiate the companies within an industry and draws them on the vertical and horizontal axes. The second approach is multidimensional by which the difficulty of selecting the best two strategic factors can be overcome by incorporating several strategic variables. The benefits of identifying strategic groups are twofold. The first is that the height of the barriers to entry and exit can vary significantly from one group to another. The second is that the choice of a strategic group determines which companies are to be the principal competitors. Despite these benefits, a number of criticisms have been made. Issues related to identifying appropriate dimensions upon which to develop groups, their number, and the dynamic versus static analysis of strategic group formation, remain problematic. While the strategic group is a useful concept, the value of that analysis is as a descriptive rather than a predictive tool. It is unlikely to offer much insight into why some firms in an industry are more profitable than others.

Competitor analysis

The objectives of competitor analysis are twofold. First, a company may have to develop a profile of the nature and success of the likely strategy changes each competitor in the market might make. Secondly, the company may have to anticipate other competitors' probable response to the range of feasible strategic moves other firms could initiate, and each competitor's probable reaction to the array of industry changes and broader environmental shifts that might occur. For competitor analysis, companies have to gather secondary data on each competitor's goals, strategies, and performance. They may also undertake primary market research with customers, suppliers, and dealers to understand the competitors' strengths and weaknesses. This is a key aspect of the strategic use of market research.[4] Recently, social media platforms have also been used for intelligence gathering.

Competitor analysis is seen as a set of activities which examine the comparative position of competing organizations in a given market. The set of competitor analysis activities organizations might undertake are:

- identifying the company's competitors
- understanding competitors' objectives

---

[4] See later in this chapter for the strategic use of market research.

- identifying competitors' strategies
- assessing competitors' strengths and weaknesses
- estimating competitors' reactions
- selecting competitors to attack and those to avoid.

In identifying the company's competitors, a company should not be restricted to its current competitors but also take into account potential competitors. Among the sources of potential competitors are firms that might engage in market expansion, product expansion, backward integration, forward integration, and the export of the assets of skills (Aaker and McLoughlin, 2010). Shell, for example, has introduced mini-supermarkets to its forecasts to compete with supermarket petrol stations and 24-hour opening for convenience. This has been countered by Tesco with the introduction of 24-hour opening at selective sites.

Once a company identifies its principal competitors, it needs to focus upon each competitor's objectives. What drives each competitor's behaviour? Is it profit maximization or some other objectives? In practice, profit maximization might be an unrealistic objective which, for many reasons, some companies are unwilling to attempt. The management of Ryanair, 'the no-frills airline', may have decided in the first three years of its launch not to adopt profit maximization as a strategic objective; instead they were interested in achieving a sustainable share of the domestic and Western European market. Each competitor has a variety of objectives, each of which has a different weight. The competitors' objectives might typically include cash flow, market share growth, technological leadership, or overall market leadership. Understanding this set of objectives allows the strategist to arrive at tentative conclusions about how a competitor will respond to a competitive thrust. For example, a firm such as Volkswagen, pursuing market share growth, is likely to react more quickly and strongly against a competitor's price cut or a substantial increase in advertising budget than a firm such as Microsoft, aiming for technological leadership.

For an understanding of competitors' strategies, a company should first identify each competitor's assumptions. These assumptions generally fall into two major categories: (a) the competitor's assumptions about the industry and other companies, and (b) the competitor's assumptions about its own business. A competitor's assumptions about the industry and other companies may well be subtly influenced by, as well as reflected in, its current strategy. Knowing what a competitor's assumptions are will guide a firm to identify the basis of the competitor's strategy, e.g. the competitor may see itself as socially aware, an industry leader, a low-cost producer, or as having the best salesforce. These assumptions will influence how the competitor behaves, the way it reacts to events, and how it formulates its own competitive marketing strategy.

Having defined the competitors' assumptions, the strategist must assess the current marketing strategy of each competitor. The firm needs to know each competitor's product features, quality, customer services, pricing policy, distribution coverage, salesforce policy, and advertising and other promotion programmes. The firm has also to think of competitors' future strategies. It is unwise to assume that an existing competitor strategy will continue to be effective. Competitors' current actions may only signal probable future actions. General Motors (GM) and Toyota competed head-to-head in the global automobile market for many decades. While GM kept the number one position longer than other automakers, it lost this position to Toyota in 2008. It took Toyota 71 years to beat GM but only 2 years for GM to regain the top spot in 2011 (Chowdhury, 2014).

The strengths and weaknesses of one's competitors are at the very heart of any marketing strategy. Understanding a competitor's strengths and weaknesses provides insight into the firm's ability to initiate and/or react to strategic moves, respond to environmental or industry events, and pursue various strategies. The Japanese car producers were able to dominate the world automobile market during the 1970s, 1980s, and 1990s by analysing competitors' strategies and appreciating their strengths and weaknesses. Such a thorough understanding enabled them to provide customers with better value than their competitors did. Competitors' strengths and weaknesses are based upon the existence or absence of assets or skills. Thus, to analyse competitors' strengths and weaknesses, it is necessary to identify the assets and skills that are relevant to the industry (Aaker and McLoughlin, 2010). For example, an intangible asset like Nike's well-known brand could present a major strength as could a skill like the company's ability to manufacture top-quality goods. Conversely, the absence of a unique asset or distinctive skill can present significant weaknesses. Several factors can make a competitor vulnerable such as the lack of cash flow, low margins, poor growth, and limited market share.

Many companies are using benchmarking to assess competitors' strengths. Benchmarking could be seen as a powerful tool for increasing a company's competitiveness. It is a process for assessing products, services, and practices against that offered by leading competitors. The UK Customs and Excise department won the 1996 European Best Practice Benchmarking Award for an innovative adaptation of benchmarking to meet the requirements of a public sector organization market testing the value of its activities.

A company's survival depends on anticipating the actions and reactions of rivals. How a competitor is likely to behave in future should be examined from two sides: first, how a competitor is likely to respond to any changes in the external environment, and second, how the competitor is likely to respond to specific competitive moves by other organizations. Four common reaction profiles among competitors in terms of type and time of response have been identified by Kotler and Keller (2012):

- **the laid-back competitor:** does not react quickly or strongly to a given assault
- **the selective competitor:** might react to certain types of assault and not others
- **the tiger competitor:** reacts swiftly and strongly to any assaults
- **the stochastic competitor:** does not exhibit a predictable pattern.

It has been suggested that firms can build competitive advantage by focusing on the actions and response profiles of their rivals in a market. A firm's response profile can simply be predicted from the manner in which it interprets and processes information. While competitors can surely be threats, the right competitors can strengthen rather than weaken a firm's competitive position in the market. Companies that learn to live with competitors and even benefit from them will clearly be better positioned for the future. Microsoft and Apple Macintosh are examples of two companies competing in the same market (personal computers) and contributing to the market development and improving customer knowledge. A good competitor is not one that performs the beneficial functions and challenges the firm not to be complacent, but one with which the firm can achieve a profitable industry equilibrium without protracted warfare. Bad competitors, on the other hand, have the opposite characteristics (Porter, 1985). Four competitors' benefits are identified: increasing competitive advantage, improving current industry structure, aiding market development, and deterring entry (Porter, 1985).

Competitive intelligence

The concept of intelligence has a rich history of more than 200 years (Juhari and Stephens, 2006). The British tea industry is an example that has its roots in collecting competitive intelligence when Mr Wickham, who worked as an agent for the English East India Company, was sent to China to gather intelligence and relayed the importance of tea to the Chinese and its potential to contribute to the British economy (Calof and Wright, 2008). For a company to undertake a valuable competitor analysis, it needs to collect various sets of information about their rivalry. Such information should be collected, organized, interpreted, and disseminated via an intelligence gathering system. The concept of intelligence as part of marketing strategy has been recognized as an effort to improve the organization's competitiveness. Competitive intelligence has been seen as a system of environmental scanning which integrates the knowledge of everyone in a company (Calof and Wright, 2008). It can also be viewed as a process for supporting both strategic and tactical decisions, and in order to support these decisions, organizations need to have processes in place to gather and analyse reliable, relevant, and timely information that is available in vast amounts about competitors and markets (Trim and Lee, 2008). It is also believed that the term 'competitive intelligence' may imply the true meaning and purpose of intelligence; that is, to gain strategic advantage (Dishman and Calof, 2008).

The objective of a competitive intelligence system is to help companies to develop and sustain distinct competitive advantages by using the whole of the organization's networks to develop actionable insights about the various components of the business environment. It uses a systematic and ethical process involving planning, collection, analysis, communication, and management of information gathered (Calof, 2008). The competitive intelligence system first identifies the vital types of competitive information and the best sources of this information. The system then continuously collects the data from the field. The information should be checked for validity and reliability before key information is communicated to relevant decision-makers. The process and functions of a competitive intelligence system are shown in Figure 3.5.

It is worth noting here that social media platforms have recently been used by many organizations as a key digital tool for monitoring and gathering information about competitors: their brands, strengths and weaknesses, and strategic directions. Some companies may even employ other specialist firms to do that on their behalf. Using social media to analyse competitors' activities and brands and compare them with the company's own activities and brands would allow the company to better understand the market in which it operates (Windels, 2013).[5]

Customer behaviour analysis via social media network platforms

The term 'consumer behaviour' refers to the behaviour that consumers display in searching for, purchasing, consuming, evaluating, and disposing of products and services they expect to satisfy their needs. Customer analysis is an integral part of the micro environmental analysis, and sometimes it is perceived to be of more importance than analysing competitors,

---

[5] Readers can refer to Chapter 2 for more detail about social media and competitive intelligence.

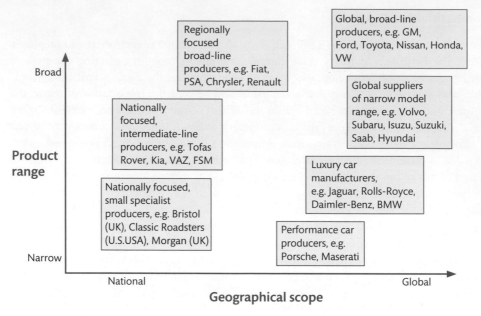

3.5 Functions of a Competitor Intelligence System

Source: Michael E. Porter (1980), *Competitive Strategy: Techniques for Analysing Industries and Competitors.* Reprinted with the permission of the Free Press, a Division of Simon & Schuster Adult Publishing Group.

especially in the markets where consumer bargaining power is relatively high. Customer behaviour analysis aims to understand how individuals make decisions to spend their time, money, and effort on consumption-related items. It includes the analysis of **what** brand they buy, **why** they buy it, **when** they buy it, **where** they buy it from, **how** often they buy it, and **how** frequently they use it. This information can help organizations in the strategic marketing process of segmentation, targeting, and positioning by identifying the customers' differences and similarities to form the basis for profiling consumers and putting them into groups. Figure 3.6 illustrates how a company such as Heineken can analyse consumer behaviour in the UK beer market using the 5Ws questions to identify different consumers' needs and preferences.

Customer analysis allows organizations to predict how consumers are likely to react to various informational and environmental cues. It is important to recognize how and why individual consumers make their consumption decisions so that organizations can make better strategic marketing decisions. A company is market-oriented if it has mastered the art of listening to customers, understanding their needs, and offering products and services that meet these needs. As mentioned earlier, Zara's tactic is to place a few items on the shelf for a brief period and then respond to their customer buying behaviour by keeping the items that fly off the shelf and removing those that don't.

Believing that this process gives competitive advantage, many companies spend millions of dollars every year on focus groups, surveys, and social media. The 'voice of the customer' reigns supreme, driving decisions related to products, prices, promotions, distributions, and positioning (Dawar, 2013).

When?

Individuals over 18 can purchase between licence times (different in Scotland). Seasonal changes: Spring—hoppy,citrus, zingy beers. Summer—light and golden ales or lagers. Autumn and Winter—darker, earthy beers or stouts. Trend more prevalent in pubs/bars/clubs than shops.On-premise beer consumption is highest on Friday and Saturday with around 53% of volume sold then.

Where?

Beer drinkers can purchase all kinds of beer on-trade and enjoyed in premises such as the pub or off-trade and enjoyed at home. Speciality world beers harder to find in licensed premises can also be bought online.

Who?

AB-InBev company research revealed five different major customer profiles:

'38% of beer consumers = Loyalists. Mostly on-premise socialising around beer and sport.; mainly on-premise socialising around beer and sports

25% - Experimenters. Have passion for beer, less price sensitive. Looking for uniqueness, variety. Craft beer drinkers.

15% -Aspirers. Ethnic groups are more dominant, they tend to drink imported beers

12% -Trend Seekers. Food/beer pairings are a popular.

10% - Sippers. Skew toward females, beer is usually not their first beverage of choice. Sippers are spurring the growth of sweeter, fruity beers'. (AB-InBev, 2010)

Why?

In a struggling economy consumers have been shown to be putting more thought into their purchases, especially in on-trade venues, and so we are seeing an increase in desire for craft beers. Those buying premium lagers or speciality craft beers prefer quality over quantity

What?

Expectations—fresh and cold beer, consistent in taste and quality, premises should have a good selection of brands and beer types.
On-trade beer purchasers—more experimental than if buying in shop.
Off-trade beer purchasers—experience not as important ,'grab-and-go', promotions and displays influential in purchases

3.6 Consumer Behaviour Analysis in the UK Beer Market

Source: Reprinted with permission of the authors. Originally produced by a group of final year marketing students for class assignment.

Traditionally, customer analysis has always been undertaken via various forms of desk and market research, including demographics and statistics analysis, consumer surveys, market observations, mystery shopping, and focus groups. Recently, many (if not all) organizations have shifted 33 their attention towards social media networks and used them as valuable platforms on which they can monitor, evaluate, and analyse consumer behaviour. Through social networking, companies can not only monitor but also interact with individual consumers. Such interactions allow companies to improve their understanding and appreciation of consumer behaviour. Using new semantic analysis technologies, marketers can detect buying signals, such as content shared by people and questions posted online. Most marketers at leading organizations have created many lively exchanges with and among customers on sites such as OPEN Forum (American Express), myPlanNet (Cisco), and Fiesta Movement (Ford), tapping into participants' knowledge, expertise, and creativity for brand development and strategy advancement. This brief discussion emphasizes the valuable contributions that social media can make to customer behaviour analysis in particular, and marketing strategy development in general.

The strategic use of market research and the role of big data

As discussed earlier, the two tasks of competitor and customer analyses form integral parts of the strategic analysis of the micro environment. To undertake such analyses a company needs to systematically gather a vast amount and various types of information, organize it, and then put it in a logical context to inform the strategic marketing decision-making process. This is the typical strategic use of market research. It aims to collect and convert raw data into meaningful information and disseminate it on a regular basis to the strategy makers for better understanding of the market in which the company operates.

This strategic use of market research includes the collection of vast amounts of information on competitors' goals, objectives, strategies, tactics, and performance. It also includes the collection of detailed information about the company's customers and their expectations, preferences, spending patterns, and demographics. Marketing research has been used strategically by many companies such as Procter & Gamble and Microsoft to identify new market opportunities. Procter & Gamble, for example, create a market advantage by spending great amounts of money on advertising and promotion to build entry barriers in the face of a new entrant. This company and others believe that market research is a useful tool in directing incremental improvements to existing products.

We must note here that not all the information from market research can be taken seriously unless it is carefully tested and validated. See Mini Case 3.2 which considers why not all information/views given by consumers in market research or on social media platforms should be taken as strictly true. When asked about the market research that went into the development of the iPad, Steve Jobs famously replied, 'None. It's not the consumers' job to know what they want.' And even if they do know what they want, asking them may not be the best way to find out.

 Mini Case 3.2 The truth about lies[6]

Why do people lie online? Whether it's on social media, in market research groups, or in product reviews, evolutionary drivers can tempt us all to be dishonest.

In consultancy work the two primary challenges are the need to get beyond any consumer's inability to be honest, and getting clients—particularly those who work in consumer insight functions—to stop believing the things that consumers tell them are true. People outside the market research world typically understand that what people say isn't true: they've usually been selectively ignoring research for years.

The thing is, everybody lies. To understand why everybody lies or, more accurately, why what everybody says is hardly ever honest, you have to consider the different routes to expressed untruths. Broadly, these take three forms.

The first are the inaccurate things people tell themselves so that they feel better about themselves—the 90 per cent of people who believe that about themselves can't all be right. Then there are responses

[6] Philip Graves, *The Marketer*, May-June 2014, p.15.

that are biased by the questions asked or the situation. And of course there are lies people tell knowingly to gain an advantage in a particular situation: customer service staff routinely encounter people who claim that they haven't used a product, or that they used it in accordance with the manufacturer's instructions, when it is entirely apparent that this isn't the case.

Online, there are lots of opportunities for people to indulge in all three types of untruth. Social media provides an ideal playground in which people can present an idealised view of themselves to the people around them: the act of choosing what aspects of your life you report to your 'friends' is inherently selective. Product reviews are often misleading because they reflect a natural polarisation of perspectives. Often they are posted soon after the product arrives, in the first floods of infatuation and excitement: you'll find it really hard to find a review for an exercise or diet that says, 'I did this for a bit and it worked; then I couldn't be bothered, so it didn't.' Yet 90 per cent of the time this will be the reality. On the other hand, people who feel let down lose any sense of perspective. Their consumer power has been violated by disappointment and, rather than recognise that a small proportion of product failures may occur, they will vent their fury by describing the product as rubbish.

Objective evaluations are rare because people are rarely objective in any situation. The temptation for some people to post fake reviews to endorse their own products or to undermine their competitors is, in psychological terms at least, understandable. It has been suggested that we've evolved with the capacity to lie because it gives us an edge over those around us. However, this all depends on not getting caught; the point at which we become social outcasts is the point at which that evolutionary benefit is lost.

For marketers interested in what they read online the clear conclusion is that while there may be a grain of truth in there, it's unlikely that what you're reading reflects the full picture with any accuracy. And for those interested in making the internet a more honest place, ensure that the likelihood of detection is sufficiently high and the consequences of being caught are sufficiently alarming to deter would-be cheats. If we're lucky, what will be left are just the lies we tell ourselves and the contextually biased reactions we give without knowing we're being economical with the truth. These are part and parcel of society and, provided that you don't base your marketing on insights that are blighted by them, reasonably harmless.

Any effective strategic use of market research depends on a number of factors, the most important of which are the quality of data sets and the quality of processing them. Collecting vast amount of data sets from various sources may present a problem for an organization when it comes to handling and processing them. This is why the new term big data came on the scene recently. 'Big data' is a term for the collection of data sets so large and complex that traditional data processing applications cannot handle them. By deriving analysis of a single large set of data it allows correlations to be found which may otherwise go unnoticed (Biesdorf et al., 2013). Exploring and processing data for market research and other business planning activity is becoming an increasingly essential source of competitive advantage. A recent survey was conducted by The World Federation of Advertisers (WFA), with 47 member companies (representing $35bn in annual marketing investment), in which they were asked for their views on big data. It was reported that 88 per cent agreed that big data is vital for current and future business decision-making; however, a worrying 74 per cent stated they were unprepared to take advantage of the opportunities offered by big data (Ward, 2014).

Although there was a general agreement among industry experts in the past few years that the term 'big data' does not fly, it appears now that marketers have started to appreciate the important role big data can play not only for marketing research purposes, but also for planning and prediction purposes. Kayyali et al. (2013) discuss in a recent article the evolution and importance of big data and its predictive capabilities in the US health care market. Biesdorf et al. (2013) state that the successful big data plan is the one that promotes strategic dialogue at the corporate top level, and helps to shape investment priorities. The success of such big data plans depend on three elements:

- assembling and integrating extraordinary volumes of new data to generate fresh views/ insights
- choosing advanced analytic models that optimize operations and predict the outcome of business decisions
- developing intuitive tools that translate the model's output into tangible business actions, and training employees on the model's use.

Despite the growing popularity of the term big data and the general consensus of its strategic importance, the strategic implications of big data have yet to be fully understood and appreciated. Many organizations are still struggling with how to utilize and invest in big data and to acquire a sustainable competitive advantage. Why is that? Because big data has been hyped so heavily that companies are expecting it to deliver more value than it actually can (Ross et al., 2013). Another reason that investments in big data fail to pay off is that the majority of companies do not know what to do with the information they already have. They do not know how to handle it appropriately or how to analyse it in a way that enhances their understanding of the situation, which can then lead them to make changes in response to new insights.

Now, most executives ask the question: 'Where is the evidence that using big data intelligently will improve business performance?' And how can the investment in data analytics create a competitive advantage? The answer to these questions is not evident so far. Interviewing a number of executives, McAfee and Brynjolfsson (2012) reported that the more companies characterized themselves as data-driven, the better they performed on objective measures of financial and operational results. The generalization of this finding is open to debate.

Strategic analysis of the internal environment

Internal analysis aims to provide a detailed understanding of those aspects of the organization that are of strategic importance. Although the external analysis is essential to success, it is not sufficient to achieve the required success unless accompanied by a thorough analysis of the organization's internal environment. The internal appraisal has a pivotal role in formulating marketing strategies and plans with which a firm can trace its success. It has been claimed that differences in performance among companies may be best explained not through differences in industry structure identified by external analysis, but through differences in the firm's assets and resources (Hunt and Derozier, 2004). It has also been claimed that a considerable amount of thinking in the 1980s on marketing strategy focused on the nature and structure of the organization's external environment and upon the ways in which this environment influences strategy development. But it is argued that the significance of the external environment has been over-emphasized and that a more practical focus for strategy development should be the organization's resource base (Collis and Montgomery, 2008).

Resource-based approach to internal analysis

The resource-based approach to internal analysis is a recognized framework for strategy development (see Figure 3.7). Figure 3.7 illustrates the role of the firm's resources as the foundation for marketing strategy formulation. This framework shows how a firm's resources and capabilities can create a competitive advantage.

The elements of this framework are: (1) defining the firm's resources that present internal strengths and weaknesses; (2) the organization's combined resources form a number of capabilities; (3) these resources and capabilities provide a sustainable competitive advantage; (4) this sustainability derives from linking the organization's unique resources to different types of strategies that exploit these resources and capability across time; and (5) the characteristics of resources and capabilities (e.g. durability, transferability, and replicability) are important in sustaining competitive advantage. Some of the resources may be unique because they are difficult to imitate (e.g. a world-class brand, patented products, or location). Capabilities develop when companies repeatedly apply their knowledge and skills to

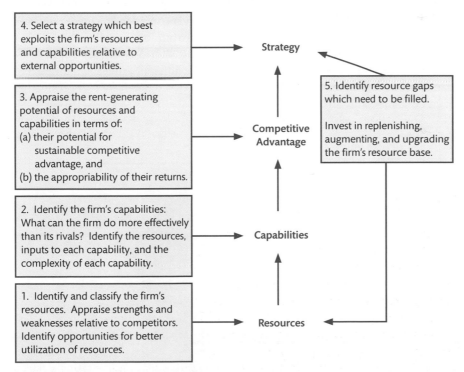

3.7 A Resource-based Approach to Strategy Analysis: A Practical Framework
Source: Robert M. Grant (1991), 'The Resource-Based Theory of Competitive Advantage: Implications for Strategy Formulation', *California Management Review*, 33(3), Redrawn by permission.

combine and transform resources in ways that contribute to achieving the firm's goals and competitive advantages (Morgan, 2012). One can tell which internal activities a firm considers to be a source of competitive advantage by how well they protect them. If a company's edge lies in its production processes, then plant visits are strictly controlled. If it believes that its R&D is unique, security around its research labs is airtight and armies of lawyers protect its patents. If it appreciates its talent, it will provide hip work spaces for employees, gourmet lunches, yoga studios, nap nooks, sabbaticals, and flexible work hours (Dawar, 2013).

Value chain approach to internal analysis

Porter (1985) has developed this framework as a way of examining the nature and extent of the synergies, if any, among the internal activities of a firm. According to Porter, every firm is a collection of activities that are performed to design, produce, promote, deliver, and support its products. These activities can be presented in five primary activities and four support activities using a **value chain** concept (see Figure 3.8). The principal idea of a value chain is examining all activities a firm performs and how they interact to differentiate a firm's value chain from its competitors' value chains. The value chain concept forces managers to think about supply chain operations and building and maintaining trust-based relationships (Trim and Lee, 2008).

Value chain analysis has been widely used as a means of analysing the internal activities of an organization. One benefit of the value chain analysis is the recognition that organizations are more than a random collection of machines, money, and people because these resources are of no value unless deployed into activities and organized into systems which ensure that products/services are produced and valued by the final customer/user. Because most companies produce several products or services there may be a different value chain for each of the company's product lines. Thus the internal analysis of the company involves evaluating a series of value chains, and can be undertaken as follows:

Porter's value chain model

3.8 Value Chain Model
Source: Michael E. Porter (1985), Competitive Advantage: Creating and Sustaining Superior Performance, Redrawn with the permission of the Free Press, a division of Simon & Schuster Adult Publishing Group.

- examination of each product line's value chain in terms of the various activities involved in producing that product
- examination of the linkages within each product line's value chain
- examination of the potential synergies among the value chains of different products.

In addition to these, it should be noted here that much of the value creation occurs not only inside the organization but also in the supply and distribution channels. For example, the quality of a car is not only influenced by the activities undertaken within the production plant but also determined by the quality of spare parts and components, and the performance of distributors.

Evaluation of functional areas

One of the simplest approaches for analysing an organization's internal environment is functional analysis. A company's resources and skills can be grouped into a competence profile according to the typical business functions of marketing, finance, R&D, and production, among others. The firm's resources include not only the financial and physical resources in each functional area but also the ability of people to formulate and implement the necessary functional objectives, strategies, and policies. Used properly, the functional resources may serve as strengths to support strategic decisions. In addition to the functional resources, the organization's culture and structure should be regarded as key parts of the organization's internal environment (Wei et al., 2014).

Performance analysis approach

One of the classical approach to internal analysis is the **PIMS program** (*Profit Impact of Market Strategy*) conducted by the Strategic Planning Institute in the USA to help pinpoint relevant internal strategic factors for business corporations. The PIMS program aims to discover empirical principles that determine which strategy variables, under which conditions, produce what results in terms of return on investment and cash flow. Specifically, PIMS research has identified nine major strategic variables that account for 80 per cent of the variation in profitability among businesses in the database (Buzzell and Wiersema, 1981; Buzzell and Gale, 1987).

There are many other ways to evaluate the performance of a business. While the most common are the financial measures, other non-financial measures can provide better understanding of long-term business health. The non-financial measures include market standing, product value, management development, and productivity. It should be noted here that an organization's strategic objectives may change over time, and so should the financial measures to use for assessing business performance. For example, at the introduction stage of a new product, the key measure to use may be sales growth, whilst at maturity stage, ROI may be used to assess the company success. Given the importance of both financial and non-financial measures, Kaplan and Norton (1992, 1996) introduced a new, and arguably comprehensive, method which evaluates a company's performance, namely '*the balanced scorecard*'. This method recognizes four perspectives which integrate the financial and non-financial measures of a company's performance: the financial perspective, the customer perspective, the internal business perspective, and the innovation and learning perspective.

Apart from categorizing the internal variables into financial or non-financial, strategic managers must look within their companies to identify the internal strategic factors that have the greatest effect (positive or negative) on the company's performance. In other words, strategic managers should identify the internal variables that may be regarded as strengths or weaknesses. A variable is a strength if it provides a competitive advantage, it is of value to the customer, and the firm does or has the potential to do particularly well relative to the abilities of existing or potential competitors. On the other hand, a variable is a weakness if it is also of value to a customer but the firm does it poorly or does not have the capacity to do it well, although its competitors have that capacity (Wheelen and Hunger, 2012). To evaluate the significance of these variables, a company has to compare the measures of these variables with similar measures of the company's past performance, the company's key competitors, and the industry as a whole.

The use of financial statements to measure a company's performance should be done carefully because of the different accounting rules that multinational corporations follow outside their home countries. For example, British firms such as M&S and BP use the term 'turnover' rather than 'sales revenue'.

'Strategic fit'—the conclusion of external and internal strategic analyses

A successful strategy arises from a firm's strategic analysis of emerging opportunities and threats in the external environment while taking into account the firm's internal strengths and weaknesses. The development of marketing strategy requires forming a strategic vision and implementing the market targeting and positioning strategies. For this purpose, the organization's strategic analysis of the macro and micro environments could be concluded by developing what is known as an 'environmental impact matrix' in which major opportunities and threats are identified, their potential impact assessed/weighted, and their implications for strategy development accounted for (see Tables 3.3A and 3.3B).

Similarly, the organization's analysis of its internal environment could also be concluded by developing what is known as a 'strategic capability profile' in which the potential strengths and weaknesses of the organizational resources and capabilities are identified, assessed, and weighted (see Table 3.4).

Table 3.3A Environmental Impact Matrix: The Macro (Remote) Environment

Factor	Impact of Factor	Potential Opportunity or Threat
Political/legal	Increased legislation on product liablity	Mild threat
Economic	Recession in key overseas markets	Major threat
Technological	Little innovation likely from competitors	Neutral impact
Socio-cultural	Increased awareness of environmental protection issues	Significant opportunity

Source: Reprinted with permission of the authors.

Table 3.3B Environmental Impact Matrix: The Competitive Environment

Factor	Impact of factor	Potential opportunity or threat
Competition	Intense rivalry in industry/market place	Critical threat (−5)
Buyers	Convergence of customer requirements worldwide	Significant opportunity (+5)
Suppliers	Few suppliers dominate industry	Critical threat (−5)
Threat of new entrants	Industry barriers to entry are low	Threat (−3)

Source: Reprinted with permission of the authors.

Table 3.4 Strategic Capability Profile Based on Resource Audit

Internal Area	Resource/Competence	Evaluation
Physical resources	New facilities incorporating latest technology	Major strength (+4)
Human resources	Highly trained technical staff	Minor strength (+2)
	Top scientists recruited	
Financial resources	High gearing	Mild weakness (−2)
Intangibles	Strong corporate image in the marketplace	Significant strength (+5)
	Well-established brand names	Significant strength (+4)
Inbound logistics/procurement	Over-reliance on a limited no. of suppliers	Significant weakness (−4)
Outbound logistics	Ineffective warehouse automation	Weakness (−3)
Human resource management	High levels of absenteeism/ poor industrial relations record	Significant weakness (−4)

Source: Reprinted with permission of the authors.

SWOT analysis is a systematic way to integrate internal and external analyses to find a 'strategic fit' between what the environment wants and what the organization has to offer, as well as between what the organization needs and what the environment can provide. SWOT is an established analytical device that appraises an organization's current situation and can be extended by linking the results of the analysis to scoring procedures and then placing the results in matrices to enhance the strategic decision-making process. The four headings of SWOT analysis (i.e. Strengths, Weaknesses, Opportunities, and Threats) can be very useful for summarizing principal elements of the internal analysis and combining them with the key issues arising from the external analysis. For example, the strengths of an organization may include a well-known brand, well-qualified labour, a unique competitive advantage, an established relationship with suppliers, customer service, and/or efficient management of overhead. One of the strengths of Wal-Mart lies in its strong brand, while FedEx's strength is based on its stellar customer service. On the other hand, weaknesses may include factors such as limited brand awareness, low market share, unstable sales figures, quality issues, and/or inefficient operations. For example, Internet companies such as Zappos.com offer a wide variety of items for sale, but have the weakness of an inefficient distribution system that cannot stand the competition from other players in the footwear market. A company like Sears, known for its household goods, has suffered from a depleted market share in recent years because of increased competition.

Organizations aim to assess whether their specific strengths and weaknesses are relevant to, and capable of, dealing with the external changes taking place in the business environment. Such changes may represent opportunities or threats. Opportunities must provide a company with a real and executable advantage to invest in. For example, the closure of some retail banking branches in the UK because of the financial crisis of 2008/09 provided opportunities for some retail stores such as Tesco and Asda to offer financial products to their customers. The major guitar retailer, Guitar Center, saw an opportunity in the wide usage of the Internet to promote and sell its brands everywhere and managed to capture market share in the musical instruments market. Threats come from various directions such as the economic situation, changes in laws, changes of government/regime, intense competition, and/or other uncontrollable variables. For example, companies that feature luxury items, such as Tiffany & Co or Bloomingdale's, had to be a little more creative as recession threatened the luxury market. Another example of unpredictable threat was the bad weather in France in 2011 which affected that year's wine production.

Performing a SWOT analysis can help organizations to identify the areas where immediate strategic decisions need to be taken either to capitalize upon strengths or to overcome a threat. The analysis can also uncover new areas a company must look at. As an example, Amazon, which has captured a large share of the Internet book market, found that it had spent serious money to gain that market share, but now has to streamline its costs to remain competitive. In that case, a new strength was offset by a new weakness that had to be addressed.

Although SWOT analysis is a well-known strategic tool, it has been subject to several criticisms because of its apparent limitations. One principal criticism is that in practice the tool can be ineptly used, which makes it of no real value. The common reason for the ineptitude is managers' tendency to list strengths, weaknesses, opportunities, and threats in a 'bullet point format' without paying sufficient attention to their real significance. The result is what academics call 'a balance sheet approach'. Another criticism is that, having done the SWOT analysis, managers often fail to identify an appropriate set of strategic choices and recommendations to improve the company's strategic position that take account of outcome of the analysis. Weihrich (1982) proposed a SWOT (TOWS) matrix which, while making use of the same inputs of the SWOT analysis, integrates them more fully into the strategic management process. This matrix, shown in Figure 3.9, illustrates the alternative ways in which an organization can use its strengths to capitalize on opportunities or to minimize threats and invest in available opportunities to overcome its weaknesses. The SWOT (TOWS) matrix is a very useful tool for creating a series of strategic alternatives that the decision-makers in an organization might not otherwise have considered.

We present here, as an illustrative example, Subway (a key player in the UK fast food market) to show how a company can operationalize the SWOT (TOWS) analysis. Figure 3.10 shows how Subway could utilize the internal and external analyses to produce a number of strategic routes/directions, and make strategic marketing recommendations the company can follow to best position its brand in the market. By combining their strengths of serving healthy fast food and flexible customization of foods with the various opportunities in the market, Subway

Internal factors (IFAS)	Strengths (S)	Weaknesses (W)
External factors (EFAS)	List 5–10 *internal* strengths here	List 5–10 *internal* weaknesses here
Opportunities List 5–10 *external* opportunities here	**SO strategies** Generate strategies here that use strengths to take advantage of opportunities.	**WO strategies** Generate strategies here that take advantage of opportunities by overcoming weaknesses
Threats (T) List 5–10 *external* threats here	**ST strategies** Generate strategies here that use strengths to avoid threats	**WT strategies** Generate strategies here that minimize weaknesses and avoid threats

3.9 The SWOT (TOWS) Matrix

Source: Adapted from Heinz Weihrich (1982), 'The TOWS Matrix—A Tool for Situation Analysis', *Long Range Planning*, 15(2), pp. 54–66.

should consider capitalizing on the increasing awareness of healthy eating habits to position the brand better in the market. Subway can also capitalize on the wide popularity of digital services to introduce a new ordering system that provides more convenient value to consumers. Such a new system may overcome one of the company weaknesses of having smaller outlet size than its competitors and may improve its competitive position in this regard.

Finally, once the analytical tool has been chosen for its strategic analysis, an organization needs to review its inputs on a regular and ongoing basis to identify how these inputs are changing and the implications of the changes on the future directions of the marketing strategy development.

The latest thinking: big data—the new management revolution

Data driven strategic decisions are better decisions as strategic managers are enabled to decide on the basis of evidence rather than intuition, and for that reason has the potential to revolutionize today's strategic management decisions (McAfee and Brynjolfsson, 2012).

Barton and Court (2012) note that big data and analytics have rocketed to the top of the corporate agenda. Most executives look with admiration at how large organizations such as Google, Amazon, and others have outperformed competitors with powerful new business models derived from an ability to utilize and exploit data. They also see that big data is attracting massive investment from leading technology companies such as IBM and Hewlett Packard. Large organizations that were born digital are already masters of big data. But

External Factors / Internal Factors	OPPORTUNITIES: Change of people lifestyle: faster lifestyle. People's view of food has changed (healthier food). Economic recession in the UK and most of Europe.	THREATS: Food quality issues, e.g. food safety and other regulations. Several competitors offering more choices to consumers.
STRENGTHS: Healthier than other fast food brands (e.g. fried fast food). Green image. Flexible sub-customization to customers (bread, toppings, salad and sauce). Clear marketing strategy (targeting specific customer groups). Introduction of drive-through. Low start-up costs	Lower the price with no change to the food quality. Extensive advertising to raise brand popularity and create a unique 'Subway experience'. Underline 'healthy message' in all promotional activities.	Expand product portfolio and offer customers more choices on the menu.
WEAKNESSES: Smaller store size compared with main competitors (e.g., KFC, McDonalds). Limited food choices to customers (only sandwich). Low market share compared with other fast food companies. Control over franchisees so that they can't respond to local tastes. Poor customer services.	Provide better training to staff to improve service quality. Improve existing outlets' interior. Allow a higher degree of localization/customization	Introduce self-ordering system to make the process more convenient and faster.

3.10 Subway SWOT (TOWS) matrix presenting strategic choices and recommendations for the UK fast food market.

Source: Reprinted with permission of the authors. Originally produced by a group of final year marketing students for class assignment.

the potential for gaining competitive advantage from it is even greater for other digital and non-digital companies. In fact, big data can transform the way organizations do business. As data-driven strategies take hold, they will become an increasingly important point of competitive advantage and differentiation. According to a study by McAfee and Brynjolfsson (2012) companies that inject big data and analytics into their operations show productivity rates and profitability 5 to 6 per cent higher than those of their rival peers.

It has been suggested that exploiting data and analytics requires three mutually supportive capabilities. First, companies must be able to choose the right data and manage multiple sources of data. Second, they should build advanced analytics models for predicting and optimizing business outcomes. Third, they must possess the ability to transform the organization's capabilities so that the data and models yield better decisions. Two important features underpin those activities: a clear strategy for how to use data and analytics, and deployment of the right technology architecture and capabilities (Barton and Court, 2012).

In research by Goyal et al. (2012) designed to understand how large organizations use big data to identify lucrative new sales spots, they interviewed 120 sales executives from companies that have significantly outperformed their competitors in revenue and profitability. They found that most sales organizations are combining and crunching the mountains of data about customers, competitors, and their own operations to dice up their existing sales regions into hundreds of 'micromarkets' to identify new-growth hot spots. The authors named this a as a 'micromarket strategy' which, in their view, is the most potent new application of big data analytics in the sales field. Micromarket strategy develops through five stages: defining the optimal micromarket size, measuring the growth potential for each, gauging the market share in each, understanding the causes of variation in market share, and prioritizing high-potential markets to focus on. Figure 3.11 illustrates and compares how big data can drive sales growth via traditional approach and 'micromarket' strategy.

Traditional Approach	Micromarket Strategy
Data management	
Sales collects customer data from internal sources (CRM, billing, customer-service databases). Data are updated and analysed quarterly or semi-annually Outside analysts provide tools, advice, and statistical services.	Sales combines very large databases of internal and external data such as demographics, social media chatter, and competitive intensity. Data are updated and analysed monthly, weekly, and daily data collection and analytics are done by in-house experts.
Resources allocation	
Sales coverage is defined by large regions and territories. Sales resources are allocated according to a region's historical performance.	Sales coverage is segmented into dozens or hundreds of micromarkets. Resources are deployed at the micromarket level according to expected future opportunity.
Resource management	
Rep (and channel partner) performance is assessed relative to other reps (and other channel partners).	Performance is assessed relative to the opportunity within micromarkets.
Collaboration	
Sales, marketing, and other departments are siloed.	Sales, marketing, strategy, customer service, and other functions are collaborative.

3.11 How Big Data Can Drive Sales Growth.

Source: Goyal Manish, Maryanne Hancock, and Homayoun Hatami (2012), 'Selling into Micromarkets', *Harvard Business Review*, 90 (July-August), pp. 79–86.

Big data seems to affect every aspect of a business, requiring a change in mindset from leadership down to the front lines. Describing such a transformation at Pioneer Hi-Bred, a DuPont agricultural products company, Alejandro Munoz, the vice president for the Americas and global production, said that 'this granular view is really a new way of thinking, and it takes time for it to become part of the company's DNA'. At Pioneer, it took years, he said, but today it guides 'how we run our commercial operations, how we invest against opportunities, and how we deploy sales and marketing' (Goyal et al., 2012).

Although the technical challenges of using big data are enormous, the managerial challenges are even greater. One of the critical aspects of big data is its impact on how decisions are made and who makes them. Big data's power does not erase the need for human vision and insights. McAfee and Brynjolfsson (2012) identified five challenging areas for management that are particularly important for organizations to gain the full benefits of a transition to using big data.

- **Leadership:** companies succeed in the big data era not simply because they have more or better data, but because they have leadership teams that set clear goals, define what success looks like, and ask the right questions.

- **Talent management:** as data become cheaper, the complements to data become more valuable. Some of the most crucial of these are data scientists and other professionals skilled at working with large quantities of information.

- **Technology:** the tools available to handle the volume, velocity, and variety of big data have improved greatly in recent years. These technologies require a skill set that is new to most IT departments, which will need to integrate the relevant internal and external sources of data.

- **Decision-making:** an effective organization puts information and the relevant decision-making rights in the same location. In the big data era, information is created and transferred, and expertise is often not where it used to be.

- **Company culture:** the first question a data-driven organization asks itself is not 'what do we think?' but 'what do we know?' This requires a move away from acting solely on hunches and instinct.

The trend towards big data is growing and strategic managers cannot afford to dismiss it as hype. As more organizations acquire the core skills of using big data, building superior capabilities may soon become a decisive competitive advantage.

Conclusion

The formulation of marketing strategy is the development of long-range plans for the effective management of the major factors and key trends in the organization's marketing environment. The development of a marketing strategy should therefore be based on a thorough understanding and effective use of environmental opportunities and threats while taking into account the organization's strengths and weaknesses. Increasing environmental uncertainty coupled with increasing pressure on organizations to create and sustain a distinctive competency means that the scanning and analysis of the internal and external environments will become an important part of every marketer's job. To remain competitive, companies need to consider various methods of gathering, evaluating, and disseminating intelligence to those who need it. The availability of market information and competitive intelligence is essential for the development and success of any marketing strategy in today's business environment.

Summary

This chapter has discussed in great detail the first part of the SMM process, namely strategic analysis. Strategic analysis is concerned with understanding the strategic position of the organization in terms of its external environment, its internal resources and competencies, and the expectations and influence of stakeholders. Strategic analysis is central for the development of marketing strategy. Without it strategic managers could be wrongly guided and the strategy formulated might not be in tune with the key trends in the organization's marketing environment. For proper conduct of strategic analysis different sets of market information and competitive intelligence should be gathered, scanned, and analysed. This analysis aims not only to identify the possible opportunities and threats in the external environment but also the organization's internal strengths and weaknesses. Many analytical models and frameworks are available to support such an analysis and strategic managers should make their choice based on their understanding of how to operationalize the selected model. To conclude their strategic analysis and to inform the subsequent decision of strategic choices, strategic managers should attempt to find a strategic fit between external opportunities and internal strengths while working around external threats and internal weaknesses.

Key terms

- **Big data:** is a term for the collection of data sets so large and complex that traditional data processing applications cannot handle them.

- **Environmental scanning:** is the process of collecting information about the forces in the environment. Scanning involves observation, perusal of secondary sources, such as business, trade, government, and general interest publications and marketing research.

- **Scenario analysis:** is the process of exploring different assumptions about the environment and its future. it involves the development of a few plausible scenarios, the formulation of strategies appropriate to each scenario, the evaluation of scenario probabilities, and the assessment of the resulting strategies across scenarios.

- **Strategic choices:** involve the options for strategy in terms of both the directions in which strategy might move and the methods by which strategy might be pursued.

- **Strategic (position) analysis:** is concerned with identifying the impact on strategy of the external environment, an organization's strategic capability and the expectations and influence of stakeholders.

- **Strategic group approach:** is an analytical device designed to aid in industry structural analysis. It is an intermediate frame of reference between looking at the industry as a whole and considering each firm separately.

- **Strategy implementation:** is concerned with ensuring that chosen strategies are actually put into action. It is the translation of strategy into organizational action through organizational structure and design, resource planning, and the management of strategic change.

- **Value chain:** is a strategic tool (model) that aims to examine the nature and extent of the synergies, if any, among an organization's internal (primary and supportive) activities.

Discussion questions

1. For a market of your choice, critically examine with examples the environmental factors that influence organizations operating in this market.

2. Refer to a company you are familiar with, and discuss the implications of the social network platforms for improving consumer behaviour analysis and intelligence gathering.

3. Discuss the major steps an organization might undertake to conduct such a competitive analysis. Support your discussion with examples and relevant model.

4. Analysing an organization's internal environment is not an easy task given the number of resource areas that need to be thoroughly assessed. Do what extent do you agree or disagree with this statement? What approach would you recommend for the management of an organization to undertake an internal audit?

Online resource centre

 Visit the Online Resource Centre for this book for lots of interesting additional material at: <www.oxfordtextbooks.co.uk/orc/west3e/>

References and further reading

Aaker, David A. and Damien McLoughlin (2010), *Strategic Market Management* (New York: John Wiley).

Ansoff, Igor H. (1991), 'Critique of Henry Mintzberg's The Design School: Reconsidering the Basic Premises of Strategic Management', *Strategic Management Journal*, 12 (6), pp. 449–61.

Ansoff, Igor H. (1994), 'Comment on Henry Mintzberg's Rethinking Strategic Planning', *Long Range Planning*, 27 (3), pp. 31–2.

Barton, Dominic and David Court (2012), 'Making Advanced Analytics Work for You', *Harvard Business Review*, 90, October, pp. 79–83.

Biesdorf, Stefan, David Court, and Paul Willmott (2013), 'Big Data: What's Your Plan?', *McKinsey Quarterly*, Issue 2, pp. 40–51.

Buzzell, Robert D. and Bradley T. Gale (1987), *The PIMS Principles*, (N.Y: The Free Press).

Buzzell, Robert D. and Frederik D. Wiersema (1981), 'Successful Share-Building Strategies', *Harvard Business Review*, 59, January-February, pp. 135–44.

Calof, Jonathan L. (2008), 'Selling Competitive Intelligence', *Competitive Intelligence Magazine*, 11 (1), pp. 39–42.

Calof, Jonathan L. and Sheila Wright (2008), 'Competitive Intelligence: A Practitioner, Academic and Inter-disciplinary Perspective', *European Journal of Marketing*, 42 (7/8), pp. 717–30.

Chowdhury, Shamsud D. (2014), 'Strategic Roads that Diverge or Converge: GM and Toyota in the Battle for the Top', *Business Horizons*, 57, pp. 127–36.

Collis, David J. and Cynthia A. Montgomery (2008), 'Competing on Resources', *Harvard Business Review*, 86, July-August, pp. 140–50.

Crittenden, Victoria L. and William F. Crittenden (2012), 'Strategic Marketing in a Changing World', *Business Horizons*, 55, pp. 215–17.

Dawar, Niraj (2013), 'When marketing is strategy', *Harvard Business Review*, 91, December, pp. 101–8.

Dibb, Sally, Lyndon Simkin, William Pride, and O.C. Ferrell (2012), *Marketing: Concepts and Strategies*, 6th edn, Cengage Learning.

Dishman, Paul L. and Jonathan L. Caloff (2008), 'Competitive Intelligence: A Multiphasic Precedent to Marketing Strategy', *European Journal of Marketing*, 42 (7/8), pp. 766–85.

Goyal, Manish, Maryanne Q. Hancock, and Hatami Homayoun (2012), 'Selling into Micromarkets', *Harvard Business Review*, 90, July–August, pp. 79–86.

Grant, Robert M. (1991), 'The Resource-Based Theory of Competitive Advantage: Implications for Strategy Formulation', *California Management Review*, 33 (3), pp. 114–35.

Hunt, Shelby D. and Caroline Derozier (2004), 'The Normative Imperatives of Business and Marketing Strategy: Grounding Strategy in Resources-advantage Theory', *Journal of Business and Industrial Marketing*, 19 (1), pp. 5–22.

Johnson, Gerry, Kevan Scholes, and Richard Whittington (2008), *Exploring Corporate Strategy*, 8th edn, (Harlow: FT Prentice-Hall).

Johnston, Michael, Audrey Gilmore and David Carson (2008), 'Dealing with Environmental Uncertainty: The Value of Scenario Planning for Small to Medium-sized Enterprises', *European Journal of Marketing*, 42 (11), pp. 1170–8.

Juhari, A. S. and D.P. Stephens (2006), 'Tracing the Origins of Competitive Intelligence throughout History', *Journal of Competitive Intelligence and Management*, 3 (4), pp. 61–82.

Kachaner, Nicolas and Michael S. Deimler (2009), 'Stretching the Strategy Process', *Strategic Decision*, 25 (1), pp. 17–20.

Kaplan, Robert S. and David P. Norton (1992), 'The Balanced Scorecard—Measures That Drive Performance', *Harvard Business Review*, 70, January–February, pp. 71–90.

Kaplan, Robert S. and David P. Norton (1996), 'Using the Balanced Scorecard as a Strategic Management System', *Harvard Business Review*, 74, January–February, pp. 75–85.

Kayyali, Basel, David Knott, and Steve Van Kuiken (2013), 'How Big Data is Shaping US Health Care', *McKinsey Quarterly*, Issue 2, pp. 17–18.

Kotler, Philip and Kevin Keller (2012), *Marketing Management*, 14th edn, Harlow: Pearson Education.

McAfee, Andrew and Erik Brynjolfsson (2012), 'Big Data: The Management Revolution', *Harvard Business Review*, 90, October, pp. 61–8.

Miles, Raymond E. and Charles Snow (1978), *Organizational Strategy, Structure and Process* (New York: McGraw-Hill).

Mintzberg, Henry (1990), 'The Design School: Reconsidering the Basic Premises of Strategic Management', *Strategic Management Journal*, 11 (3), pp. 171–95.

Mintzberg, Henry (1994a), *The Rise and Fall of Strategic Planning* (Upper Saddle River, NJ: Prentice-Hall).

Mintzberg, Henry (1994b), 'Rethinking Strategic Planning Part I: Pitfalls and Fallacies', *Long Range Planning*, 27 (3), pp. 12–21.

Mintzberg, H. and J. Lampel (1999), 'Reflecting on the Strategy Process', *Sloan Management Review*, 40, Spring, pp. 21–30.

Morgan, Neil A. (2012), 'Marketing and Business Performance', *Journal of the Academy of Marketing Science*, 40, pp. 102–19.

Porter, Michael E. (1979), 'How Competitive Forces Shape Strategy', *Harvard Business Review*, 57 March–April, pp. 137–45.

Porter, Michael E. (1980), *Competitive Strategy: Techniques for Analyzing Industries and Competitors* (New York: Free Press).

Porter, Michael E. (1985), *Competitive Advantage: Creating and Sustaining Superior Performance* (New York: Free Press).

Porter, Michael E. (2008), 'The Five Competitive Forces that Shape Strategy', *Harvard Business Review*, 87, January, pp. 79–93.

Rosenzweig, Phil (2013), 'What Makes Strategic Decisions Different', *Harvard Business Review*, 92 (November), pp. 88–93.

Ross, Jeanne W., Cynthia M. Beath, and Anne Quaadgras (2013), 'You May Not Need Big Data after All' *Harvard Business Review*, 92, December, pp. 90–8.

Trim, Peter R. J. and Yang-Im Lee (2008), 'A Strategic Marketing Intelligence and Multi-organizational Resilience Framework', *European Journal of Marketing*, 42 (7/8), pp. 731–45.

Utterback, James M. and W.J. Abernathy (1975), 'A Dynamic Model of Product and Process Innovation', *Omega*, 3 (6), pp. 639–56.

Verity, J. (2003), 'Scenario Planning as a Strategy Technique', *European Business Journal*, 15 (4), pp. 185–95.

Ward, Chris (2014), 'Smart Data: Creating a Strategy that Delivers Actionable Insights', **MyCustomer.com**, Friday 21 Feb 2014. <http://www.mycustomer.com/feature/data/getting-smart-how-create-data-strategy-develop-actionable-insights/166504>

Wei, Yinghong (Susan), Saeed Samiee and Ruby P. Lee (2014), 'The Influence of Organic Organizational Cultures, Market Responsiveness, and Product Strategy on Firm Performance in an Emerging Market', *Journal of the Academy of Marketing Science*, 42, pp. 49–70.

Weihrich, Heinz (1982), 'The TOWS Matrix – A Tool for Situation Analysis', *Long Range Planning*, 15 (2), pp. 54–66.

Wheelen, Thomas L. and David J. Hunger (2012), *Strategic Management and Business Policy: Toward Global Sustainability* (Upper Saddle River, NJ: Pearson Education).

Zenger, Todd (2013), 'Strategy: The Uniqueness Challenge', *Harvard Business Review*, 91 (November), pp. 52–8.

 End of Chapter 3 case study   Fage Yogurt: sustaining competitive advantage in a crowded market

Synopsis

This case discusses the US entry of Fage, a Greek-based yogurt company. In a pioneering move Fage introduced in the US market Greek style thick yogurt. Although initially the product satisfied a small niche market, very fast it attracted a wide popularity. However, increasing sales of Fage yogurt invited competitive entries into the market. At the present time Fage's sales are still increasing although it is not the market leader in the Greek style yogurt category any more. The challenge for Fage is to pursue the appropriate strategy to defend its market share in the US market and gain the ground that it lost from its competitors.

Themes

Branding strategy, positioning, customer relationship, marketing implementation, international market entry

Introduction

The Fage company originated as a small dairy store selling yogurt and other milk products in a neighbourhood in Athens, Greece. The original store was established in 1926 by the grandfather of the present owners of the company, Athanasios Filippou. Yogurt had always been a popular product in Greece where numerous small dairy stores were producing their own yogurt on a daily basis. The original Fage store was similar to many other stores selling dairy products in the Greek market.

In the 1950s and early 1960s, as the country was experiencing a post-war rapid economic growth, the small company invested in a yogurt wholesale network, the first of its kind in the Athens market serviced until then by small artisan yogurt stores. In the 1970s the company further consolidated its position in the Greek market and started expanding to foreign markets. The company's innovations and insistence on high quality standards, led its transformation from a small yogurt producer to a company operating in several foreign countries. Presently the company is selling its products in England, Italy, several other European Union countries, and such far-away places as Australia, Hong Kong, Ethiopia, and the USA.

Expansion to the US

Fage made its first exports to the US in 1998. The first inroads to the US market targeted the Greek American community and other ethnic communities familiar with Greek style thick creamy yogurt. In 2000, the company established a wholly owned subsidiary, FAGE USA Corporation, to import and distribute its products in the US. The sales of the company started growing rapidly as its products became popular among a wider American consuming public. By 2004, the company was selling 2000 tons of imported yogurt and it saw an opportunity to establish a production facility in the US. In February 2004 the decision was made to invest in a modern dairy facility in Johnstown, New York, in order to manufacture its products locally. The location in Johnstown was selected due to the short distance to New York state dairy farms and the close proximity to a big concentration of consumers in the large metropolitan areas of the Northeastern US. The new plant was built at a total cost of $148.3 million, a huge investment for a fairly small family business. When the plant opened in 2008 it employed 120 full-time employees. The company's products, initially distributed in ethnic markets, speciality stores, and natural-food stores, have moved to the shelves of mainstream supermarket chains.

The promotional campaign that the company used in its US expansion was extremely creative and successful. *Advertising Age*, the advertising industry trade magazine, recognized Fage for its 2007 campaign as the product that best stood up to advertising claims. The magazine noted that the company's exceptional print and out-of-home advertisements have made a wonderful impression and have sparked consumers' interest for a new product. In the following years, Fage's sales increased rapidly and it was successful in establishing Greek style creamy yogurt as a mainstream staple in American supermarkets. Total sales of Greek yogurt which were only $33.3 million in 2007 increased to $469 million in 2010. Although Fage was the first company to market Greek yogurt in the US, its main competitor, Chobani, has become the market leader. Chobani's sales in supermarkets, drug stores, and other venues totalled $257.3 million in 2010, up 225.9 per cent from the previous year. The sales of Fage were $141.7 million, an increase of 66.3 per cent. Oikos, a Danone brand, had sales of $53.8 million. Fage has approximately a 25 per cent market share of the Greek yogurt product category.

The success of Fage in creating a new product category was totally unusual and unexpected. Many observers were very surprised with the success of Greek style yogurt in the US market. It was an unanticipated success because it came out of nowhere. Bill Patterson, an analyst with Mintel, a market research company, stated that 'It wasn't as if there was an obvious sort of marketing push. Greek yogurt just kind of leapt on the scene. It truly was consumer-driven, which is really quite unusual'. In 2010, the Greek style yogurt product category accounted for approximately 12 per cent of the growing US yogurt market. Sales of Greek yogurt have doubled each year since 2006. Table C3.1 shows the growing importance of the Greek yogurt market segment.

Yogurt has been a popular product in many European and Middle Eastern countries although it was not very popular in the US until the 1970s when the French-owned company Danone entered

Table C3.1 Greek Yogurt by Numbers

$469 M	Total Greek yogurt sales last year
$33.3 M	Total Greek yogurt sales in 2007
12%	Greek yogurt's portion of overall yogurt-category sales
58%	Percentage of adults who eat yogurt
70%	Combined Greek yogurt share of two market leaders, Chobani and Fage
7.5	Number of times the average American eats all types of yogurt each month

Source: Mintel, sales figures for period ending 10/31/2010. Cited by Advertising Age

the market. Even today the average American eats yogurt only 7.5 times a month. European consumption is a lot higher, indicating that there is plenty of growth potential in the American market.

Greek yogurt probably became a successful product as health-conscious US consumers are looking for products with few ingredients. The difference between Greek yogurt and the regular variety is that the liquid is removed because it is filtered through a cloth. This results in a thicker final product which contains twice the protein of regular yogurt. Greek yogurt has been described as every person's dream: 'a yogurt with zero fat and the rich taste of sour cream'. American yogurt tends to be soupier and not as strong. The popularity of Greek yogurt has been sparked by a healthier turn in US eating habits. Greek yogurt is a product that is thicker, creamier, and fresher without the fat. It is a product that is 99.9 per cent lactose free and as a result easier to digest. As consumers perceive yogurt to be a healthier choice, many have shifted away from breakfast cereal to yogurt. The growth of Greek yogurt parallels other recent trends in the US diet as consumers are looking for foods that are healthy, organic, and functional. Greek yogurt has increased in popularity due to the recent focus on the benefits of the Mediterranean diet. The biggest selling point of Greek yogurt for health conscious consumers is that it has double the protein and half of the carbohydrates of regular yogurt. As a result it has created a loyal following among athletes trying to eat high protein foods, and among dieters, cooks, and foodies.

Interestingly enough, previous attempts to introduce Greek yogurt in the US, initially by Danone in 1942 and Stonyfield in 1983, flopped. It appears that the market was not ready for such an exotic product. However, when Fage entered the market, the high number of health conscious American consumers had created the right atmosphere for the rapid growth of the product category.

Competitive pressures

While Fage's incursion into the US market proved to be extremely successful, its success invited fierce competition by companies lured by the high profit margins of the Greek style yogurt category. Many observers state that the battle for dominance in the Greek style yogurt category is just beginning as the American public discovers an appetite for rich, creamy, protein-packed blends of yogurt.

Chobani has emerged as the main competitor for Fage in the US. In 2010 it had approximately 45 per cent of the Greek yogurt market. Agro Farma is the parent company of the Chobani brand and it was founded by Hamdi Ulukaya, a Turkish immigrant who came to the US in 1994 to attend college. He was looking to recreate the rich thick yogurt that he had enjoyed while growing up in his homeland.

Alpina, a global dairy giant with more than $800 worldwide sales and a presence in more than 20 countries, is planning to enter this popular market segment. While it is not planning to introduce a Greek style yogurt, the company will position its regular yogurt as 'indulgently creamy' and is going to target similar demographics as Fage. Its products are at the present time selling in gourmet speciality stores, but it is planning to place its products in mainstream grocery stores.

Kraft Foods, General Mills, and Danone, the companies that traditionally have dominated the yogurt market in the US, were slow to enter the Greek yogurt market. Recently, however, all three companies are planning to offer products in the segment. Danone, a major player, in the yogurt market selling such brands as Activia and Danimals, is planning an aggressive ad campaign to promote its Greek style yogurt, Oikos. Yoplait, a General Mills brand which leads the regular yogurt market with approximately $1.4 billion in sales, introduced a Greek style yogurt in 2010. Kraft Foods, which exited the yogurt market a few years ago, is introducing Greek style yogurt under its Athenos brand, its division for Mediterranean foods.

In addition to large companies entering the Greek yogurt market, private label brands are expected to follow now that Greek yogurt has gone mainstream. Private label yogurt has the largest market share in the regular yogurt market with $417 million in sales in 2010. Trader Joe's, a speciality grocery retailer, is already producing its private label Greek yogurt and other grocery stores are expected to follow suit.

Fage's reaction

In order to safeguard its position in the market and potentially regain market leadership, in 2010 Fage initiated its first ever TV campaign. The campaign includes a 45 second spot that employs poetry to position yogurt as a product with extraordinary sensory experience. Fage's competitors are also increasing their promotional budget. Chobani, the market leader, has introduced television commercials, billboards, and social media like Twitter, Facebook, and YouTube to promote its products. The Chobani campaign has concentrated on 'real consumers' to share their 'real experience' with the product. The Agro Farma company, Chobani's maker, announced that it will spend $13 million in the first quarter of 2011. This is a tremendous increase for a company that spend only $209,000 in 2009, and spent no money for promotion in the first nine months of 2010.

The question is whether Fage will be able to retain its market share in the US now that its expanding market niche has attracted the attention of food giants such as Kraft and General Mills, willing to support their brands with huge promotional campaigns. The importance of the US market has increased as Greece is experiencing a severe economic crisis and sales of dairy product are declining. In the January–September 2010 period, Fage's domestic sales declined by 12.1 per cent. In contrast, international sales increased by 40.1 per cent, with US sales going up by more than 61 per cent.

An additional question for Fage is its pricing strategy. Traditionally Greek yogurt has been priced higher than its regular counterpart because large amounts of milk are used in its production. When Greek yogurt was a niche speciality product, a higher price could be justified. However, now that it is becoming a mainstream product, price plays an increasingly important role in capturing new consumers.

Based on the uncertainty of the competitive environment Fage has to decide which strategy to follow. Should it decrease its prices, hoping to regain market share and discourage other companies from aggressively entering the market, or should it increase its prices and become the premium product in the Greek yogurt category? Considering that it still enjoys certain first mover advantages and a favourable country of origin image, this strategy may work. Another question that the company is facing is the amount of money it should spend on promotion. Should it try to match the competition or focus on specific target segments? A market diversification may also be a feasible strategy for Fage. Similarly to Kraft offering several types of Mediterranean products under its Athenos brand, Fage could introduce to the US market a wide variety of Mediterranean products, either imported or produced in the US. Whatever strategy Fage decides to undertake, it has become obvious that the company is facing fierce competition in the future.

Discussion questions

1. What were the opportunities in the external environment that allowed Fage to establish itself in the US market?

2. What are the threats that Fage is facing in the US?

3. Which strategy is the best one for Fage to pursue in the future? Why?

This case was prepared by George Nakos, Clayton State University, Morrow, GA (georgenakos@clayton.edu), Robert Moussetis, North Central College, Naperville, IL, and David Furman, Clayton State University, Morrow, GA.

Part III

Where do we want to be?

Strategic marketing decisions, choices, and mistakes

◎ Learning Objectives

1. Understand the hierarchy of strategic choices and decisions at three organizational levels.

2. Be able to identify and illustrate strategic decisions at the corporate and SBU levels such as choice of directional strategy and generic strategy.

3. Appreciate the strategic marketing decisions including products to offer, markets to target, and competitive position strategies.

4. Comprehend how marketing plan links to strategy and review the common strategy mistakes.

⊙ Chapter at a Glance

I. Introduction

1 Overview and strategy blueprint
2 Marketing strategy: analysis and
   perspectives

II. Where are we now?

3 Environmental and internal analysis: market
   information and intelligence

III. Where do we want to be?

4 **Strategic marketing decisions, choices,
   and mistakes**
5 Segmentation, targeting, and positioning
   strategies
6 Branding strategies
7 Relational and sustainability strategies

V. Did we get there?

14 Strategy implementation, control, and
    metrics

IV. How will we get there?

8 Product innovation and development
   strategies
9 Service marketing strategies
10 Pricing and distribution strategies
11 Marketing communications strategies
12 International marketing strategy
13 Social and ethical strategies

 Case study: Heineken Desperados—a sensational experience

Heineken unleashed its full arsenal of sensory, experiential marketing at several urban music festivals in East London to create awareness of the new tequila flavoured Desperados brand.

The brief

With a name that smacks of cornered bandits in a shoot-out, Desperados is positioning itself as a lager with an edge. This premium-packaged product from Heineken, aimed predominantly at drinkers aged 18 to 24, is flavoured with tequila to create a distinctive taste and image. For 2013, Desperados sought to engage influencers to encourage word of mouth, with a particular focus on East London's media-savvy trendsetters. Believing this demographic to be receptive to fresh thinking from brands, Heineken decided to offer new experiences. With integrated marketing agency Space, it set about developing an activation programme with a distinctly experiential approach.

The strategy

'In 2012, all aspects of the Desperados brand were evaluated, from taste to packaging', says Heineken brand director, world lager, David Lette. 'What emerged were the sensory characteristics: both the bottle and our marketing communications are led by bright colours and a creative, eye-catching design. The taste of the lager is intriguing and disruptive as it merges traditional perceptions of premium lager with a tequila flavour. The bottle is tactile, with embossed lettering that brings an extra dimension to the drinker's experience, while its citrusy taste and aroma set it apart from other lagers'.

Mindful of the huge importance of the sensory characteristics of the brand, the team developed 'In Every Sense' as a summary of both the sensory engagement experienced from the drink itself and the activity that immerses drinkers in the core values of the brand. 'In Every Sense' was to be delivered via London's foremost urban and alternative music festivals. Flavoured beers are just beginning to establish their place in the market and the role the senses play in their appreciation is an area Heineken wants to 'own' to help bring the brand experience to life. 'Sensory marketing is still untouched ground when it comes to brand communications', says Lette, 'so we felt it would provide the standout we were looking to achieve for brand prominence in a "noisy" category'.

Saturation of the festival timetable means younger festival-goers have become ever more discerning about which events to attend. So it was essential for the brand to target those festivals with the greatest appeal to the all-important brand influencer audience. Although big weekend festivals offer economies of scale, they are a less targeted opportunity than more local, day-long urban events. The team therefore targeted the audience at festival spaces on consumers' doorsteps in East London.

The execution

The festival kicked off with the Land of Kings festival in Dalston in May 2013. As well as being a main sponsor of the event, Desperados hosted its own outdoor stage with a line-up of newcomer acts and past masters, plus an exclusive after-show party at Arcola Studios, a local arts venue. The festival partnership continued with Field Day in Victoria Park where headline acts included Animal Collective, Four Tet and Bat for Lashes. Desperados introduced The Factory to Field Day for the first time, a fully branded bar and stage hosting a musical line-up curated collaboratively by Space and Desperados, headlined by Waze and Odyssey.

In what Space group account director Sean Kelly describes as a ground-breaking concept and global first, the team created an immersive 3D visual and aural experience for festivalgoers, surrounding them in the Desperados brand. The concept was adapted from spectroscopy—the interaction of energy and matter, such as light bouncing off objects—to push the 'In Every Sense' experience for festivalgoers. Dancehall spectroscopy was originally developed by the award-winning theoretical chemist David Glowacki in association with Bristol University.

Festivalgoers moved through an atmospheric dome that rippled with a 360 degree visual representation of themselves, triggered by their movement. Engulfed by smoke bubbles and citrus aromas that emphasized the Desperados characteristics, visitors were encouraged to interact with their own image while heavy bass beats pulsed through their bodies. The entire experience was orchestrated to amaze and engage all the senses.

A live graffiti-style street art installation sat alongside Field Day's digital graffiti wall, which the audience was invited to link to their social media sites. This activity was supported by an outdoor advertising campaign, helping to provide a combined 'opportunity-to-see' score of 7.2 million.

The outcome

Total festival footfall at Field Day was 35,300; footfall through the Desperados area was 21,000. The Spectroscopy Dome attracted 1,412 people, immersing themselves in the brand experience for an average of two minutes each. There were 51 tweets relating to Desperados at the festival. Product sampling was solid: 9,500 samples went to consumers in the Desperados area at Field Day and 7,000 branded lanyards were handed out. The Factory bar was at full capacity for most of the event.

More broadly, according to Heineken, Desperados has grown distribution by more than 6,000 accounts in the year to date in the on trade (drinks bought and consumed in pubs or bars) and has grown value in the off trade (drinks bought from retailers) at 475 per cent year on year.

Analysis

'The campaign seems to be ticking boxes for our target 18–24 year-old audience who know what they like when it comes to music and culture', says Lette. 'Working with Space has helped extend the brand's engagement with music and festivals to a deeper level, while reaffirming the brand as both inspirational and cutting edge'.

While the dancehall spectroscopy made a fitting statement about the brand and was well-executed, constraints on the number of people able to use it meant only five per cent of festivalgoers experienced it first hand, says Lette. 'The spectroscopy did, however, push the brand's "In Every Sense" line through uncharted territory with an immersive, multisensory show', he says. But leveraging the activity through social media delivered lacklustre results—perhaps Desperados is riding the right trail, but not yet with all guns blazing.

*Rob Gray, **The Marketer**, November/December 2013, pp.18–20.*

Introduction

Companies aspiring to meet the challenges of today's rapidly changing marketing environment and increasing competition require strategic management decisions to be founded on well-conceived strategies. In today's turbulent environment marketers must play new strategic roles in addition to their conventional roles of creating demand, promoting sales, and earning customers' loyalty (Joshi and Gimenez, 2014). They must be (a) strategists allocating resources to support company goals and priorities, (b) technologists capitalizing on the useful sophisticated technology, and (c) scientists experimenting for the future of their business. The strategic question that drives business today is not what companies can offer, but what more they can do for their markets and customers (Dawar, 2013).

The primary thrust of this chapter is to discuss in greater detail the second stage of the strategic marketing management (SMM) process, that is, **strategic choice** and decisions. *Strategic choice* involves understanding the bases and directions that guide an organization's future strategy, generating various strategic options and alternatives, and choosing the most appropriate ones for the organization. Drawing upon the conclusions from the strategic analysis stage, managers have to identify and assess the alternative ways in which their organization can use its strengths to capitalize on opportunities—or minimize the threats,

Strategic decisions at the corporate level
Developing mission statement
Directional strategy
Resource allocation

Strategic decisions at the SBU level
Choosing generic strategy (strategic orientation):
cost leadership strategy
differentiation strategy
Focus strategy: cost focus and differentiation focus

Strategic decisions at the functional level
Products to offer
Market segments to target
Market position tactics

4.1 Hierarchy of Strategic Choices and Decisions

Source: Drawn by the authors from various sources.

and invest in available opportunities to overcome its weaknesses. The key task is to generate a well-justified set of strategic decisions and choose the ones that will contribute to the achievement of the corporate strategic goals and objectives. Decision makers need to have two vital skills (Rosenzweig, 2013). First, they must be able to discern the nature of the decision at hand. Second, they have to respond with the right approach and tactics. The focus at this stage of SMM process is on defining the path to enhanced competitive advantage by identifying the critical business initiatives that will drive relative advantages and recognizing the internal rules of the game. These will hopefully position the company to outperform competitors and meet or exceed the market's expectations for growth, profitability, and asset utilization (Kachaner and Deimler, 2009). Figure 4.1 shows the hierarchy of strategic decisions at the three organizational levels: corporate, SBU, and functional.

Hierarchy of strategic choices and decisions

Marketing managers at different organizational levels are required to translate the outcome of strategic analyses (as discussed in Chapter 3) into a number of strategic options and choose the most appropriate ones. This does not fit all situations, but broadly it may be seen as follows.

- Strategic decisions at the corporate level involve developing a mission statement, choosing a directional strategy, and allocating resources among strategic business units (SBUs).
- At the SBU level marketing managers have to make decisions regarding the choice of a generic competitive strategy (i.e. cost leadership, differentiation, focus).

- At the functional level strategic choice and decisions are related to the various practical areas within the organization (i.e. marketing, finance, R&D, production, operations, and human resources). Within the marketing area, managers should consider such decisions as products to offer, market segment/s to target, and positioning strategies.

Collaboration across different organizational levels and integration of the proposed strategic options are needed to generate integrated and harmonized decisions. The best strategic decisions normally result from collaboration across various organizational levels (Kachaner and Deimler, 2009). For example, McDonald's regional managers in Europe (and in far Asia as well) regularly meet to discuss new products, promotional ideas, quality issues, pricing options, and recently, with considerable success, to discuss sustainability and waste matters.

Strategic choices and decisions at the corporate level

Defining the corporate mission

An organization's mission statement provides a brief description of the unique purpose of the organization. It distinguishes it from other companies, and specifies the boundaries of its operations as well as defining the primary direction and key foundations upon which objectives and strategies are based. Many marketers regard the creation of a mission statement as crucial to strategy development since it represents a vision of what the organization is or should attempt to be.

Inside the firm, the mission statement serves as a focal point for individuals to identify the organization's direction and ensure unanimity of purpose within the firm (though rarely can they recite precisely what it is!). Outside the firm, the mission statement contributes to the creation of firm identity, i.e. how the company wants to be seen in the marketplace and general public (Wilson and Gilligan, 2005).[1] A survey of 181 US companies identified nine components that are frequently included in mission statements (David, 1989):

- customers
- goods or services
- location
- technology
- concern with survival
- philosophy
- self-concept
- concern with public image
- concern with employees.

---

[1] See Hamel and Prahalad (1994: pp. 132–3) about their exercise with 15 officers of a large company who confused their mission statement with those of competitors.

The same survey also found that the company's mission is often shaped by the company's history, management preference, market environment, organizational resources, and distinctive competencies. What makes for a good mission statement? It should be short on numbers and long on rhetoric while still remain succinct!

Choosing the directional strategy

Every organization needs to decide its intention and orientation towards whether it wants to do it formally or not. The following three questions are fundamental.

1. Should we expand, cut back, or continue our businesses unchanged?
2. Should we concentrate our activities within our industry boundaries or should we diversify into other lines of business?
3. If we want to grow and expand nationally or internationally, should we do so via self-development or through external acquisition, mergers, or strategic alliances?

Executives at the corporate level normally choose a directional strategy from three general orientations, often called 'grand strategies' (Wheelen and Hunger, 2012) (see Table 4.1):

- *growth strategies*: expand the corporation's activities
- *stability strategies*: make no change to the existing activities
- *retrenchment strategies:* reduce the corporation's level of activities.

Strategic managers can then consider one or more specific sub-strategies, such as 'concentration' or 'diversification'; they might decide to concentrate their efforts on one product line or one industry, or diversify into other market segments or even different industries. It is probably best that such decisions should be based on a high degree of objectivity rather than subjectivity, though the power of instinct should not be underestimated. However, for the most part, a successful growth strategy requires careful preparation to identify attractive markets/industries and new sources of competitive advantage (Jackson, 2008). Take the case of Ford. They made a decision in the mid-1990s to acquire Jaguar and Aston Martin Lagonda in order to achieve short-term growth and expansion, penetrate new markets, and

Table 4.1 The Directional (Grand) Strategies

Growth Strategies	Stability Strategies	Retrenchment Strategies
Concentration	Pause/Proceed with caution	Turnaround
• Vertical growth	No change	Captive company
• Horizontal growth	Profit	Sell-out/divestment
		Bankruptcy/Liquidation
Diversification		
• Concentric		
• Conglomerate		

Source: Thomas L. Wheelen and David J. Hunger (2012), *Strategic Management and Business Policy*, 13th edn, Pearson Education, Inc.

acquire new skills and technologies. This decision was seen (then) as one that enabled Ford to serve new upmarket segments. A few years later, Ford sold both these companies, perhaps certainly to concentrate their resources on those market segments they knew better.

Corporate managers might select 'stability' rather than growth as a directional strategy by making no changes to current activities. This strategy is generally more applied when firms are doing well and see no reason to 'rock the boat'. While appropriate in the short run, the stability strategy can be risky in the long term. For example Tesco, the UK's largest super-store, with its wider presence and intense competition not only in the high street, but also in small towns, has threatened smaller retailers such as bakers and greengrocers who have failed to develop specific market niches. Mind you, it's not just SMEs (medium to small-sized businesses) that have felt competition from Tesco. Just think of clothing retailers and banks.

The corporate manager may also choose to pursue a retrenchment strategy if the organization has a weak competitive position in one or more of its markets. This situation puts pressure on the company to improve its performance by eliminating those product lines that are dragging down the overall performance of the company. Another example from the car market will illustrate: this strategy was adopted by BMW in 2000 after six years of owning Rover, the British car manufacturer. BMW invested $3.4 billion in Rover over six years, but failed to turn it into a profitable business. Eventually, BMW decided to sell Rover to Ford, though it retained the profitable Mini division.

Allocating resources between the SBUs

Large corporations with multiple products must decide how to allocate their resources between SBUs to ensure the organization's overall success. Portfolio analysis, which has had a colourful history in the business literature since the 1960s, is a useful tool for assessing the strength of SBU's position in the market and allocating resources between them. Ovans (2011) compiled about 20 models that changed the shape of strategy in the world; at the top was the BCG portfolio chart, a model that, despite its problems, has become an iconic part of management thinking and a tool that will show up consistently in corporate boardrooms for years to come. Recently, Cui (2013) examined the portfolio dynamics and the impact of portfolio resources dissimilarity on alliance termination.

A survey of the *Fortune 1000* found that portfolio planning approaches are widespread among large diversified industrial companies and increasingly used (Haspeslagh, 1982). Portfolio planning can take two forms: (a) product analysis and (b) business analysis. Here are some methods of portfolio analysis that are widely used by strategic managers.

- The Boston Consulting Group (BCG) matrix, which focuses on market share and market growth (see Figure 4.2).
- General Electric's (GE's) business screen, which places the SBUs in a nine-cell matrix using the attractiveness of the industry and the position of the business (see Figure 4.3).
- The Shell directional matrix, which uses two dimensions: prospects for profitability and firm's competitive capabilities (see Figure 4.4)
- Abell and Hammond's model, which is an expansion of the GE model and the Shell directional matrix, evaluates SBUs using two dimensions: business position and market attractiveness.

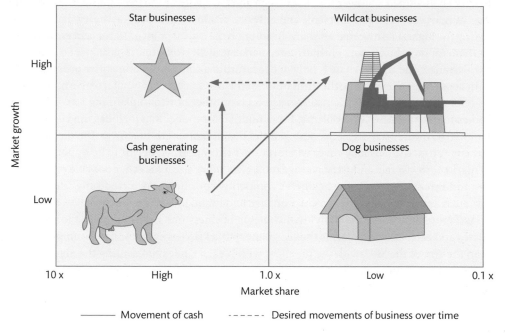

A schematic depiction of the portfolio management concept

4.2 Boston Consulting Group (BCG) Matrix

Source: Drawn by the authors from various sources (attributed to The Boston Consulting Group, 1970).

The BCG matrix is inferior to more discursive portfolios such as the GE business screen, but for many businesses it is seen as the simplest way to portray the corporation's portfolio of investments. The BCG matrix can be used with the product life cycle concept to provide a useful strategic tool for resource allocation. Figure 4.2 illustrates the four positions a business unit (SBU) can attain in a market/segment based on the market share it has and the growth rate of the market/segment. It also illustrates the movement of cash between different SBUs and desired movements of businesses over time. However, if the funds generated by a SBU cannot be freely transferred to another SBU, the portfolio will be of less help to the organization. For example, Charoen Pokphand, a major Asian agribusiness group, has cash cows in China, Thailand, and Hong Kong, but if it is not allowed to transfer funds to its new SBUs in Eastern Europe, the portfolio will then be handicapped. SBUs are expected to change their positions in the market (the four quadrants of the matrix) over time. They generally start as 'problem children—wildcats' and with successful management they move into the 'stars' category. Eventually they become 'cash cows', as the growth level of the market starts to slow down. Finally, when they begin to lose their market shares, they move into the 'dogs' stage. It has been suggested that each SBU should set up its strategic objectives based on its position in the BCG matrix. Build/ growth will be, arguably, an appropriate strategic objective for the 'stars', while hold/harvest will be appropriate for the 'cash cows'. Investment can be selected for the 'children problem', while divestment will be appropriate for the 'dogs' who are seen as having no potential.

The BCG matrix is a well-known tool with many advantages: (a) it helps organizations planning the desired movement of business over time, and (b) planning the movement of funds from an SBU where there is less need for it to another SBU where it is needed. Many limitations have been identified, however. The use of *high* and *low* to define the rate of market growth and level of market share is too simplistic and only one product can appear on the left-hand side as having the highest relative market share. In addition the cut-off point of 10 per cent growth is far too high for most businesses. Furthermore, market growth is only one indicator of an industry's attractiveness and market share is only one measure of a company's competitive position.

In an attempt to overcome the limitations of the BCG matrix, a few alternative models can be offered. General Electric's business screen is another portfolio planning tool that overcomes many of the BCG's problems. It is a multifactor model that includes nine cells based on long-term industry attractiveness and the business strength of a firm. The definition of industry attractiveness may cover whatever the firm concerned deems to be important such as market growth rate, industry average return, industry size, plus other possible opportunities and threats. Similarly, the business's competitive position may include any relevant factors such as profitability, size, product quality, and brand image (see Figure 4.3).

As Figure 4.3 shows, the individual strategic business units are plotted in the matrix as circles and each circle represents the size of the market (in terms of sales, for example) rather than the size of the SBU, with the pie slices within each circle representing the market share of the SBU in this market. The nine cells of the GE matrix fall into three categories, each of which needs a different investment strategy. For example, the three cells at the top left of the

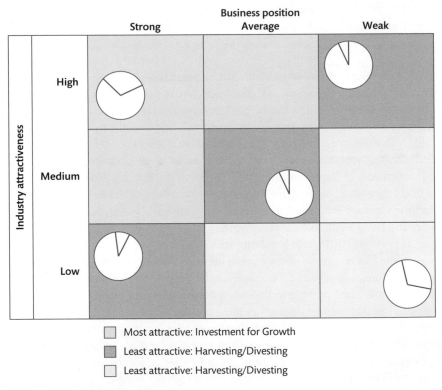

4.3 General Electric Model

Source: Drawn by the authors from various sources (attributed to McKinsey & Company for General Electric, 1970).

matrix are considered the most attractive that require an investment strategy for growth. The three cells that run diagonally from the top right to bottom left are seen as having a medium attractiveness, hence they require a greater emphasis placed on selective investment policy. The three cells at the bottom right of the matrix are the least attractive markets, and therefore require a policy of harvesting/divestment.

The advantage of the GE model lies in the use of many more variables than those used in the BCG matrix, and the recognition that the attractiveness of an industry can be assessed in many different ways rather than simply using growth rate or market share. It also allows strategists to choose any industry variables they justifiably feel are more relevant to their organizations

The Shell directional 3×3 matrix offers another alternative. It uses two dimensions: the firm's competitive capabilities and the prospects for sector profitability. It won't be dwelt on here because it is similar to the GE matrix, but with the Shell directional each dimension is divided into three categories and SBUs are plotted within the matrix to allow top management to identify the most appropriate investment strategies for each SBU. A similar matrix to the Shell directional model has been produced by Abell and Hammond (1979) (which is not illustrated here) to depict relative investment strategies. It is almost the same as the Shell directional matrix, aside from using different terms, namely market attractiveness and business position rather than competitive capability and prospect for sector profitability.

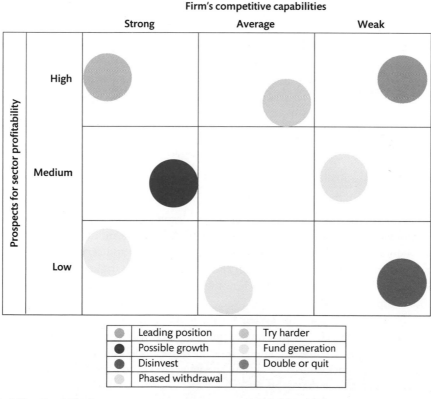

4.4 Shell Directional Matrix

Source: Drawn by the authors from various sources (attributed to Shell Chemical Co., 1975).

Nevertheless, the GE model has its shortcomings. The quantification of industry attractiveness and business's competitive position, while capturing the central issues, may be generated based on subjective judgements and may, or may not, be weighted appropriately.

Despite the wide adoption and the apparent attraction of portfolio analysis, Wilson and Gilligan (2005) note many criticisms and limitations.

- It is generally too simplistic in structure, and may lead the company to place too much emphasis on market share growth and entry into high growth businesses, or to neglect its current businesses.
- Its practical value is based on developing an appropriate definition of the industry and market segments in which an SBU competes.
- It suggests a standard strategy for each competitive position, which in some cases seems impractical.
- It uses the subjective judgements of top management and therefore its results are sensitive to the ratings and weights which can be manipulated to produce a desired plot in the matrix.
- It is not always clear what makes an industry attractive or where a product is in its life cycle.

But it should be noted here that portfolio analysis has been adopted widely because it offers many advantages (Haspeslagh, 1982).

- It encourages managers at the corporate level to think strategically, and adopt a more proactive approach to management.
- It motivates managers to evaluate the internal and external environment of each business unit to set long-term objectives and allocate resources between them.
- It furnishes companies with a greatly improved capacity for strategic control when portfolio planning is applied intelligently.
- It stimulates the use of externally oriented data to supplement management's judgement.
- It recognizes the importance of the fund generation ability of each SBU to inform the allocation of resources between the SBUs.

Another planning approach that has gained widespread adoption by large corporations and business units is the use of business models. A **business model** describes the set of coordinated activities a company performs to deliver goods and services to customers in order to ensure overall success (Wheelen and Hunger, 2012). Originating in the 1990s, the term business model was used to show how the new technology and global trade are changing how companies must do business. Every successful company operates according to an effective business model, and by systematically identifying all of its constituent parts, the company can understand how the model fulfils a potent value proposition in a profitable way. The company's executives can judge how the same model could be used to fulfil a radically different customer value proposition, and what they need to construct a new model, if required, to capitalize on that opportunity.

But one business model is not always enough for an organization (Casadesus-Masanell and Tarziján, 2012). Using more than one business model at a time is devilishly difficult, and frequently cited as a key reason for strategic failure. Despite this, situations may arise where a company might need to approach a few market segments using a separate business model for each market. In emerging markets, for example, a bank may create a separate company to offer credit to low and middle-income customers. Banco Santander-Chile has done this with Banefe. Another is the forestry company, Celulosa Arauco, which converts its trees into paper pulp under one business model, and into wood panels under another.

Business model innovations have reshaped entire industries and redistributed millions of dollars of value in the US business environment (Johnson et al., 2008). Retail discounters such as Wal-Mart and Target, which entered the market with pioneering business models, now account for 75 per cent of the total valuation of the retail sector. Also, low-cost airlines grew from a 'slice on the radar screen' to 55 per cent of the market value of all airline carriers. A survey conducted in 2005 by the Economist Intelligence Unit reported that over 50 per cent of CEOs believe that business model innovation will become more important for success than product or service innovation (cited by Johnson et al., 2008). Another survey conducted by IBM in 2008 on corporate CEOs confirmed these results.

While established companies can often launch new products and services that outperform competitors without fundamentally changing their existing business models, there are some circumstances that require new business models to be invented. Johnson et al. (2008) identified five of these strategic circumstances.

1. The opportunity to address the needs of potential customers who are shut out of a market because existing solutions are too expensive or too complicated for them.

2. The opportunity to capitalize on a brand-new technology or leverage a tested technology by bringing it to a whole new market.

3. The opportunity to bring a job-to-be-done focus when one does not yet exist. A jobs focus allows companies to redefine industry profitability.

4. The need to fend off low-end disrupters.

5. The need to respond to a shifting basis of competition.

Strategic choices and decisions at the SBU level

What is an SBU? It is a single business or interrelated businesses that can plan separately from the rest of the corporation. An SBU competes in a specific industrial sector or marketplace. It has a manager responsible for strategic planning and profit performance, who also controls factors affecting profit. The key strategic decision taken at the SBU level relates to the choice of a generic strategy; the fundamental approach to the competitive advantage a firm is pursuing which provides the context for the decisions to be taken in each functional area.

Identifying a generic competitive strategy

An appropriate generic competitive strategy will best position the company's offerings against those of competitors and give the company the strongest possible competitive advantage within its industry. Porter (2008), the eminent Harvard strategist, suggests that a

4.5 Porter's Generic Strategies

Source: Michael E. Porter (1985), *Competitive Advantage: Creating and Sustaining Superior Performance.* Free Press, a Division of Simon & Schuster Adult Publishing Group.

generic strategy can be viewed as building defences against the competitive forces or finding a position in the market where the forces are weakest. Porter (1980) originally proposed 'focus' as a third generic strategy. Yet five years later in *Competitive Advantage* (1985a) he introduced differentiation focus and cost focus as two variants of focus strategy (see Figure 4.5). Are you still following this?! Well, in a later book, *The Competitive Advantage of Nations* (1990), he dropped focus as a separate strategy and began viewing it instead as a category of competitive scope. It is appropriate to take a closer look at Porter's approach to competitive strategies.

Porter's generic competitive strategies

- **Cost leadership** is a low-cost competitive strategy that aims at the broad mass market and requires aggressive construction of efficient-scale facilities, vigorous pursuit of cost reduction, tight cost and overhead control, avoidance of marginal customer accounts, and cost minimization in areas such as R&D, service, salesforce, and advertising.

  Having a low-cost position gives a company a defence against rivals. Its lower costs allow it to continue to earn profits during times of heavy competition. Its high market share gives great bargaining power with its suppliers because it buys in larger quantities. Its low costs serve as a barrier to entry, as few new entrants will be able to match the leader's cost advantage (Porter, 1980). Note that sometimes cost leadership is confused with setting low prices. Certainly cost leaders are more able to make a profit at lower prices than rivals, but it is not necessarily part of the strategy. For example, Dell has a cost advantage with its direct business model; however, its prices are by no means the lowest.

- **Differentiation** is a generic strategy that involves the creation of a significantly differentiated offering, for which the company charges a premium. This speciality can be associated with design, brand image, technology, dealer network, or customer service. Differentiation is a viable strategy for earning above average returns in a specific business because the resulting brand loyalty lowers customers' sensitivity to price. Buyers' loyalty also serves as an entry barrier. New firms must develop their own distinctive competence to differentiate their products in order to compete successfully (Porter, 1980).

- **Cost focus** is a low-cost strategy that focuses on a particular buyer group or geographic market and attempts to serve only this niche, to the exclusion of others. In using a cost focus strategy, the company seeks a cost advantage in its target segment. This strategy is based on the belief that a company that focuses its efforts can serve its narrow strategic target *more efficiently* than can its competitors. A focus strategy does, however, necessitate a trade-off between profitability and overall market share.

- **Focused differentiation** is a strategy that concentrates on a particular buyer group, product line segment, or geographic market. The target segments must have buyers with unusual needs, or else the production and delivery system that best serves the target segment must differ from that of other industry segments. This strategy is valued because of the belief that a company that focuses its efforts can serve its narrow strategic target *more effectively* than can its competitors.

Focused differentiation and cost focus strategies are not the same. Whilst cost focus exploits differences in cost behaviour in some segments, differentiation focus exploits the special needs of buyers in certain segments (Porter, 1985a). Another comparison can be made between overall differentiation and differentiation focus strategies. These two are perhaps the most often confused strategies in practice. While the overall differentiator bases its strategy on widely valued attributes, the differentiation focuser looks for segments with special needs and meets them better.

- **Stuck in the middle:** any company that fails to pursue one generic strategy may become 'stuck in the middle' with no competitive advantage.

Support for Porter's generic strategies

Generic strategies form a simplified system and offer several important advantages for guiding the choice of a competitive strategy (Herbert and Deresky, 1987).

- They highlight the essential features of separate, situation-specific strategies, capturing their major commonalities so that they facilitate the understanding of a broad strategic pattern

- They provide guidance at the corporate level on decisions concerning business portfolio management and resource allocation

- They assist business-level strategy development by suggesting priorities and providing broad guidelines for action.

Criticism of Porter's generic strategies

Porter's typology is not without criticism. It has been argued that while Porter's generic strategies might be appealing to organizations, they have practical limitations. Generic strategy often proves inadequate for use by 'distressed' firms because it assumes that companies operate 'normally' in a competitive environment (Pretorius, 2008). Managers of troubled organizations facing turnarounds need to analyse the complex factors involved, and cannot depend on Porter's typology of generic strategy alone. Another gap is the lack of identifying what tactics are associated with each of the three generic strategies (Akan et al., 2006). Also it is not clear what tactics will warrant higher levels of organizational performance. Another criticism is that it is up to SBUs to choose from them, although the appropriate selection of a generic strategy will be dependent on the firm's resources and capabilities, the industry life cycle, and the state of competition in the market. Table 4.2 illustrates the commonly required skills and resources and the common organizational requirements for each of Porter's generic strategies.

From a marketing perspective, one criticism has been that Porter's three generic strategies are typical marketing strategies rebranded using different names. Cost leadership invariably depends upon standardization and so is equivalent to an undifferentiated marketing strategy. Differentiation is identical in both models. Cost focus and focus differentiation can be seen as variants of a concentrated marketing strategy and involve niche marketing.

Table 4.2 Requirements for Generic Competitive Strategies

Generic Strategy	Commonly Required Skills and Resources	Common Organizational Requirements
Overall Cost Leadership	• Sustained capital investment and access to capital • Process engineering skills • Intense supervision of labour • Products designed for ease of manufacture • Low-cost distribution system	• Tight cost control • Frequent, detailed control reports • Structured organization and responsibilities • Incentives base on meeting strict quantitative targets
Differentiation	• Strong marketing abilities • Product engineering • Creative flair • Strong capability in basic research • Corporate reputation for quality of technological leadership • Long tradition in the industry or unique combination of skills drawn from other businesses • Strong cooperation from channels	• Strong coordination among functions in R&D, product development, and marketing • Subjective measurement and incentives instead of quantitative measures • Amenities to attract highly skilled labour, scientists, or creative people
Focus	• Combination of the above policies directed at the particular strategic target	• Combination of the above policies directed at the particular strategic target

Source: Michael E. Porter (1980), *Competitive Strategy: Techniques for Analysing Industries and Competitors.* Free Press, a Division of Simon & Schuster Adult Publishing Group.

Alternative generic strategies to Porter

Looking at Porter's strategies in a different way, Bowman and Faulkner (1997) developed 'Bowman's Strategy Clock', which extends Porter's three generic strategies to eight, and identifies the likelihood of success for each strategy. These eight strategies are illustrated in Figure 4.6 and outlined below. However, please note, Bowman and Faulkner (1997) noted that strategy positions 7 and 8 are not sustainable positions.

1. **Low price/low value:** firms do not usually choose to compete in this category. Rather, it is a position they find themselves forced to compete in because their product lacks differentiated value.

2. **Low price:** companies competing in this category are the typical low cost leaders. These companies drive prices down to a minimum, and balance the low margins with high volume.

3. **Hybrid (moderate price/moderate differentiation):** these companies offer products at a low cost, but with a higher perceived value than other low cost competitors.

4. **Differentiation:** these companies offer their customers high perceived value, and to be able to afford this they increase their price and sustain themselves through higher margins.

5. **Focused differentiation:** these represent designer products with high perceived value and high prices.

6. **Increased price/standard product:** these companies take a gamble by increasing the prices without an increase to the brand value. If the price increase is accepted, they will enjoy higher profitability.

7. **High price/low value:** this is classic monopoly pricing in a market where only one company offers the goods/service.

8. **Low value/standard price:** companies adopting this strategy lose market share because of the low value product and unaffordable price.

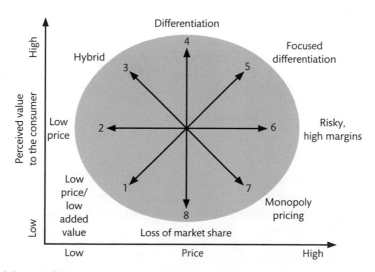

4.6 Bowman's Strategy Clock

Source: Cliff Bowman and David Faulkner (1997), *Corporate Competitive Strategy*, McGraw-Hill, Inc.

Other alternative typologies of generic strategy have been developed by Utterback and Abernathy (1975) and Miles and Snow (1978). Utterback and Abernathy (1975) proposed cost-minimizing and performance-maximizing strategic business types that may be positioned at opposite ends of the spectrum.

Miles and Snow (1978) proposed four business types of competitive strategy, which are 'reactor', 'defender', 'analyser', and 'prospector'. According to Miles and Snow, the 'reactor' is a company that has no consistent strategic approach and only drifts with the environmental events, reacting to them but failing to anticipate or influence these events. The 'defender' is an organization that concentrates on protecting its current markets, maintaining stable growth and serving its current consumers. BIC Corporation, once a leading company in the writing instrument industry, has chosen since the late 1970s to defend its substantial market share in the industry. The 'analyser' is a company that maintains its market share and seeks to be innovative. Most large companies fall into this category because they want to protect their operations but at the same time create new market opportunities. It is always suggested that IBM uses analyser strategy. The prospector is a company that is highly innovative and which constantly seeks out new markets and opportunities and is oriented toward growth and risk-taking. Johnson & Johnson could be seen as a prospector.

Strategic choices and decisions at functional level

Strategic decisions taken at this level relate to the various functional areas within an organization (e.g. marketing, finance, R&D, production). These decisions include marketing objectives to support corporate strategy, products to offer, market segments to target, and market position strategies. Other strategic decisions of other functional areas are also outlined.

Setting the marketing objectives

While a few businesses may decide to pursue a single objective, most companies will have a mixture of marketing objectives including sales growth, market share, innovativeness, customer satisfaction, reputation, and brand loyalty. Whereas marketing objectives are primarily developed to guide the overall marketing activities, they are also used for evaluation purposes. Key characteristics and guidelines for developing appropriate sets of objectives are:

- hierarchical: objectives should go from most to least important
- quantitative: in order to avoid ambiguity, marketing managers must turn objectives into measurable targets with respect to size and time
- realistic: objectives should be developed based on the result of detailed analysis of the firm's capability, competitive strengths, and external opportunities
- consistent: to avoid confusion, marketing managers have to pursue compatible marketing objectives. It is obviously unrealistic to aim for substantial gains in both market share and profitability at the same time.

If a company's strategic objectives are poorly developed, either focusing too much on short-term goals or being so general that they provide little real guidance, a planning gap might arise. When such a gap occurs, strategic managers have to change their strategies to improve performance or adjust objectives downward to be more realistic. Mini Case 4.1 illustrates how organizations' objectives should change to take account of environmental and market change including economic trends and fluctuation.

 Mini Case 4.1   Will the tide turn in 2013?[2]

'With household incomes flattening out and British exports to the emerging economies starting to take off, there are signs of hope for marketers in 2013'

A year ago it was very obvious to any decent forecaster (in other words the majority of those not working for the government) that 2012 was going to be a pretty tough year. And so it turned out. But underneath the surface, hidden by the effects of rising food price inflation, the continuing European recession and the uncertainties in the Middle East, there were some glimmers of hope for the British economy. 2012 was the first year that British exports to the emerging economies started to take off. Exports to China in Q3 2012 were 13 per cent up on a year ago and exports to South Korea 85 per cent up. Cars seem to be particularly important here, especially luxury models. The effects of this have been obscured by the European recession—for the same quarter exports to Belgium were down 14 per cent, to Germany 10 per cent and to Italy 25 per cent.

2012 also seemed to indicate an end to falling disposable incomes, with the year-on-year change in household incomes flat by the end of the year. In the context of rising food prices and a continuing squeeze on wages, this is better than it sounds. In the past five years, real disposable incomes per household had fallen by 8 per cent (for context, in WWII the fall was 13 per cent). The final positive trend has been the rebalancing of the British economy. Activity in the City of London collapsed during 2012—so much so that it fell behind New York in numbers and looks set to fall behind Hong Kong within the next three years. But even in London the jobs have been more than replaced by the 'flat white' economy—the cultural, media, consultancy and IT economy. Of course the 'flat white' economy is much more labour intensive, but pay is much lower so it will take time for its net contribution to GDP to overtake that of the City. The question for 2013 is whether it will be the first year since 2007 when the positive trends outweigh the negative.

The answer is, unfortunately, probably not quite yet. Exports are moving into a headwind of slow growth in world trade. Asia is suffering the knock-on effects of overinvestment and slowing export markets; the European recession is likely to intensify as the weakness in southern Europe spreads to France, and Germany becomes mired in the general recession. Household incomes will continue to be held back by subdued wage increases at a time when worldwide prices are rising. Food prices are likely to be up around 5 per cent in 2013 and although clothing prices should fall back with the lower price of cotton, this will make it difficult to achieve a large rise in disposable incomes. The coalition government will have to resume progress in cutting the government deficit as it reels back the problems caused by its overspending predecessor. And businesses are hardly likely to invest heavily when there is already surplus capacity, although new technologies will at least hold investment levels up. But probably the best news for the economy is that the coalition has at last grasped that if it fails to achieve economic growth, nothing else will help it—it won't even succeed in its flagship policy of reducing the public deficit.

Yet even the good news might be tempered by international events. The flare-ups in the Middle East in November remind us that our energy prices depend on the flow of oil from the Gulf and that this is a politically unstable area. One issue that the political classes are chattering about is a bust up between mainland Europe and the UK. On the continent they seem so preoccupied with their own problems (which are severe) that they seem to be pushing the UK towards the exit door. I suspect a divorce would prove much more painful for both sides than is currently imagined. But it might yet happen.

[2] *Douglas McWilliams, **The Marketer**, January 2013, p.13.*

Marketing strategy

Marketing is viewed in this book as an orientation that guides an organization's overall activities (see Chapter 2). This does not mitigate against marketing also being a distinct function. At the functional level, the major task of marketing managers is to influence the level, timing, and character of demand in a way that helps the organization to achieve its long-term strategic objectives. The marketing manager is often seen as the organization's primary link to the market and, therefore, must be particularly concerned with the development of the firm's positioning strategy and the marketing mix programmes.

The development of marketing strategy has been discussed extensively in the marketing literature. The development of marketing strategy can be seen at three main levels (Hooley et al., 2011). At the first level, the core strategy of the organization is selected, where the marketing objectives and the broad focus for achieving them are identified. At the next level, market segments and targets are chosen, and the organization's differential advantage is defined to serve the target groups of customers better than the competition. Taken together the identification of targets and definition of differential advantage constitute the creation of the competitive positioning of the organization and its offerings. At the third level, the marketing department is putting out the marketing mix programmes that can convey the positioning and the products/services to the target market.

Marketing strategy is the manner in which company resources are used in the search for a differential advantage and should be formulated with reference to the market environment and competitive conditions in which an organization operates (Cook, 1983; 1985). In a survey of 217 companies from Australia, Singapore, the Netherlands, and China, it was found that most marketing strategies appear to be useful in conditions of relatively stable environments such as placid-clustered environments (Ward and Lewandowska, 2008). In turbulent environments it does seem though that concerns for customers should be the major focus of organizations, and therefore customer-oriented strategies seem to be most effective. Competitor-based strategies are best suited to placid-clustered environments, business conditions which are favourable and attract greater competition.

Strategic decisions of products to offer and markets to target

Fundamental marketing decisions that should be considered by marketing managers are products to offer and markets to target. While the topic of segmentation, targeting, and positioning is discussed in Chapter 5, in this chapter some marketing-related strategic choices are worth mentioning. Ansoff's 2×2 matrix (shown in Figure 4.7) is a useful framework that is frequently used to guide marketing managers.

This matrix illustrates the four possible options available to any organization in relation to product/market strategy.

Market penetration as a strategic option involves selling more of the organization's existing products in its existing marketplace. Adopting this option will depend on competitor activity and the likely development of existing market segments. Market penetration is the least risky option of the four alternatives since the organization will be targeting market segments it already understands using products/services it knows. Consumer product manufacturers such as Procter & Gamble and Unilever are expert in using market penetration strategy to gain market share in a product category.

	Present products	New products
Existing market	**Penetration strategy** • Increase share of customer spending • Increase market share • Non-users to users (where both are in the same segment)	**Product development strategy** • Product modification via new features • Different quality levels • New product(s)
New market	**Market development strategy** • New markets • New distribution channels • New geographical areas	**Diversification strategy** • Joint ventures • Mergers • Acquisitions/takeovers

4.7 Ansoff's Product/Market Matrix

Source: H.I. Ansoff (1957), 'Strategy for Diversification', *Harvard Business Review*, 25, September–October, pp. 113–24.

Product development involves developing additional or new products to serve existing market segments. This strategic option is more risky than market penetration as it entails offering a new product where there is uncertainty as to how it will be perceived by current customers. The development of a new product may also create a degree of cannibalization that might affect the net growth in the marketplace.

Market development takes place when the organization focuses on the present product range, but searches for new market segments and looks at ways of marketing its existing products in the new segments. The degree of risk associated with this option is probably higher than with the previous two options. Entering a new market requires the organization to undertake a strategic analysis in order to understand the new market.

Diversification is probably the riskiest of the four alternatives as it involves the marketing of new products into new markets, though the potential return can be high. Producing new products requires an increase in resources and investment. Serving new market segments also needs further analysis of the micro marketing environment.

It should be mentioned here that the choice between the four strategic options will be influenced by a number of external and internal factors (Aaker and McLoughlin, 2010). External factors include the state of competition in the market and the critical success factors in the industry. Internal factors, on the other hand, include the product life cycle and the range of the company's product offerings. Table 4.3 sets out the critical success factors in action.

Strategic choices and decisions for competitive tactics

A tactic is an operating action specifying 'how', 'when', and 'where', a strategy is to be implemented. Compared with strategies, tactics are narrower in scope and shorter in time horizon. Tactics may therefore be viewed (like policies) as a bridge between strategy formulation and implementation. Tactics available to organizations are those dealing with competitive market position.

Table 4.3 Critical Success Factors in Action

Critical Success Factors	Strategies	Performance Indicators
Ability to achieve critical mass volumes through existing brokers and agents	● Develop closer ties with agents ● Telemarket to brokers ● Realign agents' compensation	● Policies in force ● New business written ● Percentage of business with existing brokers
Be able to introduce new products within six months of industry leaders	● Underwrite strategic joint ventures ● Copy leader's products ● Improve underwriting skills	● Elapsed time to introduce ● Percentage of products introduced within six months ● Percentage of underwriters having additional certification
Be able to manage product and product line profitability	● Segment investment portfolio ● Improve cost accounting ● Closely manage loss ratio	● Return on portfolio segments ● Actual product cost/revenue versus plan ● Loss ratio relative to competitors

Source: Richard M.S. Wilson and Colin Gilligan (2005), *Strategic Marketing Management: Planning, Implementation and Control*, with the permission of Elsevier.

Competitive position tactics

According to its position in the market a company can implement its competitive marketing strategy by pursuing offensive or defensive tactics. An offensive tactic usually takes place away from a company's position in the marketplace, whereas a defensive tactic usually takes place within it.

The two terms 'offensive' and 'defensive' are frequently defined in the business literature as two types of competitive strategy, yet they are viewed here as competitive tactics. This is for two reasons. First, by definition strategy is formulated and implemented for a long period of time, but for a firm to be defensive or offensive this will depend on the state of competition in the market at any given point in time. The state of competition, by its nature, is dynamic rather than static and, therefore, it is not required for a firm to be offensive or defensive at all times. Secondly, a firm's generic strategy should be oriented by the goal of competitive advantage rather than by a set of defensive or offensive actions that aim to protect and/or increase its market share. In other words, a firm can act offensively in one segment or geographical area and defensively in another. A brief description of the competitive tactics of four market positions is now given.

Market leader: the firm with the largest market share and, by virtue of its pricing, advertising intensity, distribution coverage, technological advance, and rate of new product introduction, it determines the nature, pace, and bases of competition. To remain number one, leading firms may implement both offensive and defensive tactics.

Market challenger: a runner-up firm that is fighting hard to increase its market share. It may choose to adopt an aggressive stance and attack other firms, including the market leader. Therefore, it will normally implement offensive tactics.

Market follower: another runner-up firm that wants to hold its share without 'rocking the boat'. It may adopt a less aggressive stance and a defensive tactic in order to maintain the status quo, but at the same time follow the leader.

Market nicher: firms that serve smaller segments not being pursued by other firms. By concentrating their efforts in this way, market nichers are able to build up specialist market knowledge and avoid expensive head-on fights with larger companies.

Figure 4.8 illustrates an overview of how market leaders might defend their current position, how challengers might attempt to seize share offensively, and how followers and nichers will act accordingly.

Competitive tactics for market leader

If a company is to remain the dominant player in a market, it needs to defend its position constantly. Three competitive tactics are considered.

- **Expanding the total market**

  The market leader needs to search for *new users, new uses, and more usage.* Search for *new users* by attracting buyers who are still unaware of the product, or who are resisting it because of its price or its lack of certain features. Search for *new uses* by discovering and promoting new ways for the use of the firm's product. Search for *more usage* by encouraging existing users of the product to increase their usage rates.

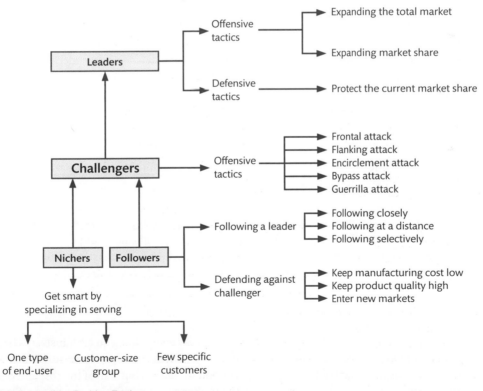

4.8 Competitive Position Tactics

Source: Drawn by the authors - adapted from various sources, e.g. Richard M.S. Wilson and Colin Gilligan (2005), *Strategic Marketing Management: Planning, Implementation and Control.*

- **Expanding market share**

  At the same time as trying to expand the total market, the market leader should not lose sight of the need to defend its market share. According to the saying 'the best defence is a good offence', the market leader may adopt an offensive tactic to increase its market share over other competitors. This can typically be done in a variety of ways including heavier advertising, improved distribution, price incentives, and new products. By doing this, the market leader increases its market share at the expense of other competitors and reaps the benefits of this increase in the form of higher profitability.

- **Protect the current market share**

  It has long been recognized that leaders are often vulnerable to attack. Therefore, a market leader has to adopt defensive tactics to protect its position. Porter (1985b) pointed out that defensive tactics aim to lower the probability of attack, or reduce the threat of attack to an acceptable level. Porter suggested three types of defensive tactics, such as raising structural barriers, increasing expected retaliation, and lowering the inducement for attack. Military analogies have frequently been used in the business literature to describe different types of defensive tactics.

  - **Position defence**, in which a company builds fortifications around its current position. Simply defending a current position or product rarely works.
  - **Flanking defence**, in which the company carefully checks its flanks and attempts to protect the weaker ones.
  - **Pre-emptive defence**, where, in contrast to a flanking defence, the leader firm can be more aggressive, striking competitors before they can move against it.
  - **Counter-offensive defence**: despite its flanking or pre-emptive efforts, a market leader company could be attacked so it needs to respond to minimize the threat. Counter-attack is particularly important in those markets that are crucial to the leader. Therefore, the leader must act decisively and swiftly.
  - **Mobile defence** involves more than aggressively defending a current market position; the leader extends itself to new markets that can serve as future bases for defence or offence.
  - **Contraction defence**: when a firm finds its resources are spread too thinly and competitors are nibbling away on several fronts, it opts to withdraw from those segments in which it is most vulnerable or in which it feels there is the least potential. It then concentrates its resources in other segments believed to be less vulnerable.

Competitive tactics for the market challenger

The challenger may take on the market leader or it may avoid doing so and, instead, challenge firms of its own size or smaller. The selection of which to challenge is thus fundamental and is a major determinant not only of the likelihood of success, but also of the cost and risk involved. Attacking a strong leader requires the challenger to meet three conditions. First, the assailant must have a sustainable competitive advantage (in cost or differentiation). Secondly, the challenger must be able to partly or wholly neutralize the leader's other advantages.

Finally, there must be some impediment to the leader being able to retaliate (Porter, 1985b). A number of possible attack tactics have been suggested in the marketing literature.

- **Frontal attack:** the challenger opposes the competitor directly using its own weapons, and trying not to expose its weak points. Frontal attacks are appropriate for large companies with substantial resources and a significant competitive advantage. The US brewing company, Anheuser Busch, adopted this tactic when competing against Danish Carlsberg for exclusive supply contracts with top restaurants in major cities in Italy.

- **Flanking attack:** as an alternative to a costly and risky frontal attack, the challenger can focus its strength against the competitor's weaker flanks or on gaps in the competitor's market coverage. This method is chosen by companies that do not have the resources to attack established competitors head-on. Honda adopted this tactic against Harley-Davidson when it entered the US motorcycle market. Initially it concentrated on small devices, leaving Harley-Davidson to focus on larger sports motorbikes. After consolidating its market position, Honda gradually introduced larger models that competed directly with those of the local competitor.

- **Encirclement attack:** involves attacking from the front and the flanks. A challenger encircles the competitor's position in terms of products or markets or both. It attacks its rivals in as many ways as possible by extensive stretching of its product lines. Casio, the Japanese watchmaker, seems to follow this tactic with a diversity of watch models in different price brackets to satisfy all the needs of all its potential customers.

- **Bypass attack:** the challenger chooses to change the rules of the game by diversifying into unrelated products, moving into new geographic markets, or leapfrogging into new technologies to replace existing products. Michelin, the French tyre producer, used to compete in the US market with its radial tyre, but other producers like Goodyear did not follow this move so as to avoid giving radials an stamp of approval. The success of Michelin's product eventually forced Goodyear to follow after they had lost big parts of their market share.

- **Guerrilla attack:** the fifth tactic open to a challenger is best suited to smaller companies with a relatively limited resource base. The challenger might use selective price cuts, executive raids, intense promotional outbursts, or assorted legal actions.

Competitive tactics for the market follower

As an alternative to challenging for leadership, many companies are content to adopt a less pro-active posture and simply follow what others do. The market follower can learn from the leader's experience and copy the leader's products and strategies, usually with less investment. There are three distinct postures for market followers depending on how closely they emulate the leader.

- **Following closely**, with a similar marketing mix and marketing segmentation.
- **Following at a distance**, so that the follower can flag up some areas of differentiation, and diminish the obvious similarities with the leader.
- **Following selectively**, both in product and market terms, so that the likelihood of direct competition is minimized.

Competitive tactics for market nîcher

A nicher is interested in a few niches, not in the whole market. The goal is to be a large fish in a small pond rather than the other way round. A market nicher can specialize in serving one type of end-user, or in serving a given customer-size group, or focus on one or a few specific customers. Although there are many advantages of niching, specialization can prove risky if the market changes in a fundamental way, leaving the nicher exposed. For this reason, there is a strong argument for multiple rather than single-sector niching.

Other functional strategies

Financial strategy

The principal goal of a financial strategy is to provide an organization with an appropriate financial structure and funds to achieve its overall goals and objective, and also to provide competitive advantage through a lower cost of funds and a flexible ability to raise capital to support a competitive strategy. Wheelen and Hunger (2012) noted that a financial strategy usually attempts to maximize the financial value of the firm by establishing the trade-off between achieving the desired debt-to-equity ratio and relying on internal long-term financing via cash flow. Such a trade-off is a key issue in any financial strategy development, which would lead to the creation of competitive advantage for the firm.

Manufacturing strategy

Manufacturing strategy can be defined as the management principles dictating how a product is manufactured, how resources are deployed in production, and how the infrastructure necessary to support manufacturing should be organized (Zahra and Das, 1993). Manufacturing strategy creates and adds value by helping a firm to establish and sustain a defensible competitive advantage, which is the unique position an organization develops vis-à-vis its competitors. The role manufacturing facilities can play in creating competitive advantage to an organization has been acknowledged in the business literature. Design for manufacturing (DFM), for example, can contribute to the creation of competitive advantage by serving as the basis for a differentiation or low cost position in the marketplace. DFM can provide differentiation through speed of delivery, quality, and variety in combination with the former two. DFM can also contribute to a low cost position by reducing scrap and rework, creating efficiencies in purchasing, assembly, and inventory, and by allowing a firm to move up the learning curve faster.

Research and development (R&D) strategy

R&D strategy principally deals with three ingredients: basic R&D, which focuses on theoretical problem areas; product R&D, which concentrates on marketing and is concerned with product improvements; and process R&D, which concentrates on quality control and the improvement of production. Companies that depend on either product or process technology for their success are becoming increasingly concerned with the development of R&D strategies that complement business-level strategies.

Research suggests that focusing on quality improvement through an effective R&D strategy is one of the best ways for organizations to improve market position and profitability, and to gain a sustainable competitive advantage. Thus, the R&D strategy that aims to improve product quality must be recognized as a significant part of a company's competitive strategy. Mini Case 4.2 shows how blending existing ideas and innovations can create great products and business opportunities.

Human resources management and other functional strategies

Strategies related to human resources management, information systems technology, and other areas within an organization are likely to play a significant role in creating

---

 Mini Case 4.2   When ideas collide[3]

'Some of the greatest new business thinking has come about by blending seemingly incompatible existing ideas and innovations'

What do you think of these proposed products—a solar-powered torch, an inflatable dartboard and a waterproof tea bag? Pretty stupid eh? But they are examples of something that I recommend marketers consider—weird combinations.

Reckitt Benckiser recently launched wasabi-flavoured Strepsils. Unilever brought out Marmite cashew nuts. HP now offers HP Guinness sauce. Leading companies are showing the way; extending their brands with bizarre blends. Unilever UK and Ireland chairwoman Amanda Sourry says, 'We continuously challenge ourselves to see how we can grow our portfolio and we identified scope for our iconic brands to stretch outside their traditional categories.' That is the point of these weird combinations—they can take your brand to new places.

Great marketing thinkers are constantly on the hunt for new ways to combine things. What can we put with this idea in order to come up with something different? Not so long ago suitcases were just suitcases. You carried them or put them on a trolley. Then someone thought that it would be a good idea to combine the suitcase with the trolley and they came up with a suitcase with wheels. Now everyone wheels their suitcase. Rob Law took the idea one stage further. He combined a wheeled suitcase with a children's ride-on toy to invent the Trunki. Before its launch, the invention featured on Dragons' Den, but was not taken up. It went on to be a big commercial success with sales all over the world.

Diageo is a master of combining and extending brands. A prime example is its Baileys Irish Cream drink, which has been combined with desserts, ice creams and other products. Britvic, which make Robinsons Fruit Squash drinks, recently collaborated with Monty Bojangles to make flavoured sweets for Waitrose.

When we consider weird combinations the concept does not only apply to products and services. It applies to organizations too. The rock band U2 performed with the opera star Pavarotti. Each brought a new audience to the other's music. Their joint concerts and CDs were a big success. When Mercedes-Benz wanted to develop an entirely new concept of town car it chose to collaborate not with another engineering company but with Swatch—a fashion watch manufacturer. Together they came up with the Smart Car—the most innovative small car since the Mini.

The idea of collaboration works for businesses large and small. A supplier of camellias co-operated with a conservatory manufacturer. He noticed that the conservatories in the showroom were empty. By putting his camellias on display there he found a great way to display his products and to enhance the look and feel of these glass constructions. If we think laterally we can see that many bizarre blends are feasible. The solar-powered torch can be left out in the sun to charge and then used at night. An inflatable dartboard would work with Velcro darts. A tea bag which was waterproof in cold water but absorbed very hot water would stay fresher for longer. Take another look at your brand. Ask what are the wheels we can put on our suitcase? Who could we collaborate with to reach new markets?

[3] *Paul Sloane, **The Marketer**, August 2011, p.13.*

and sustaining the competitive advantage. Human resources management, for example, is seen as a strategic tool to achieve the match between individuals and jobs available. This match will enhance job performance and employees' satisfaction and will properly equip employees to carry out the company's goals and objectives. Management development should be integrated with competitive strategy to enable the company to build its collective competence and to create the learning organization essential for future competition.

Information technology (IT) also has a role to play in creating and sustaining an organization's competitive advantage. To be successful in its business environment, a company needs to have access to different types of information which adds value to strategic decision-makers. This information, when analysed, will strengthen the company's competitive advantage. Information technology is necessary to ascertain what the company's competitive advantage is and how able it is to convert advantage into strategic positions, but information technologies alone are not enough to produce sustainable competitive advantage (Powell and Micallef, 1997).

Organizations have gained advantages by integrating IT with the firm's infrastructure of human and business complementary resources such as flexible culture, partnerships, integration of strategic planning and IT, and supplier relationships. For example, Dell integrated supply chain management with customer-driven order processing, complete control over the build process, logistics, delivery, a strong relationship management system, disintermediation, mass customization, etc. This led to a significant competitive advantage (none of their rivals have grown as fast). Dell has capitalized on first mover status and has managed to stay ahead of the competition by employing IT as a strategy and seeking to develop strategic alliances with others such as Microsoft.

Marketing plan and its link to strategy

A marketing plan is simply a set of detailed actions that should be based on a solid strategic foundation and a well-designed marketing strategy. If the aim of a strategy is to set a long-term direction for the business and define the key strategic goals to proceed in that direction, the marketing plan then aims to translate this organizational direction into shorter-term detailed action plans. A sound marketing plan helps organizations to identify sources of competitive advantage, set objectives and tactics, search for opportunities and threats, identify investment resources, commit resources to marketing programmes, and measure performance. Without solid strategic bases, a marketing plan may fail to contribute to the organization's overall goals and objectives. A typical marketing plan document includes the following content.

- Executive Summary
- Situational Analysis, including customer and competitor analysis
- Marketing Objectives
- Marketing Strategy, including targeting and positioning strategy
- Action Programmes (the 4Ps/7Ps operational marketing plans)

- Budgeting and Financial Forecast
- Evaluation and Controls.

Will every organization consider this content regardless of their size and capability? There are mixed views in the literature. The marketing planning capability of an organization influences the content of a marketing plan in different ways (Slotegraaf and Dickson, 2004). Companies with a strong marketing planning capability are more likely to use rationally based budgeting approaches. These companies may recognize that rationally based budgets afford more resources for the planned actions. However, companies with strong marketing planning capability do not necessarily include more comprehensive coverage of their situational analysis and marketing mix programs in the marketing plan document.

Blue Sky Clothing is a Canadian small company that was founded recently by two entrepreneurs, Lucy Neuman and Nick Russell, to design and market a line of clothing with a unique appeal to outdoor enthusiasts. The company developed a marketing plan to cover five years during which the aim was to secure additional funding for growth and inform its staff of the company's current situation and the future direction. A key objective of the marketing plan was to extend the product line and to add new lines. In addition, the marketing plan was set to explore opportunities for online sales, increase distribution, offer new products, and win new customers. The company's mission was to be a leading producer and marketer of personalized, casual clothing for consumers who love the outdoors.

Strategy mistakes and organizational failure

Mistakes and failure are a fact of life that most organizations cannot escape. General Motors and Toyota, the two giants in the world car market, had both lost the number one position in the market for several years. Why such failure to maintain their leadership positions? Strategy mistakes!

Failure may be defined as deviation from expected and desired results (Cannon and Edmondson, 2005). This includes both avoidable errors and the unavoidable negative outcomes of some strategic decisions. Taking a strategic choice perspective, one might argue that **organizational failure** is a product of repeated strategic mistakes and unsuccessful interactions between the firm's management and its external environment.

Organizational failure and/or poor organizational performance is invariably down to ineffective strategy execution (Neilson et al., 2008). It is important for organizations to identify, understand, and learn from their strategic mistakes in order to avoid organizational failure. Tesco, for example, has lost market share to the hard-discounters Aldi and Lidl, while other retailers such as Waitrose and M&S have introduced more value ranges in response to the wider competition of price cutters. As a result, Tesco's earnings and market share have fallen along with each other.

While most managers know they are always at risk of facing organizational failure, they try to ignore the subject rather than actively seek to find the reasons for failure, guard against it or, at least, be prepared to learn from it when it does occur (Wilkinson and Mellahi, 2005). The question is still open about the possible causes of strategy mistakes and organizational failure, and where they emerge from.

In an interview, Michael Porter outlined the strategic mistakes organizations often make (Magretta, 2012).

- To compete to be the best in the market and to follow the same way as everyone else, thinking that somehow you can achieve better results.
- To overestimate your strengths. A real strength for a strategy is something the company can do better than competitors.
- To define the business wrongly or its geographic scope inaccurately.
- Not to have a strategy at all. Some managers might believe they have a strategy but in fact they do not have a well-defined and rigorous one.

If strategy is defined as a means that helps to marshal and allocate organizational resources based on anticipated changes in the market, failing to evaluate the environment properly represents the most fundamental strategic mistake managers can make. Inaccurate or improper evaluation of the environment might lead to poor strategy formulation and implementation. Although external forces can, to some extent, influence how the turnaround outcome—strategic success or failure—eventually unfolds, these forces are mediated by strategic manoeuvring within the firm. Many firms have suffered because they tried to adapt to environmental fluctuations that lasted for only a brief period of time, or have based their adaptation on faulty understanding of the environment or their own capabilities. Nokia's marketing strategy may have failed because it was not based on a clear value proposition to consumers. It focused heavily on factors less relevant to consumers and did not create an effective message that should produce real results. Apple iPhone and Samsung Android did.

Porter (2004) notes that the threats to strategy are seen to emanate from outside a company because of changes in technology or the behaviour of competitors. Although this is true, the greater threat to strategy often comes from within. It is critical to our understanding of organizational survival and failure that we recognize three factors that contribute to either one: (a) the management of the firm, (b) its external environment, and (c) the way the firm's management interacts with its external environment. Magretta (2011) on a *Harvard Business Review* Blog Network suggested five strategy mistakes connected to the firm's management.

1. Confusing marketing with strategy.
2. Confusing competitive advantage with what you are good at.
3. Pursuing size—if you are the biggest, you will be more profitable.
4. Thinking that 'growth' is a strategy.
5. Focusing on high-growth markets—that is where the money is.

There are four essential points managers need to know in order to understand the link between strategy mistakes and organizational failure (Sheppard and Chowdhury, 2005):

- organizational failure is not typically the fault of either the environment or the organization, but rather it must be attributed to both of these forces, or to be more exact, failure is the misalignment of the organization to the environment's realities
- because organizational failure involves the alignment or misalignment of the firm and its environment, it is by definition about strategy

- because organizational failure deals with strategy, managers can make choices to accelerate it or avoid falling into its clutches
- because organizational failure can be avoided even after a decline—rapid or prolonged—the ultimate failure of the organization really stems from a failure to successfully execute a turnaround.

A study of a very large European telecommunications firm identified a number of strategic choices and decisions that might lead to strategic mistakes and failure (Baumard and Starbuck, 2005):

- attempted growth into a new domain without adequate skills or experience might lead to strategy failure
- projections of overestimated demand can also lead to strategic failure where organizations incurred heavy fixed costs
- transferring an old business model to a new situation might result in strategic failure if the transfer was inappropriate
- launching a new product can increase uncertainty and mobilize resources with low predictability of success
- designing new activities that are projections of core beliefs can be a version of escalating commitments to losing businesses.

Another study, analysing the battle between GM and Toyota for the top spot, offered three lessons for incumbent and budding top executives of large corporations (Chowdhury, 2014).

1. Growth and profit should be treated as mutually inclusive firm objectives.
2. Executives should carefully guard against the pitfalls associated with lock-ins and lock-outs.
3. Hubris might work differently in different contexts but may lead to the same outcome.

To prevent the reccurrence of strategic mistakes and failure, or to initiate corrective actions to minimize the damage incurred while navigating through failure, Sheppard and Chowdhury (2005) produced a list of 'what to do' in the form of strategic advice directed to managers in order to avoid strategy and organizational failure (see Table 4.4).

Managers must draw lessons and learn from past strategic mistakes and failure. Understanding the causes strategic mistakes and organizational failure requires companies to adopt a proactive approach and undertake skilful search within and outside the organization.

The latest thinking: categorizing strategic decisions

What is required from a company when it finds an opportunity to enter a new market or launch a newly modified product? A decision. Rosenzweig (2013) suggests that to make better strategic decisions, managers need to recognize how decisions differ, and how to break the universe of decisions into a few categories in order to be able to identify the best approach for each decision. Rosenzweig believes that strategic decisions vary along two

Table 4.4 Strategic Advice to Managers to Avoid Failure

Strategic Elements	What To Do
Poor strategy performance	Do not confuse a sustained decline with a brief hiccup or a series of hiccups. This delineation is critical: if confusion leads to oversight or inaction on your part, it may lead to your firm's eventual death. Recognize a decline early and that there are elements of the firm's strategy that must be changed.
Taking strategic actions	Be serious and judicious in understanding the situation you are up against and prioritize actions and execute your strategies accordingly.
Statement	Know what your firm is all about: what basic customer needs your firm can serve well; the products you sell; the customers and market segments you serve. Develop a clear identity that sends a clear signal to customers.
Addressing key stakeholders	Listen carefully to key stakeholders. Ask for their input and all-out support and mobilize them to rally around your firm's chosen course of action.
Industry dynamics	Be careful about ambiguous and incomplete environmental data, as they might lead to incorrect interpretation of the industry dynamics. Because of constantly evolving industry dynamics, an incorrect reading does not let you manoeuvre the external forces well; rather it serves as a booby trap.
Resources	Be steadfast and decisive in the acquisition and use funds needed to make the correct change in a timely fashion. The same change might need far more resources later, or the opportunity to change might have been lost for good.
Strategic capabilities	Have marketing to connect with what customers want and the financial acumen to fund needed changes.
Core competences	Make a dedicated effort to exploit where the firm can add value with rare, hard to imitate activities.
Domain selection	Be familiar with your industry's domain without defining it too broadly. Be ready to quickly adjust your domain along with changes in customer needs. Do not stick to domains that have recently seen limited success.
Implementation	Coordinate implementation of strategy elements to work together in an effective, decisive, and timely way.

Source: Jerry Paul Shepherd and Shamsud D. Chowdhury (2005), 'Riding the Wrong Wave: Organisational Failure as a Failed Turnaround', *Long Range Planning*, 38, pp. 239–60.

dimensions, control and performance, which matter most for organizations. Putting them in a 2×2 matrix creates four categories of strategic decision. Figure 4.9 shows these four categories.

Figure 4.9 shows that for organizations to make better decisions, it's important they recognize the different types. Those in the first field, where the organization has no control over outcomes and performance is absolute (the company is not competing with anyone), include consumer choices and personal investment decisions. Those in the fourth field, where the organization can influence outcomes and needs to outperform rivals, include the strategic decisions that are most challenging for managers such as launching a new product or entering a new market. Rosenzweig (2013) notes that managers should make better strategic

Control

Low   High

Third field **Placing competitive best**	Fourth field **Managing for strategic success**
First field **Making judgements and choices**	Second field **Influencing outcomes**

(Vertical axis: Performance — Relative (top) / Absolute (bottom))

4.9 Four types of strategic decisions

Source: Phil Rosenzweig (2013), 'What makes Strategic Decisions Different', *Harvard Business Review*, 92 (November), pp. 88–93.

decisions when they learn to identify which kind of decisions they are facing and develop the versatility to change approaches accordingly.

Discussing decision-driven marketing and how strategic decisions can be made more effectively, Joshi and Giménez (2014) note that when marketing collaborates with other units to execute key strategic decisions it can avoid organizational bottlenecks and get things done far more quickly and effectively. Marketing pioneers tend to inject more discipline into the decision-making processes, clarifying roles for marketing and other relevant functions and establishing decision criteria.

Most marketing decisions cannot be made by marketing alone. Some require collaboration with the CEOs; others need close interaction with sales, pricing unit, IT, product management, and/or other functions on marketing's boundaries. This is what Joshi and Giménez (2014) call 'mining the seams'. They suggest that three categories of marketing-related strategic decisions cross organizational seams.

Strategy and planning decisions involve aligning marketing objectives with business and customer strategies, and aligning the marketing and sales priorities. These decisions address such questions as:

- Which market segments and product lines we should focus our marketing support on?
- What is the appropriate level of spending, and how is it to be allocated between tools and channels?

Execution decisions relate to the proliferation of marketing tools and digital technologies that has increased the difficulty of creating and delivering offers and messages in today's ever-challenging environment. These decisions cover issues such as:

- Which product features must we flag up in our marketing efforts?
- What incentives should we give to encourage consumers to buy our offerings?
- What is the best blend of traditional and digital marketing tools?

Operations and infrastructure decisions look at the new capabilities that are important to marketing's success. They address these questions:

- How will we buy, administer, and evaluate the new marketing technologies and tools?
- What is the appropriate level of integration between digital and traditional marketing?

Joshi and Giménez (2014) concluded that companies have improved interaction and collaboration between marketing and other functions with simple tools that streamline strategic decision-making by establishing clear roles, explicit decision criteria, and well-defined processes.

Conclusion

Drawing upon the strategic analysis of the organization's internal and external environment, strategic managers have to evaluate several alternatives available to them and make strategic decisions that will define the future direction of their organization. The task is to generate a well-justified set of strategic choices and select from them the ones that will strengthen the future position of the organization in the market/s in which it has elected to compete. Figure 4.1 showed the hierarchy of strategic decisions taken at the three organizational levels: corporate, SBU, and functional. Strategic decisions that should be made at the corporate level are the creation of a mission statement, the selection of a directional strategy, and the allocation of resources between SBUs. The key strategic decision at the SBU level is identifying the organization's strategic orientation for the future, that is, one of the three generic strategies (cost leadership, differentiation, focus). Strategic decisions, within marketing, include products to offer, markets to target, and market position strategies. In this chapter, we presented and discussed each of these strategic decisions and reviewed some of the available literature that supports our discussion.

Summary

This chapter has discussed in more detail the second stage/area of the Strategic Marketing Management process (SMM), namely strategic choice and decisions. At this stage managers aim to understand the underlying bases guiding future strategy, generating strategic options, and selecting from among them. They aim to capitalize on the organization's strengths to take advantage of external opportunities and/or minimize threats, and invest in available opportunities to overcome the organization's major weaknesses. Many strategic choices and decisions are taken to contribute to the achievement of the overall corporate goals and objectives. The first set of these strategic decisions will be taken at the corporate level, the next at SBU level, and the final set at the functional level. This chapter has discussed the various sets of strategic decisions at each level and reviewed key analytical models that have frequently been used to inform the decision-making at each level.

Key terms

- **Differentiation strategy:** another generic strategy which involves the creation of a unique product or service for which the company may charge a premium. This speciality can be associated with design, brand image, technology feature, dealer network, or customer service.

- **Directional strategies:** the corporate directional strategies are those designed to achieve growth, stability, or reduction in the corporation's level of activities.

- **Focus strategy:** a generic strategy which involves concentrating the marketing effort on a particular segment and competing in this segment using cost factor or differentiation approach.

- **Low-cost strategy:** a generic strategic strategy which aims at the broad mass market and requires aggressive construction of efficient-scale facilities, vigorous pursuit of cost reduction from experience, tight cost and overhead control, avoidance of marginal customer accounts, and cost minimization in areas like R&D, service, sales force, and advertising.

- **Organizational failure:** from a strategic choice perspective, organizational failure is the product of repeated strategic mistakes and unsuccessful interactions between the firm's management and its external environment.

- **Strategic choice:** involves understanding the underlying bases guiding future strategy and generating strategic options for evaluation and selecting from among them.

Discussion questions

1. Critically assess three approaches/tools to resource allocation, and how organizations can choose from them. Which approach do you think is more suitable and why?

2. Discuss typologies of generic strategy other than Porter's. Do you agree that Porter's strategies are the most applicable in practice?

3. To what extent do you agree that marketing strategy can play a pivotal role in creating competitive advantage? Refer to a company example to support your argument.

4. Identify and discuss the different types of market position strategies. Support your answer with examples.

Online resource centre

Visit the Online Resource Centre for this book for lots of interesting additional material at: <www.oxfordtextbooks.co.uk/orc/west3e/>

References and further reading

Aaker, David A. and Damien McLoughlin (2010), *Strategic Market Management* (New York: John Wiley).

Abell, Derek F. and John S. Hammond (1979), *Strategic Market Planning: Problems and Analytical Approaches*, (Englewood Cliffs, NJ: Prentice Hall).

Akan, Obasi, Richard S. Allen, Marilyn M. Helms, and Samuel A. Spralls (2006), 'Critical Tactics for Implementing Porter's Generic Strategies', *Journal of Business Strategy*, 27 (1), pp. 43–53.

Ansoff, H. I. (1957), 'Strategy for Diversification', *Harvard Business Review*, 25 (5), September-October, pp. 113–24.

Baumard, Philippe and William Starbuck (2005), 'Learning from Failures: Why it May not Happen', *Long Range Planning*, 38, pp. 281–98.

Cannon, Mark D. AndAmy C. Edmondson (2005), 'Failing to Learn and Learning to Fail (Intelligently)', *Long Range Planning*, 38, pp. 299–319.

Casadesus-Masanell, Ramon and Tarziján Jorge (2012), 'When One Business Model Isn't Enough', *Harvard Business Review*, 90, January–February, pp. 132–37.

Chowdhury, Shamsud D. (2014), 'Strategic Roads that Diverge or Converge: GM and Toyota in the Battle for the Top', *Business Horizons*, 57, pp. 127–36.

Cook, Victor J., Jr (1983), 'Marketing Strategy and Differential Advantage', *Journal of Marketing*, 47, Spring, pp. 68–75.

Cook, Victor J., Jr (1985), 'Understanding Marketing Strategy and Differential Advantage', *Journal of Marketing*, 49, Spring, pp. 137–42.

Cui, Anna S. (2013), 'Portfolio Dynamics and Alliance Termination: The Contingent Role of Resources Dissimilarity', *Journal of Marketing*, 77, May, pp. 15–32.

David, Fred R. (1989), 'How Companies Define Their Mission', *Long Range Planning*, 22 (1), pp. 90–7.

Dawar, Niraj (2013), 'When Marketing is Strategy', *Harvard Business Review*, 91, December, pp. 101–8.

Dibb, Sally, Lyndon Simkin, William M. Pride, and O.C. Ferrell (2012), *Marketing: Concepts and Strategies*, 6th edn (Cengage Learning).

Hamel, Gary and C.K. Pralahad (1994), *Competing for the Future,* (Watertown, MA: Harvard Business School Press).

Haspeslagh, Philippe (1982), 'Portfolio Planning: Uses and Limits', *Harvard Business Review*, 60, January–February, pp. 58–73.

Herbert, Theodore T. and Helen Deresky (1987), 'Generic Strategies: An Empirical Investigation of Typology Validity and Strategy Content', *Strategic Management Journal*, 8 (2), pp. 135–47.

Hooley, Graham, Nigel Piercy, and Brigitte Nicoulaud (2011), *Marketing Strategy and Competitive Positioning* (Harlow: Pearson Education).

Jackson, Stuart E. (2008), 'Strategic Opportunism', *Journal of Business Strategy*, 29 (1), pp. 46–8.

Johnson, Mark W., Clayton M. Christensen, and Henning Kagermann (2008), 'Reinventing Your Business Model', *Harvard Business Review*, 86, December, pp. 50–9.

Joshi, Aditya and Eduardo Giménez (2014), 'Decision-Driven Marketing', *Harvard Business Review*, 92, July-August, pp. 64–71.

Kachaner, Nicolas and Michael S. Deimler (2009), 'Stretching the Strategy Process', *Strategic Direction*, 25 (1), pp. 17–20.

Kotler, Philip and Kevin Keller (2012), *Marketing Management*, 14th edn (Upper Saddle River, NJ: Prentice Hall).

Magretta, Joan (2011), 'Five Common Strategy Mistakes', *Harvard Business Review Blog Network*, December 8. <http://blogs.hbr.org/2011/12/five-common-strategy-mistakes/>

Magretta, Joan (2012), *Understanding Michael Porter: The Essential Guide to Competition and Strategy* (Watertown, MA: Harvard Business Review Press).

Miller, Danny (1992), 'The Generic Strategy Trap', *Journal of Business Strategy*, 13, January-February, pp. 37–41.

Miles, Raymond E. and Snow, Charles (1978), *Organizational Strategy, Structure and Process*, (New York: McGraw-Hill).

Neilson, G. L., K.L. Martin, and E. Powers (2008), 'The Secrets to Successful Strategy Execution', *Harvard Business Review*, 86, June, pp. 60–70.

Ovans, Andrea (2011), 'The Charts that Changed the World', *Harvard Business Review*, 89, December, pp. 34–5.

Porter, Michael E. (1980), *Competitive Strategy: Techniques for Analyzing Industries and Competitors* (New York: Free Press).

Porter, Michael E. (1985a), *Competitive Advantage: Creating and Sustaining Superior Performance* (New York: Free Press).

Porter, Michael E. (1985b), 'How to Attack the Industry Leader', *Fortune*, 111 (9), 29 April, pp. 153–66.

Porter, Michael E. (1990), *The Competitive Advantage of Nations* (New York: Free Press).

Porter, Michael E. (2001), 'Strategy and the Internet', *Harvard Business Review*, 79 (3), pp. 63–78.

Porter, Michael E. (2004), 'What is Strategy?', in Segal-Horn, Susan (ed.), *The Strategy Reader*, pp. 41–62 (Chichester: Blackwell).

Porter, Michael E. (2008), 'The Five Competitive Forces that Shape Strategy', *Harvard Business Review*, 86, January, pp. 79–93.

Powell, Thomas C. and Anne Dent-Micallef (1997), 'Information Technology as Competitive Advantage: The Role of Human, Business, and Technology Resources', *Strategic Management Journal*, 18 (5), pp. 375–405.

Pretorius, Marius (2008), 'When Porter's Generic Strategies Are Not Enough: Complementary Strategies for Turnaround Situations', *Journal of Business Strategy*, 29 (6), pp. 19–28.

Rosenzweig, Phil (2013), 'What Makes Strategic Decisions Different', *Harvard Business Review*, 92, November, pp. 88–93.

Sheppard, Jerry Paul and Shamsud D. Chowdhury (2005), 'Riding the Wrong Wave: Organizational Failure as a Failed Turnaround', *Long Range Planning*, 38, pp. 239–60.

Slotegraaf, Rebecca J. and Peter R. Dickson (2004), 'The Paradox of a Marketing Planning Capability', *Journal of the Academy of Marketing Science*, 32 (4), pp. 371–85.

Speed, Richard J. (1989), 'Oh Mr Porter! A Re-Appraisal of Competitive Strategy', *Marketing Intelligence and Planning*, 6 (5), pp. 8–11.

Sullivan, Tim (2013), 'The Tyranny of Strategy', *Harvard Business Review*, 92, December, pp. 138–9.

Utterback, James M. and W.J. Abernathy (1975), 'A Dynamic Model of Product and Process Innovation', *Omega*, 3 (6), pp. 639–56.

Ward, Steven and Aleksandra Lewandowska (2008), 'Is the Marketing Concept Always Necessary?: The Effectiveness of Customer, Competitors and Societal Strategies in Business Environment Types', *European Journal of Marketing*, 42 (1/2), pp. 222–37.

Wheelen, Thomas L. and David J. Hunger (2012), *Strategic Management and Business Policy: Toward Global Sustainability* (Upper Saddle River, NJ: Pearson Education).

Wilkinson, Adrian and Kamel Mellaho (2005), 'Organizational Failure: Introduction to the Special Issue', *Long Range Planning*, 38, pp. 233–8.

Wilson, Richard M. S. and Colin Gilligan (2005), *Strategic Marketing Management: Planning, Implementation and Control* (Oxford: Butterworth-Heinemann).

Wright, Peter (1987), 'A Refinement of Porter's Strategies', *Strategic Management Journal*, 8 (1), pp. 93–101.

Zahra, Shaker A. and R. Das Sidhartha (1993), 'Building Competitive Advantage on Manufacturing Resources', *Long Range Planning*, 26 (2), pp. 90–100.

 End of Chapter 4 case study Luxury apparel brands in a recession market: a closer look at Michael Kors and Coach

The most recent United States recession officially began in December 2007 and ended in June 2009, according to the National Bureau of Economic Research, and affected almost every aspect of the economy. Consumers were hit hard through loss of wealth due to the stock market crash and the housing bubble burst. Companies also felt the pain as demand for many goods decreased. This decline in demand was particularly acute in the luxury goods category with 83 per cent of US consumers reporting purchasing fewer high-end designer/luxury brands in 2011 and 86 per cent intending to maintain this behaviour moving forward. A year before the recession, luxury retailers were growing at 9 per cent annually, but from 2007 to 2009 their sales dropped, on average, by more than 13 per cent. The luxury apparel category was under tremendous pressure to curb declining sales, but they were faced with the challenge of figuring out how to do so at a time when consumers were cutting back, reprioritizing their needs, and rejecting the conspicuous consumption that the category represented.

Consumers within the luxury apparel market can be divided into three important segments, which were impacted to varying degrees by the recession: (1) the super-rich, for whom luxury brands are a way of life (the bedrock of the luxury market), (2) aspirational buyers, who purchase luxury goods when able, based on positive financial windfalls, and (3) premium buyers, who are tourists in the luxury market and splurge only when their finances permit. Throughout the recession, the super-rich segment tended to maintain their buying power and were largely unaffected by the economic decline, enabling them to continue their consumption of luxury goods. Conversely, both premium and aspirational buyers saw a serious decline in their buying power, resulting in an inability and a declining desire to purchase luxury products.

In response to negative sales trends, luxury apparel brands had a critical choice to make regarding the targeting and positioning of their products: (1) Should they maintain their status and focus on targeting super-rich consumers who were maintaining their luxury purchasing? Or (2) should they risk undermining their own product positioning by extending their product lines and lowering prices to reach aspirational and premium buyers who were cutting back? Both Michael Kors and Coach elected the latter approach in an effort to offset losses by increasing their overall volume of sales. From 2010 to 2011, both Michael Kors and Coach found this strategy to be successful and were able to increase sales by 57 per cent and 15 per cent, respectively. However, by electing to follow similar strategies, competition between the two brands has intensified, and they now find themselves in a battle to win preference and loyalty among aspirational and premium luxury buyers.

Michael Kors' approach

Michael Kors' efforts to make the brand more accessible to budget conscious consumers relied heavily on two strategies.

1. Expanding the Michael line— a less expensive sub-brand that targets Millennials with entry-level items such as accessories—in an effort to make the luxury apparel market more attainable so as to reduce the use of goal substitution among consumers.

2. Increasing the number of retail stores, growing from just 74 in 2009 to 191 in 2012, with a long-term goal of 400.

The financial performance of the company indicates that Michael Kors' strategy is working, with annual revenue growth from 2008 to 2012 of 43 per cent, of which the primary driving force has been store growth. As of 2012, the Michael line accounted for approximately 90 per cent of the company's total sales. Operating margin has improved as well, growing from 8 per cent in 2008 to 19 per cent in 2012.

Coach's approach

Coach's approach to driving sales volume and revenue in a time of consumer belt-tightening was three-fold.

1. Lowering prices through the heavy use of discounts and promotions.

2. Growing outlet store sales as a means to drive volume.

3. Lowering the quality of products sold in outlet stores to keep prices down and appeal to a more price-conscious consumer. Currently 85 per cent of the company's merchandise is specifically manufactured for the factory consumers, which means the majority of Coach products on the market are of a lower quality than in the past.

The company implemented these changes under the master Coach brand without creating sub-brands or new product lines. This reduction in the quality of its core brand of products combined with the lowering of consumer price expectations due to continuous promotional pricing has put the Coach brand image at significant risk, particularly in terms of product quality perceptions. While Coach sales grew between 2009 and 2011, with net sales increases of 11.7 per cent, 15.3 per cent, and 14.5 per cent, respectively, the company is currently experiencing a decline in US sales. Comparable sales growth is now at 1.7 per cent, as the company struggles to eliminate some promotional discounting efforts and is faced by increasing competition from Michael Kors' factory stores.

Conclusion

Although both Michael Kors and Coach chose the same strategic approach in response to the recession, their tactical implementation has differed, leading to greater success by Michael Kors. While Coach focused heavily on promotional discounting and outlet stores under the same master Coach brand, Michael Kors smartly created a sub-brand through the Michael line, which helps customers distinguish between its entry-level and upper-tier products. This has better enabled Kors to maintain its brand image while still offering lower priced items, making it easier for consumers who are 'trading down' to rationalize a luxury brand purchase. Additionally, by maintaining the quality and stature of its more expensive Michael Kors lines, the company has protected the perceived quality of the brand and is able to keep customers engaged with the brand for a longer period of time by graduating its entry-level customers into more expensive and prestigious products.

Conversely, Coach's use of discounting and emphasis on outlet sales has trained its customers to expect lower prices and lower quality products. As a result, the brand has devalued its image and perceived quality and is now regarded by many as an entry-level brand, from which they will graduate to other, more prestigious brands. While this approach successfully drove volume during tough economic times, as the economy improves, Coach will inevitably begin to lose entry-level customers who are regaining their ability to trade up within the luxury apparel market, but do not feel they can do so within Coach's current offerings. Additionally, as Coach decreases the use of promotional offers and heavy discounting, its new entry-level audience is troubled by what appears to be rising prices without a similar improvement in the quality of products. This is likely to negatively impact overall value perceptions of the brand.

Discussion questions

1. How would you describe the continuum of decision-making in the luxury apparel category? How might this vary by consumer segment? Provide an example of how one consumer segment might go through the decision-making process.

2. What are some possible sub-segments (i.e. age, lifestyle, race/ethnicity, gender, etc.) that Coach might target moving forward to grow the business? For example, should Coach focus on upwardly-mobile Millennials versus affluent Boomers, etc.?

Weigh the pros and cons associated with targeting each group suggested. Please use at least two reliable outside resources. Some suggested resources to help develop your answer are:

- Coach's annual report: <http://www.annualreports.com/Company/2246>
- Luxury Institute: <http://luxuryinstitute.com/blog/>
- Unity Marketing: <http://www.unitymarketingonline.com/cms/Home/White_Papers.php>

3. Based on Figures C4.1 to C4.5, what methods do Michael Kors and Coach appear to be using to motivate purchase? Discuss which human motivation Coach and Michael Kors are appealing to based on Maslow's Hierarchy of Needs.

4. Based on the financial results of Michael Kors and Coach over the last five years, who do you think has implemented the most successful strategy for growing sales during and post-recession? Why?

Develop your conclusions by focusing on revenue, gross profit, operating income and comparable store sales trends. Compare advertising spend as a percentage of net sales. Please utilize the annual reports of both companies along with any additional outside resources to develop your answer. Please show all quantitative calculations.

- Coach's annual report: <http://www.annualreports.com/Company/2246>
- Michael Kors' annual report: <http://phx.corporate-ir.net/phoenix.zhtml?c=235654&p=irol-reportsannual>.

☐ Improving outlook vs. prior period ☐ Worsening outlook vs. prior period				
	Mar 2011	**Sep 2010**	**Mar 2010**	**Sep 2009**
Optimistic about our country's economy	20%	21%	21%	27%
Having a hard time making ends meet	38%	43%	37%	48%
Living paycheck to paycheck	42%	48%	42%	51%
Somewhat or very worried about losing a job	45%	53%	54%	50%
Optimistic about ability to manage household budget	53%	49%	51%	48%
Making lifeplan changes due to declining asset values	57%	61%	73%	68%

C4.1 Declining Consumer Sentiment from 2009 to 2011

Source: McKinsey Consumer Sentiment Survey III, IV, V and VI (Sep 2009, Mar 2010, Sep 2010, Mar 2011).

Consumers intend to stick with purchasing behaviour adopted since the beginning of the downturn

Behaviour since the beginning of the downturn	Percent intending to keep behaviour[1] Mar 2011		Positive, neutral or negative +/●/– indicator of consumer sentiment vs prior wave			
			Sep 2010	Mar 2010	Sep 2009	Feb 2009
Purchase high-end designer/luxury brands *less*		86 ●	87 ●	84 ●	83 ●	81
Shop at mass merchants *more*		85 ●	84 ●	82 ●	81 +	75
Purchase private label/store brand products *more*		85 ●	84 ●	87 ●	85 +	78
Shop at dollar stores *more*		80 ●	79 ●	78 ●	82	N/A
Shop at club stores *more*		75 –	80 ●	84 ●	80 +	72
Go out to eat *less*		68 ●	71 ●	73 ●	70 ●	67

1 Consumers who would keep their new behaviour as it is now completely or for the most part

C4.2 Consumer Reaction to Economic Instability

Source: McKinsey Consumer Sentiment Survey III, IV, V and VI (Sep 2009, Mar 2010, Sep 2010, Mar 2011).

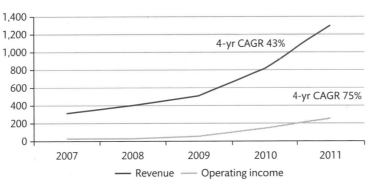

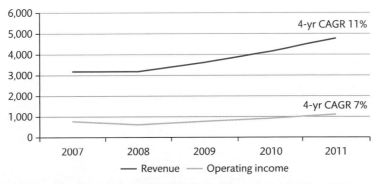

C4.3 Financial Results for Michael Kors and Coach (derived from most recent financial statements of each company)

C4.4 Coach Marketing
Sources and additional resources
Print Ad 1: <http://modadimagno.blogspot.com/2008/05/today-in-ads-pictures.html>
Print Ad 2: <http://www.fidoo.com/Brand/482>
YouTube Channel: <https://www.youtube.com/user/coach>
Twitter Page (use images): <https://twitter.com/Coach>

C4.5 Michael Kors Marketing

Sources and additional resources

Print Ad 1: <http://searchingforstyle.com/archives/8712/>

Print Ad 2: <http://zenportfolios.com/cynthialuu/>

Print Ad 3: <http://art8amby.wordpress.com/2012/01/09/michael-kors-spring-summer-2012-ad-campaign/>

You tube Channel: <https://www.youtube.com/user/michaelkors>

Goldman Sachs Global Retail Conference Presentation (Page 5):

<http://phx.corporate-ir.net/phoenix.zhtml?c=235654&p=irol-calendarPast>

This case was prepared by Allison Davis, Stacey Maniscalco, Dominic Trozzi, and Stephanie Zanin.

Segmentation, targeting, and positioning strategies

5

Learning Objectives

1. To understand the ways in which companies can segment markets.
2. Discern how marketers can measure the effectiveness of identified target segments.
3. Be able to differentiate among the various ways in which marketers can reach the identified market segments.
4. Be able to explain the importance of positioning the product in the head of the target consumer.
5. To know how to use important tools for perceptual mapping.
6. To know how to achieve a powerful position within the mind of the target consumer.

Chapter at a Glance

I. Introduction

1 Overview and strategy blueprint
2 Marketing strategy: analysis and perspectives

II. Where are we now?

3 Environmental and internal analysis: market information and intelligence

III. Where do we want to be?

4 Strategic marketing decisions, choices, and mistakes

5 **Segmentation, targeting, and positioning strategies**

6 Branding strategies
7 Relational and sustainability strategies

V. Did we get there?

14 Strategy implementation, control, and metrics

IV. How will we get there?

8 Product innovation and development strategies
9 Service marketing strategies
10 Pricing and distribution strategies
11 Marketing communications strategies
12 International marketing strategy
13 Social and ethical strategies

 Case study: Targeting children—an ethical dilemma?

For many years around the world there have been complaints about companies attempting to target their products to children. Nowhere is this more prevalent than with fast food and confectionery producers whose products are considered to be 'junk food,' high in sugar and fat content. Cereal companies have often been accused of hitting children with adverts during morning cartoon programmes, pushing children to pressure their parents to buy these products for them when they are in Waitrose or Tesco. Governments are concerned with controlling this as there is concern on both sides of the Atlantic regarding the ever-increasing level of youth obesity as children are becoming less physically active and tending towards unhealthy lifestyles. To address the obesity concern physical activity is often promoted through public service announcements with 'get out and play' campaigns using famous sports figures to motivate children to get off of the sofa and out onto the sports pitch. The problem is that while there are bans on adverts promoting unhealthy products to children (in the UK this took effect in January 2008), marketers are now using viral alternatives to reach these important consumers. Creative marketers are using websites to reach this target audience with fun and games, and mobile phone networks are reaching children with a variety of prize promotions. Coke and its Fanta brand have tried these types of campaigns in the US and the UK. Of course these methods are in addition to the heavy use of cinema and TV product placements and celebrity tie-ins. If Miley Cyrus is eating some brand of junk food, it is pretty easy to see how many star-struck children might try to eat the same thing. Luckily, Walt Disney Co. has always been concerned about conveying the 'right' messages to children, but as the company's films are creeping out of the U ratings to PG and higher restrictive ratings to get bigger audiences, the potential is there to step a bit over the moral line.

Who has made a more visible use of food tie-ins for children than McDonalds, Burger King, and KFC? The 'happy meal' tying-in of a variety of new movie-focused toys has been an issue for parents for many years. Children push to get the whole series of toys, and the parents are pressured to buy many happy meals to get all of the series of toys for their kids. At least KFC has made the move to eliminate toys from children's meal packs. Hopefully the others will follow suit. McDonalds make use of its Kid Zone on its website which offers games for children mixed in with a variety of Happy Meal adverts, and even Cadbury makes use of Bebo for promotion of Crème Eggs sweets.

In this day and age, it would appear that a better way to target your offerings would be to take the high road and opt to act in a socially responsible manner to get the parents of the kids to support your company. Of course this means that food producers must seek new healthier alternatives like cereals with lower sugar content and low-fat snack treats. Wendy's has taken the moral high road in the US by allowing parents to substitute oranges and apples and salads for fries and McDonalds appears to be close behind as good citizenship is proving to be profitable. Finally in November 2008 an agreement was reached between some of the biggest fast-food franchises in the UK to improve the fat and salt content of their products. Wimpy, Nando's, McDonalds, KFC, and Subway, among others, have committed to making their offerings more healthy. Particularly with the offering of grilled versus fried chicken and chicken sandwiches, the public are offered healthier options at these restaurants. Consumers are also regularly offered caloric/fat content information for the various food offerings, and this makes better options available for consumers. So the question that some are asking is whether the use of more 'creative' marketing campaigns to reach children should still be used if they are not breaking any laws and attempting to improve the overall quality of their products. It can be argued that it is always better to take the high ground in these matters.

Introduction

Market segmentation is vital for company success. Without a clear idea of the nature of the target segments, the firm is forced to use a scatter-shot approach to marketing strategic decision-making with little chance for success. Dividing the market up into reasonable segments is only a starting point. The firm then must develop a series of strategic goals and strategies for effectively reaching those identified segments. Targeting requires the firm not only to aim at, but hopefully to hit its target segments. The final important aspect involves the establishment of an important perceptual position in the mind of the consumer. The company whose brand comes immediately to mind when a need arises in a particular product/service class has a distinct advantage over its competitors. This chapter will present a series of possible foundations for effective segmentation and mechanisms for developing action plans for reaching those segments, and will discuss ways in which marketing strategists can enhance their product/service position inside the mind of the targeted consumer. New thinking is presented in discussions on real-time experience tracking and the creation of the 'superconsumer'.

Foundations for effective segmentation

With the vast array of different wants and needs for any product or service class, it is unlikely that any company can have the luxury of appealing to an entire market. The buying requirements for such an array of consumers would be widely varied. This might be possible in the early stages of a product or service form life cycle; however, as competition builds, the company is forced to give consumers a reason to prefer its product offerings from those of the competitors through differentiation. For this to be successful, it is necessary for the company to identify target segments of consumers and tailor their offerings to best meet the wants and needs of that particular group of consumers. It must be reiterated, however, that the initial requirement for effective segmentation is for the company to have clear strategic goals/objectives set within the umbrella of the corporate mission statement before target segments can be identified and targeted, and a positioning strategy developed.

Market segmentation involves the analysis of **mass markets** to identify subgroups of consumers with similar wants and buying requirements. These subgroups can range from quite large down to 'segments of one.' It might be possible to successfully focus on each and every customer as a viable target market (particularly for business-to-business marketers where markets are smaller by nature than for business-to-consumer marketers). The point is to maximize between segment differences while minimizing within segment differences using a variety of grouping variables. The firm is then in a position to tailor its offerings to best meet the desires of the consumers belonging to that segment. The point is for the firm to identify clusters of similar consumers that will allow for more efficient uses of resources and improve firm performance. The identification of a segment allows the firm to identify a profile of its typical desired customer, which in turn would allow the firm to develop a product configuration, pricing scheme, promotional campaign, and distribution coverage plan to best meet the needs of that identified typical consumer.

Criteria for identifying segments

The most important variables for identifying segments are as follows.

- Geography:
    - Global
    - Global Regional
    - National
    - National Regional
    - City/State
    - Neighbourhood/Local
    - Topography
    - Climate

- Demography:
  - Gender
  - Age
  - Education
  - Income
  - Occupation
  - Religion
  - Ethnicity
  - Family Size
  - Stage of Family Life Cycle
  - Social Status/Class
- Psychography:
  - Personality
  - Lifestyle
  - Values
- Behaviour:
  - Usage Rate
  - Loyalty Level
  - Event Creation
  - Key Benefits

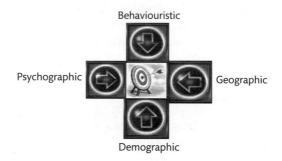

Each of these will now be discussed with illustrative examples.

Geographic bases for segmentation

Geography focuses on the where issues. It ranges from **local/neighbourhood** to **global**, and it could encompass any variation within the two extremes. Here the main mechanism for segmentation is the nature of the geographic market being covered. **Local segmentation**, often used by small firms getting their start, keeps the market confined to a manageable area of coverage until a far greater understanding of possible niches is gathered. Since these firms often are not sure who their direct competitors are or will be, they opt for a group of nearby customers to reach. Picture the small restaurant getting its first connection to potential area customers with the placing of windscreen flyers or door-to-door leaflets to tell people that they are open for business.

Global segmentation would assume that the company sees the entire world as its appropriate playing field. This would indicate that the firm sees the broadest array of customers as its potential market. The danger of this approach normally entails the potential for cultural inappropriateness without some modification for different regions or nations. The other options are all variations limited by the amount of geographic coverage. Often companies will use geographic mapping programs (like SPSS Maps) to address geographic segmentation by measuring potential trading area coverage. There are often assumptions made that if their best customers are located in a particular area, there may be important opportunities to build other strong customers in that coverage area. Kotler (2003) mentions the use by many companies of customer cloning whereby the densest geographic areas are mapped and the company assumes that if the majority of customers are located in a particular area, then the best potential customers will come from that area.

Another aspect of geographic segmentation, which often is overlooked, is **topography**. The contour of the land within a geographic area may have a bearing on effective segmentation. Topography includes such elements as rivers, mountains, lakes, and valleys which may affect population movement. The costs of overcoming physical obstacles may make a significant argument for effective segmentation. This might also apply to climatic conditions. Arid desert conditions as opposed to humid rainforest conditions can also be an appropriate mechanism for segmentation.

In practice, larger firms undoubtedly utilize a variety of different segmentation approaches given different types of products. Campbell's Soup had great success in the upper midwest of the United States with its cheddar cheese soup, but this product had little relevance for the US southwest, so the manufacturer put in jalapeno peppers to add spice to it and found great acceptance for the product as a coating for tortilla chips.

Demographic bases for segmentation

Here the overall market is subdivided using a series of demographic variables. One of the most obvious ways to segment demographically is by gender, but this is a complex term. **Gender** does not just address physical sexual make-up. It also contains a psychological component. How the individual sees themselves in terms of their sexual make-up and orientation is becoming less distinct in a variety of developed countries. Sex segmentation involves choosing males or females as the target audience. Certainly there are a variety of products that have attempted this from cosmetic companies to alcoholic beverages; however, it is more difficult now as one's feelings of masculinity/femininity affiliation may be a more appropriate segmentation tool. In the United States, Virginia Slims cigarettes were oriented to women, but it was not clear that they had no appeal to those males who felt a particular affinity for things of a feminine nature.

Age is another basis for demographic segmentation. This can be clearly seen in the segmentation being done by Sony and Microsoft for its popular computer gaming systems and hand-held systems (Sony's Playstation and PSP and Microsoft's X-Box). The aim is to reach the computer savvy youth with considerable discretionary income to spend on computer games, music CDs, and DVDs. Youth can clearly be seen in the segmentation of toys, music, cereals, clothing, electronics, and cellular telephones.

With globalization forces at work, there is an increasing opportunity for similarity of youth segments in terms of wants and needs driven strongly by world entertainment media (cinema, music, television). This would primarily apply to developed countries as income levels in developing countries would not support these types of products and services.

Elderly consumers provide another promising avenue for product/service segmentation. With life expectancies significantly increasing in many developed countries, the elderly become increasingly lucrative as a segmentation vehicle. The United States has seen a considerable increase in the segmenting of older consumers by fast food franchisers as consumers looking for places to socialize with others and as potential employees. A wide range of health-related products are being aimed at increasingly older consumers with travel and leisure products/services and low-fat and low-carbohydrate food/beverage products.

An interesting shift in focus was seen for Red Bull energy drinks in the UK, which had built a credible position targeting what was considered 'edgy youth' interested in nightclubs and extreme sports. The company shifted its segmentation target in 2004 to older consumers interested in golf, which would move the product into the mainstream. The company has plans to distribute Red Bull in UK golf clubs and will align itself with the European Professional Golfers Association Tour (Sweeney, 2004). Another attempt to shift focus can be readily seen in the recent relaunching of Burton Food's Viscount brand of biscuits. The new product is called Viscount Minis, and the new target is the younger woman who buys biscuits and confectionery to share. This is a distinct departure from the more mature female consumers who were previously seen as the key segment for the company's biscuits.

An important approach to age segmentation involves the concept of a **cohort of society** moving through the ageing process together. However, while birth age is relatively easy to use as a basis for grouping potential consumers, it has little to do with consumer motivations. Defining moments and events in late adolescence/early adulthood (17–23 years of age) provides a set of fairly stable values that stay with members of the same generational cohort throughout their lives. *Advertising Age* (January 15, 2001) presented six main generational cohorts in the US: (1) the **GI Generation** (those born between 1901 and 1924) who are conservative and civic-concerned; (2) the **Silent Generation** (those born between 1925 and 1945) who are interested in conforming and raised families at an early age and are concerned with youthfulness and vitality; (3) the **Baby Boomers** (those born between 1946 and 1964) who believe that personal acquisitions are important, have high levels of disposable income, and are concerned with value and do not want to be perceived as older; (4) **Generation X** (those born between 1961 and 1981) who are considered to be somewhat cynical, have great economic power, and who feel rather lost or alienated; (5) **Generation Y** (those born between 1976 and 1981) who are a subset of generation X, interested in an urban style, like outdoor activities, and enjoy retro-style products; and lastly (6) the **Millennials** (those born between 1982 and 2002) who are multicultural, interested in high-tech products, social media savvy, well-educated, and more used to violence and sex as a part of life.

While the idea of cohorts makes sense when thinking about similar experiential countries like the United States and the United Kingdom, any attempt to assume similar generational cohorts in a global context may not work. An interesting study examined generational cohorts in a global setting, and found that there are a number of countries which may not have the kinds of cohorts that have been found in the US (Schewe and Meredith, 2004. The research suggested that for cohorts to be formed, there are three requirements: (1) a telecommunications infrastructure that facilitates mass communications, (2) a population which is reasonably literate, and (3) the events involved must have significant social impact. These conditions can be met in all developed countries as well as India, Eastern Europe, Lebanon, and China; however, underdeveloped nations are not fertile ground for cohort segmentation (Schewe and Meredith, 2004). There are distinctly different generational cohorts in Brazil and in Russia. These cohorts provide a valuable opportunity for segmentation.

The **level of education** can also be an effective basis for segmentation. The complexity of certain products makes them more appropriate for proper evaluation and usage by individuals with higher levels of education. There are certain products which are targeted to students from primary school level (with such products as crayons, books, games, and snack products) to higher levels of education such as high school and college (with products like calculators, computers, apparel, music, and DVDs). The US has seen the advent of the SKIPPies acronym as descriptive of an important buying group (School Kids with Income and Purchasing Power). Firms like Coca-Cola, Nike, and Nabisco have all turned to in-school promotions to attract the teenage student segment.

One particularly successful in-school marketing programme in the US is offered by Channel One (Cort et al., 2004). This in-school television network broadcasts a 12 minute daily programme with two minutes of commercials to over 12,000 schools throughout the US and carries news and programming of interest to students. In return for allowing the programming during classes, the school receives television sets and receiving equipment. It is hoped that the advertiser utilization of the system will begin to build the seeds of brand awareness and loyalty in a unique environment with long-term consumer relationship potential.

A logical basis for segmentation is **level of income**, but in many countries the larger concern is the individual's level of purchasing power. The important distinction in income is found in the difference between disposable and discretionary income. For basic necessity types of product (food, clothing, and shelter), the starting point would be to examine disposable income, which is the income left over after taxes and creditors are paid. Discretionary income is what is left over from disposable income after acquiring basic necessities. The remainder is then used to buy such products/services as fashion items/jewelry, cosmetics, and fragrances, and a variety of leisure time products/services like vacations and fitness club memberships.

Occupation can also serve as an appropriate basis for segmentation. There are a series of products/services that are aimed at homemakers as opposed to professionals, students, 'white collar' workers (managers. executives, professionals) as opposed to 'blue collar' workers (labourers, tradespeople), retirees/pensioners, and the unemployed.

Religion is an important basis for segmentation particularly when religious teachings/doctrine make the consumption of certain products mandatory or prohibited. Some products may never be allowed (beef for Hindus, alcoholic beverages for Muslims) while others may depend on the time of year or even day of the week. Acceptable articles and types of clothing may be dictated by religion, e.g. coverings to be worn by women in the Middle East. In the US, the Manischewitz Company sells products which meet Jewish kosher standards.

Ethnicity equates to national country/culture of origin. In the United States, McDonald's has been particularly focused on race and ethnic heritage as a segmentation tool. Ads are run with Asian American, African American, and Hispanic American settings, which include appropriately representative models, locales, music, and language. This can also apply just as easily to any national origin and cultural extraction. The key element would involve the use of effective representations of those cultures. In many developed countries, there are significant ethnic communities with considerable purchasing power which are effective targets for segmentation strategies.

Minority and ethnic group segmentation must consider the impact of acculturation since the amount of time that individuals have spent in the society will impact their outlook (Palumbo and Teich, 2004). Parallel strategies should be developed for targeting both acculturated ethnic groups as well as those not yet acculturated. The authors suggest that this is equally applicable in the US as well as Western Europe, given the large influx of immigrants into these countries and cultures.

Family size is another segmentation variable worth considering. The existence of the extended family in many developing countries is an important consideration since there are various members of the family unit who can play a variety of roles in the product/service choice process. Kellogg's had seen problems in its Brazilian advertisements showing a father and child in a breakfast setting. It was not seen as representative of real life, since the father would not be the one normally getting the child his or her breakfast. In Brazil that would be the grandparent. The ads were changed and were received much more favourably as a result.

Family life cycle stage reflects a variety of life conditions that have a potential impact on product/service purchase decisions. If the target segment is single as opposed to married, there may be a series of preferences linked to that life state. Examples can be found in food packaging of meals for one person as opposed to two or more, dating services, and fashion and hygiene products to help the individual find a date/partner. Later life stages include young marrieds, marrieds with no children, marrieds with young children, marrieds with older children, empty-nesters (marrieds whose children have left home and are now on their own), and older marrieds or those who are older but single again. These types of segmentation mechanisms are particularly useful in terms of leisure time activity choices as one's leisure time usage is heavily influenced by the nature of the home/family situation. Automobile companies use life cycle stage segmentation quite heavily. Vans are often chosen by families with young children since they have more space for carpooling several children at a time to a soccer game or to a school programme, while small sports cars with only two seats are aimed at singles or young marrieds.

In Great Britain, the 2003 National Readership Survey (NRS Ltd) in its SAGACITY Life Cycle Groupings utilizes four distinct life cycle stages: dependent (mainly under the age of 24 and either living at home or a full-time student); pre-family (under the age of 35 and with their own household but without children); family (under the age of 65 with one or more children in the household representing as a group the main shoppers and primary income earners); and late (all adults whose children have left the home or those adults older than 35 without any children). For SAGACITY, these categories are then further divided into categories based upon previously discussed criteria (income and occupation). Here, life cycle stages are then divided into the white group (where the primary income earner works in the ABC1 occupation group) and the blue group (where the primary income earner works in the C2DE occupation group). Finally, in terms of the family and late categories, each is subdivided into two sub-categories in terms of income: better off and worse off. This combination approach leads to the identification of 12 separate and distinct categorizations for segmentation purposes. The theory here is that each subdivision reflects a group with different aspirations and behaviours.

Finally, **social class/status** can also be utilized as an effective basis for segmentation. There are six accepted grade definitions used in the UK reflecting social class (National Readership

Survey, 2003): (1) A, **upper middle class** (3.5 per cent of the population), which reflects higher administrative, professional, and managerial occupations, (2) B, **middle class** (21.6 per cent of the population), which includes intermediate levels of each of the occupations mentioned above, (3) C1, **lower middle class** (28.5 per cent of the population), which counts junior levels of each of the above-mentioned occupations along with supervisory and clerical positions, (4) C2, **skilled working class** (20.7 per cent of the population), including skilled manual labourers, (5) D, **working class** (16.5 per cent of the population), incorporating semiskilled as well as unskilled workers, and (6) E, **those at the lowest level of subsistence** (9.2 per cent of the population), including state pensioners, widows (with no other earners), casual workers, and the lowest-grade workers (Marketing Pocket Book, 2004). Each of these groups has different wants, needs, expectations, and preferences. Demographic bases are the most used of all segmentation bases since they are the easiest to measure. Often they can be determined from readily available secondary data sources. When focusing on perceptual issues, segmentation mechanisms become a bit more complex.

Psychographic bases for segmentation

Psychographic bases for segmentation centre on perceptual issues. These segments are determined by combining individuals who are psychologically similar in their orientations. These distinctions are made based upon similarity of lifestyles, personalities, and values. Psychographics are often associated with the acronym AIO, which stands for activities, interests, and opinions, and segments which are exactly the same in terms of demographics may be significantly different in terms of their psychological make-up. This is an extremely important segmentation base because of its excellent potential for effective targeting of the segment due to an understanding of how the segment members live their daily lives and the opportunity to tie products and services to their particular values and aspirations.

Lifestyle reflects the ways in which individuals choose to live their lives. What types of activities they enjoy, what life settings they desire, and who they surround themselves with are all components of lifestyle. A British company which has built its segmentation on lifestyles is the clothier, Ben Sherman, which has found a distinctive niche with a return to the look and styles of the 1960s (O'Loughlin, 2005). Two recent themes have been utilized: (1) the **Park Life** campaign (connecting their mod fashions to classic British icons like Big Ben and Hyde Park) and (2) the **Mods in the Mansion** campaign (tying affluent rock stars to country homes). In the United States there are three main lifestyle groupings that are often chosen for segmentation: (1) the arts and culturally oriented consumer, (2) the sports enthusiast, and (3) the outdoors adventurer. The arts consumer is one who enjoys attending cultural events (e.g. symphony concerts, opera, ballet), which assumes a more educated, higher social grade, and a quieter type of individual who needs cultural infusion to be happy. The sports enthusiast is seen as a younger, less educated individual, who is more outgoing and loud in voice and mannerisms. Finally, the outdoors person is one who enjoys the great outdoors. This individual enjoys a variety of ways to commune with nature, and is likely to go camping, hiking, jogging, and biking.

One study attempted to use lifestyle patterns to segment beer consumers in the US (Orth et al., 2004). Using cluster analysis with lifestyle survey respondents, the study identified eight different segments: (1) **TV-opposing moderates** (11 per cent of respondents who do things in moderation), (2) **unromantic thrill seekers** (9 per cent of the respondents who look for thrills but are not interested in social or romantic activities—predominantly male and younger), (3) **unexcited romantics** (9 per cent of the respondents who prefer quiet, leisurely, and romantic activities to thrills—predominantly females), (4) **lazy opportunists** (15 per cent of the respondents who prefer not to be active—predominantly older), (5) **interactive party animals** (15 per cent of the respondents who prefer activities which involve social interactions and shy away from activities which are done on one's own or are quiet—predominantly male and younger), (6) **introvert individualists** (14 per cent of the respondents who prefer to do things on their own), (7) **outgoing socializers** (12 per cent of the respondents who prefer social activities), and (8) **rushing adrenaline addicts** (16 per cent of the respondents who prefer activities involving excitement and motion).

Personality is another mechanism for segmentation. Kotler (2003) lists the four main variations of personality as compulsive, gregarious, authoritarian, and ambitious. Here the idea is to group people into roughly similar personality types with the underlying assumption that people will be more favourably disposed toward those of a similar personality profile. Personality has also been applied to products and services in the work of Jennifer Aaker (1997), who found that brands can be imbued with personality traits. Her research identified five different personality traits for brands: sincerity, ruggedness, sophistication, competence, and excitement. The idea is to match the brand personality with the consumer segment personality profile to establish a strong connection.

Another approach to psychographic segmentation involves the use of **core values**. The company tries to match its core values with those of its customer segments, building positive associations. The company stresses values in its products/services as well as in its corporate environment and culture, and the hope is that the segment will become loyal to the company because it embodies the core values important to the consumer. Core values are deep set in the individual by life experiences and teachings, and cannot be changed easily. The Body Shop, Ben and Jerry's Ice Cream, and Starbucks are all companies that try to resonate with the consumer by stressing concern for the environment, the use of natural materials, and human welfare. They hire people who embody these concerns, they infuse their store atmospheres and marketing communications with these values, and they back appropriate social causes, all indicating that not only do their products fit with these values but everything that they do as an organization is based on them. This creates a powerful connection with the consumer and creates strong consumer loyalty. The work of Shalom Schwartz (1994) focuses on the identification of basic cultural core values. Schwartz identified seven cultural value types: (1) **conservatism** (where the stress is placed on maintaining the status quo and system order), (2) **intellectual autonomy** (freedom of thought, curious, creative, innovative), (3) **affective autonomy** (freedom of action, adventurous, free spirited), (4) **hierarchy** (roles in society, social power, authority), (5) **mastery** (successful, ambitious, competent, confidence), (6) **egalitarian commitment** (loyalty, social justice, honesty, equality, responsibility), and (7) **harmony** (harmony of human beings and their natural surroundings along with social harmony, peace, helpfulness). When a more global view of segmentation is taken by large corporations, there may be effective bases for global segmentation found in these basic cultural values.

A multi-based approach to segmentation incorporating both individual psychological values and demographics, known as the VALS typology, was developed by a company called SRI International. The organization, which presently oversees the VALS system, is SRI Consulting Business Intelligence <http://www.sric-bi.com/VALS/>. For the US market,

SRI identified eight separate groups for segmentation purposes: (1) **actualizers** (10 per cent of the population) are successful individuals with high self-esteem and significant financial resources, and are very cognizant of their personal image as a representation of their character; (2) **fulfilleds** (11 per cent of the population) are highly educated, older individuals, concerned with maintaining order, who are satisfied with their life circumstances and make practical purchase decisions; (3) **experiencers** (13 per cent of the population) are impulsive, variety-seeking, younger, looking for more excitement, concerned with buying the latest fashions and electronics; (4) **achievers** (14 per cent of the population) are career-oriented, hard-working, family-focused, buyers of prestige goods and services; (5) **believers** (17 per cent of the population) are nationalistic, patriotic, conservative, religious, community-oriented, interested in buying national products; (6) **strivers** (12 per cent of the population) are financial under-performers, who are concerned with betterment of their lives and living conditions without self-esteem problems; (7) **makers** (12 per cent of the population) are do-it-yourselfers, with manual skills who like to be independent and self-sufficient, and like conservative governments that do not infringe upon individual rights; and (8) **strugglers** (12 per cent of the population) are elderly who are poor, lack skills, are relatively uneducated, are primarily focused on safety and security issues, and are wary consumers. The VALS system was a breakthrough in that it built on demographic variables, lifestyles, and personal aspirations, and the eight categories provided marketers with new opportunities to build relationships with key consumer segments.

A similar approach has been taken in the UK with the Social Value Group typology as developed by Consumer Insight Ltd from its 2003 Survey. This is the largest survey of social changes that has been attempted in the UK, and the segments identified are based upon values, beliefs, and motivations and linked to the various stages of Maslow's hierarchy of needs. The following are the segments which resulted from the 2003 Survey: (1) **self-actualizers** (15.9 per cent of the population), who are individualists, creative, people-oriented, relationship-oriented, looking for change without being judgmental, (2) **innovators** (9.1 per cent of the population), who are risk-takers, self-confident, want new and different products and services, and have clear goals in mind to achieve, 93) **esteem seekers** (22.3 per cent of the population), who are materialistic, looking to surround themselves with the kinds of trappings and having the kinds of experiences that would provide them with social status, (4) **strivers** (15.1 per cent of the population), who are also concerned with personal image and status, but their concern is to gain status only in the eyes of their particular peer groups, and they tend to keep traditional values, (5) **contented conformers** (14.3 per cent of the population), who are concerned with being a part of the norm, so they go along with the crowd, which provides the security they seek, (6) **traditionalists** (18.6 per cent of the population), who are conservative and do not like to take risks, who feel that traditional values and behaviours are safe and comfortable, and who are quiet and reserved, and (7) **disconnected** (4.7 per cent of the population), who live in the here and now, who are unhappy with their situations, and are somewhat apathetic. It is possible to see many similarities between the American VALS segments and the Social Value Group segments. The values and beliefs upon which these segments are built change very slowly, and they are significant drivers of consumer purchase behaviour. These segments would seem to have important implications across Europe and the US for those companies looking at identifying homogeneous segments on a global front.

Behaviouristic bases for segmentation

These bases are built around groups in which consumers have similar understandings of, uses for, and responses to particular products or services. **Usage rate** involves the amount of product that is normally consumed by the individual, and the categorizations are light, moderate, and heavy users. The wants and needs of each group may be somewhat different from each other. The issue is that heavy users are far more important for most companies than others because they consume such high volumes and because they may be more likely to be loyal to a particular brand than moderate or light users. Rewards systems like frequent flyer miles are aimed at the frequent travellers to keep them coming back to the same airlines. Many hotels and motels aim at frequent business travellers by offering a wide variety of business services (in-room Internet access, business desks with fax/printer capabilities, free *Wall Street Journals*, free continental breakfasts, etc.). One interesting attempt to segment on usage rate can be seen by Interbrew UK, which launched its half-pint can of Stella Artois in 2005 to reach those who drink primarily on special occasions rather than on a daily basis. Another example can be seen in their 2004 introduction of a draught beer dispenser for the home aficionado, which was created in a partnership with Philips Electronics.

Loyalty level is another effective base for segmentation. There are five different levels of loyalty: brand insistence, brand loyalty, split loyalty, shifting loyalty, and no loyalty (the switchers). **Brand insistence** is the highest level of loyalty, and it reflects the consumer who when faced with the favourite brand not being available, will not buy any alternative brand. **Brand loyalty** is where the consumer will buy the favourite brand if it is available, but if it is not available, another brand may be purchased instead. **Split loyalty** reflects having loyalty to more than one brand. Here the consumer may want only two of the brands available in the product/service class, but either might be acceptable on any given occasion. Such consumers do not care whether the diet cola that they drink is Diet Pepsi or Diet Coke, but they will not accept any other cola drink. **Shifting loyals** are those who are loyal to one brand for a period of time and then shift to another brand for a period of time. Finally, **switchers** are those who have no loyalty to any brand in that product or service class. These consumers are primarily deal and variety focused. Studying these different groups tells you quite a bit about your strengths as well as your weaknesses. Studying the brand insistent only tells you what you are doing right for that particular group of individuals. This will not provide any helpful insight on what you failed to do to attract others. Studying the brand loyals and the shifting loyals provides insight into who the brand's direct competitors are in the eyes of those consumers, and studying the switchers tells you what it takes to potentially attract consumers with deals and special promotions.

A study published in *McKinsey Quarterly* (Coyles and Gokey, 2002) cautioned that companies must be far more cognizant of changes in buying patterns because active management of migration patterns allows companies to stop potential customer defections and to shift consumers to higher levels of loyalty and consumption. The authors recognize six important loyalty profiles: (1) **emotive loyalists** (emotionally attached to the company and its products), (2) **deliberate loyalists** (who rationally choose the company and its products as the best possible choice), (3) **inertial loyalists** (who see the costs of switching away as too high), (4) **lifestyle downward migrators** (who may have experienced life changes and their needs are no longer being met), (5) **deliberately downward migrators** (who are prone to frequent reassessment of their needs and have found a better solution in some other company and its products), and (6) **dissatisfied downward migrators** (who are actively dissatisfied due to one or more bad experiences). The authors suggest that only studying the defectors misses more subtle buying changes which can lead ultimately to defection, when it may be too late to get them back (Coyles and Gokey, 2002).

Another type of behaviouristic segmentation involves the **creation of special events**. Florists, greetings card, and candy companies in the US have long focused on special occasions. The creation of such special days of recognition as Sweethearts' Day, Bosses' Day, Secretaries' Day, and even Mother-in-Law's Day are all examples of segmentation on the idea of a special event as opposed to everyday occurrences. Some companies have chosen the opposite approach in focusing on those types of products and services that are used every day without the need for a special occasion. Usually this type of approach is used by the company that has nurtured a connection with a particular occasion but which wants to branch out into other use occasions. Another segmentation approach using events is to focus on critical events in the consumer's life. This is the type of segmentation used by jewelry companies to promote diamond engagement rings or anniversary gifts.

Benefit segmentation is based on the assumption that consumers can be grouped in terms of the key benefits that they seek from the use of certain products or services. There can be two or more different segments who buy the same products or services but seek different key benefits from the use of the products or services. For example, McDonald's may appeal to one group because its offerings are inexpensive, to another because of the taste of its food items, to another because it offers convenience, and to another because it offers an opportunity for socialization with peer group members. Some elderly consumers have become an important constituency for McDonald's because they like to have a chance to regularly meet with friends in a social setting and a breakfast or lunch meeting at McDonald's provides this opportunity. Other elderly consumers like McDonald's for meals because of the value menu items given their limited income levels. Pomegranate growers have found that pomegranate juice contains high levels of anti-oxidants, which have been claimed to help the body ward off cancer. The key health benefits from the use of the product then provide an excellent special basis for segmentation. This anti-oxidant health benefit segmentation has also been successfully used by the growers/processors of blueberries, Concord grapes, and the growers/bottlers of red wines. Whenever there is a new medical finding that shows how the use of a particular product can add years to one's life, a new segmentation mechanism will be created. This has been seen surrounding the cholesterol-reducing capabilities of oat bran, the heart attack preventative use of aspirin, and the cold-preventative power of Echinacea.

A study that appeared in the *British Food Journal* examined two important trends that affect British food consumption: convenience and health concerns. This study found that these are really not overlapping trends as convenience food items and health-oriented food items are most effectively segmented using distinctly different segmentation variables. The authors found that household size and region of residence were the most important segmentation variables for convenience-oriented food items, and they also found that gender and age were the most important segmentation variables for health-oriented food products (Shiu et al., 2004).

Cross-border segmentation and international challenges

The nature of global expansion and spreading to new segments outside the borders of the country in which the company built its initial success creates a variety of new strategic challenges for the firm. The difficulty becomes painfully apparent when companies assume that what has been successful at home will work anywhere. Examining different product categories, it becomes clear that there are greater opportunities for similar segments to be found globally for high-tech products like computers, mobile phones, game consoles, and tablets as opposed to food products which are so highly influenced by cultural norms, tastes, and habits. Culture presents the single biggest challenge for international marketers, but the key is to study the potential segments to understand what drives their purchase decisions and to understand the trade-off that would be involved between the costs of reaching them effectively as opposed to the revenues they would generate. The most important thing for marketers crossing borders is to combine the secondary data available pertaining to the segments of interest with actual on-the-ground observation and study to determine the most attractive potential segments.

A particularly important approach to weighing the pros and cons of different consumer target segments deals with observing them in their natural state and seeing how they experience life (Madsbjerg and Rasmussen, 2014). This, of course, would apply as appropriately in a domestic context as in a new international expansion, but it makes particular sense when attempting a new international segment entry. Observing consumers as they go about their daily life can allow better understanding of the motivations of the various segments and what they are looking for in their consumption experiences. This study is often referred to as **phenomenology**, and going through these initial observational and interpretive steps might allow the company to avoid costly mistakes when entering a new culture. Of course this may be done through the use of experts and consultants whose services might be available for purchase, but nothing is quite as valuable as personal experience when seeing things in foreign settings.

Much of the need for localization would depend on what uses the target audiences would have for the products in question. The more similar the uses, the more opportunities there may be for standardizing the marketing strategies to reach the target consumers, allowing important efficiencies and economies. Providing a new fruit juice drink might sound like an interesting idea, but the tastes of local consumers when matched with the intensity of local competition may make entering the segment extremely risky. This would seem to be more appropriate for a company from a developed country to consider rather than for a company from a developing country, but there is an interesting new opportunity for companies in developing countries for building consumer segments in other countries (Kumar and Steenkamp, 2013).

The approach is called **diaspora marketing**, and it involves using immigrants from the home country to serve as the target audiences for the company's products as it enters new international markets. The study discusses the successes of companies like Haier, Lenovo, Tata, Embraer, Jollibee, Mahindra & Mahindra, and Natura, which have built strong markets in their home countries and are building international presences for themselves. The issue is that smaller companies in emerging countries do not necessarily have the resources of the bigger companies in developed countries, but these companies can tap cost-effectively into the diaspora, which means targeting certain groups of new immigrants to that market of interest from the same country as the targeting company.

The authors develop a four-cell matrix of recent immigrants to a marketplace. Based on the level of affiliation with the host culture from low to high on one axis and the level of desire to maintain home country identity from low to high on the other axis, four cells are developed.

1. **Assimilators** (high affiliation with host culture and low desire to maintain home country identity) will prefer host country to home country products, so they are a poor segment to target.

2. **Marginals** (low affiliation with host culture and low desire to maintain home country identity) will prefer products based on performance rather than where they are produced, so, again, a poor segment to target.

3. **Biculturals** (high affiliation with host culture and high desire to maintain home country identity) will purchase products from the home country, so a good segment to target.

4. **Ethnic affirmers** (low affiliation with host culture and high desire to maintain home country identity) will prefer home country products, so an excellent segment to target.

The key here is to choose the right segments of people living in the target country that are from your home country. Not all are good candidates, so studying the nature of the different segments opens two good potential target groups for segmentation.

Strategic framework for segmentation

An excellent framework for transition from the foundation to the strategic considerations for segmentation was provided by Palmer and Millier (2004). The principles of segmentation they suggest are shown in Figure 5.1. The framework is meant to be used by either B2C or B2B marketers. The segmentation can be done based on either who the buyer is or what is being bought, and if it is based on who buys, then the segmentation criteria are separated by whether they are hard (based upon hard data categorizations—socio-economic, demographic, or geographic) or soft (values, attitudes, and lifestyles).

Since the point of segmentation is to identify a homogeneous group of consumers with a high probability of interest in the product/service offered, new and creative combinations of segmentation schemes are being attempted every day. A variety of tools to help the strategic marketer with segment identification will now be discussed.

Segmentation tools

The main tools used for segmentation are cluster analysis, conjoint analysis, discriminant analysis, and multidimensional scaling. **Cluster analysis** is a group of multivariate techniques whose main purpose is to classify objects in such a way that within-group differences are minimized and between-group differences are maximized according to some grouping variable. These objects can be products or survey respondents. The goal is to create clusters that

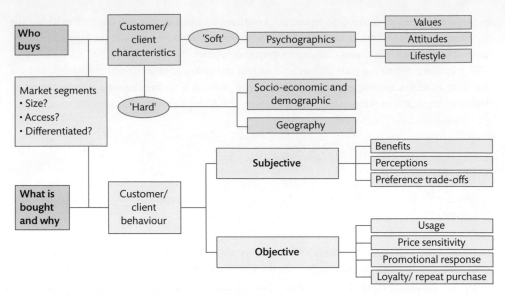

5.1 Principles of Market Segmentation

Source: R.A. Palmer and P. Millier (2004), 'Segmentation, intuition and implementation', *Industrial Marketing Management*, 33 (8), pp. 779–85. Copyright 2004, with permission of Elsevier.

are similar within and distinctly different from one another, which are clearly the goals for consumer segmentation. The best starting point for clustering is to define clear and distinct customer needs. Often this can be preceded by qualitative mechanisms such as focus groups or in-depth interviews to examine a variety of different constituent groups to determine their needs and motivations. Once these needs are identified, survey research instruments can be created and cluster analysis used to examine the nature of the respondents involved and the possibilities of grouping into meaningful and effective consumer segments. A rudimentary clustering example would involve asking a group of individuals to list in order of importance the attributes that are of concern to them in the choice of a particular product or service. What is interesting is that the overall lists of attributes that are part of the choice criteria will probably be quite similar across all of the lists, but where the differences will lie will be in the rankings of the relevant attributes. The rank orderings of attributes can then allow groupings of similar rankings. These subgroups with similar expectations regarding the important choice criteria comprise simple but quite relevant possible segments. Of course computer analyses with more detailed data will lead to more sophisticated groupings, but the mechanism for clustering is seen as quite basic and logical.

Conjoint analysis on the other hand involves the use of a series of possible product/ service attribute combinations to see which ones are preferred by survey respondents. In this case the company chooses a series of possible variations of product attributes (e.g. three types of scent, four colours, three package sizes, three different prices), and a series of attribute combinations are generated in a partial factorial design (so that consumers only respond to a subset of all possible attribute combinations making the process considerably more manageable for the respondent). The consumer can rank or rate the offerings in terms of preference and, from the various choices made, decomposition is utilized to develop a series of scores (utility part 'worths') for each variation of each attribute. From this analysis the company can see what the optimal product configuration would be for each relevant consumer target segment. Coca Cola often uses this type of analysis to assess the possibility of new can colorations (e.g. additional colours to the normal red, white, and silver) or new product flavourings (e.g. Coke with lime, vanilla Coke, cherry Coke, Coke with lemon). Using this kind of tool the company can get a good idea of potential consumer reactions to product changes or new product offerings.

The third approach to segmenting is **discriminant analysis**, which involves identifying a series of variables that help to discriminate the members of one or more groups from others in the data set. The basic idea is to examine a series of possible differentiating variables that would explain and hopefully allow prediction of different possible group memberships. One way to use it would involve including in the analysis a variety of product/service attributes and demographic data which when combined could explain what makes buyers different from non-buyers of a particular product or service. It might also be used to examine non-users as opposed to light users, moderate users, and heavy users. The technique produces formulae that can be used to explain and predict group membership. In order to test the effectiveness of the models generated, all respondents are then classified according to the discriminating functions generated and the predicted group membership is compared with the actual group membership as a check for accuracy. If there were four categories involved (non-users, light, moderate, and heavy users), the prior probabilities would be 0.25 (1 in 4), so any classification scheme that does better than 0.25 would be an improvement over pure chance.

The fourth tool is **multidimensional scaling**, which involves a variety of different techniques that can visually demonstrate how particular consumers view the various offerings in a particular product or service class. These techniques are also often referred to as perceptual mapping because the goal is to spatially differentiate the perceptions of consumers relative to their preferences for, or the similarities among, a set of objects (e.g. companies, products, services) in terms of distances in multidimensional space. These techniques allow the researcher to determine what types of attribute are most distinctively associated with their products or services. Certainly it is important for the consumer to have a clear idea of what the product stands for, and it allows the researcher to determine whether consumer perceptions match company management perceptions. The use of multidimensional scaling also provides important strategic direction if the company finds that a competitor is associated in the minds of the target market with attributes that are more appropriately associated with its own product. In this case the company can try to communicate in advertisements to its target audience to educate them on the relevance of those important attributes with its products or services. As an example, if the company found that its competitor was seen as more environmentally friendly, the company could mount an advertising campaign to show how it is working to protect and maintain the environment.

Targeting

Once the firm has identified a series of potential market segments for consideration, the next step is **targeting**. Targeting involves deciding the number of different segments to select and serve and the best action plans to reach the identified segments. The first consideration from a strategic standpoint is to decide on the type of pattern of coverage that the firm will utilize. According to one of the great marketing strategists, Derek F. Abell (1980), the firm faces the following choices: (1) **single-segment concentration** (where one product is geared towards one market segment in a niche strategy), (2) **selective specialization** (where the firm aims different product variants at different segments with the idea of one product per segment), (3) **product specialization** (where the firm aims a particular product variant to a variety of different segments), (4) **market specialization** (where the firm aims a variety of product variants at one particular market segment), and (5) **full market coverage** (where the firm uses undifferentiated marketing aiming a variety of product variants across a variety of segments).

Measuring effectiveness of target segments

Once the segments have been chosen, how do we know whether they are viable or not? Kotler (2003) presents the most recognizable series of requirements for segments to be appropriate. He suggests that they must be: (1) **measurable** (e.g. size of segment, income and purchasing power, and characteristics of the segment), (2) **accessible** (the firm can reach and is able to effectively serve the segment), (3) **substantial** (large enough and capable of generating sufficient profits), (4) **differentiable** (truly distinct from other segments in terms of composition and response to marketing stimuli, and (5) **actionable** (marketing programmes can be developed to effectively identify, attract, and serve the segment).

These criteria can be put to the test in almost every company due to the fact that within most organizations there is a trade-off involving production and marketing that must be considered when segmenting markets. In one case unrestrained marketing might identify a wide range of distinct market segments, but while there may be demand within these segments, there may be no cost-effective way to develop the necessary product variations to address the needs of all of the identified segments. On the other hand, unrestrained **product differentiation** might identify a wide variety of product variations that the firm could produce, but there may be no demand within some or all of the identified segments. This mandates that marketing and production work together to find the most cost-effective product variants to serve the most promising consumer market segments. Take for instance the situation in the United States in 1985 between the Ford Motor Company's Thunderbird and the imported Honda Accord. In an attempt to convince consumers that they could have any type of Thunderbird they might want (mass customization), they offered as many as 19,000 different possible product variations, but the problem arose particularly in how the Ford service departments would deal with all of the possible variations when handling servicing problems. What kinds of inventories of parts would be required for all of these possible segments? There is no way that there were 19,000 different viable segments for this product. It would have been surprising if more than 50 distinct offerings were in demand. The Honda Accord being shipped in from Japan provided only 34 different product variations which would suggest that they had clearly thought through the issue of viability of each of the identified consumer segments. This balancing of segmentation with differentiation is an effective integrated strategic approach to finding viable segments with cost-effective product/service variants.

Targeting improvement

There is concern that segmentation can produce a wide variety of segments which cannot effectively be reached with a targeting strategy. There is also the possibility that some market segments may be very difficult (in terms of time and money) to measure effectively. Marketing strategists can attempt to create segmentation strategies that can work even if it is hard to determine who exactly is included in the segment. Before attempting to identify and reach target customers, a viable alternative approach could be to consider whether certain collective segment traits may be associated with profitable strategies. There are three options for these profitable strategies: (1) **self-selection**, which concentrates on enabling the customer to find and select the best product as opposed to finding the appropriate customers (examples provided include different sizes of washing-up bottles and cereal packets), which is best suited for large customer bases with such small individual sales that mass customization is not viable; (2) **scoring models**, which involve the development of a series of questions to allow a quantitative scoring that would place customers into different categories depending on what is most important for those customers (e.g. credit card companies that distinguish good from bad risk customers) to allow appropriate targeting strategies to best reach those particular categorized groups of customers; and (3) **dual-objective segmentation**, which attempts to convert unreachable segments into actionable segments through a series of reclassification approaches which attempt to reclassify outliers into different categories after which follow-up profitability analyses are run (Forsyth et al., 1999). The idea is to try to place those who do not clearly fall into consumer target segments into other possible segments. It may be that the outliers become a separate segment themselves rather than becoming squeezed into inappropriate segmentation schemes, or that the outliers do not make sense for targeting at all. The idea is to step back sometimes from the comfortable segmentation approaches and look at things from a different angle to see if there are new possibilities that may work better than old ways. The key to targeting is to reach the target segment efficiently and effectively.

Positioning

Positioning refers to the placing of the product or service in a particular perceptual position within the mind of the consumer. This would follow the processes described in segmentation and targeting. We now have a specific consumer segment in mind and a specific plan to reach it, and now the idea is to ensure that the target consumer has a clear and distinctive image in mind that is consistent and positive regarding the product/service offerings being aimed at them.

Al Ries and Jack Trout, advertising executives with over 50 years of experience between them, made a strong statement in their landmark book, *Positioning: The Battle for Your Mind* (2001), that the real battle does not take place at the cash register when the consumer goes to the store to make a purchase, but in the consumer's mind before even going to the store. They argued that it is positioning that is the strategic key. If the consumer has a particular product or service name that automatically comes to mind when a need arises in that particular product or service category, that is the product or service that the consumer is most likely to buy. The point is to keep your product brand name automatically at the top of the choice possibilities (the favourite brand). As Ries and Trout explain, there is a ladder inside every consumer's head for each and every product and service class. All of the competing brands known to the consumer are therefore placed on different rungs of that ladder. The strategic goal is to get to the top rung where the consumer has chosen a particular brand as the best or their favourite. Once the need arises in that class, the top rung brand is what will normally come to mind and will more than likely be the one purchased by the consumer. For Ries and Trout, the key is to understand the ladder and develop strategies according to where on the ladder the consumer placed any particular brand.

Being on the top rung of the ladder allows the firm to enjoy consumer franchise, which is a term that was reported to have been coined by Dr Peter Sealey, Global Marketing Director for Coca-Cola Corporation, who has since left Coke to become a consultant in California. **Consumer franchise** is the ability of the firm to keep its product, brand, or company name foremost in the mind of the target consumer. It is considered to be a bankable asset since there is a psychological buffering built in for the firm that is on the top rung of the product/ service class ladder. When bad news appears regarding a particular company, if its product or brand in question is on the top rung of the ladder (the favourite or preferred brand), the psychological process known as denial can buffer the company because the consumer is put in a mental situation where it could not possibly be their favourite brand that could have done something wrong. We tend to assume that our judgement is infallible, and when something happens that questions that judgement, we step back and refuse to believe that we have made a mistake. This denial is a powerful protection for the company. No company saw more benefit from this denial and the power of consumer franchise than Coca-Cola Corporation when New Coke was introduced with a completely different product formulation than that used for the previous Coke product. As the groundswell built against Coke, with loyal consumers asking why the formula had been changed, the Corporation, sensing a problem, implemented a contingency plan and introduced Classic Coke. New Coke did not fare well in the marketplace, but Coke was not hurt because it took corrective action, and it was protected by its consumer franchise and never felt the negative effects financially or in lost market share. To illustrate how powerful consumer franchise is as a buffer, one colleague to this day claims that everything was part of a carefully designed strategic plan to offer an additional brand product, but the delay from introduction of New Coke to the introduction of Classic Coke would argue that this was not a carefully designed plan from the beginning but a mistake with little negative backlash. Of course Coke had to take corrective action, but it was able to fare well, demonstrating the power of its consumer franchise. Of course my colleague was born and raised in Atlanta, Georgia, which might explain the perceptual basis for his argument!!

Consumer franchise has two major components, one behavioural and the other attitudinal. How does a company measure whether it is the favoured or preferred brand behaviourally? By examining its market share figures and sales, it can be seen if the brand is the favoured one or not. Attitudinally, the only way to know is to do consumer surveys. In this case the consumer can be asked to indicate their favoured brand among a series of choices, or can be asked what brand would they choose if a need arose in a particular product category? The key strategic aspect to remember here is that a downturn in brand image might not immediately affect brand sales. There is usually a lag. As a result it is important

> [Convince] business managers and professionals engaged in making time sensitive decisions about international business,
>
> [That] DHL delivers on time
>
> [Because] its pickup, transportation, and delivery system is wholly owned and managed by DHL personnel, not by third party providers.

5.2 Sample Positioning Statement

for companies to track their results in the marketplace as well as their brand images so that a problem in terms of brand image can be corrected before it has a negative impact on corporate performance. If only the behavioural side is tracked, then the company may be caught in a situation where it is not sure what is causing the problem in the first place. If bad publicity is caught and corrected before it has a chance to affect consumer perceptions, any future performance problems may be eliminated before they manifest themselves.

The positioning statement

A key element of positioning is the development of a positioning statement that will serve as the foundation for all of the positioning efforts. An example of a positioning statement for DHL Package Delivery is found in Figure 5.2.

As can be seen from this example, there are three key components to the positioning statement: (1) the audience and context, (2) the value proposition, and (3) the action components that will be used by the company to deliver the value proposition to the audience in the context identified. Of course, there are many ways in which a position statement can be poorly structured, so the criteria for successful positioning are found in the four Cs as shown in Figure 5.3.

To be effective, any positioning statement must be clear. There can be no room for misinterpretation in terms of who the intended audience is and what the clear benefit/value will be for them. With the DHL example, it is very specific in its statement of which individuals are the target and in what context they fall. The positioning statement must also be consistent, so that all messages sent regarding positioning must all be consistent with each other

> • **Clarity**: in terms of target market and differential advantage
> • **Consistency**: maintain a consistent message
> • **Credibility**: in the minds of the target customer—they must believe the claim
> • **Competitiveness**: the differential advantage should offer the customer something of value competitors cannot provide (competitors should be named if possible)

5.3 The 4Cs of Positioning

so that consumer confusion is eliminated or at least minimized. If DHL, over time, sends different messages to consumers in their communications, they will lack consistency and the message will be lost. Thirdly, it must be credible, since whatever claims the company makes must be believable to the target audience. If the customer does not believe that DHL has the personnel and equipment to be able to deliver the packages on time, then no matter what is claimed, the claims will not resonate with the customer. Finally, the positioning statement must be seen as competitive so that the target audience sees it as something being offered to them by the company that cannot be provided by their competitors. If the target audience does not see DHL as superior to FedEx or UPS or other competitors, then the positioning will not be able to stick with the target audience. Two excellent examples of strong positioning statements can be found in Figure 5.4.

The next step will be to examine ways in which the company can assess its perceptual position inside the heads of its target audience. This involves the use of perceptual mapping.

Perceptual mapping

Perceptual mapping is the visual representation of the different competitive brand offerings/objects of interest in perceptual space. In other words, it represents a map of the various offerings within the minds of the target consumers. This is where 'perception equals reality' comes home to marketing strategists. The only thing that is important is what the consumer believes—not what management believes to be the case. This can only be determined via survey instruments. As previously mentioned, the attitudinal component of consumer franchise is often neglected as behaviour is the representation of what has already been done. The problem is that past purchase behaviour is no guarantee of future purchase behaviour.

Excellent examples of perceptual mapping can be seen in Figures 5.5 and 5.6, which present two different views of the confectionery market in the UK. Figure 5.5 presents a perceptual map for Mars in which four of its products are seen in perceptual space connected to key attributes in the mind of the target audience.

As can be seen here, the two Galaxy products are aimed not functionally but emotionally. Galaxy Minstrels are seen as more of a social product, while Galaxy Caramel is more

Apple offers …. the best personal computing experience to students, educators, creative professionals, and consumers around the world through its innovative hardware, software, and Internet offerings.

The Chrysler PT Cruiser is an inexpensive small car, that is versatile, fun to drive, and will appeal to active singles and young couples with children who otherwise would have bought an SUV or a minivan.

5.4 Examples of Positioning Statements

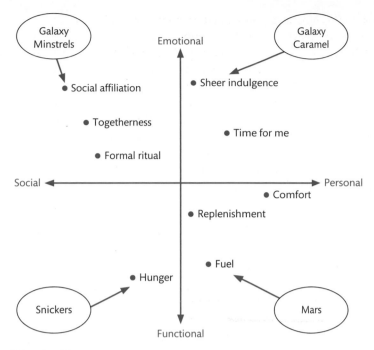

5.5 Perceptual Mapping: Mars

perceived for personal benefit. The Snickers product is aimed functionally—perceived to be a good mechanism for the satisfaction of hunger—while the Mars product is seen as something to use to get an energy boost when it is needed. These are very different perceptual positions that have been achieved, and the key is to strategically maintain the 4Cs as long as the products are holding their own performance-wise but to take possible corrective action if performance is not what was expected.

Figure 5.6 shows a perceptual map of a variety of sweets, given the perceptions of a particular market segment. Here the perceptual axes are quality and price, and there appear to be two major groupings given the particular product brands chosen for the study with the high price, high quality quadrant containing such brands as Ferrero Rocher, Belgian chocolates, and Cadbury's Roses, while the low price, low quality quadrant includes such brands as Mars, Twix, and Cadbury's Fruit & Nut.

Positioning and the importance of consistency

As positioning reflects the position that the brand or product has achieved on the product or service class ladder, the key strategic issue associated with positioning is to present a clear and consistent message to the target audience. The company that constantly tinkers with its image stands the chance of confusing its target market. If strategic decisions are made which are inconsistent from period to period, the consumer is left with potentially mixed messages which become confusing and create cognitive dissonance. The often seen use of brand extension creates a potential problem for strategic marketers as their company, which

5.6 Perceptual Map of UK Confectionery Brands

may have been clearly positioned in the past, begins to put its name on inconsistent products which set off alarm bells inside the heads of loyal customers.

As a strong example, look at the recent movement by Mercedes and Volvo to lower-priced product lines. Can the company offer products at the top end and in the middle at the same time? The problems faced by Calvin Klein when selling jeans through Sears and at the same time selling extravagantly priced designer gowns should still resonate with the marketplace today. How can a company undermine its own distinctive perceptual niche? This leads potentially to strategic suicide. Harking back to the consumer franchise discussion reminds us that there is an attitudinal side which must be periodically tracked along with the behavioural side. Inconsistencies might not be reflected in a downturn in sales until much later, and then the problem becomes image reinstatement for the brand.

The latest thinking: real-time experience tracking and how to build superconsumers

Real-time experience tracking (RET)

A recent article by Macdonald et al. (2012) in *Harvard Business Review* discusses a radical new tool for marketers to track immediate customer reactions without annoying them through the use of intrusive mechanisms. This tool is called real-time experience tracking (RET), and it allows the immediate gathering of information on customer reactions/perceptions without the problems associated with the almost immediate fading of memory as often experienced in the use of other types of marketing research techniques like survey data or potentially biased results like the use of focus groups in the hands of inexperienced moderators.

Market researchers have found that ethnography is an effective tool which involves observations and personal shadowing to gain insights. The authors explain that RET was built on two major understandings. Firstly, they realized that shadowing customers 24 hours a day is not really feasible, but their use of their mobiles is something that can be tracked without annoying them. Secondly, while customers have myriads of ways in which they can interact with a company, four key points of information related to these interactions are critical: (1) the brand, (2) the touch point, (3) the feelings of the consumer about the interaction, and (4) the level of impact of the interaction experience on future brand selection by that customer. As a result, the authors created a short SMS-based survey that can be completed when these interactions occur. The input involves a four-character text message that covers all aspects of the four key information points mentioned above.

The way the system works involves the customer filling out a survey at the beginning of the month about a particular product group, exploring their awareness, knowledge of, feelings about, and use of the various brands in that group. The participants are then instructed to use their mobiles to report any interactions with the brand throughout the rest of that particular month. These reports involve four-character texts. The first letter indicates the specific brand involved, the second reflects the type of touch point for that interaction (with over 20 types of interactions that are possible), the third is a number which reflects how positive the experience was for the individual from 1 to 5 (with 5 being very positive), and finally the last character is also a number ranging from 1 to 5 reflecting the level of impact of the interaction on future choice of the same brand. The participants are then asked to fill out an online diary with opportunity to provide more information on the encounters, including greater detailed descriptions, photos, etc. The last step in the process involves completion of a second survey reflecting changes in overall perceptions/attitude about the brand as a result of the various interactions involved. The authors found that it was not difficult for participants to provide information about a wide range of touch points, and what appeared to be relatively inconsequential interactions could have significant differences on consumer behaviour. As an example, the authors found that if the product was seen in a friend's house in passing, the individual was three times more likely to buy the product compared with those who had not seen the product in a friend's house. This technique allows the researcher to create touch point impact matrices which can compare interactions in terms of the feelings of the individual about the touch point from very negative to very positive on one axis while showing the level of impact on the likelihood to purchase the brand on the other axis. This becomes even more enlightening if several different brands are tracked and compared on the same matrices.

Why is RET so potentially valuable for researchers? Macdonal et al. (2012) explain that the data they track has a number of important benefits.

(1) Using regression with RET data shows which touch points have the greatest impact on behaviour.

(2) You can compare touch points for your brand and your competitor to see which touch points are more effective.

(3) It is possible to examine chains of touch points to find optimal paths for the greatest positive impact upon customer behaviour along with indicating weak links that need improvement.

The building of superconsumers

A recent article in *Harvard Business Review* (Yoon et al. 2014) presented an interesting strategic alternative to segmentation, examining how companies can use their very best consumers and target them for growth to become 'superconsumers'. They used the example of Kraft Foods and its Velveeta brand of cheese products, where sales had softened as a variety of global consumers shifted to natural and organic food choices from processed products like Velveeta. They found that normal consumers of the product would likely buy once or twice a year and use the product in the creation of some kind of a dip for salty snacks like potato crisps or pretzels. Probing into their consumer usage data, Kraft found that while its best customers only amounted to 10 per cent of the total of their consumer base they accounted for almost 40 per cent of total revenue and more than 50 per cent of their total profits. They called these consumers 'superconsumers' and found that these users were truly passionate about the products. The authors estimated the size of this group as 2.4 million, and the company realized that this particular group was anxious to get any new variants that they could find. As a result, the company launched both refrigerated slices for sandwiches, burgers, and sausages and refrigerated shredded Velveeta for use in salads, soups, pies, and casseroles. The new products generated more than $100 million, and the company realized its first major growth in the Velveeta brand in many years. Most competitors were assuming that light or lapsed users were the best targets for marketing efforts, but Kraft found success from growing the revenues from its best customers.

The authors mention the Pareto principle, which states that 80 per cent of revenues will normally come from 20 per cent of the customer base, which will again be discussed in the Chapter 7, and this effect is what the authors were building upon in the strategic thinking about the superconsumer. They used A.C. Nielsen scanner data and found that superconsumers, while comprising 10 per cent of the product's consumers, could account for anywhere from 30 to 70 per cent of sales and even more in terms of profit. While many companies offer amenities for these good customers, few ever looked at them as a major growth vehicle. The authors stressed that these superconsumers were not the same as 'heavy users', who are categorized strictly by the quantity of their purchases. Yoon et al. (2014) found that superconsumers are a subset of heavy users who truly engage with the brand economically as well as attitudinally. The point is that they are interested in innovative new uses and product variations. So why are supercomputers so valuable for the company for targeting? They are already buying the products, which makes them particularly easy to reach, so promotional expenditures can be more efficiently targeted. They are particularly open to digital marketing efforts since they are often connected through social media around their interests, and in particular the authors found that these select consumers are a rich focus for new product development.

Finally, the authors present a series of points debunking what they consider to be myths about superconsumers.

(1) They are not just heavy users since they spend a lot and are highly connected emotionally.

(2) Many commentators believe they do not exist, but there are many product categories that have them.

(3) Many assume that superconsumers are wealthy and eccentric, but they have logical reasons for their love of the product. They find more meaning and value in them than others do

(4) Likewise, many experts believe they are difficult to identify, but they can be identified using social media and big data

(5) Lastly, there are those who believe that since they buy so much already, they would have no need to buy more, but this is probably the most incorrect assumption of all. These consumers produce growths in sales of 30 per cent more than other groups and they have immense reach via word of mouth and the use of social media.

Conclusion

When companies approach segmentation, processing, and positioning as a series of logical steps in a process, they enhance their chances of success. Only in the rarest of circumstances is a company in the luxurious position of being all things to all customers, and as a result the company must find appropriate target consumers, understand them, effectively reach them, and grab a position of importance on the product/service class ladder inside their heads. The company then has to avoid the lure of change for the sake of change and focus on consistency. This requires keeping up with the perceptions of consumers and continuing to build and maintain consumer franchise.

Summary

Segmentation involves the identification of a distinct subset of consumers within the overall marketplace that have a desire for the products/services that the company produces. This process should follow the careful development of strategic marketing goals/objectives. There are a variety of tools and techniques that can be used for segmentation across a variety of segmentation criteria. The firm must carefully assess the different segments and choose those that have the greatest potential for success. Once the firm has identified the various segment possibilities, the next step involves the assessment of the potential for each segment so that only those with the highest chances for success are chosen. Once the particular segments are chosen, the company must decide on how it will use the various pieces of the marketing mix to reach those segments. Targeting focuses on how to most effectively reach the various market segments. The last step involves the assessment of the particular perceptual space that the product achieves within the heads of the target segment consumers to ensure that the product is on the top rung of the product class ladder. The power of this position is found in the fact that when a need arises in the mind of the consumer, the product that commands the top rung of the mental ladder of competing products is the one most likely to be chosen for purchase.

Key terms

- **Acculturation:** the exposure of a foreign visitor to a local culture and the impact that exposure will have on the visitor and their cultural make-up.
- **Cohort:** a group of consumers that go through life together and share common experiences.
- **Consumer franchise:** a term coined at Coca-Cola that refers to the ability to keep the company brand, product, or company name foremost in the mind of the consumer. It comprises a behavioural and an attitudinal component.
- **Diaspora marketing:** the using of immigrants as a foundation for identifying and targeting attractive consumer segments in new international markets.
- **Market segment:** a homogeneous subset of all consumers in a particular market.
- **Market segmentation:** the process of identifying for targeting purposes appropriate separate subsets of consumers out of all the consumers in that market.
- **Mass customization:** each individual consumer is treated separately with a product configuration to suit the needs of each consumer.
- **Mass market:** all consumers are treated the same way within a single product configuration.
- **Perceptual mapping:** the use of a variety of tools to examine the various competing products and the positions they command in perceptual space within the minds of the target market.
- **Phenomenology:** an approach to weighing the pros and cons of different consumer target segments by observing them in their natural state and seeing how they experience life.
- **Positioning:** the process involved in placing the product in the mind of the consumer in terms of a position on the product/service class ladder.
- **Price–benefit position map:** a map which builds on the primary benefit customers will see as valuable to them along with the prices of all of the various products in that specific product category.
- **Product differentiation:** production-based orientation which examines the various forms and variants of the product which the company can cost-effectively produce.
- **Psychographic segmentation:** segmentation predicated upon the activities, interests, and opinions of a particular group of people. For segmentation purposes this will normally involve such variables as lifestyle and personality.
- **Targeting:** the use of the elements in the marketing mix to reach the consumers identified in the market segmentation process.
- **Topography:** land contours that can affect the geographic grouping of appropriate target segments of consumers.

Discussion questions

1. Why is market segmentation vital for company success?
2. What is psychographic segmentation, and why is it so important for marketing strategists?

3.　What are the seven cultural values that were identified by Schwartz, and why are they important for marketing strategists?

4.　What is diaspora marketing, and why is the use of immigrants a promising segmentation vehicle for companies from emerging countries?

5.　Why is phenomenology an important mechanism for studying target consumers?

6.　What are the four different tools that were discussed for segmentation? How are they different from each other?

7.　What is the difference between market segmentation and product differentiation?

8.　What are the five different patterns of target market coverage that were discussed in the chapter?

9.　What are the five criteria that were presented by Kotler to assess the viability of various target market segments under consideration?

10.　How does consumer franchise relate to the concept of positioning, and why is this relevant for marketing strategists?

11.　What is real-time experience tracking (RET), and why is it important for tracking consumer perceptions?

12.　What are superconsumers, and why are they such an attractive potential segment of consumers for identification and targeting?

13.　What is a price–benefit position map, and why would it be useful for strategic marketers?

Online resource centre

Visit the Online Resource Centre for this book for lots of interesting additional material at: **<www.oxfordtextbooks.co.uk/orc/west3e/>**

References and further reading

Aaker, Jennifer (1997), 'Dimensions of Brand Personality', *Journal of Marketing Research*, 34 (3), pp. 347–56.

Abell, Derek F. (1980), *Defining the Business: The Starting Point of Strategic Planning* (Upper Saddle River, NJ: Prentice Hall).

Bruce, Margaret and Michael R. Solomon (2013), 'Managing for Media Anarchy: A Corporate Marketing Perspective', *Journal of Marketing Theory and Practice*, 21 (3), pp. 307–18.

Christiansen, Clayton M., Scott Cook, and Teddy Hall (2005), 'Marketing Malpractice: The Cause and the Cure', *Harvard Business Review*, 83, December, pp. 74–83.

Cort, Kathryn T., Judith H. Pairan, and John K. Ryans Jr (2004), 'The In-School Marketing Controversy: Reaching the Teenage Segment', *Business Horizons*, 47 (1), pp. 81–5.

Coyles, Stephanie and Timothy C. Gokey (2002), 'Customer Retention is Not Enough', *McKinsey Quarterly*, No. 2, pp. 81–9.

D'Aveni, Richard A. (2007), 'Mapping Your Competitive Position', *Harvard Business Review*, 75 November, pp. 110–20.

Forsyth, John, Sunil Gupta, Sudeep Haldar, Anil Kaul, and Keith Kettle (1999), 'A Segmentation You Can Act Upon', *McKinsey Quarterly*, No. 3, pp. 7–15.

Harrington, Richard J. and Anthony K. Tjan (2008), 'Transforming Strategy One Customer at a Time', *Harvard Business Review*, 86, March, pp. 62–72.

Hemp, Paul (2006), 'Avatar-based Marketing', *Harvard Business Review*, 84, June, pp. 48–57.

Keillor, B. D. and G. Tomas M. Hult (1999), 'The Development and Application of a National Identity Measure for Use in International

Marketing', *Journal of International Marketing*, 4 (2), pp. 57–73.

Kotler, Philip (2003), *Marketing Management*, 11th edn (Upper Saddle River, NJ: Prentice-Hall).

Kumar, Nirmalya and Jan-Benedict E. M. Steenkamp (2013), 'Diaspora Marketing', *Harvard Business Review*, 91, October, pp. 127–31.

Macdonald, Emma K., Hugh N. Wilson, and Umut Konus (2012), 'Better Customer in Sight – in Real Time', *Harvard Business Review*, 90, September, pp. 102–8.

Madsbjerg, Christian and Mikkel B. Rasmussen (2014), 'An Anthropologist Walks Into a Bar', *Harvard Business Review*, 92, March, pp. 80–8.

O'Loughlin, Sandra (2005), 'Ben Sherman Brings U.K. Lifestyle to Spring', *Brandweek*, 46 (2), p. 9.

Orth, Ulrich R., Mina McDaniel, Tom Shellhammer, and Kannapon Lopetcharat (2004), 'Promoting Brand Benefits: The Role of Consumer Psychographics and Lifestyle', *Journal of Consumer Marketing*, 21 (2/3), pp. 97–108.

Palmer, R.A. and P. Millier (2004), 'Segmentation: Identification, Intuition and Implementation', *Industrial Marketing Management*, 33 (8), pp. 779–85.

Palumbo, Frederick A. and Ira Teich (2004), 'Market Segmentation Based on Level of Acculturation', *Marketing Intelligence & Planning*, 22 (4), pp. 472–80.

Phou, Ian and Kor-Weai Chan (2003), 'Targeting East Asian Markets: A Comparative Study on National

Identity', *Journal of Targeting, Measurement and Analysis for Marketing*, 12 (2), pp. 157–68.

Ries, Al and Jack Trout (2001), *Positioning: The Battle for Your Mind*, 20th Anniversary Edition (New York: McGraw-Hill).

Robinette, Scott (2001), 'Best Practice: Get Emotional', *Harvard Business Review*, 79, May, pp. 24–5.

Rubinson, Joel (2010), 'What Behavioral Economics Can Teach Marketing Research', *Journal of Advertising Research*, 50 (2), pp. 114–17.

Schewe, Charles D. and Geoffrey Meredith (2004), 'Segmenting Global Markets by Generational Cohorts: Determining Motivations by Age', *Journal of Consumer Behaviour*, 4 (1), pp. 51–64.

Schwartz, Shalom (1994), 'Beyond Individualism/ Collectivism', in Kim, U.S., et al. (eds), *Individualism and Collectivism: Theory, Method, and Applications*, (Thousand Oaks, CA: Sage Publications), pp. 85–119.

Shiu, Eric C. C., John A. Dawson, and David W. Marshall (2004), 'Segmenting the Convenience and Health Trends in the British Food Market', *British Food Journal*, 106 (2/3), pp. 106–18.

Simons, Robert (2014), 'Choosing the Right Customer', *Harvard Business Review*, 92, March, pp. 48–55.

Sweeney, Mark (2004), 'Red Bull Targets Golfers in Shift to Mainstream', *Marketing*, 26 May, p. 1.

Yoon, Eddie, Steve Carlotti, and Dennis Moore (2014), 'Make Your Best Customers Even Better', *Harvard Business Review*, 92, March, pp. 23–6.

 End of Chapter 5 case study   Celebrity brands: a risky business

Introduction

This case study highlights the risks associated when companies choose a celebrity spokesperson or endorser.

It illustrates the influences a celebrity endorser may have on a product or brand image—primarily the negative consequences. Though this relationship can be mutually beneficial to both the corporation and the individual, there are risks and problems associated with celebrity branding.

An article that appeared in *Private Label Buyer* entitled 'Celebrity Exclusives: High Risk, High Reward' offers perspectives as to how corporations should go about choosing the 'right' celebrity for their brand. It describes the possible risks and rewards that companies should consider when taking on a celebrity endorser. On the plus side, a popular celebrity can help promote a brand, establish credibility, add instant recognition, and exemplify a glamorous image and an aspirational lifestyle. When celebrity endorsements work, they can influence consumers in the buying process and increase revenue. On the minus side, celebrity-based brands tend to be vulnerable to changes in popular culture which can shorten the brand lifespan. Another negative of using celebrity endorsers is the need to mitigate risk if the endorser violates an established moral code and/or behaves in a manner inconsistent with the company's brand values.

A *New York Times* article, 'Big Risk in a Brand of One Man', discusses specific incidents of celebrities making poor decisions. One key example focuses on Tiger Woods as the former spokesperson for Accenture, a global management consulting firm. A second example in the article illustrates the Olympic gold medal swimmer Michael Phelps' public misstep. Martha Stewart is another high profile celebrity who jeopardized her professional brand when she was convicted of perjury, obstruction of justice, and conspiracy related to a stock transaction.

Tiger Woods

After Tiger Woods' extramarital affairs with multiple women were publicly exposed in 2009, Accenture, a global consulting firm focused on Fortune 500 companies, ended its six-year marketing relationship with the professional golfer. Woods' other endorsers had to make urgent strategic decisions on whether or not to keep him on as a celebrity spokesperson. AT&T also ended its relationship with Woods after this public scandal. Tag Heuer and Gillette decided to limit their use of Woods in advertising campaigns. Nike, who had a $30-million deal with Woods, continued to support the professional golfer.

According to a *Brand Channel* article, when the Woods scandal broke, some marketers couldn't distance themselves from him fast enough, while others tried to weather the storm. Woods reportedly dropped around $32 million in sponsorship money as a result of the disclosure of his extramarital affairs. But some branding experts think the damage to the brand is questionable. Stephen Cheliotis, CEO of Britain's Centre for Brand Analysis, stated, 'It's difficult to quantify how much damage a scandal has caused. It would require a robust tracking method of the brand performance before and after the scandal, and proof of a direct causal link.'

If a celebrity gets injured, or suffers from scandals, rumours, or other negative press, his or her negative image impacts the company as well. Celebrities are human and make mistakes; therefore some companies are purchasing 'disgrace insurance' to protect brand image when a celebrity takes an unfortunate public misstep.

Michael Phelps

The Olympic gold medal swimmer, Michael Phelps, publicly acknowledged his transgression and apologized after a photograph surfaced of the star athlete smoking marijuana while visiting the University of South Carolina. Kellogg dropped its sponsorship of the swimmer when it decided that this behaviour was not consistent with the firm's brand image (see Figure C5.1). Phelps also received a three month suspension from competition by USA Swimming, swimming's governing body in the US. Phelps was 23 years old at the time the photograph was revealed in a London newspaper. Other companies, including Speedo, Omega, Subway, Hilton, and Visa, stood by Phelps.

Martha Stewart

Yet another example of a multi-million dollar brand resting on one person's image. In a faculty publication, *Martha Stewart and Insider Trading*, Kevin Rawls describes that in 2001 Martha Stewart owned 3,928 shares of a company called ImClone. When the CEO of ImClone, Sam Waskal, learned that a new prescription drug would not receive approval from the Food and Drug Administration, he made a call to his stockbroker to sell his shares in the company stock. The broker, who also served as a broker for Martha Stewart, notified Stewart that the CEO was liquidating company stock and that it would be in her financial interest to sell her shares too. The Securities and Exchange Commission noticed the unusual link between the selling of a large

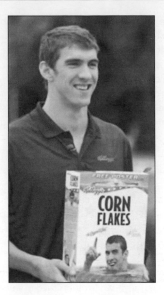

C5.1 Michael Phelps holding the Kellogg's Corn Flakes Box that displayed his image
USA Today "Celebrity endorsements tested by scandal", *<http://mediagallery.usatoday.com/Celebrity-endorsements-tested-by-scandal/G1996> Accessed October 10, 2013.*

number of shares by the CEO of ImClone and Martha Stewart and began an investigation to determine if Martha Stewart was guilty of insider trading.

Once this investigation began, Stewart created a story that she had a standing order to sell the ImClone stock if the price dropped to $60.00 per share. This action was construed as an attempt to defraud the Securities and Exchange Commission. On 4 June 2003, Stewart was indicted by the government on nine charges, including securities fraud and obstruction of justice. Stewart voluntarily stepped down as CEO and Chairwoman of Martha Stewart Living Omnimedia (MSLO), but stayed on as Chief Creative Officer.

When the ImClone stock scandal broke, Stewart's company saw revenues, profits, stock prices, and the number of ad pages slump. She went on trial in January 2004 and was found guilty in March 2004 of making false statements, obstruction of justice and conspiracy. As described in a *CNN Money* article, Stewart was sentenced in July 2004 to serve a five month term (minimum imposed under federal sentencing guidelines) at Alderson Federal Prison Camp, located in West Virginia. Stewart was also ordered by the judge to pay a $30,000 fine (maximum under federal laws). Following her stay in prison, Stewart served five months home confinement with electronic monitoring and two years of supervised probation.

If anyone could turn a five month prison stay into a 'Good Thing', it's home and lifestyle expert Martha Stewart. Following the completion of her sentence on federal criminal charges, Stewart returned to the limelight and revenue for MSLO improved.

Lance Armstrong

Lance Armstrong, considered one of the best cyclists in the world, broke many records in his athletic career as the seven-time Tour de France winner. In October 2012, however, Armstrong pleaded no contest to doping allegations (possession, use, and distribution of performance-enhancing drugs) and was banned from recognized competition for life and disqualified of his

C5.2 Le Tour de France Historical Guide from 2004

Le Tour de France Homepage, "Historical Guide", <http://www.letour.fr/le-tour/2013/us/>, Accessed October 9, 2013.

competitive results from 1998 forward. Looking at the Tour de France Historical Guide online illustrates how Lance Armstrong's results have literally been crossed out of the record books (see Figure C5.2). Consequently, Nike stopped sponsoring Armstrong, citing what it called insurmountable evidence he had used performance-enhancing drugs and misled Nike about it for more than a decade. Anheuser-Busch also ended its relationship with Armstrong.

According to a *Wall Street Journal* article, Nike supported the Livestrong Foundation, the non-profit organization that the former professional cyclist and cancer survivor created in 1997 to assists cancer patients, for a period of nine years. Following Armstrong's plea, Nike stopped selling merchandise carrying the Livestrong brand which had generated $150 million in funds annually for the charity. Proceeds from merchandise sales accounted for about 25 per cent of the charity's average yearly revenue.

In 2012 Armstrong resigned as chairman of the Livestrong Foundation and disassociated himself from the charity altogether. According to a *USA Today* article, revenue was down 19 per cent from the previous year during the first year without Armstrong at the helm of the charity Even before the resignation, Livestrong-branded clothing and exercise equipment showed poor sales results at Dick's Sporting Goods.

Adopting a celebrity endorsement strategy

The behaviour and reputation of a celebrity can heavily influence a brand. If a celebrity has an unfortunate misstep the sponsor and the public will react. Some celebrities deny allegations and others respond with apologies. Following a transgression situation some celebrity endorsers rebound and others disappoint.

It can be difficult for companies to predict how a celebrity's future actions will impact consumer opinion of the celebrity and the brand(s) represented. In an era where camera phones and social media are at the touch of every consumer's fingertips, celebrities are at high risk of exposing their failures and flaws to the world. Before endorsing a celebrity to represent the brand, the company must evaluate the benefits and risks associated with celebrity spokesperson. Unfortunately, when a celebrity receives negative publicity, both the celebrity and the company run the risk of failure. Every new case of negative publicity about celebrities raises the level of caution that businesses must adopt when considering a strategy to employ celebrity endorsers.

Discussion questions

1. Evaluate the risks a company takes when using celebrity endorsers.
2. How can companies who use celebrity endorsers avoid these risks?
3. Give an example of a celebrity endorser, not mentioned in the case, who developed a negative public image while representing a brand, and evaluate the aftermath of the effects on the company.
4. Describe how Martha Stewart had a negative impact on her company's revenue. Using Table C5.1, create a column graph showing Martha Stewart Living Omnimedia Incorporation's revenue from 1998 to 2007. Calculate the per cent change for each year. Using information from the case, label key events on the time series data.

Table C5.1 Martha Stewart Living Omnimedia, Inc. Revenue

Year	Revenue (million)	Per cent Change
1998	$ 177.20	- - - -
1999	$ 229.79	
2000	$ 282.32	
2001	$ 288.61	
2002	$ 295.05	
2003	$ 245.85	
2004	$ 187.44	
2005	$ 209.46	
2006	$ 288.34	
2007	$ 327.89	

Source: <http://subscriber.hoovers.com.ezp.lndlibrary.org/H/company360/overview.html?company Id=53053000000000Hoovers.com>.

This case was prepared by Professor Hope Corrigan, Loyola University Maryland, Baltimore, MD, together with five students, Tara Daly, Jeff Fromer, Courtney Jason, Becca Martin, and Mike Verrier.

Branding strategies

⊙ Learning Objectives

1. To grasp the complex nature of branding.

2. Understand ways in which consumers attach meaning to brands and the impact on company performance.

3. Discover ways in which brand managers can streamline brand costs and improve brand profitability.

4. Be able to identify the various ways in which brand managers can strategically create relationships between their brands and consumers and realize competitive advantages.

5. Become familiar with several strategic assessment tools that will aid the brand manager in assessing the nature of brand meaning and value and help in brand reinforcement and revitalization.

I. Introduction

1 Overview and strategy blueprint
2 Marketing strategy: analysis and perspectives

II. Where are we now?

3 Environmental and internal analysis: market information and intelligence

III. Where do we want to be?

4 Strategic marketing decisions, choices, and mistakes
5 Segmentation, targeting, and positioning strategies
6 **Branding strategies**
7 Relational and sustainability strategies

V. Did we get there?

14 Strategy implementation, control, and metrics

IV. How will we get there?

8 Product innovation and development strategies
9 Service marketing strategies
10 Pricing and distribution strategies
11 Marketing communications strategies
12 International marketing strategy
13 Social and ethical strategies

 Case study: Unilever—corporate branding for a consumer products company? Can Lynx and Dove be seen as appropriate under the same brand umbrella?

In January 2009 Unilever decided that it would start including its corporate logo on all of its consumer ads in the UK and Ireland. They had already been doing this in some of their overseas markets (Latin America and Asia), and this was seen as a good mechanism for creating consistency across the variety of different products they offer. The company decided they needed greater consistency since the person who buys one of their products is potentially likely to buy another if they know there is a corporate connection.

If one thinks through the logic behind these contentions, this seems to be counter-intuitive since the main reason that product-branding companies use individual stand-alone product names is because the main driver of purchase at that level of consumer goods is variety and price competitiveness. It is more difficult to build strong product loyalty when dealing with products which do not have a great deal of perceived consumer risk associated with them. If consumers are deal and variety prone, then the likelihood is that Unilever will have trouble keeping them loyal, so the hope is that by having an array of product offerings in each category, consumers who want another choice will shift to another of their products. This is the rationale behind Procter & Gamble offering 26 different kinds of laundry detergent. If the consumer tries another product, the likelihood is that that other product will also be one of P&G's products. For this kind of company, a stock out is far deadlier than excess inventory since a customer who cannot get what they want will potentially buy a product from another company and never come back again. If they do not increase sales, cannibalization is of course a potential danger when a company brings out a new product in a category where they already have offerings, but the increase does not have to be very large to reap efficiency benefits.

If the idea actually sounds like a good one with consistency and connections across company products improving the potential for selection in the mind of the consumer, think about the danger that goes along with tying a corporate brand to these individual branded products. First of all, the likelihood is that some new products will fail after introduction, and if a product which ties itself to a common brand fails, it has the potential to harm the corporate brand. If the product-specific brand fails, then the customer does not connect the failure to the corporate brand as there is no direct mental connection to it. The other downside to this is when the mixture of products is not perceived as consistent, even if the company believes that it is. Take, for example, the very different advertising approaches taken for Dove products as opposed to the Lynx brand. The ads run in the UK for Lynx are not at all consistent with the feminine sensitive Dove ads. The view of women as having a natural beauty all their own and the product only enhancing their own internal beauty, and the respect for different appearances and body shapes and sizes, takes an almost diametrically opposed view to the approach used by Lynx to promote the sexual animal magnetism associated with the use of the Lynx product. The idea is that when a man uses Lynx, all women will throw themselves sexually at him, and what would be particularly difficult to justify is that the women who are shown are young, fit, and attractive. Are these two disparate products consistent with each other? If not, then putting them under a common corporate brand may be really confusing for consumers who make that brand connection.

Introduction

Branding involves a complex set of perceptual components when viewed from the mind of the consumer. Getting this right is a major concern for brand managers. Brands communicate valuable information to the customer, and a thorough understanding of what the brand signifies is an essential part of marketing strategy. Whatever the company does can have an impact on customer perceptions of the brand, and the potential impact of corporate strategic decisions must be assessed particularly in terms of being consistent with the understanding and expectations of the customer.

What are the top brands today? Interbrand presents an annual assessment of brand value which attempts to place a discrete financial figure on the value of a brand, but the list primarily focuses on the biggest brands in the global arena (see Figure 6.1 for the top ten listing for 2013), so this is of little value to the small to medium-sized entity trying to deal with the complexity inherent in brand valuations.

What is particularly relevant in terms of differentiation and distinctiveness is the 'buzz' that is generated when the brand is considered by the public to be 'cool.' This kind of social cachet keeps the brand top-of-mind, and the immense publicity value pays for itself many times over for the firm lucky enough to attain this perceptual position. The Centre for Brand Analysis, the UK-based organization which collects opinion data from a variety of different countries,

	Company	Country	Value (£m)	Value (US$m)
1	Apple	US	58,738	98,316
2	Google	US	55,736	93,291
3	Coca-Cola	US	47,325	79,213
4	IBM	US	47,083	78,808
5	Microsoft	US	35,575	59,546
6	GE	US	28,048	46,947
7	McDonald's	US	25,088	41,992
8	Samsung	Korea	23,665	39,610
9	Intel	US	22,259	37,257
10	Toyota	Japan	21,117	35,346

6.1 Interbrand's 2013 Top Global Brands by Value

Source: Interbrand (2013)

released its CoolBrands listing in September 2014, and its list of the top twenty cool brands for 2014/15 is shown in Figure 6.2. To qualify as cool, a brand must meet the following six criteria:

(1) it must be thought of as stylish

(2) it must be perceived to be innovative

1	Apple
2	Aston Martin
3	Nike
4	Chanel
5	Glastonbury
6	Google
7	YouTube
8	Dom Perignon
9	Rolex
10	Netflix
11	Bang & Olufsen
12	Ray-Ban
13	Alexander McQueen
14	Instagram
15	Bose
16	Liberty
17	Selfridges
18	Sony
19	Virgin Atlantic
20	Stella McCartney

6.2 Top Twenty Cool Brands for 2014/15

Source: Centre for Brand Analysis

(3) it must be seen as an original

(4) it must be felt to be authentic

(5) it must be desirable

(6) it must be considered as unique.

These twenty were identified as the top brands out of some 5,500 considered.

The companies marketing these brands have reached powerful perceptual positions that help to reinforce the power of the brands involved. It is interesting to note that of the twenty brands listed, two are manufacturers of electronics products (Sony and Apple), three are fashion-design brands (Alexander McQueen, Stella McCartney, and Chanel), one is a sports clothing and equipment manufacturer (Nike), two are major retailers (Liberty and Selfridges), and four are powerful online-focused companies (YouTube, Instagram, Google, and Netflix). There are also six which represent global premium product manufacturers (Aston Martin, Bang & Olufsen, Bose, Dom Perignon, Ray-Ban, and Rolex). The remaining two are Glastonbury and Virgin Atlantic.

Branding and industry structure

The important questions raised in this chapter are:

(1) How can we use brand strategy to reduce our overall costs?

(2) How can brand strategy differentiate our offerings and help to build a meaningful relationship with the target consumer?

Strategic brand management in light of Porter's strategic framework, therefore, requires a sophisticated understanding of industry cost structure, brand efficiency and profitability, consumer perceptions of brand, and the potential for differentiation and sustainable competitive advantage. Both are important considerations and will be addressed in turn. The first step, however, is to briefly review the nature of branding and then lay the strategic foundation with an understanding of brand architecture.

The complex nature of brands

Branding represents one of the most important assets the company can acquire, but it must be carefully managed. It is not, as commonly defined, just a logo or a name. A brand represents different things to different constituencies, and the key to effective management of brand equity is to understand what goes on inside the heads of customers. The management of an array of products for multiple target groups of consumers raises difficult questions for brand managers who lack a sophisticated set of brand assessment tools and techniques.

Branding and functionality

So what exactly is a brand? At a base level, a brand is what identifies the company selling goods and/or services. It is information-laden and helps the consumer make the choice to fill a particular need from a series of similar offerings. Brands perform a number of functions for both the buyer and the seller (Berthon et al., 1999). For the buyer, brands help with product identification, which reduces search costs, signal particular quality levels, which reduces perceived risk, and provide social status, which reduces social and psychological risks. There are also a series of benefits for the selling company in the form of:

(1) the facilitation of customer identification and purchase, which improves financial performance

(2) the breeding of customer familiarity, which aids in the introduction of new product offerings

(3) the ability to identify specific product offerings clearly, which aids promotional efforts

(4) the differentiation of company offerings from those of competitors, which enables the use of premium pricing

(5) the distinctiveness of the product offering, which allows the identification of appropriate target segments and tailored communications/promotions, and

(6) the enhancement of brand loyalty, which promotes repeat purchases.

A brand is much more than just a signifier.

Brand identity

As David Aaker (1996a) explains in his seminal book *Building Strong Brands*, at its most basic level the brand has a core identity which is its essence and which remains constant. There is also an extended identity, which focuses on a series of psychological and physical aspects that give it nuance and texture. Brand can be thought of as having a variety of important facets that should be considered in assessing its full nature.

First of all a brand can be thought of as a product. Aaker (2004, 1996) suggests that this would entail such considerations as product scope, product-related attributes, quality/value associations with the brand, uses or applications for the brand, brand users, and brand country of origin. Companies can often be found in conflict involving the brand as product since the basic attributes and uses for the product should always be consistent with the consumer perceptions and expectations engendered by the brand. So fit between offerings and expectations becomes important in this case, given a particular brand.

Another important facet of brand deals with the connections between the brand and the company which creates it. Aaker (2004), Keller (2000), and others suggest that a brand can also be imbued with organizational attributes (e.g. innovative, young, socially responsible, etc.) and certain expectations in terms of geographic coverage (e.g. local vs. global). In this case it becomes difficult for the consumer to actually separate the brand from the company behind the brand. As many brand specialists argue, the products produced by the company should always be tied back to the company and the associated brand so that a clear message is sent to the consumer which conveys the basic meaning and message associated with the brand. The Ritz-Carlton chain of hotels brings to mind service above and beyond the normal expectations and amenities that are at the highest standards of the hotel industry. Consistent with this would be such attributes as immediate attention from hotel staff, immaculate and consistent uniforms, bedroom amenities like high count Egyptian cotton sheets, room-darkening shades, sound proofing, and room decor and hotel facilities superbly decorated and presented.

A third level of branding can be seen in the brand possibly becoming synonymous with a particular person. This would include the brand potentially taking on a distinctive personality (e.g. compassionate, responsible, athletic, etc.) or creating the impression in the mind of the customer that they have an actual relationship with the brand (e.g. seeing the brand as a friend or a mentor, etc.). This personality connection was used effectively by Accenture when it connected itself directly to the persona of Tiger Woods, known for drive, precision, preparation, and winning. While this was very effective during Tiger's ascent to the top of his game, it also demonstrates how important it is for the company using this type of association to monitor the activities of the celebrity endorser to ensure that the association is able to build a positive image for the company. Accenture was eventually forced to cut its connection to Tiger after his character was brought into question when his personal indiscretions were exposed in the media. In the use of celebrity endorsers and brand personality it is imperative for brand managers to monitor the fit between the brand and the celebrity to ensure that the fit is maintained, otherwise dissonance can quickly become a perceptual problem.

The fourth possible level of branding is for the customer to see the brand as a symbol. This would entail the brand being connected with particular visual images (e.g. the McDonald's golden arches, the Nike swoosh, etc.) as well as the brand and its history or heritage (e.g. Jack Daniel's sour-mash whiskey and its black and white ads connecting the product to its storied heritage). The idea here is to separate the product from others because it has distinctive imagery associated with it and/or because it must be good because it has been around for a long time.

Clearly, a brand means different things to different segments, and a better understanding of brand identity is an integral part of a successful brand management programme. The key is to understand the perceptions of the consumers relative to the array of company brands.

Brand equity

Another integral strategic aspect of a brand relates to the concept of brand equity. Aaker first coined the term, **brand equity**, in his 1991 book *Managing Brand Value*, and defined it as a set of assets (as well as liabilities) connected to the name and symbols of the brand that adds to (or detracts from) the value of the product or service to a company and/or that company's customers. The point is to compare brand assets with brand liabilities and maintain a strong and viable brand equity valuation. The concept involves an assumption that there are really five types of assets that should be considered when examining the brand.

- The first of these is **brand name awareness**. If the consumer is aware of the brand, then it will more likely be a candidate for their choice set, and familiarity certainly has the potential to generate positive feelings.
- The second is **brand loyalty**, which assumes that loyal customers will spread positive word-of-mouth and help attract a new set of customers. This also suggests that

loyalty will allow the greater potential use of premium pricing since this establishes a substantial barrier against new entrants.

- The third group of assets focuses on **perceived quality**, which is strongly associated with profitability.
- The fourth level involves **brand associations**, which involve the various connections and associations made by consumers about the brand.
- The fifth and last level of assets involves **intellectual rights** that support the brand like patents or trademarks.

These measures allow the brand manager to effectively assess the value of the brand as a firm asset, and the examination of brand value at regular intervals allows the brand manager to maintain a steady brand course and to take specific corrective action when downward trends are identified. Aaker (2004, 1996b) suggests that these measures can effectively be applied across a variety of products and markets.

An understanding of the complexity of brands is an essential starting point to the development of an effective marketing strategy from the perspective of brand management. Brand management involves a variety of different strategic brand choices and an assessment of the perceptual impact of those choices on various customer groups. The discussion will now focus on the strategic choices that will help the brand manager to improve the profitability of the brand, differentiate the brand from its competition, and aid in the creation and maintenance of relationships between the consumer and the brand.

Brand architecture: a strategic management framework

Firms have many different options facing them when it comes to brand choices, and it is important to lay the groundwork. The best framework to date is the concept of **brand architecture** which looks at the brand portfolio as a complex structure with a variety of different types of brand roles and relationships. The idea is that this structure is analogous to the structures designed by an architect. Aaker and Joachimsthaler (2002) present their brand architecture relationship spectrum to demonstrate the various options that are possible for brand management (see Figure 6.3). The array of brand options stretches from the **house of brands** at one extreme to the **branded house** at the other extreme. The house of brands involves a company that manages a disparate group of brands, each standing on its own. Procter & Gamble, Colgate Palmolive, and Unilever are all examples of companies which manage a house of brands. Each has the potential to own a particular niche market on its own merits and build strong brand relationships with specific target market segments. Virgin and BMW present examples of the branded house in that all of their offerings build on the name as a focal point for consumer expectation.

Another way of looking at this is the concept of **product-specific branding** as the mechanism used when a house of brands is utilized, and **manufacturer's branding** when a branded house is used. Strategically the point is that the house of brands is an array of products, each with its own brands that stand alone and are separate and distinct from each other. Why might this be important for Procter & Gamble, Colgate Palmolive, and Unilever? Because the likelihood at this level of consumer products is that some new products will

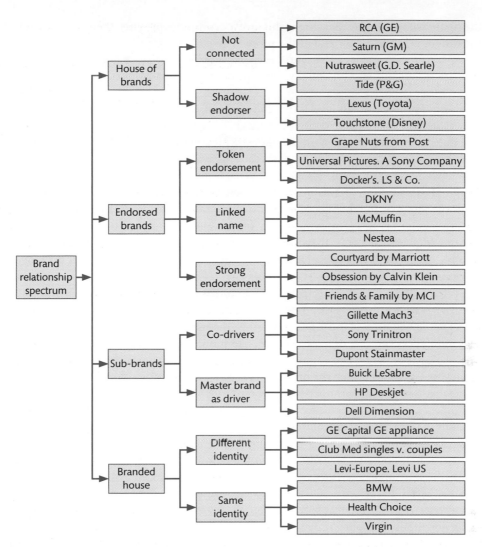

6.3 Brand Architecture

Source: David A. Aaker and Erich Joachimsthaler, *Brand Leadership* (2000a). Reprinted with the permission of the Free Press, a division of Simon & Schuster Adult Publishing Group. © 2000 by David A. Aaker and Erich Joachmisthaler. All rights reserved.

fail. Estimates suggest that as high as 80 per cent of all new products fail, and the strategic problem is that if a product fails, the company tied to the product will also be negatively affected by the failure. The failed brand would tarnish the overall brand reputation which could be disastrous for the company involved. If one thinks about the strategic options in this case, a product can fail and not harm Unilever's reputation, but the drawback is that each product starts with no consumer awareness or understanding and it will be necessary to effectively launch the product with all of the necessary marketing muscle to make the target market aware, interested, and desirous, and then to get them to try the product and hopefully adopt it. This will require a major marketing expenditure outlay. Why is this worth the financial investment? Because at this level of consumer product, there is far less loyalty than there is at the higher end of the product spectrum. From a marketing standpoint, a stock-out of the product is far worse than excess inventory since not being able to meet consumer demand may potentially send the consumer to a competitor from where they might never come back.

Another problem at this level is that consumers are far more deal and variety prone, so if they switch away from one of the company's brands, they will hopefully switch to another. The danger at this point is **cannibalization** which is where the addition of a new brand does not increase the overall sales but spreads them among a now broader range of brands, which would be unprofitable for the firm. What is important to remember, however, is that marginal sales improvements might be beneficial since they may improve overall company efficiency by improving capacity utilization rates, providing a basis for greater shelf space allocation with a greater number of brands and more chance that the consumer will buy one of your products if they want to try something new. As an illustration, Procter & Gamble has 26 different types of laundry detergent in the US market to cover the range for consumers.

On the other side of the spectrum is the **branded house** or **manufacturer's brand strategy**. This is where all company products are tied to the same corporate name, and the power of the name will pre-sell the product offering. The manufacturer's brand can be geographically limited in the case of a local brand, like John Smith's brand of Yorkshire beer, or it can be global in nature like Guinness or Stella Artois. From a positive side, the amount of money necessary to launch the product from a marketing/promotional standpoint will be somewhat less than the product-specific brand since the company name is already known. The downside of this, is that since the company name is already known, whatever the name signifies in terms of quality, features, options, and performance will set the expectation level for whatever is introduced to the market under the same company name.

Where this can be problematic is when the new product offering is not consistent with other company offerings. The new C-class of Mercedes produced by Daimler-Benz and the move by BMW to include a 100-series of vehicles are attempts by both companies to move to a lower end of the product spectrum, but the issue is that this less-expensive alternative, while potentially appealing to a much larger group of consumers, may confuse existing customers who associate premium-priced offerings with the Mercedes and BMW names. This is not the same type of offering that consumers have grown to expect from the company, and the result may be problems for these companies and their brands. Confusion, in this case, may lead to a loss of strategic advantage.

Having discussed the extremes, there are other choices that might be possible as well. Another option is the **endorsed brand** which builds on its connection to a known brand, but this connection can be strong or weak in nature. This is sometimes referred to as umbrella branding. The point is that the company may have several different key brands under its ownership that represent different quality levels and do not detract from each other, but there are great strategic synergies in the connecting of like products under the same brand umbrella. This is also sometimes referred to as family branding when the brands are all part of the same family of products. Examples would include food products like Post or Kellogg's cereal products. The point is that the brand now has its own foundation but it is tied to the endorser in a way that gives the new brand greater credibility. Aaker and Joachimsthaler

(2000) provide an excellent example of endorsement in what they call the linked name in endorsement, using such illustrative examples as the McMuffin sandwich or Chicken McNuggets for McDonalds.

Another strategic branding option involves the use of the **sub-brand**. This is a stronger connection than is involved in the endorsed brand. The point here is to connect the brand more closely to the parent brand. This can involve the tacit parenting of the company brand like HP Laserjet or Deskjet printers, where the hope is that HP is the key but Deskjet can be recognizable as well. This is also the kind of strategy followed by Sony with its Vaio computers. Sony is the key here, but the Vaio has the ability to develop its own recognition as well. If Vaio later becomes strong enough, it may become a co-driver, which is another option under sub-branding where each name has more of an equal power and footing in the combined brand. This can be seen in Sony's television sets from the 1980s and 1990s when it introduced its Trinitron sub-brand. This involved a special colour gun in the TV which would present clearer and more vibrant colour since it mixed all colours with a single projection mechanism as opposed to three different colour projections as was done in most competing brand models. Trinitron was to be clearly connected to Sony but have separate added value as well. The main benefit was to have both equally add to the name recognition and value perceptions.

One other option of note is the **private brand**, which is where the manufacturer puts another company's name on the product for them. Why would it make sense for a manufacturer to put someone else's name on their products? There are several benefits, such as using its production equipment more efficiently and increasing its overall sales, and responsibility for the products ends with production since the company it is being branded for has the responsibility for marketing the products. This is a great mechanism for retailers to gain brand followings as they have their own name which they hope will be preferred by their customers. The manufacturers and food processors who handle private branding for grocery chains like Tesco, Sainsbury, and Waitrose are the same high quality providers that also make their own branded merchandise available, so consumers can often get good quality at value prices when they buy private branded products. This allows the retailer to create relationships with target consumers that may be quite profitable over the long term.

Industry cost structure: brand efficiency and profitability

As previously discussed, strategic brand decisions can have an important impact on a firm's financial performance, and there are a number of ways in which brand managers can improve brand performance from a cost and profitability perspective. Operational efficiencies can be achieved from such mechanisms as brand leveraging and co-branding, and there are some promising new valuation mechanisms which can aid brand managers in achieving greater cost efficiencies. Each of these will be discussed in turn.

Brand leveraging

Strong brands often produce above-average returns for shareholders, and there is great pressure on brand managers to use the name recognition that accompanies a strong brand to increase potential sales and profits by attaching the name to other company offerings (Court et al., 1999).

What are the potential advantages associated with brand leveraging? Brand extension is constantly luring businesses to tie new offerings to existing brands since the name recognition is already there, and the costs to build awareness are considerably lower than would be associated with new startup names. Another point is the movement towards convergence with mergers and acquisitions and that leveraging involves a heavy focus on building relationships between customers and brands. After all, what the product has in terms of features and options is not so much an issue as the fact that consumers emotionally engage with the brand and feel a kinship.

Certainly brand leverage success can be seen in the offerings of such brands as Walt Disney, Sony, and Apple, but these companies make sure that the offerings are seen as perceptually consistent. Since the market for Disney is children and their parents, the idea of Disney putting its name on adult-content movies or alcoholic beverages would be ludicrous. Successful brand leveraging can be seen in the top-end electronic offerings of Sony with its 3DTVs, HDTVs, Blu-ray players, etc. This is also the case for Apple with its high-demand speciality electronic products like Apple Mac computers, iPods, iPads, and iPhones. What do these companies do that makes them successful? It has been suggested that what they do well is to identify a 'golden thread' which can tie together a diversified group of businesses (Court et al., 1999). Principally these are significant economies of scale and scope, and shared resources which can provide mechanisms for improving profitability. One example is Disney and its focus on 'wholesome fun', and another is Sony and its elegance of design. Such companies were also found to invest in the creation of a high credibility brand personality that can be leveraged (Aaker, 2004; Keller, 2000).

While leveraging can produce economic benefits, there is also a downside to aggressive leveraging, as was found in the unsuccessful strategies employed by both BIC and Gucci. These companies were drawn into confusing extensions with product offerings that were inconsistent with their flagship products. Inconsistent offerings can confuse loyal customers, and spreading out from their limited area of focus can be dangerous if the broadening occurs too quickly. Research has shown that the extent of damage done to the parent by a failed extension will depend to a certain extent on the involvement of the consumer with the parent brand, and in a sub-branding strategy the damage is lessened to the parent when the brand extension is given another name in association with the parent brand (Keller and Lehmann, 2006). This would argue for the use of a co-branding strategy as opposed to a straight brand extension if risk of potential failure is high. Sub-branding would also be warranted when the brand extension is quite a bit different from the parent brand product category and when fit between the extension and the parent is minimal. The sub-brand often acts as a buffer by shielding the parent from negative feedback (Keller and Lehmann, 2006).

Co-branding

Co-branding involves the bringing together of two separate company brands to be marketed together to create a new joint offering with additional value for the customer. Examples include such successful pairings as British Airways and Hertz, Adidas and the New Zealand Rugby Union, Starbucks Coffee and Barnes & Noble Bookstores, and Kellogg's Cereals and Walt Disney.

There are a number of operational benefits that can accrue to co-branding partners. Co-branding can make transactions more efficient through sharing of retail sites, for example the case of Starbucks and Barnes & Noble (Prince and Davies, 2002). Starbucks gets use of space in the bookstore and revenues from the high traffic of shoppers as a result. Barnes & Noble gets the benefit of lower expenses for overhead and up-front investments, which are being shared with Starbucks. Co-branding may be a viable strategic option, but it requires a careful assessment of the potential candidates for partnering. There will be spillover effects incurred when the brands are combined in an alliance, but much of the potential downside would be driven by the lack of congruence in image or fit involved (Simonin and Ruth, 1998).

Co-branding is an effective mechanism for global brands to be successful in local markets (Abratt and Motlana, 2002). The local brands bring high local brand equity to a global brand that may not have high local brand equity. Co-branding then becomes a great tool for introducing new consumer products. The synergies created can often produce an impression of greater value and lower the financial risk associated with a normal new product introduction. Such co-branding makes sense for acquisitions because the acquiring company develops a brand portfolio with a heritage that can help weak products.

Brand valuation mechanisms

There are a variety of tools for asset valuation from a financial perspective that may aid brand managers to achieve greater efficiencies. Two promising mechanisms are **advertising turnover** and **brand ROI** (Herremans et al., 2000). Marketing investment and advertising investment are one and the same for brand valuation purposes since advertising makes up such a large part of brand building compared with any other marketing promotional mechanisms, and as a result they suggest a ratio, advertising turnover, which examines the relationship between advertising expenditures and brand value. This measure would therefore reflect how effectively the firm has converted advertising expenditures into brand value. Advertising turnover is calculated by dividing brand value by advertising expenditures on a year-by-year basis and examining trends.

The use of brand ROI is another aspect, where the following formula for calculating ROI (sales/investment × net income/sales) is assumed, brand sales being substituted for sales and brand value for investment (Herremans et al., 2000). Thus, the formula becomes:

$$\text{Brand ROI} = \frac{\text{Brand Sales}}{\text{Brand Value}} \times \frac{\text{Net Income}}{\text{Brand Sales}}$$

The first part of the formula reflects the brand turnover (brand sales/brand value), which shows the effectiveness of brand value conversion into sales), while the second part is the brand return on sales (net income/brand sales), which indicates how well brand sales convert into operating income.

Mini Case 6.1   Delta and Northwest, Mars and Wrigley: what makes brand alliances work?

Brand alliances can provide a number of ways in which the partners can benefit from image boosts to greater efficiencies and effectiveness. One such powerful brand alliance can be seen in the takeover of Wrigley by Mars, which created the biggest sweets company in the world. What makes this a particularly synergistic alliance is that both companies are known as well-run family businesses. The names of the original founders are represented in the brand themselves. They are also seen as complementary to each other rather than as directly competitive. They also represent companies seen as similar in corporate values with strong emphases on ethicality and respect for workers and their wellbeing along with that of the environment, and both have long histories associated with building successful brands that have lasted for generations. Mars is known for global confectionery like M&Ms, Mars, Snickers, Starburst, Twix, and Milky Way, among many others, while Wrigley is known primarily for its chewing gum products like Juicy Fruit, Spearmint, Orbit, Doublemint, Hubba Bubba, and others.

Brand alliances can often be seen as a means to consolidation if both partners are faced with rapidly increasing costs, as in the example of the merger of Delta Airlines and Northwest Airlines creating a huge airline with enormous synergies in code-sharing agreements, so they are well aware of values and management structures. They achieved many of the kinds of synergies seen by Mars and Wrigley. This type of alliance where equals become partners allows the two companies to maintain their own individual brand identities and management structure for everyday operations, but the real benefits can be seen in the consistency of the two brands now being merged and the added value that brings with it. They will have a number of potential cost-savings opportunities against ever-rising jet fuel prices and the costs of IT systems and logistics, but they also see added benefit in their complementary routes and geographical coverage. This type of consolidation has been seen as particularly important in trying economic times, but the benefits that accrue will become even more valuable when economic conditions improve.

This of course assumes that there will not only be internal operating synergies between the brand partners, but also, in the eyes of consumers, perceptual consistency that will allow boosts for the co-brands. Some alliances do not provide this type of boost as can clearly be seen by the failed Daimler–Chrysler merger, which brought a certain amount of credibility to Chrysler, but the opposing nature of the quality perceptions associated with Chrysler probably did not do much good for Daimler. In fact, there is concern that the Chrysler focus on high volume has potentially clouded the consumer view of Daimler as it expands its Mercedes products downwards to a C-Class. The concern is that this may tarnish the image of the top-end products as the reach of the new, less expensive, product potentially eliminates some of the social cachet associated with being one of the few able to afford a Mercedes car. In other words, the weakness of the Chrysler brand can actually have a negative effect on the stronger brand partner in the alliance. Of course, Daimler saw the error of its ways and divested Chrysler to a private equity group, but the question remains whether the cultural change that occurred during the alliance will have a long-term negative effect upon Daimler and its Mercedes flagship.

While cost considerations are important when evaluating brand strategy, there is also the need to examine brand management from the perceptual side. The perceptions of **brand, brand personality,** and brand value are key strategic considerations that significantly improve brand strategic planning perspective in the pursuit of sustainable competitive advantage.

Consumer perceptions of brands

Brand management cannot focus on financial assessment alone. There is also an enormously important perceptual aspect. Companies are finding that brand management has an image and personality management component, which must also be carefully assessed and tracked over time. This section will focus on such image-oriented strategic issues which are customer involvement with the brand, brand perceptual reinforcement and revitalization, and the overall assessment of the brand using the brand wheel.

Customer brand involvement and perceptual connections

Companies have found that the key to brand success is to build strong relationships with customers by enhancing customer experiences with the brand, its personality, and its heritage (Joachimsthaler and Aaker, 1997). This involvement and relationship building can clearly be seen in innovative attempts to enhance customer experiences with the brand. Cadbury's theme park (Cadbury World, Bournville, England) allows the customer to experience the brand in multiple ways, creating a link between brand, brand attributes, brand personality, and the customer. What was once just a factory tour has now become an entire theme park with emphasis on the Cadbury brand heritage via a chocolate museum, a restaurant, a tour of the plant, and a big chocolate sales store. Visitors learn about the history of chocolate (with characters portraying historic figures like Cortez, Montezuma, and King Charles II of England) as well as the history of John Cadbury and his company. This idea was so successful that it encouraged Hershey to open its own version of this experience in New York City.

Another example can clearly be seen in the development of the HOG (Harley Owner Groups) clubs by Harley-Davidson motorcycles. HOGs regularly get together to ride and celebrate the history and heritage of Harley motorcycles. Nestlé has worked to develop customer groups with its Buitoni pasta products by creating the Casa Buitoni Club, which involves customers in the history of Buitoni and of pasta through visits to the Buitoni family home in Tuscany and a series of mailings of newsletters, Italian lifestyle literature, recipes, and discount coupons. Customers get continual positive brand reinforcement with the hope of building ever-increasing involvement between brand and customer.

Brand perceptual reinforcement and revitalization

Kevin Lane Keller (1999) suggests that effective brand management requires a long-term perspective with continuous reinforcement of brand meaning and, when necessary, brand revitalization. Reinforcement of brand equity occurs when tactical marketing decisions convey consistent meanings to consumers. A series of important questions raised by Keller (1999) in this regard are:

- What products are represented by the brand?
- What benefits are supplied by the brand?
- What specific needs are satisfied by the brand?
- How does the brand make those products associated with it superior?
- What distinct and favourable brand associations are made by consumers with the brand?

Keller (2013, 1999) warns that the most important consideration in brand reinforcement is the consistency of the support (in terms of both the type and amount) provided by the company to the brand. He emphasizes that price increases with inadequate marketing support are potentially disastrous. This is not meant to suggest that brand management should not make any changes to its marketing efforts for the brand, but that any changes must keep the image integrity of the brand. Some companies have been forced to come back to old themes for advertising when new creative ideas did not register well perceptually with consumers. Kentucky Fried Chicken (KFC) was forced to return to using Colonel Sanders to promote the product after eliminating his likeness as a way to modernize the company image.

Certainly there may be times over the brand's lifetime when strategic chances will be taken that may not be successful and could potentially undermine the vitality of the brand. In these instances brand managers should consider revitalizing the brand. Revitalization requires a careful assessment of brand meaning and associations so that meaningful repositioning decisions can be made. This requires the implementation of a thorough **brand audit**. The brand audit is a comprehensive examination of the various sources of brand equity from the perspective of the company as well as the consumer. Keller (2000) introduced his own tool for effective brand auditing, the Brand Report Card, which involves rating from one (extremely poor) to ten (extremely good) honest answers to the following brand equity questions (Keller 2000).

- How well does the brand excel at delivering the benefits customers truly desire?
- How well does the brand remain relevant?
- How well does the pricing strategy reflect consumers' perceptions of value?
- How well is the brand positioned in the minds of consumers as compared with competing brands?
- How consistent are the brand's marketing programmes and the messages sent to the consumer?
- Does the brand portfolio and hierarchy actually make sense?
- How well does the brand utilize and coordinate a full range of marketing activities to build brand equity?
- How well do the brand's managers understand what the brand means to consumers?
- How well does the company give proper support to the brand, and how well has this support been sustained over the long run?
- How well does the company monitor the sources of brand equity?

Keller (1999) suggests that once a brand audit has been done, the important brand associations will be better understood and the firm will be able to take one or more of the following paths:

(1) expanding brand awareness (e.g. finding additional or new usage opportunities for the brand like Arm & Hammer Baking Soda)

(2) improving brand image (e.g., strengthening positive associations and/or eliminating negative associations using such mechanisms as brand heritage/history

(3) balancing both old and new target segments (e.g. bringing in a younger customer and keeping relationships with loyal older customers at the same time)

(4) retiring and/or consolidating brands that no longer fit or would be too costly to revitalize (e.g. Procter & Gamble's merging of the White Cloud and Charmin toilet paper brands and the Solo and Bold detergent brands).

The brand audit is a vital assessment tool for effective brand management.

Key brand assessment vehicles for differentiation purposes: the brand wheel

A useful tool, given the complex nature of brands, developed by Ward, et al. (1999) can give the brand manager a reasonable view of his or her brand/ without inordinate amounts of complicated data acquisition and analysis. This is known as the 'brand wheel' (see Figure 6.4). The first level, **features**, focuses on how the brand delivers its promise. The firm owns or maintains a series of tangible and intangible assets that it could point to which are used to deliver its promise. The second layer involves the translation of the features into a series of benefits for its target audiences. The third layer, **values**, considers aspects of the firm in relation to its place in society. Now the firm must be concerned with whether its brand conveys information about the nature of its community citizenship or social responsibility. This would then examine the ways in which the brand would be suggestive of a series of social values that would add to its brand worth. The fourth layer is **personality**, which focuses on the particular personality traits that are associated with the company/brand. This is not something that is asked directly in a questionnaire. In order to examine this important aspect, the following are the types of questions that many companies use to identify associated traits.

- If this brand were a car, what would it be?
- If this brand were a person, who would it be?
- If this brand were a newspaper, which one would it be?
- If this brand were a lunch, what would it be?

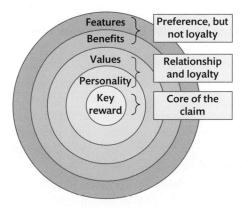

6.4 Brand Wheel

The final layer involves the **key reward**, and it is the central reason that people buy and/or use the brand based upon the four earlier levels of the brand wheel. The identification of the most important level of the brand wheel is vital for understanding and nurturing the brand, and it may be that any one or a combination of the prior levels determines the key reward. It might be that it is the benefits layer or the personality where the key reward is found, or it might be the cumulative effects of all of the layers that create the key reward. An important distinction to make here is that features and benefits may create preference, but they will not necessarily ensure loyalty to the brand. Values and personality reflect the character of the brand and therefore offer the potential for loyalty.

Given the importance of consumer perceptions about brands and the nature of the relationships built between consumers and brands, the nature of information gathering by consumers is drastically changing with the growing use and sophistication of social media. This will now be discussed in detail.

Social media and branding

No chapter on branding would be complete without a discussion of the impact of social media upon the brand and brand strategy. In a 2010 *Harvard Business Review* article, David Edelman raises some serious questions about the nature of branding in the new 'digital age' in which we live. Edelman is a co-leader of McKinsey & Company's Global Digital Marketing Strategy practice. He suggests that consumers still want what they previously wanted (distinct brand promises and value), but what has now changed is that consumers are being affected by information and influences at new 'touch points', forcing companies to learn how consumers get their information and to reach them when they are open to influence. These new touch points require a better understanding of consumer social media habits. Edelman suggests that work at McKinsey & Company has shown a major change in consumer brand choice from what was known as the 'funnel metaphor' in which consumers would start with a wide variety of possible brands to choose from and over time would weed out unacceptable options until a final choice was made. At that point the consumer would purchase the brand and use would help in the creation of a relationship between the consumer and the brand.

After studying over 20,000 consumers across a variety of industries, McKinsey found that the consumer decision process has changed. There are now four stages which the consumer goes through: (1) consideration, (2) evaluation, (3) purchase, and (4) enjoyment, advocacy, and bonding. Since consumers are bombarded with information they will now eliminate options from their initial consideration set. This will then be followed by the evaluation stage where individuals will seek a variety of information sources and then add new brands to the mix while eliminating others. The third stage, buying, is more likely now to be delayed until they can actually enter the store and get key final information to help them make the choice. This is a critical point as this will be the make or break moment for the final decision to purchase. The final stage focuses on the interaction between the consumer and the product itself where a whole new series of touch points are found which involve word-of-mouth, interactions on social media sites, gathering of information from others on their use of the brand, and their perceptions of their brand experiences.

The key for Edelman is that this is the vital time when the company must effectively use all of those touch points to reinforce the positive nature of the relationship between the consumer and the brand. The point here is that with negative input the consumer may desert the brand, but with the right amount of positive reinforcement, the consumer will enter into the enjoy–advocate–buy cycle and not need any further consideration and evaluation stages.

This research helps the brand manager to realize that consumers are finding new ways to make connections to products/brands. The strategic key for the brand manager is to understand the various ways in which the consumer gets information and has the potential for connections being built when the consumer is in a position to be influenced. This requires a careful assessment of target audience social media habits. It has been found that successful companies are effectively using social media to bond with consumers at various points along the way to purchase and advocacy (Barwise and Meehan, 2010). This applies to such companies as American Express which used OPEN Forum, Procter & Gamble and its Beinggirl.com, Fiesta Movement from Ford Motor Company, and Cisco's myPlanNet to use customer experience and to help with new product development. The point is that these types of site engage potential consumers and start or enhance existing relationships between the company/brand and customers. Brand marketers are advised (Barwise and Meehan, 2010) to:

(1) Let the brand promise guide all actions using social media

(2) Use social media to learn about customers, particularly Facebook or even company-sponsored online brand communities

(3) Strive to use social media to communicate messages to customers that reflect brand authenticity but at the same time are relevant and have high entertainment value to enhance the chances of going viral through such mechanisms as YouTube

(4) Be careful to follow the rules associated with each form of social media by monitoring discussions and only exerting influence once the company is established and accepted by the other participants in the environment.

An interesting 'take' on how firms should consider handling social media is the idea of a 'ringmaster' to handle the new media (Spenner, 2010). This is a new type of executive who is both digitally knowledgeable and has the ability to coordinate marketing as well as consumer-facing activities. The point is that this ringmaster will use their talent to bring the consumer into the picture and, interact with them seamlessly, and hopefully keep them engaged with the brand. This new executive should have three distinct capabilities.

(1) **Integrative thinking**—bringing together the knowledge of branding, communications, and social media technologies to create vibrant interactive communities of followers (like Mini and Ford have done in their creation of fans who get emotional benefits from connections with each other).

(2) **Lean collaboration skills**— as opposed to brand managers, these executives will often have to work with limited resources, and their selling abilities and persuasiveness will be key to bringing teams together throughout the company.

(3) **High speed**—these executives will be working in much shorter time frames than normal brand managers. An important ability here is the need for skilful use of digital media technology to spot potential opportunities and threats and be able to deal with them quickly.

A vital new driver of brand community engagement should 'love' the technological side, but also have extensive experience in external relationship building (Spenner, 2010). Success will be built upon the understanding of key customer touch points and the ability to focus and unify a brand voice with meaningful stories to keep the customer engaged.

Two of the most relevant social media vehicles at the present time are Facebook and Twitter. Facebook uses the mechanism of indicating likes and sharing of posts to indicate reach, and firms are jockeying to find ways to get customers to go to the company Facebook page and indicate that they 'like' it, comment on it, and share posts on the company's page. A study of more than 1,000 wall postings from 98 different global brands identified eight ways in which brand managers can increase the 'likes' that the company receives (Malhotra et al., 2013).

(1) Express things through the use of **photos** since they are personal and easily communicate with the viewer.

(2) **Remain topical** by keeping up with the times and linking to special events.

(3) **Do not hold back on promoting the brand** since consumers who visit the wall expect promotional information.

(4) **Share the brand's success stories** with the customers to solidify their willingness to become a fan of the brand as people like to hear about awards and achievements.

(5) Use the opportunity to **educate the consumer** and enhance their experience with the brand using such mechanisms as information about the brand's history and how it produces its connected products.

(6) Fans like 'living' brands, so the company should try to **make the brand human with the connection to emotions** allowing the consumer an opportunity to emotionally bond with the brand.

(7) **Humour can effectively be used to encourage likes** as people like to laugh, and effective use of art and accompanying text can create humorous pictures around the brand and its products.

(8) The brand wall should **'politely' ask for likes** as people are more apt to indicate likes if they are asked for them as opposed to when they are not asked for them, but care must be taken not to overkill on the asking.

When a visitor to the Facebook page of the brand shares a message with others, this is a concrete indication that that individual has become an actual advocate for the brand. This is an important step in building the brand interactive community of fans and ambassadors. There are also five don'ts if you want to prevent wall messages from not being liked (Malhotra et al., 2013).

(1) **Don't be long-winded**, as the longer the wall post, the less apt visitors are to indicate that they like it.

(2) **Avoid event-related posts** since the future is not where visitors want to be when they visit the wall.

(3) **Don't use the message to affiliate with particular social causes** or charities since visitors may be concerned with different charities and causes.

(4) **Don't use the message to promote contests** since visitors can quickly see through this type of promotional strategy.

(5) **Don't use the post to promote special 'deals'** as these will turn visitors off.

Facebook provides opportunities to monitor consumer comments since anyone can respond to brand posts on the wall. In fact there can be many comments directed at the company and at other visitors, setting up an important dialogue to allow information sharing and giving the company a chance to better understand the mindsets and perceptions of consumers. It is important to note that sharing on Facebook is very similar to what is known as 'retweeting' using Twitter. Many of the concerns about what will help as well as hinder liking mentioned above will also apply to tweets on Twitter. The limit on the number of characters in tweets is a major difference between the two mechanisms, and while length of message does not matter for Facebook, it does matter for Twitter as longer tweets are less likely to be retweeted than shorter ones, and tweeting pictures does not increase retweets (Malhotra et al., 2013). One major difference between Facebook and Twitter is that Twitter is more focused on location and is a better forum for event-related material, and Facebook is a better forum for engaging consumers in real-time communication. Both vehicles are important and should be built into the social media network for the brand.

The social media focused brand manager must also be monitoring the advent of new platforms which spring up regularly. Not all will catch on, but the point is that the technology and the vehicles are evolving rapidly, and the brand manager must be cognizant of the changes and adapt quickly to maintain viable connections to consumers.

Brand connections are vital, and some companies have gone beyond brand engagement to create stronger bonds through focusing on **lovemarks** as opposed to brand. This new approach is described in the following section.

Lovemarks

Kevin Roberts, Saatchi & Saatchi CEO for Worldwide Operations, introduced the idea of brand love in his 2004 book *Lovemarks: The Future Beyond Brands*, and later enhanced and expanded it in his 2006 book *The Lovemarks Effect: Winning in the Consumer Revolution*. It is Roberts' premise that branding itself is flawed since brands are not actually making strong emotional connections with people. He claims that there are six reasons for this:

(1) brands are worn out from overuse

(2) brands are no longer mysterious

(3) brands can't understand the new consumer

(4) brands struggle with good old-fashioned competition

(5) brands have been captured by formula

(6) brands have been smothered by creeping conservatism.

The issue is to build an emotional bond with the consumer to such an extent that the consumer actually feels a love for the product. Roberts believes that love goes beyond reason, and a love bond is an emotional attachment that transcends logic and reason.

Brand	Lovemark
stands for information	focuses on relationship
is recognized by consumers	is loved by people
is generic	is personal
presents a narrative	creates a love story
promises quality	presents a touch of sensuality
is symbolic	is iconic
is defined	is infused
is a statement	is a story
a set of defined attributes	is wrapped in mystery
is a set of values	is a spirit
is professional	is passionately creative
needs an advertising agency	needs an ideas company

The lovemarks approach has gained ground strategically and Roberts presents a series of brands that he believes have been elevated to lovemarks. These include IKEA, Singapore Airlines, Twinings, BBC, Snaidero, and Campbell's. In order for the Lovemark brand strategy to be integrated into marketing planning, it must have some robust metrics. A recent attempt to add metrics to lovemarks can be seen in a *Journal of Advertising Research* article by Pawle and Cooper (2006). The authors developed a measure for emotion that combines qualitative analyses with quantitative measurement. They develop a grid for measuring the level of love on one axis and the level of respect on the other (see Figure 6.5). They developed scales for measuring emotional, social, cultural, and functional relationships between consumers and brands, and combined these with qualitative projective techniques to gain insight into

6.5 Lovemarks Measurement Matrix

Source: John Pawle and Peter Cooper (2006), 'Measuring Emotion—Lovemarks, the Future Beyond Brands', *Journal of Advertising Research* (March), pp. 38–48.

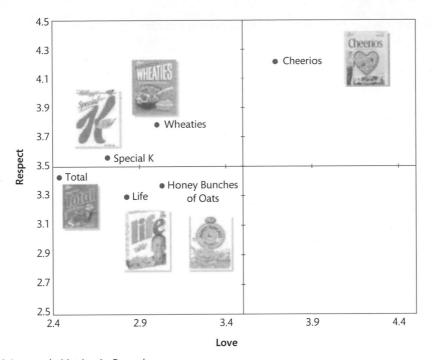

6.6 Lovemarks Metrics: An Example

Source: John Pawle and Peter Cooper (2006), 'Measuring Emotion–Lovemarks, the Future Beyond Brands', *Journal of Advertising Research* (March), pp. 38–48.

emotional relationships. An example of the application of these techniques can be seen in Figure 6.6, which indicates the results of their assessment of the US cereals market.

From their analysis, the only lovemark found was for Cheerios. This is extremely valuable and promising research. One key contention the authors make, which is supported by Roberts, is that decisions are either rationally or emotionally made and that over time functional benefits which are rationally appealing are getting narrower and narrower and emotional benefits must then take over. The way for companies to win over the consumer is to create an approach which makes the emotional connection and builds a strong emotional bond.

The latest thinking: neuromarketing and sensory branding

A great deal of interest has been generated recently around **neuromarketing**, which links neuromapping and brain function to consumer perceptions, reactions, and brand choice. Developed at Harvard University in 1990, neuromarketing involves examination of mental states and reactions to marketing stimuli (Sreedevi et al., 2013). Neuromarketing has its foundation in what is called the meme, a unit of information stored in the brain which can be used to quickly influence a particular product choice. The idea is to understand the best mechanisms for utilizing these influencers to create the most positive image and experience. A new approach to branding that involves neuromarketing is what is called **sensory branding**. It seeks to connect the brand to the customer's senses in such a way that a lasting emotional connection is built between the customer and the brand. The idea is to use the senses to influence consumer behaviour. The more senses that can be brought into the brand experience, the stronger the bond that will be forged emotionally between the consumer and the brand. Sensory branding makes use of brain imaging studies to probe the interplay between the mind and memory, and companies are beginning to use brain scans to see how consumers will react to various types of sensory stimuli and what the effect will be on brand image and preference. Promising new work is being done with the addition of smells to the brand stimuli to help create a more profound brand experience. Certain media allow more effectively for smell and touch than others, especially magazine advertising where scratch and sniff and textural experiencing might be easily accessible. Other interesting avenues involve associating brands with the kinds of scents and smells that might trigger powerful and positive nostalgic experiences, thereby adding the additional emotional warmth triggered by the connections to past experiences. A great deal more work needs doing here, but the study of brain physiology and the triggering of emotions through a multi-sensory marketing strategy offer exciting possibilities for brand managers.

Conclusion

Strategic brand management requires an understanding not only of brand costs and profitability, but also consumer perceptions of brand meaning, image, and value. Tactical brand decisions predicated upon cost savings and increased efficiencies must never be attempted without a clear understanding of the implications of how those decisions may be perceived by consumers, as brand perceptual inconsistencies may seriously undermine brand value and long-term brand equity. The company that regularly reassesses its brand equity and monitors its brand image across a variety of platforms will be in a better position to maintain its relevance with its target markets and ensure not only its long-term brand survival, but also its profitability and market leadership.

Summary

A brand is a complex entity that serves as a product and/or company identifier and provides utility for both buyers and sellers. A brand establishes important associations in the minds of target consumers, and these associations facilitate the building of a brand identity, meaning, and value. Customer perceptions of brand are an integral part of brand management and must be carefully examined, and brand refinements undertaken, to maintain relevance to the consumer. Brand managers must be able to undertake thorough brand audits to understand what the brand truly means and how it is valued, not only by the target customer, but also by the firm's management. Brand managers must constantly look for ways to improve brand efficiency and effectiveness, but must also guard against making decisions that can confuse their loyal customers and undermine the brand relationships that have been built. Successful brand managers treat brands as valuable firm assets that require constant nurturing.

Key terms

- **Advertising turnover:** a measure of the relationship between advertising expenditures and brand value. This measure reflects how effectively the firm has converted advertising expenditures into brand value. Advertising turnover is calculated by dividing brand value by advertising expenditures on a year-by-year basis and examining trends.

- **Brand:** a name, symbol, word, sign, design or combination that differentiates one or more offerings of a seller or group of sellers from the competition.

- **Brand architecture:** a complex structure of brands in a brand portfolio with a variety of different types of brand roles and relationships. The idea is that this structure is analogous to the complex structures designed by an architect.

- **Brand audit:** a comprehensive examination of the various sources of brand equity from the perspective of the company as well as the consumer.

- **Brand equity:** a set of assets (as well as liabilities) connected to the name and symbols of the brand that adds to (or detracts from) the value of the product or service to a company and/or that company's customers.

- **Brand idea:** the basic concept or meaning behind the brand. It conveys in a succinct way the nature of the brand, and it serves as the focal point for all aspects of corporate branding strategy.

- **Brand identity:** at its most basic level, the brand has a core identity, which is its essence and which remains constant, and an extended identity, which focuses on a series of psychological and physical aspects that give it nuance and texture.

- **Brand leveraging:** where the company uses the name recognition that accompanies a strong brand to increase potential sales and profits by attaching the name to other company offerings.

- **Brand personality:** the embodiment of the personality traits of the consumer in the brand itself.

- **Brand ROI:** An ROI calculation that focuses on the brand where the normal formula (sales/investment × net income/sales) is modified with brand sales substituted for sales and brand value for investment.

- **Brand story:** the brand message derived from the brand idea which should be conveyed consistently in all communications and tactical decisions made with regard to the brand.

- **Cannibalization:** where the addition of a new brand does not increase the overall sales but shifts them among a broader range of brands, which would be unprofitable for the firm.

- **Co-branding:** the bringing together of two separate company brands to be marketed together to create a new joint offering with additional value for the customer.

- **CoolBrands:** a list of the top brands as developed by the Superbrands Organization that are judged by a wide range of consumers to be stylish, innovative, original, authentic, desirable, and unique.

- **Lovemark:** a move beyond branding to where the name becomes a symbol of love to the consumer. The key is that the name triggers an emotional attachment that transcends reason.

- **Neuromarketing:** linking of neuromapping and brain function to consumer perceptions, reactions, and brand choice, involving examination of mental states and reactions to marketing stimuli.
- **Sensory branding:** connecting the brand to the customer's senses in such a way that a lasting emotional connection is built between the customer and the brand.

Discussion questions

1. What are the various benefits provided for both buyers and sellers through the use of branding?
2. What is brand identity, and why is it so important for effective strategic brand management?
3. How does the brand manager assess brand value?
4. What is brand leveraging, and what are the forces driving its use?
5. What are the benefits that can be achieved through brand consolidation?
6. What are advertising turnover, brand ROI, and brand health, and how are they helpful for strategic brand managers?
7. What is a brand audit, and why is it vital for brand revitalization?
8. How would a brand manager attempt to develop a brand personality, and how can this lead to the creation of a competitive advantage?
9. What is a lovemark, and how does it differ from a brand?
10. What makes a brand cool, and why does it matter?
11. Why should a brand manager consider simplifying the brand, and how can this be accomplished?
12. What is the brand wheel, and how can it be used by brand managers for overall assessment of the brand?
13. How can social media affect brands, and how can they be properly incorporated into a brand strategy?
14. What is sensory branding, and why is this important for brand managers?

Online resource centre

 Visit the Online Resource Centre for this book for lots of interesting additional material at: <www.oxfordtextbooks.co.uk/orc/west3e/>

References and further reading

Aaker, David A. (1991), *Managing Brand Equity* (New York: Free Press).

Aaker, David A. (1996a), *Building Strong Brands* (New York: Free Press).

Aaker, David A. (1996b), 'Measuring Brand Equity Across Products and Markets', *California Management Review*, 38 (3), pp. 102–20.

Aaker, David A. (1997), 'Should You Take Your Brand to Where the Action Is?', *Harvard Business Review*, 75, September-October, pp. 135–43.

Aaker, David A. (2004), *Brand Portfolio Strategy: Creative Relevance, Differentiation, Energy, Leverage, and Clarity* (New York: Free Press).

Aaker, David A. and Erich Joachimsthaler (2000), 'The Brand Relationship Spectrum: The Key to the Brand Architecture Challenge', *California Management Review*, 42 (4), pp. 8–23.

Abratt, Russell and Patience Motlana (2002), 'Managing Co-Branding Strategies: Global Brands into Local Markets', *Business Horizons*, September-October, pp. 43–50.

Barwise, Patrick and Sean Meehan (2010), 'The One Thing You Must Get Right When Building a Brand', *Harvard Business Review*, 88, December, pp. 80–4.

Berg, Julie Dexter, John M. Matthews, and Constance M. O'Hare (2007), 'Measuring Brand Health to Improve Top-Line Growth', *MIT Sloan Management Review*, 48, Fall, pp. 61–8.

Berthon, Pierre, James M. Hulbert, and Leyland Pitt (1999), 'Brand Management Prognostications', *Sloan Management Review*, 40, Winter, pp. 53–65.

Court, David C., Mark G. Leiter, and Mark A. Loch (1999), 'Brand Leverage: Developing a Strong Company Brand', *McKinsey Quarterly*, No. 2, pp. 100–7.

Devlin, James (2003), 'Brand Architecture in Services: The Example of Retail Financial Services', *Journal of Marketing Management*, 19 (9/10), pp. 1043–66.

Edelman, David (2010), 'Branding in the Digital Age', *Harvard Business Review*, 88, December, pp. 62–9.

Edmundson, Gail, Paulo Prada, and Karen Nickel Anhalt (2003), 'Lexus: Still Looking for Traction in Europe', *Business Week* (17 November), p. 122.

Henderson, Terilyn A. and Elizabeth A. Mihas (2000), 'Building Retail Brands', *McKinsey Quarterly*, No. 3, pp. 110–17.

Herremans, Irene M., John K. Ryans Jr, and Raj Aggarwal (2000), 'Linking Advertising and Brand Value', *Business Horizons*, May-June, pp. 19–26.

Interbrand, *Top Global Brands by Value for 2012*, Interbrand Organization.

Keller, Kevin Lane (1999), 'Managing Brands for the Long Run', *California Management Review*, 41 (3), pp. 102–24.

Keller, Kevin Lane (2000), 'The Brand Report Card', *Harvard Business Review*, 78, January-February, pp. 3–10.

Keller, Kevin Lane (2013) 'Kevin Lane Keller Speaks about Brand Marketing', *SERI Quarterly*, July, pp. 79–82, <www.seriquarterly.com>.

Keller, Kevin Lane and Donald Lehmann (2006), 'Brands and Branding: Research Findings and Future Priorities', *Marketing Science*, 25 (6), pp. 740–59.

Knudsen, Trond Riiber, Lars Finskud, Richard Tornblom, and Egil Hogna (1997), 'Brand Consolidation Makes a Lot of Economic Sense: But Only One in Five Attempts Succeeds', *McKinsey Quarterly*, No. 4, pp. 189–94.

Lane, Vicki R. (1998), 'Brand Leverage Power: The Critical Role of Brand Balance', *Business Horizons*, January-February, pp. 75–84.

McWilliam, Gil (2000), 'Building Stronger Brands through Online Communities', *MIT Sloan Management Review*, 41 (3), pp. 43–54.

Malhotra, Arvind, Claudia Kubowicz Malhotra, and Alan See (2013), 'How to Create Brand Engagement on Facebook', *MIT Sloan Management Review*, 54 (2), pp. 18–20.

Papasolomou, I. and D. Varonis (2006) 'Building Corporate Branding through Internal Marketing: The Case of the UK Banking Industry', *Journal of Product and Brand Management*, 15 (1), pp. 37–47.

Pawle, John and Peter Cooper (2006), 'Measuring Emotion—Lovemarks, the Future Beyond Brands', *Journal of Advertising Research*, March, pp. 38–48.

Petromilli, Michael, Dan Morrison, and Michael Millon (2002), 'Brand Architecture: Building Brand Portfolio Value', *Strategy & Leadership*, 30 (5), pp. 22–9.

Prince, Melvin and Mark Davies (2002) 'Co-Branding Partners: What Do They See in Each Other?', *Business Horizons*, September-October, pp. 51–5.

Rao, Akshay R. and Robert W. Ruekert (1994), 'Brand Alliances as Signals of Product Quality', *Sloan Management Review*, Fall, pp. 87–97.

Roberts, Kevin (2004), *Lovemarks: The Future Beyond Brands*, (New York Powerhouse Books).

Roberts, Kevin (2006), *The Lovemarks Effect: Winning in the Consumer Revolution* (New York: Powerhouse Books).

Simonin, B.L. and J.A. Ruth (1998) 'Is a Company Known by the Company it Keeps? Assessing the Spillover Effects of Brand Alliances on Consumer Brand Attitudes', *Journal of Marketing Research*, 35 (2), pp. 30–42.

Spenner, Patrick (2010), 'Why You Need a New-Media "Ringmaster"', *Harvard Business Review*, 88, December, pp. 78–9.

Sreedevi, V., K. V. Jayasree, and P. Lovelin Auguskani (2013), 'NeuroMarketing—An Effective Marketing Strategy', *International Journal of Marketing and Technology*, 3 (6), pp. 63–70.

Superbrands (2012), *The Top CoolBrands of 2012*, Superbrands Organization.

Vishwanath, Vijay and Jonathan Mark (1997), 'Your Brand's Best Strategy', *Harvard Business Review*, 75, May-June, pp. 123–9.

Ward, Scott, Larry Light, and Jonathan Goldstine (1999), 'What High-Tech Managers Need to Know About Brands', *Harvard Business Review*, 77 (4), pp. 85–96.

 End of Chapter 6 case study   IKEA: global brand perspectives

> At IKEA our vision is to create a better everyday life for the many people. Our business idea supports this vision by offering a wide range of well-designed, functional home furnishing products at prices so low that as many people as possible will be able to afford them.

Most of the international companies that seek global expansion face rising business management costs and decreasing growth rate due to a highly diverse global market. IKEA has, however, turned complicated enterprise management into simple principles: design products in accordance with consumption demand, spare no efforts in reducing costs to create low prices, create a healthy global supply chain and experiencing-style point of sale terminals. Even with this innovative approach IKEA is facing many challenges regarding the consumer perspective towards the brand as it attempts to expand its global presence. The big question is what can IKEA do to overcome its present 'weaknesses' and obtain a stronger position on the international markets. Given the current competition in the furniture market, IKEA needs to find the way to differentiate itself once again by adapting its marketing strategies to a cross-cultural consumer.

IKEA: the company

Background

IKEA is a home products company that is perhaps best known for selling ready-to-assemble, simplistic and stylish furniture such as beds, chairs, desks and bookshelves, appliances, kitchen cabinets, and home accessories.

Ingvar Kamprad founded the company in 1943 with money his father gave him for succeeding in his studies. The store began by selling pens, wallets, picture frames, table runners, watches, jewelry, and nylon stockings. By October 2011, IKEA had expanded to 332 stores in 38 countries (For a comprehensive history of IKEA's evolution see <http://www.ikea.com/ms/en_US/about_ikea/the_ikea_way/history/>).

IKEA follows the belief that to get quality products at an affordable price level, you have to 'do it yourself'. Its primary target is the general mass of the public, and its strategy is to select some of the critical needs of this group and hone its resources to perform exceptionally well in fulfilling those critical needs. IKEA has built its success by focusing its resources on what's important for the customer as well as constructing a strong reliable brand. Its clear focus is on product quality, price, display setting, product trial, and the canteen.

IKEA successfully markets its furniture as being cost-competitive due to technologies such as 'flat pack' which is considered unique compared with how other furniture retailers ship their products. As an indirect marketing strategy, IKEA is using the overall shopping experience in which they provide pencils, measuring tapes, store guides, catalogues, shopping carts, bags, and strollers to assist the consumer.

This retailer stands out because of its obsession with lifestyle; anyone can purchase almost anything they need for their home from an IKEA store. Mintel's brand research shows that IKEA is a brand which has strong value connotations and also a strong reputation for innovation. Their humorous and quirky marketing has also led consumers to perceive it to be a vibrant, fun, and trend-setting brand. IKEA is considered by its customers as a brand which can be trusted and one that differentiates its products in order to satisfy all of its actual and potential consumers.

The IKEA purchase experience

The IKEA stores are very well designed and provide a unique experience, even though they are generally identical. This increased level of familiarity makes shopping at IKEA really easy. Another characteristic of IKEA is the one-way direction through the store; arrows on the floor indicate that you can move only in a planned and organized manner. As you progress through the first floor of the store, you realize that everything is placed in a context: dining room, living room, kitchens, exactly as they would be placed in the customers' homes.

The two levels of each IKEA shop can be differentiated: the first level is for those who know what they are looking for; the second is for those not entirely certain about what they need.

One way that IKEA stores differ from their competitors is the self-service type atmosphere, but you're not alone. People are there to help you and answer questions, but not to pressure you into a sale.

IKEA around the globe

Europe

In recent decades IKEA has become one of the leaders in the European furniture and home-retailing market, dominating through competitive prices achieved mainly by immense economies of scale. Their products attract a wide range of consumers, but especially those who furnish their first home. The business concentrates its selling on mass-produced flat-pack furniture whilst maintaining an edge in design associated with its Scandinavian roots. The European operations represent more than 75 per cent of the overall business. The problems IKEA faces in the European market are not customer-related any more, so the company goal at this point is to increase the brand visibility.

United States

IKEA opened its first store in 1985 and since then has grown to 38 stores in the United States and continues to plan openings in strategic locations. Within the American market IKEA competes with brands such as Pottery Barn, Sears, J.C. Penney, and Ashley Furniture. IKEA considers itself a high quality/low cost provider, a critical aspect when breaking into the US market which still remains part of IKEA's current marketing strategy.

IKEA has had a few problems with their integration into the US market mainly due to a lack of market research. Their products are in metric units which cause issues with US designed homes that are built around imperial units. Also, European serving sizes are smaller than the typical US consumer is accustomed to.

IKEA's US consumers realize very fast that almost everything they purchase from the store will require some assembly; however, a common complaint is the amount of time spent assembling the furniture. Even so, most US consumers see the value in the IKEA brand in spite of the assembly required and European design style.

China

IKEA entered the Chinese market in 1998. The company currently operates just ten stores in the country, with the first two in the cities of Shanghai and Beijing. IKEA has plans to open three new stores in 2013, despite the negative economic outlook on the horizon.

Owing to the rapid economic growth of China, home ownership has increased exponentially in the last 15 years. Many new owners don't have a good understanding of how to furnish or decorate a home, so IKEA educates consumers by presenting its unique home furnishings in Western-style showrooms that model bedrooms, dining rooms, and living rooms.

The low price of IKEA household goods has not been a factor in this market, and customers are confined to some middle-class consumers even though IKEA has made efforts to lower prices year by year. The majority of visitors go to its stores only to buy small household goods or experience the shopping atmosphere. The Chinese consumer wants to buy unique designs and is willing to pay higher prices; they believe that if too many people purchase the same IKEA furnishings, then they are not considered as special anymore.

India

IKEA is currently planning the eventual building of 25 stores in India with a short-term goal of ten stores over the next decade. The task of expansion into the country has proved somewhat difficult due to the perfect dichotomy of its population when it comes to attitudes about foreign retailers. The younger generation embraces foreign retail while the older generation remains obstinate in its stance against outsiders who threaten the culture of the 'mom-and-pop' shops across the country. In addition, IKEA faces challenges breaking into India because of government policies designed to make it difficult for the entry of foreign retailers.

Promotion

The IKEA catalogue

The first IKEA catalogue was published in 1951 and has been printed annually ever since, being the company's primary marketing tool. The 2013 catalogue will be shipped all over the world with a projected 200 million copies in 62 different versions. In most versions of the catalogue the greater part is identical, but the images are revised to suit the preferences of the specific local market.

Recently IKEA experienced criticism regarding the catalogue published for the Saudi market, specifically that no images of women were used (Figure C6.1). IKEA has issued an apology for this adaptation stating, 'We should have reacted and realized that excluding women from the Saudi Arabian version of the catalogue is in conflict with the IKEA Group values'.

Despite the recent hiccup in the IKEA catalogue, the exciting development of 2014 is the IKEA Catalogue App, available for all Apple devices (iPhone, iPod, and iPad) and Android, that will allow customers to interact with the publication (Figure C6.2). Users will be able to view additional photos, videos, and 3D models by scanning pages in the printed catalogue where they see the smartphone icon.

Strategic campaigns

In addition to the annual catalogue, IKEA is now leveraging strategic alliances and product placement agreements to further advertise their products and change consumer perceptions.

'Fix This Kitchen' is an A&E TV series where home chefs have their kitchens upgraded and remodelled with IKEA products. The show seems to resonate in a favourable way; 60 per cent of viewers believe that 'IKEA offers high-quality materials', and 'two of three viewers said that they would visit IKEA if they were considering a kitchen renovation'.

Another strategic development is the recently launched Share Space, which allows people to upload photos of rooms they've decorated and to tag the IKEA products used, as well as view the rooms that other users have uploaded and posted. Share Space also includes a design blog where users can interact with IKEA designers and read their posts on a variety of design-related topics.

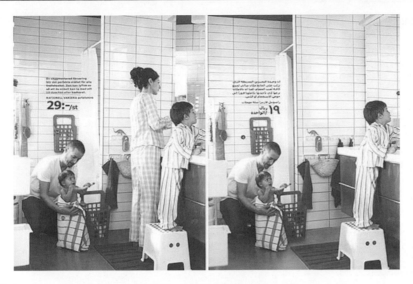

C6.1 Catalogue Images: Standard Version versus Saudi Version

Source: Anna Molin (2012), 'IKEA Regrets Cutting women from Saudi Ad', *Wall Street Journal*, 1 October.

Leveraging creativity

IKEA is also leveraging their famous creativity when it comes to experiential and guerilla marketing. They have developed numerous campaigns that bring the brand to life in non-traditional ways. Earlier, in 2012, IKEA launched 'The IKEA Apartment—54 Square-Metre Ideas to Life' in Paris—a campaign meant to illustrate the use of their products in particularly small living spaces. Five small 'apartments' were constructed in a Paris subway station open for the public to view, furnished with IKEA products. They then brought in volunteers to live in the apartments for one week, showcasing the effectiveness, flexibility, and utility of the IKEA products in such tight quarters (Figure C6.3).

C6.2 IKEA Catalogue Apps

Source: iTunes

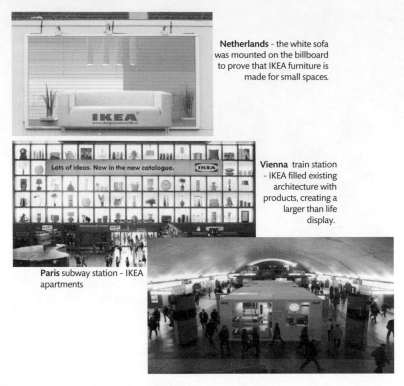

Netherlands - the white sofa was mounted on the billboard to prove that IKEA furniture is made for small spaces.

Vienna train station - IKEA filled existing architecture with products, creating a larger than life display.

Paris subway station - IKEA apartments

C6.3 IKEA Guerilla Marketing Campaigns

Brand extension possibilities

Inter IKEA Group is the company that owns the IKEA intellectual property rights under which all IKEA franchises operate. The overall purpose of the Group is to secure independence and longevity, and through Inter IKEA Systems B.V. to control, safeguard, and develop the IKEA Concept. 'We seek to contribute to the IKEA vision "to create a better everyday life for the many people"'.

The Property Division (Inter IKEA Group Divisions, <http://inter.ikea.com/en/divisions/decentralised-operation/>) recently announced that it is planning to open 100 hotels all across Europe, initial focus being on two hotels in Germany with planned opening in 2014. Following these, other locations will include Belgium, the Netherlands, the Nordic countries, Britain, and Poland. The hotels will be designed and built around IKEA's philosophy of good quality at a reasonable price, but they will not trade under IKEA's name or brand the furniture. According to Harald Muller, a business development manager of Inter IKEA Group Property Division, the hotels will have a Scandinavian feel as the interiors will be made by Nordic designers: 'Aside from that, guests won't really recognize IKEA in it at all'. Muller further commented 'It's a continuation of our normal investment activities in real estate'.

Discussion questions

1. IKEA continues to grow and expand across the globe. Compare Hofstede's dimensions of culture measurements (Figure C6.4) and suggest how IKEA can adapt their marketing strategy to various cultures. What further suggestions do you have for the United States, China, and India?

2. Using the Multi-Attribute Attitude Model (MAAM), construct the attitude functions towards IKEA and another three competitors from the market and compare the results obtained. What are the

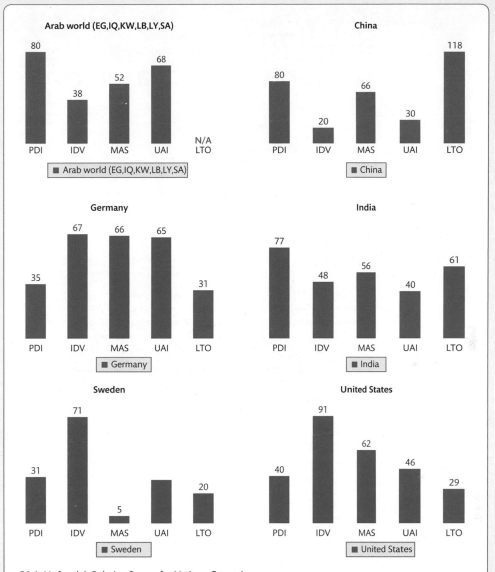

C6.4 Hofstede's Relative Scores for Various Countries

Source: http://geert-hofstede.com/

differences/similarities between the four brands? How can IKEA overcome its weaknesses given the results of the model? In order to construct your MAAM use at least five criteria that you consider to be the most important ones and a +/−1 to +/−9 scale for your attribute ratings.

3. Currently, the IKEA advertising strategy is mainly based on their catalogue and strategic campaigns. What are the recurrent motives that can be identified from the IKEA promotion strategies?

4. Provide and discuss a few possible brand extensions which IKEA might want to consider. Will launching low budget hotels in Europe extend or dilute IKEA's brand? Why? Would low budget hotels, similar to what is planned in Europe, work in the United States?

This case was prepared by Professor Georgiana Graciun at the University of Pittsburgh together with four students, Justin Ledger, Melanie Olar, Gabriela Sava, and Mike Thompson.

Relational and sustainability strategies

Learning Objectives

1. Understand the importance of developing relationships with customers.

2. Discover ways in which marketers can assess customer desirability and rank customers in terms of customer value to the firm.

3. Be able to identify the various ways in which marketers build loyalty with customers.

4. Understand the importance of customer relationship management systems and grasp the differences between CRM for consumer marketers (B2C) and industrial marketers (B2B).

5. Be aware of various approaches to the building of customer databases with which to strategically address customer relationship building strategies while also explaining the potential pitfalls inherent in ill-designed and ill-conceived data mining approaches and relationship management systems.

6. Be able to explain the strategies that will help the firm to create long-term relationships with its customers which can create competitive advantage and can be sustained.

Chapter at a Glance

I. Introduction

1 Overview and strategy blueprint
2 Marketing strategy: analysis and perspectives

II. Where are we now?

3 Environmental and internal analysis: market information and intelligence

III. Where do we want to be?

4 Strategic marketing decisions, choices, and mistakes
5 Segmentation, targeting, and positioning strategies
6 Branding strategies
7 **Relational and sustainability strategies**

V. Did we get there?

14 Strategy implementation, control, and metrics

IV. How will we get there?

8 Product innovation and development strategies
9 Service marketing strategies
10 Pricing and distribution strategies
11 Marketing communications strategies
12 International marketing strategy
13 Social and ethical strategies

 Case study: Faux relationships—companies that go through the motions to build customer relationships only hurt themselves in the long run

During the growth stages of life cycles, firms are often able to build revenues merely by offering their products or services. But it requires a major change of corporate thinking when things begin to slow down as maturity stages take over. Intense competition forces companies to stand out from the crowd, and one way that companies hope to do this is by opening up to customers and becoming their 'friends'. They want to really understand their customers and cater to them and build meaningful relationships, but this is not as easy as it sounds because it means making major changes in how customers are communicated with and personally handled. Many companies facing this change in orientation try to do it by asking their service personnel to be more friendly and outgoing in their dealings with customers, but they try to handle the situation with a minimum of expense and as little change trauma as possible. The problem is that trying to cater to relationships with customers requires different types of resource commitments on the part of the companies involved. Service providers have had more trouble with this issue than product manufacturers since the service involves an experience which is provided for the customer by the service personnel, and the best way to build repeat purchase behaviour is to create an experience that the consumer believes is what they were looking for and want to experience again. Many service providers, especially banks and health-care providers, have been slow to pick up on the subtleties of personality compatibility and relationship maintenance programmes. This requires looking at your employees in a different way and hiring for different sets of skills and capabilities. The banking industry in the United States provides an excellent window into the growing pains and strategic mistakes that can be made by industries being forced to change their marketing strategic focus.

During the early period of modern banking, employees were hired who went through training programmes to move into managerial positions. Lending officers would be hired and trained in company policies regarding loans and risk management, and they would slowly move up the seniority ladder and find ways into management responsibility. Branch management programmes would focus on putting all hirees into teller positions to learn the procedures involved and then move them into management positions after proving themselves as tellers. What was clearly not understood was that these tellers were the front line of personnel dealing with customers on a daily basis, and how they treated the customer would have a major impact on how the customer felt about that bank. These employees really were the bank, and if they did not have pleasant dealings with customers, customers would not develop good feelings about using the bank. With greater intensity of competition, customers end up with a great deal of choice, which means that they do not have to continue dealing with poor service provision for very long.

The real issue here is that personnel being put into the front line of customer-facing positions were not being hired to be tellers as a career end goal, so people being kept in teller positions were actually not achieving their desired positions as branch managers and were often frustrated by this. So they might take it out daily on the customer. As one can readily see, this is an unacceptable way to advance, but it is difficult to shift to a customer orientation unless you hire people who have certain personality traits that make them more likely to be compatible with customers. If counter positions of this type have proper incentive systems and rewards and promotion possibilities, people who like the job and what it entails will open many new opportunities for creating positive impressions and pleasant service experiences.

For services businesses, going through the motions of becoming more 'friendly' to customers will never be sufficient. These service firms must reorient themselves to become the providers of choice because the customer prefers them for the nature of the service experience they provide for their customers. There is nothing more frustrating than entering a bank or health-care facility or beauty parlour or restaurant where the personnel are merely acting out a friendly approach without emotional involvement. In banks a staff member may be asked to greet every new customer who comes in the door, but saying 'hello' does not, by itself, build relationships. This is obvious if the customer looks up to see who said hello and does not see anyone actually making eye contact. Just saying that you are customer oriented (maybe in your promotional materials) does not make it so. Unless the employees really like what they are doing and enjoy the relationships they are involved in, there will be no real warmth in that exchange, and the customer will quickly see through the charade. Being told to greet each and every customer does not make a relationship. Without an emotional bond being built, there really is no relationship involved.

Introduction

Marketing strategy has gone through a pronounced paradigm shift over the past decade as B2C companies have changed their focus from transaction-based to relationship-centred. This has occurred as companies have recognized that one-time purchases do not single-handedly keep companies in business. It is repeat purchases that are the key to success. The United States saw a number of industries during the 1960s and 1970s add significantly to their new business development capabilities, but what they did not realize was that the focus on new business development neglected the real lifeblood of the company, its loyal customers. Important accounts that are assumed to be a given are often taken for granted, and if all efforts are placed on the more fickle customers (who are also less profitable), then how much time is there left to spend paying attention to the needs of the loyal customers?

As telecommunications companies like AT&T analysed their marketing activities and assessed their customer make-up, they realize that a good portion of their marketing efforts and expenditures were aimed at the smaller and more problematic accounts. They were one of the earlier companies to realize that **the 80–20 rule** did have merit. This rule suggests that on average an industry can expect that 80 per cent of its revenues will come from 20 per cent of its customer base (for many industries it can be 90–20 or even 95–5). If one takes the time to carefully consider this ratio, the reciprocal suggests that 20 per cent of revenues then come from 80 per cent of the customer base. A more appropriate goal might be to spend 80 per cent of the time nurturing the relationships with that important 20 per cent of the customer base, leaving only the remaining 20 per cent of the time and effort devoted to the more problematic accounts. Support was empirically provided for this relationship by Frederick Reichheld in his 1996 book *The Loyalty Effect*, in which he reported that it is five times more costly to bring in a new customer than to keep an existing one.

Customer lifetime value (CLTV) has recently become a vital consideration for many companies as they recognize that happy customers are loyal customers who not only spread their satisfaction by word of mouth to friends, colleagues, and relatives, but also spend increasing amounts on the purchase of particular products/services over time (see also Chapter 14). CLTV is the present value of the future profits that will accrue from the customer's lifetime purchases. The company must attempt to measure future earnings from the customer as well as be able to subtract from those earnings the cost of acquiring and maintaining the relationship with the customer. The key issue is to determine CLTV for each individual customer or group of customers so that each group can be assessed to determine the proper investment necessary to make in each customer to build meaningful relationships and retain customers. This sets up an important future revenue stream that cannot be overlooked. General Motors Cadillac division has analysed CLTV, and it has determined that a Cadillac customer will spend approximately US$350,000 over their lifetime (Best, 2005). This would include both the purchase of automobiles and maintenance. One can see how problematic it can become to lose that customer early in their product purchase life cycle. Each lost customer represents hundreds of thousands of dollars of lost revenue. According to Best (2005), research in the US has shown that the acquisition of a new credit card customer costs the credit card company approximately $51 per customer. These new customers will generate an average company profit in the first year of $30; this escalates to $42 in the second year and will grow to $55 by the fifth year. The obvious goal should be to retain the customer since bringing in each new customer generates an initial loss each time.

Companies should be careful to make CLTV calculations based on realistic options, and Schoder (2007) suggests that the best way to do this involves a five-step process: (1) estimate the probability of purchase and dollar amounts expected to be spent for a set of customers using the RFM (recency, frequency, and monetary value) approach; (2) then calculate costs amassed per customer per period; (3) both the amounts generated in steps (1) and (2) should be used to estimate the profit contribution for each customer over the time horizon of interest; (4) then for each period the key will be to determine whether the expected future profit contribution will be negative; and finally (5) calculate the CLTV that includes the option value (i.e. the value of dropping the customer). The point is to assess by reasonable calculation what the savings might be if the customer were dropped at any particular period of time.

Relationship marketing in the B2C context

What is **relationship marketing?** It is the development of long-term and intimate relationships between buyers and sellers. It involves open communications and the ability to know the customer or client so well that changes in wants and needs can be anticipated before they become critical. This means that companies really have to communicate effectively and often with their customers or clients. The problem is that all customers are not equal. One of the best frameworks in which to discuss the nature of different customers is the loyalty ladder as envisioned by Adrian Payne (2000). Payne's ladder (see Figure 7.1) includes the following designations from least to most desirable: suspects, prospects, customers, clients (hostages/ mercenaries/terrorists), supporters, advocates, and partners. This framework presents an effective mechanism for discussing relevant costs and communications strategies.

Suspects

Suspects are individuals who are not yet even mildly warm leads for the selling company. They are possibly prospects, but they are not yet interested in your products or services. These are probably not the kinds of individuals that companies should spend much time or effort to develop relationships with. There are some industries that simply do not lend themselves to customer or client relationships and retention. In the used-car industry, the fickle

7.1 Loyalty Ladder for B2C Marketers

Source: Adapted from M. Raphel (1980), 'Ad Techniques Move Customers up the Loyalty Ladder', *Bank Marketing*, 12 (11 November), pp. 37–8.

nature of these customers would argue against spending time and effort building rapport and friendship since they will likely go where they get the lowest price in future transactions. The cost would most certainly outweigh the benefits. The firm must develop some kind of mechanism to determine whether the suspect is worth spending time with. One tried and true approach is the use of **customer equity** (Blattberg and Deighton, 1996).

Customer equity

From a financial standpoint, marketing budget setting becomes the job of balancing what is spent on customer or client acquisition with what is spent on retention. This has been referred to as the customer equity test (Blattberg and Deighton, 1996), and in order to estimate this amount, a firm needs first to measure each customer's expected contribution to offsetting the company's fixed costs over their expected lifetime. Then, expected contributions to net present value are discounted at the rate set by the company as its target rate of return for any marketing investments, and finally the company adds together all of the discounted expected contributions across all of the company's current customers. The authors suggest that it is quite similar to assessing the value of a real estate portfolio.

    An excellent overview of the relationship process was proposed by Slater et al. (2009) in a recent issue of *Marketing Management* magazine. The process is shown in Figure 7.2. The key steps in the process are as follows: (1) **identify high potential customers or clients**, (2) **develop a customer acquisition strategy**. There are four generic acquisition strategies that should help balance investment with returns: (a) full throttle or low

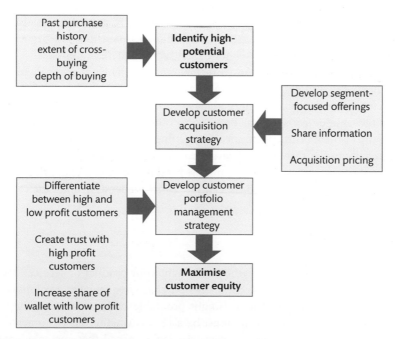

7.2 The Relationship Marketing Process

Source: Reprinted with permission from *Marketing Management*, published by the American Marketing Association, Stanley F. Slater, Jakki J. Mohr, and Sanjit Sengupta , 2009 (January/February), pp. 37– 44.

risk/high return; (b) slingshot or high risk/high return; (c) pay as you go or low risk/ low return; and (d) divest/restructure or high risk/low return). Then (3) **develop the customer portfolio management strategy**, and (4) **maximize customer equity** (Blattberg et al., 2001).

Gupta et al. (2004) show that profitability can be found in relationship building with their demonstration that a 1 per cent increase in customer retention produces a 3–7 per cent increase in profitability. This, of course, has shifted many companies to managing their firms as a portfolio of customers or clients rather than as a portfolio of different products/services. The problem, however, is that very few companies have a systematic way of identifying the best customers for relationship building and of developing effective customer or client acquisition and retention strategies (Slater et al., 2009).

From the customer equity standpoint, the suspect is probably a poor candidate for the time and effort that would be required for acquisition, and there would be little guarantee of profitability.

Prospects

A better candidate would be found in the prospect. This is a warm lead, who has interest in your product but who has not yet made a purchase. Customer equity would probably be higher for the prospect than for the suspect. Interest is, however, not a guarantee of purchase, and the other question that should be asked is what the probability of purchase is. This is not a regular buyer of your products or services, and the problem is that the costs of acquiring and retaining the prospect may far outweigh their potential lifetime value. The old methods of adding product selection and/or cutting prices to attract prospects may be highly problematic, as adding new products/services adds to excessive inventory and cutting prices reduces margins and intensifies competition across sellers. This argues for greater focus or expertise to increase the likelihood of attracting interested prospects. If prospects are a major focal point for the company, direct marketing can help to reach them where they live. It also helps to have salespeople interact with prospects and get known and recognized. The reason for this is that relationships are based upon familiarity and trust. Spending too much time focusing on prospects as opposed to others higher on the loyalty ladder may be problematic as there is little assurance that getting them to buy will lead to a lifetime of loyalty, especially in the case of lower-level consumer products where customer or clients may be more deal and variety prone. Again, the need is to clearly identify the various levels of customers served by the firm and concentrate efforts depending upon the value of those different customers.

Customers

A customer, of course, is someone who has bought your product or service. The game is to try to enhance that individual or company's purchase frequency and volume over time, so that the customer becomes increasingly profitable and valuable to the company. The important question, which really must be asked, is whether all customers are 'good' customers. Many firms in the service industries have learned that customer interactions can be problematic. Service providers are finding that it is necessary to manage the service experience very carefully to ensure it meets the expectations of key customers. This requires that important customers do not interact with those who might negatively affect customer value perceptions. Imagine the restaurant that becomes an important setting for a romantic evening for an affluent couple when the maître d' brings a loud and hard-drinking group to a nearby table. Loud voices and interactions could certainly destroy the ambience for the romantic setting. The restaurant must understand who its important customers are and keep others from participating in the service who might harm the service quality perceptions of those key customers. This would mean turning some customers away. In the example above, however, it is not immediately clear who are the most important customers. The restaurant would have to have this clearly understood and handle things accordingly. If the loud and obnoxious group are regulars and spend £500 per month dining at that restaurant, they would be seen as potentially far more important than the romantic couple who come once a year and spend only £80.

This raises the question of how to deal with different and potentially incompatible consumers. Compatibility management is a concept from the services literature that is quickly gaining support for use in dealing with the mixing of different types of customers.

Compatibility management

Much depends on a thorough understanding of the target customers and spending patterns. This is referred to in the services literature as **compatibility management** and is an important consideration for service businesses where customer interactions can significantly affect the service experience. Some companies can adjust for different customers by using different pricing and different venues to keep incompatible customers from interacting with each other. Sporting events and concerts provide opportunities for wealthier patrons to separate themselves from others through differential pricing. Paying top prices allows closer access to the sports pitch or to the acts on the stage. The idea, of course, is to provide the best experiences for those who are desirable and keeping them happy.

What becomes particularly meaningful once the company has a viable customer base is to examine the variety of customers served and decide on a hierarchy of those customers. Especially in the B2C world of myriad customers, relationships with all customers might not be efficient or effective. If customer lifetime value (CLTV) can be calculated for each relevant customer group, then the profitability of each customer group can be assessed. As a result, one particularly relevant approach to ranking or prioritizing customers is based upon the impact that that specific group of customers has on firm profitability. The **customer profitability pyramid** has also gained wide acceptability (Zeithaml et al., 2001).

Customer profitability pyramid

Zeithaml et al. (2001) proposed the creation of a customer pyramid based upon profitability for firms trying to improve long-term performance. The argument is that ranking based upon profitability has become a high priority, especially for service firms like FedEx, Bank of America, The Limited, Hallmark, and GE Capital Corporation. This would also have value for consumer and industrial products companies. This is a natural extension beyond segmentation that was covered in Chapter 5. The authors suggest that profitability ranking allows the company to manage the customer mix for maximum profitability. The firm can build stronger associations between service quality and profitability as well as provide an effective tool for optimal resource allocation. The point is to match up customized services and products to customer utility, ultimately producing greater customer value, which in turn would lead to higher profits. The authors suggest that there are four necessary conditions that must be met to allow the use of customer tiers. First of all, **profitability tiers must vary and have identifiable profiles**. Profile descriptions will lead marketers to identify optimal marketing activities to reach different tiers. Secondly, **customers in different tiers must view service quality differently**. Different customer expectations of service quality allow the company to develop optimal bundles of attributes to offer the various tiers. Thirdly, **different factors must drive customer acquisition and increases in purchase volume**. As a result, the company can acquire new customers and stay with them as they move to higher profit tiers over time. They can meet perceptual service quality expectations in different ways as the customer moves to subsequently higher tiers. The point is to get the customer early and stay with them as they move up. Lastly, **improvements in service quality should have different profit impacts for different customer tiers**. Theoretically, higher tiers should see greater customer responses from improvements in perceived service quality in terms of new customer development, business volume, and the average profit level for each customer.

A customer pyramid with four different levels based upon gradation in metal values (Zethaml et al., 2001) proposes four tiers as follows (from the least to the most profitable): (1) the **Lead Tier**—the bottom of the pyramid—includes those customers who are costing the company money rather than bringing in any profits; (2) the **Iron Tier**—second from the bottom—provides volume for the company but does not buy enough to warrant any special treatment; (3) the **Gold Tier**—second from the top—volume is high but profits may be limited due to desire for price discounts; and (4) the **Platinum Tier**—the top of the pyramid—customers who are heavy users, loyal, profitable, and not price sensitive.

Using the alchemy analogy, the authors suggest that strategic relationship building can move customers into higher and more desirable tiers of the pyramid. So the authors suggest that **to turn gold customers into platinum customers** the following strategies are recommended: (1) become a full-service provider—if the customer can get everything they need from the firm, they will become better customers; (2) provide outsourcing—taking on something that the customer used to have to do for themselves; (3) increase brand impact through line extensions—tying additional complementary offerings in with the company's umbrella of offerings; (4) create structural bonds—providing customized services that utilize technology and can help the customer be more productive; and (5) offer service guarantees—making sure the customer is always satisfied by making it right.

In order **to turn iron customers into gold customers**, the following strategies are recommended: (1) reduce the customer's non-monetary costs—reduction of search costs; (2) add meaningful brand names—adding brands to the offering lines that are perceived to be better quality than the others normally carried; (3) become knowledgeable about the customer using technology—building databases that can add customer knowledge and pinpoint recommendations; (4) become knowledgeable about the customer by leveraging intermediaries—using dealers to gather information about the local needs of customers; (5) develop frequency programmes—the higher the use, the more accrued benefits for the customer; and (6) create strong recovery programmes—finding out when customers are disappointed and correcting the problem before losing them.

Finally, with lead-level customers, the authors suggest that a firm should only attempt to **move customers up from lead to iron if there is good future potential**. Otherwise, it might be best to send these customers on their way looking for a different provider. If there is strong potential, the authors suggest the following strategies: (1) raise prices—adding prices for services that customers previously received free; and (2) reduce costs—find less expensive ways to deal with these customers, such as remote automated sites.

One problem is that more research is needed connecting the profitability pyramid to CLTV. While there is usually strong support for the argument that higher levels of loyalty will be associated with greater customer lifetime value, there are still a few gaps in the research. In particular, it is not yet clear as to whether the advocate is any more profitable than the mercenary (client). More work is clearly needed.

Clients

Clients are regular customers. Customers become clients when they have some level of trust in the seller and believe the seller's offerings will be beneficial to them. This is the first development of a relationship between the buyer and seller; however, it is not necessarily a relationship that will last forever, and it may not be a relationship that remains mutually beneficial for both of the parties involved. Some clients might begin to feel as though they are **hostages** to the seller due to some leverage the seller utilizes over them (Paine, 2000). The loss of a feeling of mutual benefit raises questions about the life expectancy of that relationship, and the client may look for any opportunity to jump to another seller that appears. For a relationship to properly exist, there should be mutual benefits that are achieved by the parties to the relationship.

Another type of problematic client is the **mercenary**. This type is one that appears to have loyalty to the relationship, but may hold the tenuousness of that relationship over the seller's head to maintain some kind of leverage over the seller. The idea is that this kind of client is not involved in a meaningful relationship and, again, one-sidedness in a relationship creates instability. The issue with the mercenary is that they can easily be attracted by the 'better deal' from someone else in the industry.

The other type of client that becomes a serious problem for the seller is the **terrorist**. Now the client is in a position to hold the company as a hostage rather than the reverse situation. What kind of client becomes a terrorist? An unsatisfied client! When companies can make unhappy customers pleased, they can raise their loyalty level significantly over what it was before the complaint. In the services literature this is known as the recovery paradox. The customer who has a problem but is handled successfully by the company to alleviate that problem becomes even more committed to the relationship than they were before the problem occurred. The point to be made here is that even your best customers might at one time become unhappy with you for whatever reason. The key is to open the doors of true communication with your good customers to ensure that they are remaining satisfied with the relationship. A client who has a problem which is not immediately rectified stands the chance of becoming a severe problem. One unhappy client can tell anywhere from seven to eleven others about their dissatisfaction, not only negatively affecting other existing clients, but also discouraging others from becoming new clients (Pruden, 1995). Ritson (2003) found in a study of disgruntled US consumers that dissatisfied customers took steps to undermine the company involved by creating 'symbols of defiance' out of company logos. Examples include Shell's logo being changed to Hell, and Greenpeace's modification which changed Esso to E$$O. These active detractors can wreak a certain amount of havoc on target companies.

Monitoring of client satisfaction becomes an important barometer for measuring the potential for changes in relationships so that proper corrective action can be taken to shore up the relationship. Of course the use of marketing for the sake of marketing is not necessarily a good way to handle this situation. As Pruden (1995) stated, relationship strategists must be careful not to let 'frequency marketing' take the place of 'aftermarketing'. Both of these can be considered as relationship marketing. **Frequency marketing** is a strategy aimed at identifying best customers, keeping them, and increasing their expenditures through the development of intimate long-term relationships (Pruden, 1995). On the surface this would appear to mirror relationship marketing; however, there is an important difference. Relationship marketing should be more like 'aftermarketing,' which focuses on the retention of more than just a small percentage of best customers. Aftermarketing involves long-term relationships being built in which the firm actively attempts to move customers up the loyalty ladder and tries to minimize the outflow of unhappy buyers. This may not be practicable for all businesses. While direct merchants can effectively utilize frequency marketing, aftermarketing is preferable for manufacturers of products and services who depend upon mass distribution (Pruden, 1995).

Is the customer always right?

A relevant question to raise here is whether the company should rush to coddle all clients who appear to have a problem. It is possible that a client's needs may have changed over time, and that the company is not able to cost-effectively cater to that client's new needs. In that situation, it may be preferable for the company to look at outsourcing that customer rather than catering to them in a way that might prove detrimental to other more profitable clients. The key is to continuously monitor the relationships to see what is happening. Some customers can be effectively re-energized while others cannot. The company is best served by realizing that some clients may no longer be as profitable and beneficial as they once were and in a positive way move them to another provider (with the hope of keeping them from becoming a terrorist). The idea is to help the customer remain satisfied while being moved to another supplier. The point is to make the transition as smooth and painless as possible.

What about unfair customers? An **unfair customer** is one who does not act in a manner in which decency, care for the welfare of others, and reasonableness are guiding principles (Berry and Seiders, 2007). These customers can hurt the company and its employees while not actually doing anything illegal. There are five particular types of problematic customer (Berry and Seiders, 2007): (1) **verbal abusers** who take their frustrations out on company employees in disrespectful and offensive ways, thereby presenting a problem not only for the service employee involved, but also for other customers in the vicinity hearing the complaints; (2) **blamers** who take aim not at the employees but rather at anything the company does and are particularly problematic in services contexts since as co-producers they take no share in the blame for any failures; (3) **rule breakers** who apply their own rules to the company and its employees rather than following the policies and procedures established by the company; (4) **opportunists,** out for their own gains by creating problems and demanding compensation for their difficulties; and (5) **returnaholics** who are part opportunists and part rule breakers, excessively creating problems so that they can continually return products.

How should the company deal with these unfair customers? Berry and Seiders suggest the following strategies for dealing with them. First they suggest that **the company should manage customers according to a standard of behaviour.** Companies should have environments for dealing with anyone in which respect is an integral part and managers will need to manage customers just as they manage employees. Secondly, **fair customers should not be penalized.** Unfair customers must be dealt with fairly but firmly in a system which is built around the fair and ethical majority. Thirdly, **managers need to plan for possible unfair situations involving unfair actions on the part of customers and be ready for them when they occur.** This involves training employees and managers systematically how to deal with inappropriate actions. Finally, **managers need to deal fairly and firmly with customers and not allow inappropriate actions to be rewarded.**

Managers should prepare themselves when assessing the potential for customer dissatisfaction by asking the following four questions (McGovern and Moon, 2007). (1) **Are the most profitable customers the ones who have the greatest reason to be dissatisfied with the company's performance?** If so, these customers are clearly not getting the appropriate level of value from the company's offerings. (2) **Does the company have rules that they want customers to break so that they can generate excess profits?** For example, having premiums associated with passing some procedural limit which will be important to establish. (3) **Does the company make it difficult for customers to follow the rules and do they help the customers to violate them?** If yes, this will lead to problems for customers that will grow over time. (4) **Does the company rely on legal contracts to keep customers from leaving?** This will also lead to problems.

Supporters

Supporters are those who buy everything you produce that they can use. But while they are supportive of your company and its products and services, and while they will spread good word-of-mouth for you, they will not necessarily be motivated to the level of an advocate. They will not go out of their way to recruit others to your company. You convert a client to a supporter through the provision of great service. The idea here is to start to find ways to reward clients for their purchases and loyalty to move them to supporters. The idea is to find ways to provide extra value and benefits for the buyer. In terms of communications at this point, the job of the marketer is to avoid the danger of over-promising. The customer has to have their expectations met—and, if possible, surpassed. Over-promising sets up the potential for disconfirmed expectations. Strategically, however, the profitability to the business of the supporter must not be exceeded by the cost of providing the extra value that motivates them to become more than clients.

Advocates

The advocate is a coveted position. It is the consumer who buys your products and services and actively recruits others to do the same. They are valuable commodities. These are the individuals that you particularly want to keep happy. One way to do that is with the kinds of incentives that loyalty schemes carry with them.

Loyalty schemes

Loyalty schemes are programmes that are established by companies to provide added value to the regular purchaser as opposed to the irregular customer. They provide increasing benefits for increasing levels of company loyalty. In the UK two loyalty schemes have been particularly successful. One is Tesco and its use of the Clubcard, and the other is the loyalty scheme created by Nectar, which is believed to boast the largest number of cardholders in the UK. The idea is to build up points or credits for purchases which allow the consumer to get rewards like discounts off a series of special products or announcements about new offerings that no others receive. Frequent flyer miles programmes for the airlines are also loyalty programmes, whereby travellers build up miles that can be used to upgrade classes of service or even for free airline tickets. There are a number of airlines and other organizations which offer their own credit cards that can build reward points which can be used every time a purchase is made using that credit card. These programmes are all designed to keep the customer satisfied and loyal and to entice them to increase their use of the company's products and services.

Loyalty schemes have their drawbacks as well (Brierley, 2012). Rewards may now actually be based on the wrong metrics. When the American Airlines programme was established back in 1981, the rewards were based upon the number of miles flown. This was a mistake. The problem is that the number of miles flown does not accurately reflect the price differences in actual fares. For example, 'Hilton Honors' bases rewards on the money being spent, which makes them more appealing to the travellers and hotel management. Another problem is that airline programmes have been rewarding future mileage travel perks for their past high mileage efforts. Many retailers are now rewarding scheme members who shop this month with rewards in the upcoming month (rather than on yearly bases) which generates repeat store visits. Brierley (2012) found one programme was seeing the redemption of rewards increase profits by almost US$100 million. A third problem is that rewards schemes often over-reward the top users while not doing much for lesser and yet still loyal customers. This relates to the 18–55 rule which states that the 18 per cent of customers that make up the second tier (rather than the 2 per cent who comprise the top tier) usually produce somewhere around 55 per cent of revenue.

The point is that in the airline industry the most rewarded group are the 2 per cent who constitute only 25 per cent of total revenue. It does not make sense to reward the top tier and make the majority of good customers feel less important. Good customers will grow in their usage over time and many will ultimately become elite users. A final point is that those who signed on early when the first schemes were created (back in the early 1980s) will eventually tail off in their use of the company's services or products, and it might be necessary to create some kind of 'emeritus' status for those who helped the company become successful as they age and scale back. This way the baby boomers will not feel lost and unwanted.

In addition, loyalty schemes can reasonably be expected to do several things for the companies that use them (Nunes and Dreze, 2006): (1) keep customers from defecting, (2) win a greater share of the wallet, (3) prompt customers to make additional purchases, (4) provide insight into customer behaviour and preferences, and (5) create profit. The five key mistakes to avoid when using loyalty schemes are: (1) avoid setting up a new commodity (do not just use discounting to promote greater degrees of disloyalty); (2) do not provide rewards for those who are not loyal (like grocery stores who provide membership cards who end up merely rewarding those who own cards rather than bringing in new customers to get the cards); (3) do not provide awards solely for volume and not for profitability (do not just track purchase quantity as it does not necessarily reflect profitability); (4) avoid giving away too much (do not cut into profits if costless rewards can make the customer happy); and (5) do not promise something that you ultimately cannot deliver (the lower bounds of premium service must never look worse than standard service). Loyalty schemes can still be very effective, but company management must keep a close watch on the scheme development and implementation and must be willing to drop the programme if it does not live up to expectations (Nunes and Dreze, 2006).

The point is to convert the supporter to an outright advocate. As they are important to the company, they need to be communicated with even more than the lower-level consumers on the ladder. These individuals need to feel as though they belong to the company. They are the platinum customers on the profitability pyramid. They need to be treated in a special way. If things are done correctly, the supporters will want to become advocates as they see that there are additional benefits associated with reaching that higher status on the ladder. These are also the individuals who make great testimonial spokespersons to reach others who want to be like them. Peers can significantly affect the opinions of others like themselves. These individuals need to be fully engaged by the company in almost every aspect of the business from R&D to website design (Lindstrom, 2005). This creates that personal sense of ownership which helps to make a person a true advocate for the company. The power of word-of-mouth at this level can be seen in the results of NOP World's 2004 Global Brand Advocacy Survey, which surveyed 30,000 consumers worldwide and found that the highest levels of brand advocacy in the world were for Mercedes Benz with 59 per cent of those surveyed considering themselves 'active brand advocates' (Brand Strategy, 2004). Other brands with high levels of advocates were BMW (53 per cent), Toyota (51 per cent), Nokia (50 per cent), and Sony (46 per cent). Word-of-mouth is believed by many consumers to be the best mechanism for recommendation for a company.

Partners

Partners are the ultimate level of relationship as they share in everything. For the B2B situation, this is where the buyer and seller enter into a joint position of commitment, where for example the partner modifies their way of working or behaviour to accommodate the seller. For example, a company may buy a payroll software system from a consulting firm and have to alter its processes in making payments to its staff. Obviously this will produce the highest level of commitment to the relationship. Few B2C settings lend themselves as well to this kind of a relationship, though it may be seen for example when Microsoft brings out a new version of Office and users have to learn new ways of working that they then get used to. An example in the B2B market is Allegiance Healthcare. The company shrink-wraps its medical supplies and labels them specifically for the destination within a hospital. This eliminates the need for hospitals to have a dedicated system to direct general incoming supplies to the

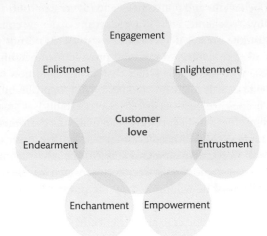

7.3 Customer Love

relevant wards where they are needed. Thus supplies are shrink-wrapped by Allegiance and sent direct to the ward that requested them.

When buyers are made to feel a part of the company, we are verging on partnership territory. In a partnership both parties have a vested interest in the continuation of the partnership along with the commensurate trust and commitment made.

Customer love

What is the ultimate level of bond with the customer? Building an emotional bond that verges on love (Bell, 2002). This suggests that it is no longer sufficient to just have a relationship with your customer; you need to develop the love of your customer. This is what has made such companies as Starbucks, Ritz-Carlton Hotels, and Harley-Davidson so successful. There are seven important steps in building customer love—the 7Es (Bell, 2002) (see Figure 7.3): (1) **enlistment: customers care when they share**—the key is knowing exactly when and how to include customers, since bringing them in as co-producers of a service makes them more loyal; (2) **engagement: the power of straight talk**—since customers who have a problem and complain spend twice as much as customers who have a problem and do not complain, the company must find a way to listen to and talk straight with customers in such a way that customers believe that their input made a difference; (3) **enlightenment: growing customer love**—educating and keeping customers up to date helps to build their loyalty and commitment; (4) **entrustment: affirming the covenant**—reliability is vital for trust, so to convince the customer that you can be trusted, you must be seen as caring for the customer to get them to care for you; (5) **empowerment: customer control through consistency**—customers feel in control when they have an offering that is consistent so keep the core offering intact; (6) **enchantment: making the process magical**—service which surprises adds the sizzle and not showing how keeps the mystery and builds devotion; (7) **endearment: gifting**

without a toll—showing generosity to the customer if backed by authenticity says that you really care about them, not just a concern for profit.

The key benefits to the achievement of customer love are: (1) customers who love you go out of their way to take care of you, (2) customers do not just recommend the company to their friends, they insist on their friends using the company, (3) they both forgive you for mistakes (once you have earned their love) and they try to back you up to others who have had bad experiences, (4) they will give helpful candid and forthright feedback when they see a problem, (5) they do not take legal action against you, and (6) they will pay more for what you offer because they feel that your offering is worth it. These are powerful benefits, and the analogy of social/human relationships applied to buyers and sellers is a helpful strategic perspective. With the bar being ever raised on customer expectations, keeping up with the customer and keeping them happy in their devotion is a key to long-term viability and success.

Relationships and loyalty in B2B markets

So how do things differ when B2B marketing is involved? When compared with B2C markets, B2B markets are characterized as dealing with fewer customers, larger transactions, customized products, negotiated prices, values often determined by usages, and brands not often as critical as the relationships that are built between the buyers and the sellers. In this case, selling is far more complex as buyers may be groups instead of individuals; these target markets are often made up of one instead of thousands or even tens of thousands of individual customers. Selling teams may be important, although often there is a key sales person who deals with a key customer and these potential relationships are critical. The problem is that using the same types of mechanisms as are used in B2C markets to build relationships are often not effective in B2B market situations. Many B2B marketers spend too much time trying to figure out ways in which they can create value for customers rather than on communicating the various benefits that they can provide to their customers (Narayandas, 2005). One effective way to handle this is to develop a list of the various benefits that can be provided, link it to the corresponding key executives within the target firm that want these benefits, and rank them in terms of importance. Practice indicates that usually each member of the buying group of executives will be looking for one specific primary benefit, so the strategic approach should be to match up the key benefit to the particular executive and make sure that he or she is effectively educated on that particular offering. In that way the company enhances its chances of success in getting the contract and potentially keeping it over a long period of time.

One of the biggest problems faced by B2B marketers is that they seem to focus much too heavily on satisfaction scores, just as B2C marketers do, but in the B2B case these are misleading indicators. More than 80 per cent of B2B marketers use these scores to measure loyalty levels, but there is little correlation, if any, between satisfaction and loyalty in B2B markets (Narayandas, 2005). More savvy B2B marketers are realizing that better indicators would involve composite measures that include satisfaction scores along with more reliable indicators like recommendations and repurchase ratings. The best way to address the issue is to think of a B2B loyalty ladder as shown in Figure 7.4. This ladder helps by providing strategic insight that may not be gained from use of the B2C loyalty ladder shown in Figure 7.1.

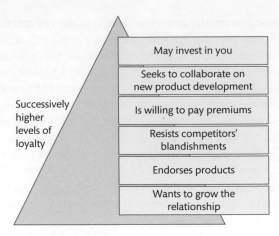

7.4 Loyalty Ladder for B2B Marketers

Source: Das Naryandas (2005), 'Building Loyalty in Business Markets', *Harvard Business Review*, September, 2005. Reprinted with permission of Harvard Business Publishing. All rights reserved.

Within the B2B loyalty ladder, the different segments deal with increasingly higher levels of loyalty, and the amount of time and effort spent by the company on relationship building and maintenance should be commensurate with the levels on the ladder. Beginning at the bottom and moving up the ladder, customers move through a series of behaviours as they become increasingly loyal, and these characteristics must be carefully nurtured by B2B marketers. As the customer displays the next level of loyalty, the revenues will increase. Perhaps there are only four kinds of buyer (see Figure 7.5), and their position on the buyer matrix will suggest whether they are good candidates for investment, maintenance, or divestiture. Each of these customer groups will now be discussed and strategic suggestions provided.

Commodity buyers are only interested in basic offerings, and are primarily interested in shopping at the lowest prices. These tend to be large volume types of customers, and the strategic focus should not be on trying to sell them high value added services, but to strip service costs to the bare minimum.

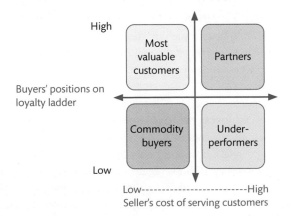

7.5 B2B Buyer Matrix

Source: Das Naryandas (2005), 'Building Loyalty in Business Markets', *Harvard Business Review*, September, 2005. Reprinted with permission of Harvard Business Publishing. All rights reserved.

Underperformers tend to be those prestigious accounts that were acquired to build credibility by luring them with very low prices or even free services. The hope is that by acquiring them with low fees/prices they can later be traded up, but this is not usually the case. The best way to deal with these accounts is to try to move them to commodity buyers by cutting those services provided that are not essential, to move them to partners by having them pay more for services they need, to offer standard products, or to divest them. This is a difficult strategic choice, but it may be the best option if the customer is costing more to keep than the revenue they generate.

Partners are customers who want everything provided for them since they don't have the in-house capability to handle these needs. The key is to provide them with the latest and best products available—price premiums will not be a problem for them. They can be helpful in new product development. The issue is that these customers can be lost if the product evolutionary cycles are short (as in high-tech offerings), and if the supplier doesn't stay on the leading edge of product innovation.

The final category, **most valuable customers**, are loyal and do not cost as much to maintain as the partners. In these cases the customer has often taken over some of the things originally provided by the supplier, but is still willing to pay premium prices for the offerings in honour of past services provided. These customers will also be strong proponents for the supplier. One strategic imperative here is for the suppliers to consider moving these customers to the partner category if new technologies are created or new competitors enter the market with the offering of new services (Narayandas, 2005).

One of the most promising new findings for B2B marketers is the identification of a taxonomy of different relationship types found in business markets. This is based on data from both buyers and sellers in B2B markets and, using cluster analysis, produces five distinct types of relationship (Wong et al., 2010).

1. **Disgruntled followers**—accounted for 19 per cent of the relationships studied and were characterized as competitive/opportunistic relations with the buyer maintaining dominance with larger, more frequent, standardized transactions involved. The average length of these relationships was 13 years.

2. **Manipulative leaders**—accounted for 27 per cent of the relationships examined and were characterized by the seller being the dominant party. These are also competitive/opportunistic

3. **Benevolent independent relationships**—accounted for 17 per cent of the relationships involved and were characterized by lower levels of opportunism with less communication taking place with easy to replace products/services involved. The average length of these relationships was 7.3 years. These are seen as beneficial to both parties with little conflict. Successful relationships based on the products and services involved which are needed but not vital for the buying firm's survival.

4. **Arm's length relationships**—accounted for 14 per cent of the relationships included. These were high on opportunism with power being unbalanced between partners. These were the shortest relationships, lasting on average 4.9 years. These relationships involve smaller transactions with many substitute products/services seen as available. There is little communication involved and there is more conflict found here than for other types of relationship. Eventually there will be a breakdown and movement to another supplier.

5. **Close relationships**—accounted for 25 per cent of all relationships studied. These have high levels of mutual benefit, and there is high commitment and trust involved along with interdependence. Very little opportunism is found in these relationships. These will last on average 11 years. These have the highest evidence of transaction satisfaction with frequent communication and little, if any, conflict.

The relationships identified should be helpful to B2B marketers from either side of the partnership and they offer opportunities for strategic shaping of the relationships over time and the use of tools that will aid in relationship diagnosis.

Customer relationship management

Having examined the nature of relationship marketing, the loyalty ladder, and customer valuation, the next logical step would involve an examination of the mechanics of relationship management. Customer retention is obviously an important goal for any company, especially in light of the costs necessary to acquire a new customer as opposed to keeping an old one. Kotler (2003) explains that there are two ways to strengthen customer retention: (1) to create high switching barriers (the price of looking for another supplier, evaluating them, switching to them, and potential loss of customer discounts which are loyalty based, or (2) to deliver ever-increasing levels of customer satisfaction. Kotler suggests that this is preferred since switching barriers are difficult and costly to erect. So how does the company deliver appropriate levels of customer satisfaction? The corporate solution is the creation of a **customer relationship management** (CRM) system. CRM is a process by which a firm gathers information about the wants and needs of its customers to enable it to adjust its offerings to better fit those wants and needs. It involves data gathering, storage, and dissemination to those who need it. Often this involves the acquisition of relationship management software and data mining techniques, which promise to effectively track customers and build large customer storehouses of data for use by the company in building long-term relationships. The foundation of this system is the database of information, often referred to as the **customer information file** (CIF).

There are five major areas of content that make up the customer information file (Winer, 2004): (1) basic descriptions of the customers, usually in terms of demographics, and names and addresses; (2) customer purchase histories—records of all purchases made by the customer in terms of price paid, purchase location, and product variant purchased; (3) customer contact histories—records of all customer contacts with company personnel; (4) customer response information—records of customer reactions and responses to various marketing promotions and activities; and (5) customer value—an estimate of the monetary value of the customer. The customer information file then serves as the basis for analysing customers to find out how to build better relationships and make them more profitable.

Successful companies carefully monitor all customer touch points and find ways to offer superior service so their customers are continuously impressed (Favilla, 2004). One example was Starwood Resort Hotels which had to handle over 14 million calls each year using 900 call centre agents across various cultures. Starwood implemented an automated customer interaction recording and performance evaluation mechanism that created a consistent customer experience, improved reservation sales volume, helped supervisors improve call centre productivity, and improved customer service quality ratings. Another example involved Hewlett Packard (HP), which was trying to deal with 10–12 different methodologies for handling common service processes which led to very high employee frustration levels and to customers becoming confused by a variety of inconsistent responses. HP corrected the situation through the development of a single global, help desk mechanism to improve service delivery, which reduced overall cost per employee and improved tracking and trend analysis. Another excellent example was that of the South African Revenue Service which had to deal with taxpayer information kept in eight different systems. Different IT systems were utilized based upon a series of taxpayer subcategories. To correct the situation the Revenue created an integrated multiple-taxpayer system, using a team of companies including Accenture, IBM, and Siebel Systems. The result was a saving of almost $12 million per week and significantly improved response time to taxpayer questions.

While touch points certainly matter to customers, one cannot lose sight of the overall journey the customer makes (Rawson et al., 2013). The company can focus too much on touch points to maximize consumer satisfaction at those moments and this may overstate just how happy the customer is, given that the journey they will take does not only involve those emphasized touch points. The most successful companies are those that have managed the entire customer experience, producing greater customer satisfaction levels, improved employee satisfaction levels, and increased revenue. Companies are often adept at handling individual interactions with customers but spend little time understanding the entire customer experience involving both the purchase and afterwards.

Companies need to do things differently (Rawson et al., 2013). They need to build customer journeys into their operational thinking in four ways: (1) they need to identify the journeys that matter to their customers, and that requires data using top-down as well as bottom-up analyses—the idea is to carefully assess the most important journeys and the points at which there are discrepancies between the promises made and the service delivered; (2) each key customer journey should be studied to determine the nature of current performance—this is a good time for blueprinting to understand the nature of the sequential interactions between the customer and various service personnel along the journey which will show any discrepancies from the service the customer expected and allow corrective steps to be taken; (3) they then need to redesign the experience and engage front-line personnel, which normally will involve cross-functional teams to see the problems and design the solutions to fix them; and (4) they need to implement the changes through the development of change leadership teams with executives in charge to allow break-away from functional mindsets and blockages of needed improvements.

The ability to break away from functional biases is necessary for firms to properly handle the entire customer journey, and with this change the firm can expect to increase revenue, cut costs, and improve innovative capabilities, besides increasing customer and employee satisfaction.

One can easily see the benefit inherent in getting information in a B2B marketing situation, since industrial marketers have fewer customers to deal with on a regular basis than B2C companies. It gets trickier with companies aiming at large groups of customers, especially when they have many competitors with what appear to be very similar offerings. One important question is how B2C companies can build meaningful intimate relationships with hordes of individual consumers (Fornier et al., 1998). Part of the problem is that many customers of consumer goods companies get bombarded with surveys which ask for information to help the company build a database of customer information. The biggest difficulty for the consumers is that they keep giving out information but do not see anything coming back to them for their efforts. They are often tired of filling out surveys and hearing nothing in return. They feel disconnected rather than part of an intimate relationship. The authors caution that developing customer intimacy requires the company to take a holistic view to create 'life satisfaction' for the customer rather than merely customer satisfaction. They suggest that this would require in-house controls of toll-free customer call numbers, regular Internet monitoring, trend analyses to understand consumer lifestyle trends, and the tracking of customer perceptions to avoid negative customer backlash.

An important issue is to set up appropriate mechanisms for data collection, which allow the firm to understand its consumers more effectively and to keep them trusting and committed (Davenport and Klahr, 1998). It is important to manage customer support knowledge and ensure that front-line personnel get the knowledge whenever needed to help customize the offering to the needs of the most profitable customers. This kind of knowledge would include information on known customer problems and solutions, regular customer questions that have been asked and their answers, and customer product/service questions and a series of recommendations.

There are a number of benefits that accrue from this kind of customer support knowledge (Davenport and Klahr, 1998): (1) improved solutions for the customer, (2) consistency of solutions provided, (3) improved handling of problems on the first call rather than later, (4) reduced costs per call, (5) reduced calls to the customer service support desk, (6) reduced costs of field service calls, (7) the ability to hire front-line personnel for their people skills as opposed to technical expertise, (8) improved quality and speed of on-the-job training, (9) increased front-line staff satisfaction, and (10) increased overall customer satisfaction.

Data mining has become an important tool in customer relationship management. Data mining is the analysis of consumer databases to look for possible new relationships that can provide direction for innovative customer relationship strategies. Since the early findings of synergies in reservations among airlines, hotels, and car rentals in the SABRE reservation system utilized by American Airlines, customer data have been analysed to look for possible relationships that researchers never knew existed. The trouble is that data being gathered for the sake of having data to add to the customer knowledge system may create its own problems. Many companies have been investing in customer transaction tracking systems which have built very large databases, but with few helpful insights into who their customers really are (Davenport et al., 2001).

The problem is that many companies rely on raw data rather than really observing and getting to know their customers. The problems mentioned previously suggest that just asking customers for information isn't really enough. The evidence from interviews of personnel from 24 leaders in customer relationship management found that the 'best' companies went out of their way to combine transaction data with human data (Davenport et al., 2001).

CRM pitfalls to avoid

Companies can easily get caught up in spending enormous amounts of money on a variety of customer relationship management schemes, but many of these will fail (Rigby et al., 2002). The first of the pitfalls is **the implementation of CRM before a customer strategy**

has been developed. The first step to CRM must be for the company to develop a customer strategy. This will require a clear identification of the customers that the firm wants to build relationships with. These identified customers must then be categorized into different groups ranging from the most profitable down to the least, which will allow a clear delineation of actions and responses and efforts for the various segments. The customer strategy must involve debates involving the following five questions.

1. How must our present value proposition change to gain greater customer loyalty?
2. How much customization is appropriate and profitable?
3. What is the value to be gained from increasing customer loyalty, and would this vary by customer segment?
4. How much time and money can we invest in CRM at the present time?
5. If customer relationships are important to us, why aren't we already building a CRM programme, and what might we be able to do in building customer relationships without investing in technology?

CRM may not be the answer if the company concludes that cost reductions or the handling of all customers in a standardized way makes more sense.

The second CRM pitfall is the **implementation of a CRM programme before the organization has become a customer-focused entity**. The danger here is that the company says it wants a CRM programme but has not restructured its processes to better meet customer needs. Often company executives do not see the need for internal system and structure changes since they assume that CRM affects only processes that involve face-to-face interactions with the customer. Successful companies work for years to modify their structures and processes before ever attempting CRM initiatives.

The third hazard is the **assumption that more CRM technology is always to be preferred**. Often executives will assume that CRM must be technologically intensive. But this may not be the case. It may make sense to provide incentives to motivate company employees to better track customer needs as opposed to investing enormous sums of money into buying the latest and most complex technology. The authors suggest that excellent CRM programmes are comprised of a variety of technologies from low to high. Managers really need to ask themselves where their CRM needs fit on the technology spectrum. The best way to deal with the complexity issue is to start with low-tech alternatives and then assess whether more is needed.

The fourth and final danger is the **potential to stalk your customers rather than woo them**. Managers often end up trying to build relationships with the wrong customers, or trying to build them with the right customers but in the wrong way, because they forget that the types of relationships will depend on what your company stands for and what types of relationships it wants to build with its customers. As the authors describe the situation, relationships involve two sides. A company may want to build stronger ties to affluent customers, but those customers may not want closer relationships with the company. It may also be that the company does not build a relationship with customers who value relationships, and these customers will undoubtedly be lost to competitors.

Another challenge is building relationships with those customers who do not want them, where the company may be seen as an irritant. The use of loyalty programmes can often fall into this pattern. Having the ability to contact customers does not mean that the company should contact them. It depends on the customer strategy mentioned earlier, rather than the CRM programme.

Sustainability of relationships and competitive advantage

The key to relationships is to convert them into long-term partnerships between the buyer and seller, whether B2C or B2B, so that the two parties become co-dependent on each other. The hope is that the relationship will become so comfortable that the commitment level will remain as high as possible. It is based on the expectation that switching costs will increase over time, making dissolution of the relationship no longer a possibility. Of course this will require true trust, commitment, and confidence on the part of both partners. This will undoubtedly become more of a challenge for B2C than B2B marketers as loyalty becomes increasingly difficult as the price of the product/service decreases, but there are opportunities for those firms who nurture these relationships to shift them from short-term to long-term to create the potential for competitive advantage. The question is whether this type of advantage is sustainable or not.

Judging sustainability

In the B2B literature, recent research has proposed the imperative to manage buyer–seller relationships for the long term. There has been a major paradigm shift for B2B marketers in that now relationship marketing has shifted from a short-term to a long-term focus to be effective (Ryu et al., 2007). As a result, the measurement of the relationship management's long-term orientation (LTO) is vital for ensuring success. Practice suggests that there can be no LTO without the existence of trust. In turn, trust is affected by relational norms and satisfaction with the performance of the suppliers.

The perceived level of power of the manufacturer has been found to be a moderator in the link between trust and the long-term orientation of the supplier, which underscores the fact that the power structure is important for the creation of a viable competitive advantage. In a turbulent resource environment firms involved are hesitant to enter into long-term relationships thinking that suppliers might not be counted on to ensure a smooth flow of raw materials needed for the final products. Of course the longer the two partners have worked together and built trust in one another, the more commitment to the relationship will remain.

Managerially, there is an important lesson to be learned. Trust on the part of one partner is usually formed as a result of the proven abilities of the other to offer proper solutions and adapt to changing circumstances while also openly exchanging information. As a result, the supplier should regularly measure, share, and also manage all aspects of the exchange process (even what would seem to be implicit rather than explicit) so that the buyer will want to develop a long-term relationship.

An important consideration is that for a short-term relationship to become a long-term relationship it is imperative that the engagement between the firms or between the firm and the customer becomes an emotional one (Noble and Kumar 2008). Obviously this goes beyond the development of trust to a level of emotional attachment, which would be more akin to love than to mere attachment. This next level of attachment will bring with it commitment and at the same time raise the switching costs involved, creating a situation where the customer will not want to leave the relationship, thereby creating a sustainable asset for the company. What may seem counter-intuitive is that wowing the customer may not be the way to build meaningful relationships as will be discussed in the next section. The old adage of KISS, or 'keep it simple, stupid', may really be the best strategic option for relationship management.

Latest thinking on customer relationships: the customer effort score and the 29 variations in types of customer relationships in B2C settings

Several recent developments in customer relationship management are worth reporting. Many companies have focused on adding every amenity possible to take customers beyond liking to delight, but this may not be the right way to handle things (Dixon et al., 2010). Companies have become so focused on 'over-the-top' service that they have missed the real need of the customer, which is to have their problems solved. Customer loyalty is driven by how well companies deliver their basic customer promises. Adding additional elements to raise the service to 'dazzling' levels may get farther away from the basic offer. This may lead companies to spend far more than they need to and potentially lose sight of what the customer wanted or was willing to pay for.

A study of 75,000 individuals who had spent time with service company representatives dealing over the phone or through a variety of social media mechanisms found that delighting customers does not build loyalty while reducing the effort that the customer has to expend to receive the service does build loyalty, (Dixon et al., 2010). Eighty-nine out of 100 customer service managers indicated that their primary strategy was to exceed customer expectations. On the other side, 84 per cent of customers reported that their expectations had not been exceeded. Companies are focused so heavily on customer expectations because customer satisfaction scores are the most important mechanism for measurement. The issue here is that there is little direct connection between satisfaction and loyalty. The authors suggest that companies are better served focusing on ways to reduce the effort that customers have to expend to get the service that they need. The goal is to make things as easy for the customer as possible.

Another interesting breakthrough in relationship research indicates that if you want to be able to build meaningful connections with your customers in a B2C context, it is imperative to understand the types of relationships that are important for customers (Avery et al., 2014). Some companies are spending a 'fortune' on CRM, but without any deep understanding of what drives relationships. Assuming a one-size-fits-all approach is a road map for confusion and disaster. Companies often frustrate customers by not knowing what they want. Relationship types range from old friends, colleagues, buddies, team-mates, business partners, best friends, marriage partners, next-door neighbours, close siblings, love–hate relationships, ex-friends, former friends, marriage-on-the-rocks, online friends, to one-night stands, flings, secret affairs, enemies, fleeting acquaintances, casual acquaintances, complete strangers, annoying acquaintances, stalker–prey, dealer–addict, guru–disciple, star–groupie, teacher–student, master–slave, and finally villain–victim. There are two important steps to follow to properly understand your customers and the types of relationships that they are looking for (Avery et al. 2014).

(1) Use surveys and interviews to understand the types of relationships currently expected by your customers (helpful mechanisms here involve web-crawling and data mining mechanisms to identify relational data).

(2) **Understand which rules when broken can destroy the relationships** (the company can look to create an ideal mix of relationships given its strategic goals and customers can be shifted toward more desirable relationships strategically over time).

What becomes important over time is that the company begins to think of these relationships as long-term assets, and the most successful companies are actually structuring their marketing around relationships and allowing marketing information to be shared throughout the organization in all areas that touch customers in some way.

Conclusion

Once companies have gone through the process of segmentation, processing, and positioning, they must look to the creation of meaningful relationships with those customers. Customer acquisition is far more costly than customer retention, and the building of intimate relationships with key customers allows the firm to keep in step with changes in their wants and needs and to be able to take corrective action in refining product and service offerings to retain those customers. But relationships with the wrong customers can be problematic since some customers can cost far more to retain than they are worth in additional potential revenue generation. The firm must carefully assess which customers to build relationships with and work to keep those valued relationships. The use of customer relationship management systems is an important approach to managing customer relationships, but committing to a CRM system requires careful preplanning and a commitment throughout the organization to being customer oriented. Putting a system in place for the sake of having one usually leads to serious problems over time as the system may not fit with the company outlook and environment.

Summary

Relationship marketing is important for company success. Normally a company will not be successful trying to focus on single transactions since companies depend on repeat purchases for long-term success. Taking care of important customers is vital, especially in light of the 80–20 rule that states that in most industries 80 per cent of the revenues come from 20 per cent of the customer base. Spending an inordinate amount of time and effort to bring in problematic customers is both inefficient and ineffective especially since there is less time remaining to take care of the mainstay customers. The issue is that key customers must be nurtured to remain loyal to the company and continue to buy its products. Relationship building requires the acquisition of relevant customer information, the storage of that information in databases, and the use of that information to adjust company offerings.

Key terms

- **80–20 rule:** the rule which is built on the understanding that 80 per cent of the company's revenues come from only 20 per cent of its customers.

- **Aftermarketing:** long-term relationships being built in which the firm actively attempts to move customers up the loyalty ladder and tries to minimize the outflow of unhappy buyers.

- **Compatibility management:** the management of different groups of customers to ensure that there is no interaction that could devalue the service for important customers.

- **Customer equity test:** the firm first measures each customer's expected contribution to offsetting the company's fixed costs over their expected lifetime. Then, expected contributions to net present value are discounted at the rate set by the company as its target rate of return for any marketing investments, and finally the company adds together all of the discounted expected contributions across all of the company's current customers.

- **Customer information file (CIF):** another name for the customer database built by the firm to better understand customer wants and needs so that stronger ties can be built with the customer. The CIF contains such information as descriptions of the customer, their purchase histories, the various contacts the customer has had with company personnel, information on how customers have reacted to marketing activities, and measures of customer value.

- **Customer journey:** the entire set of possible touch points between the customer and the service personnel during the provision of the service. The idea is to holistically understand the various pathways, judge how important they are to the consumer, and make sure that discrepancies between what is promised and what is actually delivered are eliminated.

- **Customer lifetime value (CLTV):** the present value of the future profits that will accrue from the customer's lifetime purchases. The company must attempt to measure future earnings from the customer as well as be able to subtract from those earnings the cost of acquiring and maintaining the relationship with the customer.

- **Customer love:** where the firm goes beyond building a relationship with its customers to the point where there is a strong emotional bond between the company and the customer. This is where the customer believes that the supplier cares about their well-being.

- **Customer profitability pyramid:** a ranking of customers in a pyramidal design with customer groups positioned on the pyramid by profitability for the firm. The top of the pyramid contains the platinum customers, the second tier contains the gold customers, the third tier is comprised of the iron customers, and the base of the pyramid is made up of the least profitable customers, the lead customers.

- **Customer relationship management (CRM):** a process by which a firm gathers information about the wants and needs of its customers to enable it to adjust its offerings to better fit those wants and needs. It involves data gathering, storage, and dissemination to those who need it.

- **Data mining:** the analysis of consumer databases to look for possible new relationships that can provide direction for innovative customer relationship strategies.

- **Frequency marketing:** a strategy aimed at identifying the best customers, keeping them, and increasing their expenditures through the development of intimate long-term relationships.

- **Loyalty schemes:** programmes that are established by companies to provide added value to the regular purchaser as opposed to the irregular customer. It provides increasing benefits for increasing levels of company loyalty.

- **Relationship marketing:** the development of long-term and intimate relationships between buyers and sellers. It involves open communications and the ability to know the customer so well that changes in wants and needs can be anticipated before they become critical.

Discussion questions

1. Why are repeat purchases so important for company success?
2. What is relationship marketing?
3. What are the differences between B2C and B2B relationship marketing?
4. What is customer lifetime value (CLTV), and how is it measured?
5. What is compatibility management, and why is it important for marketing strategists?
6. What is the customer pyramid? Which customers would the firm consider retaining, and which ones would it make sense to offload?
7. What are loyalty schemes, and why have they been criticized by strategic marketers?
8. What is data mining, and why is it important for building customer relationships?
9. What are the five general rules for gathering and managing data from a series of customer encounters that were presented by Davenport et al. (2001), and why are they important?
10. What are the four major pitfalls that must be avoided in the use of CRM that were presented by Rigby et al. (2002)?
11. How can relationships with customers be built into competitive advantage?
12. What is customer love, and how does it differ from customer relationships?
13. What is wrong with trying to delight your customer? Why might this be a problem?

Online resource centre

 Visit the Online Resource Centre for this book for lots of interesting additional material at: <www.oxfordtextbooks.co.uk/orc/west3e/>

References and further reading

Avery, Jill, Susan Fournier, and John Wittenbraker (2014), 'Unlock the Mysteries of Your Customer Relationships', *Harvard Business Review*, 92, July-August, pp. 72–81.

Bell, Chip R. (2002), 'In Pursuit of Obnoxiously Devoted Customers', *Business Horizon*, March-April, pp. 13–16.

Berry, Leonard L. and Kathleen Seiders (2007), 'Serving Unfair Customers', *Business Horizons*, 51, pp. 29–37.

Best, Roger J. (2005), *Market-Based Management: Strategies for Growing Customer Value and Profitability*, 4th edn (Upper Saddle River, NJ: Prentice Hall).

Blattberg, Robert C. and John Deighton (1996), 'Manage Marketing by the Customer Equity Test', *Harvard Business Review*, 76, July-August, pp. 136–44.

Blattberg, Robert C., Gary Getz, and Jacquelyn Thomas (2001), *Customer Equity: Building and Managing Relationships As Valuable Assets* (Boston, MA: Harvard Business School Press).

Bold, Ben (2004), 'John Lewis Backs Card with Rewards Scheme', *Marketing*, 1 April, p. 8.

Brierley, Hal (2012), 'Why Loyalty Programs Alienate Great Customers', *Harvard Business Review*, 90, July-August, p. 38.

Davenport, Thomas H. and Philip Klahr (1998), 'Managing Customer Support Knowledge', *California Management Review*, 40 (3), pp. 195–208.

Davenport, Thomas H., Jeanne G. Harris, and Ajay K. Kohli (2001), 'How Do They Know Their Customers So Well?', *MIT Sloan Management Review*, Winter, pp. 63–73.

Dixon, Matthew, Karen Freeman, and Nicholas Toman (2010), 'Stop Trying to Delight Your Customers', *Harvard Business Review*, 88, July-August, pp. 116–22.

Dowling, Grahame R. and Mark Ucles (1997), 'Do Customer Loyalty Programmes Really Work?', *MIT Sloan Management Review*, Summer, pp. 71–82.

Favilla, Emmy (2004), '10 Strategies for Customer Service Success', *Customer Relationship Management*, 8 (6), pp. 38–45.

Fournier, Susan, Susan Dobscha, and David Glen Mick (1998), 'Preventing the Premature Death of Relationship Marketing', *Harvard Business Review*, 78 (2), pp. 42–51.

Gupta, Sunil, Donald R. Lehmann, and Jennifer Ames Stuart (2004), 'Valuing Customers', *Journal of Marketing Research*, 41 (1), pp. 7–18.

Keiningham, Timothy L., Lerzan Aksoy, Alexander Buoye, and Bruce Cooil (2011), 'Customer Loyalty Isn't Enough. Grow Your Share of Wallet', *Harvard Business Review*, 89, October, pp. 29–31.

Kotler, Philip (2003), *Marketing Management*, 11th edn (Upper Saddle River, NJ: Prentice Hall).

Kumar, V., J. Andrew Petersen, and Robert P. Leone (2007), 'How Valuable is Word of Mouth?', *Harvard Business Review*, 85, October, pp. 139–46.

Lindstrom, Martin (2005), 'Extreme Loyalty: Show Off Your Brand Tattoos', *Media* (25 February), p. 24.

McGovern, Gail and Youngme Moon (2007), 'Companies and the Customers Who Hate Them', *Harvard Business Review*, 85, June, pp. 78–84.

Meyer, Christopher and Andre Schwager (2007), 'Understanding Customer Experience', *Harvard Business Review*, 85, February, pp. 117–26.

Nambisan, Satish and Priya Nambisan (2008), 'How to Profit from a Better "Virtual Customer Environment"', *MIT Sloan Management Review*, Spring, pp. 53–61.

Narayandas, Das (2005), 'Building Loyalty in Business Markets', *Harvard Business Review*, 83, September, pp. 131–9.

Nobel, Charles H. and Minu Kumar (2008), 'Using Product Design Strategically to Create Deeper Consumer Connections', *Business Horizons*, 51, pp. 441–50.

Nunes, Joseph C. and Xavier Dreze (2006), 'Your Loyalty Programme is Betraying You', *Harvard Business Review*, 84, April, pp. 124–31.

Payne, Adrian (2000), 'Relationship Marketing: The UK Perspective', in Sheth, J. and Pravatiyar, A. (eds), *Handbook of Relationship Marketing* (Thousand Oaks, CA: Sage), pp. 39–68.

Pruden, Doug R. (1995), 'There's a Difference Between Frequency Marketing and Relationship Marketing', *Direct Marketing*, 58 (2), pp. 30–1.

Rawson, Alex, Ewan Duncan, and Conor Jones (2013), 'The Truth About Customer Experience', *Harvard Business Review*, 91, September, pp. 90–8.

Reichheld, Frederick F. (1996), *The Loyalty Effect* (Boston, MA: Harvard Business School Press).

Rigby, Darrell K., Frederick F. Reichheld, and Phil Schefter (2002), 'Avoid the Four Perils of CRM', *Harvard Business Review*, 82 (2), pp. 101–10.

Ritson, Mark (2003), 'Brand Terrorists Offer an Insight into How the Public Interpret Ads', *Marketing* (27 November), p. 18.

Ryu, Sungmin, Jeong Eun Park, and Soonhong Min (2007), 'Factors of Determining Long-Term Orientation in Interfirm Relationships', *Journal of Business Research*, 60, pp. 1225–33.

Schoder, Detlef (2007), 'The Flaw in Customer Lifetime Value', *Harvard Business Review*, 85, December, p. 26.

Slater, Stanley F., Jakki J. Mohr, and Sanjit Sengupta (2009), 'Know Your Customer', *Marketing Management*, January-February, pp. 37–44.

Staff (2004), 'Brand Strategy Briefing: Land Rover Case Study—Customers at the Wheel', *Brand Strategy* (3 November), p. 54.

Ulwick, Anthony W. and Lance A. Bettencourt (2008), 'Giving Customers a Fair Hearing', *MIT Sloan Management Review*, Spring, pp. 62–8.

Winer, Russell S. (2004), *Marketing Management*, 2nd edn (Upper Saddle River, NJ: Prentice Hall).

Wong, Charles, Ian F. Wilkinson, and Louise Young (2010), 'Towards an Empirically Based Taxonomy of Buyer-Seller Relations in Business Markets', *Journal of the Academy of Marketing Science*, 38, pp. 720–37.

Zeithaml, Valarie A., Roland T. Rust, and Katherine N. Lemon (2001), 'The Customer Pyramid: Creating and Serving Profitable Customers', *California Management Review*, 43 (4), pp. 118–42.

 ### End of Chapter 7 case study   The relationship chain

A promising way to examine relationship building and marketing strategy focuses on the relationship chain. It involves an examination of the incremental stages required in building lifetime customer value through a loyalty marketing programme, from initial investment through to lifetime relationship. Relationship chain methodology includes an analysis of incremental sales and increasing levels of retention which can be tied back directly to the company's loyalty programme, even from the very beginning. The problem is that some approaches to analytical tools are usually involved at later stages of the chain, and, as a result, companies miss valuable information in the early stages that might have improved retention. Higher levels of involvement/engagement for members in loyalty programmes lead to increased sales and improvements in retention rates, but companies need better indications early in the process to evaluate the effectiveness of their loyalty programmes.

Shortly after the launch of the loyalty programme, relationship chain methodology would utilize an analysis of customer activity involving such measures as increases in customer retention, levels of brand engagement, and levels of customer spending. Another important measurement would involve reductions in customer turnover. These types of measurements can then be used as helpful predictive inputs to see whether customers are properly on track to becoming loyal long-term customers, with the supplier's ability to take corrective action if necessary to get customers back on track or to let those with poorer potential fall out of the programme rather than spending too much time or money on them. This approach to treating relationship-building as a series of incremental stages is a promising new approach. The basic idea here is that as the customer moves from one stage to the next in the process, their relationship becomes increasingly valuable to the firm as CLVT increases and the ROI associated with the loyalty programme improves.

There are four basic stages involved in the relationship chain. The first is the stage in which the company ensures that it enrols the right customers from the very beginning. Knowing which are the best candidates is a key step in the right direction in the proper design of the relationship chain. Who are the customers we value most? How do we design our programme in such a way that we can grab their interest and stimulate their involvement? How will we reward them for their value to us? This starts the process rolling and helps the designers to work with specific individuals who have a high probability for success, and the entire programme can be designed with them in mind to enhance the chances for attraction and retention, but at least the fact that the relationship is seen as incremental in nature allows the firm to assess what information it needs and when to take corrective action along the way.

The second stage involves the actual development of customer interest. The key here is to build an open communication mechanism with the customer to stimulate their response and involvement. Only through reaching customers and starting the engagement process can they be moved along the relationship chain, so the issue here is to find the right mechanisms for reaching them and actively involving them. What do we want our customers to do once they have seen our message? How do we get them to communicate with us regularly? This is where heavier uses of websites, call centres, and social media will be invaluable.

Stage three looks beyond initial contacts to regular participation in the loyalty programme. Here, the firm looks for activities that go beyond regular transactions. This would involve tracking such activities as placing of telephone orders, participation in sweepstakes, filling out of surveys, responses to pinpointed offers, bidding on items up for auction, and the number of times that the person checked their cumulative point balances. These types of activities would indicate that there is a growing interest beyond the norm, and these individuals would be seen as prime candidates for relationship development, while others might be seen as appropriate to cull out. What can we do to give them added value? How can we cross-sell to them? Increasing participation will translate to increases in CLTV and improved retention rates.

Stage four then looks to the stimulation of multiple redemptions. So the key is to get them to take advantage of the programme. This is where the real value is in the loyalty programme. It is the measure of what the customer feels about the continuing value of the programme, so what is important is not just that they redeem their accrued benefits but that they do it more than once, since doing it once does not indicate engagement and commitment. If a frequent flier uses air miles once, that really does not indicate commitment to the airline, but if they do it every so often once they reach a certain level of air miles, then there is a better indication of the value of the entire loyalty programme for the consumer. The question here, therefore, is how do we get them to use the programme benefits on multiple occasions? Examples could include such things as attendance at certain members-only functions or the redemption of coupons for special discounts for better customers.

So what kinds of metrics are helpful in connection to this relationship chain? Certainly key metrics would include such measures as the amounts involved in the redemptions used by the customer, along with the number of times the customer has sought redemptions, along with the time periods between redemptions. The company would also want to look at the number of non-redeemers as well. Also, the trend to multiple redemptions is important, since the company needs to determine how to predict heavier future redemption. Are there certain signs that we can use to tell when some are more on the path to multiple redemptions than others? Other important metrics would include looking at those who had actually enrolled in the programme and whether they were the ones that were the targeted audience. Also, it would be important to track those who move from one group to another along the way from enrolment to regular redemption to see if they are progressing as quickly as we have expected. Do we have different categories established from high potential to high value? Are we seeing the proper movement across these segments? Are there hold-ups at any point along the chain? We would also want to examine what the actual customer transaction value is on an annual basis and compare this with the chain and see if the proper improvements are being seen. If not, then we would assess why and how we might correct for the hold-up. It would also be important to track cross-selling as well as trading up in sales to see again if there is any indication of value improvement. Of course, it would be important to address CLTV as well and to link it to a series of predictive measurements such as improvements in retention and increased redemptions. Finally, it would be beneficial to check the lost participants to see who is leaving the programme and attempt to determine why.

One of the most important things to remember strategically is that no single measure should serve as a panacea for everything. Relationship chain methodology should be incorporated into a series of mechanisms to get the most accurate and appropriate data for strategic decision-making. What is promising is that this may allow marketers to ensure that their efforts are paying off in the right ways and improve overall firm performance while reducing waste and inefficiency.

Discussion questions:

Apply the relationship chain to hotel usage.

1. How would you suggest the loyalty programme for the hotel chain be structured, drawing upon the relationship chain?

2. How might you identify the different target segments for your hotel chain?

3. What metrics would you suggest be associated with each of the stages of the chain and why?

4. Assess how you might know whether you were successful or not.

This case was prepared by John Ford, Old Dominion University, Norfolk, Virginia.

Part IV

How will we get there?

I. Introduction

1 Overview and strategy blueprint
2 Marketing strategy: analysis and perspectives

II. Where are we now?

3 Environmental and internal analysis: market information and intelligence

III. Where do we want to be?

4 Strategic marketing decisions, choices, and mistakes
5 Segmentation, targeting, and positioning strategies
6 Branding strategies
7 Relational and sustainability strategies

V. Did we get there?

14 Strategy implementation, control, and metrics

IV. How will we get there?

8 Product innovation and development Strategies
9 Service marketing strategies
10 Pricing and distribution strategies
11 Marketing communications strategies
12 International marketing strategy
13 Social and ethical strategies

8

Product innovation and development strategies

Learning Objectives

1. Appreciate the role of innovation and product development in marketing strategy.

2. Absorb the range of innovation and product development objectives.

3. Be able to assess the two main adoption theories and their implications for marketing strategy.

4. Understand the main options for market and innovation strategies.

Chapter at a Glance

I. Introduction

1 Overview and strategy blueprint
2 Marketing strategy: analysis and perspectives

II. Where are we now?

3 Environmental and internal analysis: market information and intelligence

III. Where do we want to be?

4 Strategic marketing decisions, choices, and mistakes
5 Segmentation, targeting, and positioning strategies
6 Branding strategies
7 Relational and sustainability strategies

V. Did we get there?

14 Strategy implementation, control, and metrics

IV. How will we get there?

8 Product innovation and development strategies
9 Service marketing strategies
10 Pricing and distribution strategies
11 Marketing communications strategies
12 International marketing strategy
13 Social and ethical strategies

 Case study: Brands and the Red Queen Theory

In 1973, Leigh Van Valen came up with the **Red Queen Theory**, which sums up the theory of evolution in one simple quote:

'It takes all the running you can do, to keep in the same place.'

Alice Through the Looking Glass: Lewis Carroll

Each species must constantly fight to stay in this world. Why? Because we face infinite and dynamic competitive pressure. Sex is the mechanism by which we ensure our survival, adapting our genetic makeup to help fight off any existing threat. Of course, the problem is that the competition is doing exactly the same. Germs and viruses, for instance, are endlessly mutating in a bid to crack our resistance. But it's all a game of poker. Neither side can predict how the other will adapt. Evolution has no mission statement, no brainstorming sessions —but there is also no stasis. Constant change is imperative. Mutations are random, evolving every millisecond of every day.

Scientists at the University of Liverpool have shown that evolution is driven most powerfully by interactions between the species, rather than environmental conditions, and that the Red Queen Theory is correct: 'We used fast-evolving viruses so that we could observe hundreds of generations of evolution. We found that for every viral strategy of attack, the bacteria would adapt to defend itself, which triggered an endless cycle of co-evolutionary change.'

Brands and sex

What is sex? When you break it down, sex is just the random mashing up of DNA to create something new, something that is different from the parent DNA. In other words, sex is the means by which change happens.

In the same way species have learned to evolve for survival, brands need to be dynamically seeking improvement in a constantly changing market. If they do not evolve, they will die. Brands that embrace the sex principle—that change is good—will gain a competitive advantage over their rivals. But change must happen fast, with less planning, bolder strategic thinking and more urgency.

Evolved thinking

Many years ago, I read zoology as my first degree, of which evolutionary zoology was a core part of the course. Over the years, I have often used evolutionary principles to understand how brands can best innovate to deal with competition. This has also led me to the discovery of agile development. I have seen how agile and evolution, while operating on different timescales, are complementary partners when it comes to innovation.

Agile is a methodology that comes out of software development, based on iterative and incremental development. Agile uses adaptive planning and evolutionary development—solutions 'evolve' rather than being delivered up-front as a fully formed whole—and requires rapid and flexible response to change.

Agile and the anti-journey

People often see evolution as a process of sequential, linear development and improvement—as in the familiar 'monkey to man' graphic. In fact, evolution is directionless and random. Sometimes it works, sometimes it doesn't. It's not a pre-defined journey. There is no setting of long-term goals.

You could say evolution is an anti-journey. And that's how agile comes into play. By endlessly experimenting with new products or changes to an existing product, a brand will find the innovations that work. Google, Amazon and Asos work this way—and very successfully. And perhaps surprisingly, it's the way that most successful banks work as they digitalize their business. They are constantly and endlessly tweaking their product, selecting what works, dropping what doesn't.

Does it apply to all brands? Yes, but with the caveat that not all products benefit from constant iteration but they do benefit from speedy innovation and testing across the myriad of ways they use to get the brand into the hands of consumers.

Evolution's secret weapon

A surprising principle of sex is that 'it stores genes that are currently bad but have promise for re-use. It continually tries them in combination, waiting for the time when the focus of disadvantage has moved elsewhere'.

It's not big changes that lead to survival but lots of little changes, many of which aren't successful today but might well come in useful tomorrow. The business world is just as ruthless and dynamic as the natural world but can you imagine a brand or organization storing the things that are bad, putting aside for later the things that don't work?

In Japan, *chindōgu* is a concept that involves coming up with 'un-useless' inventions by combining products or objects that are unrelated, to create inventions that are at best unusual, often ridiculous, but which may fulfil a purpose. Take, for example, the household duster/cocktail-shaker for a cheeky reward while doing the household chores, or the chindōgu baby mop, an outfit worn by babies to clean the floor as they crawl about. This art movement uses the absurd to satirize modern day society but at the same time it shows how the 'cross-pollination' of ideas can lead to disruptive thinking.

Staying alive

To ensure their survival, businesses, brands and organizations need to keep making changes, even small ones. Without losing the essence of their brand, they need to keep mixing up their DNA. It doesn't need to be an obvious change. It doesn't need to be THE BIG INNOVATION. For some brands making too big a change too fast can be counter-productive. Some ideas will work today. Some won't. But therein lies the secret of staying alive.

Graham Thomas *is the co-founder of two digital businesses: Radical, a company that creates innovative digital products for its clients, and Join SAM, the world's first on-line money service just for kids and their families. Before founding these, he spent many years working for Saatchi & Saatchi.*

Introduction

From a strategic perspective, innovation is based upon technological superiority and posits that buyers will seek goods and services that provide the greatest interest along with performance, features, quality, and value for money. Innovation is an integral part of marketing strategy owing to its ability to reduce costs and/or differentiate. The 'and' part of the sentence has provided one of the biggest challenges to Porter's cost-differentiation framework in that in many markets, the 'name of the game' is both to reduce costs AND to differentiate. Buyers have become increasingly demanding and no longer see a contradiction between product innovation and development and falling prices. For example, mobile phone manufacturers such as Apple and Samsung offer superior products every year at similar or below previous prices (with the concurrent effect of reducing long-term profits).

Given that most theories of business eventually become obsolete, the key competency for any organization that wants to survive is the ability to innovate. Firms that cut their support for research and development (R&D) activities have been found to have significantly lower future stock market valuations (Mizik, 2010). Indeed Drucker and Maciariello (2008: p. 30) argued that, 'because the purpose of a business is to create a customer, the business enterprise has two—and only two—basic functions: marketing and innovation. Marketing and innovation produce results; all the rest are costs'. As well, firms that have a reputation for innovation have been found to build up considerable 'licence' amongst consumers to deviate from the normal marketing strategies in their markets (Barone and Jewell, 2013).

For example, an innovative car brand may be given leeway if it deviates from the norms of fuel efficiency in its category—it is less likely to be penalized for atypical strategies compared with products from less innovative firms.

Innovation often brings previously unrelated companies into competition as competitive boundaries become blurred and companies have to trust their staff to exploit the 'small world' networks that they work within (Fleming and Marx, 2006). Take the case of telecommunications. Previously separate sectors such as computing, entertainment, telephony, and utilities are now locked in fierce competition. Thus, in the UK, BT has developed alliances with content providers to offer a variety of services over broadband, most notably covering football, including BT Vision, which competes with Sky and Virgin media. Similarly, Siemens, Sony, and Panasonic have entered the photographic marketplace using digital technology, and Tesla has come out of nowhere to compete in the car market with its ground-breaking premium electric car range featuring the Roadster and Model S.

Innovation can be used to find 'comfort zones' in the marketplace. The best strategic place for any organization is to occupy a space that rivals have no interest in or cannot easily emulate. Jaeger-LeCoultre uses established technology to build classic watches, while Seiko uses innovation to produce digital watches with kinetic energy. Innovation and development only has strategic value if appropriately positioned. Jaeger-LeCoultre likely has no interest in advances in Velcro strap technology!

Consider BMW's 'The Ultimate Driving Machine' pitch to the market. Here is a company saying that it will not use technology that makes driving a car like 'sitting on a sofa'. Also, take the case of the controversial alcopops market, which is extremely fashion-oriented, based upon innovation with a rapid turnover of flavours. This has led to a variety of product innovation and development strategies achieving differentiation within a largely traditional sector. For example, the Hooch brand specializes in limited-edition lines such as lemon, orange, and blackcurrant beers. Product and service innovation and development offer all organizations an important means to gain a competitive advantage: innovation and development is a strategic issue.

This chapter is divided into three sections. The first looks at setting objectives for innovation and development and is followed by one looking at targeting issues. Finally, an examination of overall product innovation and development positioning is considered. However, the first task is to examine how to define innovation.

What is innovation?

Innovation is a noun with a definition along the lines of 'the introduction of something new' or 'a new idea, method, or device', as with Google Glass, the Teslar Model S, or Evian's Smart Drop (a WiFi-enabled refrigerator magnet that allows you to order more water instantly). Strictly speaking, the difference between innovation and invention is that invention applies to things that are new-to-the-world, whereas innovation refers to subsequent changes and adaptations. An obvious example would be Alexander Graham Bell's 'electrical speech machine' of 1876. Looking back, we can see that the telephone was the precursor to the Internet, but it would be a 'stretch' to say that Bell invented the web. So we recognize that both the telephone and the web were new-to-the-world, despite the myriad of innovations that can be traced back to the telephone. When it comes to competitive marketing strategy, the talk is mainly of innovation rather than invention; for example adding a little more cleaning power to a laundry detergent or a better flavour to a toothpaste. These provide what, for example, P&G calls 'er' benefits: 'better', 'easier', and 'cheaper'. These are all important factors to sustaining share among current customers and getting new people to try a product (Brown and Anthony, 2011).

Disruptive business models

A **disruptive technology** fundamentally shifts the production paradigm and often how a product or service is used. For example, digital technology has changed a number of markets, from cameras to radios to telephony (Christensen, 1997). People still take pictures, but the dominance of the 35-mm film market has evaporated. People still listen to radio, but not solely by tuning to a channel on a radio. Hardbound copies of the *Encyclopaedia Britannica* ceased in 2012 after 244 years of production, faced with Internet competition though the company continues to thrive with a web presence in various markets (Cauz, 2013). However, in recent years, the scope of the disruption debate has been widened to include disruptive business models (Markides, 2006) such as discount shopping, low-cost airlines, and online businesses such as Expedia (see also Christensen and Raynor, 2003). It might be argued that there is another category: a disruptive design innovation (Verganti, 2006; Noble and Kumar, 2008). However, design in this chapter is treated as part of disruptive product innovation. For example, the Tobii Gaze is a USB device that allows the movement of your eyes to substitute for pushing a mouse around a pad; after a quick one-time calibration it lets you select items and scroll just by looking at them.

First, a quick review of a business model is in order (see also Chapter 4). The term 'business model' arose in the early 1990s and is used to express the nature of the activities and processes a company performs to deliver goods and services to customers. Every company operates according to a business model, which may or may not be effective; for example, the different business models in terms of strategy and implementation between a high-street shop selling physical CDs and a website offering music downloads. A disruptive business model is the discovery of fundamentally new ways of doing business in an existing market. New business models attack existing markets by emphasizing different product or service attributes than the established competitors do. The kinds of new attributes might, for example, be:

- price
- convenience
- speed of execution
- design
- selection
- location
- ease of use.

New business models offering such attributes have appeared in such markets as bookshops and travel, for example with Amazon and easyJet, respectively. However, established firms often find it very difficult to respond to new business models because the 'architecture' of their business throws up a variety of barriers (Johnson et al., 2008; Wessel and Christensen, 2012). So, if a low-cost no-frills competitor comes into the market, it is often not easy to respond as it would probably mean renegotiating wage and supply contracts. Another issue is that new business models are often seen as unattractive in the early phases of market adoption, so the incumbents often have very little incentive to respond.

There are some distinct differences to disruptive technologies; new business models rarely completely overtake the traditional ways of competing. Waterstone's still exists in the face of the might of Amazon, and books are still traded and read despite the existence of e-book readers. Indeed, Markides (2006) estimates on average that new business models capture no more than 20 per cent of markets. The reason is that new business models are rarely superior to existing ones; instead, they are normally complementary and most market incumbents do not find them attractive. The next section will examine disruptive products (see Figure 8.1).

 Mini Case 8.1   China innovation survey

264 respondents participated in the annual Booz & Company survey, which shows that that innovators in Mainland China are gaining rapidly in competitiveness compared with companies in Europe, United States, and other regions. This year, nearly two-thirds of respondents at MNCs operating in China said some Chinese competitors are at least as innovative as their own companies, a strong increase since last year.

According to Booz & Company's study on innovation, all innovative companies fall into one of three categories.

- **Need Seekers** – first movers who proactively discover their customer needs and then use this understanding to shape new products.
- **Market Readers** – second movers who focus on incremental improvement in already existing products.
- **Technology Drivers** – deliverers of new technological achievements, who realize both breakthrough and incremental change but have less direct contact with customers.

Although each of the strategies can be highly successful, analysis from Booz & Company's study shows that following a Need Seeker strategy, although difficult, offers the greatest potential for superior performance in the long term. This year's China Innovation Survey shows that a much higher share of Chinese companies are following the Need Seeker strategy.

Key findings of the survey

- Some 64 per cent of the respondents at non-Chinese companies said some Chinese competitors are equal to or better than their own companies at innovation—a strong increase from 48 per cent in the 2012 survey.

- More than two-thirds of respondents in 2013 said they are now conducting product development for the rest of the world in China, up sharply from 41 per cent in 2012. Even more expect to be doing so in the future; 88 per cent of Chinese companies said they will be doing global R&D in China by 2023

- In 2013, fully 44 per cent of the Chinese companies surveyed see themselves as conducting activities that make up the Need Seeker strategy, compared with the Global Innovation 1000 average of 27 per cent

- China is on its way to becoming a true global innovation hub for MNCs from developed markets; 66 per cent of respondents conduct R&D in China for foreign markets—an increase from 51 per cent last year

- The survey results show that Chinese companies are still focusing on core innovation capabilities such as platform management and production ramp-up, and are also moving away from reverse engineering as the sole source of innovation. The MNCs in China are more formal and process driven, and focus on capabilities related to government relationship management and understanding the market potential.

Appendix 1: Top 10 Innovative Companies in Mainland China (Chinese Company)

Rank	Company Name
1	ALIBABA GROUP
2	HUAWEI INVESTMENT & HOLDING
3	TENCENT HOLDINGS LTD
4	LENOVO GROUP
5	SANY HEAVY INDUSTRY CO., LTD.
6	CHINA MERCHANTS BANK
7	BAIDU INC.
8	HAIER ELECTRONICS GROUP CO., LTD
9	360 BUY GROUP
10	WANXIANG GROUP

Appendix 2: Top 10 Innovative Companies in Mainland China (Non-Chinese Company)

Rank	Company Name
1	3M
2	APPLE
3	SAMSUNG ELECTRONICS
4	GOOGLE
5	ABB (CHINA) LIMITED
6	PROCTER & GAMBLE (GUANGZHOU) LTD
7	VOLKSWAGEN GROUP CHINA
8	MICROSOFT
9	LG ELECTRONICS
10	BOSCH (CHINA) INVESTMENT LTD

Michelle Wang and Meng Du, *21st Century Business Review*

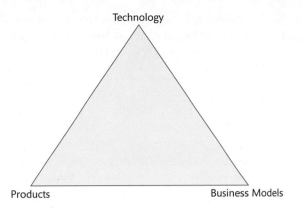

8.1 Scope of Disruption

Source: Constantinos Markides (2006), 'Disruptive Innovation: In need of Better Theory', *Journal of Product Innovation Management*, 23, pp. 19–25

Disruptive products

Launching disruptive goods and services is a risky business, especially if the technology is discontinuous (requiring a significant change in behaviour and/or in complementary technology); e.g. DVD recorders cannot play VHS tapes, as opposed to Blu-ray, which can play DVDs. If it goes wrong, the costs can be enormous. Consider the early problems with the Boeing 787 Dreamliner involving fires from within its lithium-ion batteries (as well as fuel leaks) which led to the US Federal Aviation Administration ordering a review of the design and manufacture of the innovative aircraft. Shortening the new product development (NPD) process can be a formidable competitive weapon. Xerox is a case in point; it recaptured its lead in the copier market by reducing its seven-year NPD process to two.

The following marketing strategies form the 'umbrella' of product innovation activities pursued by organizations and are based on the original NPD typology developed by Booz Allen Hamilton (1982) (see Figure 8.2). They are activities conducted by market leaders,

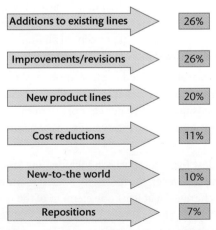

8.2 Booz Allen Hamilton Typology

challengers, and niche players who use innovation as a competitive tool in the marketplace (followers tend to introduce innovation once the risk has been reduced).

- **Additions to existing lines:** for example, when Heinz added 'Green' to its range of ketchups. Or take the trend for secret menus for devotees of fast food chains. For example, McDonald's offers a secret menu including an 'MC 10:35', a fusion between an Egg McMuffin and hamburger which can only be ordered during the crossover from the breakfast to the standard menu at 10:30. Studies show additions to be about 25 per cent of all marketing innovation and they are valuable in offering new choices to loyal as well as new customers, thereby increasing overall sales. For example, Harley-Davidson's introduction of an electric motorcycle called the LiveWire with a range of 210 kilometres (perhaps to be known colloquially as e-asy rider!) aimed at young riders rather than their current 40+ age group of the HOG' (Harley Owners Group) fanbase.

- **Cost reductions:** cost reductions, as with the introduction of cheaper flights to Europe by easyJet and Ryanair and SouthWest Airlines in the US. These account for slightly above 10 per cent of all innovations. Such airlines have introduced new processes and ways of doing business to fill a gap in the marketplace for cheap foreign travel. Cost reductions can open up new markets for companies and provide relatively safe spaces to operate within, as long as established rivals are unable to change their processes sufficiently to match.

- **Improvements/revisions:** for example, when Kellogg's introduced a foil wrap for its cereals to improve freshness. Improvements and revisions tend to account for about 25 per cent of all marketing innovation and are particularly useful at maintaining loyalty and distancing from rival and often me-too products. Thus, in the case of Kellogg's Corn Flakes, the foil wrap distinguishes the brand from supermarket own labels.

- **New product lines:** for example, when the engineering and transport company Atkins added management and project services to its range of design and engineering solutions or when Asus added the Google Nexus 7 tablets to its computing range. Vodafone even considered becoming a bank, given that so many of its customers make payments via their mobile apps, and even took out a banking licence in Italy (they abandoned the idea on the basis that it required a skill set they simply did not possess). Indications are that new product lines account for about 20 per cent of all innovations and can be successful in increasing the spend of loyals and in enhancing loyalty.

- **New-to-the-world:** Motorola invented the first 'mobile' phone in 1973, but it wasn't until 1985 that they first came to market in a format that would be recognized as mobile. New-to-the-world makes up about 10 per cent of all innovations and can provide significant market advantages in the intervening space before rivals can introduce their own versions.

- **Repositions:** in its widest form, a reposition includes any kind of reposition, albeit just a change in advertising. However, more strictly related to innovation and development, it involves significant changes in at least one element of the mix—be that product, price, place, promotion, or people. For example, Lucozade was repositioned in 1985 from an energy drink for the sick to an energy replacement for sports people. The advertising used Daley Thompson with the claim: 'Lucozade Replaces Lost Energy'. Tablets and cans were introduced to enable greater portability, but no change was made to the formula of the drink. Studies indicate that repositions account for slightly less than 10 per cent of marketing innovations a year and are especially used by companies faced with ageing markets and/or declining sales to revitalize the brand (e.g. Brylcreem).

Whatever the form, NPD and innovation are central tenets of marketing strategy for many companies. They underpin cost reductions, such as the web delivery of insurance and banking, as well as differentiation, such as the iPhone with its various applications.

Aside from repositioning, all of the above innovation strategies require that a new product or service be developed. The following section will examine the NPD process, market preparation and branding, and product rollovers.

NPD (new product development)

Process

New ideas have been traditionally developed by a three-stage process (see Figure 8.3).

1. **Idea generation** involves activities like problem analysis (Spradlin, 2012), listing attributes and changing combinations, suggestion boxes, brainstorming, and customer requests. Ideas are then screened by their market attractiveness and market competitiveness. For example, Ferran Adrià closed the famous Barcelona elBulli restaurant, which was considered by many to be the best in the world, for six months each year to develop and test new recipes such as sea urchin foam and curry ice cream.

2. **Business screening analysis** involves identifying positioning, creating a concept, and attempting to predict market behaviour.

3. **Development and test marketing** involves sales forecasting, product development, market tests, possible marketing mix, and break-even analysis. Success for many products depends on how consumers learn to use them. This research suggests that initial product trial may lead to jumps in consumer learning with the implication for marketing managers to structure initial trials in a manner conducive to exploration, and insight-driven learning (Lakshmanan and Krishnan, 2011).

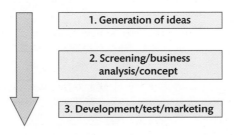

8.3 NPD Process

One interesting finding has been that transcendence, whereby staff are allowed some unfocused free time at work (for example, the 20 per cent time policy at Google) to detach themselves from everyday activities, has been shown to be an important factor in breakthrough innovations (Waytz and Mason, 2013). Whatever the approach, once a company has established the qualitative and quantitative nature of its objectives it has to ensure that there is a process in place to enable innovation to happen and to transplant innovative ideas into manageable projects. It may help to break the process into stages.

From an organizational perspective, the whole process might be driven **functionally**: the new product passes sequentially between departments and ends with marketing. Alternatively, a **parallel** approach might be adopted, where all the elements are developed in tandem so that marketing has involvement from the generation of the idea onwards. Alternatively, Bonabeau et al. (2008) advocate separating the early stage of NPD from the later with two completely detached organizational structures. They argue that the first phase is for 'truth-seeking' to identify prospects or eliminate bad bets. The second is to focus on maximizing the value of products that have made it through the first stage. They broadly estimate that between 60 and 80 per cent of candidate new products will be eliminated at stage 1 and around 70 per cent will go to market launches. Organizations need not fully commit to any of these processes.

Toolkit strategy

The toolkit strategy enables customers of NPD companies to undertake their own innovation and is an important example of the direction in which the NPD process is moving (see Figure 8.4).

At its core, the basic problem of NPD is that the 'need information' side of the equation resides with the customer while the 'solution' information resides with the manufacturer. Take the case of BBA, which develops speciality flavours to bolster and enhance the taste of processed foods. A traditional project might start with a client requesting a single sample of a 'meaty flavour' for a soy product. The shipment is then made within six days. After three

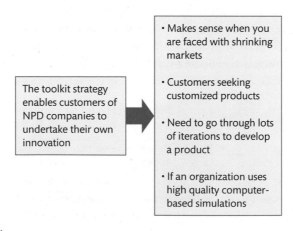

8.4 Toolkit Strategy

weeks, the client might respond with: 'It's good, but we need it less smoky and more gutsy' (Thomke and von Hippel, 2002). BBA then attempts to modify the flavour in two days. Several more iterations may occur before they get it right. BBA bears most of the development risks, with R&D costing from around £600 for a minor tweak to £160,000 for an entirely new flavour. Furthermore, on average, most clients only accept about 15 per cent of new flavours after full market evaluation, with 5 to 10 per cent eventually making their way to the marketplace.

In response, BBA has shifted more innovation activities to their customers. They have developed an Internet-based tool containing a dataset of flavour profiles. Customers are able to select information and manipulate it on-screen and send the new flavour design directly to an automated machine (often located at the clients' site) and the product is made within minutes. After tasting, if needed the flavour can be manipulated and tweaked again.

Take another case, the custom computer chip industry. Traditionally, manufacturers were only able to undertake projects for companies wanting high volumes, given the high cost of developing bespoke chips for such uses as robotic circuitry. Companies such as LSI Logic have transformed the process by providing both large and small customers with DIY tools to design their own chips. Such developments are based on companies taking their knowledge, developed over decades, and incorporating it onto sophisticated CAD/CAM (computer-aided design/computer-aided manufacturing) programs that contain libraries of design options to solve numerous problems using graphical interfaces. They also enable testing through computer simulations to build virtual prototypes easily and quickly. By standardizing transistor design and adding LSI's solution information, the customer toolkit can function.

When to develop such toolkits? Customer innovation and toolkits make sense when you are faced with shrinking markets and customers seeking customized products. They are also useful when you need to go through lots of iterations to develop a product. Another pointer is if an organization uses high quality computer-based simulations to develop new products and has computer-adjustable production processes.

Systematic inventive thinking

Product developers are constantly striving for the 'innovation sweet spot'. This is the point when a new product idea is different enough from the existing product to attract customer interest and at the same time close enough to the company's existing position and capabilities that it makes sense to customers and can be delivered by operations.

'Systematic inventive thinking' (SIT) provides a highly disciplined approach to new product idea generation that represents the interests of both customers and the company (Goldenberg et al., 2003) and is worth particular mention (see Figure 8.5).

The starting point for SIT is to list all the main elements of a product in terms of physical components and attributes such as colour and expected useful life. The next stage is to identify the immediate environment, again in terms of physical components and attributes (e.g. ambient temperature and type of user). Finally, five innovation patterns (based on the work of Russian engineer Genrich Altshuller) may be manipulated to develop a new product idea.

> **Subtraction** is about removing components or attributes
>
> **Multiplication** involves adding elements like developing a double waste bin unit that can be used for rubbish
>
> **Division** is the breaking-down of an existing product into its component parts such as the replacement of the integrated hi-fi into modular systems involving speakers, amplifier, tuner, tape, and CD
>
> **Task unification** concerns assigning a new task to the product such as when Rubbermaid placed assembly instructions for storage cabinets on the packaging rather than on a separate enclosed sheet
>
> **Attribute dependency change** involves the relationship between the attributes of a product and the attributes of the immediate environment as with the development of male and female razors

8.5 Systematic Inventive Thinking

(*Source*: Jacob Goldenberg, Roni Horowitz, Amnon Levav, and David Mazur (2003), 'Finding Your Innovation Sweet Spot', *Harvard Business Review* (March), pp. 120–9.

The five patterns of innovation are subtraction, multiplication, division, task unification, and attribute dependency change.

- **Subtraction** is about removing components or attributes to make products simpler and more specific such as a dedicated GPS device rather than part of a bundle within a mobile.

- **Multiplication** involves adding elements like developing a double waste bin unit that can be used for rubbish and recycling or a double-bladed razor that lifts whiskers when shaving. (Note the need for qualitative change rather than just straight multiplication.)

- **Division** is the breaking down of an existing product into its component parts, such as the replacement of the integrated hi-fi into modular systems involving speakers, amplifier, tuner, tape, and CD, or Motorola's Atrix mobile phone that separately docks with and runs a 'laptop' consisting of just a keyboard and screen—the phone becomes the 'heart' of the laptop.

- **Task unification** concerns assigning a new task to the product, such as when Rubbermaid placed assembly instructions for storage cabinets on the packaging rather than on a separate enclosed sheet.

- **Attribute dependency change** involves the relationship between the attributes of a product and the attributes of the immediate environment, as with the development of male and female razors.

One case was the development of a new business card for a company (Goldenberg et al., 2003). Having examined conventional business cards, it was decided to choose the pattern of 'subtraction'. A business card was developed without a job title and, instead, a hole was cut in its place. It demonstrated clearly that the company was non-hierarchical, but it presented several challenges: it undermined the primary function of a business card; it might make junior employees insecure without a title; it might seem inadvertent; and the meaning of the hole was not obvious. The next stage was 'task unification', which involved the assignment of a new task to the product. One idea was to use the hole as a window to frame additional information such as different job titles, trade association memberships, weekend activities, and intellectual interests. This demonstrated a lack of hierarchy while appearing to be innovative and offered a multifaceted view of an employee. It left a problem of how to provide a variety of role definitions. The final solution was to shrink the card to accommodate a standard rotating 'wheel' made of card that could be turned to show the multifaceted job functions, roles, relationships, and interests of the card bearer. A new product!

Market preparation and branding

Having developed a new product, market preparation is about 'warming-up' the marketplace for the innovation. In the case of high-tech products, cooperative strategies with rivals are becoming the norm (Easingwood and Koustelos, 2000). This is because alliances and licensing help signal to consumers that this new technology will not leave them marginalized, as happened with the high definition optical disc format war in 2006–8 between the Blu-ray Disc (Sony) and the HD DVD optical disc (Toshiba) standards for storing high definition video and audio, which was won by Blu-ray largely because Sony had licensed the majority of movie studios with 70 per cent of rentals at Blockbuster coming from Blu-ray. Many lessons have been learnt and operating standard agreements, which enable planning and stability, have mushroomed.

An innovative product may have its own brand, for example Netflix, or be an endorsed brand like the Asus Google Nexus 7, or be a sub-brand such as the Samsung Smart TV. As such, a brand provides the potential for an organization to 'own' an innovation in the minds of buyers (Aaker, 2007), which means that even if competitors copy the innovation they will have to work harder to make an impact. Moreover, in sophisticated markets, a branded innovation says to consumers 'the benefits are such that we thought it was worth branding'. This enables a company to add credibility and legitimacy to a claim, as with Gore-Tex linings to clothing and shoes. Brand names are highly visible and make communications more efficient. From a communications stance, PR on the forthcoming release is crucial. Intel always releases details of all its new chips, such as Celeron, which helps develop anticipation and excitement in the market. Crucially, the PR appears far enough along the process so that rivals cannot react with copycat products in time, given that Intel does not seek alliances. PR can also be used by companies to 'educate' the market about the new technology, but this is often a longer-term process. This does not mean that everything should be branded. The product innovation has to be a significant advance and newsworthy, or buyers will see through it very quickly.

Product rollovers

Short product life cycles increase the frequency of 'product rollovers', the displacement of old products by innovations (Billington et al., 1998). Ideally, existing innovation would be sold out just at the introduction of a new one, but this rarely happens. The Osborne II replacement of the Osborne I, the first successful portable computer, is a classic example. Adam Osborne announced the forthcoming Osborne II in late 1982. Market response was

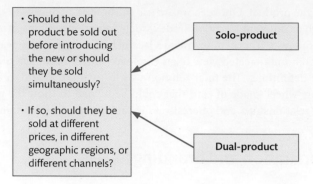

8.6 Product rollovers

(*Source*: Corey Billington, Hau L. Lee, and Christopher S. Tang (1998), 'Successful Strategies for Product Rollovers', *Sloan Management Review* (Spring), pp. 233–30.

quite logical: people decided to cancel orders for the Osborne I and wait. However, the slump in sales for the mark I severely reduced Osborne's cash flow and made investment in the mark II hard to sustain and what is more, owing to technical problems, the introduction of the mark II slipped. The company eventually had to file for bankruptcy in late 1983. It is an extreme product rollover case, but it demonstrates the point that a strategy is required.

Should the old product be sold out before introducing the new one or should they be sold simultaneously? If so, should they be sold at different prices, in different geographic regions, or through different channels? The two strategic options are *solo-product roll* and *dual-product roll* (Billington et al., 1998), as shown in Figure 8.6.

Solo-product roll

This aims to have the entire range of old products sold out at the planned introduction date (e.g. HP's 5Si series was succeeded by the 8000, and later by the 8100 and 8150 which brought higher resolution and faster printing). This is a high-risk and high-return strategy. It can prove to be expensive if the old product is sold out too early or there are high inventory levels in place, as potential sales may be lost.

Dual-product roll

This is where both old and new products sell simultaneously for a period, for example Pentium compatible processors such as the Celeron, the Core, the Xeon (high-end version used in servers and workstations), and the Atom. It is less risky than the solo option, but requires the marketing of both old and new products, with the consequent risk of confusing the marketplace. Geographic rolls can reduce confusion (e.g. Daimler Benz first introduced its Smart cars in Europe and then in North America). Another angle is to differentiate by channels (e.g. Nike introducing new models at premium retailers while selling older models through discounters). Dual pricing may also be utilized, as with the aggressive pricing of older computer chips. A fourth strategy is the so-called 'silent' approach, which is to quietly introduce a new rollover without any fanfare (Sony and new hi-fi models). The

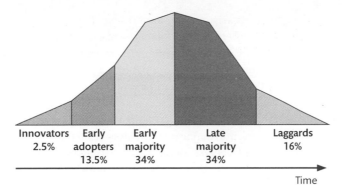

8.7 Adopter Categorization by Relative Time

Source: Everett M. Rogers (1983), *Diffusion of Innovation* (New York: Free Press).

point is to manage new products and the process of displacement of old products *jointly* rather than separately.

It is worth mentioning that there is a partial alternative strategy known as the 'lean launch'. This is where the firm makes small commitments of resources with slow manufacturing 'ramp-up' and limited commitment of inventory during rollout to reduce risk. It has been found that a lean launch can be successful if the timing is neither too soon to take advantage of market readiness for the technology nor too late to miss the market opportunity (Calantone and Di Benedetto, 2012).

Disruptive technologies

The following section will examine the two main frameworks of Rogers (1983) and Moore (1999, 2004a), which address disruptive technologies.

Rogers' perspective

An innovation strategy without any idea of buyer behaviour is a non-starter. Everett M. Rogers' (1983) seminal work on the adoption of innovation was the first to compellingly categorize consumers' readiness to adopt disruptive technologies. Rogers identified five adopter types: innovators, early adopters, early majority, late majority, and laggards (see Figure 8.7).

- **Innovators:** risk-takers and willing to try new ideas.
- **Early adopters:** respected opinion-leaders in the product field who are more cautious.
- **Early majority:** do not seek leadership, but are more likely to adopt than the average buyer.
- **Late majority:** more risk-averse and will adopt an innovation after there has already been a sizeable take-up.
- **Laggards:** highly risk-averse and traditional. Once an innovation has reached 'traditional status' they will come into the market.

There are a variety of implications arising from Rogers's typology.

In order for an innovation to enter from the left of the market and move to the right it will need to have a relative market advantage. This might involve quality or convenience or anything that avoids the 'bad bits' of what it aims to supersede. For example, Recaro introduced a leading-edge child seat for Porsche and Aston Martin drivers.

Strategically, it will also help if it maximizes compatibility with the existing marketplace in terms of physical space (e.g. a relatively large home computer would no longer be a viable option for most customers), is able to hook into the current inventory of alternatives, can link up to other similar products, and needs no or few behavioural changes. For example, attempts to introduce non-QWERTY keyboards have met with universal failure. As noted above, convergent standards are important issues. Companies introducing new digital phones increasingly make them compatible with US, Asian, and European standards. One interesting variation on this theme used by Luz Engineering installs industrial solar-heaters costing between £1 million and £3 million at no initial cost to buyers. Instead, they are required to take out a twenty-year contract at a discount rate to buy steam at 350°F with the local power company, which aids adoption considerably.

It also helps if the innovation is not too complex, can be communicated readily, and can be tried and tested. Finally, Rogers argued that perceived risk needs to be as low as possible—in particular regarding uncertainty of performance, consequences of failure, financial cost, physical health concerns, and effects on self-image.

Moore's perspective

Rogers' view of adoption largely held sway until the late 1990s, when Geoffrey A. Moore introduced his ideas of the 'chasm strategy' (Moore, 1999, 2004a, and see 2004b). Moore pointed out that innovative products do not normally slide in from the left-hand side and work their way steadily across to the right. Instead, they often meet with failure, which he categorized as falling into 'the chasm' (see Figure 8.8).

Studies indicate that only about 10 to 12 per cent of new products make it to market. Though before going any further, the point must be made that most disappear because of internal rather than external market processes:

- about 40 per cent disappear after **business screening**
- a further 20 per cent of innovations evaporate in **development**
- around 10 per cent are dropped after **test marketing**.

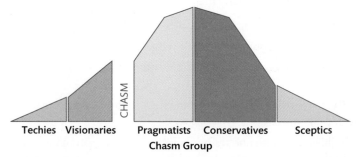

8.8 The Chasm Early/Late Markets

Source: Geoffrey A. Moore (1999), *Crossing the Chasm: Marketing and Selling Products to mainstream Customers* (Oxford: Capstone Publishers).

Once introduced to the marketplace, around 30 to 50 per cent of all new products fail to meet with commercial success, and for high-tech products the position may be considerably worse. The key problems are often that a company does not have the resources to support fast growth, in practice the new product falls short of its claims, the product is not that different in reality, not enough is invested in educating consumers to its value, or there is simply no market for the innovation (Schneider and Hall, 2011).

Crossing the chasm

Moore has argued that the fundamental issue for success in crossing the chasm is to understand the difference between the early and late markets. His perspective is oriented towards B2B rather than Rogers' B2C view, although the implications of chasm-marketing may be equally applicable to B2C markets (see Figure 8.9).

- **Techies:** companies that are largely motivated by technology. They do not particularly reference the behaviour of other companies and are willing to purchase high-tech products at a relatively low price and assume the risk of debugging any problems. They are not bothered if the supplier is a market leader but will need considerable training, especially with a discontinuous technology. Integrated marketing communications (IMC) to this group should stress 'newness'.

	Techies	Visionaries	Pragmatists	Conservatives	Sceptics
Motive	Tech	Personal vision	Business	Competition pragmatists	Only option
Ref Group	None	Other visionaries	Other pragmatists	Pragmatists	None
Pricing	Low	High	Market/med	Market/low	Low
Leadership	None	Potential	Strong contender	Market leader	Monopoly
IMC	New	Innovation	Safe/easy/ effective	Safe/easy/ effective	Only choice
Services	Train	High level consultancy	Some	Few	None

8.9 Chasm Strategies

Source: Geoffrey A. Moore (1999), *Crossing the Chasm: Marketing and Selling Products to Mainstream Customers* (Oxford: Capstone Publishers).

- **Visionaries:** companies that are looking to get ahead of rivals. They are not interested in technology for its own sake; rather, they see new technology as a way of getting ahead. They reference other visionaries, will accept relatively high pricing, and will need high levels of consulting training. Communications to this group should stress innovation rather than newness and they are likely to respond better to companies that exhibit signs of potential leadership of the new technology. If a company is unable to establish a business value for its innovation with visionaries, it is unlikely to cross the chasm.

- **Pragmatists:** on the other side of the chasm sit the pragmatists. The failure of most high-tech products rests on their inability to resonate with the pragmatic company. Pragmatists are looking to fix a 'broken business process'. Essentially, the problem posed by pragmatic companies is that if the innovation fails to fix something that they perceive as 'broken', they will simply not purchase the technology. They reference other pragmatic companies (not Techies or Visonaries), are prepared to pay a market price, and may need some training services. However, Pragmatists are looking to buy from companies that they see as strong contenders for market leadership in the technology. They do not want to be left holding innovations from companies that prove to be 'also-rans' and will need communications stressing that the technology is proven, safe, easy, and effective. If you have it, a particularly safe execution is to emphasize market leadership. The new high-tech product is launched in an 'all out' way that leaves customers in no doubt that you intend to push your product into the marketplace. Microsoft's launch of Windows was a classic case of a concentrated approach to execution, with a massive coordinated campaign across the globe with little expense spared.

- **Conservatives:** behind the Pragmatists sit the Conservative companies that, as you can guess, are much more risk-averse than Pragmatists. They see themselves in competition with Pragmatists whom they also reference. However, their risk-aversity means that they tend to wait to see whether or not the technology 'stays the course' and also what standards develop and which market leaders emerge. Pricing to this group needs to be at market or lower and the communications required are broadly similar to that to the Pragmatists: safe, easy, and effective. Case studies work particularly well with Conservatives. Given the penetration of the technology by this point, Conservatives need few services.

- **Sceptics:** are similar to Rogers' 'Laggards'. Sceptics are the companies at the end of the curve that have to be dragged 'kicking and screaming' into the market. They tend to buy when there is no alternative. What they have has broken down and they have to replace it, and the new technology is the only alternative. For example, a small firm of solicitors may be running its business with five-to-ten-year-old computers. They do the job and there is no reason to replace them except when they are uneconomic to operate. They do not reference other companies, need low prices, will tend to buy from the leading company in the market, and are unlikely to need much in the way of communications or training services.

Two marketing campaigns

Moore suggests that the best strategy for crossing the chasm is to conduct two marketing campaigns. The early market involves Techies and Visionaries. Techies can be used to make sure the innovation works and to 'iron out any bugs'. Visionaries should then be targeted and used to develop the whole product (see Figure 8.10), including pre- and post-sales and software and peripherals. Visionaries will enable the company to find the competitive advantage within the technology and establish the basis of the appeal for the Pragmatists. For example, QR codes (short for Quick Response) were invented in 1994 by Denso-Wave, a Japanese corporation, initially to track parts in vehicle-manufacturing using bar-code technology. These special bar codes have migrated to the consumer market and allow shoppers to swipe a packet of tomatoes, for example, and see such facts as the size and location of the originating farm. They have grown to cult status in Japan and have begun to appear in the UK, but can, of course, only be read by mobile phones with cameras. The technology is poised to cross the chasm from Techies and Visionaries to Pragmatists as Pepsi placed QR codes on 400 million products in late 2008, offering consumers access to games, videos, websites, and prizes at the swipe of a phone.

How might such technology as QR codes cross the chasm? Moore argues that as Pragmatists reference each other a 'bowling alley strategy' is required to make headway. The idea is to target and dominate a specific market that has influence over other markets—hence the bowling-alley analogy—one pin goes down and (hopefully) also knocks down several other pins too. Thus, when USDC developed an active-matrix flat-panel screen, with each pixel linked to its own transistor, it targeted the world's leading air forces which it knew had a pressing need to adopt paper-quality screens (Easingwood and Koustelos, 2000) and would influence outside commercial markets. Another example of targeting was NTT's Digital Photo System. The system enabled the transmission of digital pictures via mobile phones and was targeted at newspapers and insurance companies and later migrated out to other industries. Having penetrated the Pragmatic market and crossed the chasm, the Conservatives will then enter the market, buying from market leaders. Thus, industry opinion-leaders

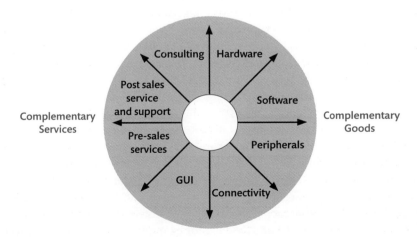

8.10 Whole Product

have been successfully used by Compaq and NEC. Doctors are commonly used by pharmaceutical companies to influence general practitioners.

There has been a recent question over the chasm. Is it a chasm or might it be a 'saddle'? A saddle is a sudden, sustained, and deep drop in sales of a new product after a period of rapid growth following initial take-off, followed by a gradual recovery to the former peak. Chandrasekaran and Tellis (2011) tested for the applicability of the saddle across products and countries using empirical data. They found on average the saddle occurs nine years after take-off at an average market penetration of a third and lasts for eight years with a drop in sales of just under a third in depth. Depending on specific circumstances they explained the phenomenon as being the results of the nature of chasm consumer adoption behaviour and the combined effects of both business and technological cycles.

Horizons of growth

An important element in managing product innovation and development is to recognize the stage of development of the business concerned. Baghai et al. (1999) have argued that there are three 'horizons' to consider: Horizon 1 (H1), Horizon 2 (H2), and Horizon 3 (H3). H1 businesses are mature and established and for most businesses provide the bulk of profits and cash flow. H2 are businesses on the rise and experiencing rapid growth. H3 businesses are emerging ones with potential.

Because each horizon has its own distinctive strategic and operational requirement, businesses encapsulating more than one horizon need more than one management system. H1 businesses need traditional management strategies and operations, and can be measured by productivity and efficiencies. H2 businesses require disciplined risk-taking and significant resources to capitalize on growth opportunities and so should be judged by revenue growth and market share, whereas H3 businesses are fledgling and need to be run by champions and inspiring leaders who can create new strategies and business models. The main measure appropriate to the H3 horizon is the ability of the business to make progress in converting new ideas into workable businesses. The advantage of the approach is that it fits nicely with Moore's ideas of the chasm (H3 is before the chasm; H2 at the growth stage; H1 at maturity), and provides a framework for managing innovation and development on a coexistent basis within large organizations, along with focusing management attention on the particular needs of fledgling businesses.

If you aren't the market leader

Innovation strategies that stress market dominance (Horizon 2 above) are all very well for the leading players in such markets, but what do you do if you are a smaller player in the marketplace? Quite often it is possible to be the leader in one market and a small player in another (see Mini Case 8.2). Yoffie and Kwak (2002) have identified what they call 'judo' strategy—an approach particularly well-suited to small players in innovative markets (see Figure 8.11 and Mini Case 8.2 for examples of small-scale innovations in India).

Mini Case 8.2   A snapshot of small-scale top innovators in India

Godrej Group

Godrej crowdsourced rural villages for design input on its small, affordable ChotuKool refrigerator. It can work on the mains or a battery, consumes just 62W of power, and is lightweight and easy to carry.

Indian Premier League

The IPL has introduced a new business model that has transformed cricket by restructuring, revamping, and tailoring the game to short attention spans and the need for entertainment infrastructure. As such the IPL is expected to generate revenue of over $2 billion over the next decade based upon revenues from ticket sales, TV, sponsorship, franchise sales, and theatrical rights to screen games in cinemas across India.

Narayana Hrudayalaya

Known in India for its low-cost heart surgeries, the company has launched 'Integrated Telemedicine Project' which aims to extend the hospital's health-care reach to 53 African countries through fibre-optic networks and satellite.

Sarvajal

In villages and urban slums, clean water is hard to come by. Sarvajal' (which in Sanskrit means 'water for all') has developed RFID-equipped ATMs to dispense purified water at a nominal cost through prepaid cards or coins, and harnessed technology to track usage, technical problems, and efficiency of its purifiers for villages and urban slums. Locals are encouraged to start their own water ATM franchises with over 150 franchises for over 70,000 people in rural areas.

Selco

Helped by the falling prices of panels, Selco has introduced solar lighting systems to more than 100,000 rural households with limited or no access to electricity.

Skymet

Skymet has introduced daily weather forecasts at local village level to farmers in 13 Indian states and streams data from 60 weather stations to its corporate clients. It has set up more than 2,000 weather stations in Maharashtra with a public–private partnership and streams forecasts to Indian TV, press, and radio.

VNL

A telecom for the rural poor using solar-powered base stations that can be fitted onto a village home's rooftop without much skill being required and hooked to a mobile service provider within about five or six hours.

Judo strategy is an approach to competition based on skill rather than size or strength and uses the three principles of 'movement', 'defining space', and 'speed' (see Figure 8.11). One of the key tactics in *movement* is the 'puppy dog play'. In essence, keep a low profile until you are strong enough to fight. For example, developments in mobile technology and apps didn't catch the attention of Microsoft until the market was well established. The next judo tactic is to *define the competitive space*. This boils down to keeping the product simple and uncluttered and easy to understand. The first apps for the then 'Android Market' in 2008 were simple and straightforward to use utilities and games that offered functionality and entertainment and helped define the space. The next tactic is to *follow through fast*. As Microsoft began to enter the mobile marketplace with apps for its Windows Mobile it has been faced with enormous competition (Google Play's open platform has 1.2m apps on offer compared with proprietary Windows Marketplace at some 160,000). There is little doubt that Microsoft will catch up and develop its app offerings to consumers and businesses, but Google's judo play of leveraging the power of the open source Android Java-based operating system has given it a considerable early advantage—classic judo strategy.

Innovation 'modes'

Despite strongly contended cases to the opposite by such companies as Sony, very little technological innovation is developed without some sense of a strategy. Once a new innovation or development has reached the market, people's perceptions and expectations are often changed (as with flat-screen televisions or photocopying) and often reshape how people live or work. Market success normally requires an overall strategic framework.

Overall, companies learn from markets, and the customers learn from new technologies. For any organization, the degree of focus on either innovation and/or the customer can vary. There are, therefore, as shown in Figure 8.12, four strategic options of low/high market orientation, matched with low/high innovation orientation (framework modified from the work of Berthon et al., 1999).

Isolate mode

The so-called 'isolate' mode (bottom left of the quadrant in Figure 8.12) is where an organization has a low innovation orientation as well as market orientation. The flows between customer and technology are almost non-existent, and technology either stagnates or is developed for its own sake. Stagnation or evolution occurs separately from the market. Such organizations are introverted and may be exemplified by the British automobile and motorcycle industry of the late 1960s and throughout the 1970s. British Leyland introduced innovations, but these were often tangential to market needs and preferences.

Movement
One of the key tactics in movement is the 'puppy dog play' **Keep a low profile until you are strong enough to fight**

Define the competitive space **Establish the positioning of the product and keep it simple**

Follow through fast
Maintain innovation with a focus on design, functionality, **and low prices**

8.11 Judo Strategy

Source: David B. Yoffie and Mary Kwak (2002), ' Mastering Strategic Movement at Palm', *MIT Sloan Management Review* (January), pp. 47–53.

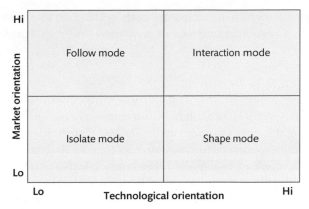

8.12 Options for Innovation

Source: Pierre Berthon, James M. Hulbert, and Leyland F. Pitt (1999), 'To Serve or Create: Strategic Orientations Toward Customers and Innovation', *California Management Review*, 42 (1), pp. 37–58.

Follow mode

The low innovation but high market orientation organization is in the 'follow' mode of the quadrant (top left in Figure 8.12). Here, technology is used in response to the needs and wants of the customer and may be seen with the development of Japan's Shiseido Company's 'White Lucent' which is used to lighten the appearance of skin discoloration due to sun exposure. This product line relies on Japanese botanicals and vitamin C esters. This is an example of a company designing products based on what customers want.

Shape mode

Organizations in the high innovation but low market orientation mode are in the 'shape' part of the quadrant (bottom right in Figure 8.12). Shaping is where a company applies a technology that defines human needs and determines the nature of customer demand. A recent shaper in the market would be the Apple iPod—a technological entrant that has disproportionately influenced the criteria by which later entrants, such as the Creative Zen, have been judged. Berthon et al. (1999) suggest two distinct forms of shaping. 'Definers' lead the market, as with Chrysler's minivan of the early 1980s, and Compaq's forging of the server market in the 1990s. 'Influencers', on the other hand, shape markets but do not define the market or dominate it. For example, the Apple Macintosh shaped expectations of computers without leading the market.

Interaction mode

Organizations that achieve a high market orientation married to high innovation are in the 'interaction' mode of the quadrant (top right in Figure 8.12). This is where a true dialogue occurs between an organization's application of technology and what customers want. Such interaction occurred before mass markets arose, of course, for example with men's and women's tailoring. However, interaction is being applied apace with the concept of one-to-one marketing, where companies such as Dell.com and iTunes allow customers to prepare their own specifications of computers and compilations of music CDs, respectively.

Strategic choice

Which mode to choose? It is difficult to be normative as each one has its good points—even isolation might have its proponents in some circumstances! A 'shaping' strategy would suit a rapidly evolving technology such as genetics, but given the power of large supermarkets, suppliers of fast-moving consumer goods (FMCG) might be best to 'follow'. Overall, it is likely that interaction would win the popular vote. In particular, interaction is the most likely of the four to maximize prices and profitability. Organizations that use technology in an interactive way and develop customized offerings reduce customer price pressures. For example, with **customization** car dealers would likely reduce the need to offer discounts to close a sale. As such, this strategy will be focused upon and the factors that affect an organization's ability to offer customization will be explored in the next section.

Customization

Customization and 'mass customization' are especially relevant to innovating and developing new services. It is worth bearing in mind that most of the product innovation and development research has been focused upon products rather than services, though products and services are on a continuum rather than on any fixed points. Nevertheless, relatively few researchers have examined the challenges of service NPD, or might it be termed NSD (New Service Development)? The difficulty is that services are fluid, dynamic, and co-produced in real time with buyers, whereas many of the invention/innovation techniques are focused on tangible 'hard' technologies (Bitner et al., 2008). In particular, Bitner et al. recommend deconstructing a service into its component parts (a technique they call 'service blueprinting'), including physical evidence, customer actions, onstage/visible contact employee actions, backstage/invisible contact employee actions, and, finally, support processes and most importantly keeping the focus on the customer throughout to find potential sources of innovation. Customization and adaptation are the foundations of NSD.

Customization from a marketing strategy context inevitably leads to an assessment of mass customization, which is similar to mass production in terms of its basic structure, with some significant differences. Instead of selecting one variety of product or service, the buyer provides unique information so that the product or service can be tailored to varying degrees. This means that the production process has to be flexible in order to tailor the product or service in the required way. Take the car industry. Only about 7 per cent of cars in the US are 'customized', or, as it is known in the car industry, 'built-to-order' (BTO). By contrast, in Europe BTO cars account for about 20 per cent of all cars sold. This is partly a reflection of the smaller dealer footprints in Europe (given land prices) and the higher proportion of premium sales.

One major benefit for following a customized innovation strategy is that there are no finished goods inventories for producers. On the other hand, customers inevitably have to wait longer than they might otherwise. Technologically, the differences between mass customization and mass production are only matters of degree. The key differences are the requirements for richer information flows and added process flexibility. Unfortunately, these provide significant barriers to the growth of mass customization as a primary innovation strategy for most organizations. There are essentially four key capabilities in mass customization (Agrawal et al., 2001; Swaminathan, 2001; see also Duray et al., 2000), namely 'elicitation', 'process flexibility', 'logistics', and 'inventory', that form the boundaries to any organization's strategy to mass customize.

Elicitation

Elicitation requires some means of interacting with customers to find out their requirements and is a difficult process. In order to elicit information, companies are presented with problems of enabling customers to decide what they want. Customers are sometimes certain about what they want, but often they are not. People make selections from menus. However, depending upon the nature of the product concerned, they might find the process frustrating and give up without buying anything. This is particularly likely with low-priced and standardized everyday products. Physical measurement makes elicitation more difficult. For example, when Levi Strauss experimented with the mass customization of women's jeans, their sales staff had to take measurements in stores as body-scanning equipment is still some way away. There is some experimentation with prototypes but the technology remains fraught with difficulties. Having said that, such things as three-dimensional views of sofas and three-dimensional body images that enable people to 'try on' clothes online from catalogues have been developed (see: <http://www.myvirtualmodel.com>).

Process flexibility

Process flexibility involves the use of production technology so that the product can be tailored according to the customer's information and presents another challenge. One-dimensional processes are relatively straightforward. For example, a bicycle frame can be customized by size and easily cut as required. Two-dimensional printing and printing-like technology are also relatively easy to undertake, as printing and patterns involve zero-dimension dots, one-dimensional lines, and two-dimensional patterns. However, three-dimensional processes are much less flexible. Robots are slow and expensive, so three-dimensional mass customization, such as for car parts, is a long way off.

Logistics

Logistics involves the processing and distribution stages so that the identity of each customer is maintained right through to delivery of the customized product and can present a considerable constraint to customization. Thus, Levi Strauss took several years to develop washable bar codes to customize jeans and sew and wash them in bulk, while tagging each order.

Inventory

Customization raises the question of how much inventory to carry to guarantee required service levels. How will the equipment cope with capacity? What levels of components will be needed? How do you manage the large number of suppliers required? With the shorter product life cycles in customization, how do you manage inventory phasing, marketing, and bringing on suppliers?

On the demand side, the key implication for inventory relates to sales forecasting. Establishing aggregate demand for product A (e.g. a Toyota Yaris) is one thing, but establishing accurate forecasts for subset configurations of product A (e.g. a Yaris Hybrid Icon Plus Model with Bluetooth) is another. Problems mount when there are several products (B, C, D, …) with their own possible configurations, especially when each product's sales could have an effect on the sales of others.

The car industry

The car industry presents an interesting case for customization and demonstrates the pros and cons for marketing strategy better than the headline cases like computers or the music business. A car company using customization as its main innovation strategy would have to leave plants idle during troughs of demand and operational changes would also be required. For example, it is standard practice across the industry for paint shops to process cars in batches for each colour to reduce costs and to minimize emissions and waste. Such economies and environmental benefits would be lost if colours were customized. Additionally, customization would also require shipping a mix of components according to individual orders rather than thousands of components as a batch.

US dealers might also resist BTO changes as they mainly feel that large numbers of cars on a lot show that they are 'healthy' and open for business. BTO would also require radical changes to labour organization and IT systems that might be painful to implement. Finally, from a customer perspective it remains unclear as to how far they are willing to trade-off delivery times of up to six months against customization.

Implementing customization

There are five primary approaches to implementing mass customization, differentiated by the degree of standardization.

- **Partial** customization is the most common approach. However, it can lead to a degree of cannibalization if noticeable. For example, two cars might share the same wire harnesses, whereas consumers would easily notice if the dashboards were the same.

- **Process** customization requires firms to store inventory in a semi-finished form to be customized to the specific order. For example, Honda redesigned its cars so that saloons, 4×4s, and sports models all come off the same production line.

- **Product** customization involves offering a large variety while stocking relatively few and thus being prepared to substitute higher specifications. For example, Avis and other rental companies substitute higher-end cars when lower-end ones are out of supply.

- **Procurement** customization is where there is commonality in part and equipment purchasing across a wide variety of products. For example, PC manufacturers can aggregate their demand across a wide variety of products.

- Finally, an ingenious alternative is to offer '**virtual customization**' (Swaminathan, 2001; Papathanassiou, 2004). This involves setting up a network via the Internet or distributive channel. For example, in the case of the car industry, if customers can be offered access to dealers' cars, cars in transit, cars on the assembly line, or cars scheduled for production, the chances are that they will find the one with the right colour and options for them. Thus, customization or BTO is replaced by the ability to 'locate-to-order'. Customers do not care whether the product was especially built for them or not, or where the product is found in the supply chain, as long as it has the features that they want. Virtual customization via shops or the Internet may be a strategy with considerable appeal not restricted to the car industry.

Conclusion

Innovation can be a winning component of any marketing strategy. The vast majority of today's brand leaders have introduced breakthrough innovations at some point in their histories. This chapter has focused on the use of innovation and product development, but the reality is that the vast majority of companies do not see it as the panacea in the marketplace. To be fair, unplanned and untargeted innovation simply leads to what has become known as 'innoflation'—a position where new products and services are launched into the marketplace at a frenzied pace with very little impact. Consumers just get confused, company supply chains overheat, and the end result is a poor return on investment. Study after study has shown that, at heart, most consumers are loyal to a core of products and services in most markets and so, if there is to be any innovation, it needs to be focused upon existing brands. Today, too many organizations take a risk-averse stance and would rather stay with the tried and tested and buy out any competitors who appear to have hit upon 'blockbuster' innovations in the marketplace.

As Airbus, Dell, Dyson, eBay, easyJet, Indigo (Indian low cost airline), and Tesco have shown (to name but a few), challenging or reinventing what you offer through innovation can hold the key to market success. This chapter has shown that what is required is a measured and planned approach to innovation and its potential impact on costs and/or differentiation in the marketplace. As such, it is to be hoped that more companies will reduce their concentration on immediate competitors and consider wider lateral innovation based upon new definitions of market needs and wants. For many companies, the wisest strategy would be to include innovation within their marketing strategy rather than to focus on best value alone. At the bare minimum, all companies should regularly review their innovation strategy against current and anticipated market needs and wants.

Summary

Product innovation and development can play a pivotal role in marketing strategy. Central to this is the concept of new product development (NPD), a creative activity towards which there are many different approaches, such as systematic invention thinking. Particular strategic issues to consider are market preparation and product rollovers, which can have a dramatic impact on product innovation and development. Strategic frameworks that can provide considerable insight include Rogers' product adoption curve and Moore's concept of 'crossing the chasm'. Smaller players in the market should consider the judo strategy. An organization's overall innovation mode is worth giving careful thought to. Customization is becoming an increasingly important area of marketing strategy.

Key terms

- **Adoption patterns:** differences in the propensity of customer types to adopt innovations.
- **Customization:** tailoring products and services to suit individual needs and wants.
- **Disruptive technology:** a technology that fundamentally shifts the production paradigm and often how a product or service is used.
- **Innovation:** subsequent changes and adaptations to 'new-to-the-world' introduction. *Innovare* is the Latin verb meaning to change or to alter.
- **Judo strategy:** an innovation strategy used by relatively small companies to outwit larger rivals based upon skill rather than size or strength.
- **Market preparation:** market strategies to ensure that new-to-the-world products do not shock consumers.
- **New-to-the-world:** significantly new product or service market introductions that are often discontinuous.
- **NPD:** new product development.
- **Product rollovers:** displacement of existing products by new ones.
- **Systematic inventive thinking:** an NPD system based on the work of Genrich Altshuller to manipulate idea generation and stimulate relevant creativity.
- **Toolkit strategy:** enabling customers to take significant control over the NPD process.

Discussion questions

1. Briefly outline and describe the umbrella of activities included in product innovation and development.

2. Are there any particular kinds of innovation that are more important than others or does it depend upon market conditions?

3. Toolkit strategy is a growing trend amongst B2B product developers. Do you think such an approach to innovation might work in any particular B2C markets?

4. Apply the five patterns of systematic inventive thinking (subtraction, multiplication, division, task unification, and attribute dependency change) to the iPad. Can you create what you regard to be a viable new product that adds value?

5. Can you name two or three products that have recently failed to cross the chasm? To what extent do you think lack of interest from Pragmatists was the problem?

6. What are the major advantages and disadvantages of customization?

Online resource centre

 Visit the Online Resource Centre for this book for lots of interesting additional material at: <www.oxfordtextbooks.co.uk/orc/west3e/>

References and further reading

Aaker, David (2007), 'Innovation: Brand It or Lose It', *California Management Review*, 50 (1), pp. 8–24.

Agrawal, Mani, T. V. Kumaresh, and Glenn A. Mercer (2001), 'The False Promise of Mass Customization', *McKinsey Quarterly*, 3, pp. 62–71.

Baghai, Merhrdad, Stephen Coley, and David White (1999), *The Alchemy of Growth: Practical Insights for Building the Enduring Enterprise* (London: Orion).

Barone Michael J. and Robert D. Jewell (2013), 'The Innovator's License: A Latitude to Deviate from Category Norms', *Journal of Marketing*, 77, January, pp. 120–34.

Berthon, Pierre, James M. Hulbert, and Leyland F. Pitt (1999), 'To Serve or Create: Strategic Orientations Toward Customers and Innovation', *California Management Review*, 42 (1), pp. 37–58.

Billington, Corey, Hau L. Lee, and Christopher S. Tang (1998), 'Successful Strategies for Product Rollovers', *Sloan Management Review*, Spring, pp. 23–30.

Bitner, Mary Jo, Amy L. Ostrom, and Felicia N. Morgan (2008), 'Service Blueprinting: A Practical Technique for Service Innovation', *California Management Review*, 50 (3), pp. 66–94.

Bonabeau, Eric, Neil Bodick, and Robert W. Armstrong (2008), 'A More Rational Approach to New-Product Development', *Harvard Business Review*, March, pp. 96–102.

Booz Allen Hamilton (1982), *New Product Management for the 1980s* (New York: Booz Allen Hamilton).

Brown, Bruce and Scott D. Anthony (2011), 'How P&G Tripled Its Innovation Success Rate: Inside the Company's New-growth Factory', *Harvard Business Review*, June, pp. 64–72.

Calantone, Roger J. and C. Anthony Di Benedetto (2012), 'The Role of Lean Launch Execution and Launch Timing on New Product Performance', *Journal of the Academy of Marketing Science*, 40, pp. 526–38

Cauz, Jorge (2013), 'How I did it…Encyclopaedia Britannica's President on Killing Off a 244-Year(-Old Product', *Harvard Business Review*, March, pp. 39–42.

Chandrasekaran, Deepa and Gerard J. Tellis (2011), 'Getting a Grip on the Saddle: Chasms or Cycles?', *Journal of Marketing*, 75, July, pp. 21–34.

Christensen, Clayton M. (1997), *The Innovator's Dilemma: When New Technologies Cause Great Firms to Fail* (Boston, MA: Harvard Business School Press).

Christensen, Clayton M., and Michael Raynor (2003), *The Innovator's Solution: Creating and Sustaining Successful Growth* (Boston, MA: Harvard Business School Press).

Drucker, Peter F. and Joseph A. Maciariello (2008), *Management: Revised Edition* (New York: Harper Collins).

Duray R., P. T. Ward, G. W. Milligan, and W. L. Berry (2000), 'Approaches to Mass Customization: Configurations and Empirical Validation', *Journal of Operations Management*, 18 (6), pp. 605–25.

Easingwood, Chris and Anthony Koustelos (2000), 'Marketing High Technology: Preparation, Targeting, Positioning, Execution', *Business Horizons*, 43 (3), pp. 27–34.

Fleming, Lee and Matt Marx (2006), 'Managing Creativity in Small Worlds', *California Management Review*, 48 (4), pp. 6–27.

Goldenberg, Jacob, Roni Horowitz, Amnon Levav, and David Mazursky (2003), 'Finding your Innovation Sweet Spot', *Harvard Business Review*, March, pp. 120–9.

Johnson, Mark M., Clayton M. Christensen, and Henning Kagermann (2008), 'Reinventing your Business Model', *Harvard Business Review*, December, pp. 50–9.

Lakshmanan, Arun and H. Shanker Krishnan (2011), 'The Aha! Experience: Insight and Discontinuous Learning in Product Usage Success', *Journal of Marketing*, 75, November, pp. 105–23.

Markides, Constantinos (2006), 'Disruptive Innovation: In Need of Better Theory', *Journal of Product Innovation Management*, 23, pp. 19–25.

Mizik, Natalie (2010), 'The Theory and Practice of Myopic Management', *Journal of Marketing Research*, 47, August, pp. 594–611.

Moore, Geoffrey A. (1999), *Crossing the Chasm: Marketing and Selling Technology Products to Mainstream Customers* (Oxford: Capstone).

Moore, Geoffrey A. (2004a), *Inside the Tornado: Strategies for Developing, Leveraging, and Surviving Hypergrowth Markets* (New York: Harper Business).

Moore, Geoffrey A. (2004b), 'Darwin and the Demon: Innovating within Established Enterprises', *Harvard Business Review*, July–August, pp. 86–93.

Noble, Charles H. and Minu Kumar (2008), 'Using Product Design Strategically to Create Deeper Consumer Connections', *Business Horizons*, 51, pp. 441–50.

Papathanassiou, E. A. (2004), 'Mass Customisation: Management Approaches and Internet Opportunities in the Financial Sector in the UK', *International Journal of Information Management*, 24 (5), pp. 387–99.

Rogers, Everett M. (1983), *Diffusion of Innovations* (New York: Free Press).

Schneider, Joan and Julie Hall (2011), 'Why Most Product Launches Fail: Getting Attention for a New Offering is a Big Challenge. Five Causes of Flops—and How to Avoid Them', *Harvard Business Review*, April, pp. 21–3.

Spradlin, Dwayne (2012), 'Are You Solving the Right Problem?: Most Firms Aren't and That Undermines Their Innovation Efforts', *Harvard Business Review* September, pp. 84–93.

Swaminathan, Jayashankar M. (2001), 'Enabling Customization Using Standardized Operations', *California Management Review*, 43 (3), pp. 125–35.

Thomke, Stefan and Eric von Hippel (2002), 'Customers as Innovators: A New Way to Create Value', *Harvard Business Review*, April, pp. 74–81.

Verganti, Robert (2006), 'Innovation through Design', *Harvard Business Review*, December, pp. 114–22.

Waytz, Adam and Malia Mason (2013), 'Your Brain at Work: What a New Approach to Neuroscience Can Teach Us About management', *Harvard Business Review*, July–August, pp. 102–11.

Wessel, Maxwell and Clayton M. Christensen (2012), 'Surviving Disruption: It's not enough to know that a threat is coming. You need to know whether it's coming right for you', *Harvard Business Review*, December, pp. 56–64.

Yoffie, David B. and Mary Kwak (2002), 'Mastering Strategic Movement at Palm', *MIT Sloan Management Review*, January, pp. 47–53.

Zipkin, Paul (2001), 'The Limits of Mass Customization', *MIT Sloan Management Review*, 42, Spring, pp. 81–7.

Key article abstracts

Vorhies, Douglas W. and Michael Harker (1999), '**Capabilities and Performance Advantages of Market-Driven Firms**', *European Journal of Marketing*, 33 (11/12), pp. 1171–202.

This is a useful paper. It places NPD and innovation within the context of the marketing mix and for assessing the relationship to marketing orientation.

Abstract: Although progress has been made in understanding market-driven businesses from a theoretical perspective, relatively few empirical studies have addressed the capabilities needed to become market-driven and the performance advantages accruing to firms possessing these capabilities. One of the barriers faced has been in defining what is meant by the term 'market-driven'. This paper develops a multi-dimensional measure useful for assessing the degree to which a firm is market-driven. The paper presents evidence that market-driven business units developed higher levels of six vital marketing capabilities (in the areas of market research, pricing, product development, channels, promotion, and market management) than their less market-driven rivals, and significantly outperformed these rival business units on four measures of organizational performance.

Hart, Susan (1993), '**Dimensions of Success in New Product Development: An Exploratory Investigation**', *Journal of Marketing Management*, 9 (1), pp. 23–41.

This paper indicates that there is not much evidence that NPD success or failure is measured financially.

Abstract: As a key element in survival and sustaining growth, the constant development and redevelopment of products has been the subject of many academic and consulting group studies. The specific focus of these studies has often been to identify and describe those factors which determine the outcome of new product developments, the critical success factors in NPD. In order to fulfil their objectives, the studies have focused on many aspects of the management of new product development programmes in companies, and attempted to relate them to a number of alternative outcomes. This has called for the measurement of 'success' itself. Unfortunately, there is very little consensus amongst the authors of the studies regarding how best to operationalize 'success', and researchers have employed a variety of measures, focused on different levels of analysts, sought data from different sources, and used different data-collection methods. This paper examines the performance measures used in several major NPD studies and shows how success 'measures' have been treated as financial and non-financial. In addition, attention is drawn to the problems inherent in the different definitions of success. Finally, using data from an empirical survey, the relationship between financial and non-financial outcomes is examined.

Haenlein, Michael and Barak Libai (2013), '**Targeting Revenue Leaders for a New Product**', *Journal of Marketing*, 77, May, pp. 65–80.

Traditionally marketers have placed emphasis on opinion leadership. This paper reminds us of the importance of the value of the customer and the recognition that customer connectivity necessitates a 'network view' of customer decision-making and profitability. The authors suggest including the value created by high value customers (revenue leaders) as well as opinion leaders in any new product strategy.

Abstract: Historically, when targeting potential adopters of a new product, firms have tended to focus first on people with disproportional effect on others, often labeled 'opinion leaders.' The authors highlight the benefit of targeting customers with high customer lifetime value (CLV), or 'revenue leaders.' The authors argue that targeting revenue leaders can create high value both by accelerating adoption among these customers and because of the higher than average value that revenue leaders generate by affecting other customers with similarly high CLV. The latter phenomenon is driven by network 'assortativity' (whereby people's social networks tend to be composed of others who are similar to themselves). Analyzing an agent-based model of a seeding programme for a new product, the authors contrast revenue leader seeding with opinion leader seeding and compare the factors that influence the effectiveness of each. They show that the distribution of CLV in the population and the seed size play a major role in determining which seeding approach is preferable.

End of Chapter 8 case study   Amazon instant video

Introduction

Consumer appetite for streaming video consumption is increasing, and a number of companies are competing for market share. Netflix, the clear current market leader, has reigned over this industry, as it introduced a streaming video product as an extension of its DVD rental by mail offering and by most accounts provided the first viable commercial streaming video service to carry mainstream movies and television series programming. Amazon, the titan of Internet shopping, has realized the market potential of this blossoming industry, and, given its wealth of knowledge and experience in Internet-based technologies, has taken a product to market that directly rivals Netflix's. It is now faced with the challenge of obtaining market share from entrenched 'first-movers', as well as spurring adoption of this product by their existing customer base.

In considering the uphill battle in which Amazon is engaging, one must take into account a number of factors pertaining to consumer behaviour, from brand equity and impact of promotions on brand switching, to brand loyalty and consumer adoption of innovative products. This case will detail the established research on such topics and address a few of Amazon's early strategic attempts to gain market share as it enters an increasingly competitive streaming video market.

Context

Streaming video on demand (SVOD) products established their genesis in the mid-1990s with rudimentary pioneering broadcasts that served to showcase the advent of new Internet-based technology. Given the explosion of smartphone and other mobile media device sales, SVOD products are now a mainstay of the consumer media delivery mechanisms. Companies such as Netflix and Amazon have commercialized this technology by providing customers with mainstream video content acquired via contracts with the major production studios and visual media conglomerates that create the first-rate cinematic blockbusters and popular television series broadcast on major networks.

This relatively recent media delivery method has amounted to a significant paradigm shift in media profitability. A greater number of consumers are interested in finding ways to rid themselves of increasingly exorbitant cable TV costs, while still retaining accessibility to comparable high-quality content. Netflix entered the media arena by offering monthly subscription service for mail-delivered DVD movie rentals. Advances in technology-based logistical modelling allowed them to send and receive DVDs frequently and rapidly with highly predictable delivery windows. By establishing a part-virtual/part-tangible business model, Netflix was able to eliminate all serious bricks-and-mortar competition, as it operated at a fraction of the overhead costs of their rivals. Consumers gleaned greater value from a firm offering a selection wider than that of a video rental store, orchestrated the pick-up and drop-off of their rentals, and eliminated the concept of late fees.

Given the warm reception consumers expressed toward this model of media delivery, Netflix expanded on its delivery options by offering SVOD products, which eliminated time lag between requesting movies and actually viewing them, as well as reduced costs associated with DVD delivery. Netflix aims to appeal to the masses and has leveraged its prior connections to content-producing entities in bolstering its available streaming content. It retains the majority of the SVOD market despite catastrophic membership losses in 2011 following a failed DVD/SVOD business divergence plan that alienated some consumers. It would appear that Netflix is set up to maintain this advantage for years to come, given that the full capacities of SVOD delivery have not yet been realized and that their history of industry experience and Internet technologies predisposes them to success as demand for this type of product trends upward.

Beginning in September 2006, Amazon has cautiously participated as a 'second mover' in the SVOD industry. Amazon has made some high-profile strategic content acquisitions since the unveiling of 'Amazon Prime Instant Video' in January 2011. By combining yearlong two-day shipping on all Amazon-based purchases, access to SVOD resources, and monthly e-book rental benefits, Amazon is attempting to lure market share from Netflix by way of a 'value-added' model that enhances the original Amazon Prime offering that only included two-day shipping. Presently, Amazon doubles its quantity of SVOD titles every nine months, and their library is presently comparable with that established and currently offered by Netflix (Figure C8.1). Additionally, Amazon is pursuing ventures aimed at developing its own original content, as opposed to solely contracting with other networks and production outfits. Further capitalizing on consumer desire for SVOD on a mobile platform, Amazon recently began selling its newest portable media device, the Kindle Fire HD, which will reinforce its efforts to penetrate the SVOD industry.

It is notable that a distinct 'information advantage' is held by companies whose products are tried first, as they gain experience from which to determine subjective value. Even though consumer loyalty diminishes as the number of comparable competitive brands increases, consumers tend to express greater loyalty to 'pioneering brands', such as Netflix. One application of this theory that companies may pursue is to appeal to the target segments via free trials and promotional opportunities, which research has shown to be the most effective trigger for motivating consumers considered likely to be brand-switching in nature.

Amazon's ease of use and available free trials for select demographics support its market potential. Research has shown that free trials are a useful tool in enticing customers into adopting a new product. While the use of free trials aids the adoption process, it does not necessarily guarantee long-term adoption. Rather, a consumer's free trial period is followed by significant evaluation of the experience, then adoption. Companies, such as Amazon, should follow up and provide any necessary assistance during this evaluation period in order to promote the likelihood of 'positive product confirmation,' which increases the chances of truly on-boarding an 'adopter' for the long-term.

Now that Amazon has positioned itself as a contender in the SVOD arena in terms of content and delivery platforms, the only obstacle remaining between implementation and successful execution is the marketing strategy. By battling Netflix head on, Amazon is fighting an uphill battle to shift the market share distribution away from the entrenched leader, and success largely depends on enticing consumers to switch brands from Netflix to Amazon Prime Instant Video.

Segmentation and current marketing strategy

Firstly, it is important to define the market segment that Amazon seeks to attract toward its Amazon Prime Instant Video product. Its targets include both men and women—generally young, given their disproportionately large and generally accepted affinity for technology and

Internet-based shopping and media delivery platforms compared with other age segments. Current Amazon Prime promotions are tailored specifically toward college students and new mothers, both of whom are considered by Amazon to be high-frequency purchasers (i.e. text books for students, infant and baby necessities for mothers) and therefore potential Amazon Prime customers, even if solely for the shipping benefit. Given their previous extensive experience with Amazon, these segments are likely to try new offerings it provides, and, if satisfied, they serve as powerful brand and product ambassadors through word-of-mouth advocacy with their peer groups.

This segment seeks convenience as a major factor in determining a product's valuation. While older segments may seek video content via Netflix's original DVD mail delivery system or Redbox kiosks located adjacent to convenient retail locations, Amazon's target segment seems to place a greater emphasis on and desire for stay-at-home, on-demand, convenience. For college students and new mothers, it seems that Amazon is attempting to acquire their purchasing power based on convenience in conjunction with economy. While many may already have utilized Amazon Prime for shipping benefits, the new Amazon Prime offer (with Instant video and e-book rental) provides a bundle of services obtained through one simple transaction. The same concept was applied to smartphones. In order to edge out proximal competitors, smartphone manufacturers increased the number of device features available. By bundling the features, these improved smartphones have the potential to significantly impact PC and laptop sales and have decimated the digital camera industry.

Amazon seeks to do the same: bundle SVOD products with other features and effectively eliminate the need for consumers to acquire separate services via different vendors and provide the perception to their customers of deriving greater value. Amazon's current offering saves time by eliminating interfacing with superfluous vendors for duplicate services, as the idea of a 'one-stop-shop' aligns squarely with their needs. Adding to the convenience of Amazon's offering is use of the singular annual fee, versus the monthly billing practices utilized by Netflix. Instead of having to regularly 'manage' their SVOD account, Amazon Prime customers pay once to enjoy the benefits for an entire year. As a benefit for Amazon, this subscription structure essentially 'locks in' their customers for that duration and prevents brand switching.

As Amazon's SVOD product represents an 'innovation' to some extent, given its bundled nature, it is important and relevant to detail previous research associated with new product adoption. One model for new products and the resultant acceptance by consumers categorizes products in terms of their likelihood of success based upon new product benefits versus the degree to which consumers must change their current behaviour. 'Sure Failures' provide very little benefit compared with current market offerings and require exorbitantly high degrees of behaviour change, 'Long Hauls' yield substantial benefit but also require a significant behaviour change in the consumer, 'Easy Sells' provide ample benefit and require little change on the part of the consumer, and 'Smash Hits' result in copious benefit in conjunction with a minimal consumer-required behaviour change.

To illustrate these innovation types, consider where current market offerings in the SVOD arena exist presently and suppositions of future offerings. Market leader Netflix requires very little in terms of consumer effort and the benefit is substantial. A consumer does not need to purchase any new equipment to enjoy Netflix's content, and the 'on-demand' convenience of their delivery system is a notable benefit. This would squarely fall into the 'Smash Hits' category. Amazon could be considered an 'Easy Sell' by virtue of its benefits and the small amount of change required to realize them. Given general acceptance of SVOD products, Amazon's offering (in comparison with other SVOD providers) only requires the consumer adapt to using a new, unfamiliar user interface. Even though it is necessary for a consumer to expend effort to attain Amazon's benefits, the investment is decidedly minimal. However, in the context of a demographic that has yet to adopt SVOD technology, all SVOD providers' offerings may perceptually be considered 'Long Hauls.' To this group, SVOD may represent a foreign departure from comfortable technology, and they may prefer more tangible media formats, such as DVDs. While they may not dispute the benefits of SVOD, the personal investment they must make to change consumption formats may seem quite large, slowing the pace of adoption in this type of group. Finally, should an SVOD provider create a product that requires its own exclusive hardware, it risks falling into the 'Sure Failures' category. Requiring consumers to pay additional costs in terms of equipment and failing to provide benefits greater than those that are already available from other SVOD products essentially creates its own entry barriers and certainly increases the likelihood of product failure.

Conclusion

Amazon has made substantial advancements in developing its SVOD product and determining its target segments. Since Amazon is a 'second-mover' in this industry, and therefore trails significantly behind other SVOD providers in terms of market share, it will have to apply concepts pertaining to consumer behaviour in order to compete successfully in this burgeoning industry, which has revealed no near-term indicators of reaching maturity. By examining factors that encourage (or discourage) brand loyalty, brand switching, and new product adoption, Amazon will greatly increase their odds of supplanting Netflix as the market leader and be much more prepared in responding to competitor reactionary manoeuvres.

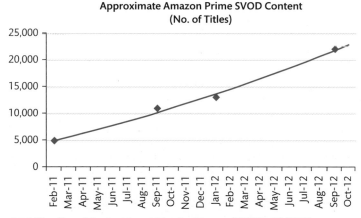

Approximate Amazon Prime SVOD Content (No. of Titles)

C 8.1 Timeline of Content Acquisition by Amazon (2/2011–10/2012)

Since February 20011, when Amazon announced the pairing of Amazon Prime shipping benefits with value-added Instant Video, content available to consumers has essentially doubled every 9 months.

Discussion questions

1. As a second-mover in the SVOD market, is Amazon Prime making a sound strategic decision by targeting college students and young mothers?

2. What adopter categories with respect to consumer behaviour do these targets fall in to?

3. Is there another audience that would be more beneficial to capture in order to gain market share?

4. Explain who this audience would consist of and the adopter categories that should be targeted.

5. List three reasons for and against changing the marketing strategy to capture these users.

Source: This case was prepared by Matthew Protulipac, Evan Goldstein, Lauren Kanick, Alyssa Roffol of the University of Pittsburgh. The case is solely for the basis of class discussion and is not intended to illustrate effective or ineffective management or administrative situation or any form of endorsement.

Service marketing strategies

 Learning Objectives

1. Grasp the nature of services.
2. Discover the relationship between service quality and customer satisfaction and profitability.
3. Be able to apply the service dominant logic to both services and manufactured goods.
4. Be familiar with ways in which services can streamline operations and improve productivity and profitability.
5. Understand the nature of the customer service experience.
6. Be able to appreciate the relationship between customer value and sustainable competitive advantage.
7. Acquire several strategic tools for fine assessment of the service process and the delivery of customer value.

 Chapter at a Glance

I. Introduction

1 Overview and strategy blueprint

2 Marketing strategy: analysis and perspectives

II. Where are we now?

3 Environmental and internal analysis: market information and intelligence

III. Where do we want to be?

4 Strategic marketing decisions, choices, and mistakes

5 Segmentation, targeting, and positioning strategies

6 Branding strategies

7 Relational and sustainability strategies

V. Did we get there?

14 Strategy implementation, control, and metrics

IV. How will we get there?

8 Product innovation and development strategies

9 Service marketing strategies

10 Pricing and distribution strategies

11 Marketing communications strategies

12 International marketing strategy

13 Social and ethical strategies

 Case study: India's Mumbai dabbawalas bring new meaning to service excellence

A recent article in *Harvard Business Review* (2012) by Stefan Thomke focused on the incredible service that is provided by a corps of 5,000 individuals known as dabbawalas who carry meals made by customers at home to their places of work in metal pails called dabbas and then return the empty pails each day to the customer's home. The amazing thing is that there are roughly 130,000 lunch pails moved each day throughout the year during a six-hour period of time, six days each week across the city of Mumbai. The feat that these poorly educated workers accomplish is quite remarkable given that they do it at a minimal expense without high technology. Thomke reports that the dabbawalas were formed back in 1890 and have survived many major obstacles including wars, riots, storms, and disease. The goal for the entire process is on-time delivery, and the major vehicle is the Mumbai Suburban Railway. The way that the system works is that delivery personnel use bicycles to move between homes and offices and between train stations. Office workers find restaurants expensive and want their own home cooking, so they prefer cooking their own meals and then having them delivered to their offices.

This complex system requires the pail to be picked up from the customer's home and taken to a nearby train station where it is put on a pallet according to where in the city it is being sent. The pallets are then transported to another train station and taken to the offices. At this point it is sorted out again and taken by a dabbawala to the office before lunchtime. The afternoon is spent carting the empty dabba from the office back to the customer's home. As Thomke reports, the dabbawalas have created 200 separate units comprised of 25 persons per unit to carry out the delivery process, and each unit has its own control. The whole process is enormously efficient with a charge per customer of somewhere between £5 and £6 per month. Everything is geared around the train schedule with workers having to load and unload the crates of pails in as little as 40 seconds at major stations and only 20 seconds in lesser stops. This tight scheduling forces discipline into a potentially chaotic situation. If one of the dabbawalas is late, or makes a mistake, it is obvious to all involved and is rectified quickly. It is interesting to note that the dabbawalas manage themselves, and all are expected to contribute to a fund used for insurance and financial help for emergency situations. For example, broken or stolen bicycles can be replaced using resources from this fund.

Each dabbawala negotiates prices for delivery with their customers, but there are price rules and guidelines set up by a governing body of dabbawalas. The relationships that are developed between the dabbawalas and their customers are often long term in nature with a great deal of trust being built between the individuals involved. There is then a strict code of conduct where no other dabbawala is allowed to try to steal the business for themselves. The afternoons allow the opportunity to communicate with their customers about their schedules, pending concerns, and to collect their fees. Thomke reports that if someone wants to join a unit, the rest of the members will see if there is sufficient demand to allow a new member to join. The members then take responsibility for training the new participant over a probationary period of six months, and they charge the individual the equivalent of ten times their expected monthly income to buy a share in the operation. After ten years of experience the individual can become a supervisor, and individuals are chosen from each unit by the members to serve on the managing committees.

This fascinating system works because strict rules and processes are adhered to. The dabbawalas feel a sense of belonging to their unit, and the shared identity brings with it a pride of workmanship and service. They wear a uniform, and most of them are poorly educated. They understand exactly what their core service proposition is and live by it. It has kept them viable in many challenging times when many other services have failed. The point is the attention to the process that works so very well.

One interesting point of information is that the team from *Top Gear* (the popular BBC car show) went to India to see if they could improve on the delivery system used by the dabbawalas by driving a number of dabbas to their appointed destinations through the city. Jeremy Clarkson, Richard Hammond, and James May are known for their driving abilities, but in this instance they failed miserably in trying to better the efficiency of the Mumbai Suburban Railway and demonstrated very effectively just how well this system works.

Introduction

There is little doubt that the service sector is the fastest growing sector of the world economy. In the countries of the OECD (Organization for Economic Co-Operation and Development (OECD), services now account for almost 70 per cent of gross domestic product (GDP), and service jobs make up the largest category of all employment opportunities with nearly 65 per cent of all OECD country workers employed in activities related to services (OECD, 2010). Even in the emerging economies, services are rapidly growing and often comprise more than 50 per cent of GDP (World Bank, 2013).

Services are by nature intangible, heterogeneous, inseparable, and perishable, and they create unique strategic challenges. While an understanding of industry structure can aid the service strategist to streamline service delivery and improve profitability, it is also important to achieve sustainable competitive advantage (SCA) through customer satisfaction and the creation of perceived value (Frei 2008). Services cannot be protected in the same way as manufactured goods with property rights such as patents, so they are easily copied, unless the company has built a perceptual bond with its customers. To beat competitors, the service firm must continually meet and/or exceed customer expectations (Stuart, 2006; Ford et al., 2001). This forces the firm to continually monitor the wants and needs of its target customers and to strategically refine its offerings to enhance customer value.

The focus on customer value is not just relevant for service firms. Many global industries are presently being forced toward standardization of offerings as life cycles mature. The road to parity creates enormous strategic turbulence as firms attempt to differentiate their offerings from those of competitors. Manufacturers can differentiate through the development of value-laden complementary services, but the key is to ensure that these complementary services are perceived by target customers as adding real value to the overall offering (Cohen et al., 2000).

The challenge for service firms is to create a position of perceptual value and power that cannot be easily copied by competitors. This requires a constant balancing of operational efficiency, perceived differentiation, and customer relationship building. This chapter will focus on the nature of services, set the foundation of the general service experience, and then focus on operational efficiency and profitability and the building of relationships with customers that enhance differentiation and perceptions of customer value.

The distinctive nature of services

There are four readily accepted distinguishing characteristics for services that create strategic challenges (see Figure 9.1). Briefly, each of these will be examined, the 7Ps of services will then be examined, and the stage will be set for the experience associated with the service.

Intangibility

Services are seen as being intangible so that customers cannot hold them, touch them, and try one out before buying. A key strategic issue is that even the most intangible services (pure services like consulting projects or executive seminars) have certain tangible aspects to them that can be used to convey perceptions of service quality. Consulting personnel can dress in a manner to convey professionalism, the consulting offices where meetings with the client take place can be managed to convey success and professionalism through various atmospheric components (e.g. furniture, floors, walls, lighting, colour, music, etc.), and the various promotional materials, communications, and project reports can be presented in such a way as to exude quality. Even the most intangible service can be made more tangible in creative strategic ways.

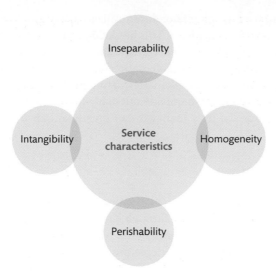

9.1 Service Characteristics

Heterogeneity

This focuses on the fact that each time the service is provided there will be differences due to environmental variation or changes in attitude, mood, or emotion on the part of either the provider or recipient. It is therefore important for the services marketer (given the heterogeneity of service interactions) to ensure as much consistency as possible. While total consistency is impossible, there are mechanisms that can be utilized to reduce inconsistencies. One involves the design of the service in such a way as to make it as uniform as possible. This might be accomplished via automation where possible or by training service personnel to follow strictly controlled guidelines. Hand-in-hand with this approach would go the need for effective employee selection, motivation, and retention. No matter how sophisticated the service is, there is no substitute for hiring the right people, training them effectively, and putting them into an environment that nurtures their success. Many service providers have found that another strategic approach is also necessary to eliminate the problems inherent in heterogeneity—the use of money-back guarantees. If the firm expects that even with tight controls, there will be the chance of a disgruntled customer, the offering of a money-back guarantee may alleviate any post-production dissonance that might arise due to service provider–customer interactions.

Inseparability

In the mind of the service customer the service cannot be separated from the provider of the service. This creates challenges. Companies can foster a more proactive involvement on the part of the customer. Another way to deal with this issue is to look at the location issue. The production must be brought to the customer, so providing additional locations for the service provision and training personnel to effectively handle greater demand for the service is critical, arguing for greater decentralization and employee empowerment to ensure the highest service quality level. This has helped build loyal followings for easyJet, Virgin, and Apple Computers. Another strategic approach that could help involves training service personnel to deal with problematic customers so as to reduce the potential for customer dissonance. Vocal problematic customers can negatively affect other customers involved, and moving them quickly out of a public area into an office where their difficulties can be addressed by a manager can greatly enhance the experience for all concerned.

Perishability

Since services cannot be stored in inventory, they are perishable. Dealing with the peaks and valleys of demand can only be handled through either flexing capacity or shifting demand. There are a number of ways that have been found over the years to synchronize supply and demand. These include (1) differential pricing to shift demand to slower/quieter time periods (e.g. off-peak prices for hotel rates), (2) new services provided to customers while waiting (movies on TV screens while queuing), (3) new service opportunities in off-peak time periods (free oil change if your car is serviced at off-peak times), (4) the use of reservations systems (keeping better track of supply and demand), (5) flexing capacity to have more staff on duty during peak times and fewer at slower times (like McDonald's, KFC, or Pizza Hut), (6) increasing the use of the customer as co-producer (customer packs up their own pots and pans before moving services arrive to pack up the rest of their household furnishings), and (7) developing services that can be shared by other service providers (reservations system to help a variety of service providers).

The 7Ps of services

In addition to the normal marketing mix elements (product, price, place, and promotion), services are normally associated with three additional mix elements: people, process, and physical evidence.

People refers to the fact that those service personnel who interact with the customer become integrally linked to the service in that interaction. In the eyes of the customer these people become the service, and it is not possible to separate the service from the service provider representative. How the customer actually feels about that service experience is shaped by the interaction, so the company must hire personnel who can do their job and enhance the customer service experience. Strategically this focuses on hiring and retaining the best people for the provision of the service, and trusting and empowering them sufficiently to allow them to provide the best customized service to meet the expectations of the customer. Service personnel are boundary spanners between the company and its customers, and they serve an important function in conveying customer expectations to management and facilitate the delivery by enabling the customer to become a co-producer of the service.

Process reflects the fact that there is a process utilized to provide the service to the customer. This requires the company to step back and examine that process looking at all of the interactions between customers and service personnel to see if the process is as smooth and efficient as possible. A proper process assessment will also examine the support personnel and processes that operate out of the customer's view to quality-control the delivery.

Blueprinting is an effective mechanism for this kind of assessment, and the company is able to identify potential red flag areas when the entire delivery process is carefully examined. The point is to ensure that the customer gets the best experience as efficiently and effectively as possible when they want it. Banks can easily benefit from this blueprinting by seeing all the steps that a customer goes through once they enter the bank, and they can see where any potential stumbling blocks might be in the provision of the various bank offerings. What is particularly helpful is that the non-contact service personnel are also included along with the background supporting processes (e.g. the cleaning services who come after hours, the IT support staff, the ATM maintenance personnel, etc.). All aspects of the service can be examined to ensure that the service provision is smooth and error free.

Physical evidence focuses on the various visible attributes that affect the delivery process and customer satisfaction. This can involve the layout of the shelving and aisles in a Tesco or Waitrose store, the colours painted on the walls, the music playing in the background, the carts that are being pushed by customers for their food items, the uniforms worn by store personnel, the end-of-aisle displays, the use of posters on the walls to inform customers, etc. The point is that each of these may add to the overall service experience, and the key is to find the best experience to make the customer happy and get them to come back again. The **servicescape** is the pictorial representation of the physical evidence associated with the service, and it provides an excellent mechanism for additional service performance evaluation. If the physical components of the service are inconsistent with the expectations of the customer, there is increased potential for service failure and customer loss. Can you imagine dirty tablecloths at a restaurant owned by Gordon Ramsay? Every aspect of a service environment can affect the perceptions of the quality of the service.

Customer experience strategies

In order to be successful, service strategists should try to understand exactly what the consumer is looking for when they 'experience' the service in question. Each customer will have a set of expectations regarding the service experience that must be met to ensure his or her satisfaction. How is customer satisfaction ensured? Research has consistently shown that the key to service firm success is keeping the customer happy. Fulfilment appears to be the key ingredient in the concept of customer satisfaction (Grenci and Watts, 2007). If a service meets or exceeds the customer's expectations, they will enjoy a sense of fulfilment and will be satisfied with the service consumption experience. The job for the service strategist therefore is to determine how to measure service quality.

SERVQUAL: measuring the quality of the customer experience

Parasuraman et al. (1991) have done extensive work examining the concept of service quality, and they found that service quality is a multi-faceted construct with five distinctive dimensions: reliability (dependability and accuracy), responsiveness (helpfulness and promptness), empathy (customer understanding and individualized attention), assurance (employee competence, courtesy, and trustworthiness), and tangibles (condition of physical evidence). The authors created a survey instrument to assess customer perceptions of service quality along these five dimensional lines that they named SERVQUAL, which has been used in many settings to compare the expected service delivery with the actual customer perceptions of service delivery to provide an excellent service process evaluative tool. The various questions that make up the SERVQUAL questionnaire are shown in Figure 9.2.

The way that SERVQUAL works is that there are three sections to the survey instrument. The first section asks the respondent to respond to the various items listed in Figure 9.2 with regard to an ideal provider of the type of service directly in question. Using 7-point scales with anchors of strongly agree and strongly disagree, respondents then indicate their perceptions of the offerings of an ideal service provider across the 22 items in terms of their level of agreement with the statements. The second section of the instrument uses the same 22 items, but this time the statements are written with regard to the specific service provider being assessed. There is also a third section in which the respondent is asked to indicate

Tangibles	Reliability	Responsiveness	Assurance	Empathy
• This service has modern-looking equipment. • This service's physical facilities are visually appealing. • This service's employees are neat-appearing. • Materials associated with the service (such as pamphlets or statements) are visually appealing.	• When this service promises to do something by a certain time, it does so. • When you have a problem, this service shows a sincere interest in solving it. • This service performs the service right the first time. • This service provides its services at the time it promises to do so. • This service insists on error-free records.	• Employees of this service tell you exactly when services will be performed. • Employees of this service give you prompt service. • Employees of this service are always willing to help you. • Employees of this service are never too busy to respond to your requests.	• The behaviour of employees of this service instils confidence in customers. • You feel safe in your transactions with this service. • Employees of this service are consistently courteous with you. • Employees of this service have the knowledge to answer your questions.	• This service gives you individual attention. • This service has operating hours convenient for all its customers. • This service has employees who give you personal attention. • This service has your best interests at heart. • Employees of this service understand your specific needs.

9.2 SERVQUAL Survey Items

Source: A. Parasuraman, Leonard L. Berry, and Valarie A. Zeithaml (1991), 'Understanding Customer Expectations of Service', *Sloan Management Review*, 32 (3), pp. 38–49.

their priorities regarding the five different groupings of SERVQUAL statements, allowing 100 points to be divided up across the five groupings of items (empathy, tangibles, assurance, responsiveness, and reliability). This then indicates the relative importance of each of the groupings.

The use of SERVQUAL allows the service provider to do a gap analysis, which allows researchers to see whether the expectations of customers are being met or not. Each of the 22 items can be compared in terms of the ideal setting (or the expected level of performance) and the actual performance they received. If the expected score is subtracted from the actual score, and the result is a negative number, then the customer expectations are not being met. This is the gap in question. Of course, if the result is positive, then it means that the customer is getting more than they expected in that case. The reason for the third section becomes obvious if one considers only addressing the gaps involved, since one would assume that the statements that reflect the biggest gaps would strategically be the ones most in need of revamping.

A potential problem could therefore arise if the items that have the biggest gap scores associated with them are considered to be the least important in the overall assessment of the service offering. This has often been the case when SERVQUAL has been applied to university education since the items that are often associated with higher gap scores tend to be the tangibles category (classrooms, campus, etc.) while these items are considerably less important than assurance items reflecting, say, the quality of the professors and lecturers the students are learning from. Strategically it would not make sense in that case to put large expenditures into plant and equipment due to the limited importance that those have for the students involved. SERVQUAL research has shown many times over that perceptions of service quality lead ultimately to better firm performance.

Why is this set of relationships so important? Because perceptions of service quality lead to customer satisfaction, which in turn leads to positive purchase intentions, which leads on to sales and profits. The point is that satisfied customers are likely to come back and spend more in the future while also passing the word to others. Many researchers have found that the longer a service company is able to retain its customers, the more they will spend on the services the company offers.

Service-dominant logic: enhancing the customer experience through the customer as co-producer

Much of the early work on services focused heavily on the distinctive nature of services and the fundamental differences between services and manufactured goods. While this was helpful for service strategists at first, a new perspective has appeared in the marketing literature which takes a very different look at marketing products and services. From the definition of product in marketing, most now interpret this to mean anything that has value for the consumer. This could relate to a product, a place, a person (e.g. a political candidate), or a location (holiday destination), as well as a service. Assuming that products are separate and distinct from services may be somewhat of a problematic perspective since a service component beyond the actual manufactured product is a key ingredient in the ability to attract and retain customers. As a result, Vargo and Lusch (2004) have introduced a valuable new perspective for marketing which they call **service-dominant logic** (see Figure 9.3) in which the firm uses the customer as a co-producer of the service or good created. This perspective suggests that this can be used with anything that has value to facilitate the exchange process.

The key terms in this approach are **operand resources**, which refer to **resources which are acted upon or operated upon to produce an effect**, and **operant resources**, which are **resources which are used to act upon operand resources**. In other words, operant resources are resources that actually produce effects. So from the operand resources perspective, customers are acted upon, while from the operant resources perspective, the customer becomes an actor in something else (e.g. a co-producer). The customer is the actor rather than what is acted upon, an important distinction in this emerging perspective. Eight different foundational premises differ between goods-centred and service-centred logic (Vargo and Lusch, 2004).

FP1: The application of specialized skills and knowledge is the fundamental unit of exchange.

FP2: Indirect exchange masks the fundamental unit of exchange.

FP3: Goods are distribution mechanisms for service provision.

FP4: Knowledge is the fundamental source of competitive advantage.

FP5: All economies are services economies.

FP6: The customer is always a co-producer.

FP7: The enterprise can only make value propositions.

FP8: A service-centred view is customer-oriented and relational.

The point behind the new paradigm is to not consider goods and services as separate and distinct as has been suggested for so long. The key is that in this era of relationship marketing, all marketers must focus on using a services-centred dominant logic to avoid the problems inherent in acting upon the customer rather than acting with the customer to create something of perceived value. The eight foundational premises, if applied to all marketing output, will not only increase perceived value in the output for the customer, but will also ensure competitive advantage for the firm. A more fundamental comparison between goods-dominant and service-dominant logic can be seen in Figure 9.4. This shows the basic differences and further explains why the service-dominant logic approach is the higher road to take for strategic marketers to build meaningful relationships with their customers.

From service-centred dominant logic it can be seen that what will help ensure success for service firms involves meeting or exceeding customer expectations, and it is this perceptual position in the head of the customer that serves as the basis for sustainable competitive advantage.

Service delivery as drama

An important step in service delivery and enhancement of the customer experience can be seen in the burgeoning interest in viewing services through the lens of **dramaturgy** (Grove and Fisk, 1983; Grove et al., 1992). In other words, it involves thinking of the service delivery and experience as the performance of a drama with its main elements being

Resources	Traditional goods-centred dominant logic	Emerging service-centred dominant logic
Primary unit of exchange	People exchange for goods. These goods serve primarily as *operand resources*.	People exchange to acquire the benefits of specialized competences (knowledge and skills), or services. Knowledge and skills are *operant resources*.
Role of goods	Goods are *operand resources* and end products. Marketers take matter and change its form, place, time, and possession.	Goods are transmitters of *operant resources* (embedded knowledge): they are intermediate 'products' that are used by other operant resources (customers) as appliances in value-creation processes.
Role of customer	The customer is the recipient of goods. Marketers do things to customers: they segment them, penetrate them, distribute to them, and promote to them. The customer is an *operand resource*.	The customer is a co-producer of service. Marketing is a process of doing things in interaction with the customer. The customer is primarily an *operant resource*, only functioning occasionally as an operand resource.
Determination and meaning of value	Value is determined by the producer. It is embedded in the *operand resource* (goods) and is defined in terms of 'exchange value'.	Value is perceived and determined by the consumer on the basis of 'value in use'. Value results from the beneficial application of *operant resources* sometimes transmitted through *operand resources*. Firms can only make value propositions.
Firm–customer interaction	The customer is an *operand resource*. Customers are acted on to create transactions with resources.	The customer is primarily an *operant resource*. Customers are active participants in relational exchanges and co-production.
Sources of economic growth	Wealth is obtained from surplus tangible resources and goods. Wealth consists of owning, controlling, and producing *operand resources*.	Wealth is obtained through the application and exchange of specialized knowledge and skills. It represents the right to the future use of *operant resources*.

9.3 Goods-Dominant vs. Service-Dominant Logic Perspectives: Resource Use

Source: Stephen L. Vargo and Robert F. Lusch (2004), 'Evolving to a New Dominant Logic for Marketing', *Journal of Marketing*, 68 (January), pp. 1–17.

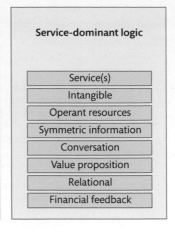

Goods-dominant logic	Service-dominant logic
Goods	Service(s)
Tangible	Intangible
Operand resources	Operant resources
Asymmetric information	Symmetric information
Propaganda	Conversation
Value added	Value proposition
Transactional	Relational
Profit maximization	Financial feedback

9.4 Basic Differences in Logic Paradigms

Source: Robert F. Lusch, Stephen L. Vargo, and Alan J. Malter (2006), 'Marketing As Service-exchange: Taking a Leadership Role in Global marketing Management', *Organizational Dynamics*, 35 (3), pp. 264–78.

the stage, the actors, and the audience. Each will be discussed in turn, followed by a discussion of excellence in performance and the enhancement of emotional engagement with the customer.

The stage: servicescape

The servicescape is the physical evidence associated with the service offering. The stage is set for the service experience and the greater the fit between the expectations of the customer and the appearance of the physical setting, the greater the potential for a positive service experience. Think of the appearance of a restaurant in terms of the cleanliness of the tables, the floors, etc. There is also the matter of the colours of the paint on the walls, the amount of light from the lighting fixtures, and the soft music playing on the sound system. These components make up what is referred to as an ambience, and it can make or break a service experience even when the personnel involved are doing everything they can to make the experience as positive as it can be.

All of these servicescape elements add to or detract from the customer's experience, and the need to understand the expectations of the target customer is imperative for the enhancement of the service experience. How many tables are spread across the room, the nature of the tablecloths and the types of chairs, and whether fine china and crystal are involved can affect the view of the customer regarding the delivery of what they expected or not. Walt Disney World washes down their servicescape every night to ensure that it is spotless for the visitors the next day.

The actors: service personnel interactions with each other

The actors are the various service personnel who come into contact with the customer during the service experience. As with a stage performance, the actors have to be in synch with each other. Is a romantic play believable if the two romantic leads have no chemistry with each other? If the waiter in a restaurant argues with another waiter or other staff members, does this enhance the service experience? So the actors themselves have to be working together to make the experience a memorable and satisfying one for the customer.

The better that the cast gets along, the better will be the experience for the audience. It is also important that there is a connection between the actors and the audience. If the audience does not sympathize or empathize with the characters on stage, the experience can be less than positive. The more that the audience buys into the cast and feels comfortable with them, the better the service experience is likely to be for the audience.

The audience: customer interactions during the service experience

While the actors have to be in synch with each other as well as with the audience, the audience members need to be compatible with each other to enhance the experience. When customers are surrounded by people that they do not feel comfortable around, this can detract from their enjoyment of the experience. Compatibility management is the monitoring of the customer interactions with other customers to ensure compatibility. Active management of the fit among a variety of customers is a strategically relevant issue for service providers. One way to accomplish this is by means of differential pricing. This approach has been used in many major cities with opera companies charging significantly higher prices for opening night than for other performances.

Imagine the romantic evening that involves a couple being seated next to a loud and obnoxious table of partying diners. This might certainly ruin the ambience that they had hoped for. Other ways of addressing compatibility issues can involve having dress and behaviour codes, or different venues with different environments and prices. The point is to maximize the enjoyment of the experience by matching the various parts of the service to the expectations of the various customers involved.

Great performances and emotional engagement

So how can service provision as drama be used to make service companies profitable and ensure their success? Any old performance will not create the appropriate emotional engagement with the customer to build an emotional bond; the service provider must ensure that the presentation creates a 'great performance' (Stuart, 2006). The idea is that customer loyalty, which is imperative for long-term profitability and gains in market share, is something which is fostered not by perceptions of service quality, but by very high levels of customer satisfaction and service reliability. This need to go above and beyond suggests that service managers look to wow their customers with the overall experience that they provide.

The misunderstandings amongst service managers include the following (Stuart, 2006): (1) the belief that the delivery of a memorable service experience is the same as an understanding of the customer's perception of the service, (2) the re-labelling of current performance is the same as a memorable experience, and (3) making sure that they save the very best part of the service experience for the last to account for recency effects are not stand-alone mechanisms for offering great and memorable performances. He suggests that it is the ability to design a comprehensive experience which integrates a wide range of individual elements.

The following seven steps for use by service managers to offer not just a good, but an outstanding service experience can be suggested (Stuart (2006).

Step 1 is never to lose sight of the main stage. This means that the service provider must be careful not to offer inconsistent offerings and confuse their audiences. Service managers should keep the service concept clear and focused. For example, Canada's low-cost airline WestJet lost sight of its mission and began to experiment with inconsistent offerings like leather seats, satellite televisions, and expanded legroom.

Step 2 is to communicate extensively with visual cues. The need in this step is to create a common direction and sense of purpose as well as a shared vision among all personnel within the organization which should be reinforced through all manner of visual cues and not just by spoken words and phrases. For example, the Lieutenant Governor of British Columbia focused on renovating historic stable grounds into tourist attractions but faced community resistance. The approval of the plans was facilitated through the effective shared vision and visual cues in the form of artists' renderings of what these facilities would look like once renovated, which brought everything together.

Step 3 is to continuously strive for authenticity and integrity. This focuses on the importance of creating a realistic and authentic environment for the service in all aspects and to develop a service delivery system and environment that is totally in synch with the service concept. The idea here is that the service firm's theme should be vital for provision of an outstanding offering. Examples include Outback Steakhouses focusing on the authenticity of the Australian theme and experience in all facets of their offerings.

Step 4 involves integration and communication. Here the idea is to make sure that there is integration and communication across all facets of the service delivery environment. All disciplines and functions should be integrated using both formal and informal means with the purpose of supporting the needs of the front line service personnel. Take the case of the Fairmont Hotel chain in Canada and the difficult lesson that was learned when trying to focus on guest name recognition and its impact upon customer satisfaction and the potential for repeat business; there were inconsistencies across the various hotels in implementing, which was further exacerbated by differences in technological capabilities and departmental structuring.

Step 5 is to use experimentation to move towards excellence. In this case the idea is to use constant innovation and experimentation to find the best ways to delight the customer in their service experience. A great deal of this process of development is never explained or shown to the customer. Look at Tim Horton's, which tried to gain market share in the lunchtime market by offering fresh soups and sandwiches. They did not work through the process correctly and found many problems in terms of the nature of the soups and sandwiches, and long queues arose due to the wide variance in service deliveries to different customers.

Step 6 is to not only play the part, but to become the part in every way. The idea is that the delivery process is not something that should be attempted without careful practice and preparation. Walt Disney provides a great example with their training programmes in which employees are encouraged to act their parts with great sincerity so that all will believe that they are who they appear to be.

Step 7 is to fire the director and hire the facilitator. This means that in order to truly integrate the varying processes that are needed to deliver a memorable performance, a facilitator and not a director is really needed. This requires a special individual who can see beyond the superficial. This is where it all comes together, and the examples point to the dangers of not having that facilitator to bring the disparate components of the service offering together properly.

Having established the key foundations of services, the chapter will now focus on the strategic issues that surround services. Given the Porter focus adopted for this book, the key questions are: (1) how can we use our service strategy to reduce our overall costs and (2) how can service strategy differentiate our offerings and help to build a meaningful relationship with the target consumer?

Operational efficiency and profitability

Since services are basically intangible, difficult to protect legally, and have relatively low barriers to entry, they are easy to copy. Operational excellence is one way in which service firms can achieve strategic success. Operational excellence can be garnered in two important ways, **streamlining** and cost-cutting, and also through creative strategic alliances. Strategic successes provide excellent opportunities for service firms to improve operations and raise profit margins. A series of effective mechanisms for operational improvement will now be discussed and illustrated with company examples.

Streamlining and cost cutting

Many service providers have found the need to improve operations to eliminate inefficiencies and improve profit margins. To a certain extent customer value is enhanced when firm cost-cutting can be passed along with visible savings for the customer. Four major trends have forced service providers to focus on cost-cutting: (1) ever-intensifying competition as industry regulations open competition to new and varied types of competitors (e.g. deregulation and the sanctioning of new and creative strategic alliances), (2) slowing industry growth projections, (3) increasing levels of parity across providers, and (4) increasing levels of customer expectation. Service firms must satisfy customers at ever-decreasing cost levels (Arnold et al., 1998). Service providers have recently embraced some of the cost-cutting benefits that were experienced by Western manufacturers attempting to remain competitive with the Japanese during the 1990s (Swank, 2003). This recent use of 'lean service management' focuses on re-engineering operations to improve profitability. However, service providers always need to measure any improvements in performance and productivity from the customer's perspective (Swank, 2003). Whatever is attempted should not detract in any way from perceptions of customer value, otherwise competitiveness would be severely eroded. So what are specific ways in which services can improve their productivity? Friedman (1998) makes the following suggestions.

1. Operate with fewer workers by providing supporting equipment and systems or helping employees do more (e.g. automation for efficiencies like scanners for supermarkets and ATMs for banks).

2. Eliminate certain elements of a process (e.g. check-in and check-out processes for hotels and rental car companies).

3. De-skill certain jobs to allow the use of a broader pool of workers (e.g. point-of-sale machines that do not require skilled employees to oversee).

4. Take non-customer work requirements from frontline service personnel and delegate them to others within the organization (e.g. moving international currency exchange capabilities out of neighbourhood bank branches to special regional offices).

5. Determining those tasks that must be performed close to the customer as opposed to those which can be done far away (e.g. regional as opposed to local customer service centres).

6. Offloading certain work requirements to suppliers (e.g. hospitals and prepackaged surgery kits).

7. Changing customer expectations in terms of their involvement in the process (e.g. self-service filling stations and customers filling their own soft drink cups at fast-food restaurants).

Jefferson Pilot Financial provides an excellent example of service **streamlining** by successfully transforming itself into a lean service management enterprise (Swank, 2003). The company implemented a number of changes that improved efficiency while reducing costs. Process employees were moved into closer proximity with each other after having been previously structured along functional lines. Customer files were then more efficiently moved along from group to group. Procedures were also standardized with all files being stored alphabetically, and process employees were housed in similar settings to ensure consistency and allow substitute employees to work efficiently when needed. It was also found that previously there had been feedback loop-backs where applications might go back to previous processing stages and cause delays. These were eliminated. Another improvement involved setting common work tempos for employees so that higher application per hour completion goals could be set. This type of process re-engineering proved to be extremely beneficial for Jefferson Pilot Financial, allowing the company to charge lower premiums and handle applications more quickly.

In addition, services must redesign the jobs of the personnel involved in the service delivery process (Metters and Vargas, 2000). Sometimes technologies become available that allow cost-cutting across the entire service while improving the level of the quality of the service provided. When these technologies exist, they should be adopted immediately. When these technologies are not available, they suggest that management should consider **decoupling** service tasks to gain efficiencies. Decoupling involves removing certain low customer contact tasks from frontline or front office personnel, standardizing them, and moving them into remote back office locations. They present four different competitive approaches to decoupling (see Figure 9.5) and provide illustrative examples for each.

The first category presented is the **Cost Leaders** (companies that compete on price and decouple for the main purpose of lowering costs). The focus here is to take complex jobs with multiple tasks and make them simpler through standardization with the use of specialized labour and new technologies to achieve economies of scale. The decoupling of complex jobs allows the reduction of work variance. The discount stockbroker Charles Schwab & Co. and the insurance company GEICO are firms which have eliminated localized personnel who were high customer contact and paid by commissions, which was the standard of their industries. The standardization of certain basic components of the customer delivery process significantly streamlined operations and improved profitability.

The second type is the **Cheap Convenience** company which attempts to make their service offering more convenient while maintaining a relatively low cost structure. This is known as a 'kiosk' strategy, where the firm utilizes multiple service units in different locations to provide easy customer access but offers only a limited range of both back-office and front-office work. Examples of successful competitors in this category include Dollar General, 7-Eleven (Southland Corporation), and Edward D. Jones stock brokerage services. These firms compete against the Cost Leaders by offering many convenient smaller product-line outlets. Key to success for these firms is the development of easy-to-use software and the use of tightly scripted service encounters between customers and service personnel.

The third category is the **Dedicated Service** firm that decouples to support front-office personnel with cost reduction as a secondary concern. Here tasks are separated by

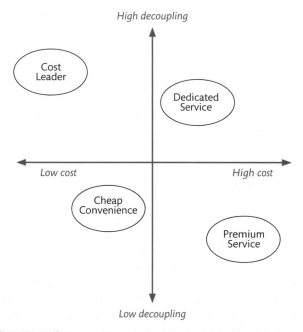

9.5 Service Decoupling Approaches

Source: Richard Metters and Vicente Vargas (2000), 'Organizing Work in Service Firms', *Business Horizons* (July-August), pp. 23–32.

personality type and ability. Decoupling here allows more variety and flexibility to enhance employee morale and customer service experiences. The driving concept is worker suitability with matching of service work to personality type. Back-office tasks are centralized by region or particular back-office contacts are specified for each group of front-office workers. Long-term relationships are built between back and front office to help the service delivery process flow smoothly. This approach requires more staff and potentially higher costs. Many traditional hospitals and insurance companies follow this kind of service strategy. The key here is to set up proper reward structures based on how well the back-office personnel support the front-office workers.

The final decoupling approach is the **Premium Service** firm where less decoupling is used in order to maximize responsiveness and customization. Here the strategic goal is to provide personalized service at premium prices. Intimate relationships are built between customers and service personnel. Frontline personnel are given power to customize a variety of offerings to meet the specific needs of each customer, while back-office personnel are minimally decoupled. The US firm Krispy Kreme Doughnuts has successfully positioned itself as a Premium Service firm in comparison with Cost Leader Dunkin' Donuts (Metters and Vargas, 2000). A sound differentiating device for hospitals can involve the development of specialized maternity (e.g. the Tennessee Birthing Center) or paediatric orientations (Children's Hospital of Philadelphia).

Creative strategic alliances

A creative strategic way to improve service profitability involves strategic partnering between different service providers, since alliances can effectively be used to strengthen brands and cut costs. These alliances can take the form of co-branding, co-marketing, outsourcing, licensing, or distribution agreements, to name a few. Examples can readily be seen in the strategic partnerings of airlines like the Star Alliance, Northwest Airlines and KLM, and United Airlines and Lufthansa, as well as in the offering of T-Mobile WiFi hotspots at Texaco stations, Starbucks coffee on United Airlines flights, and UK mobile operator 3 offering BMG music videos for download to its customers with mobile phones. These alliances offer another approach to differentiation of service offerings by allowing partners to retain their own independent brands and financial control while cutting costs and improving profits. Savings are facilitated through sharing of assets and/or business processes or through the outsourcing of components of the offering.

Nevertheless, partnering must ensure that there is no erosion of each partner's core service concept (Ernst and French, 1996). There are two main types of strategic alliance for services: brand-sharing alliances and asset-sharing alliances. Brand-sharing alliances involve the increase of customer benefits through joint offerings with minimal system integration.

The idea is to create greater value for the consumer by offering complementary services rather than to achieve enormous cost savings. Citibank developed a relationship with American Airlines to offer its credit card users benefits in the form of frequent flyer miles. This required only a minimum of coordination and integration, but both brands enjoyed brand enhancement. Asset-sharing alliances look to business system integration for the purpose of significant cost savings. These alliances can involve the sharing of real estate, computer systems, equipment, and technology. 7-Eleven (Southland) has asset-sharing relationships with Citgo filling stations to share the cost of real estate. This has also been seen with the use of Little Caesars pizza offerings in K-Mart stores and McDonald's food offerings in Wal-Mart stores. Some of these alliances can become more like mergers than strategic partnerings as the partners become integrally linked with one another. This can be seen in the airline industry with such pairings as USAir and British Airways, with common hubs, maintenance, and ticketing facilities. It has been estimated that this alliance has resulted in cost savings and increased revenues for the partners of over $100 million per year (Ernst and French, 1996).

Instrumental to the issue of strategic alliances is the burgeoning area known as **coopetition** (Kirchner et al., 2007). This focuses on a continuum between cooperation and competition, and great promise is seen for the small service firm, particularly for non-profit and charitable organizations, which are asked to accomplish much with extremely limited budgets. In the instance of regional and local arts and cultural organizations, with extremely limited operating budgets and depending upon donations from corporations and individuals for their survival, combining forces for the creation of shared events has great potential for improving their reach and aiding in their achievement of their missions. The fact that they will share resources for event creation, but not in any way for fund-raising, demonstrates that these alliances are not open in all ways; thus they are both cooperating and competing at the same time.

Partnering also requires the assurance that there is a tight fit between partners in terms of customer demographics and brand image. Customers must readily see the benefit in the pairing of services. Ernst and French (1996) provide the following suggestions for managing alliances.

1. Prepare for an alliance as you would for a merger.
2. Mechanisms must be established for strategy development, organizational decision-making, and assignment of financial accountability in the new alliance culture.
3. Both partners must move quickly and effectively to manage the transition.
4. Budget sufficient time for alliance work.
5. Monitor progress on a weekly basis, at least at the beginning.
6. Build-in mechanisms for conflict resolution and decision-making.
7. Consider exit options.

Another approach to alliances that can have synergies for service firms and aid in the cost-cutting process is **outsourcing**. It has been reported that more than 90 per cent of all US service firms have outsourced some of their service offerings (Allen and Chandrashekar, 2000). This potentially allows firms to get goods and services at a lower cost and a higher quality by relying on firms that specialize in certain components of service delivery. Anything that the firm believes is not part of their core competency becomes a candidate for outsourcing. This enormous trend toward outsourcing began with IT as a functional area with providers like Andersen Consulting, but it has spread to all kinds of service businesses. Hotels outsource concierge services, restaurant services, and cleaning services. Airlines outsource cleaning and maintenance and reservations services. Almost anything can be outsourced, provided that it does not potentially erode firm core competencies and confuse the customer. A good overview of outsourcing possibilities based on the levels of service provided by the service contractor can be found in Figure 9.6.

Level of contractor contribution

	Labour contracting	Mixed outsourcing	Complete outsourcing
Contractor provides...	• Some employees	Some or all of the following: • Employees • Materials • Process and systems • Technology and equipment • Facilities • Management/supervision	• Employees • Process and systems • Technology and equipment • Materials • Facilities • Supervision
Host firm provides...	• Some employees • Process and systems • Technology and equipment • Materials • Facilities • Management/supervision	Some or all of the following: • Employees • Materials • Process and systems • Technology and equipment • Facilities • Management/supervision	• Programme management

9.6 Categories of Service Outsourcing

Source: Sandy Allen and Ashok Chandrashekar (2000), 'Outsourcing Services: The Contract Is Just the Beginning', *Business Horizons* (March-April), pp. 25–34.

Outsourcing must be carefully managed (Allen and Chandrashekar, 2000). First, the management of outsourcing requires a shift for managers from the management of people to the management of contracts. The wording of the contracts becomes the focal point rather than the governance of personnel. An important first step in the process should be to clearly define the expectations for the use of outsourcing. A key point that the authors make is that outsourcing should not be used as a method for eliminating a problem area for the firm if the real problem stems from something that is systematic within the firm itself. Outsourcing often involves the combination of contract workers with regular service personnel, and there is always the challenge of dealing with divided loyalties and employee role conflict. Outsourcing managers must deal with potential conflicts between these two different types of worker. While cohesiveness of the workforce is challenging, with proper open communications and thoughtful strategic planning, outsourcing can be a powerful mechanism for service streamlining.

Streamlining service operations and improving productivity are excellent strategies for improving profitability, but the other side of the equation, which is equally important, is to ensure that the customer experience is the best that it can be. In order to continually meet or exceed customer expectations it is imperative that service strategists understand exactly what the consumer expects to be delivered by the service. This next section will focus on differentiation and the nature of customer service expectations and the achievement of sustainable competitive advantage.

Effect of Internet/digital/technology on expectations

Service provision must now adapt to the extensive consumer reliance on various social media mechanisms. They affect what customers expect in a variety of ways. The stage is often set for consumers in terms of service experience through the use of a variety of apps which are readily available for mobile telephones, laptops, iPads, and other tablets. These apps facilitate access to airline ticketing, hotel reservations, car rentals, and restaurant reservations, as well as tickets for orchestral concerts, plays, operas, motion pictures, and a wide variety of sporting events. These apps give customers valuable information about availability and pricing, and people are now able to use their mobiles to get through airport security as their boarding passes or tickets are shown on their screens. One of the most valuable aspects of Amazon's various websites is the ability for interested buyers to play small sections of the music that they are interested in to 'sample' the merchandise before they buy it.

While samples of haircuts and cosmetic makeovers are not readily available online, testimonials and pictures of customers experiencing satisfying service encounters are readily available via apps and websites. These apps are geared towards increasing purchases among customers and breeding loyalty, but they also provide helpful information for consumers such as reviews from other customers to reinforce their satisfaction and maintain loyalty. The easy access to a wide variety of blogs and Google-identified websites gives customers a great deal of information before the actual service experience is provided. While this is helpful for consumers to draw them to particular service providers, it also adds pressure on the service providers to do everything in their power to ensure that the service experience is the best that it can be since digital hype can raise expectations to a challenging level.

In the United States banking has changed significantly through the availability of customer apps. Bank of America touts an app which allows the customer to deposit money by merely taking pictures of endorsed checks with their mobile phone. There is no longer a need to actually go to a bank branch to do some of the things necessary to handle their banking needs. While they will still have to go to an ATM to withdraw actual cash, they can go to a wide variety of self-service locations at any time of day or night to get their funds. The idea of customer convenience is now taken to an even higher level. Customers can also move funds from one account to another easily via a website or mobile app.

Many airlines now make things as easy as possible for consumers. Delta, British Airways, Qantas, Japan Airlines, and many others provide frequent-flyer-oriented apps which allow easy access to flight reservations, flight upgrades, and seat changes, along with hotel reservations and car rentals. Tying these with their own personal credit cards (Delta has its gold American Express frequent flyer credit card which gives the user 30,000 additional frequent flyer miles with the first expenditure of $500.00 on the credit card. Airlines are also providing quick means to add additional miles to frequent flyer totals with additional changes which allow access to the next major free flight point totals. All is at the immediate fingertips of interested customers.

In order to maintain visibility and top-of-mind-awareness among consumers, social media vehicles are also in heavy use with banks, television and radio stations, and restaurant among a wide variety of service providers. Barclays Bank has a range of different Twitter accounts for each area of its business operations, sponsorships, and services. They presently have 20 of these accounts. Of course the largest following is associated with its sponsorship of Barclays Premier League football. This site, @BarclaysFooty, has well over 100,000 followers, and it regularly posts information about EPL teams and matches along with contests to win match tickets. Barclays is particularly focused on its @BarclaysOnline account to handle customer service, and there are presently over 16,000 followers of this account. This account will answer customer queries using Twitter from Monday to Friday from 8:00 a.m. to 8:00 p.m., and while they try to respond quickly, especially to complaints, there can be problems with queries and complaints received after 8:00 p.m. as they will not be responded to until the next morning or even after the weekend. Of course the limit on the number of characters limits the ability to convey complex messages, but if things can be worked out via Twitter, they may satisfy customers so that they don't need to turn to email to get their concerns voiced. With the changing nature of social media, customer access to Twitter may be far easier than resorting to email.

Barclays also makes heavy use of Facebook, which it again uses to communicate with customers from Monday to Friday between 8:00 a.m. and 8:00 p.m., but the same concerns with after-hours access apply. Barclays regularly updates their Facebook page, and they have shown well over 300,000 likes. The company uses Facebook to promote many of its offerings and competitions. Another company which has found value in Facebook is Carnival Cruise Lines. The company has developed a partnership with a digital marketing company, Razorfish, to develop and launch a new Facebook app which provides an easy comparison tool for cruise passengers to gather information on Carnival cruises and share with their Facebook friends. So the Facebook network associated with that cruise passenger can be used to help them plan their upcoming cruise and even allow them to invite some of the Facebook friends to join them on their cruise. The app allows the ability to select cruises by destinations, duration, and types of stateroom available. Delta Airlines allows customers to book flights directly through its Facebook page through its ticket window, which is quickly being copied by other air carriers.

Twitter and Facebook are not the only social media vehicles being used. Barclays also has a Linkedin presence, but its main function is to help with company recruiting. They also have a Linkedin Groups presence. In addition to these three vehicles, other vehicles that are regularly being used are Pinterest and Instagram. The challenge is to stay on top of the various new media and monitor interest and usage levels.

 Mini Case 9.1   Shopbots: comparison websites give customers valuable information

The UK, among many countries, is quickly taking to the use of price-comparison websites, which makes particular sense in the tougher economic times experienced since 2009. These comparison sites are also referred to as shopbots, and they earn their money when you click on a retailer that they are featuring (e.g. Boots or John Lewis) or by getting a small amount from each sale. The most popular shopping comparison site in late 2013, according to Hitwise, was <www.ciao.co.uk> with more than 2,600 online retailers included. Another popular site is <www.pricerunner.co.uk>, which is particularly easy to use and even offers information on things like delivery charges, while <www.moneysupermarket.com> includes services from the financial industry, travel, motoring, broadband, and utilities. Heavy advertising on TV is raising the visibility of competing sites like Gocompare.com, comparethemarket.com, and MoneySavingExpert.com, to name a few. Now others are considering taking advantage of this opportunity and jumping into the fray. In particular, one company interested in competing is Tesco. These sites allow consumers to see the offerings of various competitors, what is being offered and the prices for these offerings, so that they can make the best decisions. Consumers are more willing to use these kinds of platforms than ever before, and service marketers are realizing that if they don't participate, they will lose valuable customers to more creative competitors. Increasing numbers of British as well as Americans are using comparison sites as the first step in the buying process. If a company wants to have their products potentially in the consumer's choice set, they must be visible in the mix when customers start at the comparison site. This then incites company site visitation, but, in the end, the customer may return to the comparison site for final alternative evaluation and final choice. What seems to be happening here is that the lowest prices do not always get the customers to buy. If a company has the lowest price but is not known to the consumer, they may choose a more expensive alternative if the brand is fairly well known. Obviously there is reluctance to accept an offer when there are no personal experiences to draw upon.

One-stop shopping is valuable to consumers. They are happy to see what is available and make timely comparisons, but consumers want to be able to trust the information that they see provided. This was of concern early on for such companies as Amazon.com, but quality controls observed by the site have eliminated consumer concerns. By expanding the mix of products and brands offered via Amazon, consumers have grown to trust the information provided. The customer-based review process helps to add credibility to these sites as consumers show their level of satisfaction increasing consumer confidence and trust. Trailblazing was also undertaken in the travel industry with the successes of <www.Expedia.com>, <www.Travelocity.com>, <www.Priceline.com>, and <www.TravelZoo.com/UK>.

As more of these comparison sites become available, the marketers are being forced to consider limiting the number of sites on which to make their product information available. Things have particularly heated up in the insurance industry, and some insurance providers have decided to try their own approach to providing comparative information. In particular, Aviva has actually dropped out of using price comparison sites and has launched its own site which provides details about its products as well as those of competitors. What is innovative about this site is that its own products may not be the lowest-priced offerings, but it makes them available anyway. Several similar sites have proven to be effective marketing tools for insurance providers in the US. Progressive.com has found great success in the US by asking visitors to structure their insurance policies as they want and then compare quotes across a variety of competing offers; the consumer then sees which makes the most sense for them given the price and their specific needs. Why would Aviva and Progressive provide prices if their own company offerings are more expensive than other competitors? They believe that they will be seen in a better light through honesty and integrity, and that even when a competitor might undercut them, the consumer might still choose to stay with them because they project a better image and reputation than the competitors. It also provides a mechanism for outsourcing those consumers who would not be profitable for them to carry. It appears to be a win–win situation.

So how can companies provide great customer service to mobile customers? There are three important things to consider (Allen, 2013).

1. **Find out what is important to the mobile customer.** In other words dig deeply to find out what is really important to your customers and then build a mobile presence accordingly. In most cases they will want immediate access to information, so any website or mobile presence will need to be built for speed of access. How many clicks will it take to get to the information in question? Does the site look appealing on a mobile screen? Are company location and hours of operation readily available? Can the customer communicate with you quickly?

2. **Do you have an app?** Do you have a downloadable app that provides a two-way flow of communication? This should be significantly different from your website and should be geared around the limitations of the mobile devices involved. Can the customer immediately contact you through the app and get questions answered or convey important information about an upcoming event? Again, this depends on what the customer expects to be able to do with the app.

3. **Pay close attention to customer activity patterns and data.** Look at the usage patterns for mobile app use versus website use. Which is used and in what sequence? Do all those who downloaded the app actually use it, and if not, then why? What are the patterns of use of the app and the website in connection with actual purchases? Did customers respond to sales events and offers?

Mobile customers can be quite fickle, so companies need to monitor their behaviour and use carefully and adapt to changes as quickly as possible. But the key to services is the creation of value in the mind of the consumer. This value can be the basis for a powerful competitive advantage.

Customer value and sustainable competitive advantage

Since service firms do not have the benefit of patents and other high barriers to entry, competitive advantage for them lies in continually exceeding customer expectations (Ford et al., 2001) and building a perception of exceptional value to the customer.

If the customer believes that the quality they are receiving is the best that it can be, there is no reason to switch to the offerings of another provider. So how does the service firm ensure that it can provide value to the customer and achieve sustainable competitive advantage? One consideration is the definition of the target customer in question. Many service firm failures point to the impossible nature of being 'all things to all customers'.

Successful segmentation is a necessity for service success. It has been found that global wireless communications companies were suffering from this 'all things to all people' malaise, and they found that the few successes were based upon clear segmentation strategies (Arnold et al., 1999). Firm success was facilitated by a four-pronged approach to segmentation: (1) identify the most attractive customers to serve, (2) restructure business systems to cater to these customers as efficiently as possible, (3) create a basis for sustainable perceptual differentiation, and (4) establish an organizational entity that stays focused on the appropriate customer segments and applies metrics to ensure that the proper segments remain satisfied. Of course it is important not to differentiate for the sake of differentiating, but to base differentiation on specific sets of viable customer needs.

Relationship building with customers

Service strategists are quickly accepting the importance of relationship building with customers, which can be facilitated through effective segmentation. Zeithaml et al. (2001) found that a number of successful service firms have created customer pyramids which differentiate customers by profit potential and recognize that different groups of customers have different sets of expectations. These firms (like Fedex and Bank of America) cater to the more profitable customers and downplay the strategic efforts to reach the less profitable segments. The authors make the following suggestions regarding when firms should utilize this customer pyramid.

1. When service resources, including employee time, are limited.
2. When customers want different services or service levels.
3. When customers are willing to pay for different levels of service.
4. When customers define value in different ways.
5. When customers can be separated from each other.
6. When service differentials can lead to upgrading customers to another level.
7. When they can be accessed either as a group or individually.

Probably the most useful lessons come from observations of the most successful service providers. Companies like Walt Disney, Southwest Airlines, Marriott International, and Ritz-Carlton are all known for their service excellence in handling both sides of the service equation. They constantly refine and improve operational performance while continuously monitoring and providing customer value. There are several lessons that can help any service firm to maximize customer value perceptions and ensure a strong perceptual position in the head of their customers (Ford et al., 2001).

1. Base decisions on what the customer wants and expects.
2. Think and act in terms of the entire customer experience.
3. Continuously improve all parts of the customer experience.
4. Hire and reward people who can effectively build relationships with customers.
5. Train employees in how to cope with emotional labour costs.
6. Create and sustain a strong service culture.
7. Avoid failing your customer twice.
8. Empower customers to co-produce their own experience.

9. Get managers to lead from the front, not the top.

10. Treat all customers as if they were guests.

As mentioned above, one of the ways in which companies can make customers feel more of a relationship with the service is through their greater involvement as co-producers of the service creation and delivery (Grenci and Watts, 2007). This carries with it a shift from the usual push strategies (where the sales and service personnel have been the forces to 'push' the service on the consumer) to pull strategies, where the consumers are more integrally involved and actively seek the service that best fits their needs or 'pull' it to themselves. This is reflective of the shift from consultative selling to customer-driven buying, whereby the customer knows more about what they actually want, and the service person must have the expertise to work with the customer to customize the offering to the customer's expectations (Carter, 2003). The point is that customers are brought into the process more actively, and this opens the door for stronger customer involvement and the potential for stronger customer–service provider relationships being built. This is particularly promising for consumer services offered via the Internet (Grenci and Watts, 2007).

Successful service firms must understand the nature of the service experience and set up operating systems that continuously ensure that customer expectations are not only being met, but exceeded. The good news is that services of any size can gain sustainable competitive advantage if they set up effective service cultures that give the appropriate customers what they want while creating an internal environment that ensures employee satisfaction and loyalty.

Customer service as a basis for differentiation

When a service company uses customer service as its sole focus for differentiation from its competition, it may face perceptual difficulties. If everyone stands for service, then there is no distinction in centring on customer service as the main foundation for differentiation. The question is whether such companies as BT, British Gas, and British Airways can build strong brands by centring on customer service in their advertising campaigns. These companies all stressed customer service in their advertisements in 2003, and Lloyds TSB is preparing to do the same thing by emphasizing relationships with its customers as the 'heart of its brand.' Most services build from the standpoint that offering great service is a foundation for creating loyal customers. If people are treated well, they should not want to go anywhere else. So an important question is why these kinds of major corporations would stress customer service in their advertisements.

It has been suggested that BT, British Gas, and British Airways have built differentiating positions in very competitive markets by honing their delivery of customer service (Smith and Gray, 2004). But the question is whether customer service should be the main message in all company communications. Some of the criticisms raised by industry experts include the fact that customer service is not a strategy in and of itself, customer service as a sole focus for differentiation may miss key elements that helped to build the company credibility and success in the first place, and the fact that research has indicated that consumers don't see customer service as particularly interesting—it is perceived to be boring and lacks imagination. As noted in a study of 5,000 companies, there is a need to continually exceed their past offerings and set new standards in their offerings of customer service to stay ahead of the competition (Wiersema, 2001). Merely offering customer service is not enough; offering incomparable service is the key to success.

Such catch phrases as 'the way to fly', 'more power to you', and 'do the right thing' are too nebulous to mean very much to customers (Smith, 2004). Good customer service may be a necessary requirement to be a serious competitor in a service industry, but the company had best focus on other differentiators when building its image. Service should be improved to compete against strong rivals; however, service is a weak platform for true differentiation. If everyone is for excellent customer service, then no one is differentiated perceptually.

The latest thinking: the Chief Experience Officer

In a recent article by James Merlino and Ananth Raman (2013) in *Harvard Business Review*, the authors describe significant improvements in patient-satisfaction surveys at the Cleveland Clinic in Cleveland, Ohio. The Clinic's proportion of patients giving it the highest scores for overall satisfaction had climbed from 55 per cent in 2008 to 92 per cent. This was reported by a study of over 4,600 US hospitals. How was this accomplished? The improvement was attributed to the development of a new organizational officer, the 'Chief Experience Officer' (CExO). This person heads up the 'Office of Patient Experience', with an annual operating budget and a sizeable staff including project managers, data analysts, and service training specialists.

The first thing that the CExO did was to acknowledge past service problems, and he set out to study and understand the needs of a variety of different types of patients. He felt that it was imperative that all employees of the Clinic understood the patient experience. It was not just the relationship between the doctor and the patient that was critical, it was all interactions that patients had with service personnel. The previous discussion of blueprinting is an important mechanism for service organizations to use to see all contacts that occur. The Clinic found that every one of the interactions was important to the patient, and the Chief Experience Officer realized that all employees were caregivers and played an important role in the hospital experience.

Furthermore, Cleveland Clinic established a service culture within the organization understood by all employees and practiced daily. The CExO developed systems for tracking patients' comments with the focus on identifying the underlying causes of complaints, and electronic dashboards were established that presented ongoing information to management reflecting current data on various aspects of the patient experience and the correction of identified problems. He also set up a special department charged with identifying the best practices of various units within the Clinic. Many problems were quickly identified and corrected.

An important element of the successful system that was created at the Clinic involved a programme to celebrate outstanding caregivers, which was effective in engaging and motivating employees with financial rewards.

Finally, the CExO realized that an important part of the Clinic experience was to educate each patient about what to expect during their hospital stay, and patients were asked to help with the service provision by respecting the needs of other patients in the facility with special needs and reporting any noted service deficiencies.

This dramatic improvement in the patient experience should resonate for other types of service offerings as well since the more that the service organization and its employees understand the expected experience for the customer, the better able they will be to deliver properly on those expectations and keep the customer happy and engaged.

Conclusion

Services may not be as different from manufactured goods as once was thought. And the need to apply service strategies in non-service settings increases as the service-centred dominant logic perspective becomes increasingly relevant. Service consumption involves an experience that must be understood by the service strategist so that the service that is offered not only meets, but exceeds, the expectations of the customer. Customer satisfaction from a fulfilling service experience will lead to loyalty and profitability, but it is imperative for the service strategist to monitor changes in the expectations of consumers so that continuous service quality improvements can be facilitated. It is also important to streamline where possible to build on company strengths and minimize weaknesses. The firm that keeps offering the most enjoyable service experience for their customers, while eliminating inefficiencies, will stay ahead of the competition. It is also worth remembering that customer service as a means for service firms to differentiate may not be a sound strategy and that other defining characteristics may be more viable.

Summary

Service strategy is totally dependent upon the customer receiving the service experience they expect. Market research examining the expectations of customers provides a necessary foundation for service design and implementation. Successful services have managers who understand the wants and needs of customers and have the courage to empower their employees to be able to adapt service offerings to the special situations faced by customers. Customer focus becomes the key strategic consideration for all service employees, and it helps when there is a supportive service culture that puts the customer first with profits following. This is a difficult stand for management to take as profitability is such an important driver, but those willing to be bold will potentially reap the kinds of reward that service pioneers like Virgin, BskyB, the Cleveland Clinic, Southwest Airlines, Ritz-Carlton Hotels, and Marriott International have come to enjoy.

Key terms

- **Blueprinting:** the mapping of all the steps that a customer goes through once they enter the service, allowing service management to examine the whole process of delivery to identify any problem areas.

- **Coopetition:** the balancing between competition and cooperation that allows a sharing of assets and maximizing the impact of limited budgets, particularly appropriate for small service firms.

- **Decoupling:** where the service provider removes certain low customer contact tasks from frontline or front office personnel, standardizing them and moving them into remote back office locations. The decoupling of complex jobs allows the reduction of work variance.

- **Dramaturgy:** the approach to the provision of a service as the performance of a play with three essential and interconnected components: the actors, the audience, and the stage.

- **Heterogeneity:** the aspect of services that focuses on inconsistencies brought on by changes in mood states and emotions that can cause differences in interactions between service provider personnel and consumers.

- **Inseparability:** the service interaction takes place in a meeting of the customer and service provider personnel. The interaction creates the service experience. This means that customers are co-producers/designers of the service.

- **Intangibility:** the fact that services cannot be held in the hand, felt, and touched. This presents a challenge for strategic marketing decision-making as competitive differentiation has to be experienced by users and there really are no strategies for product disposal of unsold stock.

- **Operand resources:** resources which are acted upon or operated upon to produce an effect. From the standpoint of product-centred logic, customers and products are operand resources. They are both acted upon by marketers.

- **Operant resources:** resources which are used to act upon operand resources. The customer works with marketers to produce value as co-producer, so the customer is not acted upon but becomes part of the action on something else to produce value.

- **Outsourcing:** where the service provider looks to contract out service components to outside suppliers. Anything that the firm believes is not part of their core competency becomes a candidate for outsourcing. It potentially allows firms to get goods and services at a lower cost and a higher quality by relying on firms that specialize in certain components of service delivery.

- **Perishability:** the fleeting life of a service offering. Once the service is provided, it is consumed at that time. Since a service cannot be stored, there is a need to synchronize supply and demand.

- **Service-dominant logic:** the perspective that services as well as products should be thought of as being produced in the same way. The marketer in this perspective collaborates and works with the customer to create value as opposed to being mainly an actor upon the customer to create value in the product-centred or goods-centred perspective.

- **Servicescape:** the pictorial representation of the physical evidence associated with the service. It provides an excellent mechanism for additional service performance evaluation.

- **SERVQUAL:** a survey instrument developed by Berry et al. (1988) to measure service quality which compares customer perceptions of ideal service provision to actual service delivery perceptions for a range of service process characteristics.
- **Streamlining:** where the service provider looks to improve operations through the elimination of service inefficiencies and thereby improve profit margins. The ultimate effect will be to pass along savings to the customer.

Discussion questions

1. What are the four distinguishing characteristics of services and what challenges do they create for the services strategist?
2. What is service-dominant logic and how does it compare with goods-dominant logic? What does this mean for marketers?
3. What is SERVQUAL, and how can it be used by service strategists?
4. Describe ways in which services can streamline and improve operational efficiency and profitability?
5. What is the service experience and why is it so important for services strategists?
6. Why is the use of dramaturgy (the drama metaphor) beneficial for services strategists?
7. Why is customer segmentation important? What is needed for successful segmentation?
8. What is the customer pyramid, and how do you know if a service firm should make use of it?
9. What are the ten strategic lessons learned from the most successful service providers?
10. What lessons have been learned from theatre companies that can help service managers build sustainable profitability?
11. What is the Chief Experience Officer, and how has the creation of this position been helpful to the Cleveland Clinic in their service provision?
12. Will self-service always be important for customers when evaluating a service choice? When would self-service not be beneficial?

Online resource centre

Visit the Online Resource Centre for this book for lots of interesting additional material at: **<www.oxfordtextbooks.co.uk/orc/west3e/>**

References and further reading

Allen, Errol (2013), 'Marketing in a Mobile World—Three Factors to Consider', *Houston Business Journal Online*, 30 August.

Allen, Sandy and Ashok Chandrashekar (2000), 'Outsourcing Services: The Contract Is Just the Beginning', *Business Horizons*, March-April, pp. 25–34.

Arnold, Scott, Byron G. Auguste, Mark Knickrehm, and Paul J. Roche (1998) 'Winning in Wireless', *The McKinsey Quarterly*, No. 2, pp. 18–32.

Arnold, Scott, Greg A. Reed, and Paul J. Roche (1999), 'Wireless, not Profitless', *The McKinsey Quarterly*, No. 4, pp. 112–21.

Berry, Leonard L. and Neeli Bendapudi (2003), 'Clueing in Customers,' *Harvard Business Review*, 81, February, pp. 100–6.

Berry, Leonard L. and Kent D. Seltman (2007) 'Building a Strong Services Brand: Lessons from Mayo Clinic', *Business Horizons*, 50, pp. 199–209.

Bitner, Mary Jo and Stephen W. Brown (2007), 'The Service Imperative', *Business Horizons*, 51, pp. 39–46.

Carter, R. (2003), 'How to Let Your Prospects Sell Themselves,' *American Salesman*, 48 (12), pp. 19–21.

Cohen, Morris A., Carl Cull, Hau L. Lee, and Don Willen (2000), 'Saturn's Supply-Chain Innovation: High Value in After-Sales Service', *Sloan Management Review*, Summer, pp. 93–101.

Ernst, David and Thomas D. French (1996), 'Coffee and One Way to Boston', *McKinsey Quarterly*, No. 1, pp. 165–76.

Ford, Robert C., Cherrill P. Heaton, and Stephen W. Brown (2001), 'Delivering Excellent Service: Lessons from the Best Firms', *California Management Review*, 44, No. 1, pp. 39–56.

Frei, Francis X. (2008), 'The Four Things a Service Business Must Get Right', *Harvard Business Review*, 86, April, pp. 70–80.

Gray, Robert (2004), 'Customer Service is not a Strategy', *Marketing* (21 July), pp. 32–4.

Grenci, Richard T. and Charles A. Watts (2007), 'Maximizing Customer Service via Mass Customized e-Consumer Services', *Business Horizons*, 50, pp. 123–32.

Grove, Stephen J. and Raymond P. Fisk (1983), 'The Dramaturgy of Service Exchange: An Analytical Framework for Services Marketing', in Berry, Leonard L., Shostack, Lynn C., and Upah, Gregory D. (eds) *Emerging Perspectives on Services Marketing* (Chicago, IL: American Marketing Association), pp. 45–9.

Grove, Stephen J., Raymond P. Fisk, and Mary Jo Bitner (1992), 'Dramatizing the Service Experience: A Managerial Approach', in Swartz, T.A., Shostack, L.G., and Upah, G.D. (eds) *Advances in Services Marketing and Management: Research and Practice*, Vol. 1, (Greenwich, CT: JAI Press), pp. 91–121.

Hemp, Paul (2002), 'My Week as a Room-Service Waiter at the Ritz', *Harvard Business Review*, 80, June, pp. 50–62.

Kirchner, Theresa A., Edward P. Markowski, and John B. Ford (2007) 'Relationships Among Levels of Government Support, Marketing Activities, and Financial Health of Nonprofit Performing Arts Organizations', *International Journal of Nonprofit and Voluntary Sector Marketing*, 12 (2), pp. 95–116.

Merlino, James I. and Ananth Raman (2013), 'Health Care's Service Fanatics', *Harvard Business Review*, 91, May, pp. 108–16.

Metters, Richard and Vicente Vargas (2000), 'Organizing Work in Service Firms', *Business Horizons* (July-August), pp. 23–32.

Naumann, Earl and Donald W. Jackson Jr. (1999), 'One More Time: How Do You Satisfy Customers?' *Business Horizons*, May-June, pp. 71–6.

Organisation for Economic Co-Operation and Development (2010), *Innovation and Productivity in Services*, Paris: OECD.

Parasuraman, A., Leonard L. Berry, and Valarie A. Zeithaml (1991), 'Understanding Customer Expectations of Service', *Sloan Management Review*, 32 (3), pp. 38–49.

Reinartz, Werner and Wolfgang Ulaga (2008), 'How to Sell Services More Profitably', *Harvard Business Review*, 86, May, pp. 90–6.

Rothenberg, Sandra (2007), 'Sustainability Through Servicizing', *MIT Sloan Management Review*, 48(2), pp. 83–91.

Smith, Craig (2004) 'Customer Service Is No Basis for a Brand,' *Marketing* (21 July), p. 30.

Stuart, F. Ian (2006) 'Designing and Executing Memorable Service Experiences: Lights, Camera, *Experiment, Integrate*, Action!', *Business Horizons*, 49, pp. 149–59.

Swank, Cynthia Karen (2003), 'The Lean Service Machine', *Harvard Business Review*, 81, October, pp. 123–29.

Thomke, Stefan (2012), 'Mumbai's Models of Service Excellence', *Harvard Business Review*, 90, November, pp. 121–26.

Vargo, Stephen L. and Robert F. Lusch (2004), 'Evolving to a New Dominant Logic for Marketing', *Journal of Marketing*, 68, January, pp. 1–17.

Wiersema, Fred (2001), *The New Market Leaders*, New York: Free Press.

World Bank (2013) *World Development Indicators* 2013, Washington, DC: World Bank.

Zeithaml, Valarie A. and Mary Jo Bitner (2003), *Services Marketing: Integrating Customer Focus Across the Firm* (3rd edn), Boston: McGraw-Hill Irwin.

Zeithaml, Valarie A., Roland T. Rust, and Katherine N. Lemon (2001), 'The Customer Pyramid: Creating and Serving Profitable Customers,' *California Management Review*, 43 (4), pp. 118–42.

End of Chapter 9 case study United Parcel Service: courier and express delivery services

Introduction

United Parcel Service, Inc. (UPS) is the world's largest package delivery company, transporting more than 15 million packages and documents per day. This courier and express delivery company provides logistics support, supply chain operations, freight trucking, customs brokerage, fulfilment, returns, and distribution services in over 220 countries. UPS has its headquarters in Atlanta, Georgia, and employs 399,000 people, 323,000 in the US and the rest internationally.

According to the company's Annual Report, in 2012 UPS earned $54.1 billion in annual revenue and $807 million in net income, and showed 1.49 per cent in net profit margin. UPS operates a fleet of approximately 96,000 ground vehicles and utilizes over 500 aircraft to provide express, ground, domestic, international, commercial, and residential pickup and delivery services. It maintains air hubs in the United States, Europe, Asia/Pacific, Latin America/Caribbean, and Canada (UPS Investor Relations).

Brand equity

UPS is one of the most recognized and admired global brands. In 2010 the company changed its slogan from 'What can Brown do for you?' to 'We ♥ Logistics'. The company updated its worldwide communication and marketing strategy to focus on logistics and inform customers that UPS can provide more services than ever before. This slogan is used in all types of media formats including print, television, web, and mobile.

Competition

UPS competes with many different local, regional, national, and international companies. Direct competitors include FedEx, DHL Express, TNT Express, Deutsche Post, and the US Postal Service. These companies offer similar services to UPS and also maintain trucks, planes, and other vehicles. Larger companies in this industry benefit from economies of scale, network size, and the ability to invest in new technologies.

Technology

UPS invests $1 billion per year on information technology to grow the business. The company has implemented many leading-edge innovations, such as mainframes, personal computers, handheld devices, wireless and cellular networks, delivery information acquisition devices (DIAD boards), global positioning systems, and satellite tracking, to move information and packages. Sophisticated technology and skilled computer programmers allow the company to track package locations throughout the entire shipping process. Enhanced technology provides customers with critical time-sensitive information on the status of a delivery during each step of the supply chain.

Based on a global report prepared by UPS, 'Pulse of the Online Shopper', the company collected data to learn how customers across the globe feel about e-commerce. UPS learned that online shoppers want the following:

(1) integrated mobile, online, and in store experiences

(2) flexible shipping options and costs

(3) convenient returns.

The report described how global consumers are connected to preferred merchants' social media channels and respond positively to promotions from retailers. The study measured how long consumers in different regions of the world were willing to wait for purchases to arrive. Results from this marketing research study of 14,000 frequent online shoppers in the US, Canada, Europe, Asia, Australia, and Mexico will help UPS support higher volumes of online sales, shipments, and returns.

Growth

UPS has been pursuing a global expansion strategy through acquisition and investment. Recently the company invested in new logistics distribution facilities in Chengdu and Shanghai to meet emerging demand in China. Between 2011 and 2013, UPS spent $200 million to expand its air hub at Germany's Cologne/Bonn Airport. This renovated hub is the company's largest expansion outside the US in its 104-year history.

Not all of the company's growth strategies have been success stories. As described in a *Wall Street Journal* article, the company experienced a setback when European Union (EU) regulators blocked UPS's plans to merge with the Dutch firm TNT Express NV. The deal was rejected because of anti-trust issues related to reducing competition in the European express delivery sector. The company plans to appeal this decision through the EU's General Court in Luxembourg, which can be a lengthy process. The planned acquisition of TNT Express would have increased UPS's international business in Europe, Asia, the Middle East, and South America and made the company less dependent on the US market.

Holiday demand

During the busiest day of the holiday rush (five days before Christmas) UPS was Santa's biggest helper and delivered 28 million packages. The company's airline scheduled more than 400 additional flights to successfully manage peak demand. UPS delivered more than 135 million packages around the world during the peak week leading up to Christmas 2012. This was a record-setting holiday season for UPS with a 4.1 per cent growth in sales over 2011. The firm handled two million returned packages after the holiday. Every year UPS prepares a year-end holiday calendar to inform customers about the last days to ship packages so that gifts will arrive by the holidays (Holiday Rush).

Discussion questions

1. Describe how package delivery services offered by UPS are distinguished from goods. Consider consumers and organizational buyers.

Intangibility	
Inconsistency/Uniformity	
Inseparability	
Inventory/Perishability	
Client Relationship	
Customer Effort	

2. How would you classify delivery services at UPS in terms of equipment-based vs people-based?

3. How do customers judge the quality of UPS's services?

4. Calculate the per cent sales from each of the following UPS service categories to fill in Table C9.1. Create a pie graph with this data and include per cent sales values and service category labels around the graph. What per cent of revenue is from US, international, and supply chain operations?

Table C9.1 United Parcel Service, Sales by Service Category

United Parcel Service Service Category	2012 Sales (millions of US dollars)	Per Cent of Total Sales	Per Cent US Operations
US Ground	23,052		
US Next Day Air	6,412		
US Deferred	3,392		Per cent International Operations
International Export	9,033		
International Domestic	2,531		
International Cargo	560		Per cent Supply Chain Operations
Supply Chain and Logistics	5,977		
Supply Chain and Freight	2,640		
Other	530		

Source: 'United Parcel Service: 2012 Products and Operations', Hoover's, Inc. <http://subscriber.hoovers.com.ezp.lndli-brary.org/H/company360/productsOperations.html?companyId=40483000000000>, Accessed 15 October 2013.

5. Plot historical revenue for UPS in a column graph. Use this data to examine the growth trend and make a projection for the revenue for 2013. Explain how you made your forecast. Calculate the per cent change in revenue for each year.

Plot the historical net profit margin in a separate column graph. Calculate the per cent change in profit for each year.

Plot the historical stock high/low in a third column graph.

Exhibit 2 United Parcel Service, Historical Financials

Year	Revenue (millions of US dollars)	Revenue Per Cent Change	Net Profit Margin	Net Profit Margin Per Cent Change	Stock High	Stock Low
2003	33,485	---	8.65%	---	$74.86	$ 53.00
2004	36,582		9.11%		$89.11	$ 67.22
2005	42,581		9.09%		$85.84	$ 66.10
2006	47,547		8.84%		$83.99	$ 65.50
2007	49,692		0.77%		$78.99	$ 68.66
2008	51,486		5.83%		$75.08	$ 43.32
2009	45,297		4.75%		$59.75	$ 37.99
2010	49,545		7.04%		$73.94	$ 55.77
2011	$3,105		7.16%		$77.00	$ 60.74
2012	54,127		1.49%		$81.79	$ 69.56

2013 Projection(s)

Source: 'United Parcel Service: 2003 to 2012 Historical Financials', Hoover's, Inc. <http://subscriber.hoovers.com.ezp. lndlibrary.org/H/company360/financialHistory.html?companyId=40483000000000>, Accessed 15 October 2013. This case was prepared by Professor Hope Corrigan, Marketing Department, Sellinger School of Business and Management, Loyola University Maryland, Baltimore, MD.

10 Pricing and distribution strategies

 Learning Objectives

1. Grasp the separate and complementary roles of pricing and distribution to marketing strategy.

2. Be able to assess pricing mindsets and strategic options.

3. Understand the buyer's perspective of distribution and its implications for strategy.

4. Perceive the role of pricing and distribution amidst the drive towards the commoditization of products and services.

Chapter at a Glance

I. Introduction

1 Overview and strategy blueprint
2 Marketing strategy: analysis and perspectives

II. Where are we now?

3 Environmental and internal analysis: market information and intelligence

III. Where do we want to be?

4 Strategic marketing decisions, choices, and mistakes
5 Segmentation, targeting, and positioning strategies
6 Branding strategies
7 Relational and sustainability strategies

V. Did we get there?

14 Strategy implementation, control, and metrics

IV. How will we get there?

8 Product innovation and development strategies
9 Service marketing strategies
10 Pricing and distribution strategies
11 Marketing communications strategies
12 International marketing strategy
13 Social and ethical strategies

 ## Case study: Two pieces of the marketing jigsaw—pricing and distribution

Pricing and distribution are linked in a couple of unusual ways. Firstly, both of them have become significantly more complex in the last decade. And secondly, all too often, due to the fact that pricing and distribution tend to be at the end of the value offer, they are considered late in the day. Wrong! Both require serious analysis and creative thought early in the process.

They do often tend to be considered, but should not be separated from the other strategic decisions that need to be made. Marketers have to consider each element, be it product or price or communication or whatever, both separately and together. It is the complex interaction of all the marketing drivers that makes the whole. Dell's distribution strategy is not an afterthought! It is at the heart of their business model. Aldi's price promise drives the whole mix.

So we must consider each element separately. And we must consider each element as a key part of a coherent marketing approach. Each piece of the jigsaw has integrity but must contribute to the bigger picture.

Pricing

This is especially true of pricing. Pricing has been seen as an afterthought far too often. We have designed the product, built the brand promise, the routes to market and the audience are defined, the communications compelling. Now... what price shall we sell it for!

This is obviously marketing nonsense. Price is both strategic and tactical. For price can dictate the positioning and the communications. 'Never knowingly undersold' (John Lewis) or 'reassuringly expensive' (Stella Artois).

By understanding competitor pricing, we can determine a competitive strategy for our brand. All strategy is competitive strategy and pricing can be a key ingredient in the process. When Halifax launched its current account, it could afford to price it very competitively knowing that the established players could not easily respond as it would cost them a small fortune. To compete, existing players with huge volumes of customers would need to improve the value/reduce the price for their existing 'book' as well as for new customers.

Pricing strategy can drive the brand's positioning and indeed its service model. Ryanair is genuinely no-frills and everything is orientated towards low price after they identified a gap in the market. Everything is subjugated to their pricing strategy. This is equally apparent with high price luxury brands.

We also need to consider the role of price in the overall business model. In general, cars tend to be priced very keenly and the margin is made in the extras, spare parts and in the service packages. Similarly in the professional services industries, advice is often provided free or at low price to begin with and the margin is derived later. Current accounts at banks are notoriously unprofitable (and free); all the margin is in cross-sales driven by the relationship, data, and brand.

And, of course there is the loss-leader approach beloved of retailers, which is when pricing becomes more tactical and less strategic. Imagine the complexity of the pricing strategy for a supermarket with 25,000 lines (SKUs) and all the factors affecting price—at both the tactical level as well as the strategic positioning of the supermarket.

In fact, pricing decisions, both strategic and tactical, are such an integral component of any coherent marketing plan that it should be regarded as part of the marketing budget. Striking the right balance between the value proposition, the communications, the promotion and the price is a distinct skill. Any fool can drop the price till it sells—achieving the right balance that aligns the interests of the marketing team, the salesforce, the commercial imperative and the key stakeholders is the real prize.

Having said that, one small bit of advice in passing. It is far more difficult to increase a price than it is to reduce it—so err on the high side to give yourself competitive flexibility.

The last observation worth dwelling on is that we marketers are steadily losing control of pricing with the growing power of retailers, the development of aggregators and comparison sites, the free universal, access to information, and the fact that the customer genuinely is now king. (At last!)

The result of these forces (and others) means that staying in control of both the pricing strategy as well as its implementation is increasingly difficult and the inexorable rise of commoditization erodes price differentials.

So what are the key messages?

- Pricing strategy is a critical part of the marketing mix and can determine the marketing platform and business model.

- It is a strategic driver.

- It is not an afterthought that can be left till later.

- In and of itself it can dictate a brand's positioning.

- We need to understand the role that price plays in the business model and determine how to use it competitively and coherently.

- Stay in control of price.

And so to distribution

Distribution is a fascinating topic and needs to be given as much attention, analysis, and creativity as any of the other key marketing components. Indeed, many of the key observations that have been made about pricing apply also to distribution.

But what exactly do we mean by 'distribution'? At its most simple, distribution is the process of ensuring that our product or service is in front of the buyer when they are in the market to buy. This can be the physical distribution or the Internet or the sales force (or whatever).

Marketers increasingly tend to think of distribution as the way of putting the product or service in front of the potential customer, albeit virtually, and then allowing the fulfilment to follow the more traditional physical process. Consider selling a product via a web retailer, or indeed one's own website. The distribution of the product is via the website, but the physical distribution can be via another channel altogether or can be via the website itself (printing off a ticket or downloading software).

Furthermore, the channel used for distribution is often a service channel and a communication channel at the same time. Take, for example, a supermarket. Obviously it is a critical distribution point for many products, but it is also a giant opportunity for marketing communications, both inside and outside the store.

The same is true for the Internet—the website or the rich banner can be distributing the product, providing service, delivering information, building the brand saliency and marketing ... all at the same time.

There is increasing complexity in any analysis of distribution strategy, fuelled by the increasing complexity of the customer journey (which needs to be carefully mapped to truly understand the distribution strategy). Customer Journey analysis is a giant topic in its own right and sits naturally with any discussion about distribution. It starts with the first interaction between the customer and the brand and plots the many and varied connections that lead to purchase, fulfilment, and beyond (complaints/repeat purchase/service/etc.).

Gone are the days when we simply took the product to market and transacted with the end customer. Now, the shopper considers a product in-store whilst checking on their portable device that the price is competitive and whether they can get better value or service elsewhere. Having purchased something, they then communicate this with friends and family—or are certainly encouraged to!

There are also, frequently, many stages to the distribution process, using different channels for that single purchase. Reflect for a moment on the process for distributing mortgages, or a new car. The car is considered, the brochure ordered, the website visited, the dealer contacted, the test drive taken, and so it goes on. Mortgages (and many other products) are even more complicated with regulation entering the distribution process as well.

Pricing and distribution

The way price and distribution interact also needs to be considered. In old marketing economics, one could nuance the price to the customer according to the cost of distribution. Electrical retailers, banks and holiday companies (to name but three examples) would price the product and service depending on the channel. Bricks and mortar were more expensive. The Internet cheaper. You even had examples of banks actually charging customers extra for going to the branch to transact!!

Those days are over. The customer will not tolerate this kind of simple differential pricing.

But at the same time, unless the right price is charged, some means of distribution can no longer be afforded and are withdrawn. Importantly, as part of this process, the *role* of the distribution channels subtly alters. The branch or store becomes an advice centre—and the online brand that claimed it would only ever distribute direct, starts opening stores.

So, what are the key messages? Many of those we discussed under the subject of pricing are true for distribution. Additionally, it is worth stressing:

- distribution is now firmly intertwined with communications and service and it is difficult to consider separately
- it is becoming increasingly complex

- we must plot carefully the full 'customer journey' to truly understand distribution
- price and distribution interact strongly, but it is increasingly difficult to price according to the cost of the channel.

Tim Pile is Chairman of Cogent Elliott, a large independent marketing agency. Prior to this role, he has variously worked for Sainsbury's where he was the CEO of the Bank, on the Operating Board, and ran the marketing academy; for Lloyds TSB where he was Marketing Director; Alliance & Leicester where he was Retail and Strategy Director; and he has worked with numerous fabulous marketing-orientated businesses such as P&G, Mars, and Jaguar Land Rover (to name but three). He continues to work with a huge variety of organizations either as a consultant or as a board member.

Introduction

Pricing and distribution are distinct yet complementary elements in marketing. Strategically they are difficult to separate. A premium priced watch cannot be sold at discount jewellers. A tractor producer that wants a specific mark-up is going to find it difficult to control margin if it sells through intermediaries. Pricing and distribution strategies are separate but complementary decisions. This chapter will view the options individually and then examine the issues where decisions meet head on.

Traditional marketing strategies of cost or differentiation do not provide any intrinsic logic on pricing or distribution. Porter was talking about 'cost' and not 'price'. He argued that relatively low costs provide a potential advantage over rivals in profitability. Put simply, you could charge the same price as rivals and make more money.

The price of anything and the route by which it is distributed simply reflects its value. Certainly a low cost producer is positioned to offer lower prices or discounts, but it is far from certain that it would do so. For example, Dell has attained cost leadership in the industry with its direct-to-customer web distribution process. Nothing is built that hasn't been ordered, so inventories are reduced and with direct sales there are no intermediaries to take a share of the profit. Yet Dell's prices are not the cheapest. What it has been able to do in a hyper-competitive market is to combine cost leadership with customized one-to-one products (the ultimate differentiation) and direct-to-customer distribution which is a powerful value-added offering. By contrast, Sony offers greater design differentiation at similar prices, but while it has 'Sony Direct' it mainly distributes its computers via authorized dealers and its own (largely franchised) network of retail Sony Centres and does not offer Dell's bespoke build model.

The moral is that customers look for value when they buy rather than absolute price. Value is a perceptual concept, as for example with the supermarket chain Asda. Asda has entered into an intense price war with Sainsbury's, Tesco, Morrisons, and Waitrose, while Aldi and Lidl have continued to prosper. Middle-class shoppers have increasingly joined the ranks of bargain-hunters and are taking a more 'mercenary' view. However, most companies approach price setting from a basis of covering their costs plus a profit mark-up, and there is no denying the general logic of covering costs (at least in the longer term) however defined! This chapter will review these and other issues in pricing and distribution. It begins with an assessment of pricing strategy.

Pricing

Definition

Pricing has generally been seen as tactical rather than strategic and considered much easier than creating the product in the first place. Essentially it has been the 'Cinderella' of marketing. When it boils down to it, a price is just a number. Given that prices affect sales, all things being equal, a small increase or decrease can have a disproportionate impact on profitability compared with any other marketing decision. For illustration see Table 10.1 which shows how a 10 per cent increase in prices outweighs the effect on profitability of reductions in costs.

Pricing strategy involves deciding more than this: the key decisions are how much, where, when, and how a buyer will pay. This is what holds together individual pricing decisions based upon an organization's objectives and how they want to set their 'numbers' within the market. Most managers face enormous pressures on prices, especially during a downturn. Nevertheless, customer needs may change; it is still important to align the price–benefit offering. There are several elements in pricing strategy to consider (Schindehutte and Morris, 2001) whatever market conditions prevail: value, variable, variety, visible/invisible, and virtual (see Figure 10.1).

Value: Price is fundamentally about value. Customers place prices within the context of perceived value. For example, when people pay more for sitting in the front row of a theatre they still see the same play as everyone else, but get the benefits of being closer to the actors.

Variable: Prices can be changed in a number of ways apart from the absolute level, such as by time form or terms of payment. For example, it has been found that when consumers perceive there will be a 'hassle period' with a product (e.g. when taking out a contract with a new Internet broadband supplier) they expect to get a cheaper initial price (Lambrecht and Tucker, 2012).

Variety: Prices can be set at different levels across multiple products and services to achieve different objectives for positioning and contribution as with bundling or unbundling items. Unilever famously came up with the sachet solution with its value proposition in

Table 10.1 Effect of Price

XYZ PRODS			(Assume no volume change)[*]	
Sales	$m	$m *200*		$m
Materials	50		Price +10%	20
Labour	50		Materials −10%	5
Mkt & Adv	10		Labour −10%	5
R&D	10		Mkt & Adv −10%	1
Other variables	20		R&D −10%	1
Total Variables	*140*		*Variable −10%*	*14*
Total Fixed	*40*		*Fixed −10%*	*4*
Net Profit		*20*		

*Falls in volume will also lead to higher profits with a 10% price increase up to a 20% drop

> **Value:** Price is fundamentally about value. Customers place prices within the context of perceived value
>
> **Variable:** Prices can be changed in a number of ways apart from the absolute level, such as by time form or terms of payment
>
> **Variety:** Prices can be set at different levels across multiple products and services to achieve different objectives for positioning and contribution, as with bundling or unbundling items
>
> **Visible/invisible:** Prices may be open and visible or hidden and confusing for customers
>
> **Virtual:** of all the decisions marketers make, a price change is arguably the easiest and quickest decision to make. It might not prove to be successful but the decision to raise or lower a price can be made quite straightforwardly in most organizations

10.1 Key Elements to Pricing

Source: Miner Schindehutte and Michael Morris (2001), 'Pricing as Entrepreneurial Behaviour', *Business Horizons*, 44 (4), pp. 41–9.

India. Traditional bottles of shampoo and boxes of detergent and similar sized fast-moving consumer goods (FMCG) are generally too expensive for rural consumers in India. Unilever came up with the idea of selling single sachets of these products at a very low price (one rupee) and the whole sachet-sized marketplace subsequently took off.

Visible/Invisible: Prices may be open and visible or hidden and confusing for customers. In the US, Sprint demonstrated invisible pricing when it offered 4,000 call minutes for $39.99 a month which appears to be a cent a minute (Ayres and Nalebuff, 2003). Unfortunately, only 350 are 'anytime', with the rest (3,650) restricted to evening and weekend. Go over your 350 limit and you have to pay 35c a minute.

Virtual: of all the decisions marketers make, a price change is arguably the easiest and quickest to make. While it might not prove to be successful, the decision to raise or lower a price can be made quite straightforwardly.

Strategic mindset

Pricing can be a 'mindset' for many companies and the consequences of the wrong mindset can be dire. This has been demonstrated in an experiment involving managers by Joel Urbany (2001) at Notre Dame. He gave 60 managers a straightforward choice: you sell sunglasses for $10 with a unit cost of $7 and you are thinking of cutting the price by 50c. According to the best sales estimate (a) if you hold the price you will have a 100 per cent chance of selling 1000 units and (b) if you cut the price to $9.50 you have an 80 per cent chance of selling 1250 units and a 20 per cent chance of selling only 1000. Statistically both options are identical as each produces a $3,000 profit. However, option (a) is risk free and so might seem to be the logical choice. Despite that, most of the 60 managers opted to reduce the price. Even when they were told competitors would match the cut, they still chose to do it. Furthermore, most continued to want to reduce the price in the face of new evidence that the cut would lead to lower profits!

The case of Polaroid demonstrates (Shantanu et al., 2002) another kind of problematic pricing mindset. Polaroid was the first company to develop digital imaging technology, but decided not to run with it. The reason was that Polaroid had relied on the 'razors-and-blade' approach to business in that it sold cameras cheaply and made money on the film. Digital imaging did not fit into this paradigm and so it gave up its lead with the technology. While this is an extreme case, it does demonstrate how an innovative company lost out because it lacked the appropriate pricing strategy.[1]

The company versus societal perspective may only be a factor in a minority of cases but is worth a mention, perhaps most prominently with antibiotics. There is widespread antibiotic resistance and thousands of people die each year from infections that would have been treatable years ago. What is the incentive for drug companies to develop new antibiotics? The answer is unfortunately: 'Not much'. Developing antibiotics for the relatively small number of people (at the moment) who are resistant simply doesn't make economic common sense to drug companies, without government support, given the research and development investment needed.

Strategic options

Successful pricing means that the prices set have to complement the company's overall marketing strategy and ideally strike a balance between maximizing revenues and offering customers value (Rusetski et al., 2014). With the latter point, prices need to be coordinated across any business. The whole process has to be holistic. Dolan (1995) suggests eight stages to pricing strategy (see Figure 10.2). This will be followed by a review of the alternative approach of price mapping (D'Aveni, 2007) and then a discussion of several options aimed at maintaining price points.

Dolan's eight options

Reverse cost-plus to value pricing

The first stage is to reverse the traditional cost-plus-based pricing approach (Indounas, 2006). This can be achieved by assessing the value that buyers place on a product or service, which is an 'outside-in' rather than an 'inside-out' approach and requires considerable

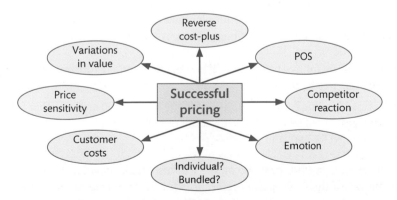

10.2 Dolan's Strategic Options

[1] Polaroid has since embraced digital technology with its Bluetooth enabled PoGo Digital Photo Printer which uses Zero Ink (Zink) technology, and has developed wi-fi cameras and instant print cameras.

intelligence gathering either formally (e.g. market research) or informally (e.g. comments from the salesforce).

Value-based pricing

Having considered this, it is then best to look for variations in how buyers value products. Wherever possible try and separate markets (e.g. both companies and individuals use Post-it notes and may be prepared to pay different prices) and segments (e.g. heavy, medium, and light users) and charge accordingly. Even in a recession there are significant opportunities to apply value pricing. Performance will have different values to different buyers—pest control is more valuable to a restaurant chain than it might be to an exhaust fitting centre.

Price sensitivity

Beneath the value that buyers place on product or service performance is price sensitivity. Buyers can differ greatly in their price sensitivity based upon their overall elasticity. Much will depend on who bears the cost; for example a flight might be purchased by an individual or their company. Also, what percentage of total expenditure does the product represent? Obviously people and organizations tend to be less price sensitive when the percentage is lower. Another factor is the buyers' ability to judge quality, as with a watch or a lawyer. To what extent can buyers compare prices and how time critical is the purchase? Are there switching costs? A bank might increase its charges for a current account, but regular customers are unlikely to move owing to perceived high switching costs. Thus, the music streaming service Napster charged its UK users nearly twice the amount it charged in the USA. Napster argued that their pricing reflected the cost of the content, and VAT was included in the UK package, unlike in the USA.

Single or multiple?

Having considered these issues, the next stage in the strategy is to identify the formal pricing structure. Should prices be single or multiple? Take the case where the optimal price for a product is £100 and there are two notional buyers, A and B.

- Buyer A is looking for five units and will buy the first one at £100, but will not buy again unless the price drops to £50.
- Buyer B is also looking for five units and will buy one at £100 and a further four if each subsequent unit is priced at a sliding discount of £10 each time (i.e. the second unit for £90 and the third for £80, and so on).

If the seller sticks to a £100 price he or she will only make two sales for a total of £200. However, knowing Buyer B's price preferences for further units it would be possible to sell both buyers two units for a total of £200 plus a further four units to B on the sliding scale of £300 (90 + 80 + 70 + 60) for total sales of £500. Assuming the seller can still make a profit with the lowest sliding £60 price, in this instance multiple prices would make sense.

Competitor reaction

The key issue now is to consider how competitors will react to any price changes. Just ask whether if the company puts up the price by 5 per cent competitors would do nothing, match the increase, reduce their prices, or change some other element of their mix? Competitors generally react to a lower price by lowering their prices as well. Sometimes regulation has to be used when predatory pricing is suspected. The European Commission fined Amazon €1,000 per day that it continued to offer free delivery after action brought about by the French Booksellers' Association (Syndicat de la Librairie Française) which accused Amazon of offering illegal discounts on books—and even of selling some books below cost. Amazon chose to keep paying the fine and sending books out for free.

Point of sale (POS)

Towards the end of the process it is important to monitor what prices are realized at the point of sale. If a list price is agreed, it needs to be established whether this price is fixed or open because if prices are subsequently reduced by the sales department to close a sale, it can lead to confusion. To implement a holistic approach it might be necessary to change the internal incentives. If you are distributing through an intermediary (e.g. Star Bazaar supermarkets in India or ParknShop in Hong Kong), there may be discounts given for early payments, rebates on volume, negotiated discounts, etc. A company may also need to consider margins in line with the product returns, service guarantees, damage claims, and so on. These should all be taken into account with the price.

Emotion

Research may be needed to assess a buyer's emotional response to a price because over time people develop price points they see as fair. For example, consider the furore in the UK over the price increases by the top six utility companies over the past few years. Good deals may reduce margins, but they can produce good word-of-mouth in the marketplace. One interesting example is transparent pricing where the costings that make up the price are clearly presented. Transparent pricing has been found to work when consumers are willing to relax inherent self-interest in gaining a deal and often make counter-intuitive choices (Carter and Curry, 2012). Transparent pricing says: 'Here is why we set these prices'. For example, in one of its advertising campaigns, Starbucks provided information on the various costs involved in the business to justify its prices to consumers. The ad cited the cost of the beans, the training of staff, the provision of health insurance, and the furnishings and leases of their stores. Emotion may well play a part in promotions such as free gifts (Laran and Tsiros, 2013). It has been found that when people make emotional decisions to purchase products they can be swayed by uncertain offers (e.g. 'You may receive a free set of floor mats for a car'). However, unsurprisingly, when the decision is viewed more logically, the promotion has to be more certain (e.g. 'You will receive a free set of car mats').

Customer costs

Finally, wherever possible a company needs to decide whether the returns justify the costs in serving buyers. In relationship marketing this has led to a move by many companies to focus on who they regard as their most profitable customers. This can be a socially and politically charged issue, as when banks have occasionally been found to send out directives to their branches on who to encourage or discourage from opening an account. One bank advised its branches to discourage anyone aged over 40 from opening a current account as by this stage of life most people had made their key financial decisions and would be less likely to provide much profit. The decision led to considerable negative publicity when the story was leaked.

Maintaining price points

Every business-to-business (B2B) or business-to-consumer (B2C) buyer or client knows that the price paid for a product or service can vary at any time or place. It might be the result of promotions such as bonus packs, temporary price cuts, coupons, circulars, on-pack coupons, or an end-of-aisle display (Davey et al., 1998). However, in the retail context, there is some doubt as to how effective promotions are other than for a few related products (Leeflang and Parreño-Selva, 2012). Furthermore, some policies can mask price while others highlight it. A £10 cash transaction for a book feels quite different to a £100 one, yet the same transactions by credit card feel identical as both involve the same process with a pin number or signature. Not surprisingly, theatres find that pre-booking cash-paying customers are much more likely to turn up for shows than credit card ones!

How can a company at least maintain a price? Potter (2000) suggests mounting **bundling** benefits. As the price of the standard product falls, the price may be maintained by including previous options as standard. On the other hand, unbundling benefits is where a product or service that was a standard feature is removed and becomes an option. There has been some interesting work by Alexander Chernev (2012) at the Kellogg School of Management on the issue. Apparently because of 'categorical reasoning' people classify products as either expensive or inexpensive and this influences how they judge them. People are more inclined to buy an expensive product when offered alone rather than bundled with a cheaper product. For example, Chernev found that people were willing to spend $225 on one piece of luggage and $54 on another, but when they were offered as a package (no pun intended!) they were only willing to pay $165 for both. The cheaper product exerted a halo effect on the more expensive one when considered together, while there was no subtraction effect when considered individually.

Alternative quality/service levels can also be offered at different price points. The idea here is not to offer discounts across the board because as the economy improves buyers get so used to these lower prices that it becomes impossible to reinstate the pre-discount price (Mohammed, 2011). Instead introduce lower-priced budget versions of products (e.g. the Waitrose 'Essential' range of products) or use promotions to avoid dropping prices across the board (e.g. Expedia offering a 14 day holiday in Brazil for the price of a 10 day one). Assurances may also play a role. In a recession, no matter how cheap a good or service is, people may not buy for fear of over-stretching themselves. Hyundai came up with a novel solution. They offered buyers the option of returning their vehicles if for any reason they could no longer make the payments. It proved highly successful with sales increases far outstripping returns.

Linking future purchases to current transactions is another strategy to explore. For example, car manufacturers often sell to rental companies with an agreement to repurchase the cars after a set period. The car rental companies get new cars at a keen price and the car manufacturers are in a favourable position to re-negotiate new contracts when the rental companies rotate the cars.

Another strategy is to **change the price effectiveness period**. The aim is to lock in potentially volatile customer volume or to obtain a higher price when it is expected that prices will fall. For example, many credit card companies have lengthened the time when new customers can benefit from low levels of interest on debt. Similarly, mobile phone companies offer discounts on long-term contracts, given the likelihood of future price falls.

Having made these points, an important factor in the level of consumption of any product or service is its cost. Thus, in the long run, strategies to maintain or raise prices may cause considerable upset and disloyalty. Consumption has been found to increase the chances of loyalty, and the more customers appreciate prices the more likely they are to consume. **Higher consumption helps develop long-term relationships** as customers are more likely to repeat the same patterns in the future. For example, in a field study, health club members who worked out four times a week were much more likely to renew their memberships than those who worked out once a week (Gourville and Soman, 2002).

The **timing of a payment** has been found to be important as well. For example, people who pay large sums for memberships of health clubs 'up-front' tend to use the facilities regularly in the first few weeks after payment. However, as the sunk (economic term for a cost that cannot be recovered) cost effects dissipate, they tend to treat their memberships as if they were free and work out less and less. By contrast, members who pay on a monthly basis are much more likely to attend regularly. It has also been found that people who buy tickets for a series of plays at festivals are much less likely to attend each play than people who buy tickets separately for each performance. By bundling, consumers lose sight of the cost of each ticket. In this case, the advice would be to introduce itemized billing as much as possible, so that customers get a better sense of price rather than bundling.

Overall, when considering price maintenance, there are some basics. Rises or falls in the price of raw materials—especially raw materials that are widely diffused throughout the economy, such as petrol—will affect a lot of organizations. Government policies will play a role, particularly with interest rates and purchase taxes.

Online pricing

Baye et al. (2007) suggest a number of strategies for online pricing. One of the key differences they point out is that online retailers increasingly compete at the product level rather than on such aspects as range, choice, and service, and so incremental costs need to be considered.

Click-through rates (the number of times people click on advertisements on line—often abbreviated to CTR) tend to be product specific as people check prices across a number of sites. The fees for CTRs can be considerable when aggregated (they range from about 15p to £1) and on average only about 1–3 per cent of click-throughs result in sales. This means that assuming a CTR of 2 per cent, an average of 50 CTRs will be needed to produce a single sale which might cost a site between £7.50 (50 × 15p) and £50 (50 × £1) on top of the wholesale price. Baye et al. suggest that the best strategy is to increase the mark-up when the number of competitors is low and reduce the mark-up when high. Quite a simple proposition really.

Given that competitors can use the web to stay constantly informed about pricing, price elasticity is a key consideration. Keep it unpredictable: Pixmania makes it very difficult for competitors to predict its pricing policy and so extremely hard to undercut. Given the ease with which competitors can track prices, Baye et al. suggest a 'hit and run' strategy by under-cutting prices for a relatively short period followed by a return to a higher price point to avoid being stuck in the middle. This is because companies with only slightly lower prices have been shown to achieve around 60 per cent more sales on price comparison sites such as Kelkoo. Slightly lower prices attract price-sensitive (mercenary) shoppers who account for just over 10–15 per cent of all online shoppers. If such price reductions are spasmodic (and thus unpredictable), competitors seldom see the need to respond, so a price war is rarely triggered. Yet during the price reduction a company can achieve an enormous increase in sales. Setting prices slightly above the lowest price will not attract the price conscious and margins will be greatly reduced amongst less deal-based shoppers.

Another consideration with online sales is the use of dynamic pricing (Weisstein et al., 2013). This involves differential pricing from the same seller for the same product, as is commonly used in the airline business. Technological advances increasingly mean that sellers can personalize online prices. For example sophisticated algorithms may be employed that take into account overall demand along with a buyers' characteristics, such as the frequency of purchase, the amount spent, and how recently they purchased; the price may then vary between individuals. Social media have highlighted such practices as followed by companies like Amazon and various airlines.

Pricing cross-subsidization on the web also needs to be considered. Commentators have coined various terms to encapsulate the phenomenon such as the 'free economy' or 'freeconomics' (see Mini Case 10.1).

 Mini Case 10.1 What's the price? It's free!

According to Chris Anderson, editor in chief of the Wired website and author of *Free: The Future of a Radical Price* (2009), new business models are being developed and a new generation of consumers, mostly under 35, are increasingly getting used to the idea that they don't have to pay for a lot of things.

The idea of free dates back to King Gillette who had the idea of selling disposable razor blades after finding he could no longer sharpen his standard cut-throat razor. In the first year (1903) Gillette only sold around 50 razors and 170 blades. After a series of marketing tactics, he finally bundled the razors with as many groceries as he could negotiate including coffee, tea and spices. In giving away the razors, he cleverly created demand for the disposable blades. Essentially the pricing model was one of cross-subsidization and has been applied to things like mobiles and service agreements and to video consoles and games.

Fast forward to today and so much information and music is available free to a new generation of consumers that cross-subsidy pricing no longer applies (Papies et al., 2011). Radiohead and a clutch of other bands have offered their albums for free on MySpace. Music can be freely listened to on Spotify. An endless stream of organizations provide free news. The pricing model here is much more akin to the one adopted by commercial television and radio. By attracting an audience, income can be generated by advertisers wanting to reach that same audience. Take the case of Google—just about everything it offers, including search, is free (e.g. Gmail, Google Earth, and Picassa). The company is not alone: Yahoo Mail offers unlimited storage totally free and Freeview offers just under 50 TV channels and 24 radio channels for free after the purchase of the set top box. The reality is that the marginal cost of digital information is coming closer to zero as networks are reaching larger and larger audiences. A new viewer on YouTube adds nothing to the cost of the operation.

Two trends are thus at work: on the one hand Gillette's razor and blade subsidy pricing model, as with Ryanair seeing itself as a travel agent rather than an airline; on the other, digital networks are reducing costs of transactions down towards zero, hence the drive amongst utility companies and banks to move people to Internet billing. Such services aren't really free, but they are so cheap as not to matter.

Unfortunately, consumers see a big difference between incredibly cheap and free. Give something of value away for nothing and it will navigate the web at warp speed. Charge a penny for it and the take-up is likely to be abysmal. The difference between zero and a penny, from a psychological perspective, is quite different than between one penny and two pennies. It can be the difference between a mass market and nothing at all. On the web, winners tend to be the first ones who go free.

What should an incumbent do who is suddenly faced with a competitor's free offering for the value they offer to the market? What should Microsoft do with the pricing of its Office suite, for example, in the face of free Google Docs and Oracle's Open Office? The trick is to figure out whether the competition are offering a free version of the existing offering or a new free product that appeals to new users (Bryce et al., 2011). Generally, responding sooner rather than later is the best strategy as when Quicken personal finance software purchased Mint.com in 2009, after Mint had acquired two million web users in just three years with its free software. Alternatively, an incumbent can offer a better free offering as when Auto Trader UK fought off rival car classified sites by introducing its own site that is free to users.

According to Bryce et al. (2011) the four basic strategies to compete and make money in a free market are as follows.

- *Up-sell*: offer a basic version and charge for a premium version (e.g. wetransfer.com).
- *Cross-sell*: sell other products not directly tied to the free product (e.g. Spotify sells artistes' merchandise such as T-shirts and posters).
- *Charge third parties*: provide a free product to users and charge a third party for access (Facebook selling advertising).
- *Bundle*: offer a free product with a paid offering (e.g. a free Nexus 7 with a subscription to the *Financial Times* newspaper).

Giving stuff away doesn't mean that no money is being made. Marketing has traditionally viewed price as an exchange between a buyer and a seller. This basic view has shifted to a broader view with often many parties involved and where pricing occurs between only some who exchange cash. This system has been around for years. Commercial television airs for free and the cover price for newspapers is heavily subsidized: advertisers pay to reach the audiences. These are examples of a three-way market: in this case, (1) media owner, (2) reader/viewer, and (3) advertiser (who pays the price).

New product pricing

Companies too often overplay the benefits of their new products and set unrealistically high prices (Marn et al., 2003). The first step in pricing a new product is to understand its true nature. 'Me-too' products or services need a clear target market and pricing needs to be set in line with existing offerings. Evolutionary products or services that offer relatively small enhancements need to be priced a little higher than existing offerings to avoid a price war, whereas truly evolutionary ones that can create their own markets can price at a premium.

A more novel approach to new product pricing is target pricing. The idea here is to develop products and services from the design stage onwards with a final target price objective for a particular market (Cooper et al., 1996). The strategy was pioneered by leading Japanese electronics and car manufacturers and has since spread widely. The main benefit is that target pricing is a disciplined approach that brings the reality of the marketplace throughout the entire process from idea conception to eventual output of the product or service. The process starts with targeting the most attractive segments in a market. Next, the level of quality and functionality is determined for success given a particular price. The organization finally undertakes the design, sourcing, production, and delivery process for the product or service that will enable it to achieve the desired profit level with this target market, rather than the other way around. Camera manufacturers provide a good example of the approach. The Canon EOS Rebel digital SLR camera incorporates a host of cost-saving technologies to produce a camera that is around half the price of rivals but with similar features. However, target pricing is more difficult to achieve when a company does not have much control over the design and supply of components. Komatsu has demonstrated a viable approach in cooperation with its suppliers. In order to implement target pricing Komatsu had to provide its suppliers with the parameters required to meet its required margins from early sub-assembly of its heavy equipment. Thus, the company 'sub-contracts' the target pricing objectives to its suppliers to fit the overall targeted price. The idea is not to compromise the quality of the product, but rather to balance the value equation between what is produced and what buyers demand. Engineering is pressed to the limit to meet the targeted price.

Implementing pricing strategy

To implement pricing strategy three 'capitals' are required: human, systems, and social (see Figure 10.3). Companies need to invest in all three capitals for pricing strategy to work.

Human capital

Human capital means training and hiring people who understand pricing across a range of products or services, customers, suppliers, and competitors. For example, Roche has an internal university to increase knowledge about pricing among its employees (Shantanu et al., 2002).

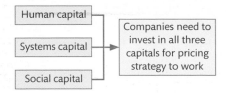

10.3 Three Capitals of Pricing Strategy

Systems capital

Systems capital relates to the hardware and software to process and implement pricing decisions. Sophisticated systems are also used by many manufacturers in B2B markets in a variety of ways such as helping sales reps understand the profitability of a deal. In using such systems sales reps can quote prices to customers almost immediately instead of having to go back to the office to calculate the price, which means that deals can be done much more quickly.

Yield management systems (YMS) were first developed in the mid-1980s in the airline industry and have migrated into other areas such as hotels, rentals, and all kinds of events (Desiraju and Shugan, 1999). Marketers have developed complex YMS algorithms with the objective of adjusting price over time to maximize available capacity at a profit. In practice it generally boils down to partitioning prices by time periods with discounts early on so that a hotel might charge £80 bookings six months away, but as the hotel fills up on these dates and the space becomes scarcer the YMS automatically raises the price. This is a further example of the impact of technology on marketing strategy, which now increasingly turns on a set of rules of behaviour rather than being based on strategic insight.

Social capital

Social capital is the 'glue' that coordinates and holds together the many participants in a pricing decision, which may be broadly designated as vertical (top-down) or horizontal (across departments) (Homburg et al., 2012). Internally it may involve, for example, persuading divisions to accept its pricing policies. According to Shantanu et al. (2002), in one case it took two years for the manufacturer concerned to replace divisional managers with ones who were willing to accept the pricing strategy.

Distribution

Definition

Distribution strategy is a vital element in creating value and has a direct bearing on pricing, promotion, packaging, salesforce logistics and delivery, installation, repair, and servicing, as well as outbound logistics of order processing, warehousing, and inventory. It's about making the supply of something available to people—be they buyers or users. It can be (1) physical, such as supplying hard copy of an accounting software package to a customer in a box, or (2) a service, such as supplying a training session for an accounting package, or (3) virtual, such as uploading an accounting package to a customer via the Internet. It is intrinsically linked to pricing for most companies as the mark-up of distributors can account for a significant amount of the price, normally at least 50 per cent. This section will now go on to examine the key strategic marketing elements in distribution.

Buyer's perspective

The strategic marketing perspective on distribution involves asking the central question: What do buyers want? Of course what buyers want will vary, but their main wants are:

- availability
- speedy delivery
- reliable supply
- range of choice
- empathy when supply is interrupted
- convenience
- service and support
- a good price.

However, people are increasingly 'leisure time poor' in both B2C and B2B markets and keen to trade off shopping time against leisure, so, of all the items on the list, convenience is the primary concern for most buyers (Seiders et al., 2000). As a consequence, convenience has driven just about every innovation in retailing such as supermarkets, department stores, shopping malls, the web, and self-scanning in the pursuit of providing what customers want. Despite this, few managers define convenience from the customers' point of view or have a systematic convenience strategy. Instead, 'convenience' has become a generic term for a bundle of attributes such as product assortment, salesperson expertise, speed of checkouts, hours of business, service levels, layout, and parking.

Perhaps the accolade of the best distribution systems in the world for convenience should arguably be given to the dabbawalas of Mumbai (formally known as the Mumbai Tiffin Box Supplier's Association). A cooperative organization, the dabbawalas deliver around 175,000 home-cooked meals to mainly office workers in Mumbai using carts, bicycles, and the train network—and a coding system. They have a six sigma record; that is, they make no errors to speak of, are always on time, and have a 100 per cent safety record. Fantastic.

From the customers' point of view, convenience means 'speed and ease'. Speed and ease consists of four elements—'access', 'search', 'possession', and 'transaction' (see Figure 10.4). Access is about being easy to reach; search is about enabling customers to speedily identify what they want; possession relates to the ease of obtaining products; and transaction is about the ease of purchase and return of products. What is clear is that convenience is a dynamic construct; 24 hour photo processing is no longer fast and renting a video is now seen by many as a task.

As with all aspects of convenience, **access** is relevant to both store and non-store shopping. Accessibility factors include parking, location, availability, hours of opening, and proximity to

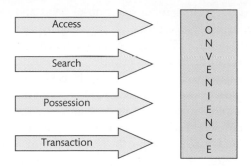

10.4 Primary Concerns of Buyers

other outlets, as well as telephone, mail, and Internet. Convenience simply does not exist without access. This often explains the alliances being formed between organizations (e.g. eBay customers being able to collect their purchases from local Argos stores or Waitrose customers being able to collect their groceries from designated tube stations in London). Customers increasingly want access to products and services as fast and direct as possible with very little hassle. However, what can be offered often depends on government regulation and the available infrastructure. For example, Tesco has been badly hit by curbs on opening hours in South Korea, which were imposed in an effort to support small retailers.

Search convenience, identifying and selecting the products you want, is connected to product focus, intelligent outlet design and layout, knowledgeable staff, interactive systems and product displays, packaging, and signage, be they physical or virtual. One example of good practice is the German discount chain, Adler Modemärkte GmbH, which uses colour-coded tags to help customers quickly spot their sizes. Also, training can prepare sales staff to act more like personal shoppers by anticipating choices and matching the merchandise to the shopper.

Possession convenience is about having merchandise in stock and available on a timely basis. For example, Nordstrom clothing store guarantees that advertised products will be in stock and Lens Crafters prepares glasses on the same day, generally in one hour. But while there are numerous examples of good practice, possession convenience has its limitations. In particular, while the Internet scores highly in search convenience, it is generally low when it comes to possession convenience. Shoppers might save a trip to the store but invariably they have to wait for their purchases. Sometimes this can cause significant problems for suppliers. To illustrate, there was the case of the Need a Cake bakery who offered 12 cupcakes for £6.50 via Groupon instead of the normal price of £26.00 (the price was below cost). The offer was taken up by 8,500 people, necessitating hiring extra temporary staff and working flat out to fulfil the order. Need a Cake almost went bust over it. Though please bear in mind the international context with this discussion. In many parts of the world the road infrastructure is extremely poor, making physical distribution quite a challenge. FMCG companies such as P&G, Unilever, and Colgate often rely on handcarts, bicycles, and mopeds for difficult to reach rural areas in countries such as Ghana. Generally known as 'hub and spoke' systems, they consolidate stock in larger centres and then distribute in a piecemeal manner in the best way possible to more remote areas.

Transaction convenience is the speed and ease with which consumers can effect or amend transactions before and after the purchase. There have been a variety of innovative approaches in recent years, such as robot selection of items and self-scanning in outlets like Waitrose (the latter being a process which is perceived by shoppers as faster despite the time it takes to scan each item). Well-designed service systems can mitigate the peaks and troughs in store traffic, as with Sainsbury's use of electronic sensors to track customer traffic to predict checkout requirements. Single queues used by banks and post offices can be effective but owing to lack of space cannot be replicated by supermarkets. Some stores empower employees to take a customers' word on the price of an unmarked item (within reason) to keep queues moving. Transaction convenience is a significant issue on the Internet. Many Internet shoppers drop out when completing the first page of the billing form. Internet sites often require too much personal information, frequently designed to increase their advertising revenues. Furthermore, customers are not properly prepared for shipping and handling costs. Pure Internet retailers also have problems with returns compared with bricks and mortar counterparts. Generally, is not that easy to return items via the post and often shoppers have to pay the non-refunded postage. Unconditional guarantees go a long way, but Internet retailers are generally at a disadvantage when it comes to returns.

Navigation

At the heart of the buyer's perspective is navigation. Navigation is the process of steering between the mass and variety of information and choices in both physical and e-commerce. For example, no one reviews all the possible options in buying a shirt or pair of shoes. Instead consumers rely on suppliers and retailers to help them navigate (Laffey, 2007). Navigation is the key to profit potential. For example, Amazon.com started out as an online bookseller but has broadened its offering to include music, DVDs, games, electronics, computing and office, homes and gardens, toys, children and baby, jewellery and watches, clothing and shoes, sports and leisure, health and beauty, and DIY and tools. Where will it end? Amazon had its roots in the publishing industry; the unknown limits to the domain in which Amazon.com is the preferred navigator is the reason why the company is now worth more than the entire publishing industry.

Navigation has four dimensions: 'reach', 'affiliation', 'richness' (Evans and Wurster, 1999), and 'range' (Wells and Gobeli, 2003) as shown in Figure 10.5. Each of these will now be considered in turn.

Reach is the extent to which a retailer can manage its value chain to connect to its customers. It is not just the ability of customers to reach the firm, but also the firm's ability to reach the customer with its products and services. This also often applies with a 'co-distribution'

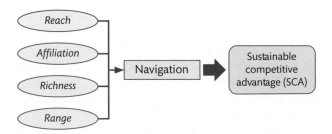

10.5 Navigation

approach in countries such as China and India where people in isolated rural areas will often make the effort to travel considerable distances to larger centres to purchase consumer durables like TVs and electric fans because they get greater variety of choice and better prices. They might take them home precariously balanced on a bike or a moped, but this is seen as preferable to taking what might be offered locally. The manufacturer obtains reach partly on the basis of the effort by the consumer.

Affiliation is about transparency and trust between retailers and their customers. The difference on line is that customers cannot tangibly evaluate the physical space of the shop or office concerned (Reicheld and Schefter, 2000). Images and promises are all that they have, and if they do not trust the company concerned, they will shop elsewhere. John Lewis became a leading department store in the UK by creating one of the most reliable and trustworthy shopping experiences. In the online world, customers in their millions allow Amazon to store their names, addresses, and credit card details so that they can make repeat purchases with just the click of a mouse.

Richness is the degree to which a retailer can match customers' exact wants and needs. For example, the interaction between a local tailoring shop and its customers is extremely rich as the tailor can easily observe preferences and produce a customized product. Physical retailers have always had the ability to collect and use information about their customers, but the Internet greatly enhances this aspect. For example 1-800-flowers.com maintains a customer-specific file with anniversary and birthday information and a record of gifts sent. Customers can be alerted to an impending birthday and particular flowers suggested. Furthermore, data mining techniques can be applied to browsing behaviour as well as purchasing history and building relationships. Purchasing behaviour can be compared between similar customers and played back to similar profiled customers. Richness is one area where producers have an edge compared with retailers when related to customer information. Retailers, be they physical or electronic, have most information on consumers, but no-one knows the goods or services better than suppliers.

Range relates to the breadth and degree of products offered by retailers. It might be category-specific (narrow) as with Dell, which can offer high customization. It might be cross-category (broad) like Companhia Brasileira de Distribuição in Brazil, which offers breadth with hypermarkets, supermarkets, wholesale supermarkets, and household appliances stores, but minimal specialization or customization. The digital retail medium allows the seamless integration of complementary products and services that were previously difficult or impossible to manage. Thus, travel portals like Aviasales.ru in Russia can offer tickets, car rentals and hotel reservations, and travel planning in one cohesive package. The essence of customization is to add value. If customization is used effectively, both B2B and B2C markets can be populated by highly loyal customers for retailers.

Retailers that offer thousands of products across hundreds of categories often pick one supplier to be a 'category captain' to manage a particular category—including rivals' brands—on their behalf (Gooner et al., 2011). Such retailers generally lack the resources and capabilities to manage a wide range intensively, but the worry is that influential 'captains' will be opportunistic and that the benefits of intensive category management will be lost. Such an issue brings into focus the consideration of how to manage distribution.

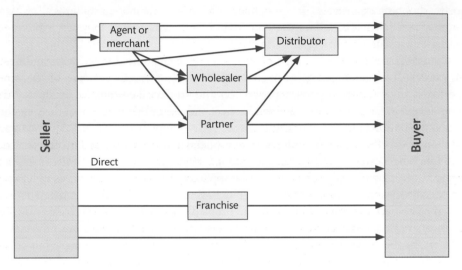

10.6 Distribution Options*

*More limited for services

10.7 Principal Channels

Distribution options and principal channels—buyer's perspective

Having discerned what buyers want, the strategic imperative of any distribution system should be to satisfy these wants in the most effective manner. There are a number of options for a seller to reach a buyer (more limited for services), but these can be broadly broken down into three choices: direct, salesforce, or intermediary as shown broadly in Figure 10.6 and in more detail in Figure 10.7.

Direct/online

Going direct to a buyer can be achieved by using the Internet, telephone, mail, catalogue, some form of direct advertising (press, DRTV, or radio), or own distribution network. Direct channels can provide a reliable supply and a good price, and can be extremely convenient by saving the physical requirement to shop. They are, however, prone to problems of availability, speedy supply (no instant purchases can be made aside from digital products), range of choice (e.g. companies like Bullrush Clothing Company in Australia only offer their own branded clothes), empathy when supply is interrupted, and service and support (especially if items have to be returned).

It is a gross simplification, but on the whole direct channels are best when the strategy is cost focus for niche or mass markets. Buyers are often prepared to sacrifice negatives like speedy delivery for the benefits of a lower price. Strategically such channels may also work with highly differentiated items that cannot be obtained elsewhere. For example, Air China used Facebook as a promotional tool in Sweden (Facebook is blocked in China) via Swedish ad agency Rodolfo, who took advantage of local Asian restaurants in Stockholm. Customers were invited to check in at these restaurants for a chance to win plane tickets to Asia. A lot of buzz was created and it enabled Air China to reach a large number of potential buyers cost efficiently.

On the web shoppers can access price comparison sites and 'shopbots'—websites for finding the cheapest online deals for a range of items. They make money by having commercial relationships with most of the shops they list and get paid per click or via a small percentage of whatever is purchased which means that each shopbot may cover a different range of retailers. There are well-known generalists such as Kelkoo, Pricerunner, MoneySuperMarket.com and Alibaba (China), as well as a number of specialists such as Quaffers' Offers (wine), FindDVD, CheapPerfumeExpert, and mySupermarket.

From a wider perspective, going direct provides suppliers with considerable control over the mechanics of distribution, and revenues and reliability of supply are directly linked to production so there is no formal need to motivate a channel. However, it requires logistical expertise even if many of the supply chain relationships are contracted out (e.g. delivery), and so the investment required may be relatively high.

Having made these points, the main question with direct distribution is why would an organization choose any other way? The reason is largely down to discrepancy of assortment—most suppliers have a small number of products and services whereas consumers desire variety of choice and ease of purchase, especially in B2C markets. Few people would buy their groceries from individual suppliers as it would be too time-consuming (more manageable through intermediaries like Tesco). Thus direct distribution, which has many advantages for suppliers, is largely confined to specialist single-item purchases and B2B markets where consumers are willing to trade off any disadvantages for cheaper prices or highly differentiated (or often unique) products or services. However, the Internet has accelerated the process by driving down transaction costs and made direct supply a lot easier for both seller and buyer.

Salesforce

An alternative to going direct is to use a salesforce. The alternatives are to (1) set up your own, (2) use another organization, or (3) hire on a contractual basis. The use of a salesforce in the B2C marketplace is largely no longer viable and very few companies have continued to use one. That is not to suggest that the use of a salesforce in B2C markets was ever that common; since the 1950s it has been largely confined to a relatively small group of industries and companies such as vacuum cleaners and financial products. The problems of using a salesforce strategy in most B2C markets have been the fragmentation of households and rise of overall employment, and the increase in car ownership and alternative means of shopping means that door-to-door selling just does not have much appeal in B2C markets.

The B2B marketplace is quite different and operates with active salesforces across just about all markets. Sustaining a longer-term customer relationship requires developing a close personal bond between both parties. Salespeople tend to liaise regularly with a distinct and small group of senior managers, whatever the size of the company. However, the decision to select, continue, or terminate a purchase or contract at larger corporations has long been known to be the product of joint decision-making processes, involving a large number of decision-makers and influencers. Furthermore, with increasingly decentralized management structures amongst companies, many salespeople find that they are increasingly isolated from key decision-makers.

Salespeople increasingly use social media for prospecting, qualifying leads, and managing relationships (Giamanco and Gregoire, 2012). The reality is that B2B buyers are doing things like reading blogs, holding online discussions about buying products, scanning YouTube, using Google, and tweeting. Social media can be used for prospecting by salespeople by looking out for a discussion on a Facebook page, complaints on Twitter, or perhaps an invitation on LinkedIn. This can be much more productive than cold-calling. Leads can be qualified on social media by using IBM's guide of 'BANT': following companies and assessing their potential **budgets**, whether their contact has the **authority** to buy, whether there is a **need** for a product, and whether the potential **timeline** for delivery fits what the customer might want. Social media have become part of relationship management with many reps having a wide base of 'friends' or 'followers', as long as the content has sufficient value for buyers.

Having your own salesforce clearly provides the optimum control and ability to motivate them and to build relationships with buyers and potential buyers, but comes at a price. Such decisions are often determined by the margins at stake. For example, it is not uncommon for a company like Tata Aerospace to employ a salesperson for 5–15 years without making a single sale in some markets. It might take this long to develop the relationships with government agencies and defence companies and other buyers, and there is no prospect of contacting this person outside of the business. If a sale is made it might be worth several £100 million and, therefore, ultimately worth the effort. Strategically there is no substitute for having a salesperson(s) in such markets.

Intermediaries

An intermediary channel has to be used when it is difficult or impossible for a supplier to 'meet' its customers. There is an ownership issue here. If you own a shop and sell your products through it, it would not be classified as an intermediary. However, if you sell your products through an identical shop that you do not own, that shop would be classified as an intermediary. There are several different types of intermediary: agent, distributor, franchiser, merchant, and wholesaler. An agent acts as principal intermediary between the seller and supplier of a product or service and finds buyers without taking ownership. A merchant performs the same but does take ownership. Wholesalers stock products (not services) before the next level of distribution. Distributors do just that—they distribute the product within a market. Franchising is where a company offers a complete brand concept, supplies, and logistics to a franchisee who invests an initial lump sum and thereafter pays regular fees to continue the relationship (e.g. O Boticário is a popular retailer of bath, body, and beauty products in Brazil with over 3,252 franchises).

Strategically, intermediaries enable firms to offer just about everything buyers want: availability, speed of delivery, reliable supply, range of choice, empathy when supply is interrupted, convenience, and service and support. From a customer's perspective there are few, if any, downsides aside from the kind of B2B customer identified in the previous section WHO is involved in a measured choice and needs to deal with a salesperson.

One problem with an intermediary is the lack of control. Suppliers are often at the mercy of intermediaries as to where their products are placed on shelves, how they are finally priced and the consequent effect on sales and margins.

Intermediaries are markets in their own right and require considerable resources to support and develop relationships with—hence the importance of branding. Take a brand like Sony. Despite product parity in many electronic markets, Sony remains the premium electronics brand in the B2C marketplace. Any electrical retailer without Sony products is going to be less of a destination for most shoppers as they will expect to see the brand. Sony has supplier power and can negotiate higher margins and better shelf positioning and stocking for its products than its rivals.

Multi-channel marketing

It is all very well considering the main three channel options of direct/online, intermediaries, or salesforce, but increasingly a **multi-channel marketing** strategy is required for buyers who use more than one channel when interacting with an organization. A good example is when customers go online for information but then go offline to complete a purchase, or the process might be reversed where someone goes into a shop to get some information about a product but then goes online to buy it.

Multi-channel shoppers are now in the majority; studies indicate they account for just under two-thirds of all shoppers and they also spend significantly more than single-channel shoppers. The tendency for multi-channel shopping will rise as wireless devices and mobile phones increasingly offer new ways to enter a market and associated services. Weinberg et al. (2007) suggest three cohesive actions for developing an effective multi-channel strategy, and each will be reviewed in turn.

Value proposition

Rather than take a tactical view of distribution, the idea with assessing the value proposition is to appreciate the value offered by each channel, including strengths, weaknesses, and synergies. Organizations need to review all the potential customer touch points, and spend on the things that are working and downplay things that are not. The underlying approach is: the channels that are most valuable to the customer are the ones most valuable to the brand. Bearing in mind the increasing tendency to try out products and then buy online, a number of companies are experimenting with new experiential retail outlets (see Mini Case 10.2). According to Rigby (2011) digital retailing has morphed into something that perhaps needs a new name, which he suggests should be 'omnichannel retailing'. Retailers are now able to interact with customers through countless channels—websites, physical shops, kiosks, pop ups, direct mail and catalogues, call centres, social media, mobile devices, gaming consoles, televisions, networked appliances, home services, and many more. Rigby suggests that unless conventional retailers integrate disparate channels into a single seamless 'omnichannel experience',

⊡ Mini Case 10.2 'Try before you buy'

Back in the 1960s and 1970s music shops offered booths where customers could pop on some headphones and sample a single or album before deciding to buy it. These became redundant and went out with the ark. However, 'try before you buy' did not die as a concept. Sample Lab in Tokyo's downtown is a members-only shop that invites consumers to sample and test new products. The Sample Lab doesn't make any money from its products; instead companies pay them to have their items stocked there so that they get consumer feedback on their products and the potential buzz. The Sample Lab's 'Lcafe' is a way to reach Japanese women in their 20s and 30s with information about new products. The women must first register using their mobile phones and provide personal information, including their age, birthday, and marital status, in order to become members. Registered members get a barcode sent to them on their mobiles, which helps Sample Lab track who got what sample. Once registered, they get tokens based on the amount of food or drink they order. These tokens can be redeemed for more samples such as pretzel sticks with flavours like cheese, apple, or tomato, along with assorted skincare products. The Lab sends out questions to see how a member liked a particular item and those who answer get extra tokens for more samples.

Another example is provided by Villeroy & Boch Bubble Shops in Utrecht, The Netherlands. The shop enables potential consumers to experience bubble baths in two secluded luxury rooms along with a private outdoor area for open air spas so they can try out the various Aqua & Air systems or steam shower cabins. It's free with no strings attached and sessions in the shop can last for up to an hour with a capacity of around four to six appointments a day.

Panasonic offers a 'try before you buy' service for their top of the range Lumix DMC-GH3 with 12–35 mm lens camera. Customers can borrow the GH3 kit for 48 hours (excluding delivery and collection time) from a number of retailers, with no obligation to purchase. This allows them to explore and try the camera in their own setting before deciding to purchase or not. Barney Sykes, the Lumix G Camera Product and Marketing Manager, said: 'The GH3 is by far the most advanced system camera we have ever launched and we recognize customers may want to "road test" this product before committing to such as high value purchase'. Panasonic Power Tools also offer 'try before you buy' demonstrations within designated builders' merchants in workbench settings. Trade professionals are able to try out a variety of power tools in settings close to what they would experience when completing projects.

Another example is tastingroom.com which attempts to take the guesswork and uncertainty out of shopping for wine. Their innovative wine-tasting kit contains six selected wines from around the world, packaged in small, taste-test-sized (50ml) bottles. They use a system designed for the purpose of transferring wine directly from standard 750ml bottles into mini bottles that is oxygen-free. You follow the instructions with the kit and learn about the types of wine that suit your taste. Once you've rated your wine samplers, the company (Lot 18) applies an algorithm to generate your Wine Profile—a detailed explanation of the types of wine that match your profile—with the intent of then supplying you with your preferred wine types.

What is the 'try before you buy' trend all about? Perhaps it is simply tapping into people's basic behaviour? People like trying things out, they love being first with new things, and they also enjoy being part of an exclusive community. Bingo! 'Try before you buy' provides the perfect fit.

they are likely to be swept away. One caveat is there is evidence that while there are 'learners' who are keen to try new channels, there are also 'stayers', more than likely to be older customers, who are resistant to change and who generally stay with the tried and tested (Valentini et al., 2011). This is reinforced by a study by UCL in 2006 which found that trying new things employs the upper reaches of the brain and needs effort, whereas falling back on the familiar fires up the brain's pleasure centres (Scammell-Katz, 2012).

Organizational structures and incentives

Conflicts can arise in channel relationships with perceived unfairness having the greatest negative impact on cooperation and flexibility (Samaha et al., 2011). Problems can arise vertically, that is between sequential members in a distribution network such as agents and distributors over carrying a particular range or over price increases. Horizontal conflicts may arise between the same members of a channel such as between agents or between distributors where competition may be deemed to be unfair. Within any channel there is often collision of interests, given that all channel members naturally seek to maximize their profits and resources.

Occasionally 'silos' can exist within an organization. For example, data and information may not be shared between the Internet group and the bricks and mortar channel. Another angle to consider is the ownership of the product. Hagiu and Wright (2013) suggest the fundamental strategic decision in retail is to choose between being a reseller (like a supermarket), which acquires and then resells products, or operating as a multisided platform (like eBay), connecting buyers and sellers without controlling or owning the offerings being sold. Or should the two models be blended? Hagiu and Wright point out that the past ten years have seen a multisided-platform (MSP) bubble led by the success of the success of eBay and of Rakuten and Taobao, eBay's counterparts in Japan and China, respectively. The problem is that retailers who just sit between suppliers and consumers, adding no value, are losing their purpose–hence the demise of well-known high street names like Comet and Jessops.

Create metrics

The third and final element suggested by Weinberg et al. (2007) is to choose the right metrics to evaluate a holistic multi-channel approach. It is a highly complicated area, given issues of loyalty, customer satisfaction, and how the metric might be used. The authors suggest that organizations measure the synergistic impact of no more than two channels at a time, such as a website and direct mail, and focus on how well they interact. Only once the synergies have become better understood should they include a third channel.

Grey marketing

One final aspect to consider is **grey marketing** where distributors purchase goods such as fluid pumps or drill bits in one market, either from an authorized dealer or directly from the manufacturer, and resell the same goods in another market at a higher price. This has happened in mainland China with Apple's 5C phones reportedly smuggled in from Hong Kong and undercutting the prices of the authorized dealers by up to 30 per cent. Such activity is not necessarily illegal, but can fall foul of license agreements or be counter to trade regulations. Companies that find their goods being distributed by grey marketers face a mix of problems aside from lost profits. For a start, price discounting can affect their image, and relationships with authorized dealers can become strained as they watch their markets being eroded. Furthermore, they might face legal challenges as unauthorized imports might not meet local safety or import regulations. Moreover, forward planning becomes difficult as they no longer have full knowledge of sales patterns and their reputation may be further damaged if grey marketers fail to provide a decent level of service. Regions particularly badly affected by grey markets are Western Europe and the Pacific Rim, followed by Latin America.

One worthwhile strategy is to coordinate distribution channels horizontally (Myers and Griffith, 1999). What this means in practice is the sharing of information such as sales databases with distributors. If one distributor notices unfamiliar sales activities it can alert both manufacturer and distributors in nearby markets and thereby flag potential problems. Distributors should also be encouraged to update and input data on changing regulations in their markets. This will help manufacturers and other distributors to forecast potential grey market activity. For example, the EU might significantly change tax arrangements for a particular good between members and non-members of the community, and there may be consequences for grey markets. Another consideration is to restrict the power of salespeople and lower-level managers to set different prices for particular customers. Wide price margins within markets encourage buyers to seek lower prices if they cannot access the 'deals' they see on offer.

Price and distribution strategies meet

Appropriate strategies for price and distribution will depend on a variety of factors, but should be synchronized. Clearly, it would be a mismatch to distribute high-priced luxury handbags in discount stores and would only confuse potential buyers. Along with market position such as sales databases, the inherent brand position and direction must be taken into account. Bearing these three points in mind, a number of observations can be made on price and distribution.

Market leader

Just about every market has an acknowledged market leader—a firm with a dominant market share that sets the standards or rules in the market place. Obvious examples are Google and search engines, Tesco and supermarkets, and Starbucks and coffee shops. The market leader has a lot going for it, but has to be ever vigilant to the activities of close rivals constantly looking

Market leader	Market challenger
• Distribution in place • Price main weapon • Premium price • Variety of options	• Focus on flanks • Direct or indirect attack
Market follower • 'Cloning' • Set lower prices	**Market niche** • Stay with markets • Add niches • Premium price • Selective distribution

10.8 Price and Distribution Strategies

to grab the top position for themselves. Leading brand names in the consumer, business, and not-for-profit market place have retained their leadership surprisingly well over the past 30–50 years and have been the subject of much academic research as to their viability and longevity.

Dominant market leaders need to expand the total market as much as possible as they are the ones most likely to benefit, given their leadership position. They can achieve this with strategies for market usage and new applications as well as considering developing any niche markets previously neglected. Their distribution networks are usually fully in place, which leaves price as their main weapon. They might directly attack challengers by price reductions. However, if attacked by a challenger aggressively dropping its price, a leader is generally advised to 'take stock of the situation' before deciding on the best form of counter-attack. This is because market leaders normally have enough strength to wait and decide on the best response, which is often to hold off matching such drops. For example, Sony has generally been able to maintain its premier price differential in the television marketplace despite the challenges of Samsung.

Market leaders have several attacking or defensive options in declining markets. As leaders, they have the greatest visibility in the market and by reducing their prices they can encourage rivals to rapidly exit from the market place. Alternatively, they may decide to milk their position, maintain their prices, and steadily withdraw and re-allocate their resources to other markets where they consider they have better prospects.

Market challenger

The market challenger is the main reason for the nervousness of the market leader. Unlike market followers, market challengers are substantial firms or institutions in their own right, with sufficient resources and skills to occupy the market leader spot. Any marketplace is dynamic and firms' fortunes can go up or down. Hoover's dominance of vacuum cleaners was rocked by Dyson, and Sainsbury's lost its market leadership to Tesco. Market challengers normally do not wipe out the business of the market leader, but they can edge their way towards equality or gradually overtake the leader. Market challengers have little alternative but to attack leaders either directly or indirectly. They need to make better use of pricing and distribution to help do this and attack the leader's strengths or its weaker spots (flanks). A concentrated all-out attack on a leader may be the best way forward to take the high ground with lower prices.

Attacking other challengers, followers, or smaller niche players in the marketplace, rather than leaders, can be a way to launch indirect price attacks on leaders. Such tactics will result in the challenger discreetly building share, without going head-to-head on price with the leader, by picking off weaker geographic markets or segments in so-called 'bypass' attacks. In this way Swatch managed to outmanoeuvre Seiko in the fashion segment. Relatively smaller challengers may adopt 'guerrilla' tactics by picking off smaller markets intermittently. But unless backed up by some wider and deeper campaign at some later point, small-scale price tactics will never topple a leader.

Market follower

Market followers, as their name implies, make a conscious decision to chase and emulate the market decisions of leaders and/or challengers. They may clone prices and distribution and trade successfully upon the 'leftovers' of other companies. Generally they build distribution behind leaders and challengers and set their prices somewhat lower. Their profitability emanates from their decision to forego investing in uncertain new product development or in educating consumers in new ways of thinking in favour of simply following the actions of leaders or challengers in the market place. Followers, by their nature, do not seek leadership or to overtly challenge a leader. They can make good profits simply by providing imitations of leader or challenger products from which the only inhibitor is legal, such as the use of patents in the drug industry. Service sectors like banking and hotels are particularly prone to followers, as it is impossible to copyright a service provision, as are capital-intensive sectors in the business marketplace like fibre optic cables and steel. Typical examples of followers would be Virgin Money, Marks & Spencer jeans, Acer laptops, Holiday Inns, and the Motorola or HTC smartphones. By definition, a market follower needs to stick to its title. They need to follow leaders and challengers and not launch price or distribution attacks. If they launch attacks, they will become challengers and will need the requisite resources and skills to survive such combat.

Market niche

The application of the market niche brings the discussion of pricing and distribution full circle. The reason is simple: a market niche is the application of market leadership to a small and/or distinct part of the market place. The micro policy is based upon the macro one. Success with a niche policy is based upon the reality that market leaders or challengers have little or no interest in niches. Thus, Bang & Olufsen can survive extremely well in its high priced, selectively distributed, and upmarket style-conscious (but not expert) hi-fi market place, knowing that the likes of Sony or Marantz would have great difficulty in stretching their image to challenge them. Similarly, in the brewing, fashion, and cosmetics markets a host of small players continue to make good profits exploiting niche market opportunities that neither leaders, challengers, nor followers would want to occupy. Thus, most major breweries are just not interested in developing products to rival microbreweries with their wheat, herbal, and chocolate beers (to name but a few!). The secret of successful sole niching is to operate within a niche that has very little appeal for major players in the wider market place. The basis of the market niche strategy, be it a sole strategy or one adopted by leaders or challengers, is to specialize. Market niche strategies may be based upon goods or services, segments, channels or promotional images.

Best practice for sole nichers is to develop more than one market niche so that the company or institution is less vulnerable to attack from a rival. It is essential that a sole nicher is not seen as a potential rival to a leader or challenger, which might lead to a direct attack. An ideal position for a sole nicher would be one where just about everyone else in the market place regards their niche as too much effort to bother with. That way they can charge premium prices and develop selective and discreet distribution channels. A company marketing high priced organic non-dairy chocolate products only through delicatessens and health food shops is unlikely to have much trouble from the likes of Cadbury's! Turning to leaders or challengers—they can use niches to either entrench their positions or as a form of attack. As discussed above, in the hands of leaders or challengers a niche can provide a basis for market growth or to indirectly attack a rival's market position.

Conclusion

The reality for most marketers is that the pricing and distribution 'dice' have been 'thrown' by their companies. L'Oréal's dermatological skincare range Vichy was delisted by Boots in 2003 because Boots preferred to stock the brand on shelves, but Vichy would rather position the brand closer to behind-the-counter products. It is now back at Boots, but at the time Vichy was reluctant to compromise on its international distribution strategy, which positions the brand as a specialist pharmacy product rather than a mass-market or premium skincare range. Thus, for the most part, strategies have to be developed in line with historic price points and distribution structures.

In many markets pricing and distribution strategies meet in conjunction with positioning and customer wants. Take the case of the petrol companies and supermarkets. The supermarkets moved into the retailing of petrol in the early 1990s, undercutting the prices of petrol companies and offering volume discounts based on how much people spent on their groceries. In response the petrol companies transformed their garage operations into convenience stores offering many of the same staple products as the supermarkets but with much longer opening hours. In response several supermarkets, in particular Tesco, have extended their opening hours (selected stores open for 24 hours Monday to Saturday).

Overall, intensive distribution is largely found for low-priced convenience or impulse products or services where the opportunity to buy is important. Exclusive distribution is generally used for high-priced luxury items in order to achieve superior brand image, product support, better sales effort, and control over price. Selective distribution tends to work well for speciality producers (e.g. sewing machines) where knowledgeable dealers are needed and buyers are prepared to seek them out.

Undoubtedly the Internet has provided both the biggest challenge and opportunities to suppliers and bricks and mortar channel members. The problems faced by marketers overall are that a multitude of individual and combined methods for pricing and distribution are possible. The key challenge for marketers is how to price and distribute in a way that supports a chosen position and fends off the drive to commoditization (Bertini and Wathieu, 2010). This is especially, though not exclusively, what is happening in many B2B markets. Take the case of handling and storage products (e.g. hand trucks, stackers, pallet trucks) made by companies like Caterpillar, BT Rolatruc, Komatsu, and Jungheinrich. They are used to stack and manoeuvre products in warehouses and for deliveries etc. Such products are fast approaching commodity status and traded on the web with increasingly small margins as a result, which in turn leaves the companies with fewer resources to invest in R&D for future differentiation, and there is no easy solution to the problem. Given that it is less easy to evaluate a service than a good, commoditization of services is less of a problem. However, it has happened with reasonably transparent and highly competitive services such as house conveyancing, where solicitors often charge similar standard prices.

Summary

Value holds the key to both pricing and distribution. Buyers are savvy and smart, most markets are mature with products and services near (or at) parity, and distribution channels are varied and largely accessible physically and/or virtually. Any strategies attempting to 'rip off' or overcharge will fail and longer-term trust will evaporate. As a consequence of these challenges, price and distribution are likely to remain key issues in marketing strategy in the immediate future.

Key terms

- **Bundling:** grouping together features or goods or services to form a single price.
- **Channel conflict:** potential or existing disputes between different forms of distribution, for example BA ticket sales via its website and its travel agent network.
- **Elasticity:** a measure of the relationship between the percentage change in demand for a product or service and the percentage change in price. For example, if the price of a brand of coffee rises by 10 per cent and demand falls below 10 per cent, the brand would be inelastic. However, if the price were to rise by 10 per cent and demand fall by more than 10 per cent, the brand would be elastic.
- **Grey marketing:** distributors purchasing products or services in one market and reselling them in another at a higher price.
- **Intermediary:** any distributor operating between seller and buyer who may or may not take ownership of the product or service.
- **Multi-channel marketing:** a strategy for buyers who use more than one channel when interacting with an organization.
- **Price at POS:** the price realized at the final transaction between seller and buyer.
- **Target pricing:** the development of goods and services with a specific price at POS in mind.

Discussion questions

1. In what ways might an organization's pricing 'mindset' act negatively on its pricing strategy?
2. If you could only follow two of Dolan's eight stages for pricing strategy, which ones would you choose and why?
3. What is the role of price in loyalty? What pricing strategies can be used to enhance loyalty and repeat purchases?
4. Assess the impact of the web on pricing strategies.
5. Evaluate the pros and cons of a bricks and mortar company offering the same or different prices on its website.
6. To what extent do you think systems-based rules will take over pricing strategy decisions?
7. Convenience has come to the fore as the key element on which to base distribution. Assess the arguments for and against focusing on convenience over other core wants such as range of choice.
8. Why is the salesforce so important to B2B marketing strategy and so unimportant to B2C?
9. Which of the three marketing actions prescribed by Weinberg et al. (2007) for multi-channel marketing mindsets (value propositions, structures and incentives, and metrics) do you regard as key and why?
10. What strategies would you recommend to an organization faced with intense grey marketing distribution in one of its markets?

Online resource centre

 Visit the Online Resource Centre for this book for lots of interesting additional material at: **<www.oxfordtextbooks.co.uk/orc/west3e/>**

References and further reading

Anderson, Chris (2009), *Free: The Future of a Radical Price* (London: Random House).

Ayres, Ian and Barry Natelbuff (2003), 'In Praise of Honest Pricing', *MIT Sloan Management Review* 45 (1), pp. 24–8.

Baye, Michael R., J. Rupert J. Gatti, Paul Kattuman, and John Morgan (2007), 'A dashboard for online pricing', *California Management Review*, 50 (1), pp. 202–16.

Bertini, Marco and Luc Wathieu (2010), 'How to Stop Customers from Fixating on Price', *Harvard Business Review*, May, pp. 84–91.

Bryce, David J., Jeffrey H. Dyer, and Nile W. Hat (2011) 'Competing Against Free,' *Harvard Business Review*, June, pp. 104–11.

Carter, Robert E. and David J. Curry (2010), 'Transparent Pricing: Theory, Tests, and Implications for Marketing Practice', *Journal of the Academy of Marketing Science*, 38, pp. 759–74.

Chernev, Alexander (2012), 'Pay More for Less', *Harvard Business Review*, June, pp. 30–1.

Cooper, Robin, Bruce W. Chew, and Bernard Avishai (1996), 'Control Tomorrow's Costs Through Today's Designs', *Harvard Business Review*, 74 (1), pp. 88–99.

Davey, K.K.S., Andy Childs, and Stephen J. Carlotti (1998), 'Why Your Price Band is Wider than it Should Be', *McKinsey Quarterly*, 3, pp. 116–27.

Dolan, Robert J. (1995), 'How Do You Know When the Price Is Right?', *Harvard Business Review*, 73 (5), pp. 174–9.

Dutta, Shantanu, Mark Bergen, Daniel Levy, Mark Ritson, and Mark Zbaracki (2002), 'Pricing as a Strategic Capability', *MIT Sloan Management Review*, Spring, pp. 61–6.

Giamanco, Barbara and Kent Gregoire (2012), 'Tweet Me, Friend Me, Make Me Buy', *Harvard Business Review*, July-August, pp. 88–93.

Gooner, Richard A., Neil A. Morgan, and William D. Perreault Jr (2011), 'Is Retail Category Management Worth the Effort (and Does a Category Captain Help or Hinder)?', *Journal of Marketing*, 75, pp. 18–33.

Gourville, John and Dilip Soman (2002), 'Pricing and the Psychology of Consumption', *Harvard Business Review*, September, pp. 91–6.

Hagiu, Andrei and Julian Wright (2013), 'Do You Want To Be an eBay?', *Harvard Business Review*, March, pp. 102–8.

Homburg, Christian, Ove Jensen, and Alexander Haiin (2012), 'How to Organize Pricing? Vertical Delegation and Horizontal Dispersion of Pricing Authority', *Journal of Marketing*, 76, pp. 46–69.

Indounas, Kostis (2006), 'Making Effective Pricing Decisions', *Business Horizons*, 49, pp. 415–24.

Laffey, Des (2007), 'Paid Search: The innovation That Changed the Web', *Business Horizons*, 50, pp. 211–18.

Lambrecht, Anja and Catherine Tucker (2012), 'Paying With Money or Effort: Pricing When Customers Anticipate Hassle', *Journal of Marketing Research*, 49, pp. 66–82.

Laran, Juliano and Michael Tsiros (2013), 'An Investigation of the Effectiveness of Uncertainty in Marketing Promotions Involving Free Gifts', *Journal of Marketing*, 77, 112–23.

Leeflang, Peter S. H. and Josefa Parreño-Selva (2012), 'Cross-category Demand Effects of Price Promotions', *Journal of the Academy of Marketing Science*, 40, pp. 572–86.

Marn, Michael V., Eric V. Roegner, and Craig C. Zawada (2003), 'Pricing New Products', *McKinsey Quarterly*, 3, pp. 40–9.

Mohammed, Rafi (2011), 'Ditch the Discounts', *Harvard Business Review*, January-February, pp. 23–5.

Myers, Mathew B. and David A. Griffith (1999), 'Strategies for Combating Grey Market Activity', *Business Horizons*, 42 (6), pp. 71–5.

Papies, Dominik, Felix Eggers, and Nils Wlömert (2011), 'Music for Free? How Free Ad-funded Downloads Affect Consumer Choice', *Journal of the Academy of Marketing Science*, 39, pp. 777–94.

Potter, Donald V. (2000), 'Discovering Hidden Pricing Power', *Business Horizons*, 43 (6), pp. 41–8.

Reichheld, Frederick F. and Phil Schefter (2000), 'E-Loyalty: Your Secret Weapon on the Web', *Harvard Business Review*, July-August, pp. 105–13.

Rigby, Darrell (2011), 'The Future of Shopping', *Harvard Business Review*, December, pp. 64–76.

Rusetski, Alexander, Jonlee Andrews, and Daniel C. Smith (2014), 'Unjustified Prices: Environmental

Drivers of Managers' Propensity to Overprice', *Journal of the Academy of Marketing Science*, 42, pp. 452–69.

Samaha, Stephen A., Robert W. Palmatier, and Rajiv P. Dant (2011), 'Poisoning Relationships: Perceived Unfairness in Channels of Distribution', *Journal of Marketing*, 75, pp. 99–117.

Scamell-Katz, Siemon (2012), *The Art of Shopping: How We Shop and Why We Buy*, London: LID.

Schindehutte, Miner and Michael Morris (2001) 'Pricing as Entrepreneurial Behavior', *Business Horizons*, 44 (4), pp. 41–9.

Seiders, Kathleen, Leonard L. Berry, and Larry G. Gresham (2000), 'Attention, Retailers! How Convenient is Your Convenience Strategy?', *Sloan Management Review*, Spring, pp. 79–89.

Slywtotzky, Adrian J., Clayton M. Christensen, Richard S. Tedlow, and Nicholas G. Carr (2000), 'Perspectives: The Future of Commerce', *Harvard Business Review*, January-February, pp. 40–1.

Urbany, Joel E. (2001), 'Are Your Prices Too Low?', *Harvard Business Review*, 79 (9), pp. 26–8.

Valentini, Sara, Elisa Montaguti, and Scott A. Neslin (2011), 'Decision Process Evolution in Customer Channel Choice', *Journal of Marketing*, 75, pp. 72–86.

Weinberg, Bruce D., Salvatore Paris, and Patricia J. Guinan (2007), 'Multichannel Marketing: Mindset and Program Development', *Business Horizons*, 50, pp. 385–94.

Weisstein, Fei L., Kent B. Monroe, and Monika Kukar-Kinney (2013), 'Effects of Price Framing on Consumers' Perceptions of Online Dynamic Pricing Practices', *Journal of Marketing Science*, 41, pp. 501–14.

Wells, John D. and David H. Gobeli (2003), 'The 3R Framework: Improving E-Strategy Across Reach, Richness, and Range', *Business Horizons*, 46 (2), pp. 5–14.

Key article abstracts

Avlonitis, George J., Kostis A. Indounas, and Spiros P. Gounaris (2005), **'Pricing Objectives Over The Service Life Cycle: Some Empirical Evidence,'** *European Journal of Marketing*, 39 (5/6), pp. 696–714.

The service sector tends to be somewhat neglected in the pricing literature. This paper redresses the balance by assessing pricing objectives at different stages of the services life cycle and provides empirical evidence on practice.

Abstract: Purpose—To explore the pricing objectives that service companies pursue along with the extent to which these objectives are influenced by the stage of the services' life cycle. Design/methodology/approach—Reviews the existing literature and analyses data from 170 companies operating in six different services sectors in Greece in order to achieve the research objectives. Findings—The literature on pricing of services reveals the complete lack of any previous work endeavouring to examine empirically this potential influence. The study concludes that the objectives are mainly customer-oriented aimed at improving the companies' financial performance in the market. Furthermore, the stage of these services' life cycle along with the sector of operation seems to have an influence on the pricing objectives pursued. Research limitations/implications—The context of the study (Greece) is an obvious caveat to the research findings suggesting the need for further replication of the current study in different national contexts. Practical implications—The practical implications of the findings refer to the fact that managers might have much to gain by adopting a 'situation specific approach' when setting prices. Thus, different pricing objectives should be set as a service passes from one stage of its life cycle to another, while different services necessitate also a different pricing approach.

Mayukh, Dass, Piyush Kumar, and Plamen P. Peev (2013), **'Brand Vulnerability to Product Assortments and Prices'**, *Journal of Marketing Management*, 29 (7/8), pp. 735–54.

The range within product categories tends to be narrower in convenience stores compared to supermarkets and hypermarkets. It means that brands like Milky Way might compete against Twix at one location whereas it might be Milky Way against a different brand at another if Twix is not stocked there. The implication for pricing strategy is that marketers may be forced to adjust their pricing strategies in relation to location-specific characteristics to compete effectively. Overall pricing strategy needs to be flexible enough to take into consideration the assortment of products at the point of sale at different locations as needed.

Abstract: The assortment of brands that a specific brand competes against varies from one point of sale to another. The competitive landscape changes further because of within-assortment price variations at each location. The joint variation in assortment composition and pricing creates a complex set of scenarios under which a brand needs to compete. In this paper, we develop an approach to assess changes in a brand's vulnerability under alternative assortment and price configurations. We specifically propose that, in market environments with high variability in the competitive set and prices, it is more appropriate to assess a brand's strength relative to alternative assortment configurations rather than against individual competing brands. We build a model that depicts a brand's vulnerability in latent assortment space rather than the traditional brand space. The results from an illustrative model application are used to draw inferences about changes in brand vulnerabilities under shallow and deep promotions.

Narus, James A. and James C. Anderson (1996), **'Rethinking Distribution: Adaptive Channels'**, *Harvard Business Review*, July-August, pp. 112–21.

This paper examines how many companies have rationalized their channels and moved from multiple to fewer distributors in an attempt to raise quality. Examples are cited for different company types and countries. It is argued that the successful use of distribution in marketing is, to a large extent, based upon some degree of experimentation.

Abstract: To solve distribution problems, a handful of forward-looking companies are experimenting with their distribution channels to make them more flexible and responsive. Although the scope of the experiments and the specifics vary widely, each embraces a concept the authors call adaptive channels. The potential benefits of these new arrangements come from the opportunity to leverage resources and share capabilities within the channel. To learn more about innovative distribution practices, the authors conducted an extensive research study in 1994 and 1995 of 27 US, European, and Japanese organizations that are considered to be leaders in distribution. These companies' initiatives can be divided into three broad categories. In the first, the distribution channel is designed to ensure that the members are routinely able to cope with unexpected or unusual demands for products and services. In the second, the new arrangements focus on meeting customers' growing demands for broader market offers. In the third, the objective is to improve the quality of service throughout the distribution channel by substituting the superior capabilities of one member for the inferior capabilities of another.

Ross, Elliot B. (1984), **'Making Money with Proactive Pricing'**, *Harvard Business Review*, November-December, pp. 145–56.

This paper examines the concept of 'proactive pricing': taking advantage of pricing opportunities in the marketplace. Topics covered include pricing strategy and tactics, developing a pricing framework, the influence of decision-makers in pricing, changing, and setting prices, and the importance of timing.

Abstract: Although the roots of capitalism stretch back many centuries, setting prices remains an inexact science. The pricing decision, one of the most important in business, is also one of the least understood. Many industrial companies, according to the author, habitually set prices reflexively on the basis of simple criteria: to recover costs, to maintain or gain market share, to match competitors. As the author shows, however, some companies have discovered the benefits of thinking more shrewdly about pricing. The rewards of a better understanding of pricing strategy and tactics can be substantial. By carefully studying pertinent information about customers, competitors, and industry economics and by selectively applying appropriate techniques, proactive pricers can earn millions of dollars that might otherwise be lost. Across a spectrum of industries ranging from lighting equipment to computer software, customers are gaining power at the expense of suppliers. Competitive intensity is increasing, causing specialty products to evolve into near-commodities. Computerized information systems enable the purchaser to compare price and performance factors with unprecedented ease and accuracy. Improved communications and increased use of telemarketing and computer-aided selling have opened up many markets to additional competitors.

End of Chapter 10 case study Uniqlo: the next ten years

Introduction

In August 2010, Fast Retailing, the parent company of the Uniqlo brand and apparel chain, officially became the largest seller of clothing by value in Japan. Today it is the fourth largest apparel retailer in the world and operates stores in 17 different countries. The company is already Japan's most internationalized distribution firm, but now aims to become the world's leading company in its sector with target sales of ¥5 trillion by 2020.

Fast retailing: brief history

Fast Retailing was incorporated in 1963. It began as a single family-owned men's wear shop in Ube City, 950 km south of Tokyo. The company's main brand is Uniqlo, today accounting for around 50 per cent of total turnover globally and some 70 per cent of sales in Japan alone. The name Uniqlo was derived from 'unique clothing'.

In 1997, Fast Retailing adopted the so-called SPA system of supply chain management already pioneered by western companies such as Benetton and Gap. Under the system, Fast Retailing controls every aspect of its supply chain, from designing the clothes, procuring raw materials, contracting factories for production, and outsourcing logistics for both raw material supply and finished product supply to its stores. In November 1998, it opened the first Uniqlo store in Harajuku in central Tokyo and began to expand into other major urban centres. This corresponded to the launch of its first range of fleece jackets, a product that in 2001 one newspaper estimated was owned by 75 per cent of all Japanese.

In 2001, sales turnover and gross profit reached a new peak, and to huge acclaim from the Japanese press, Uniqlo launched its first overseas venture in the UK. It began with four stores in London, growing to around 16 stores around the country over the next year or so. At roughly the same time, it established Fast Retailing (Jiangsu) Apparel Co. Ltd in China, opening its first Chinese Uniqlo outlet in Shanghai. Today, Uniqlo and Fast Retailing's smaller brands are sold in 17 countries around the world, and the business employs close to 40,000 people, more than half overseas, and in 2013 had turnover of more than ¥1.14 trillion.

Acquisition strategy

Since 2000, Fast Retailing has acquired a number of companies and brands both at home and overseas. The willingness and ability of Fast Retailing to acquire volume could be a key if it is to achieve its goals. Major acquisitions up to 2012 include:

- Link Theory Holdings (USA)
- Helmet Lang (Germany
- Onezone (Japan)
- Comptoir Des Cotonniers (France)
- Petit Vehicule SAS (France), owners of the Princesse Tam Tam brand
- Cabin (Japan)
- J Brand (USA)
- Executive Team: Tadashi Yanai.

Fast Retailing has always been a family business, with the majority shareholding still owned by the Yanai family and with Tadashi Yanai listed by Forbes as the richest individual in Japan. Tadashi Yanai has masterminded the success of the company since taking over from his father, and it is widely expected that leadership of the company will pass to one of his sons in due course.

Uniqlo's implementation of the SPA distribution model

SPA is a commonly used term in Japan's apparel sector, standing for speciality-store/retailer of private-label apparel—basically the business model made famous by Gap and Benetton which is now used, in several forms, by the majority of large apparel retailers in the world. In the SPA system the entire supply chain is planned and controlled by the retailer. This generally means that the retailer is the brand and store operator, but that also it designs the merchandise range, sources raw materials, and arranges factory production. It then arranges logistic supply from factory to store.

The system is particularly suited to the apparel sector because of the constantly changing nature of fashion and the relative simplicity of clothing as a product category.

SPA as used by Uniqlo

Until recently, the Uniqlo product was manufactured entirely in China, where the company has long-term relationships with key suppliers. Recently the rising cost of production in China has led Fast Retailing to move some production to other Asian countries, notably Bangladesh, Cambodia, and Vietnam. In many cases, the companies running the new factories in these areas are the same Chinese companies the chain has worked with for many years rather than new companies local to the new production centres.

Role of Mitsubishi

In addition, Fast Retailing has close links with the Mitsubishi Shoji trading house. Mitsubishi handles much of the logistics, warehousing, factory management oversight, and quality control administration required for Uniqlo's supply chain, a common model for all kinds of imports into Japan. Mitsubishi, along with other partners such as fabric manufacturer Toray, also contributes to merchandise planning and trend consulting.

Quality control

From an early stage, Uniqlo established its own quality control centre in Japan. It was one of the earliest and best examples of direct control of manufacturing quality by a Japanese company sourcing in China. By not simply relying on locals or other intermediaries to establish finished quality, it could justifiably say that its products were of the quality suitable for Japanese markets. This is a stance it maintains today and one that provides minimum quality guarantees for products sold elsewhere in the world.

Overseas expansion and ambitions

Fast Retailing could be said to be Japan's most ambitious and aggressive retailer and aims to be the world's largest fashion retailer. In 2010, it was number four, and still only about half as large as Inditex, but overseas expansion is rapid and helps drive the large-scale production model the company relies upon. With some 800 stores at home, by 2013 there were well over 400 more stores overseas, with long-term plans to have double the sales outside Japan than at home—currently overseas sales account for around 45 per cent of the total. In 2012, Fast Retailing made English the in-house corporate language of choice.

Marketing strategy

Fast Retailing is undoubtedly one of the best retail marketers that Japan has ever seen. Although aspects of its sales promotion and business model are clearly not unique, the company has increasingly shifted to develop its own characteristics. It is a marketing-driven company as a whole, an early user of TV ads as a retailer, and now a power-user of social media and GPS tracking.

Merchandise lines

While Fast Retailing today offers a range of brands, around three-quarters of sales come from the Uniqlo brand alone. Uniqlo's initial success arose thanks to the mass production and sale of good quality fleece jackets and other fleece items in the early 2000s. The over-saturation of both this type of product and the Uniqlo brand in 2001–2 led to a reversal of fortunes that year.

Since then, Uniqlo lines have been greatly expanded, although fleeces remain a core part of the chain's winter ranges. In particular, post-2002, Uniqlo began to move away from its historical stance as a unisex clothing company and increase differentiation between men's and women's lines.

The brand continues to rely on high volume sales of particular lines. In the Heat Tech range of cold weather underwear lines, developed in partnership with Toray, Uniqlo scored another major hit with sales targets for 2013 reaching 300 million pieces for a single year. It has since added Airism (formally called Silky Dry) as a similar underwear range targeted at warm weather. Other successful products have included:

- stretch leggings: leggings and spats in a very large range of designs aimed at women
- UV blocking cardigans: women's cardigans using UV reducing fabrics to protect against tanning
- UT: high quality, logo designed T-shirts, featuring everything from Disney characters to anime, and famous food brand logos
- UJ: higher quality denim jeans
- down jackets: made exceptionally thin and lightweight
- bra-tops: sold in summer 2009, these are camisole tops with built in bras. This was a particularly popular product and one of the few summer lines to score a hit
- second-tier brand: GU.

The number of successful ranges at Uniqlo has continued to grow, but opportunities for expansion of the Uniqlo brand in Japan are now limited due to saturation. Consequently, the company has introduced a second-tier brand called GU. GU was originally developed as an in-store corner concept to open in large general merchandise stores, but has since evolved into a lower priced, fun-fashion brand in its own right. Fast Retailing has increased the number of GU stores in recent years and the brand is set to reach sales of ¥100 billion in 2014, becoming another part of the company's overall international strategy too.

Pricing

Uniqlo maintains a distinctive pricing policy. It has a series of prices for various ranges, rounding to the nearest ¥10 JPY. This is much simpler and easier for customers to understand than is typical for many retailers in Japan.

As merchandise ranges come in large range blocks, for example fleece tops or designer T-shirts, standard prices are implemented across the range. In addition, prices can be marked down uniformly to sell end of season stock and provide short-term sales promotions on some items, for example at weekends.

Uniqlo's core marketing message of 'Low price, reasonable quality' has been the key to its positioning success in Japan where lower price apparel tends to mean lower quality, with much of the market offering good quality at correspondingly higher prices. This position has eroded somewhat over the past decade as chain stores have moved into a similar position, but the Uniqlo brand has maintained its high value position through good price–quality balance, while at the same time introducing lower-priced ranges through the GU brand.

Discussion questions

1. How would you describe the positioning of the Uniqlo brand?

2. What are the strengths and weaknesses of the company and what opportunities and threats does it face?

3. How should it adjust specific elements of its strategy to enhance its strengths and correct weaknesses?

4. Based on its current objectives, how might Uniqlo be adjusted in order to meet its goals and to compete in an international market?

5. How might Fast Retailing adjust its pricing and distribution strategy in international markets?

This case was prepared by Roy Larke of the University of Waikato, New Zealand. The case is solely for the basis of class discussion and is not intended to illustrate effective or ineffective management or administrative situation or any form of endorsement.

11 Marketing communications

Learning Objectives

1. To be able to assess where marketing communications (MARCOMS) sits within overall marketing strategy.
2. To know the key elements in the MARCOMS process.
3. To possess a strategic view of MARCOMS with a focus on the creative brief.
4. To understand what are the key issues in media choice and use.
5. To grasp the operational issues in implementing a MARCOMS strategy.

Chapter at a Glance

I. Introduction

1 Overview and strategy blueprint
2 Marketing strategy: analysis and perspectives

II. Where are we now?

3 Environmental and internal analysis: market information and intelligence

III. Where do we want to be?

4 Strategic marketing decisions, choices, and mistakes
5 Segmentation, targeting, and positioning strategies
6 Branding strategies
7 Relational and sustainability strategies

V. Did we get there?

14 Strategy implementation, control, and metrics

IV. How will we get there?

8 Product innovation and development strategies
9 Service marketing strategies
10 Pricing and distribution strategies
11 Marketing communications
12 International marketing strategy
13 Social and ethical strategies

 Case study: A CRISP approach to brand and communications strategy

Over the years I've seen briefs perfectly written, creative work that responds to that brief, and brilliant on-target marketing communications strategies defined. Yet still many of these run into trouble when introduced. Why? Because many fail to apply a few very simple criteria to judge the strategy and ideas by.

We've devised a short number of criteria to use when both planning marketing communications strategies as well as creative campaigns. We use it when we are reviewing the ideas and work. We've turned these criteria into a short acronym—CRISP. Consistent, Relevant, Intimate, Simple, and Persistent. Five criteria that if most, or better still all, are incorporated we know will have a dramatic difference on the potential success of the strategy or campaign in resonating with the target audience.

Being consistent

Great consumer brands teach us that whatever strategy and tactics we might use and wherever the message appears, it has to be deployed in a consistent fashion. Consistency goes to the heart of branding.

Do we go to McDonald's for the best food in the world? Despite what my twelve year old son thinks, possibly not. But we do know what to expect wherever in the world we visit a McDonald's. Its brand is all about consistency. As a company they are incredibly consistent globally not just in managing their communications but as importantly in managing products and customer experience. Wherever the brand touches consumers it's consistent. Whatever you are going to do, do it consistently.

Finding relevance

When it comes to the positioning and marketing approach you take for your brand, it also has to be relevant to your brand's offering as well as relevant to the audience you are talking with. Gaining attention is relatively easy: show a picture of a man standing on his hands walking down a street. But unless the product stops coins falling out of your pocket it's not relevant. The Energizer Bunny has been bopping around our television screens since 1989 and has been used by the Energizer Company of St Louis, Missouri, to demonstrate the company's claimed superior battery life. The little pink bunny with its motto of Keep Going perfectly communicates the relevance of this message. The campaign has resonated with the public so well in fact that the bunny has his own personal website where he (and I'm assuming despite his colour preferences it's a metrosexual he rabbit) lists a number of personal facts. Relevance is everything in brand building.

Get emotional. Get intimate

Intimacy or emotional connections are central to brand building. We all make our choices based on a mix of both practical, functional reasons as well as emotional ones. Great brands know that you have to leverage emotional intimacy. I love holding workshops with engineers; indeed some of my closest friends are engineers. The wonderful thing is that they are very logical, left brain people and often claim never to have acted out of emotion in their lives. Everything comes down to specification, performance, and cost. I'd love to have seen some of these people propose to their wives or husbands. 'Well, you seem to be the best available model for your age. I reckon you're a fair catch for what it's going to cost me. Now would you like to get married?' Don't think so.

These logic driven individuals also claim that, frighteningly, their customers are just like them. Again it's about cost and specification. Now I've observed a number of times these are the same people who drive up in a BMW or a Mercedes. They are the same people who stand there with a Mont Blanc pen tucked in their shirt pockets. When I see this, I always offer to swap my Pilot ball pen, which is a fine pen having cost me all of €3, for their Mont Blanc but they never seem to want to take me up on the deal. Strange really. I reckon my Pilot works equally well. The truth is we all buy things for a mix of both practical as well as emotional reasons. To get people to love you and your brand you need emotional intimacy. It's not all pure logic. Thank goodness. Get close to your consumers and get intimate.

Keeping it simple

However clever the products or services, the idea at the centre of any brand strategy will also need to be very simple, to cut through the media noise we are all increasingly surrounded by every day. Simple ideas are normally powerful ideas. The remarkable Sam Goldwyn said: 'If you can't write your movie idea on the back of a business card, you ain't got a movie'. This same sentiment is equally applicable to any great idea. In essence, they have to be simple. Apple is one of the best known brands in the world, and its advertising always goes right to the heart of the issue with its simplicity. Great brands make a habit of keeping things simple.

On and on and on. Persistence pays off

Finally, if we are going to be serious about gaining some traction and awareness from our marketing efforts, we will also need to be incredibly persistent over a long period of time. Great brands keep on going, driving the same strategy over an extended period of time, and refreshing the execution. Take Coca-Cola as an example. One of the keys to the success of the brand has been the persistence shown by the company since it was started back in 1886 by Dr John S. Pemberton. Apart from a little blip in the 1980s with new Coke, the brand has been incredibly persistent over the years—a persistence that has helped keep them the number one soft drinks brand globally. Being persistent—it's the real thing.

So acronym for the day—CRISP. Consistent, Relevant, Intimate, Simple, and Persistent. If applied when judging a marketing strategy or a campaign, it can really help provide a simple set of criteria.

Julian Stubbs is founder and CEO of UP THERE, EVERYWHERE, the global Cloud-based consultancy group. His first business book, titled *Wish You Were Here*, explores the branding of places and destinations as well as his work for the city of Stockholm, where Julian created the brand positioning and tag line 'Stockholm, The Capital of Scandinavia'. Today Julian is working with a number of brand and identity assignments.

Introduction

According to the American Association of Advertising Agencies, IMC (integrated marketing communications) is:

> an approach to achieving the objectives of a marketing campaign through a well-coordinated use of different promotional methods that are intended to reinforce each other.

The idea is to combine all four primary media to provide a holistic and integrated approach. Figure 11.1 provides an example of IMC integration with the 'Go on, Get on' campaign for Arriva. The campaign utilized **advertising**, **direct marketing**, **sales promotion**, and digital media to persuade infrequent, non-bus users to 'Catch the Bus'.

One particularly important aspect of IMC is that it elevates the status of internal marketing, an oft-neglected aspect of marketing communications (MARCOMS). For example, the target audience for LaSer UK's 'Be the Difference' campaign was internal. Communicating directly with staff, the message is strong and direct—each of you can make a difference to your customers (see Figure 11.2). Employees, especially those interacting with customers, need to be kept informed and able to contribute towards an organization's communications. If service quality is about reducing the gap between a customer's expectations and perceptions of service, it is generally advisable to show staff previews of forthcoming campaigns, as well as involve them in development whenever possible and appropriate. Relevant media include ambient media (e.g. sticking a notice or some such on hand-drying machines in toilets), email, intranets, newsletters, staff seminars, voicemail, and sometimes creative placements, such as within monthly salary statements. There are several cases in marketing history where campaigns have failed because no one thought to tell the staff what was happening, such as when Clerical Medical Investments decided to reposition the brand in the early 1980s.

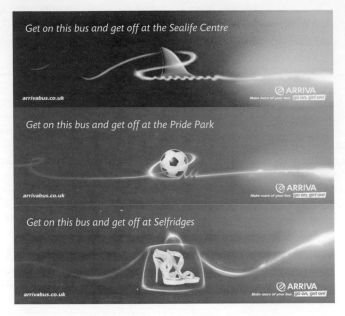

11.1 Integration: 'Go on, Get on' Campaign

Source: By permission of Arriva Group plc and Cogent Elliott

MARCOMS overall are central to Porter's (1980) generic cost-differentiation focus strategies framework (see Chapter 2) and refer to four central types of media: advertising, direct marketing, public relations (PR), and sales promotions (see Figure 11.3). There are two layers to explore in using these four media in MARCOMS strategy relating to what the client wants to 'say' as opposed to execution, which relates to 'how' you say it. The Marketing Birmingham strategy is to promote the city region as a destination to visit, to meet, and to do business. This is best shown in the film at <http://birminghamtoolkit.com/resources/films/this-is-birmingham>(see Figure 11.4).

Strategy needs to be clearly agreed between client and agency (if an agency is being used) at the beginning of the campaign process. The interpretation of the strategy by the agency

11.2 'Be Inspired' Campaign

Source: By permission of LaSer UK and Cogent Elliott

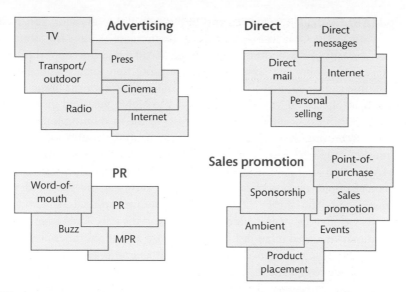

11.3 IMC Tools

becomes the executional layer and often has to entertain or be creative in some way, to stand out from the clutter of communications people are exposed to.

Can MARCOMS be used to reduce **costs**? The answer is largely 'No' for the short-term, but 'Yes' when a longer perspective is taken. The basic profit formula is:

Profit = (price – cost) × volume

11.4 'Introducing Birmingham' Campaign

Source: By permission of Marketing Birmingham and Cogent Elliott

How do MARCOMS fit in terms of a cost in the formula? In the short run, a client can spend money on MARCOMS to **help justify a price increase** or **increase volume**, but this will only add to costs. In the medium to long term, MARCOMS can support price through **brand preference** and provide some competitive protection for a brand. Furthermore, increased volume can be encouraged by pointing out **new uses** for the brand or by **targeting new markets**. Successful MARCOMS can lead to higher sales and in turn economies of scale. MARCOMS can also directly reduce costs in the medium to long term **through replacing (or increasing the efficiency) of an organization's routes to markets and in reducing market research costs**. A company with a large salesforce and/or call centre may find that MARCOMS can create an environment where they can reduce the number of staff required. For example, customers can manage their accounts and track orders (CMR—customer managed relationships), fill out surveys, customize products, and find answers to their questions via advertising and direct marketing and the web. Some commentators predict that customer-managed relationships will increase a hundred times over usage today. Eventually, benefits will be designed for segments of 'one'. Additionally, successful **public relations** may reduce costs. Take the case of Shanghai's Guangyin Yoga Club which received widespread coverage at a cost of about £80. The event consisted of placing one of the club's yoga masters in a wooden box that was placed in various locations across Shanghai. The yoga master would pop his hand out of the box with the club's business card to surprise passers-by: simple, effective, original—and widely talked about. Even sales promotions, which largely increase costs when they involve price discounting and bonus offerings, can sometimes reduce costs. For example, by directly inducing a customer to try a product with a free sample, the adoption cycle can be fast-tracked.

Differentiation is central to spending on MARCOMS. Despite the conventional wisdom that lots of products and services are at parity, there are probably more differences in offerings today than ever before. If you take any consumer or business market, the amount of choice is substantial and often impossible for buyers to process cognitively. MARCOMS provides organizations with **the possibility of establishing their position within the market and asserting their distinctiveness**. While there are a great deal of 'me-too' communications, at heart all organizations—be they for-profit or not-for-profit—seek to establish a point of difference.

Shift from push to pull

Technology is enabling consumers to perform marketing tasks and functions which were once the preserve of advertisers and their agencies. They buy and sell on auction sites such as eBay—generically known as C2C (customer-to-customer), they advise each other on products and services on sites such as Facebook, Amazon, and ePinions, and they are even redesigning and manufacturing products for themselves and others. Advertisers will increasingly find themselves in the content and entertainment business to help provide people with their '15MB of fame'.

Broadly speaking, this significant shift can be categorized as a move from 'push' to 'pull'. Applied to MARCOMS, push is when a message is placed in order to influence members of an audience (e.g. a TV commercial), whereas pull is when the audience pulls information towards themselves, for example 'Googling' or in more extreme cases making their own content, such as with uploading their own versions of commercials on YouTube. As noted by Berthon et al. (2008:7), 'The traditional distinctions between producer and consumer and between mass communications and individual communication are dissolving' with the advent of user generated advertising (UGA). UGA is advertising developed by members of the public in isolation from advertisers and uploaded to social media sites (YouTube in particular). It is developed with a variety of intentions, but mainly to offer parodies which may be negative, neutral, or positive about the brand concerned.

The result has been a general shift away from the above-the-line analogue media of TV, press, billboards, radio, and cinema (so called because agencies 'drew a line' between media that gave commission and those that did not) towards digital and interactive media, often along with attempts to create 'buzz' (Thomas, 2004; Mohr, 2007). However, it must be noted that TV remains far and above the most popular of all media, although new marketing strategies have been developed to respond to the seismic changes sweeping through the marketplace. Part of the shift to digital media has involved a change in mindset: that content should be free—free music, free videos, free news, and the like as with free newspapers (e.g. the London *Evening Standard*) and magazines (e.g. *Time Out*).

The implication for many brands is that they are becoming what might be termed 'conversation platforms', where consumers using websites such as Blogger, Facebook, Flickr, Tumblr, Twitter, and YouTube are influencing the behaviour of many prominent companies. For example, Nestlé was forced to respond to a spoof 'Gorilla Fingers' KitKat viral by Greenpeace slating the company's use of non-sustainable sources of palm oil that rapidly gained over 300,000 views on YouTube. Nestlé announced that it would only buy palm oil from suppliers who can demonstrate that they use sustainable sources. The company may well have been going along that route anyway, but the viral is increasingly showing that credit cards are the new ballot boxes. This is not a new phenomenon, with a number of historic boycotts of brands over the past forty or so years involving banks, clothing companies, supermarkets, etc., and even countries. What has changed is the phenomenal power of consumers and non-governmental organizations (NGOs) to set off such boycotts with simple acts such as the posting of a viral.

Television companies have undoubtedly lost some audience share to digital media; although shows such as *Downton Abbey* can still set the agenda, the business model for ITV has been to reach out to the audience beyond the basic content of the show to drive response and deliver competitive return on the investment by advertisers. And it has been very successful at doing so. People are still mainly watching television programmes but the the mode of delivery has changed from dependency on the traditional living room television set to include digital and mobile viewing via computers, tablets, and smartphones.

The major media have fragmented at a rapid rate. Most profoundly, the role of above-the-line media has shifted to some extent from being the primary element in any campaign to often playing a supporting role, as with the use of TV commercials to point people towards websites rather than for stand-alone brand development. 'Guerrilla' approaches are increasingly common to build audiences, as is done in product placement in TV shows (e.g. HP placed their products in the US version of *The Office*) and films (e.g. the Bond *Skyfall* film featured, amongst others, Aston Martin, Audi, Beretta, Caterpillar, Citibank, CNN, Coca-Cola Zero, Courvoisier VSOP, Heineken, Jaguar, Land Rover, Mercedes, Omega, Range Rover, Royal Doulton, Scrabble, Sony, Sony VAIO, Sony Xperia, Swarovski, and the

11.5 Facebook/Twitter 'Be A Happy Bunny' Campaign

Source: By permission of redspottedhanky.com and Cogent Elliott

Volkswagen Beetle). There are also a variety of other ways to reach consumers, such as attempts to raise interactivity with the use of voting for brand competitions using text messaging (though product placements are not new and date back to the nineteenth century and before). A MARCOMS campaign that does not consider the role of Google and social networking sites like Bebo, Facebook, and MySpace would be rare today. For example, redspottedhanky.com (Figure 11.5) used social media during their 'Be A Happy Bunny' campaign to amplify the TV campaign, driving record levels of traffic to the website and social media channels.

Strategically things have not always panned out exactly as expected. One of the biggest fears amongst retailers is the problem of 'showrooming', when shoppers view merchandise in store and then go onto the Internet to buy the goods. A number of retailers have had and still have great concerns about it. But in a survey of 3,000 social media users in the US and the UK, Sevitt and Samuel (2013) found that while just over a quarter of shoppers admitted to showrooming, over two-fifths practised 'reverse showrooming'; they browsed merchandise online and then purchased in stores because they found shopping in person more convenient.

It is also worth remembering the increasing power of own label. It is quite common for people to replace leading branded products with a cheaper supermarket own-label product regardless of the price difference, such as Coca-Cola for Sainsbury's Cola or Doritos for Tesco Cool Tortilla Chips. Given the economic environment, lots of shoppers have been forced to think more carefully about the cost of their choices, and have traded down and put the money saved towards the 'must-have' brands such as Marmite or Heinz Ketchup.

Supermarkets have plugged the low-price message in a continuous price war supported by nearly £500m in spending over the past five years. The UK's horsemeat scandal though has alerted people to the fact that you get what you pay for. Hence a recent change with own labels such as Asda and Tesco launching campaigns promoting the quality, as well as the price, of their products.

Services

One particular strategy has been to abandon overt marketing messages in favour of **services**; that is, something useful or entertaining that embeds itself much deeper into everyday life and has led to communications that do not feel like traditional advertising (Bernadin and Kemp-Robertson, 2008). For example, Tesco has a grocery delivery business in South Korea called 'Home Plus'. The company places life-size and high resolution photos of products on Tesco store shelves complete with QR codes that can be scanned with a smartphone (Gupta, 2013). South Koreans are then able to shop and arrange for delivery while waiting for their trains.

Wrangler provides another example. The brand felt it was not resonating with European youth, partly because its advertising was not in the places where its audience was spending time. In response, Wrangler set up 'guerrilla laundromats' at a number of music festivals. After leaving their dirty clothes for a free service wash, festival-goers were given Wrangler-branded jumpsuits to wear for the rest of the day until they could pick up their clean clothes.

Communities

A number of consumer goods companies have developed 'brand communities' which enable consumers to communicate with each other, with the aim of building differentiation through relationships (McWilliam, 2000). A leading example is giffgaff <http://giffgaff.com>—a mobile phone community (part of the O2 group) where there is minimal to no direct contact with the company. Customers purchase and register their phones and sim cards via the gifffgaff website and receive the products via the mail. Thereafter they deal with registered agents or members of the giffgaff community of users where they can ask questions and find the answers to frequently asked questions. Shell, with their LiveWire forums and groups <www.shell-livewire.org/>, offers opportunities to discuss any issues related to entrepreneurship for people aged 16–30. Ensuring that brand activity is relevant to the core audience of a social network is crucial if a brand wants to establish a dedicated site (Brown et al., 2007). For example, back in 2009 over 20 million people had registered a PlayStation Network (PSN) account and by 2014 it had grown to over 110 million with 100,000 people involved in its community forums. Discussions go in many directions on the PlayStation forums about the various products. For example, one member asked: 'Does Silent Hill actually scare you?' General interest issues can also arise such as the following controversial posting: 'Marijuana being sold recreationally in Colorado'.

People like online social networks as they can easily socialize without much effort, and they also seem to be a considerable leveller as it has been found that opinion leadership within Internet social networks is not a function of expertise or charisma so much as a function of human nature—influence is something that we all seem to have when it comes to a social network on the Internet (Smith et al., 2007). Cova et al.'s (2007) edited collection of work provides a compelling case for tribalism as a phenomenon beyond the usual conventions of sub-cultures, brand communities, and cultures of consumption. Consumer 'tribes' arise where consumers collectively determine, largely on the web, to what extent they will be manipulated or manipulate brands.

User groups, of course, have been around for years, especially in B2B markets like banking, insurance, and property. Outside of B2B, enthusiasts have formed a variety of clubs, especially around car and motorcycle marques (most notably, Harley-Davidson at <www.harley-davidson.com>). In Harley's case, some of the indigenous Harley chapters (clubs) threatened the image of the company and so they formed the official Harley Owner's Groups (HOGs). While spontaneous and independently formed user groups pose a risk, they do offer a number of attractions. Such groups can be contacted for opinions on things like new designs and product enhancements, and for product tests. As well, they can act as important opinion leaders. Recently social media has been used to attack the customer service provided by many banks, the profits of utility companies, and the tax avoidance policies of big corporates such as Starbucks and Google.

There are two points of view to successful community sites—the participants and the managers. From the consumer perspective, one key aspect is that a site should provide a forum for the exchange of common interests. For example, iVillage UK <www.ivillage.co.uk> has message boards for women covering such topics as money and finance and working at home, along with a social network where women can upload their profiles and make contacts (see also Mumsnet.com).

Coca-Cola, Nutella, and Pringles have all built communities of over a million on Facebook, mainly by taking a long-term view and offering value to users. Coca-Cola's site is particularly interesting as the group was first established completely independently of the company as a space where people could talk about the brand and the drink. Coca-Cola took over the running of the site when it reached 1.5 million and has since expanded it to over 82 million likes. The success of the site was in essence based upon the existing buzz about the brand. Companies have also begun to provide links wherever possible, particularly by linking Twitter to Facebook groups with micro-blogs. For example, Skittles has replaced its traditional home page with a live Twitter feed, along with content from YouTube, Google+, flickr, and Facebook. Apparently red and strawberry Skittles are being tweeted about 39 times a minute with around 130,000 followers.

There have been some stunning examples of how not to do it, though. One of particular note was the efforts of Chevrolet to engage with people by offering user-generated advertising content. People were welcomed onto Chevrolet's site and, using the video content and audio and text tools provided, could create their own commercial for the Chevy Tahoe 4×4 and upload it onto the site. Unfortunately, the missing mechanism from the process was a moderator. Depending on everyone's goodwill proved a mistake as users generated commercials that blamed such large 4×4s for things like global warming and killing thousands of people driving smaller cars, pedestrians, and cyclists. Not quite what the brand had in mind.

Blogging might be regarded as a kind of viral marketing tool as it uses social networks, is user-generated, and uses interactivity to spread the message (Singh et al., 2008). Blogging originated amongst project management 'techie' companies in the 1990s to facilitate cooperation between teams. The practice has now spread widely, and the blogosphere (the collection of all blogs on the Internet) is made up of over 165 million individual blogs which all have their followers. For example, Katy Perry has nearly 58 million followers, Barack Obama over 48 million, and Lady Gaga just over 42 million.

People join such networks largely by choosing people similar to themselves (homophily) and so social network sites vary in popularity by regions of the world as people opt for people similar to them—for example, Friendster in Asia, Orkut in Brazil, and IRC-Galleria in Finland. People often choose those who know more than them (expert power) to join their networks (Dwyer, 2007). After all, the content generated in a network is the main draw, with little regard as to who the originator was. TripAdvisor (see Figure 11.6) allows people to share experiences of hotels quickly and easily. Club Med's excellent service and beautiful resorts mean that they are always top of the ratings, one of TripAdvisor's most loved holidays.

Professional social networks offer a different type of value to users and are based on relevance. They enable people to search specific criteria such as industry type, a specific company, or people interested in a particular topic. Professional networks are especially valuable for event planners, recruiters, suppliers, and venture capitalists (e.g. putting entrepreneurs in contact with financiers), as well as all groups whose businesses rely upon the ability to capitalize on relationships such as accountants, consultants, and lawyers. LinkedIn is a professional network for business people with over 300 million members across the world and revenues in the region of about $2 billion (though yet to make a profit).

11.6 TripAdvisor Campaign

Source: By permission of Club Med and Cogent Elliott

Instead of formal pathways and structured navigation, social networks provide users with hyperlinked and unstructured navigation. Also, social media has thrown some 'wobblies' at the whole process from the organization's perspective. For example, Edelman (2010) reported that a global bank discovered that one of its customers, who would normally qualify for the lowest level of service given their business with the bank, had 100,000 followers on Twitter. The bank in question had no strategy in place and no formula for adapting what they should do for such customers.

MARCOMS strategic process

Audit

The MARCOMS strategic process can be seen in Figure 11.7. The process starts with an audit of the marketplace such as can be used with the PESTLE (political, economic, social, technological, legal, and environmental) assessment. The aim is to establish the key overall trends in the market, their importance and likelihood, and what aspects to focus upon for the MARCOMS plan.

The next stage is to examine the competitors in the marketplace. Four questions need to be answered.

1. How many competitors are there and what share does each have?
2. What positions do they take up? Why?

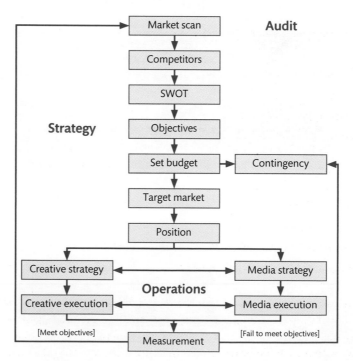

11.7 MARCOMS Strategic Process

3. Are any doing well or badly? Why?

4. How important is their presence in this market?

A SWOT (or something similar) then needs to be carried out, detailing the strengths, weaknesses, opportunities, and threats. The key issues identified need to be related to communications, such as how well or poorly first name and prompted mentions of the brand are, the brand's share of category spending, and attitudes towards the brand. Strengths and opportunities need to be leveraged and weaknesses and threats addressed.

Establishing the strategy

The next phase of the MARCOMS strategy process is to identify the central strategy (see Figure 11.7 again). Most of the following topics in the rest of this chapter feature in what agencies call the **creative brief**, a written summation of the MARCOMS task that will manage and stimulate the development of creative work to address that task.

The brief generally starts with agencies isolating in a few simple sentences what the aim of the communications is—the strategic intent. Bear in mind that the creative team in most agencies (the copywriter and the art director) are not business strategists. There might be hundreds of pages of research defining and explaining the task, with an elaborate SWOT which they will never read (or ever want to read). What they want is something succinct and to the point. Tasks should be focused, measurable, and capable of inspiring the creative team to do good work (see West and Ford, 2001). Broad examples of tasks include:

- announce launch
- build/rebuild corporate reputation
- generate leads
- increase sales
- increase/maintain share
- justify a price or price increase
- stop a decline.

An example of the suite of materials used to announce a launch can be seen in Figure 11.8 for the iconic Range Rover Evoque.

However, tasks can be articulated and a stronger direction indicated. Examples of specific tasks would be:

- Pepsi wants to be the badge of a generation
- Coca-Cola wants to be the classic choice.

Both tasks are easy to comprehend and distinct, and do not need to be complicated by further elaboration. If you think about it, all the documentation and briefing in the world can be given before a major sports event, but the task for all the players is simply to win the game. In the same vein, with the Apollo programme, NASA's objective was to get a man on the moon. In the context of MARCOMS, tasks are often stated as strategic intent, which can be broadly summarized in five formats, starting with product superiority.

11.8 Announcing the launch of the Range Rover Evoque
Source: By permission of Land Rover and Cogent Elliott

Product superiority could be the central strategy of the campaign. The intention of the strategy here is to communicate that a product or service can fix a problem or fulfil better a desire. There is an adage in the communications business that if you throw ten balls at someone they will not catch a single one. If you throw just one, it has a much greater chance of being caught. The implication is that objectives should be single-minded and focused, as suggested by the unique selling proposition (USP):

> To gain a purchase, an advertiser must persuade the potential buyer that there is a unique benefit from the product.

(Reeves, 1961)

Tangible performance benefits such as those involving technology or design can often give an edge, but can be short-lived if easily copied. This has led to the variation of the ESP, which stands for **emotional selling proposition**. Thus, the Co-op, with its banks and supermarkets, adopts an ethical stance in the marketplace and communicates this through its MARCOMS. You might not get a better deal, product, or service; you feel good because your money is part of an ethically aware organization. The Nationwide Building Society, given the uncertainty over the leading banks, has advertised itself in full-page national press advertisements as: 'Solid. Stable. Dependable. Suddenly, they're the most exciting words in a saver's vocabulary'.

11.9 World Cup Betting

Source: By permission of Coral and Cogent Elliott

The **cultural identification** strategy is about making the product, service, or organization part of the consumer's world. For example, HP Sauce ran a campaign featuring the use of the sauce by various 'tribes' in the UK such as 'white van' drivers and women out on a hen night. In a similar attempt at cultural identification, Unilever's Pot Noodles brand caused considerable controversy over a campaign promoting the brand (whose main target audience is young men) as the 'Slag of all Snacks' and associating the brand with infidelity. Pot Noodle has revisited the 1980s recently with a campaign developed by brand manager Cheryl Calverley at Unilever (Mother advertising agency) with an un-PC TV campaign. It features two young comedians singing how they wished women were as simple as the 'just-add-boiling-water' to a Pot Noodle snack. The brand has also remained topical, with such campaign themes as the credit crunch. For an example of cultural indentification see Figure 11.9 which demonstrates how Coral has used the 2014 World Cup in Brazil effectively. Not an official sponsor of the event itself, it has instead used iconic ex-player and commentator Alan Brazil as a figurehead and the line 'Proud sponsors of Brazil'.

Salience is the main concern of the **product definition** strategy. How can new products or services be made salient? Or, how can a product that has lost its salience regain it? This strategy is about finding something to say that will rekindle a brand that has lost its shine and esteem in the market. Perhaps one of the most high profile cases in the UK is Marks & Spencer. While the food part of the business continued to prosper, the clothing had lost market share to cheaper supermarket alternatives such Asda's George range and also to more design-oriented labels such as Liz Claiborne, Hobbs, Monsoon, and Jil Sander. M&S embarked on a bold Christmas TV campaign focused on design, style, and new ranges and featuring Rosie Huntington-Whiteley, David Gandy, and Helena Bonham Carter. Also, as Figure 11.10 illustrates, new technical innovations such as the Aga Total Control and Wi-Fi have helped redefine the iconic Aga cooker for the 21st century.

Possibly the most difficult of all strategies to engage in is the **paradigm shift**. Here, the aim is to alter the consumer's definition of a brand and/or category. One of the most

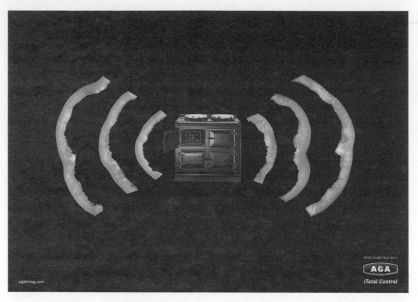

11.10 Product Superiority: Aga Total Control

Source: By permission of Aga and Cogent Elliott

successful UK attempts at a paradigm shift in recent years has been Volkswagen's campaign for the Škoda. The campaign has shown, in a variety of amusing executions, disbelief amongst the public and motor trade that the car concerned is a Škoda. The Škoda heritage may mitigate against the car being seen as the equivalent of a Volkswagen in the immediate future, yet the campaign has undoubtedly contributed towards the repositioning of the car as a sensible purchase rather than a joke.

The next stage is to translate the strategic intent into specific objectives. MARCOMS objectives are normally only applied to communications activities. Examples are:

- 'Exposure message to… '
- 'Create 40% awareness amongst… '
- 'Create attitude/opinion that… '
- 'Increase preference amongst… '
- 'Encourage trial amongst… '
- 'Reinforce loyalty amongst… '

There are three levels to MARCOMS objectives: 'exposure', 'awareness', and 'attitudes/relationships'.

Exposure represents the lowest level of objective. David Ogilvy once famously noted that: 'You cannot save souls in an empty church' (Ogilvy, 1987). Thus, exposure is simply an objective related to the desired level of OTS (all MARCOMS are only ever 'opportunities to see', as you cannot force an audience to listen and/or read your communications) and coverage to achieve the MARCOMS objectives. Most agencies seek an average of two to three

OTSs amongst the target market in order to give the MARCOMS a chance to work, given that some repetition is needed for full comprehension and remembering. An example of an exposure objective might be to cover 40 per cent of the target audience with an OTS of three. Unfortunately, a campaign might effectively cover its chosen audience with the hoped-for OTS and still have little impact if people do not respond. A higher-level objective involves 'awareness'.

Awareness can be measured at two levels: 'spontaneous' and 'prompted'. Spontaneous awareness often involves open-ended questions such as:

- 'Tell me, of all the major supermarkets that you have heard of…'
- 'Any more?'
- 'Is that all?'

Prompted awareness, as the name implies, provides the prompts. For example, you might ask: 'Which one or ones of the following supermarket chains have you heard of?'

- Aldi
- Asda
- Lidl
- Jeffrey's
- Marks & Spencer
- Morrisons
- Sainsbury's
- Tesco
- Waitrose

Note that in the list there is a little known supermarket chain called Jeffrey's, though, to be honest, Jeffrey's does not exist! Quite often, a fictitious prompt is provided to gain an understanding of how seriously the questions have been answered. If 5 per cent of the sample say, 'Yes, I have heard of Jeffrey's', you can broadly discount these respondents as the indications are that they would say 'Yes' to any name.

Nevertheless, you could have extremely high awareness and yet your brand might still be performing badly. Famously, the Strand cigarette was launched with a TV campaign in the late 1950s, showing Terence Brooks, a Frank Sinatra lookalike, lighting up a cigarette on a lonely street corner. The accompanying caption said, 'You're never alone with a Strand', with Cliff Adams's haunting instrumental playing in the background. The ads were hugely popular, Terence Brooks became a teenage pin-up, and the 'Lonely Man Theme' was a huge hit. Yet Strand became associated with loneliness and unsociability, and the brand soon disappeared from the market.

The highest level of MARCOMS objectives concern **attitudes** and **relationships**. Attitudes are positive or negative views of an object, such as an organization, product, service, or idea, that lead to the formation of relationships. Generally, marketers recognize the difference between 'opinions' and 'attitudes', between pre- and post-purchase. People hold opinions about products and services pre-purchase, but once they have tried them they have attitudes.

You might feel that an Aston Martin is a great car, but not buy one because you either do not have the resources or it simply is not a priority.

Target market

The next stage is to review the various potential segments and decide upon the specific **target market(s)** that the communication is aimed at. Given the lack of business strategic background of most creative teams in agencies (West, 1993, 1994), this is not normally a technical description. What is required is a description of a person or a group that goes beyond report format and is based upon what is, or is not, important. For example, a target description for a campaign aimed at frequent international flyers or organizational travel buyers would not point out all the details. Instead, the brief would mention such things as frequent flyers needing a good rest or sleep en route before business meetings, while travel buyers are looking for deals with leading airlines and the need to justify costs. What kind of cars might such people drive? What kind of papers or magazines do they read?

Position

The next thing to consider is how to **position** the client (see Ries and Trout, 1981). A position is how potential buyers see the product and it is expressed relative to competitors. This is what you want to achieve and should be measurable and achievable, otherwise it is not worth stating. Generally, it tends to relate to rational or emotional aspects. For an MP3 player, it might be to position the product as having the capacity for the number of songs you want to carry and that it is 'cool'. The issue here is how MARCOMS might help position the player. MARCOMS might also address **repositioning**, which involves changing the identity of a product relative to the identity of competing products. There is also the potential for **de-positioning**, i.e. attempting to change the identity of competing brands relative to the identity of your own brand in the minds of the target market.

Creative strategy

Having decided upon the position required, what communications **proposition** will do this? The proposition spells out what you want to say. At this stage, agencies look for what they call 'big ideas'. The term, originating with the advertising business, has been co-opted by various groups in recent years, most noticeably by politicians. MARCOMS big ideas require collaboration and hard work, often making difficult choices and judgements, and the exclusion of product facts. They have to be sold and defended and may change (a lot) in execution, but they are central to the strategy. For example, Hozelock use a range of 'Garden Ambassadors' from worms to flowers to bring the garden to life which have been used across multiple platforms (Figure 11.11).

Some key questions to ask of a proposition to judge whether it stands up as a big idea or not:

- Does it have staying power?
- Does it spark dramatic creative ideas?
- Is it credible?

11.11 The 'Garden Ambassador' Campaign

Source: By permission of Hozelock and Cogent Elliott

- Is it distinctive?
- Is it focused and single-minded?
- Is the promise meaningful?

Some potential sources of a proposition are:

- brand image characteristics
- direct comparisons with rivals
- disadvantages of non-use
- generic benefits
- how the product/service is made
- newsworthiness
- price characteristics
- product/service characteristics
- product/service comparisons
- product/service heritage
- satisfying psychological/physiological needs
- surprising points about the product/service
- user characteristics
- ways of using the product/service.

The key issues to consider are: Is the proposition relevant? Does it relate to the target audience's problems or desires? Strategically, is it competitively different? Can it be expressed in a single-minded execution?

You know if you have a good proposition if it **gives the creatives an 'angle' or 'way in' to develop some good creative work**. It does not need to be liberating, as restricted propositions can lead to exceptionally creative work (West and Berthon, 1997; West, 1999; West et al., 2013). It should also force a strategic choice or direction in the marketplace by being single-minded rather than all-encompassing. It goes without saying that any chosen proposition should be based on truth (rational or emotional). Thus, a recent B2B campaign by IBM extolling the benefits of on-demand processes in business used a variety of scenarios that, while fictitious in themselves (e.g. the demand for pink or white dresses being instantly fed back through the supply chain from the moment of sale at the cash register), effectively demonstrated the nature of IBM's proposition. Propositions to avoid are ones that communicate very little to the creative team such as:

- 'A wide range and good value'
- 'Stylish and modern'
- 'The best car on the market'
- 'The right food for your dog'.

None of the above would give a creative team much of a clue of what was required. However, to say that a particular mayonnaise 'takes the humdrum out of everyday food' or that a particular washing machine is 'the family workhorse', gives the team a much better steer on what is required. Bear in mind, that, for many brands, the role of the proposition in MARCOMS strategy is changing with the advent of social media. Increasingly, the job is to develop audience insight and enter into so-called 'engagement', where consumers directly influence the positioning of a brand rather than respond to a proposition. In 2012 GE launched its global marketing initiative 'GE Works' based upon its strategic mission to focus on how businesses use and benefit from technology—the outcomes—rather than the technology itself. Using social media such as Instagram, Pinterest, SocialCam, and Viddy, with photo and video content and strong data visualization, GE was able to communicate its core business. Its popular 'Juice Train' video is a good example—following a train delivering orange juice from Florida to New Jersey in a time-lapsed video showing the on-board analytics provided by GE.

Having decided upon the proposition, it remains to consider if the claim can be **supported**. If you cannot support the proposition, you cannot have it. Why should anyone believe such a message if it cannot be supported? What are the key facts or figures that provide the evidence? None of this has to appear in the execution, but it must appear in the creative brief, otherwise the proposition will be simple puffery. Thus, if the proposition states that a tyre will continue to perform even when punctured, what is the evidence? Has it been tested and is it true? The evidence does not need to appear in the ad; the claim, however, cannot be made without it. Take the case of McDonald's campaign focusing on the feeling of happiness in China aimed at urban white-collar workers with the slogan that roughly translates to 'Happiness is zero burdens'. The campaign suggests that true happiness is when you let go of the burdens of everyday life. It features the popular Chinese actress and director Jane Wu with people giving their thoughts on what happiness is related to McDonald's.

Some potential **problems** that can arise at this stage of strategy development are:

- confusing the client's concerns with their customers' concerns
- lack of focus
- lack of a meaningful target audience
- lack of a position
- making support of the product the promise
- restating objectives as the proposition.

The next creative strategic issue is how to reflect the **brand's character**. This is a key strategic issue for any brand, as the wrong character may at best add little value and at worst severely damage its market standing. In the broadest sense, brand character reflects how the brand is positioned. Does the brand's character exude fun or is it serious? Does it set out to shock or reassure? Is it modern or traditional? Take the case of the Amul dairy cooperative in India featuring the 'Utterly Butterly girl'. The Butterly girl first appeared in 1967 and is the longest running campaign ever. Amul's chubby moppet in a classic polka dotted dress and a red and white bow is usually featured in a spoof of current affairs with Amul Butter in her hand (the Amul website claims that the ultimate compliment to the campaign came when St Ivel launched their dairy spread calling it 'Utterly Butterly'). Highly controversial, the ads include comments on an Indian Airlines strike and the Naxalite uprising in West Bengal, and one ad depicted the Amul butter girl wearing a Gandhi cap.

In tangent and often in parallel with the development of the creative strategy comes the development of the media strategy (see Table 11.1 for an overview of MARCOMS options). Three questions need to be answered:

1. Where is the communication(s) going to appear?
2. How frequently?
3. How much is to be spent?

The answers to these questions can vary greatly, depending upon the strategy (Piercy, 1986; Farris and West, 2007; Prendergast et al., 2006). Media strategy is about attempting to ensure that a client's message is seen or heard by the right people, in the right place, in the right environment, with the right frequency and weight, and at the right price. British Airways chose to wrap up a building to publicize its flat beds for Club Class passengers. In a commercial that continues to baffle commentators Chanel N° 5 featured Brad Pitt standing in a corner saying:

> It's not a journey. Every journey ends, but we go on. The world turns and we turn with it. Plans disappear. Dreams take over. But wherever I go, there you are. My luck, my fate, my fortune. Chanel N° 5. Inevitable.

The commercial's impact and frequency of the schedule raised awareness and influenced attitudes towards the brand on a scale that a smaller spend could never have matched and reached just under three million people in three days.

Table 11.1 MARCOMS Options

Medium	Definition	Horizon	Form	Scope
Advertising	A paid-for communication by an identified sponsor with the aim of informing and influencing one or more people	Mainly long term	Cinema, digital, Internet, mobile, posters, press, radio, social media, SMS, TV	Awareness, attitudes
Direct marketing	The recording, analysis, and tracking of customers' direct responses in order to develop loyalty	Short and long term	Digital, direct mail, DRTV/radio, inserts, leaflets, mobile, telemarketing, press, social media, SMS, Web	Mainly retention, but also acquisition
PR	The formulation, execution, and sustained effort to establish and maintain goodwill and mutual understanding and reciprocal goodwill between an organization and its stakeholders	Short and long term	Community relations/CSR, corporate advertising, crisis management, events, internal communications, investor relations, media relations, public affairs, lobbying, social media, sponsorship, web, digital	Credibility, visibility, and reputation
Sales promotions	An incentive for the customer, salesforce, or distributor to make an immediate purchase	Mainly short term	Consumer: coupons, contests, trial, mail-in offers/refunds, group promotions, self-liquidations, in-store promotions, point-of-sale, web, digital, SMS. Trade: dealer merchandise, contests' advertising, allowance, trade allowance/staff incentive, web	Consumer: trial, re-trial, extended trial, build database Trade: gain a listing, increase distribution, increase inventory, improve shelving space/position

Spend has to be targeted by buyer characteristics, geography, and season. After gathering information, the classic approach is the four W's.

- **Who:** define the exact audience (e.g. '34–45-year-old women').
- **Where:** determine the geographic area (e.g. 'every major urban market').
- **When:** decide upon the time of purchase (e.g. 'prior to most house moves').
- **What:** establish creative material (e.g. 'describe the time-saving ability of a new washing-machine').

In this case, the most efficient choice might be the selection of newspapers, TV, posters, and online, focused between May and June. However, the solution is rarely that simple. Normally, a mix of media are used and media planners/buyers normally use past experience along with research. For example, sponsorship might be used to provide a direct and immediate inducement supporting the service or product to the salesforce, distributors, or consumers. A portfolio approach is often required, which considers how different media work with each other. For example, television might be used to point people towards a website as used by Samsung to invite potential consumers to explore the brand's offerings on the web. Thinkbox and the Internet Advertising Bureau (IAB) have recently shown that using TV and online together in advertising campaigns is significantly more effective for advertisers than using either in isolation.

Two choices need to be made in media strategy between **media classes** and **media vehicles**. A media class refers to the vertical decision involving media type, e.g. press or TV. The primary choices are:

- cinema
- direct mail
- mobile
- posters/billboards
- press
- public relations
- radio
- sales promotion
- social media
- sponsorship
- TV
- web.

Operations

The final stage of MARCOMS strategy is operational: the implementation of the strategy. This involves creative and media execution, pre-testing, contingency, and post-testing (El-Murad and West, 2003, 2004).

Creative execution

The **creative execution** stage is where the chosen strategy is translated into a piece of communication (West et al., 2008). If the strategy were to be based on user characteristics, perhaps a chocolate eaten by 'macho men', it would be stated as the proposition. Take the case of the Yorkie bar which was originally conceived as a more solid alternative to the Dairy Milk bars. Yorkie bars campaigns originally featured truck drivers to emphasize their 'macho' nature. However, in 2001 the advertising agency JWT updated the campaign with a risky 'It's Not For Girls' tagline. The roots of the campaign are unclear, but likely to be based on the increasing ambiguities about the role of men in society. The campaign was highly controversial and ran for over ten years when it was replaced with a much more balanced sense of humour approach. 'Shopping Bags' was the first execution involving a young man able to carry all of his shopping from the car to the house in one go. He treats himself to a Yorkie bar on completion of the feat as his female partner looks on with bemusement.

Media execution

Media vehicle choice concerns the choice within the chosen class. For example, if the press is chosen, will it be *The Times* or the *Sun*? Or, if TV is chosen, what programmes will be targeted? The choice of media vehicles will depend on a number of quantitative and qualitative issues. Media planners and buyers will seek the most effective vehicles for their clients within the chosen medium. Decisions cannot be left to numbers. Thus, the numbers might suggest a particular tabloid 'red-top' newspaper for a luxury car advertiser. However, qualitatively, the car company's brand might not benefit from the association with the 'red top', and a quality daily (with a less cost-effective audience than the red top) will be the preferred choice. Also, editorial content and positioning count with media vehicles. It's fashionable to write off the traditional or 'old media' vehicles from the mix, but they are not without their own digital developments.

Targeted TV advertising is a relatively straightforward technology that may, nonetheless, have far-reaching effects. The way it operates is that a comprehensive library of commercials is stored on a household's digital box or made accessible via video-on-demand services (e.g. Sky+ or Virgin Media). Audience research panel data can then be used to tailor content to a household's demographics or behaviour. Thus, a household with a young baby might receive an added weighting of baby-product commercials. Difficulties may arise in households with mixed demographics and behavioural segmentation options (think parents and teenage children). Also, viewers may balk at issues involving any perceived invasion of privacy. People won't watch more TV because the ad breaks are more entertaining; however, the trade-off between privacy and the greater relevance of commercials may be one that people are prepared to make, given that the segmentation data concerned are non-specific and broad in nature. Being able to target smaller groups will add to production costs, but the impact of being able to use specific messages to niche markets on advertising effectiveness could be enormous.

Finally, outdoor media should not be written off. For a start they can be highly creative like Network Q's 'Fill your Boots' campaign. This campaign coincided with May's Bank Holidays when families traditionally 'fill their boots' and head off for weekends away (see Figure 11.12). Furthermore, outdoor media have joined the digital age with digital screens, touch screens, and thin film 'e-paper' or 'e-ink displays'. While these technologies have largely dominated the thinking and spending, **Bluetooth** short-range wireless **poster sites** have been largely ignored. There are certainly good reasons for this. Many advertisers would regard Bluetooth as too unwieldy and expensive, and think that it takes too much effort and the communications produced are too creatively restrictive. The way it works is that as you pass by a Bluetooth-enabled poster, you are invited to enable your Bluetooth device and accept the download. Some of the keenest users target where people are waiting, such as railway stations or foyers (cinema chains, for example, use their six-sheet Bluetooth-enabled sites in foyers to offer film news and deals). The beauty of the technology for outdoor advertisers is that the impact goes beyond the immediate sight of the poster. Time will tell if the potential for greater engagement and interaction will outweigh the cumbersome nature of the set-up for Bluetooth and the degree of planning required.

11.12 'Fill Your Boots' Outdoor for Network Q

Source: By permission of Network Q and Cogent Elliott Advertising

Overall, it may be too soon to write off the old media. Digital technology offers a number of opportunities to prolong their life further than many analysts have predicted. As well, consider the wider international context. Take Africa, for example, where many businesses rely on the traditional mass media in order to promote their goods and services, such as the radio, television commercials, and newspaper ads. However, in rural areas, which tend to be less developed, posters and mobile are widespread methods of advertising. Thus it is important to recognize the economic diversity that exists across the world and not to assume the same media have the same relevance everywhere.

Measurement

It is extremely difficult to be precise about the effect of MARCOMS on behaviour using aggregate data like sales, market share, and profits or individual purchasing behaviour (see Vakratsas and Ambler, 1999). The problem is that MARCOMS effects are dependent on other factors in the marketing mix and so it is difficult to know the impact of MARCOMS alone. As such, MARCOMS measurement is normally undertaken using what are known as 'intermediate effects'—what happens to the minds of people following exposure. Aside from neurological research, there have been few radical changes in the intermediate MARCOMS effectiveness measures used in the past thirty years. The overall process of intermediate effects measurement (shown in Table 11.2) consists of:

- research prior to development
- research during development
- pre-testing
- post-testing.

Table 11.2 MARCOMS Measurement

Approach	Method	Objective	Type	Measure
Research prior to development	• Focus groups • Interviews	Discovery and understanding	Qualitative	• Attention measures • Little or no evaluation of the effectiveness of final MARCOMS
Research during development	• Concept testing • Consumer panels • Dummy media and copy • Readability of copy	Discovery and understanding	Qualitative	• Attention measures • Little or no evaluation of the effectiveness of final MARCOMS
Pre-testing	• Theatre/hall testing of commercials • Physiological tests, e.g. pupil dilation, eye tracking, skin response, neurological (e.g. EEG testing) • Focus groups	Selection, development, evaluation, comparisons	Qualitative and quantitative	Attention and processing measures: • Likeability of MARCOMS • Attitude towards MARCOMS • Credibility of MARCOMS • Brand recall • Brand recognition • Brand benefit belief • Brand attitude • Brand purchase intention
Monitoring	• Continuous tracking and testing • Recognition tests • Interviews • Questionnaires	Development, evaluation, comparisons	Qualitative and quantitative	Processing measures: • MARCOMS recall • MARCOMS recognition • Brand recall • Brand recognition • Brand benefit belief • Brand attitude • Brand purchase intention • Brand behaviour (purchasing)

The move to Web 2.0 has opened up a new wave of research (generally known as 'analytics') powered by the integration of big data, cloud computing, and new statistical methods (Nichols, 2013). Instead of measuring advertising's impact in media like TV, the press, and the Internet, the aim is to measure the interactions between such media. For example, a TV ad might spark a Google search. Nichols advocates a three-pronged approach starting with *attribution*, the process of quantifying the contribution of each element of advertising; then *optimization*, by developing media plans; and finally, *allocation*, distributing resources across different media in real time according to the optimization plan.

It doesn't stop there either. Post-purchase consumers often enter into open-ended relationships with the brand and share their experience online (Edelman, 2010). New media enables consumers to evaluate and advocate (or denigrate) brands via social media.

The latest thinking: lean advertising

The advertising of sports shoes by brands such as Adidas and Nike in recent years has been highly creative and impactful. However, the strategic approach by DC Shoes, a company that makes shoes for skateboarders, has been strikingly different. The company shoots videos featuring the driving skills of its founder, Ken Block, driving a race car doing stunts around closed-off airports, theme parks, and cities. Sometimes the video lasts for up to nine minutes. Collectively the videos have achieved more than 180 million views on YouTube. According to Thales Teixeira (2013), paying for this kind of exposure would have cost around $5 million. Teixerira calls the strategy 'lean advertising' and it is particularly salient for small companies with accompanying small MARCOMS budgets.

Lean advertising is largely motivated by cost savings. It can often cost anywhere from £100,000 to up to £1 million to develop a TV campaign and then there is the cost of placing between programmes, whereas a DIY campaign launched on YouTube would cost a fraction of this. While there are numerous examples of extremely successful lean campaigns such as for DC Shoes or Tom Dickson's viral campaign for Blendtec (the videos feature putting items such as iPads in blenders), which have achieved millions of hits, in reality just 3 per cent of YouTube videos are viewed more than 25,000 times. In order to improve the chances of a lean advertisement Teixerira suggests the following.

1. *Outsource production*: often this can be done via crowdsourcing sites such as tongal.com and helps ensure a sound strategy

2. *Search engine optimization*: appoint an inbound marketing agency such as HubSpot to maximize search engine optimization in order to improve visibility.

3. *Outsource distribution*: use the services of a social media syndication firm, such as Mekanism, who tap into influential online networks.

The problem is of course that it is impossible to exert any control over lean advertising. Despite all the efforts of the accompanying professionals listed in the three points above, the fate of an advertising campaign in the 'lean world' is in the hands of the ether. Nevertheless, it won't stop companies trying to bypass the major media with lean approaches and attempting to achieve the 'holy grail' of a highly successful viral YouTube campaign.

Conclusion

Advertising and direct marketing have the largest impacts on brand value by building relationships with customers, whereas PR (and increasingly MPR—marketing public relations) helps construct visibility, raising credibility, and ultimately building reputation. Sales Promotions can have strategic effects, but in practice are largely used for short-term inducements to purchase with, the evidence suggests, little long-term effect. The process of undertaking a MARCOMS strategy involves conducting an audit, developing the central strategy, and then deciding upon the appropriate creative and media choices. The key issue facing international organizations is the extent to which they can and should standardize or customize their communications. This can be particularly difficult in countries such as India where advertisements have a large and diverse audience and have to reach out to people of varied ethnicity, language, religion, and culture.

Summary

MARCOMS primarily consist of four media–advertising, direct marketing, PR, and sales promotions–which can be used in marketing strategy either singularly or holistically with IMC (integrated marketing communications). While MARCOMS can enable organizations to reduce costs in the medium to long term, their main strategic use is in helping to differentiate and position.

Key terms

- **Advertising:** a paid-for form of communication using a medium with an identified sponsor. Generally of long-term impact.
- **Creative brief:** a summation of the MARCOMS task in order to manage and stimulate the development of creative work to address the task.
- **Creative execution:** translation of the proposition to a tangible form.
- **Direct marketing:** an activity involving the recording, tracking, and analysis over time of customers' responses to specific communications. Generally used to build relationships with stakeholders (key ones being customers, suppliers, and staff).
- **IMC:** a concept that recognizes the added value of a comprehensive plan that evaluates the strategic roles of a variety of communications disciplines holistically.
- **Medium class:** a type of medium such as TV, newspapers, or direct mail.
- **Medium vehicle:** a choice of medium or media within a class, such as the choice between the *Daily Mail* or the *Daily Mirror* newspapers in the UK.
- **Proposition:** a single-minded and concise statement of what is to be communicated about the product or service in the MARCOMS.
- **Public relations:** a planned activity to establish and maintain goodwill and mutual understanding between an organization and its immediate and wider stakeholders.
- **Sales promotions:** an offer or incentive of extra value for a product or service to staff, distributors, or the buyer. Generally of short-term impact.

Discussion questions

1. What are the pros and cons of approaching MARCOMS strategy from an IMC perspective?

2. Over the past ten years there has been a significant shift from 'push' to 'pull' international marketing communications strategies. Evaluate why this has happened and what the impact has been on the marketing communications business.

3. Think of two recent MARCOMS campaigns that featured the campaigning organization's values. What insight do you think the client had to use such an appeal from the brand wheel?

4. Identify three brands that you consider to have high awareness but are performing relatively badly in the marketplace. What would you recommend from a MARCOMS standpoint?

5. 'User-generated advertising is here to stay'. Do you agree?

6. Select one of the leading supermarket chains and develop five different potential propositions for the brand based upon: (a) user characteristics; (b) surprising points about the service; (c) price characteristics; (d) disadvantage of non-use; and (e) direct comparison with rivals. Which one would you choose to base a campaign upon and why?

7. You have a local cinema as a client. Examine the case for spending their advertising budget in a concentrated burst versus a drip campaign.

Online resource centre

 Visit the Online Resource Centre for this book for lots of interesting additional material at: **<www.ows.co.uk/orc/west3e/>**

References and further reading

Berthon, Pierre, Leyland Pitt, and Colin Campbell (2008), 'Ad Lib: When Customers Create the Ad', *California Management Review*, 50 (4), pp. 6–30.

Brown, Jo, Amanda J. Broderick, and Nick Lee (2007), 'Word of Mouth Communication within Online Communities: Conceptualizing the Online Social Network', *Journal of Interactive Marketing*, 21 (3), pp. 2–20.

Cova, Bernard, Robert Kozinets, and Avi Shankar (2007), *Consumer Tribes* (Oxford: Butterworth Heinemann).

Dwyer, Paul (2007), 'Measuring the Value of Word-of-Mouth and its Impact in Consumer Communities', *Marketing Science Institute Report*, No. 06-118.

Edelman, David C. (2010), 'Branding in the Digital Age: You're Spending Your Money in All the Wrong Places', *Harvard Business Review*, March, pp. 62–9.

El-Murad, Jaafar and Douglas C. West (2003), 'Risk and Creativity in Advertising', *Journal of Marketing Management*, 19 (5-6), pp. 657–73.

El-Murad, Jaafar and Douglas C. West (2004), 'The Definition and Measurement of Creativity: What Do We Know?' *Journal of Advertising Research*, 44 (2), pp. 188–201.

Farris, Paul and Douglas C. West (2007), 'A Fresh View of the Advertising Budget Process', in Gerard J. Tellis and Tim Ambler (eds), *The SAGE Handbook of Advertising* (London: SAGE), pp. 316–32.

Gupta, Sunil (2013), 'For Mobile Devices, Think Apps, Not Ads', *Harvard Business Review*, March, pp. 70–5.

McWilliam, Gil (2000), 'Building Stronger Brands Through Online Communities', *Sloan Management Review*, Spring, pp. 43–54.

Mohr, Iris (2007), 'Buzz Marketing for Movies', *Business Horizons*, 50, pp. 395–403.

Nichols, Wes (2013), 'Advertising Analytics 2.0', *Harvard Business Review*, March, pp. 60–8.

Ogilvy, David (1987), *Confessions of an Advertising Man*, 2nd edn (New York: Macmillan).

Piercy, Nigel F. (1986), *Marketing Budgeting* (Dover, NH: Croom Helm).

Porter, Michael E. (1980), *Competitive Strategy: Techniques for Analyzing Industries and Competitors* (New York: Free Press).

Prendergast, Gerard, Douglas West, and Yi-Zheng Shi (2006), 'Advertising Budgeting Methods and Processes in China', *Journal of Advertising*, 35 (3), pp. 165–76.

Reeves, Rosser (1961), *Reality in Advertising* (New York: Alfred A. Knopf).

Ries, A. and J. Trout (1981), *Positioning: The Battle for your Mind* (New York: Warner Books/McGraw-Hill).

Sevitt, David and Alexandra Samuel (2013), 'How Pinterest Puts People in Stores', *Harvard Business Review*, July-August, pp. 26–7.

Singh, Tanuja, Liza Veron-Jackson, and Joe Cullinane (2008), 'Blogging: A New Play in Your Marketing Game Plan,' *Business Horizons*, 51, pp. 281–92.

Smith, Ted, James R. Coyle, Elizabeth Lightfoot, and Amy Scott (2007), 'Reconsidering Models of Influence: The Relationship between Consumer Social Networks and Word-of-Mouth Effectiveness', *Journal of Advertising Research*, December, pp. 387–97.

Teixeira, Thales (2013), 'How to Profit from "Lean Advertising"', *Harvard Business Review*, June, pp. 23–5.

Thomas, Greg Metz, Jr (2004), 'Building the Buzz in the Hive Mind', *Journal of Consumer Behaviour*, 4 (1), pp. 64–72.

Vakratsas, Demetrios and Tim Ambler (1999), 'How Advertising Works: What Do We Really Know?' *Journal of Marketing*, 63 (1), pp. 26–44.

West, Douglas C. (1993), 'Cross-national Creative Personalities, Processes and Agency Philosophies', *Journal of Advertising Research*, 33 (5), pp. 53–62.

West, Douglas (1994), 'Restricted Creativity: Advertising Agency Work Practices in the US, Canada and the UK', *Journal of Creative Behavior*, 27 (3), pp. 200–13.

West, Douglas C. (1999), '360° of Creative Risk: An Agency Theory Perspective', *Journal of Advertising Research*, 39 (1), pp. 39–50.

West, Douglas C. and Pierre Berthon (1997), 'Antecedents of Risk-taking Behavior by Advertisers: Empirical Evidence and Management Implications', *Journal of Advertising Research*, 37 (5), pp. 27–40.

West, Douglas C. and John Ford (2001), 'Advertising Agency Philosophies and Employee Risk-taking', *Journal of Advertising*, 30 (1), pp. 77–91.

West, Douglas C. Arthur J. Kover, and Albert Caruana (2008), 'Practitioner and Customer Views of Advertising Creativity: Same Concept, Different Meaning', *Journal of Advertising*, 37 (4), pp. 35–45.

West, Douglas, Albert Caruana, and Kannika Leelapanyalert (2013), 'What Makes Win, Place, or Show? Judging Creativity in Advertising at Award Shows,' *Journal of Advertising Research*, 53 (3), pp. 324–38.

Key article abstracts

Barnes, Bradley and Maki Yamamoto (2008), 'Exploring International Cosmetics Advertising in Japan', *Journal of Marketing Management*, 24 (3/4), pp. 299–316.

This paper suggests that the Japanese market needs a greater degree of localization than might be the case in the UK. As such, agencies need to take extra care when designing cosmetics advertisements and focus more on an indirect soft sell in order to appeal to the emotional needs of the image status of the Japanese consumer.

Abstract: The Japanese cosmetics market is the second largest in the world and in 2003 was valued at approximately 1.9 trillion yen. The sector is also the largest consumer of advertising in Japan (receipts exceeding 35 million yen in 2003). Despite its size and significance, research in this area is somewhat scant. To bridge the gap, the research reports the findings of an investigation designed to explore the impact of cosmetics advertising on female Japanese consumers. The findings reveal that, despite their frequent usage in ads, celebrities fail to influence purchase decisions. Specific reference groups, including experts, friends, and female family members have varying degrees of influence. However, the sample of female Japanese respondents appears to be unconvinced when such reference sources are adopted in advertising. There was some preference for Western brands and music, but not models. Magazines represent the most suitable media for influencing Japanese women, while TV is less effective, despite its relatively high cost.

de Mooij, Marieke and Geert Hofstede (2010), 'The Hofstede Model: Applications to Global Branding and Advertising Strategy and Research', *International Journal of Advertising*, 29 (1), pp. 85–110.

Geert Hofstede's dimensional model of national culture has been applied to various aspects of global branding and advertising and theories of consumer behaviour. This paper examines the famous Hofstede dimensions of cultural distance in relation to advertising and provides guidance about using the scales. For example, the picture of a family in an advertisement is assumed to be a reflection of collectivism, but paradoxically it can also be a reflection of individualism where people are afraid that family values are disappearing. In collectivistic cultures advertisers may even feel a lesser need to depict families because the family is part of one's identity; it is not the desirable.

Abstract: Recent years have seen increasing interest in the consequences of culture for global marketing and advertising. Many recent studies point at the necessity of adapting branding and advertising strategies to the culture of the consumer. In order to understand cultural differences, several models have been developed of which the Hofstede model is the most used. This article describes elements of this model that are most relevant to branding and advertising, and reviews studies that have used the model for aspects of international branding and for advertising research. It provides some cautious remarks about applying the model. Suggestions for more cross-cultural research are added.

Kitchen, Philip J. and Don E. Schultz (1998), 'IMC—A UK Ad Agency Perspective', *Journal of Marketing Management*, 14 (4/5), pp. 465–86.

This paper explores a number of themes related to integrated marketing communications. In particular, the difficulties of measuring its effect, the problems of integrating the PR function, and its value in providing consistency, impact, and continuity.

Abstract: This paper concerns integrated marketing communications (IMC) in terms of its theoretical background, and by providing initial findings from an exploratory study of IMC within a judgement sample of UK advertising agencies (total estimated billings—£3.5 billion). We consider arguments put forward by academics and practitioners in relation to what IMC is perceived to be, and whether it offers significant value to ad agencies and their clients in the dynamic MARCOMS marketspace leading toward the next century. Research findings show that IMC is not a short-term managerial fad, nor is it just a reformulation of existent praxis. Instead, IMC offers a clear response by advertising agencies and their clients driven by a constellation of factors: new forms of information technology (including development and usage of databases), media fragmentation, client desires for interaction/synergy, and global and regional coordination. The paper concludes by stating that IMC is a fundamental, probably irreversible, shift in both the thinking and practice of ad agencies and their clients, as reflected by advertising executives. IMC is driven by technological development, customers, consumers, and by organizational drive to properly allocate finite resources to the key element of creating exchanges—marketing communications.

Percy, Larry (2004), 'Advertising and the Seven Sins of Memory', *International Journal of Advertising*, 23 (4), pp. 413–27.

Effective communication inevitably confronts the problem of memory. This paper examines Schacter's framework and provides a series of suggestions on how to overcome the hurdle. Suggestions include ensuring a consistent look and feel to your advertising over time and using distinctive cues not associated with long-term memory.

Abstract: A positive intention may be formed as a result of exposure to an advertisement, but if a memory malfunction interferes with that intention, the advertising will be ineffective. This paper considers the implications for advertisers of Daniel Schacter's 'seven sins of memory': transience, absent-mindedness, blocking, misattribution, suggestibility, bias, and persistence. Each of the 'sins' is explained in detail and advice provided for advertisers on how to avoid these pitfalls.

 End of Chapter 11 case study   Cookie turns 100: how a successful heritage brand updates the product, packaging, and advertising

The Oreo cookie recently celebrated its 100th birthday and this brand has had successful growth along the way. Oreo's product, packaging, and advertising have evolved over time to match continuously changing consumer demands. After years of success in the US, and in an effort to grow through market development, Oreo was launched globally. One key international target country for expansion was China. At first, Oreo was not well received in China, but over time, Kraft Foods adapted Oreo to fit the needs and wants of Chinese consumers. After ten years of being in China, Oreo became the number one best-selling cookie in the country. Much of Kraft's success outside the US can be attributed to the company's ability to adapt a brand's product, packaging, and advertising to the desires of local markets.

Product

Oreo was first created in 1912 and consisted of two chocolate wafers, embossed with a thin wreath on the outer edge with the 'Oreo' name in the centre of the cookie, filled with a crème middle. Over the past 100 years, Oreo has grown to be a major success for Nabisco (now owned by Kraft Foods), both domestically and abroad. The 2012 *Market Share Reporter*, stated that Oreo owns 11 per cent of the US market (Figure C11.1) and was the number one selling cookie in the world.

Today, Oreo cookies are available in over 100 countries with the US and China being number one and two markets, respectively. The Asia Pacific market consumes over four billion kilograms of biscuits (cookies) per year (Biscuits Industry Profile). Furthermore, the projections are that this number is expected to increase from year to year and reach six billion kilograms by 2015 (Figure C11.2). Additionally, the Asia Pacific market makes up 22 per cent of the global biscuit market (Figure C11.3), and China makes up 13.3 per cent of the Asia Pacific biscuit market (Figure C11.4), giving Kraft an opportunity to reach a significant market size.

The Oreo brand has been expanded both through product line extensions (new flavours), and by being incorporated into other food items such as Oreo O's breakfast cereal, Oreo ice cream, Oreo Jell-O, and Oreo pie crust. Successful flavours of the Oreo cookie include the traditional chocolate wafer cookie with a crème middle as well as green tea ice cream, dulce de leche, trio chocolate, fruit duos (raspberry and blueberry or orange and mango), strawberry, vanilla, chocolate, blueberry ice cream, orange ice cream, golden vanilla, double delight (chocolate and peanut), cookies and cream, dark fudge, and white fudge.

Packaging evolution

The Oreo package has changed many times throughout the century. Oreos were initially sold in bulk tins with glass tops (Figure C11.5A), which allowed consumers to be able to see the contents inside. The tin was bulky, so it was changed to a rectangular shape in 1915 (Figure C11.5B). This version was also made of tin but, instead of having a glass top, it had a tin top. As such, consumers were now unable to view the product. Nabisco did, however, include an image of the cookie on the top of the packaging. By 1923, the packaging was long and thin and was made of paperboard instead of tin (Figure C11.5C). This version only had text on the box to describe what was inside and did not display an image of the product. During the 1940s, the packaging was yellow as opposed to the blue colour that most people recognize today. However, it was around this time that the package evolved to be a blue box and images of the cookie were put on the package to make the contents inside recognizable to consumers.

Changes to the Oreo package continued throughout the second half of the century. In the 1950s, the Oreo package became a blue rectangular paperboard box with a cellophane section in the middle, allowing the consumer to view the contents inside (Exhibit 5D). By the 1960s, Oreo packages contained several rows of cookies in one box, but the cellophane was no longer part of the packaging (Figure C11.5E). From 1975 until 1995, Oreo used a modified version of the 1960s packaging. It included several rows of cookies, but also included cellophane (Figure C11.5F). In 1995, the packaging changed to show less of the cookies and more of the Oreo brand name and logo (Figure C11.5G). Today's Oreo package is slightly different from the 1995 version in that it still consists of a thin plastic wrap that covers the cookies, but on the newest packaging there is no clear cellophane for consumers to view the product. It contains the Oreo label, nutrition facts, and other important information (Figure C11.5H). It also has a re-sealable pull tab in the top centre portion of the package so consumers are not only able to open the package easily, but also to easily re-seal the package to preserve the contents.

China

The Oreo cookie was first introduced in China in 1996, but Kraft struggled for years and at one point considered leaving China. The logo, font, and copy of the Oreo package were all written in Chinese. However, the package did not appeal to local consumers. Some Chinese consumers felt that the equivalent of $0.72 for a package of 14 Oreos was too expensive. Additionally, Chinese consumers did not care for the taste of the Oreo (*Businessweek*). The problem was that Kraft offered the same type of Oreo in China as it sold in the US. Sanjay Khosla, Kraft's president of developing markets, stated 'there was a belief that what was good for the US was good for the world'. As Kraft began marketing research with Chinese consumers, they found that the traditional Oreo was too sweet for the locals and the package contained too many cookies for small Chinese families.

In 2006, after testing 20 different Oreo prototypes, Kraft reformulated both the packaging and the taste of the Oreo cookie to better suit the locals. The newer packages were smaller and contained about six servings for $.29. Kraft worked with a panel of consumer taste experts from around the world to identify the characteristics of the Oreo, including colour, crunchiness, and bitterness. The new recipe created a cookie that was slightly smaller in size and slightly less sweet than the traditional Oreo. To test the new recipe, hundreds of Chinese consumers tasted the new Oreo. Making changes to the Oreo recipe was not easy. Lorna Davis, head of Kraft's global biscuit and cookie businesses, stated 'when you have a brand that's 100 years old, you don't mess with the recipe thoughtlessly'. However, it was not until Kraft began actively engaging with Chinese consumers about taste and packaging that Oreo sales began to take off.

Wafers are particularly popular throughout Asia, so in 2006 Kraft also began selling the Oreo as a wafer. The purpose of offering the Oreo as a wafer was to help familiarize more Chinese customers with the brand. Today, Kraft offers a variety of Oreo flavours in China, including the following (Figure C11.6):

- Oreo green tea ice cream: Oreo cookie with green tea ice cream flavour crème with a cooling sensation that simulates ice cream (Figure 11.6A)
- Oreo wafers: Oreo in a traditional wafer cookie form that is popular in China (Figure 11.6B)
- Oreo double-fruit in orange and mango or raspberry and blueberry crème (Figure 11.6C)
- Oreo minis (Figure 11.6D)

The green tea ice cream Oreo cookie has been particularly popular in China. As stated by Sheeba Philip, Global Brand Director for Oreo, 'since parts of China can reach temperatures well over 100 degrees... this popular cookie in China combines a local flavour with a cool treat'. There is a cooling sensation within the crème of the cookie to evoke eating ice cream.

Advertising

Kraft used several different advertising methods to introduce the 'reinvigorated' Oreo cookie to Chinese consumers. Chinese consumers desire interaction with national celebrities and enjoy digital media, so Kraft used this knowledge to its advantage. Based on an IBM publication,

From Stretched to Strengthened, Kraft used Chinese native and NBA basketball star Yao Ming as a brand ambassador (YouTube videos b and c).

> Using online gaming, the company encouraged younger consumers to 'compete' with Yao Ming in Oreo 'Twist, Lick and Dunk' contests. Mothers in China, the ultimate audience, were encouraged to share their 'Oreo Moments' in an online diary on China's popular QZone social network.
>
> *Source: Stretched to Strengthened*. Publication. IBM, <http://knowledge.wharton.upenn.edu/papers/download/11032011-IBMCMOStudy.pdf>

These two advertising methods were a major hit. Kraft has also used a variety of television commercials as a means to teach the Chinese how to eat an Oreo cookie, some of which feature Yao Ming (YouTube videos a, b, c, and d).

Success

In 2006, Oreo became China's number one selling biscuit. There has also been success in other emerging markets such as Argentina, India, Indonesia, and Mexico. According to Kraft, 'Indonesia ranked as one of the brand's biggest and fastest growing markets in 2010'. Also, 'Argentines have loved Oreos since the cookie was introduced in 1995'. *Forbes* article, 'Oreo Cookie Celebrates 100th Birthday with Sprinkles and World Domination' states:

> While the original sandwich remains a bestseller, Nabisco has never held back from evolving its product. The brand's inordinate global success is largely due to its maker's understanding of taste sensibilities of its various markets, and openness to craft versions of Oreos to suit regional palates, while always maintaining a nod to the original.
>
> *Source:* Nadia Arumugam, 'Oreo Cookie Celebrates 100th Birthday With Sprinkles And World Domination'. Forbes.com, *Forbes Magazine*, 8 March 2012 <http://www.forbes.com/sites/nadiaarumugam/2012/03/08/oreo-cookie-celebrates-100th-birthday-with-sprinkles-and-world-domination/>

Thanks to Kraft's overseas push in China and other emerging countries, Oreo sales grew nearly 25 per cent in 2011. Because of the ability to adapt to local markets in emerging countries, the Oreo cookie is still successful after 100 years.

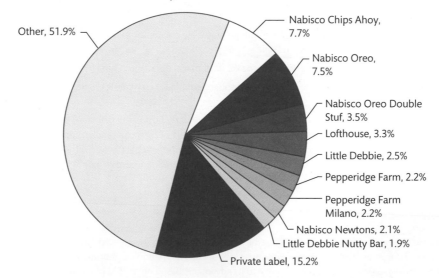

C11.1 Market Share of Top Cookie Brands in the US (2011)

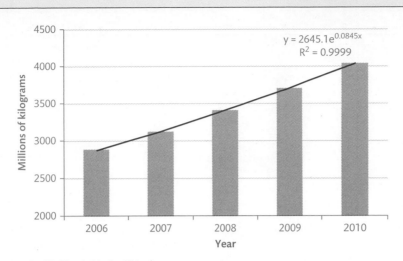

$$y = 2645.1e^{0.0845x}$$
$$R^2 = 0.9999$$

C11.2 Asia Pacific Biscuit Market Volume

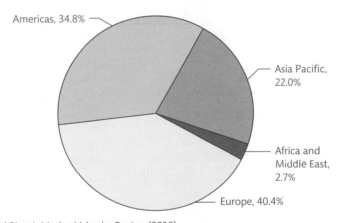

C11.3 Global Biscuit Market Value by Region (2010)

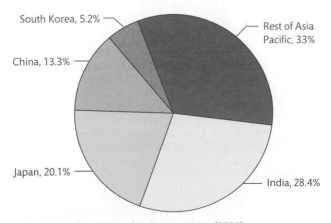

C11.4 Asia Pacific Biscuit Market Geographic Segmentation (2010)

	Image	Year / Description
A		1912: Oreos were originally sold in large tins with clear tops.
B		1915: The packaging was made more rectangular and made of tin on all sides. Consumers were no longer able to see the contents inside the package but Nabisco included an image of the product on the outside.
C		1923: The boxes were long and thin and were made of paperboard as opposed to tin. However, the packaging only had text on the box to describe what was inside as opposed to an image of the product.
D		1951: Oreo packaged the cookies so that the consumer could see the stacks through the cellophane wrapper. The package was a blue rectangular paperboard box with a cellophane section in the middle, allowing the consumer to view the contents inside.
E		1969: Oreo packaged several rows of their cookies in one box, but the cellophane section was no longer part of the packaging.

Image	Year / Description
F 	1975: Oreo used a modified version of the 1960s packaging. It contained several rows of cookies, but also included the cellophane area.
G 	1995: Oreo modified its packaging again by updating the blue colour as well as the OREO font. With this package, the consumer could see less of the cookies inside and more of the Oreo logo.
H 	Present: Today's packaging consists of a thin plastic wrap that covers the cookies containing the Oreo label as well as the nutrition facts and other important information. It also has a re-sealable pull tab so consumers can easily open the package but also preserve the contents.

C11.5 Packaging Images and Descriptions

A: Green Tea Ice Cream Oreo

B: Oreo Wafers

C: Double Fruit Oreos

D: Oreo Minis

C11.6 Current China Packaging Images (2011, 2012)

YouTube Videos

a. Oreo Commercial – Double Fruits Flavor China (includes English subtext) <http://www.youtube.com/watch?v=8hlXjrKjnc8>

b. Oreo TV Commercial China 2010 Yao Ming (does not include English subtext) <http://www.youtube.com/watch?v=TNOqyRBphA4>

c. Oreo TV Commercial China 2011, Mini & Yao Ming (includes English subtext) <https://www.youtube.com/watch?v=KhRpb1H4jcs>

d. Oreo TV Commercial China 2012 Ice Cream Flavor (includes English subtext) <http://www.youtube.com/watch?v=vPbt_VIHz2Q>

Discussion questions

1. Analyse the communication, functional and perceptual benefits of the current the Oreo cookie package with a focus on communication, functional and perceptual benefits.

2. Evaluate what Kraft had to do in order to be successful in China in terms of promotion and packaging redesign.

This case was prepared by Megan Ward and Jani Willis under the supervision of Hope Corrigan, Marketing Department, Sellinger School of Business and Management, Loyola University Maryland, Baltimore, MD (hope.corrigan@verizon.net). The case is solely for the basis of class discussion and is not intended to illustrate effective or ineffective management or administrative situation or any form of endorsement.

International marketing strategy

Learning Objectives

1. To become familiar with the concepts and definitions of international marketing strategy.
2. To be able to evaluate the potential of foreign country markets and identify international marketing opportunities and challenges.
3. To be able to compare and assess the foreign market investment (entry) modes and appreciate how organizations choose from them.
4. To understand the firm's international marketing mix decisions and strategies.
5. To appreciate the latest thinking on international marketing.

I. Introduction

1 Overview and strategy blueprint

2 Marketing strategy: analysis and perspectives

II. Where are we now?

3 Environmental and internal analysis: market information and intelligence

III. Where do we want to be?

4 Strategic marketing decisions, choices, and mistakes

5 Segmentation, targeting, and positioning strategies

6 Branding strategies

7 Relational and sustainability strategies

V. Did we get there?

14 Strategy implementation, control, and metrics

IV. How will we get there?

8 Product innovation and development strategies

9 Service marketing strategies

10 Pricing and distribution strategies

11 Marketing communications strategies

12 International marketing strategy

13 Social and ethical strategies

 Case study: HSBC Expat

With a handy hints and tips website aimed at wealthy Brits moving abroad, HSBC Expat proved that a niche target market should not be overlooked.

The brief

A move abroad is a major life step. And the to-do list is often focused on finding the right job, accommodation, and schools—keeping track of finances is often missed. When HSBC Expat looked at customers in this situation it became clear that a wealth of information on moving abroad could be found online, but less informal advice was available. So the company decided to set up a hints and tips website. The aim was to raise awareness of HSBC's expat offerings and create new business leads. 'We wanted to talk to customers about what they were worried about, while also raising awareness of our Expat offerings', says HSBC Expat digital marketing and social media manager Richard Fray.

The strategy

The small marketing team lacked the necessary resources to create a large amount of content about life abroad. 'People wouldn't necessarily believe us—where's the credibility in a bank talking about finding a good nursery in Spain?', Fray asks. From several years' experience running an expat survey and a blog that receives regular expat submissions, the brand knew that its target audience was eager to share information to assist others. 'It's almost like you become part of a club of people who successfully challenged themselves to try a new life abroad. People are willing to share their knowledge with people who haven't made that move', he says. The team contacted expat bloggers, relocation companies, and larger corporations with international employees. HSBC's own multinational employees were encouraged to add their tips.

Fray can't disclose the exact budget of the campaign, but 70 per cent was spent on building the site, 20 per cent on organically promoting it, and 10 per cent on paid social media through promoted updates and tweets. 'We wanted to create content that people will share and attract others to it, rather than spending on advertising. It was about trying something different', he says.

The goals around increasing awareness were clear: 20,000 unique visits to the HSBC Expat Hints and Tips site, reaching 50 countries and over 500,000 people on social media. HSBC Expat set a target of 800 individual submissions—content that would otherwise have cost £22,000. The tips submitted had to be of high quality, shareable, and useful. But HSBC Expat also wanted new leads, with improved search engine rankings. 'It wasn't a sales campaign, but we wanted to measure if we were getting new business from those interacting with the site. So, we also wanted our website to come up on wider searches, including on topics that aren't necessarily related to banking'.

The execution

The site was predominantly promoted through earned and owned media. HSBC Expat used website banners, an email campaign, and Twitter. It took promotional tweets to target professional people who had already shown an interest in living abroad. 'We identified the most popular organic tweets and promoted them to a wider audience. The way we managed the paid and organic tweets was very dynamic', Fray says.

The brand worked with two separate agencies to develop and promote the website. Digital agency Heath Wallace helped with the strategy and the development of the website, while PR and social media agency Hill and Knowlton developed its social strategy and connected with bloggers.

Measuring the results proved challenging. 'There is a long lead time from one considering moving abroad to actually opening a bank account, so we needed to create special reports to let us see the long-term impact of the website. We used web and social media analytics, extracting more than one billion data points for bespoke dashboards. We then pieced together how customers found our site', Fray says.

HSBC Expat wanted to ensure that it boosted sales and adopted a soft-sell approach. 'I think the ongoing challenge in content marketing is about finding the right balance between being useful and helpful while also selling services to customers. It overcame this problem by not directly promoting products, but providing links to other useful content that is further down the sales funnel. It eases the customers in by taking a gentle approach', he says.

The outcome

To measure the campaign's return on investment the team analysed the value of content created against the number of people who followed through after engaging with the website. 'But we didn't only want to see direct leads, but also uplifts elsewhere. We looked at our organic search rankings of the site. We had an incremental number of leads through organic search, where even though we couldn't track that they had used the tool, our search rankings had gone up', Fray says. Three months after launching the website, there was a 31 per cent increase in search traffic to the site and a 52 per cent increase in new business leads. 'In the three months prior to launching the tool we had relatively flat organic search traffic, then a spike coinciding with the website's launch, and then in the three months afterwards that we tracked it', he says.

The website attracted more than 25,530 visitors, 28 per cent over the target. Visitors to the website were spread across 174 countries, exceeding its target by 248 per cent. More than 1,080 tips were collected from 56 separate countries, 36 per cent higher than estimated. HSBC Expat's Twitter account subsequently became the second most followed HSBC Twitter channel worldwide, with its Twitter followers increasing by 57 per cent. New business leads directly from users of the tool exceeded targets by 51 per cent. 'Three times as many leads were generated by users of "Hints and Tips" on subsequent visits than in the same visit—indicating that we successfully engaged with users earlier in the research process. This part of the website created more leads than any other informational content on the site', Fray says.

The analysis

Fray believes the campaign was value for money. 'The website has become self-perpetuating in terms of ongoing traffic and sharing. It has given us valuable content that we can use in many ways', he says. HSBC Expat is now planning to adapt a different storytelling strategy. 'We're looking at how to reuse personal content, maybe through the use of videos to create a more emotional experience'.

Leonie Roderick, The Marketer, May/June 2014, pp. 20–22.

Introduction

It has become difficult for organizations to focus their attention on their home markets alone. While a company may confine its activities to the local market, that market is unlikely to be so restricted and may be served by firms headquartered in, or operating from, a number of other foreign countries or regions. Knowledge of the critical factors in international marketing is of vital importance to organizations whether they are actively involved in foreign markets or not. Going international, companies face wider groups of consumers, higher risk, and complexity. This is because of the increased uncertainty arising from operating in diverse and less 'controllable' environments. Developing an **international marketing strategy** is for obvious reasons a more difficult and complex task than designing a marketing strategy for the well-known domestic market.

The chapter's design is guided by the strategic marketing management process which covers the three areas of (1) strategic analysis, (2) strategic choices, and (3) strategy implementation (see Chapter 3, Figure 3.1). The SMM process has been translated here into an international-oriented model that includes the relevant international marketing activities

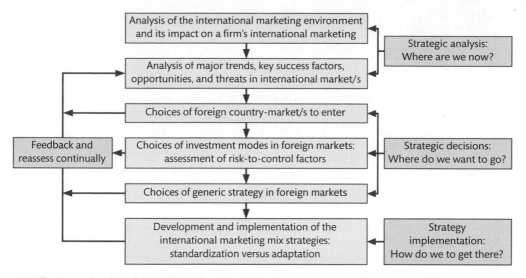

12.1 The International Marketing Decision-making Process

Source: An extended version of the strategic marketing management process, drawn by the authors.

through to design and implementation. Many organizations employ the following process in their planning and execution of international marketing strategy at three levels:

(1) *macro*: what foreign country selection decisions

(2) *national*: what foreign market investment (entry) decisions are made

(3) *market*: what international marketing mix decisions are made.

Organizations need to identify and assess key opportunities and threats in the international marketing environment and so managers must be equipped to administer the challenges emerging from the diverse economic, political, legal, cultural, technological, and competitive forces in the international environment. Emphasis should then be placed on choosing a foreign country to serve based on an assessment of that market's potential and attractiveness. Once a company has identified a target country market/s, it is next confronted with the strategic decision of choosing an appropriate investment (entry) mode/s for operations in the foreign market/s. The choice amongst the investment modes is a key component since the decision will impact the costs, risks, and return of the firm's international expansion and overall performance. Finally, emphasis at the market level should be placed on the firm's ability to design and implement the marketing mix strategies in a complex environment.

International marketing strategy

Marketing strategy has previously been defined as 'a process to viably align an organization's resources to the current and future needs of its customers in light of the environment'. Should this definition be rephrased to suit the international marketing purpose, or do we need to think of a different definition? Some researchers believe that international marketing strategy is 'a product of translating the domestic marketing solutions internationally'. Others suggest that international marketing strategy is a product of a 'sophisticated' process of international analysis and planning and not just a 'replant' of what a company does in its home market. Perhaps this stance is preferable? This is because of the large number of factors and challenges that international marketers face when they operate outside their domestic markets.

Scope of operation

- The size and breadth of the global marketplace
- The resources required for international involvement
- The varying goals/targets in each foreign market

Complexity

- The diverse and multicultural consumers in international markets
- The varying levels of economic development across foreign markets
- The varying powers of international competitors and suppliers
- The difficulty in obtaining information from foreign markets

Risk

- The many more 'unknown' and 'uncontrollable' variables
- Regimes/political and economic forces vary in stability
- Tariff, quota, and currency fluctuations are more numerous

Orientation

- 'Psychological distance' and 'self-reference criteria' may act negatively
- The stereotyping of countries may influence managers' decisions
- The necessity of managers having internationally-oriented mindset

Admittedly talking in sweeping terms, until 2008 going global seemed to make sense for many Western companies. Western markets were extremely competitive, population expansion had slowed, incomes had flattened, and corporate operating costs were rising (Bremmer, 2014). Developing economies, by contrast, had significant population growth, rising salaries, relatively low wages, and a welcoming climate for foreign investment. It made perfect sense for Western companies to seek opportunities abroad, particularly in developing economies. But in the aftermath of the global recession a different phase has been introduced. Governments of many developing nations have become wary of opening more industries to multinational companies and increasingly seek to protect local interests.

For example, in February 2013, India's Patent Office revoked Pfizer's patent for its cancer drug and granted a domestic manufacturer, Cipla, the right to produce a cheaper generic version. The government of China established price ceilings on essential drugs in 2009 and lowered the ceiling by 30 per cent in 2011, and it has pledged to expand the list of essential drugs to more than 500 medications by 2014. It's not applicable to all markets everywhere, but such moves pose major challenges and risks for multinationals, such as pharmas like Pfizer and others.

Such geopolitical factors cannot be controlled and can thereby add to the difficulties faced by managers when planning their marketing strategies for foreign markets. To reduce the effect of such challenges (and many others of course), a systematic approach to the development of an **international marketing strategy** is necessary. The following definition of international marketing strategy is thus offered.

> It is the process of planning and implementing marketing functions and activities across foreign country markets in order to position and strengthen the company presence in the international marketing environment.

Marketing managers have to consider the following principal questions.[1]

- Should the company expand globally, and with what benefit?[2]
- Which foreign market/s should be targeted, and why?
- What is the investment mode utilizing the company's resources?
- How best to create and sustain the company's competitive advantage?

International marketing analysis

The international marketing decision-making process begins with a series of strategic analyses of the international marketing environment. Managers need to understand and make sense of the international marketing environment, which is generally described as 'very dynamic, uncertain, increasingly complex, and difficult to control'. This analysis involves routine gathering of information and continuous monitoring of the international macro (remote) environment and the international micro (competitive) environment. The aim is to identify the major trends and key success factors in international markets that influence the company's operation.

For example, the key trends for growth in the global banking industry suggest it will follow the same growth rate as the GDP (Dietz et al., 2013). Some of the international trends in the market are low banking penetration in countries such as India, Russia, and Mexico, falling penetration in countries such as China, and high penetration in countries like Brazil. Trends in the international marketing environment are as follows (for brevity this is by no means an exhaustive list):

- rapid speed of technology change in developed countries
- intensifying competition, especially in the free trade areas
- regulated industries, particularly in Europe and the USA

---

[1] Please read these questions as a translation of the four classic strategic questions we presented in Chapter 3: 'Where we are now? Where do we want to be? How will we get there? Did we get there?'

[2] Reasons for organizations to go international include; saturation in the domestic market, intensifying competition at home, having excess capacity, searching for comparative advantage in skills, resources, or technology abroad, and geographic diversification.

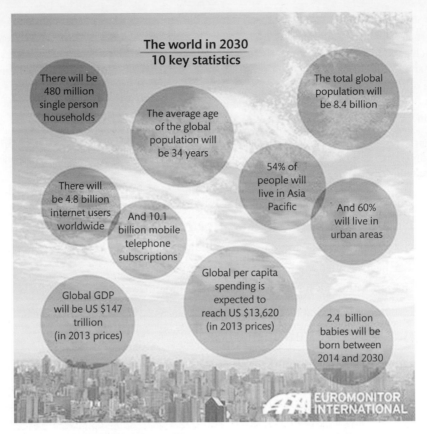

12.2 The Ten Key World Statistic Trends in 2030

Source: Euromonitor International, 2014

- instability of political regimes, for example in the Middle East and Africa
- counterfeiting and piracy in the emerging economies in Asia.

Figure 12.2 presents the forecast of ten key statistics of the world in 2030 as predicted by Euromonitor International.

In addition to identifying the major trends, marketing managers need to analyse the international marketing environment to find out what marketing opportunities exist and what are the associated challenges. For example, the availability of advanced technology in developed countries such as the USA and Japan could be seen as a major opportunity for foreign companies that can afford to invest in technology. However, it could still be seen as a threat by companies that compete on a low-cost basis.

To analyse and investigate the international macro environment, the PESTLE model we saw in Chapter 3 can be usefully employed here with a few alterations to analyse the country, regional, and global environments. Figure 12.3 shows 'PESTLIED' factors: political, economic, social, legal, international, environmental, and demographic.

Culture can be defined as 'the sum total of learned beliefs, values, religion, and customs that serve to direct customer behaviour in a particular country market'. It includes factors

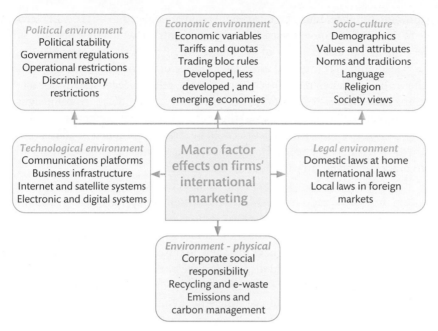

12.3 Macro Factors in the International Marketing Environment

Source: Drawn by the authors from various sources.

such as language, religion, and customs, each of which will affect the firm's operation and promotion of its products in foreign markets. For example, McDonalds and Burger King made significant changes to their menu items and the ingredients of all items in all Muslim countries they operate in to adhere to these consumers' religions and beliefs. Coca-Cola changed the translation of its brand name in China into 'Kee Kou Keele' to avoid the inaccurate meaning of the original name for Chinese consumers. MTV Networks provides mixed content of Western and localized materials to its target audience in the Middle East to avoid angering religious and conservative locals.

Tariffs, quotas, spending per capita, and currency exchange are four of the important economic factors that most companies assess when analysing the international marketing environment. Economic stability coupled with the high spending per capita in countries such as the USA, the UK, France, Germany, Australia, and Japan make these economies very attractive for international players. By contrast, the economic instability, currency fluctuations, and lack of incentives in less developed countries often deter foreign investment from all but the canniest of international players. Just think of the possible implications of the financial crisis in 2009 and onwards on the world car market in general, and on Mercedes-Benz Europe in particular? Can you also consider the impact of the same circumstance on Tata, the Indian car producer? Should we expect similar findings? Definitely not! The Indian market has boomed while Western markets have stagnated and are only now showing signs of recovery.

The international legal environment includes the legal system in the company's home market, the general laws and business legislation in the foreign countries, and the international laws that govern cross-nation transactions. This will make the analysis of the international legal environment much more complicated than that for a firm's domestic market.

Companies intending to enter the European Union are obliged to observe EU laws as well as those in the legal system within each European country in which they operate. Such laws will affect the design and delivery of the marketing mix as well. For example, the regulations for packaging, warranty, and after-sales service of a product vary from one country to another, which requires more investigation of the relevant legal system in each foreign market. The same applies to the content of marketing communications campaigns and in particular the regulation of direct marketing between member countries. What is legally allowed to be broadcast in open societies could be strictly prohibited in conservative ones. No doubt the international and local legal systems can significantly impact an organization's ability to market its brands in particular overseas markets.

What about the physical environment in foreign countries? Environmental issues, such as carbon management, recycling, e-waste, and sustainability, have emerged as important factors in many countries. Corporate social responsibility is also an important factor and has a strong influence on many consumers' attitudes towards a company and its brands. In Germany, for example, companies have to adhere to the environmental legislation by taking full responsibility for retrieving and disposing of the packaging waste of their products and using recyclable materials. Take the case of Scotland too. Environmental sustainability was a key element of the international marketing strategy of 'VisitScotland' a few years ago to promote the country and its attractions.

It could be argued that the concept of 'fair trade' was originally developed to protect workers in the developing countries as well as the environment. Using the Fair Trade logo on products may contribute to a company's success in foreign markets. For example, Starbucks, with its promotion of the fair trade concept, may gain a positive response from local consumers in countries such as Kenya, Ethiopia, and Sri Lanka.

Any international market analysis usually also covers the competitive (micro) environment. Understanding the structure of a given market's competitive environment and analysing the strengths of relevant competitors are very important to any company aiming for success. Also of high importance are the analysis of the competitive forces and an assessment of the market entry/exit barriers, including tariffs, quotas, and other barriers. The elements of market structure include the number and size of firms, entry conditions, and the extent of differentiation. Marketing managers need to know whether the foreign market they plan to enter is concentrated or fragmented, oligopolistic or monopolistic, in order to develop a suitable competitive strategy. The imperfectly competitive structure has close similarities to realistic market conditions where some monopolistic competitors, monopolists, oligopolists, and duopolists are dominant. What a list!

Once the competitive structure has been analysed, the firm should assess its relevant competitors in the foreign market. Analysis of local and foreign competitors is essential. For example, the 'new' nature of competition in the retailing industry in emerging markets has led to multinational retailers having to revise their strategies lest they become vulnerable to competitors, particularly local ones, who know how shoppers in emerging markets think, what they need, what they crave, and how they buy (D'Andrea et al., 2010).

Other competitive forces in a given foreign country or region should also be considered. Porter's five forces model is a useful framework here that is still applicable to assess the competitive forces and key players globally, regionally, or locally.[3] The task of assessing the firm's rivals involves:

- identifying the leading competitors globally and in the foreign country where the company plans to compete
- mapping their competitive positions based on geographical spread, entry mode, market shares, global branding, and so on
- assessing their objectives and strategies in each foreign market
- appraising their core capability in each foreign market/s
- predicting their likely response towards a new market entrant/s.

Relevant competitors will include not only local and international providers of the same products, but also suppliers of substitute products which may satisfy the same customer needs. British Airways not only considers other airlines such as EasyJet, Lufthansa, and Iberia as their competitors in the short-haul European market, but also takes into account other service providers, principally ferries, Eurostar, and coaches.

Threats do not only come from existing competitors. They might come from new entrants—some big players in the world market that have not served the chosen foreign market before, but might in the near future. Organizations have to take into account such possible moves and assess the current entry barriers in the relevant foreign market. The higher the entry barriers are, the lower the number of new players that can enter the market. Marketing managers should also assess the exit barriers in case they may have to withdraw from the market for some reason. In 2006, Carrefour, the French retailer, sold 16 stores in South Korea to E-Land and exited the market due to the adverse situation. Recently, Carrefour exited the Singapore market and Aeon Co. Ltd bought Carrefour Malaysia and its subsidiaries and rebranded them as 'Aeon Big'. Exit barriers can be economic, legal, technical, or even emotional. The government of Kuwait is still subsidizing the national carrier Kuwait Airlines to stay in the aviation market despite its losses in recent years.

 Mini Case 12.1 Russia—is it a solid BRIC member?

It was predicted in the last decade that the largest developing economies—Brazil, Russia, India and China (BRICs)—will overtake the G7 in size by 2050. Goldman Sachs has recently noted that this will probably happen much earlier—by 2018. The BRICs' total GDP amounts to nearly $11 trillion and their economies see phenomenal growth and rising wealth.

Russia has the largest land mass in the world and its natural resources plus its other endowments generated a GDP of around $1.5 trillion in 2010, slightly larger than that of India's $1.4 trillion, but smaller than Brazil's $2.2 trillion and China's $5.7 trillion. However, the income per capita in Russia in 2010 was about $10,522, slightly larger than that of Brazil, twice that of China, and nine times that of India.

Russia's growing economic stature has earned the country membership in the G8 industrialized nations. The country is an energy giant, being number one in the world in gas reserves and number two

---

[3] Readers can refer back to Porter's five forces model presented in Chapter 3.

in oil reserves, and supplying 25 per cent of Europe's energy. Russia is also a major exporting nation with exports amounting to over 30 per cent of GDP in 2009, in contrast with 26 per cent for China, 25 per cent for India, and 13 per cent for Brazil.

In early 2011 the Russian government established a $10 billion fund, managed by Goldman Sachs, to be used in attracting foreign investment. Russia's outward foreign direct investment has increased substantially and averaged almost $50 billion for 2007 to 2009, and the $203 billion in stock of those assets owned by Russian multinational enterprises in 2008 was larger than that of any other BRIC nation, with Brazil's being $162 billion, China's $148 billion, and India's $62 billion. In 2010, President Medvedev and the State Duma adopted a programme intended to make Russia an innovative economy over the next two decades, including creating a major centre for innovation in Skolkovo, as well as numerous technoparks and favourable economic zones throughout the country.

Despite these developments and its powerful position in the global economy, Russia received the least attention of the four BRIC nations from the media and the wider community around the world. This lack of emphasis might be because its population is the smallest of the BRICs and thus it has a smaller labour force and a limited domestic market size. Russia still has the potential to play a substantial economic and political role on the global stage, and as such it should be seen as a solid BRIC member, if not the most powerful.

International marketing choices and decisions

Based on the international market analysis and the intended strategic goals, a firm then has to consider many **international marketing choices** to position and strengthen its presence in international markets. The overall aim of these choices is to direct the organization's investment towards countries where investment opportunities exist. Recent research on the African market reveals a mismatch between supply and demand for financing that could point to investment opportunities in this area. Take the growth of capital demand and investment opportunities across Africa; the continent-wide demand for capital should increase by 8 per cent a year between 2014 and 2018, and $50 billion in total investment is possible over the next decade (Green et al., 2014).

Choice of foreign country market/s to enter

Three principal international marketing choices and decisions that any organization has to take will now be discussed.

1. Which foreign country/ies to enter?
2. How best to invest in (enter) the market?
3. What generic strategy to pursue in foreign market/s?

Choosing a foreign country requires a systematic information-based approach to assess the company's options so as to be able to choose the most attractive foreign market/s that will fit with the company's resources, capabilities, and international objectives. Cities in emerging markets will probably host many of the world's major new companies and become thriving hubs for capital, innovation, and talent (Dobbs et al., 2013). The forecast is that the number of Fortune Global 500 companies whose headquarters are located in developing countries will increase to 45 per cent by 2025, and China could be the home to the headquarters of more large companies than the USA or Western Europe.

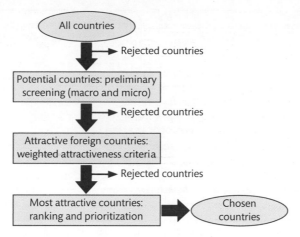

12.4 Country Screening Process

Source: Drawn by the authors from various teaching materials.

Many research studies have examined the challenges of international market selection decisions (Papadopoulos and Martin, 2011). How can such a decision be made? Consider the hypothetical example of a small Singapore-based company specializing in the development of a technique to aid automation of the primary screening stage in cervical cancer. The management want to expand internationally, but are not sure whether to consider only countries in the far Asian region or whether to target European markets, or even the USA, as well. The **country screening** process is a useful tool in this regard (Figure 12.4).

The operationalization of this process starts by forming an initial list of the possible foreign countries to enter. This list is subjected to further investigation to assess the potential of each foreign country. The shortlist of countries is then evaluated for its attractiveness, and finally prioritized using a weighting system. The task concludes by assessing the match between the company's strengths and capabilities, and the attractiveness of the foreign country. Figure 12.5 summarizes this process.

The country screening process can now be applied to the hypothetical example of the Singaporean company.

1. Preliminary list of possible foreign country markets: at this stage the company identifies a list of all countries where the cervical screening testing is legally available and foreign companies are allowed access.

2. List of potential foreign country markets: at this stage the management applies environmental factors to shorten the preliminary list and identifies potential foreign countries, for example by assessing:

- the size of female population (age 15–80)
- the GDP per capita
- the culture/society view on female cervical screening
- the legal and tariff restrictions
- the structure of competition.

  This list of potential countries may include France, Italy, Germany, Canada, Australia, USA, Japan, South Korea, and China.

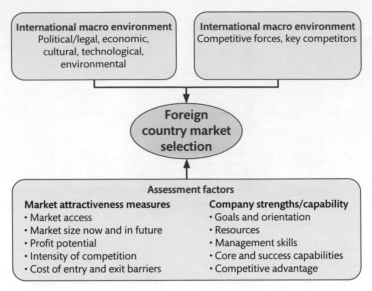

12.5 Selecting Foreign Country Markets to Enter

Source: Drawn by the authors from various sources.

3. **Shortlist of attractive foreign country markets:** at this stage the management has to use a relevant set of criteria to assess the attractiveness of potential markets, and may also apply a scoring system to prioritize these countries (note that the weights assigned are for illustration only):

- market accessibility and entry barriers (20% weighting)
- market size of medical equipment industry (25% weighting)
- health care spending per capita (25% weighting)
- level of imports of medical equipment (20% weighting)
- infrastructure and distribution system (10% weighting).

   This list of attractive countries is obviously shorter than the original one and may include, for example, the USA, Japan, Germany, France, and China.

4. **List of the most attractive foreign country markets;** at this stage the firm will use the weighting scores to put the attractive countries in a priority order.

   The calculation of the above weighting scores may result in a shorter list of only four countries in the following order: USA, Germany, France, and Japan.

5. **Final choice of foreign country markets to enter:** at this stage the management aims to find the best match between the company capabilities and the foreign marketing environment in the four shortlisted country markets.

   The compatibility assessment may guide the company to focus on the second or third market in the priority list (Germany or France in this example) as this might be a better match for the company's resources than the first market on the list.

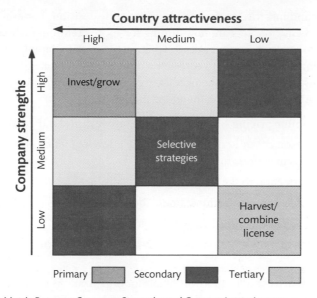

12.6 Compatibility Matrix Between Company Strengths and Country Attractiveness

Source: Gilbert D. Harrell and Richard O. Kiefer (1993), 'Multinational Market Portfolios in Global Strategy Development', *International Marketing Review,* 10(1), pp.60–72.

Harrell and Kiefer (1993) developed a scale for measuring foreign country attractiveness and company strength profile, and plotted the results in a 3 × 3 matrix that matches the company resources with specific country market requirements. This matrix (which is reminiscent of Chapter 4's portfolio analysis discussion) is shown in Figure 12.6.

- **Primary markets:** countries which fall in the upper left are the best for the company's long-term investment due to the high attractiveness and the high ability of the company to match the market requirements. These markets should generally receive further funding for growth.

- **Secondary markets:** countries falling on the lower-left to upper-right diagonal will require selective strategies as they are normally perceived to be risky despite the opportunities identified.

- **Tertiary markets:** countries in the lower right are areas to harvest or divest—or to ignore if no operations have been started. These are the countries which some companies may find suitable only for short-term investment (opportunistic approach).

Choice of generic strategy for foreign countries

Having chosen the foreign country to enter, the marketer needs to consider a generic strategy to pursue—that is, low-cost, differentiation, or focus.[4] Although this decision is most likely to be influenced by the organization's competitive advantage, external factors

---

[4] For detailed review of Porter's Generic Strategy, readers can refer to Chapter 3.

such as the demand in a foreign country may affect the decision. For example, consumers in the fastest-growing markets are now aiming for more premium or luxury automobiles (Gabardi et al., 2013). Premium car sales in China are increasing rapidly, which might influence multinational car producers to consider a differentiation strategy when competing in the Chinese market, if they have the necessary capabilities. Companies pursuing an international differentiation strategy are, therefore, more likely to:

- command premium pricing—highly adaptable rather than standardized
- invest greater resources in R&D and new product development to satisfy specific customers' needs in various foreign markets
- pay particular attention to the varying service quality across nations
- invest in corporate and international brand identity
- make heavy use of international advertising and social media
- have greater need for distribution control—wholly owned distribution.

One can argue that it could be more profitable for organizations to pursue the same generic strategy abroad as they adopt at home. For example, companies like Nike, Levi's, and Sony tend to compete across several international markets, adopting the same differentiation strategy to what they do normally. However, other companies may pursue a different generic strategy in a foreign market than the one they adopt at home. Ford, which is known for marketing low-cost cars in Europe, has been competing in the Middle East and the Gulf States adopting a differentiated product strategy. Non-traditional competitive strategies can have advantages for multinationals from emerging markets to help win the market both at home and abroad (Ramamurti, 2012). Although some observers believe that such firms have no competitive advantages to compete globally, it's simply that they have become sufficiently creative at cost reduction to deliver products at the price points that emerging market customers can afford. Although logically, that is an advantage!

Choice of foreign investment (entry) modes

Foreign investment (entry) modes are the various options an organization chooses from to operate in a foreign country market. Some writers assess entry modes along the continuum of low versus high involvement/commitment (Efrat and Shoham, 2013); that is, a decision can be based on the commitment level they are willing to make. But they could also be assessed along the risk to control continuum, so instead of specifying a desirable investment mode, it could be based on the degree of risks to control they are prepared to take for their investments. Foreign investment (entry) modes are described briefly in Table 12.1 (Young et al., 1989), and discussed under three broad categories of **exporting**, contractual arrangements, and **foreign direct investment (FDI)**.

Exporting is a mode of entry by which an organization sells its domestic good(s) abroad without any major modifications. Indirect exporting normally offers the lowest cost and risk when entering a foreign market, and is used by organizations that aim to benefit from casual opportunities abroad. For example, Mackie's Ice Cream of Scotland made its first step abroad via an unsolicited order from a trader in Seoul, South Korea, in 2002.

Table 12.1 Detailed Description of Foreign Investment (Entry) Modes

Exporting	Transfer of goods and/or services across national boundaries via indirect (domestic purchase, export house, trading company, piggybacking, etc.) or direct (agents, distributors, company export salespersons, sales subsidiaries) methods
Licensing	Contracts in which the licenser provides licensees abroad with access to one, or a set of, technologies or know-how, in return for financial compensation
Franchising	Contract in which a franchiser provides a franchisee abroad with a 'package' including not only trademarks and know-how, but also exclusivity and management and financial assistance and joint advertising
Management Contract	An arrangement under which operational control of an enterprise, which would otherwise be exercised by a board of directors or managers elected and appointed by its owners, is vested by contract in a separate enterprise which performs the necessary management functions in return for a fee
Turnkey Contracts	Contracts in which a contractor has responsibility for establishing a complete production unit or infrastructure project in a host country
Contract Manufacture/ International Subcontracting	A contractual agreement in which a company (the principal) in one country places an order, with specifications as to conditions of sale and products required, with a firm in another country.
Contractual Joint Ventures	Contracts formed for a particular project of limited duration or for a longer-term cooperative effort with the contractual relationship commonly terminating once the project is complete. May relate to co-production, co-R&D, co-development, co-marketing plus co-publishing, consortium ventures by banks to finance large loans, etc.
Equity Joint Ventures	Arrangements which involve the sharing of assets, risks, and profits, and participation in the ownership (i.e. equity) of a particular enterprise or investment project by more than one firm.
Wholly owned Subsidiaries FDI	Operations which are 100 per cent owned abroad. May be manufacturing or sales/services ventures. May be formed through acquisitions or greenfield operations.

Source: Summarized and Tabulated by authors from Young et al (1989), pp.1–2

Direct exporting is normally adopted by organizations wishing to have a more permanent position in a foreign market. Organizations that have opted for indirect exporting in the first place often change to direct exporting for more control and less risk to their international operations. Mackie's Ice Cream has now adopted a proactive approach to international markets and expanded its presence in a wider number of foreign markets (principally Taiwan, Singapore, Ireland, and the Gulf States).

Contractual agreements include licensing, franchising, management contracts, turnkey contracts, and so on. **Licensing,** as defined earlier, is a business contract between a licenser and a licensee which allows firms with relatively limited resources to exploit competitive advantages if they are legally protected or difficult to imitate. Licensees gain exclusive rights to produce and market a product within an agreed area for a period of time in return for a royalty. Fiat used to have licensing agreements with many car assembly companies in the Middle East and Asia such as Al-Nasr Co. in Egypt and TOFS Co. in Turkey.

Franchising is a two-party contract that provides a 'business package' to a franchisee. The franchisee runs a controlled business using the reputation and techniques of the franchiser,

Mini Case 12.2 Exports and emerging markets

Small businesses could be growing faster if they stuck to their marketing plans for exports to emerging markets and expansion in the services sector

Businesses could be missing out up to £122bn in sales by allowing marketing plans to slip off the radar, according to Pitney Bowes research. There are signs that the UK economy is gradually returning to life, but UK businesses need to look further afield for growth opportunities. Improved marketing focus could also help businesses to take off.

The Grant Thornton Business Confidence Monitor showed business confidence has picked up. While the eurozone is still mired in recession and unemployment across the single currency area is now at a record high of 12.2 per cent, other parts of the global economy, such as Africa, the Middle East and South East Asia, are incredibly vibrant. Are UK businesses taking due advantage of these global growth hotspots? How can they do more?

The UK tends to import more than it exports, but there are signs that businesses are redressing the balance by exporting to faster-growing markets. For the first three months of 2013 goods exports to non-EU countries matched exports to the European Union. In March 2013, UK exports to China grew by 16 per cent compared with a year earlier, and exports to South Korea by 36 per cent year on year. Compare this with a 1 per cent decline in exports to the EU over the same period. But there is no doubt the UK can and needs to do more.

While large multinational businesses are typically the most prolific exporters, small and medium sized enterprises (SMEs) can play a vital role, especially when it comes to future growth. The latest survey by the Federation of Small Businesses (FSB) showed that just 23 per cent of small businesses export anything, while an increasing share is hopeful of achieving export growth.

The FSB survey results suggest that more small businesses expect to see exports grow over the coming three months. During the first quarter of 2013 more than one in ten small businesses, or 11.4 per cent, said they expected to achieve rapid growth in exports of more than 5 per cent. So which sectors are excelling and how can the UK's businesses better realize such ambitions?

The UK is a world leader in the services sector: exports over the past year totalled £187bn. Indeed, London's services-based economy is thriving; according to recent Office for National Statistics research, employment levels in London have grown by around 200,000 over the past year. With the financial services sector still under pressure following the financial crisis, underpinning this growth in London are traditional business services, such as accounting, legal and administrative services, and the emerging technology-based businesses of the 'flat white economy'—media, information, and the creative industries.

The most recent official estimate put UK exports of communications, computer and information services at £15.6bn and growing at 12 per cent year on year. But marketing could be critical for many. Research carried out by Pitney Bowes in March showed that 87 per cent of British SMEs acknowledge that marketing has a positive effect on sales, but businesses are failing to take full advantage of effective marketing campaigns. The survey showed that the average SME only achieves 39 per cent of its planned marketing activity.

When business owners were asked to predict the effect on sales produced by increased marketing activity, the survey pointed to possible growth of 9.2 per cent. In theory, this means businesses could be missing out on up to £122bn in sales by allowing marketing plans to be forgotten. This is a big number and in practice couldn't be achieved overnight, but it serves to demonstrate how improved marketing could help. There is a clear gap between planned marketing activity and the reality of what takes place.

More than three-quarters, or 77 per cent, of SMEs surveyed recognized that marketing is important to the success of their business, but 11 per cent admitted to doing none of the marketing they had planned. When asked what was holding them back, 21 per cent of owners cited time and 36 per cent money as their main challenge. Investment and delivering on well-planned marketing campaigns is the best way to build on the burgeoning success of the services sector and success stories in the creative, information and media sectors. The shifting global economic centre of gravity creates massive opportunities and the UK is starting to take advantage of this by growing emerging market exports. But much more remains to be done.

Charles Davis, The Marketer, CIM publication, July-August, 2013 p.13.

Table 12.2 Differences Between Licensing and Franchising

	Licensing	Franchising
Payment	Consists of 'royalties'; may be negotiated	Consists of management fees; standard fee structure; less likely to be negotiated
Coverage	A product or products	May concern the whole business package
Uptake	Well-established firms; mainly in manufacturing	Tends to be younger firms; primarily in the services sector
Duration	Tends to be for 15–20 years	Tends to be for 5 years; renewable and longer term
Selection	Often self-selecting	Selected by franchiser
Benefits	Concerns specific existing products	Benefits of on going research passed on to franchisee

Source: Summarized by the authors from Young et al. (1989), p. 148.

usually as part of a wider chain. McDonald's, KFC, and Pizza Hut are examples of successful franchising in the fast-food market. Some of them had to adapt their menus to meet local customers' expectations and demands. For example, McDonald's had to remove pork and ham items from its menus in Islamic countries and replace them with halal beef. Pizza Hut found that corn sold better than pepperoni in Japan. The differences between licensing and franchising are illustrated in Table 12.2.

A **management contract** is an entry mode that allows a company to undertake the management activities of a business for a fee. The Hilton, Sheraton, and Marriot hotels are examples of companies that sign contracts with governments or individual owners to run the business for them for a fee. Energy corporations such as Aramco or Shell are examples of businesses that provide access to technology, skills, and management experience to countries in the Gulf area that have many oil fields, but lack the managerial expertise to run them.

Turnkey contracts are where a chosen contractor has responsibility for establishing a complete production unit and/or infrastructure project in a host country. This mode is commonly used by firms that undertake large capital projects (e.g. new airports, underground systems, water treatment, and nuclear energy plants).

Foreign direct investment (FDI) is an entry mode that involves a high level of involvement and commitment in a foreign market. Foreign direct investment can take the form of a wholly owned subsidiary, a merger, or an acquisition. For example, in July 2011, Volkswagen AG acquired a 55.9 per cent voting stake and 53.7 per cent of the share capital in MAN SE, pending regulatory approval. Volkswagen planned to merge MAN and Scania to create Europe's largest truck-maker. Regulatory approval was granted and the takeover completed in November 2011. Companies from developing countries may use mergers and acquisitions as fast ways to acquire some well-known brands to boost their presence in international markets. Aspen Pharmacare, a South African drug company, has taken over Sigma Pharmaceuticals, Australia's biggest drug distributor by market share, to expand in Australia. Drivers for FDI include resource seeking, efficiency seeking, new market seeking, and knowledge/relationship seeking. In 1991, the Volkswagen Group opened a plant in Bratislava to take advantage of the cheap labour and resources.

The Internet as an entry mode: besides the three traditional outward-bound modes of international investment, the Internet can now be added as a virtual mode of

Table 12.3 Internet-based Internationalization—'Internetization'

Benefits to Organizations	Limitations
Instant, 24/7, low cost access to global markets, even for small firms	Images and gestures have different cultural connotations across countries
Particularly beneficial for internationalizing SMEs, as it reduces some of the traditional barriers	Language differences and the need for website translations
Facilitates coordination and communication across the many operations/subsidiaries of MNEs	Fluctuation of computer literacy, access, and ownership of PCs across nations
Helps firms avoid some of the regulations/restrictions arising from physical presence abroad	Security and payment concerns (reluctance in sharing financial details across countries because of the threats of hackers and viruses)
Cost-effective in international marketing research and communications, e.g. interacting with customers at both the pre-sale and post-sale end, and obtaining detailed consumer purchase information	Limited applicability to certain types of products (video, software, music, and other information-based products) but not to certain high-tech products, services, or projects
	Distribution challenges particularly relating to non-digitizable products

Source: Extracted by the authors from various teaching materials.

internationalization. Many organizations go international and/or expand globally using the Internet. Some observers refer to the internationalization process via the Internet as **'internetization'**. Take, for example, the well-known company Amazon, nicknamed the 'Earth's Biggest Bookstore', which has achieved its remarkable global growth driven by the Internet. There is no doubt that the Internet has contributed greatly to world trade in the past decade. Table 12.3 shows the benefits and limitations of internetization as an entry mode.

Choosing a foreign investment mode is a relatively sophisticated decision that is influenced by a number of internal and external factors (Efrat and Shoham, 2013). Factors influencing entry mode decisions are:

- company goals and objectives in international markets
- financial and non-financial resources available to the organization
- managerial skills and motivations for international marketing
- previous experience and involvement in foreign markets
- nature of competition in the chosen foreign market
- extent of entry barriers—tariff and non-tariff
- feature of the product and its competitive advantage
- timing of entering a foreign market.

In addition to these factors, a firm can choose an investment option based on the desired level of commitment and involvement, and on the degree of control versus risk. Figure 12.7 shows the different levels of commitment and involvement as well as the degree of risk and control of foreign entry modes.

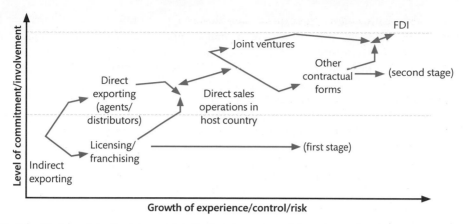

12.7 Entry Modes and the Firm's Internationalization: Assessment of Commitment/Involvement and Risk/ Control

Source: B. Dawes (ed.) (1995), *International Business: A European Perspective* (Cheltenham: Stanley Thornes)

In making the choice of foreign investment mode, managers may follow one of three approaches (Root, 1994, pp.159–60).

- **The Naive Rule:** companies are said to follow the naive rule when they consider only one way to enter foreign markets (e.g. 'we only export') or when they don't really think through the entry mode decision. This rule oversimplifies the task, which might cause the firm to miss significant chances and opportunities.

- **The Pragmatic (Stage) Rule:** firms adopt an incremental approach to foreign markets, gradually deepening their commitment and investment as they gain in market knowledge and experience. This approach suggests that different entry options are more appropriate at different stages of the firm's internationalization.

- **The Strategy Rule:** entry mode decisions are made in the context of the firm's overall strategic choices, and guided by the analysis of a relevant set of internal and external factors.

International marketing mix strategies

One of the fundamental challenges any organization undertaking international marketing has to face is whether to pursue a high degree of standardization of the marketing activity or allow substantial adaptation if needed to meet consumers' requirements in the local market/s. The **standardization** approach enforces similarity and reduces variations of the marketing mix across markets and nations. **Adaptation** is an approach that promotes flexibility by varying the marketing mix elements across markets and nations to satisfy local tastes and conditions. Levitt (1983) referred to these two approaches in his seminal article 'The Globalization of Markets' with his slogan 'think global, act local'.

Given that adaptation involves additional resources, the essential question is: When do you have to adapt? Given a choice, the vast majority of international marketers would prefer to standardize as this minimizes expenditure. However, environmental conditions may be such that it is impossible to 'replant' abroad what a company does in its home market. As mentioned above, McDonald's and Burger King have decided to adapt their marketing mix in the Middle East in the light of local tastes and religious beliefs. The key drivers and motivations for standardization and adaptation are as follows.

Standardization drivers

- Pushing for economies of scale benefits
- Increasing the cost of product development relative to its life span
- Growing standardization of tastes in some product areas
- Increasing convergence in consumer demand
- More homogenous markets and identifiable consumer segments

Adaptation drivers

- Culture and usage differences across nations
- Government and regulatory influences
- Differing consumer behaviour patterns
- Resistance from the company's local subsidiaries in foreign markets
- Local competition rules/conditions

In many respects standardization can be viewed as the 'want to' and adaptation as the 'must do' of the two choices. The debate over the extent of standardization versus adaptation has dominated the international marketing literature for a long time. Schmid and Kotulla (2011) have reviewed the research on international standardization and adaptation in the past 50 years and provided a theoretical framework that aims to enhance that decision. It should be stressed here that any marketing manager's challenge is not whether to choose solely between standardization and adaptation, but how to find the optimal balance between these two strategies (Vrontis et al., 2009). In some circumstances, marketing managers have to adhere to the local laws/regulations. For example, the European Union imposes some 'local content' requirements on cars imported into the region. Take another case: the USA stipulates that all imported spirits must be in metric measures and specific bottle sizes. Similarly, both Norway and Denmark insist that all beers and soft drinks should be sold in returnable containers. And in a final example, Japan requires that all imported pharmaceutical products must have been tested in Japanese laboratories.

International product decisions

International marketing success depends primarily on offering suitable and acceptable value to local consumers in any foreign market. There is nothing worse than introducing a product to a foreign market where it has no or little value to consumers. Certain products such as alcohol and pork are outlawed in many Muslim countries (though alcohol consumption may be covertly tolerated). Products such as central-heating systems and fireplaces are clearly unsuitable for countries that have hot weather all year round.

In assessing product acceptability and suitability for foreign markets, managers have to examine relevant issues such as product benefits, product features, and a product's perceived value. This can be done by answering the following set of questions for each market.

- How likely is it that the existing product will meet customer expectations and gain a level of acceptance?
- Does the product possess a clear competitive edge over rival offerings?
- What potential does the product have for generating profits?
- What level of investment is needed to market the product?

Marketing managers may also have to consider other issues. These include new product development, international private leased circuits (IPLCs), international branding, and the extent of brand standardization versus adaptation.

The issue of standardization versus adaptation is still open to debate in the literature. Rather than one or the other the question becomes how much can be standardized and how much has to be adapted? In Nigeria all Internet routers have to have batteries along with the standard mains electricity connection. Why? Because the electricity supply is frequently intermittent or shut down. So without a battery getting on the web would be extremely frustrating. This is an example of a product that is primarily standardized in build, but has been adapted with the addition of a battery to fit the local environment.

When considering the extent of standardization or adaptation of a brand, managers do not focus only on the core benefits of the product; they also think of other aspects that the international brand offers such as features, size, colour, packaging, warranty, guarantee, delivery, and after-sales service (see Figure 12.8). While some product aspects such as the core benefit, image, and brand name can be easily standardized, other aspects such as delivery, warranty, and after-sales service are relatively difficult to standardize. Large white goods companies normally offer three to five years manufacturer warranty in countries where consumers are generally literate and well educated. Such warranties are reduced to only one year in countries where consumers are less familiar with the product because they have been shown to be much more likely to cause damage through misuse.

International branding is an essential aspect that contributes significantly to the positioning of a product in international markets. A brand with a global reputation may earn customers satisfaction quickly in foreign markets because it assures them of specific benefits such as quality ingredients, performance, price, status, warranty, and after-sales service. Consumers normally associate certain geographies—especially developed countries—with the best brands. Take, for example, French wine, Italian sports cars, and Swiss watches. On the contrary, brands from other countries—especially developing markets—are perceived as less authentic. Brand-building in emerging markets is a long-standing problem (Rohit, 2010). Firms from developing markets sometimes cannot command a fair price. Lowering the price, in turn, reinforces the idea that their offerings are not comparable with those from developed countries. It is a 'catch-22' that leaves companies such as El Rey chocolate in Venezuela, winemaker Concha y Toro in Chile, IT consultancy Infosys in India, refrigerator maker Arcelik in Turkey, and many others unable to price their brands in a way that generates the revenue needed to fuel global growth.

Standardization

Core benefit

Performance

Brand name

Quality

Design

Features

Size and colour variants

Packaging

Delivery

Guarantees

After-sales service

Adaptation

12.8 Standardization/Adaptation of Products, Elements, and Attributes
Source: Drawn by the authors from various sources.

Global brands obviously vary in how they highlight their benefits and deliver values to consumers in international markets. For example, Ferrari promotes superiority and uniqueness, while Mercedes-Benz is known for quality and prestigious image. A brand such as Nike is associated with fashion and quality, while Wal-Mart's promise is delivering lower price. The principal international branding typologies are as follows.

- **Umbrella branding:** the whole set of products are led by a single brand name (e.g. Cadbury's).

- **Family (line) branding:** a group of products that are closely related (because they function in a similar manner) are sold to the same customer groups, are marketed through the same types of outlets, or fall within given price ranges. For example, Nike produces several lines of athletic shoes across the world.

- **Range branding:** consists of all the product lines and items offered internationally. For example, Avon's product range consists of cosmetics, jewellery, fashion, and household items.

- **Individual product brands:** these are used with individual products in a particular market (e.g. P&G's Pampers).

Product image (known in marketing as **COO or country of origin**) is one of the most powerful advantages of differentiation. The image is 'the way the public perceives the company and its offerings'. Past research has provided evidence that buyers tend to associate particular countries and their products with certain national (stereotypical) images for attributes such as quality, reliability, durability, taste, and price (Koschate-Fischer et al., 2012; Xuehua and Yang, 2008; Ibrahim and Sothornnopabutr, 2006). Consumers may also associate the COO of a product with status, authenticity, and exoticness. This allows a price premium to be obtained (e.g. French perfume, Italian designer clothes).

COO cues are like other extrinsic cues, such as brand name and retailer reputation, in that they can be manipulated without changing the physical product. Some global brands can benefit from positive COO (e.g. Mercedes-Benz of Germany, Sony of Japan, Scottish whisky, Levi's and the USA), while other brands may have to overcome negative perceptions of COO, especially if they come from less developed countries (e.g. Tata cars). Overcoming the negative perceptions is a challenge for international marketers. This challenge becomes even greater if the product is designed in a country and manufactured in another, while the headquarters of the company is in a third. This might create image confusion in the consumers' mind. Samsung Electronics, for example, is a company that has its headquarters in Suwon, South Korea, which is not associated with a high positive COO effect, and has assembly plants and distribution networks in 88 countries, some of which are associated with a very positive COO effect. The brand is promoted world-wide, capitalizing on the 'latest technology' and 'quality' that overlie the COO effect.

International pricing decisions

International pricing strategy is vital for positioning the company's offerings in foreign markets. When setting the price for international markets, managers face a wider set of factors compared with the domestic market. Pricing for the domestic market is influenced by relatively controllable cost factors compared with the highly fluctuating additional costs that are associated with international pricing. Most of these additional costs are not in the company's control zone. These include:

- tariffs and taxes
- currency exchange rate fluctuations
- cost of freight, insurance and local transportation
- cost of local management and communications
- possible price caps in some foreign markets due to purchasing power or government policies.

The variation and fluctuation of costs across foreign countries make it difficult for organizations to standardize their prices. Although pricing standardization may seem possible in theory, it is rarely achievable in practice. Price adaptation is therefore more likely in international markets. When developing a pricing strategy, management should analyse the price dynamics of its products in various country markets. Also important is assessing the product necessity to consumers. If the product is essential, then price changes may affect the company's revenue, especially in less developed countries, while the effect could be unnoticeable in well developed countries. The management should also assess the frequency with which consumers buy the product. Other price dynamic issues that need to be assessed include the perceived value of the brand, switching cost between brands, and the demand elasticity.

In addition to the price dynamics, marketing managers should also consider other external factors such as:

- **cultural:** consumers' tactics towards price (haggling, bargain-seeking, etc.)
- **economic:** transfer price, inflation, spending power, business cycle stage
- **legal:** government constraints and quotas, black market, credit system

- **state of competition:** market structure, market growth, entry barriers
- **technological:** market readiness, consumer willingness to pay for high-tech goods.

These factors vary from one country to another, and therefore pricing decisions may vary across foreign markets. Despite these differences, individual pricing strategies within a wider region should be harmonized to contribute to the achievement of the organization's overall objectives, and hence company success in international markets.

International distribution decisions

International distribution management focuses on how to ensure that the value exchange in international markets occurs in the right place, at the right time, and in a way that will increase the attractiveness of the company's offerings. International distribution strategy is not only about organizing the flow of products from the home market to foreign ones. It involves a wider range of decisions to support the company's international strategic position. These decisions are strategic in nature compared with the other 4Ps, and normally involve a long-term commitment to the foreign market which may not be easily changed without cost. Signing a long-term contract with a foreign intermediary might not be legally terminable or adaptable without compensation within the time period. These decisions may also influence the firm's ability to develop new markets and affect the level of control over the business.

International distribution strategy will be influenced by the company's international goals and should also be consistent with the type of generic strategy and entry modes adopted. This strategy is also affected by the other marketing mix elements, especially the product nature and features. Large organizations aiming for mass markets arguably pursue intensive distribution strategies to ensure wide market coverage. Pepsi, Mars, Nescafé, and Dove are examples of the brands that are intensively distributed world-wide. On the other hand, companies that produce differentiated products such as Prada and Patek Philippe tend to adopt selective distribution strategies which require a relatively smaller number of foreign intermediaries and/or foreign outlets.

In addition to the internal factors, international distribution strategy is affected by external influences such as:

- infrastructure and transportation systems
- technology development
- economic development
- culture and consumer literacy and perceptions of warranties, delivery, insurance, and after-sales service.

For an effective international distribution strategy, international marketers have to consider the following:

- choosing/designing a distribution system
- selecting and building a relationship with foreign intermediaries
- managing the logistics of physical distribution
- managing the challenges facing the distribution system
- Internet adoption levels.

In general, an organization can choose either an integrated or an independent distribution system. In an **integrated distribution system** the goods go directly from the company to its customers. The company's salesforce or outlets generate sales, administer orders, and deliver the products to the end users. This system is adopted when the products require a high level of after-sales service or the company wants to have full control and the appropriate mechanisms are in place such as Internet ordering and credit cards. On the other hand, an **independent distribution system** allows goods to go indirectly from producers to final customers via a more complex international network that employs many intermediaries and foreign outlets. This system allows firms to benefit from specialist distribution agents in foreign countries.

Many companies find and appoint intermediaries in a foreign market through advertisements in local newspapers or trade journals. Other companies may use local or international exhibitions to assess and select potential intermediaries. When selecting intermediaries, the company should first establish criteria based on its international position, its local position in the foreign market, and the intended distribution strategy. Each company will have its own selection criteria. However, some of the general criteria relate to the intermediary's ability in relation to market coverage, control of the channel activities, financial capacity, and the number of functions provided. A list of 11Cs of the possible factors an organization may consider when selecting the intermediaries has been suggested (Czinkota and Ronkainen, 2013):

- company objectives
- characters of the market
- competition
- culture
- customer characteristics
- coverage needed
- cost
- capital required
- control
- continuity of functions provided
- communication effectiveness.

Managing channels and building relationships with its members in multiple countries can be a challenging task because of the varying business cultures. Motivating channel members is also perplexing as it does not depend on the monetary rewards alone, but includes other activities such as personal training, technical assistance, and offering promotional materials. The company must also establish a communication system to enable channel members to share information and assess the contribution of each member.

International marketing communication decisions

Communication between the company and its stakeholders in a foreign market is particularly challenging because it is influenced by many factors including culture, the customers' literacy level, regulations, technology, infrastructure, and society's view towards foreign companies and their brands. The purpose of international marketing communication is to best position the company and its brands in the foreign market/s. This purpose can be translated into detailed objectives; some of which are product-related while others are for sales generation.

Brand-related objectives in foreign markets

- Introduce and increase level of awareness
- Influence consumers' perceptions of the company and its brand
- Position or re-position the firm's product/brand
- Increase the brand value and enhance product image

Sales-related objectives

- Create and defend market share
- Contact/approach potential consumers in the target segments
- Encourage responses to international promotional campaigns
- Counter-attack or soften competitors' impact

These objectives are achievable if international marketing communications tools and activities are integrated to communicate the corporate identity (where relevant) and brand image through consistent messages, style, and presentation. The Body Shop, for example, promotes its products world-wide with a consistent message showing the company's principal philosophy of opposing testing on animals and sourcing natural products, though it does occasionally focus on specific causes such as anti-weapons testing; for example, nuclear testing by France in the South Pacific has been highlighted by The Body Shop in New Zealand.

Having defined its communication objectives for international markets, the company needs to fulfil these objectives. The regular choice is between a push or a pull strategy. In a **push** strategy, the company directs its promotional activity to retailers and wholesalers to force the product down the distribution channel, while a **pull** strategy aims to contact local consumers directly through advertising, the company website, sales promotion, and social media.

A push-oriented strategy is used when:

- media availability is limited in the foreign market
- the communications budget is limited for international markets
- a market has a variety of languages and ethnic and racial groups
- the channel length is short
- industrial products are directed at intermediaries.

A pull-oriented strategy is used when:

- the channel length is long
- the communications budget is relatively high
- a wide media choice is available
- the market is characterized by self-service shopping behaviour
- consumer goods are directed at the end users.

The debate on the standardization/adaptation of international marketing communications is evident in past research (Andreas and Bowman, 2007; Vrontis et al., 2009; Fastoso and White-lock, 2007, 2012). When considering standardization for communication campaigns, market-ers should think not only about the campaign's content, but also about the concept and media choices. **A standardized campaign** is one which is run across nations using the same concept, setting, theme, appeal, and message, with the possible exception of minor translations or chang-es of colour. Red Bull, for example, uses a fully standardized campaign in all international mar-kets it serves. It uses comic drawings with the same message: 'Red Bull gives you wings'. Only the language in the background may be changed. Some other companies tend to appreciate cultural differences and local tastes and in response alter their campaigns to suit foreign markets. For example, Nestlé uses an adapted campaign when promoting its Nescafé brand in non-Western cultures. Instead of designing the message around the taste and aroma attributes, the drink was promoted as a way to relax and unwind. This campaign proved successful in many Asian and Middle Eastern markets. Other companies may standardize their communication campaign in some countries and adapt it in others. Figure 12.9 shows an example of this approach, with dif-ferent print images of Absolut Vodka adapted to appeal to consumers in different cities rather than countries, with one global image that goes to the whole world.

It can be argued that there is no universal formula that could help organizations to decide whether to standardize or adapt their international communication campaign. A campaign that uses well-known symbols, trademarks, and/or celebrities with some form of back-ground music may prove to be successful in a number of foreign markets. On the other hand, when the use of a specific language (spoken or written) and humour are essential parts of the campaign, then it may not travel. A campaign that refers to a specific theme, person, or event, which is particularly related to a single country, may also not travel.

Social media and international marketing strategy

The advanced technology of the twenty-first century has brought both opportunities and chal-lenges to the global and boundary-less world. These technologies have created three major changes: a shift in activity location from the desktop to the web, a shift in locus of value produc-tion from the firm to the citizen, and a shift in locus of power from the firm to the individual and to communities. There are five axioms (Berthon et al., 2012) to help international market-ing strategists make effective use of social media and constructively engage creative consumers related to the interactivity of web 2.0, social media, and creative consumers.

1. Social media is a function of the technology, culture, and government of a particular country.
2. In the age of social media, local events seldom remain local.
3. In the age of social media, general issues seldom remain general; that is, macro issues tend to be (re)interpreted locally.
4. The actions and creations of creative consumers tend to be a function of the technology, culture, and government of a particular country.
5. Technology tends to be historically dependent; that is, technologies in different countries evolve along unique trajectories due to inertia rather than because they are the optimal solution.

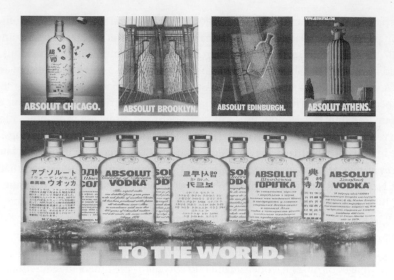

12.9 Standardization/Adaptation of Ad Campaigns

Source: Grouped and tabulated by the authors with permission from The ABSOLUT Company.

In the digital era, marketers are international by nature. Web, social media, email, video, and mobile have no borders. Time zones and distance are no longer barriers to growing businesses globally. Lara Fawzy (2013) provides five tips for success in today's multinational digital marketing, shown in Table 12.4.

The measurement of the effective use of social media in marketing should not rely on traditional metric measures such as ROI (Hoffman and Fodor, 2010). Instead, marketing managers should consider customer motivation to use social media and then measure the customer investments made as they engage with the marketers' brands. Thus the returns from social media investments should not be measured in monetary terms, but in customer behaviour tied to particular applications of social media. Hoffman and Fodor proposed four key motivations (4Cs) that drive customer use of social media: connections, creation, consumption, and control.

Finally, a few words on the successful implementation of an international social media strategy. Berthon et al. (2012), cited earlier, highlight some important barriers.

1. **The attitude and language of engagement is one major barrier**. Marketers will have to listen and learn, rather than preach. In doing so, they will need to adopt the right tone, take the right actions, and learn to engage with (not bully) customers and to take a personal (not an officious) tone in conversations with consumers.

2. **The successful implementation of social media plans has to do with technology**. There is a paradoxical situation in many of today's organizations where they are attempting to engage stakeholders by means of social media, while at the same time prohibiting their own employees from using social networking tools at work.

3. **Bureaucracy is an impediment to the implementation of social media plans**. Social media strategy requires speed and flexibility, but bureaucratic rules can stifle the successful implementation of effective social media plans.

Table 12.4 Five Tips for Success in Multinational Digital Marketing

Listening	The best way to have a conversation in social media is to listen to existing conversations. The same is true for doing business in new markets. Many multinational or large companies have withdrawn from new international markets because they haven't taken the time to understand them. Making assumptions about markets, generalizing, or just not doing the necessary research can be detrimental to the brand and company profits. International marketers need to listen by working with local agencies, sales teams, partners, or research firms, learn from marketing efforts. They also have to test localized integrated campaigns for results on a small sample of the target audience and learn from real-time or speedy results. Finally, they should listen and monitor conversations about their industry and market via social media, have their own channels, and make the listening a priority and acting upon it.
Getting involved	International marketers must not be afraid of getting involved with local initiatives. They may have to enjoy new ways of working with locals and enjoy the involvement in new cultures. They should avoid stereotyping effect and enjoy new experiences whether working virtually or in the local market.
Understand the unspoken rules, be sensitive and aware	Marketers should take time to understand the culture if they are serious about doing business in an international market. They must understand the norms, what's expected, ways of doing things, and what may potentially offend locals.
Localize	The colour red symbolizes luck in China, purity in India, but it symbolizes danger in many Western countries. Nothing with regard to brand acceptance is simply black and white. International marketers must aim to localize the company's campaigns. They must appreciate the local culture, customer pain points, cultural sensitivities, and produce content that resonates with the local audience. The imagery, colours, and copy in local language are the tip of the iceberg, before that comes the proposition, the messaging, and the meaning. Leading social networks like Twitter, Facebook, and LinkedIn allow marketers to use local languages, but for international marketing, hiring a social media manager who's fluent in the local language is advisable.
Superiority	Many emerging markets (e.g. Qatar, UAE) are transforming from natural-resource-based economies to various industries such as real estate, services, and tourism. Businesses in this and other developing countries are seeking to hire marketers from developed countries and to import professional digital skills, so international marketers may import their skills but should not import with it an attitude of superiority.

Source: L. Fawzy (2013), 'Global Thinking: Five Tips for Multinational Digital Marketing', <http://www.mycustomer.com/feature/marketing/global-thinking-five-tips-mutlinational-digital-marketing/164738>

4. **The lack of IT and communication skills is an obvious barrier to social media plan implementation.** If these skills are not included in fundamental training, a company's reputation can easily be at risk on social media. There is a clear consensus among social media experts that establishing social media guidelines and training employees within those guidelines is paramount to running a successful company.

5. **Many organizations are still oblivious of what has been termed the 'digital divide',** a situation in which many parts of the population—even in developed countries—do not have access to basic computing tools such as desktops and broadband Internet access, let alone more sophisticated social networking tools.

6. **Senior decision-makers in some organizations still see social media as the wasteful pastime of teenagers.** For social media plans to succeed, they need the buy-in and support of senior managers.

The latest thinking: 'guarded globalization'

Policy-makers in many developing countries are intervening to create 'uneven playing fields' that give domestic players an advantage over foreign competitors. The governments of those countries perceive many sectors to be of great strategic importance and deter foreign companies from entering them. State capitalism distorts the workings of free markets and thus affects globalization considerably (Bremmer, 2014). Bremmer has defined this phenomenon as a new era of 'guarded globalization', and reviewed the new risks associated with it.

- Governments monitor and dictate prices in key industries.
- Many emerging market governments, worried about the flow of information, keep tech companies under their thumb.
- Telecommunications is seen as a highly strategic industry, so is controlled by local players.
- Many countries rely on the domestic banking system to finance budget deficits, so they fear that deregulation will have a destabilizing effect.
- Politicians may try to use multinationals to promote personal agendas or deflect public anger.
- Challenges to foreign companies can now come from state-backed investigative journalists.

Anticipating the risks in foreign markets and developing creative strategies that combat them will become increasingly important capabilities in the next decade. Bremmer (2014) proposed some international strategies/approaches to help multinationals to manage the risk of 'guarded globalization'. These are outlined in Table 12.5.

In the same vein, Lou Cooper (2010) suggested five strategies that can help multinationals embrace the new challenges of globalization.

1. **Build a strong consistent brand culture.** In the past, a rigid corporate structure was an important element of the global brand. However, in recent years building a consistent and strong brand culture that remains familiar to consumers wherever it is in the world has become a priority.

2. **Be borderless in your marketing.** With the abundance of digital platforms, it is no longer possible for brands to follow different brand strategies in different countries. Companies are being forced to adopt a more unified marketing approach. Marketers need to rethink the slogan of Theodore Levitt's (1983) 'think global, act local'. It doesn't work in a digital age in the same way.

3. **Build yourself an internal hub.** The need for a unified marketing team is more important than ever. Involving marketers from across the global brand in the overall marketing strategy will engender overall cohesion.

4. **Adopt a 'glocal' structure.** Two major global brands have recently challenged the local marketing structure that has become the norm. Instead, they are adopting a more

regional structure in a bid to become more unified. Coke has scrapped its GB marketing director and simplified its operations in Europe by reducing the number of business units it has from ten to four. Similarly, Kraft has decided that while a GB marketing director position will exist, marketing will be led centrally from Europe.

5. **Make consumers your co-creators.** Durex's Anna Valle thinks that social media has helped to create the perfect environment for interactions: 'It's all about consumers advising each other, talking to each other, as well as talking to the brand. It all happens on a global scale and it all happens at the same time'.

With brands increasingly crossing international borders via the Internet, marketers may need to fine tune their strategies to ensure that their brands are making the most of the global market.

Table 12.5 International Strategies for Managing the Risk of 'Guarded Globalization'

Stay at home	While the importance of keeping out of foreign countries is obvious for companies in the defence industry, the strategy is spreading to other sectors, such as retail, which have become politically sensitive in many emerging markets.
Become more 'strategic' at home	Some companies choose to boost their value to their home government instead of looking to create value abroad. They campaign for the state to view their sector or products as strategic so that they can keep out foreign competition or boost profits by striking a closer relationship with the government.
Use the state to fight other states	Some companies may have the means to use government-to-government relations to sort out problems. For example, BP, which had operated in the UAE since 1931, ran into trouble in 2012 when British politicians and officials publicly criticized the UAE for closing the offices of pro-democracy groups and arresting political activists. The dispute undoubtedly contributed to the July 2012 decision by the UAE government to exclude BP from the 2014 licensing round of the largest onshore oil concession.
Strike alliances	Although joint ventures haven't been popular for some years, many companies will need to partner—and share profits—with local players in return for safe passage.
Add value to the state	A single-product company must often find a new way to add value in the host country. Just a few years after entering China, IMAX volunteered to help China's state-run media achieve global production values. It's hard to imagine that Beijing doesn't remember that assistance when deciding which foreign films can enter China and how many new theatres IMAX can open.
Become too diversified to fail	Many developing countries offer so many opportunities that a multi-business strategy can be compelling for multinationals. GE, for example, has dozens of investments in China, spanning different sectors and time horizons.
Build it so that you can stay	Fast expanding sub-Saharan African countries (e.g. Nigeria, Ghana and Kenya), which continually deal with traffic congestion, blackouts, and other infrastructure failures, work hard to attract private investment into infrastructure sectors.
Capitalize on state capitalism	Another useful strategy to withstand new levels of scrutiny by host states is to commit to hiring local workers and using local materials. The Brazilian government expects large projects to source components from local producers, and it favours domestic manufacturers in public procurement bids. In Africa, there are less stringent benchmarks for local jobs and sourcing, but countries across the continent want their citizens to share in the gains from foreign investment.

Source: Summarized and tabulated by the authors from I. Bremmer (2014), 'The new rules of globalization', *Harvard Business Review*, 92(1/2), pp. 103–7.

Conclusion

International marketing strategy aims to position a company and strengthen its presence in the international marketing environment. Taking a strategic approach to international marketing is necessary for organizations to ensure effective operations. The international marketing decision-making process is a systematic approach that relies upon information-based frameworks to guide the organization's development and implementation of appropriate and relevant strategy. Part of this process is the selection of foreign country markets to enter and the choice of investment (entry) mode/s. At the heart of the process is the design and implementation of international marketing mix strategies. One of the fundamental challenges an organization faces when developing its international mix strategies is the extent of standardization/adaptation of the marketing functions and activities. The challenge to managers is rarely whether to choose standardization or adaptation, but more normally how to find the optimal balance between these two approaches.

Summary

This chapter has discussed in detail the international marketing strategy covering the key marketing activities that organizations should undertake when going international or expanding their businesses across borders. It presented the key factors an organization needs to investigate when considering expansion in international markets. Then a discussion was presented on the three most important international marketing decisions of what foreign countries to enter, what generic strategy to adopt, and how best to invest in these countries. A review was also provided about international marketing mix strategies and the standardization versus adaptation debate. It was pointed out that designing and implementing international marketing mix strategies varies from one organization to another depending on the international goals and the level of commitment afforded to the international market/s concerned. The chapter concluded with a detailed discussion of social media and its impact on international marketing strategy.

Key terms

- **Adaptation:** an approach to international marketing that aims to promote flexibility by varying the marketing mix elements across markets and nations to satisfy local tastes and conditions.
- **Country of origin (COO):** the perception and attitudes of consumers towards products, brands, or services based on the country of origin where these brands were originally invented and/or produced.
- **Country screening:** a process that aims to produce a shortlist of potentially attractive markets that offer the greatest potential for a company's profitable expansion in international markets.

- **Exporting:** a foreign entry mode that an organization uses to sell its products, manufactured in its home market without any major modifications and/or adaptation, in a foreign market.

- **Foreign direct investment (FDI):** an entry mode that involves the highest level of involvement and commitment by a company to manufacture and market its product offerings in an individual foreign market or region.

- **Foreign investment (entry) modes:** the various approaches available to organizations to invest in the chosen foreign market/s.

- **Franchising:** a type of contract in which a franchiser provides a franchisee a 'package' including not only know-how and trademarks, but also exclusive rights to use logos and brand names, financial and management assistance, and joint advertising.

- **International marketing analysis:** a key area of the international marketing decision-making process that aims to examine the international marketing environment to identify where the key opportunities exist and the challenges associated with them.

- **International marketing choices:** a key area of the international marketing decision-making process that aims to guide organizations through the various international marketing decisions/choices in order to strengthen their competitive position in foreign markets.

- **International marketing strategy:** a process of planning and implementing the marketing functions and activities across foreign country markets in order to position and strengthen the company presence in the international marketing environment.

- **Standardization:** an approach to international marketing that aims to enforce similarity and reduce variations of the marketing mix across markets and nations.

Discussion questions

1. Critically evaluate the pros and cons of the country screening process and assess its validity in real business world.

2. Comment on the current debate of standardization/adaptation in international marketing and provide evidence to support your view.

3. What are the factors influencing a company's choice of foreign investment (entry) modes?

4. To what extent do you think that a standardized advertising campaign can travel well around the world? Why?

5. What is your own perception of the Fair Trade concept? Comment on its validity in less developed countries.

Online resource centre

Visit the Online Resource Centre for this book for lots of interesting additional material at: <**www.oxfordtextbooks.co.uk/orc/west3e/**>

References and further reading

Berthon, Pierre R., Leyland F. Pitt, Kirk Plangger, and Daniel Shapiro (2012), 'Marketing Meets Web 2.0, Social Media, and Creative Consumers: Implications for International Marketing Strategy', *Business Horizons*, 55, pp. 261–71.

Birnik, Andreas and Cliff Bowman (2007), 'Marketing Mix Standardization in Multinational Corporations: A Review of the Evidence', *International Journal of Management Reviews,* 9(4), pp. 303–24.

Bremmer, I. (2014), 'The New Rules of Globalization', *Harvard Business Review*, 92(1/2), pp. 103–7.

Cooper, Lou (2010), 'Five Strategies for a Successful Global Brand', *Marketing Week*, (1 July 2010), <http://www.marketingweek.co.uk/analysis/essential-reads/five-strategies-for-a-successful-global-brand/3015220.article>

Czinkota, Michael R. and Ikka A. Ronkainen (2013). *International Marketing*, 10th edn (Boston, MA: Cengage Learning).

D'Andrea, G., D. Marcotte, and G.D. Morrison (2010), 'Let Emerging Market Customers Be Your Teachers', *Harvard Business Review*, 88(12), pp. 115–20.

Dietz, Miklos, Philipp Härle, and Tamas Nagy (2013), 'A New Trend Line for Global Banking', *McKinsey Quarterly*, No. 2, pp. 18–19.

Dobbs, R., J. Remes, and S. Smit (2013), 'The Shifting Global Corporate Landscape', *McKinsey Quarterly*, No. 4, pp. 16–17.

Efrat, K. and A. Shoham (2013), 'The Interaction Between Environment and Strategic Orientation in Born Globals' Choice of Entry Mode', *International Marketing Review*, 30(6), pp. 536–58.

Fastoso, F. and J. Whitelock (2007), 'International Advertising Strategy: The Standardisation Question in Manager Studies. Patterns in Four Decades of Past Research and Directions for Future Knowledge Advancement', *International Marketing Review*, 24(5), pp. 591–605.

Fastoso, F. and J. Whitelock (2012), 'The Implementation of International Advertising Strategies: An Exploratory Study in Latin America', *International Marketing Review*, 29(3), pp. 313–35.

Fawzy, L. (2013), 'Global Thinking: Five Tips for Multinational Digital Marketing', <http://www.mycustomer.com/feature/marketing/global-thinking-five-tips-mutlinational-digital-marketing/164738>

Gabardi, E., T. Huang, and S. Sha (2013), 'Getting to Know China's Premium-car Market', *McKinsey Quarterly*, No. 3, pp. 18–19.

Gaston-Breton, C. and O. M. Martín (2011), 'International Market Selection and Segmentation: A Two-stage Model', *International Marketing Review*, 28(3), pp. 267–90.

Green, A., C. Kehoe, and F. Sedjelmaci (2014), 'Uncovering Hidden Investment Opportunities in Africa', *McKinsey Quarterly*, No. 1, pp. 24–5.

Harrell, Gilbert D. and Richard O. Kiefer (1993), 'Multinational Market Portfolios in Global Strategy Development', *International Marketing Review*, 10 (1), pp. 60–72.

Hoffman, Donna L. and Marek Fodor (2010), 'Can You Measure the ROI of Your Social Media Marketing?', *MIT Sloan Management Review*, 52(1), pp. 41–9.

Ibeh, Kevin, Essam Ibrahim, and Patrick Ezepue (2007), 'Factors Stimulating Initial Export Activity: any Difference for Sub-Saharan Firms?', *Journal of African Business*, 8(2), pp. 7–26.

Ibrahim, Essam and P. Sothornnopabutr (2006), 'Country-of-Origin and Consumer Evaluation of Mobile Handsets: a Comparative Study of Scotland and Thailand', *Journal of Customer Behaviour*, 5(2), pp. 167–96.

Koschate-Fischer, N., A. Diamantopoulos, and K. Oldenkotte (2012), 'Are Consumers Really Willing to Pay More for a Favorable Country Image? A Study of Country-of-Origin Effects on Willingness to Pay', *Journal of International Marketing*, 20(1), pp. 19–41.

Levitt, T. (1983), 'The Globalisation of Markets', *Harvard Business Review*, 61, pp. 92–101.

Papadopoulos, N. and O. M. Martín (2011), 'International Market Selection and Segmentation: Perspectives and Challenges', *International Marketing Review*, 28(2), pp. 132–49.

Ramamurti, Ravi (2012), 'Competing with Emerging Market Multinationals', *Business Horizons*, 55, pp. 241–9.

Rohit, Deshpandé (2010). 'Why You Aren't Buying Venezuelan Chocolate'. *Harvard Business Review*, 88(12), pp. 25–7.

Root, Franklin R. (1994), *Entry Strategies for International Markets* (San Francisco, CA: Jossey-Bass).

Schmid, Stefan and Thomas Kotulla (2011), '50 Years of Research on International Standardization and Adaptation—From a Systematic Literature Analysis to a Theoretical Framework', *International Business Review*, 20(5), pp. 491–507.

Vrontis, Demetris, Alkis Thrassou, and Iasonas Lamprianou (2009), 'International Marketing Adaptation Versus Standardisation of Multinational Companies', *International Marketing Review*, 26 (4/5), pp. 477–500.

Xuehua Wang and Zhilin Yang (2008), 'Does Country-of-Origin Matter in the Relationship Between Brand Personality and Purchase Intention in Emerging Economies? Evidence from China's Auto Industry', *International Marketing Review*, 25(4), pp. 458–74.

 End of Chapter 12 case study   Branding Las Vegas internationally

Introduction

Las Vegas is one of the most famous vacation destinations in the world, hosting nearly 40 million visitors in 2012, including over 6 million international tourists. Las Vegas is known as an exciting city where visitors can gamble in casinos, relax with friends and relatives, attend business conventions, revel at nightclubs, enjoy luxury shopping, and watch first-rate entertainment. There are also popular places nearby for sightseeing, including the Hoover Dam, the Grand Canyon, and Lake Mead.

Gaming revenue and the percentage of occupied hotel rooms both showed positive growth between 2010 and 2012. Gaming revenue grew from $8.9 billion in 2010 to $9.4 billion in 2012. The US national average hotel occupancy rate was 61.4 per cent in 2012, and the Las Vegas hotel occupancy rate was considerably higher at 87.4 per cent for the same year. Figure C12.1 shows the time series data for the number of visitors to Las Vegas between 2000 and 2012.

Competitive environment

Las Vegas faces competition from numerous alternatives with the increase of national and global gaming. Macau in China and Singapore are two emerging locations where gambling is growing as a destination. The legalization of online gaming in the US has also changed the competitive environment for casinos in Las Vegas. During the recent economic recession, Las Vegas saw a decrease in tourism as gamers chose to visit local and regional casinos.

Travel to Las Vegas

McCarran International Airport serves the Las Vegas area and is the fastest growing airport in the US. In 2012 the airport opened a new $2.4 billion state-of-the-art international air terminal, with 14 gates. This is the largest capital improvement project in the airport's nearly 64 year history. This airport expansion supports the growth in the number of hotel rooms and non-stop flights arriving in Las Vegas. Between 2000 and 2012 the city's hotel room inventory grew by over 26,000

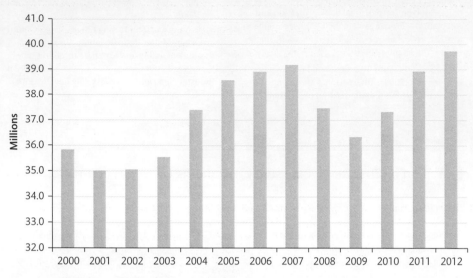

C12.1 Las Vegas Visitors, 2000 to 2012

additional rooms. McCarran International Airport receives passengers on 144 non-stop flights from 16 foreign cities.

Growth strategy

International visitors are important to Las Vegas's growth. According to the Las Vegas Casino and Hotel Market Outlook, the total number of visitors in 2012 grew to 39.7 million, 17 per cent of whom were international tourists. The Las Vegas Convention and Visitors Authority (LVCVA) promotes the Las Vegas brand globally with the support of 15 partner offices representing more than 70 countries, and set a goal to increase the international traveller's market share to 30 per cent over the next 10 years. Table C12.1 lists total visitors and percentage international visitors to Las Vegas between 2007 and 2012.

Based on data from the LVCVA, the average domestic traveller spends $590 during their trip to Las Vegas, compared with $1,146 by foreign travellers. When it comes to shopping, domestic visitors spend an average of $99, while international visitors spend $291. In 2012, 70 per cent of foreign visitors to Las Vegas were from Canada, Mexico, and Great Britain. Las Vegas planners also hope to bring in more visitors from Brazil, Russia, India, and China. Demand is strong for tourists from the UK to visit Las Vegas, and both BA and Virgin Atlantic offer direct flights to McCarran International Airport. Australia, Germany, France, China, and South Korea each showed marked visitor increases in 2010.

Travel constraints

According to a *Las Vegas Sun* article, international destinations like Las Vegas face a challenge in attracting overseas tourists due to stringent visa regulations. In developing markets such as Brazil and China, tourists who want to travel to the US are forced to wait an average of 90 days or more to have an in-person interview at the American consulate to apply for a tourist visa. Extra costs and long waits for the visa process discourage international travellers from visiting US cities such as Las Vegas.

Brand USA, a public–private partnership with the mission of promoting international travel to the US, has proposed alternatives to the in-person interview process to obtain a US travel

Table C12.1 Las Vegas Tourism

Year	Total Visitors Millions	Per Cent International Visitors	International Visitors Millions
2007	39.20	12%	4.70
2008	37.48	15%	5.62
2009	36.35	14%	5.09
2010	37.34	18%	6.72
2011	38.93	16%	6.23
2012	39.73	17%	6.75

visa. The group was established after President Barack Obama signed the Travel Promotion Act in March 2010. Brand USA has proposed three ways to increase inbound international travel that include: visa waiver programmes, visa video-conference interviews, and better resource allocation. As of 2012, 36 countries, primarily in Europe, have visa waiver programmes. Tourism data illustrates that countries with visa waiver programmes have the highest number of travellers to the US.

Las Vegas advertising programme

The iconic advertising slogan' What happens in Vegas, stays in Vegas' celebrated its tenth anniversary in 2012. The humorous tag line exemplifies the exuberant Las Vegas experience as an escape from everyday norms that makes this location different from other destinations. The award-winning 'What happens here' promotion has been the most successful and popular ad campaign for the LVCVA for driving tourist traffic. The ad campaign utilizes a multimedia approach that includes television, print, online, and social media.

Exporting the Las Vegas ad campaign

According to an article in *Adweek*, the Las Vegas brand faces a challenge when communicating in global markets with its message of risqué adult abandon. Tourism officials learned it was necessary to adjust marketing campaigns to align with local mores and values. Focus groups with international travellers were used to understand how to tailor the message for global audiences. Results illustrated that the current ads were not risqué enough for the UK. It was also found that the campaign needed to be more conservative in Mexico and worked well in Western Canada. The marketing firm that handles the Las Vegas account, R & R Partners, customizes the volume of edginess up or down depending on the cultural sensitivities in a target region.

Discussion questions

1. Develop a SWOT analysis for Las Vegas based on its international marketing strategies.

Strengths	Weaknesses
Opportunities	Threats

2. Using the Las Vegas visitor volume data in Table C12.2 (plotted in the column graph in Figure C12.1), calculate the percentage change for each year and make a prediction for 2013. How did you make this forecast?

Table C12.2 Las Vegas Visitor Volume

Year	Las Vegas Visitors Millions	Percentage Change
2000	35.8	--
2001	35.0	--
2002	35.1	--
2003	35.5	--
2004	37.4	--
2005	38.6	--
2006	38.9	--
2007	39.2	--
2008	37.5	--
2009	36.4	--
2010	37.3	--
2011	38.9	--
2012	39.7	--
2013		

3. How can the Las Vegas Convention and Visitors Authority attract a greater percentage of international tourists?

Source: This case was prepared by Professor Hope Corrigan, Marketing Department, Sellinger School of Business and Management, Loyola University Maryland, Baltimore, MD, USA

Social and ethical strategies

Learning Objectives

1. To appreciate the nature of social marketing and its implications.
2. To be able to differentiate between the interests of shareholders as opposed to the firm's stakeholders.
3. To see the importance of environmental/green marketing and social marketing as firm initiatives.
4. To be able to discuss ethics and moral judgement and the firm's actions as a morally responsible organization in society.
5. To be able to describe the various facets of corporate social responsibility.
6. To be able to recognize philanthropic activities and initiatives and cause-related marketing strategic choices.
7. To know the ways in which a firm can get involved in socially responsible activities to improve its standing as a hands-on and caring community citizen.
8. To be able to describe the various forms of greenwashing and appreciate ways in which countries are demanding substantiation of environmental claims.
9. To be aware of the ways in which the CSR strategist can make social responsibility meaningful for the firm by making it a strategic imperative as opposed to an act of compliance.
10. To be able to use the virtue matrix as a means of judging the profitability associated with social activism.
11. To have a grasp of the various issues involved with the new landscape of social media.
12. To appreciate the newest initiatives for CSR strategists to improve their performance involving the UPS model for sustainability and how to make cause marketing work.

Chapter at a Glance

I. Introduction
1 Overview and strategy blueprint
2 Marketing strategy: analysis and perspectives

II. Where are we now?
3 Environmental and internal analysis: market information and intelligence

III. Where do we want to be?
4 Strategic marketing decisions, choices, and mistakes
5 Segmentation, targeting, and positioning strategies
6 Branding strategies
7 Relational and sustainability strategies

V. Did we get there?
14 Strategy implementation, control, and metrics

IV. How will we get there?
8 Product innovation and development strategies
9 Service marketing strategies
10 Pricing and distribution strategies
11 Marketing communications strategies
12 International marketing strategies
13 Social and ethical strategies

 Case study: Watch out in the afternoon when the moral slope gets slipperier

A recent article by Maryam Kouchaki (2014) in *Harvard Business Review* focused on a study that she undertook with a colleague, Isaac Smith, to study ethical decision-making at different times of the day. The study was undertaken as a decision-making study, but it really focused on individuals and their potential use of dishonest behaviour. It was set up in such a way that the test subjects could actually make money if they lied. The original finding was that 43 per cent of all participants actually lied to achieve monetary gains in the morning while 65 per cent lied in the afternoon. Dr Kouchaki then replicated the experiment and found that people were 20–50 per cent more likely to be dishonest in the afternoon as a result of the depletion of the necessary resources for maintaining self-control. What she found was that increasing levels of fatigue could break down the walls of moral defences. In particular she found that people who usually behave more ethically were the most susceptible to moral failure. People get tired out after all the stress associated with their daily corporate activities, so by the afternoon they are tiring and lower their moral walls. Kuchaki recognizes that there are both morning people and afternoon people. Morning people tend to be more alert in the earlier hours of the day, while afternoon people may not get going and get into their stride until the afternoon. The law of averages points to the fact that most people face the slippery slope of moral judgement and potential unethical activity and are more likely to slip in the afternoon. What seems to matter most is that when self-interest conflicts with the drive to be ethical, it is self-control which is necessary to maintain moral and ethical behaviour. The ironic thing is that those who are more morally challenged are less affected by this natural depletion than those with high moral standards. The point is that those with lower moral standards have less to lose. This obviously raises serious questions about long work days with insufficient breaks.

What does the company do as a result of these findings? Isn't hard work a sign of commitment to the company and a show of loyalty and devotion? Shouldn't hard work be rewarded? One possible way to handle this problem is to ensure that those job tasks that contain important moral components should preferably be moved to the morning rather than to the afternoon. At the very least, Kuchaki says that, these should not be assigned as late-in-the-day activities. The point is not necessarily to establish a series of onerous rules of behaviour but to limit the opportunities for immorality at the times when they are most likely to occur. She points out that in a variety of cultures afternoon breaks are a normal part of the work day. Breaks can actually serve as opportunities for replenishing diminished energy levels. As she explains, self-control acts somewhat like a muscle and needs to build up its strength again after use. Suggestions for companies involve providing breaks, rest opportunities, and even afternoon snacks.

Introduction

Individuals and their respective companies do not compete against others in a vacuum. The wants and needs of society and the importance of doing business in an ethical and non-harmful manner are important contextual considerations. Firms must not only produce excellent goods and services and keep customers happy, but must also be concerned with their relationship with society at large as well as with the environment. The marketing concept has evolved into market orientation, and firms are more heavily focused on the wants and needs of consumers, but this is no longer sufficient. There is a broader context in which the firm operates, and the health and well-being of society and consumers must be taken into consideration for the firm to be seen as a good community citizen. Consumers not only expect that corporations will operate legally and fairly, but they also want them to act ethically, help charitable causes, clean up the environment, and improve conditions for citizens locally, regionally, nationally, and in some cases internationally. Sustainability has become a necessity along with managing the carbon footprint.

The firm and its role in society

An important starting point for understanding corporate responsibilities in a societal context is the determination of whom the firm is actually serving with its operations. Is it the shareholder or is it a wider variety of publics? This determination will lead the company to undertake very different strategic initiatives.

The nature of the firm's stakeholders

One can see in all of this a potential conundrum in that on the one hand there are those who follow the philosophy that the social responsibility of the firm is to make the most money it legally can for its **shareholders**. The other side argues that being a good citizen and giving money to needy organizations or undertaking community improvement projects by nature reduces profits or forces firms to increase retail prices to cover the incurred costs. To understand the potential benefits of **corporate social responsibility** (CSR), one has to be careful to examine all of the relevant constituencies affected by the firm's actions (Snider et al., 2003). The important distinction here really lies in whom the firm sees as its important constituencies. If shareholders are the only public they are concerned with, then all actions undertaken must be done in a way that will maximize return for shareholders. This perspective would argue strongly against any expenditure without proven profitability. One could argue that any community investment expenditure or donation to a charitable organization would be seen as a potential drain on company financial performance. If, on the other hand, the firm considers that there are a variety of publics that must be considered, then it might strategically make a very different set of choices.

Stakeholders are all those groups or publics that interact with and are affected by the operations of the firm. These publics include employees, partners, suppliers, customers, community members, governmental agencies, and social activist groups. If the firm takes the view that all of these groups have a stake in the operations of the firm, then their concerns must also be considered in corporate strategies and CSR initiatives. It may be that value perceived by some of these stakeholder groups may precede and in some cases drive improvements in shareholder wealth (Snider et al., 2003). As a result, stakeholder theory serves as a better framework for examining how the corporation can effectively position itself in its social context. The various stakeholder constituencies are shown in Figure 13.1.

13.1 Various Company Stakeholders

Social issues with regard to marketing have three important facets which will be discussed in this chapter: the use of marketing to reduce societal problems (social marketing), the need for the firm to operate in an ethical manner, and the importance of the company and its representatives acting in socially responsible ways (corporate social responsibility). Each of these will be discussed in detail.

Social marketing

Social marketing is the application of marketing principles and practices to help with the resolution of public health and social problems. This involves the use of marketing to help public policy-makers change public behaviours and practices considered to be harmful to health and societal well-being. The first suggestions for this appeared in the marketing literature in the early 1970s, and today there are a vast number of public awareness and improvement campaigns in evidence in many different countries. Public service announcements (PSAs) abound in the UK, the US, and Australia, to name a few. In the UK, for example, media audiences are constantly being exposed to campaigns which raise awareness of various health issues like cancer risks and self-examination, the dangers of drink-driving, the problem of teenage pregnancies, the need for children and adults to exercise and eat healthy to stay fit, and the harm associated with drug use. These are common societal problems, and public policy-makers in these countries have turned to marketing tools to get their messages to their constituencies to encourage healthier lifestyles and improved living conditions. Why has this come about? Two driving concerns for businesses have been dictated by public policy-makers concerned with safety and well-being. These concerns are the health and well-being of the consumer and the protection of the environment.

Consumerism and marketing

Two important facilitators for social improvements have been the internal pressures in a variety of countries to address consumerism and environmentalism. In the 1950s, when the marketing concept first appeared in the literature, the concern was to shift the focus to satisfying the wants of consumers and their need to be able to differentiate one firm from its competitors, and to ensure consumer choice. This made appealing to the consumer a first priority, but major criticisms of the marketing concept centred around the fact that profit was the overriding purpose rather than consideration of the welfare of the consumer.

It's a highly controversial area. One person's consumerism is another person's needed good or service. Also, the correlation might work the other way. Marketing might be a by-product of consumerism! There is no doubt that historically some form of consumption has played a central role in political, social, and economic development. Setting aside such contentious thoughts(!) there is no doubt that consumerism became an important topic particularly after a variety of books appeared touting the potential harm to the consumer that could be brought about by corporate mistakes. The seminal book *The Hidden Persuaders,* by Vance Packard, discussed the potential of marketers to manipulate the consumer by affecting consumer choice with such unsavoury methods as subliminal manipulation (affecting consumers' perceptions when they were not consciously aware that this was happening). The book was published in the late 1950s, and despite its lack of empirical evidence or scientific approach, the outcry from the public led to the suggestion that marketers were potentially able to brainwash consumers to do what they wanted them to do. While subliminal manipulation was never proved to have a significant effect on subconscious consumer choice or to be widely practised (it is outlawed), the mere idea was so onerous that any evidence found suggesting the use of it proved highly controversial.

The Hidden Persuaders was followed in the 1960s by the book *Unsafe at any Speed*, by Ralph Nader, which highlighted the dangers inherent in the use of the Chevrolet Motors Corvair, which had caused injuries or death for a number of users. This was evidence-based, unlike *Hidden Persuaders*, and made the powerful point that consumers were potentially being harmed by using unsafe products. This was not just grounds for concern, but in a number of countries governmental watchdog agencies were established to protect consumers from these 'untrustworthy' corporations. How has this helped the consumer? This vigilance on the part of companies and public policy-makers has raised the quality of consumer goods and made the safety of consumers a primary issue. However, it remains an issue in developing markets such as India, China, and Brazil, where government and industry regulation is often lighter and where consumers are less savvy and knowledgeable about marketing.

Environmentalism, sustainability, and marketing

This wave of building consumer protectionism was further fuelled by concerns over the environment since the 1960s. The 'pumping' of pollutants into the environment and the use of non-biodegradable materials in packaging roused further outcry from the public. Environmentalism became a major governmental concern in many markets across the world, and again watchdog agencies were created in many countries to monitor the activities of businesses.

Organizations have been rightly held liable for actions which would potentially harm the environment, and green or environmentally sound marketing has become a major strategic initiative. What exactly is **environmental/green marketing**? Green marketing involves the actions undertaken by the firm or donations that are aimed at improving or preserving the environment surrounding the firm. Green marketing focuses on the idea of keeping the environment clean and green. This often entails reducing or eliminating corporate pollution. 'It pays to be green.'

One can see many examples where the concerns of the environmentalists are being strategically built into corporate plans. McDonalds was criticized for using non-biodegradable styrofoam packaging. The company began to replace the plastic with paper packaging and was seen as more environmentally friendly.

Take the case of the New Zealand government. It decided that since it was known for its clean and green environment, anything made or connected with New Zealand would benefit from that association. So fruits, vegetables, lamb, agricultural equipment, and other products were automatically tagged with the 'Made in New Zealand' label, which signalled environmental responsibility. There was great synergy strategically in undertaking this, since New Zealand found that its competitive advantage lay in its agriculture.

Firms have been obliged to examine the extent of their 'carbon footprint' as well as to seek ways to replenish resources depleted by their production processes. This focus on replenishment and minimizing harm to the environment is referred to as 'sustainability'. Setting marketing strategies that create sustainable environmental uses are vitally important for corporate success.

Sustainability can lead to profitability (Haanaes et al., 2013).

- The Egyptian firm Sekem, founded in 1977, was the first organic farm. The company focused on improvement of cultivation practices and moved into growing organic cotton in 1990. The timing was excellent as worldwide demand for organic products was beginning to catch on. Sekem's farming methods helped to reclaim land from the Sahara which had been spreading into the Nile Delta. These practices allowed the absorption of greater amounts of carbon dioxide from the atmosphere which reduced the level of greenhouse gases, and they found that cotton crops actually required anywhere from 20–40 per cent less water.

- Another example is the Zhangzidao Fishery Group in Dalian, China. They went back to past practices and adapted them to create an integrated multitrophic aquaculture (IMTA), which created economies of scale by systematizing sealife farming by combining different species into a balanced ecosystem. This combining of scallops, sea urchins, abalone, and sea cucumbers, along with other species, allowed the company to cut down on the amount of fish food required, which reduced costs while seeing significant gains in overall yields. The company experienced a compound annual growth rate of 40 per cent.

- Then there is Florida Ice & Farm, located in San Jose, Costa Rica, their largest beverage bottler. The company saw great benefits from its regular monitoring and repair of water leaks in its production system which allowed it to eventually become completely water-neutral in the short span of four years. The company saw a compound annual growth rate from 2006 to 2010 of 25 per cent.

- What about Shree Cement Company from Beawar, India? The company began by looking for ways to reduce electricity needs for production, and eventually they were able to find ways to improve the effectiveness of their kilns while also recycling hot exhaust to fuel an electrical generating plant. As a result of its innovative efforts, Shree now uses 9 per cent less energy than other Indian manufacturers and almost 15 per cent less than the global average. The company experienced a compound annual growth rate of 50 per cent from 2005 to 2009.

- Finally, there is New Britain Palm Oil in Mosa, Papua New Guinea, which processes organic oils, sugar, and meat products. The company was concerned about its reliance on dangerous pesticides and developed a series of natural alternatives while increasing production yields. An expansion plan undertaken involved leasing fields from farmers rather than purchasing them outright, and this helped reduce the poverty levels of the country while building strong relationships with the local communities. Its efforts have allowed a reduction of almost 50 per cent in the amounts of pesticides used while increasing yields at 1.6 per cent per year for the past 30 years. This resulted in a compound annual growth rate of 30 per cent for 2006–2010.

These are great examples of businesses in developing markets focusing on sustainable practices and seeing significant improvements in environmental conditions while producing profits and meaningful economies of scale. But environmental causes and actions on behalf of consumers may not by themselves be sufficient, or fit with corporate strategy. Companies will not only need to act as stewards of the environment and protect consumers, but they must also ensure that they act in an ethical manner.

Corporate ethics and ethical codes of conduct

At one time being a good corporation meant that you operated in a reasonable manner, adhering to laws and regulations, but as corporations like Enron, MCI, Parmalat, and Credit Lyonnais were seen as violating public trust, the issue of ethicality was added to the set of requirements for businesses. A 2002 Gallup poll found that 90 per cent of Americans surveyed felt that those running corporations could not be trusted to look after the best interests of their employees (Handy, 2002). Only 18 per cent of those surveyed believed that companies spent a significant amount of effort looking after their shareholders, and 43 per cent perceived that senior executives were only concerned with their own well-being. Moreover a British survey found that 95 per cent of respondents surveyed believed that senior executives were looking after their own self-interest.

Evidence has been found that as many as 40 of the Fortune 100 most important US businesses had committed actions that would be considered to be unethical (Clement, 2006). These actions included anti-trust practices, fraud, discrimination, patent infringement, making unreported payments to executives, and various other infractions. This is representative of a potentially much wider serious problem, and the first step in eliminating the problem involves companies taking a harder stance on acting in an ethically responsible manner.

What is 'ethics'? It is the set of moral principles or values that shape the actions of either an individual or a group of individuals. Ethical principles therefore set a standard for behaviour in a society. Legality sets the foundation for what behaviours are seen as lawful or unlawful, but ethics focuses more on moral judgement, and the question becomes 'is something the right thing to do from a moral standpoint as opposed to whether it is lawful or not'. The difficulty is that certain activities that are seen as lawful may not actually be seen as ethical or morally appropriate, and certain activities that are seen as unlawful may not be morally inappropriate.

Why do we need ethics? Because there are a number of examples of businesses that have acted in ways that have damaged public trust. Scandals throughout the global business community have served to weaken consumer trust and belief in big business. Ethicality and the adoption of codes of ethical conduct serve to signal to the public that the companies that adopt them will not countenance unethical behaviour. With ethics the question is not whether an action is legal or illegal, it is whether the action is morally right or wrong. Morals are basically sets of rules derived from cultural norms. Moral judgement is the framework of beliefs upon which the individual makes judgements on whether an action is morally appropriate or not. Different cultures have achieved different levels of moral judgement, which affects their views on whether certain actions are ethical or unethical.

Cultural differences in ethical predisposition can be seen clearly when collectivist cultures are compared with individualistic cultures (Ford et al., 1997). Japanese managers coming from a collectivist orientation must undertake actions that benefit the group as a whole before they can even think about their own personal aggrandizement. Individualistic

American managers look towards benefiting themselves first and secondarily looking to benefit the group. These differences in perspective and expectation can create difficulties when addressing the issue of the ethicality of certain actions. As an example, a Japanese firm may use individuals to do intelligence gathering about competitor actions using any means necessary to find information that will help their company, but if the organization is put in a better position as a result of the information gathering, even if the actions were not morally defensible, the group benefits—and the individual benefits because the group benefits. The danger would be if the Japanese employees were actually caught in the act of using inappropriate means to get the information; they would actually bring shame upon the company and be fired. This shows the potential complexity in the determination of right or wrong when judging the ethicality of certain actions or practices.

Does the end justify the means, or do the means justify the end? These are fundamental philosophical arguments, and different cultures may approach ethical responsibility from different perspectives. In some cultures if the group benefits as a result of the action, that is the only thing that matters. In other cultures doing things the right way will ensure that the outcome is also morally defensible. What is ethical is a complex subject.

So how does a company approach ethical actions and ensure that it acts in an appropriate manner? It sets up a set of ethical guidelines for behaviour. All employees of the organization are asked to adhere to these guidelines in their actions. These guidelines often become formalized into a code of ethical conduct. It is expected that all individuals employed by the company will follow the code. Developing ethical guidelines or codes of conduct provides companies with the following advantages (Lamb et al., 2005).

1. Employees learn to identify with what the company recognizes as acceptable business practices.
2. The guidelines can serve as an effective internal behavioural control mechanism.
3. A written code eliminates any confusion as to whether a practice is ethical or not for decision-making purposes.
4. The formulation of the code of ethical conduct allows for the discussion among the firm's employees as to what is appropriate or not and produces better decision-making.

Corporate social responsibility

So what exactly is corporate social responsibility (CSR)? Is it **corporate philanthropy**? Is it helping the local community? Is it helping third-world countries? The answer is that all of these are examples of CSR tactics, but each may be insufficient on its own. It is a multifaceted construct that is more complex than once thought. It is really all things that the firm can do to be a good and responsible citizen of the world community, and it incorporates everything previously mentioned in this chapter along with a series of additional strategic choices to ensure that the company is a caring and contributing member of society. **Corporate social responsibility is the actions of the company to behave in a socially responsible manner to protect and enhance the various stakeholders that have an interest in the company, the community in which it operates, the environment which surrounds it, and society.**

13.2 Corporate Social Responsibility Activities

The various components of corporate social responsibility are shown in Figure 13.2. Two of these have already been discussed in this chapter and the additional two will now be considered. One important caution for global companies at this point is that different cultures may have different perceptions of the importance of different levels of corporate social responsibility initiatives.

It has been found that there are significantly different CSR responsiveness orientations when comparing US and French managers (Ibrahim and Parsa, 2005). In general, American managers are legally and ethically driven in terms of their orientation to corporate social responsibility, while the French were found to be more driven by the economic and philanthropic components. These types of cultural difference can have a significant bearing on the success of global CSR initiatives, and understanding the potential for differences in perceptions helps prepare CSR strategists for alliances with foreign firms and organizations. Clearly, this research is in its infancy, and with the growing importance of CSR, more research is needed. The two initiatives that will now be discussed are corporate philanthropy and **social activism**.

Non-profit issues and corporate philanthropy

Corporate philanthropy is primarily focused on corporate giving to charitable organizations. While most companies feel that they should give to charities, most do not know how to do it well (Porter and Kramer, 2002). What many corporations consider to be strategic philanthropy is often far more opportunistic than strategic or, worse, done for the sake of doing it rather than tying giving to anything meaningful. Philanthropy is more like public relations or advertising that works to enhance a company's image by attaching the name to **cause-related marketing** or charitable sponsorships.

The key question to ask is whether corporations should even consider philanthropic giving (Porter and Kramer, 2002)? If by philanthropy one is referring to a variety of small cash payments to local charities or universities, this may or may not be appropriate, depending on the motives. What is needed is the connection of these payments to a series of sound social or business objectives.

Bear in mind that charitable giving can be used to improve the 'competitive context', which may encompass such issues as the quality of the business environment where the company does business. Philanthropy may be used to merge social and economic goals which would allow the company not only to give money but also to leverage relationships and capabilities in the active support of charities.

To accomplish this, there are changes that would have to be made in the way the business approaches charitable giving. A company may need to refocus where it should spend its money as well as how. The first requirement is to choose the best grantees for charitable donations. Who will benefit most from the company's donations? Who fits with the company's mission and capabilities? These are important questions to be answered first before anything else is attempted. The second step entails signalling other funders as to what is a good recipient for donations; by attracting the interest of other donors, overall philanthropic spending can be increased and also spread more effectively across a number of givers. Step three involves the improvement of recipient performance, which will not only benefit society but will also increase the impact of the monies given. This will then lead to the fourth step, the advancing of knowledge and practice, setting up what Porter and Kramer identify as a 'virtuous cycle'.

Another variant of charitable giving is what has become known as cause-related marketing or CRM (not to be confused with customer relationship management!). **Cause-related marketing involves a linking between the corporation and a particular charitable cause. There are two ways that this can happen, the company can make unconditional donations on a regular basis to a particular charitable cause, or it can link its donations to customer purchase behaviour.**

The company that makes a donation to charity once a consumer has made a particular purchase allows the company to receive its benefit before the charitable organization receives its donation. Intuitively, one would expect that this could leave the consumer feeling that the activity is not as altruistically motivated as unconditional donations would be. However, one study has found that when comparing consumer perceptions of conditional and unconditional donations to charitable causes, there was little negative effect from using conditional donations (Dean, 2003, 2004). This study also examined the idea of whether long-term donor relationships between businesses and charities were more important than single donations to charities, and found the following.

1. Firms with excellent reputations for social responsibility gain little from single-instance charitable donations.

2. Firms with poor reputations for social responsibility may significantly improve consumer perceptions from single-instance charitable giving.

3. Firms with average reputations may or may not see improvements in consumer perceptions with single-instance giving.

4. Firms that are perceived to be socially irresponsible will not be thought of as excellent community citizens by a single charitable donation. It will take time and effort to significantly change perceptions.

Ultimately, if the firm is interested in charitable giving, it must note that there are concerns associated with donations (Endacott, 2004). One is that causes, like products or services, may be subject to changing consumer preferences. What is the hot cause or charity today may lose resonance with your consumers tomorrow, so the donor company must be careful to track the perceptions of its consumers periodically to see if their feelings towards a particular charity or cause have changed. Significant events like hurricanes, terrorist attacks, tsunamis, and other disasters can divert consumer interests and force the company to shift its focus to a different charitable organization. The selection of a cause must be done carefully since the cause or causes must resonate with your consumers and have a logical association with your company brand. Finally, for multinational companies, there are very few global charities but there are many global causes, so the multinational must be careful to choose wisely and realize that consumers in different countries may have significantly different perceptions of the same charitable organization or cause.

Corporate managers should carefully consider the basic trade-offs before committing any valuable corporate resources to social causes (Sasse and Trahan, 2007). But merely giving to or lining up in an affiliation with a charitable organization may not be sufficient. Another possibility involves focusing on improving the environment. This may have social consequences certainly, but the concern is for the improvement of the environment. Strategically this may be a better choice for companies that have been criticized for polluting the environment or cutting down forests. It may be a necessary step to improving a damaged image.

Social activism and community involvement

One important type of CSR activity involves the firm in an activist role in attempting to improve the community in which it operates. **Social activism** includes the actions undertaken by a firm, individuals, or a group that are aimed at making the quality of life in society better for all the inhabitants. From a business strategy perspective, this would often involve some kind of proactive role in improving the community in which the firm operates. An important approach to this can be seen in what is known as corporate social initiatives (CSIs). Many companies in the UK as well as in the US are now focused on building corporate images as good community citizens. A great deal of financial resources are being invested in community involvement projects. These projects range from locally focused education and training for youth and adults to improve their employment potential, to global projects involving aid for developing countries. The various levels and mechanisms for corporate social activism are found in Figure 13.3.

A pointed example of social involvement can be seen in the US in the efforts of Home Depot to bring company employees into community service. In 2004, 50,000 of Home Depot's 325,000 employees donated two million hours to community service (Grow et al., 2005). Home Depot's CEO, Robert L. Nardelli, has been trying to encourage other companies to follow its lead. In May 2005, Nardelli invited executives from 24 different companies

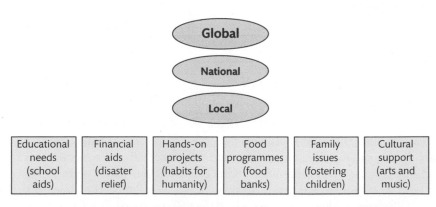

13.3 Varieties of Levels and Mechanisms for Corporate Social Activism

and foundations to come to Home Depot's headquarters in Atlanta, Georgia, to discuss community service initiatives. In September 2005 these executives kicked off a 'Month of Service', a plan developed with a community group known as the Hands-On Network which entails 2,000 different community projects across the United States using corporate volunteers. This is certainly a reflection of the importance of changing the focus from shareholders to stakeholders, as Nardelli argues that the firm must be accountable to its suppliers, customers, employees, community members, and social activists.

The use of the Hands-On Network is reflective of the fact that there is an increasing importance to the partnering possibilities with **non-governmental organizations** (NGOs). NGOs are organized around shared values, principles, or beliefs (Spar and LaMure, 2003). They are activist organizations that work for particular causes of interest. Examples include Greenpeace, Earthwatch, PETA (People for the Ethical Treatment of Animals), and the Free Burma Coalition. These organizations can bring strong pressure to bear upon target businesses. When faced with NGO pressure, companies have three strategic options: (1) pre-emption, (2) capitulation, or (3) resistance (Spar and LaMure 2003). Some firms become proactive and develop a dialogue with NGOs, which can lead to a partnership, while others give in to pressure or fight. The costs of resistance can be high both financially as well as potential damage to image.

A good example of partnering with NGOs can be seen in the recent partnership announced between Cadbury Schweppes and two NGOs to work together on a project to improve biodiversity levels of cocoa farms in Ghana and help the country establish its first cocoa farm eco-tourism initiative (*Corporate Responsibility Management*, 2005). The key to success for these kinds of proactive partnerings is to understand what each party wants to get from the partnership and see how this can be accomplished. Cadbury paired up with Earthwatch and the Ghana Nature Conservation Research Centre (NCRC), and the three worked together to find common ground. The partnership helped ensure benefits for each of the three partners. It helped develop strong relationships for Cadbury with cocoa farmers in Ghana, improved the conditions for the farmers, fostered agricultural improvements that aided the environment, and created new natural habitats for wildlife. All round it was seen as a beneficial relationship. It seems clear that social activism, social projects, and community involvement are important mechanisms for CSR.

Hess et al. (2002) present four critical suggestions for companies when approaching the development of CSIs.

1. The firm must connect the CSIs to its mission statement and core values, with top management integrally involved in CSI programme development, implementation, and evaluation.

2. Firm's management must be in sync with marketplace expectations of social responsibility so that alienation and reputation loss will not occur.

3. CSIs must be tied directly to the core competencies and primary resources of the company.

4. The company must set clear objectives for CSI programmes and have specific mechanisms for measuring success.

So how should the successes in terms of our CSR initiatives be measured? There is a growing concern in Europe and the United States over the need for social auditing, accounting, and reporting (SAAR). This is a necessary evolutionary development as there must be measurement of a firm's success in terms of social performance for it to be able to effectively report that performance to stakeholders. Social reporting improvements have recently been seen in the creation of the Global Reporting Initiative (GRI) and the Institute of Social and Ethical Accountability (ISEA). These types of initiative will help companies better communicate their successes to important stakeholders.

Greenwashing

If CSR is so important and widespread, why is there still so much confusion around it? Because too many firms are doing it just to be able to say they do it, and they do not have any true commitment to it. CSR must be made an integral part of the strategic planning process. A recent problem involves the conscious misrepresentation of company efforts to help the environment, which is known as **greenwashing**. Companies making statements without facts to back them up about their efforts on behalf of the environment are producing concerns among consumers about the real nature of so-called environmental corporate initiatives and their effects. This is fuelling concerns about corporate social responsibility and the driving corporate commitment to sustainability and the reduction of the firm's carbon footprint. The problem is that many claims are made to create an impression, and if these are too general in nature it is almost impossible for consumers to see how the firm is actually delivering on its claims.

Deceptive practices can stretch from the simplest level with firms putting their products in 'green' packages and claiming the packaging is biodegradable when in fact it is not (De Jesus, 2009), to such practices as sponsoring green events or giving to environmental causes when in fact their operations and products can be extremely harmful to fragile ecosystems. Another example is printing corporate or product brochures in green colours and using such wording as 'eco-friendly' and 'sustainable', but with no visible evidence of how they are doing anything for the environment.

In a number of developed countries there are environmental watchdog groups that can identify unsubstantiated claims and make companies correct them, but this is not necessarily the case in developing countries (De Jesus, 2009). In these countries it will take proactive governmental action to control this problematic practice, such as in the Philippines with the creation of the Green Building Council and the Green Building Initiative, and in Singapore which has established the Green Mark for rating green buildings. These actions are not sufficient of and by themselves to stem the use greenwashing, but are important steps in the right direction.

The point is that with government proactivity and vigilance, consumers can be better protected from bad company practices, and recognition of this seems to be gaining strength in the developing countries as problems such as the safety of workers are brought to light in countries like Cambodia (with strikes by garment workers) and Bangladesh (with the loss of over 1,000 textile workers in a factory fire at the Rana Plaza in 2013). Making these problems visible helps to raise awareness and levels of concern among global consumers so that they can properly assess the claims made by companies before buying their products.

In many countries companies have to substantiate their claims in order to alleviate the concerns of their various stakeholders (Junior et al., 2014). For example, the Australian Centre for Sustainable Business and Development, based at the University of Southern Queensland, represents a new array of educational centres focused on assurances in sustainability reporting, and this trend has raised the visibility of the need for proper reporting of sustainable practices. The proportion of companies listed in the Fortune Global 500 issuing yearly sustainability reports increased from 47 per cent in 2000 to 85 per cent in 2010.

One way to cut down on the potential for unethical greenwashing practices is to clearly identify those actions that are considered to be inappropriate. One interesting source is TerraChoice Environmental Marketing, a Canadian organization that reports the use of what it calls the Seven Sins of Greenwashing (Canada NewsWire 2009).

1. **The Hidden Trade-Off** where one environmental issue is emphasized at the expense of potentially more serious concerns.

2. **No Proof** where environmental assertions are not backed by objective third-party certifications.

3. **Vagueness** where claims are so nebulous they are meaningless.

4. **Worshipping False Labels** where the suggestion is made of proper certifications by a legitimate certifier though in fact this is not the case.

5. **Irrelevance** where an environmental issue is stressed which has no connection to the product produced by the company.

6. **Lesser of Two Evils** where environmental claims make consumers feel they are being green with regard to a product category that is actually lacking in real environmental benefits.

7. **Fibbing** where environmental claims are patently untrue.

These 'whistle-blowing' organizations are important, and big corporations may be forced to comply, but the problem remains that a number of smaller companies and companies from non-compliant countries are still making unsubstantiated claims and still potentially deceiving consumers. This raises the issue of how to make CSR an integral part of the strategic direction of the company.

Moving CSR from compliance to strategic imperative

If the company is to move beyond using CSR to play-act at being a community citizen, it becomes imperative to find ways in which the firm can truly live out what it is preaching. This, like strategic planning itself, can be done in a way that lets the organization say it has completed the process so as to tick off one more box on the list of things to do. As has been discussed previously in this chapter, CSR is not just about giving money to charitable organizations. It incorporates such important issues as human rights, environmental stewardship, family-friendly work conditions, and community development and nurturing. It is a multifaceted construct, which should be thought of as an integral part of business strategy. What firms are now finding is that corporate citizenship leads to competitive advantage.

Intense competition in a variety of industries presents companies with the possibility that all of them will be seen externally as the same, potentially undermining perceived competitive advantages (Epstein and Birchard, 1999). A reputation for good corporate citizenship serves as an effective point for differentiation. One can certainly argue that firms like Ben & Jerry's and The Body Shop have made names for themselves with their corporate citizenry. As the authors argue, good reputations attract investors, customers, and better job candidates, and nurturing environments help keep employees from leaving. There are also tax benefits that can accrue to those good corporate community members, and, above all else, a strong reputation is not easily undermined by competitors. Well, how do we know that corporate citizenship really pays?

There are now four prevailing justifications for CSR (Porter and Kramer, 2006):

(1) moral obligation (it is the duty of good citizens to act in a morally responsible way)

(2) sustainability (we should be good stewards of our environment and our communities)

(3) license to operate (we must get formal approval from governments and other important stakeholders to operate as a business entity)

(4) reputation (if we improve our company image through good works, we will improve our overall image, our morale, and our stock value).

All four of these justifications are limited since they centre more on the discrepancies between the business and society than on the codependency of the two. As a result no single justification from this list is sufficient. In order to further advance CSR, companies must recognize that they and society are interrelated and that if they do well, society will do well, and vice versa. The most important point made by the authors is that the real test for whether a social initiative makes sense to pursue is whether it presents the chance to create some kind of shared value. This requires a meaningful benefit for society that is also valuable to the company. **An appropriate social agenda for a company should not try to solve all of the problems faced by society, but it should fit with and reinforce company strategy through social advancement.** This is the key to success (see Figure 13.4).

Responsive CSR, where the company acts as a good corporate citizen is not the real answer. It is by elevating CSR to strategic CSR where the company chooses a unique position for itself which improves company performance from an internal operations perspective as well as an external perspective in not only better serving its customers but also making incremental improvements for society and interconnecting itself with society. This cannot be a short-term fix used by a company as a stop-gap measure. In terms of the move to strategic CSR, the only way to do this significantly is to make a long-term commitment to strategic CSR since it should be carefully planned, supervised, and evaluated (Falck and Heblich, 2006).

Generic social issues	Value chain social impacts	Social dimensions of competitive context
• Social issues that are not significantly affected by a company's operations nor materially affect its long-term competitiveness.	• Social issues that are significantly affected by a company's activities in the ordinary course of business.	• Social issues in the external environment that significantly affect the underlying drivers of a company's competitiveness in the locations where it operates.

13.4 Prioritizing Social Issues

Source: Michael E. Porter and Mark R. Kramer (2006), 'Strategy and Society: The Link Between Competitive Advantage and Corporate Social Responsibility', *Harvard Business Review*, 84, December, pp. 78–92.

Strategic dimensions	Traditional CSR	Traditional strategy	Strategic CSR
Visibility	Irrelevant: doing good is its own reward—and is profitable in the long run.	Build customer awareness of product and brand	Build customer and stakeholder awareness of product with CSR value added
Appropriability	Irrelevant: doing good is its own reward—and is profitable in the long run	Manage supplier, customer, and competitor relations to capture value added for firm	Manage stakeholder relations to capture value added for the firm
Voluntarism	Participate in social action beyond that demanded by the firm's interests and the law	Firm innovation based on ability to learn: non-deterministic behaviour	Participate in social action beyond that demanded by law
Centrality	Irrelevant: doing good is tied to social need and not to core business mission	Create value via product/service innovation	Create value via product/service innovation linked to social issues
Proactivity	Anticipate changes in social issues	First-mover advantage	Anticipate changes in social issues that present market opportunities

13.5 Comparison of Traditional CSR, Strategic CSR, and Traditional Strategy

Bryan W. Husted and David B. Allen (2007),' Strategic Corporate Social Responsibility and Value Creation Among Large Firms: Lessons from the Spanish Experience', *Long Range Planning*, 40, pp. 594–610.

One study has compared traditional CSR, strategic CSR and traditional strategy and addresses the differences across five important strategic dimensions (Husted and Allen, 2007). It highlights the need for *visibility* (the extent to which social actions can be seen by stakeholders), *appropriability* (the ability of the firm to gain economic benefits from the social activity), *voluntarism* (taking into consideration the differences between market activities and CSR projects), *centrality* (the connection to the core business mission), and *proactivity* (the extent to which the company is forward thinking and acting rather than reactive) (see Figure 13.5).

The virtue matrix

An excellent tool for corporate strategists to calculate the potential profitability of acting socially responsibly is called the virtue matrix (Martin, 2002). The idea behind this concept is that corporate managements must deal with a series of obstacles when attempting to position their companies as better community citizens. If companies commit to community projects that are not undertaken by competitors, they risk losing their competitive position. If they welcome the involvement of the government in overseeing the projects, they face the possibility of new regulations being passed, obliging them to spend significant resources in compliance while realizing only limited social benefits. Finally, if companies adopt wage scales and working conditions in newly emerging markets that match those in developed nations, this may force the outsourcing of those jobs to countries with less restrictive stand-ards. Martin presents corporate social responsibility as a product or service that is subject to market forces, and his virtue matrix allows the user to understand the forces that affect supply and demand.

Martin's version divides corporate social responsibility into two components,: instru-mental and intrinsic, modified for this book as foundation and frontier. Foundation CSR involves such activities as the support, either by choice or by regulation, of charities and arts/cultural organizations that serve the interests of shareholders as well as the inter-ests of society and the community. Frontier CSR includes those actions and initiatives that are altruistic by nature but which may or may not resonate with shareholders. These are actions which are undertaken because management believes that they are the right thing to do but may not sufficiently serve shareholder interests. Incorporating both of these aspects into the matrix provides a better framework for managers to evaluate CSR opportunities.

The matrix is divided into four quadrants (see Figure 13.6). The two lower quadrants com-prise the civil foundation, which incorporates laws, regulations, customs, and norms. The left lower one includes corporate conduct that is undertaken by choice to adhere to norms or customs, while the right lower one includes those actions that are mandated by regula-tions or laws and are therefore labelled as actions of compliance. Martin suggests that many

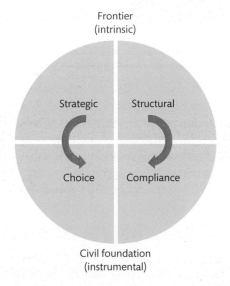

13.6 The Virtue Matrix

CSR actions begin by entering the bottom left quadrant, but as they become more the norm rather than the exception, they eventually become the basis for laws or regulations and move to the lower right quadrant. The key aspect to the civil foundation is that the upper limit of involvement is not fixed. In developed economies one can expect that new social initiatives will often become norms and later be codified. In developed economies one can expect the limit to extend upwards, while in less developed and less broadly-based economies it might actually move downwards.

The upper quadrants involve those activities that are intrinsic by nature, which shareholders in the business may or may not see as beneficial over time. These actions are undertaken by a corporation because its management feels they are the correct actions to take. One would certainly expect that if these are seen as valuable to shareholders, other companies would imitate them, and, over time, upper quadrant initiatives may move downwards and become part of the civil foundation. The upper left quadrant is the strategic frontier, which includes activities that may be expected to add to shareholder value if supported by customers, employees, and governmental agencies.

The upper right quadrant is the structural frontier, which includes those actions that are intrinsic and clearly not in the interests of shareholders. Here the idea is to bring benefits to society rather than immediately to the company. The line separating these two upper quadrants may in practice be fuzzy because some CSR initiatives fall in the middle between actions that would be seen as directly beneficial to the corporation's owners and those the same owners might well see as inappropriate. It becomes clear when examining the matrix that there would be potentially innovative and beneficial initiatives that would be stifled because management would not want to take the risk of attempting something which competitors would not emulate and shareholders would not value.

The biggest barrier to corporate virtue is the lack of vision inherent in company management (Martin, 2002), but this can be corrected by providing support for businesses and leaders who undertake innovative and risky actions. Consumer agitation can help in this regard. Peer encouragement can help as businesses that achieve success can communicate that success and encourage other companies to follow suit. The lack of any economic incentives is problematic regarding corporate initiatives that fall in the structural frontier because here the rewards are not necessarily visible to consumers, so consumer agitation will not help and peer encouragement will be absent since the risks may appear to be too high. As a result, it may have to be governmental agencies that step in and validate the actions undertaken to help initiatives shift from the upper to the lower quadrants.

The virtue matrix is one of the most interesting and innovative approaches developed to help corporate managers understand the forces inherent in positioning their companies as good community citizens. Companies and their innovative managers can indeed find ways in which to better both society and their own shareholders as well as create a competitive advantage and greater profitability for themselves if they understand the forces involved and the potential barriers that have to be overcome. The virtue matrix provides an excellent tool for strategic decision-making.

One question often raised when companies look to being a good corporate citizen is how they can actually get out into the community and 'make a difference'. How would this be achieved? The firm must act in a socially responsible manner.

Issues related to new media: privacy, security, etc. and their relation to strategy

The explosion of social media has presented a new array of opportunities for ethical problems to appear in the corporate landscape. Today, comments by employees via social media can create serious issues for companies. Giving away important company information, making information available that threatens the security of company employees, and the frustrations of an employee voiced via social media can seriously damage company reputation and negatively affect company performance, not to mention the potential harm that it could bring to personal safety and security. These are creating problems for many companies, and it argues for the vital nature of setting clear company policies with regard to the use of social media by all employees and their family members.

Reputational risk is the single biggest example of how social media can negatively affect the company if it does not set codes of conduct for its employees in their use of social media (McMullen, 2013). What seem to be innocent uses of social media by company employees can create major problems. One example could be an attempt by a company employee to make negative comments about a competitor, which could lead to the competitor suing for defamation of character.

Officials using social media to monitor employees and potential employees can also lead to legal problems. Imagine the 'snowballing' through Twitter and Facebook that is possible when an unsubstantiated comment about a problem with a company's products exponentially spirals out of control, setting the stage for a serious blow to the company's brand image. One example cited in *PR News* (1 July 2013) mentioned how John Mackey, the CEO of Whole Foods Market, used a false name to post disparaging comments about a competitor, Wild Oats Markets, which Whole Foods was trying to purchase. Undoubtedly he was hoping to reduce the purchase price as much as possible before the completion of the transaction, but the identification of the problem backfired for Mackey. This type of damage can take enormous efforts and financial resources to correct. Another area of concern is the use of social media by one employee to harass another within the same firm.

Another serious issue in this ever-developing cyber world involves security breaches from 'creative hackers'. Obviously these types of problem have to be recognized and policies carefully created to govern social media usage along with the construction of effective hacker firewalls.

A recent trend known as **tweetjacking**, where the tweets sent out by a company in an attempt to spread good news about itself are turned against it, is worth mentioning (Lyon and Montgomery, 2013). For example, a 'media disaster' was created in 2012 when McDonald's launched a Twitter campaign to allow customers and vendors to share positive information about the farmers growing ingredients used for Big Macs and Chicken McNuggets. It was immediately subverted by a series of tweets involving poor working conditions, animal mistreatment, and food poisoning. The company was forced to drop the campaign only hours after it was initiated.

What this suggests is that the speed of social media in relation to CSR is 'lightning' fast, and when companies do things that people see as wrong, they can react immediately and negate any good that the company might have tried to project. This tweetjacking example is a great lesson for companies to protect themselves by carefully testing their proposed campaigns on a limited front first before opening things to the world. The underlying issue that this highlights is that there is a growing scepticism among the public that companies are prone to twist things to make themselves look good. The problem of greenwashing mentioned earlier in the chapter has exacerbated this situation since many of the unsubstantiated claims made by companies have created an impression among many social media users that companies simply cannot be trusted. Ninety-eight per cent of the companies making environmental claims about their products have been found to have committed at least one of the seven sins previously listed (Canada NewsWire, 2009).

Is it any wonder the public is concerned? The good thing is that this wariness on the part of the public keeps companies on the straight and narrow, but strategically it becomes essential that the company can back up its claims with facts to allay the negative reactions of the public.

The latest thinking: UPS and sustainability, and making cause marketing work

UPS and sustainability

In a recent article in *Harvard Business Review* (Kuehn and McIntire 2014), the authors wrote about the successes with sustainability they found at United Parcel Service (UPS). UPS created a sustainability steering committee with the underlying belief that companies have the responsibility to aid society and the environment, and company investments must always return some kind of value to the company. They realized that sustainability programmes must be carefully financially evaluated. Their key finding was that the programmes that have the greatest impact not only match with company strategies but also move in conjunction with their activities. It suggests that companies should use their momentum to accelerate societal and environmental change. The authors describe the process followed at UPS as one in which there are five key steps.:

1. **Assess your strengths**. Examine your core competencies, infrastructure, and relationships as part of sustainability strategy development. This should produce the identification of strengths that charitable partners often lack:

   (a) capital
   (b) specialized knowledge and experience
   (c) relationships
   (d) processes
   (e) physical assets, personnel, and infrastructure
   (f) business acumen.

2. **Choose your spots**. You must narrow the field and get insights from external stakeholders and internal managers.

3. **Find momentum**. Focus on where company energy is already in motion and where company actions could actually make a significant difference.

4. **Build productive partnerships**. To ensure a productive relationship it is important to clearly articulate that the hope for the business is to leverage its strengths to accelerate change. This usually leads to a sharing of organizational strengths and weaknesses as well as shared values. Then strategic plans can be developed with clear goals and objectives, timelines, and performance assessment metrics.

5. **Convene other sources of strength**. Large companies develop significant networks, which allows them to bring in other players that may help accelerate the momentum for change in a good sustainability cause.

The authors end the article with a discussion of the problems associated with executives who are supportive of sustainability programmes but who do not want to discuss in detail return on investment for the programmes since that would be seen as insincere. The problem here is that an ROI analysis is not always possible for the following reasons.

1. **You may not have all of the data**. Internal systems and process metrics may not be able to get access to all relevant data along with the fact that NGOs and other community organizations may not use standard accounting mechanisms.

2. **Much of the return is intangible**. Most benefits of sustainability programmes involve imprecise intangibles. The development of company goodwill, the inspiration of company employees, and the development of corporate leaders must be evaluated in other ways.

3. **Payback is on a different time frame**. Sustainability programmes require longer payback time periods.

The authors suggest that it is not unreasonable for executives to want to see positive returns for their sustainability programme expenditures, but their basic assumptions must be rethought. They suggest the analogy of advertising in that there is still a lot of concern on exactly how much a company should spend on advertising, but there is no doubt that it is vitally important for the firm to advertise, but this has led over time to the search for better ways to make the necessary benefits become measureable. These have now been found for advertising, and the same will happen for measuring the ROI for sustainability programmes. One attempt to move in this direction is seen in the work of Virgin Mobile USA as will be discussed in the following section.

Making cause marketing work

A recent article by Echo Montgomery Garrett (2013) discussed how companies have been able to use cause marketing effectively to improve their financial performance. She discusses the example of Virgin Mobile USA which in 2006 decided to become more cause-focused; in order to make the right decision, the company called together a panel of its main customers, teens and young adults, to examine their feelings about social issues. They suggested teen homelessness as an important cause to address, which they felt was virtually invisible as a social problem. The company launched the RE*Generation campaign, and then, with the help of pop-singer Jewel, lobbied the US Congress to designate the month of November as National Homeless Youth Awareness Month. The company followed this up with the launch of the Virgin Mobile FreeFest in Baltimore, MD, in 2009, which has now become a popular annual music festival which attracts as many as 50,000 attendees. Virgin uses the event to ask all of the concert-goers to donate their time to help with teen homelessness or to give $5.00 to help with the cause. This has led to donations of over $750,000 with which it has built Youthwork, a living space for transitional homeless youth aged 16–20 in Washington, DC. This led in 2013 to a commitment by Lady Gaga to offer a portion of her ticket sales to homeless youth organizations operating in cities where she performs.

Garrett suggests that companies must be careful to communicate transparently and clearly regarding their cause-related efforts. Tara Olivier is a director of Cone Communications, a marketing and public relations firm in Boston, MA. Cone created the terminology 'cause branding', and she suggests that while many companies are trying to engage in social causes, it is the companies which live out their social cause efforts effectively which earn the trust of consumers. Cone reported in its *2012 Corporate Social Return Trend Tracker* that 82 per cent of consumers felt they would be likely to buy the products or services of a company that showed clearly how its efforts have actually helped the cause they were aligned with. Garrett (2013) reports that what is now a necessity for corporate investors is to believe that the alliance is heartfelt. Some alliances seem inappropriate to consumers, like the disastrous alignment of Kentucky Fried Chicken (KFC) with breast cancer, which is strongly linked to the consumption of fatty foods and obesity. Garrett presents a series of points on how to make cause marketing successful, given the experiences of companies like Cone Communications.

1. Establish clear business objectives for your cause marketing.
2. The societal need chosen should be a natural extension of your brand equity and core values and competencies.
3. Do not spread yourself too thin by tackling too many challenges at the same time.
4. Share your results on how your efforts have helped the cause with your consumers.

The point here is that consumers want companies to be involved in social causes, but they also demand that the company shows results for their efforts. Lip service will no longer suffice.

Conclusion

Companies must carefully consider their 'place' in the world around them. What role will they play in society? What social initiatives must they undertake to be considered a good community citizen? These are important questions that must be answered. Firms can no longer think of themselves in isolation from the forces and publics around them. Gone are the days of just satisfying shareholders. The company of today must pay attention to a number of relevant publics including employees, suppliers, partners, community groups, and social activists. CSR managers must weave initiatives into the basic fabric of the organization, and CSR must be a process that is endorsed by top management. When done the right way it will not only improve the image of the firm, it will also improve productivity and profitability. Good corporate citizenship is well worth the effort, but it must be genuinely tied to the skills, abilities, competencies, and values of the firm to be sure of doing the right thing.

Summary

Corporate social responsibility comprises a number of important components. The firm has an economic responsibility in that it must maximize shareholder value. The firm also has a legal responsibility to operate according to society's rules and regulations. Beyond law and economics, social responsibility also encompasses ethics. The firm must act in a fair, just, and moral way in its operations. Finally, corporate social responsibility entails a discretionary/ philanthropic level that entails such diverse social responsibilities as donating money and hands-on help to charities, the community, the environment, and in some cases developing nations. Being a good community citizen carries great responsibilities with it. It signifies being a good steward of the investments made by the shareholders; it means operating within the legal system not only of the location of the headquarters but also wherever else the firm has operations; and it entails ensuring that the firm, its employees, and its management always do what is fair and morally defensible. It also demands that the firm act in a responsible way to help the local community, make the environment cleaner and safer, and protect community citizens. But being a good citizen is not just doing things that appear to be altruistic for the sake of being able to say that you are a good community citizen. The things that are done, the aid given, and the corporate presence in different activities and initiatives must be tied to the mission, values, and essence of the organization and its leadership. Corporate social responsibility must be treated as an integral part of strategic market planning. Only when the company sees itself as a vital member of its various communities will it act in the most appropriate ways and ensure its viability. Hopefully, with the strategic knowledge that this text provides, the reader will be better prepared to make the most informed decisions as the firm operates in its various markets.

Key terms

- **Cause-related marketing (CRM):** the commitment of a corporation to a particular charitable cause. There are two ways that this can happen, the company can make unconditional donations on a regular basis to a particular charitable cause, or it can link its donations to customer purchase behaviour. The company that makes a donation to charity once a consumer has made a particular purchase allows the company to receive its benefit before the charitable organization receives its donation.

- **Corporate philanthropy:** the act of giving to a charitable recipient.

- **Corporate social responsibility (CSR):** the actions of the company to act in a socially responsible manner to protect and enhance the various stakeholders that have an interest in the company, the community in which it operates, the environment which surrounds it, and society in general.

- **Environmental/green marketing:** the actions undertaken by the firm or donations that are aimed at improving or preserving the environment surrounding the firm. Green marketing focuses on the idea of keeping the environment clean and green. This often entails reducing or eliminating corporate pollution.

- **Ethics:** the set of moral principles or values that shape the actions of either an individual or a group of individuals. Ethical principles therefore set a standard for behaviour in a society. Legality sets the foundation for what behaviours are seen as lawful or unlawful, but ethics focuses more on moral judgements, and the focus becomes the right thing to do from a moral standpoint as opposed to whether it is lawful or not.

- **Foundation CSR:** the types of activities undertaken by the company in support of charities and arts/cultural organizations, either by choice or by regulation, that serve the interests of shareholders as well as the interests of society and the community.

- **Frontier CSR:** actions and initiatives that are altruistic by nature but which may or may not resonate with shareholders. These are actions which are undertaken because management believes that they are the right thing to do but may not sufficiently serve shareholder interests.

- **Greenwashing:** the conscious misrepresentation of company efforts to help the environment.

- **Moral judgement:** the framework of beliefs upon which the individual makes judgements on whether an action is morally appropriate or not.

- **Non-governmental organizations (NGOs):** organizations created around shared values, principles, or beliefs. They are activist organizations that work for particular causes of interest. Examples include Greenpeace, Earthwatch, PETA (People for the Ethical Treatment of Animals), and the Free Burma Coalition. NGOs can bring strong pressure to bear upon target organizations.

- **Shareholders:** those individuals who have purchased stock in the company. They have a vested interest in the operation of the firm. They expect the company to be a good steward of their investments.

- **Social activism:** the actions undertaken by a firm, individuals, or a group aimed at making the quality of life in society better for all the inhabitants. From a firm strategy perspective, this would often involve some kind of proactive role in improving the community in which the firm operates.

- **Social marketing:** the application of marketing principles and practices to help with resolving health and social problems. This involves the use of marketing in a great many countries to change public behaviours and practices considered to be harmful to health and societal well-being.

- **Stakeholders:** all the groups or publics that interact with and are affected by the operations of the firm. These publics include employees, partners, suppliers, customers, community members, governmental agencies, and social activist groups.

- **Tweetjacking:** where the tweets sent out by a company intended to spread good news about the company are turned against it.

Discussion questions

1. What is the difference between company shareholders and stakeholders, and why would this matter when determining appropriate CSR strategy?

2. What is moral judgement, and how does it affect ethical decision-making?

3. How do French and American managers differ in their views of corporate social responsibility, and why would this be important for a CSR strategist?

4. What is cause-related marketing, and what are the two variations of cause-related giving that were discussed in the chapter?

5. What are corporate social initiatives, and what are important considerations when they are being developed?

6. Does corporate social responsibility create profits for the firm? How do we know?

7. What is the virtue matrix? Explain how it works, and why is it important for the CSR strategist?

8. What is greenwashing, and why is it a major problem for corporations? What can be done to correct this problem?

9. What is tweetjacking? What can companies do to protect themselves from image problems with social media?

10. What are the five key steps in the UPS approach to financially evaluating sustainability programmes?

Online resource centre

 Visit the Online Resource Centre for this book for lots of interesting additional material at: <**www.oxfordtextbooks.co.uk/orc/west3e/**>

References and further reading

Beard, Alison and Richard Hornik (2011), 'It's Hard to be Good', *Harvard Business Review*, 89, November, pp. 88–96.

Clement, Ronald W. (2006), 'Just How Unethical is American Business?', *Business Horizons*, 49, pp. 313–27.

Dean, Dwayne Hal (2003/2004), 'Consumer Perception of Corporate Donations: Effects of Company Reputation for Social responsibility and Type of Donation', *Journal of Advertising*, 32 (4), pp. 91–103.

De Jesus, Amado (2009), 'What You Should Know about Greenwashing', *Philippine Daily Inquirer*, 17 April.

Endacott, Roy William John (2004), 'Consumer and CRM: A National and Global Perspective', *Journal of Consumer Marketing*, 21 (3), pp. 183–9.

Falck, Oliver and Stephan Heblich (2007), 'Corporate Social Responsibility: Doing Well by Doing Good', *Business Horizons*, 50, pp. 247–54.

Ford, John B., Michael S. LaTour, Scott J. Vitell, and Warren A. French (1997), 'Moral Judgment and Market Negotiations: A Comparison of Chinese and American Managers', *Journal of International Marketing*, 5 (2), pp. 57–76.

Garrett, Echo Montgomery (2013), 'Good Cause and the Effect', *Arrive*, May-June, pp. 57–9.

Grow, Brian, Steve Hamm' and Louise Lee (2005), 'The Debate Over Doing Good', *Business Week*, Issue 3947, 15 August, p. 76.

Haanaes, Knot, David Michael, Jeremy Jurgens, and Subramanian Rangan (2013), 'Making Sustainability Profitable', *Harvard Business Review*, 91, March, pp. 110–13.

Hess, David, Nikolai Rogovsky, and Thomas W. Dunfee (2002), 'The Next Wave of Corporate Community Involvement: Corporate Social Initiatives', *California Management Review*, 44 (2), pp. 110–125.

Husted, Bryan W. and David B. Allen (2007), 'Strategic Corporate Social Responsibility and Value Creation among Large Firms: Lessons from the Spanish Experience', *Long Range Planning*, 40, pp. 594–610.

Joachimsthaler, Erich and David A. Aaker (1997), 'Building Brands Without Mass Media', *Harvard Business Review*, January-February, pp. 39–50.

Junior, Renzo Mori, Peter J. Best, and Julie Cotter (2014), 'Sustainability Reporting and Assurance: A Historical Analysis on a World-Wide Phenomenon', *Journal of Business Ethics*, 120, pp. 1–11.

Kayes, D. Christopher, David Stirling, and Tjai M. Nielsen (2007), 'Building Organizational Integrity', *Business Horizons*, 50, pp. 61–70.

Kouchaki, Maryam (2014), 'In the Afternoon, the Moral Slope Gets Slipperier', *Harvard Business Review*, 92, May, pp. 34–5.

Kuehn, Kurt and Lynette McIntire (2014), 'Sustainability a CFO Can Love', *Harvard Business Review*, 92, April, pp. 66–74.

Lamb, Charles W., Jr, Joseph F. Hair Jr, and Carl McDaniel (2005), *Essentials of Marketing*, 4th edn (Mason, OH: South-Western Publishing).

Lyon, Thomas P. and A. Wren Montgomery (2013), 'Tweetjacked: The Impact of Social Media on Corporate Greenwash', *Journal of Business Ethics*, 118, pp. 747–57.

McMullen, Darin (2013), 'Effectively Managing Social Media Risks', *Mondaq Business Briefing*, 17 December.

Martin, Roger L. (2002), 'The Virtue Matrix: Calculating the Return on Corporate Responsibility', *Harvard Business Review*, 80, March, pp. 68–75.

Porter, Michael E. and Mark R. Kramer (2002), 'The Competitive Advantage of Corporate Philanthropy', *Harvard Business Review*, 80, December, pp. 56–67.

Porter, Michael E. and Mark R. Kramer (2006), 'Strategy and Society: The Link Between Competitive Advantage and Corporate Social Responsibility', *Harvard Business Review*, 84, December, pp. 78–92.

Reinhardt, Forest L. (1998), 'Environmental Product Differentiation: Implications for Corporate Strategy', *California Management Review*, 40 (4), pp. 43–73.

Ritson, Mark (2005), 'Nike Shows the Way to Return from the Wilderness', *Marketing*, 20 April, p. 21.

Sasse, Craig M. and Ryan T. Trahan (2007), 'Rethinking the New Corporate Philanthropy', *Business Horizons*, 50, pp. 29–38.

Snider, Jamie, Ronald Paul Hill, and Diane Martin (2003), 'Corporate Social Responsibility in the 21st Century: A View from the World's Most Successful Firms', *Journal of Business Ethics*, 48 (2), pp. 175–84.

Spar, Debora L. and Lane T. LaMure (2003), 'The Power of Activism: Assessing the Impact of NGOs on Global Business', *California Management Review*, 45 (3), pp. 78–102.

Staff (2009), 'Greenwashing Affects 98% of Products Including Toys, Baby Products and Cosmetics', *Canada NewsWire*, 15 April.

Staff (2005), 'Communication Key to Cadbury–NGO Partnership', *Corporate Responsibility Management*, 1 (4), pp. 8–9.

Staff (2004), 'CSR Activities Generate Higher Performance—Official', *Women in Management Review*, 19 (5/6), p. 280.

 ### End of Chapter 13 case study: Nespresso's sustainability challenge

In December 2012, Mr Winkler, product manager of Nespresso Austria, was holding a pack of the biodegradable capsules from the Ethical Coffee Company (ECC) in his hands. Although the ECC capsules themselves were only one of the problems Mr Winkler was facing at the moment, he had the impression that the market entry of this new competitor had simultaneously made other company issues surface as well. It seemed that ECC was one step ahead and had the finger on the pulse of time with its sustainable business approach. Mr Winkler realized that Nespresso could no longer afford to rest on its laurels but needed to come up with a conclusive response to this new challenge.

Nespresso's history

Nespresso is commonly considered to be one of the most successful and innovative products the Nestlé Group has ever launched. Interestingly, the foundation for the first capsule system ever had already been laid in 1970 when Eric Favre invented a coffee capsule filled with fresh ground coffee and an appropriate technique which enabled the coffee brewing process under high pressure. Six years after Favre's invention, the first patent application was filed for the Nespresso system, i.e. the interaction of both the capsule and the machine.

Nespresso was founded in 1986 as a wholly owned, but autonomous, subsidiary of the Nestlé Group with headquarters in Lausanne, Switzerland. In 1988, Jean-Paul Gaillard became Chief Executive Officer (CEO) of the company. Under his management, both the positioning of Nespresso and its target group were re-specified. Gaillard's goal was to place the single-serve coffee system as a luxury brand for household use, thereby targeting consumers with a high affinity for gourmet coffee. Furthermore, he was convinced that a premium product such as Nespresso should be supported by a service module, so the Nespresso Club was created, with automatic membership with the purchase of a Nespresso machine. Although Nespresso was starting to be successful in the mid-1990s, Gaillard left the company in 1998 after ten years as CEO. He had put Nespresso on the right track due to his own entrepreneurial style and had ingrained in the organization the positioning of Nespresso as a lifestyle product with distinctive marketing, namely exclusive distribution and the Nespresso Club as a customer relationship management (CRM) tool.

Although profitable, Nespresso was still not a big market player due to the fact that the portioned coffee segment, especially for capsules, was not yet fully developed. This changed, however, when Nespresso opened its first boutique in Paris. The brand with all its inherent meanings and the coffee experience became tangible for consumers and accessible by simply visiting the boutique. Nespresso stores gradually opened in all countries of operation; by 2007 there were 117 boutiques worldwide. The system and brand gained additional popularity because in 2000 the first Nespresso commercials went on air on European television. In 2004, a new Boutique Bar concept was launched with the first being opened in Munich. This new retailing format was distinct from the former boutiques as it subdivided the store in several areas to accommodate different levels of experience with the brand and to facilitate navigation for consumers. The new retail concept was a complete success and responsible for revenues exceeding one billion Swiss francs for the first time in 2006. In the same year the public election of a testimonial for Nespresso took place for which George Clooney was chosen as brand ambassador. The engagement of Clooney was worthwhile right from the outset: Nespresso's CEO stated that an astonishing 'one quarter of our [Nespresso's] growth we owe to him [George Clooney]'.

Business model

Nespresso SA has two business divisions: Nespresso and Nespresso Business Solutions. For its business-to-consumer (B2C) business, Nespresso offers a range of six machine models with various functions at different price points. The capsule assortment consists of 16 coffee varieties; each capsule is made of aluminium and contains 5–6 grams of fresh ground coffee. Whereas the original Nespresso system was targeted at private households, the company started to diversify early and set up a business-to-business (B2B) unit in 1993, which mainly serves the aviation industry, the office sector, and the hospitality industry. To meet their needs, Nespresso Business Solutions provides a range of four machine models and eight coffee varieties. The ground coffee is packaged in aluminium pods instead of aluminium capsules. The B2C machines and capsules, are not compatible with the professional system or any other external competitive system—Nespresso is a proprietary system. This proprietary system, i.e. the interaction of the machine and capsule is protected with roughly 1,700 patents. Yet Mr Winkler was aware that many of those patents were set to expire in 2012, therefore providing less protection from competitors.

Branding and marketing

The Club and boutique concept communicate an image of exclusivity and specialness. This is successfully supported by the other marketing activities of Nespresso which convey premium quality and luxury at all customer touch points along the value chain from product presentation through sales to customer service. The high price points of the system's components as well as the exclusive B2B partners also support the notion that Nespresso is a premium product. Nevertheless, Nespresso is priced in such a way as not to exceed the threshold of affordability and thus constitutes a luxury item everybody can afford, i.e. the brand is 'selective, yet inviting'. Finally, the engagement of George Clooney as endorser was a stroke of luck for Nespresso because he embodies perfectly what the brand wants to stand for, namely elegance, sophistication, and smartness with a hint of mischievousness.

The impact of the brand's equity is seen when comparing the prices of Nespresso coffee with those of the competition. A single Nespresso capsule contains an average of 5.5 grams of ground coffee and costs between €0.35 and € 0.39. Therefore, one pound of Nespresso coffee costs between € 31.81 and € 35.45. In contrast, one pound of regular ground coffee, which is for sale in retail and not packaged individually, costs around € 5.49. Yet consumers are willing to pay the price differential because of the unique combination of Nespresso's business model, marketing, and branding which gives the company a competitive advantage. Nevertheless, Nespresso is facing a dilemma: on the one hand its business model and branding are centred around exclusivity and uniqueness, but on the other the company is pursuing ambitious growth rates which are in direct contrast with these aspects. Mr Winkler was pondering if the Club, and in fact the entire marketing strategy, were at risk of losing eventually credibility.

Sustainability at Nespresso: Ecolaboration

Like most companies Nespresso has made sustainability a top priority on its business agenda. Nespresso has realized that sustainable practices in the coffee growing regions are a prerequisite in order to provide customers with a high quality coffee. At the same time it is the company's goal to mitigate 'the economic, environmental and social impacts' of the entire value creation process.

Nespresso started its sustainability efforts quite early with the introduction in Switzerland in 1991 of a capsule recycling system consisting of 34 collection points. In 2003 Nespresso introduced the AAA Sustainable Quality Programme which was intended to organize the coffee procurement process more sustainably. The company's diversified sustainability programmes were finally consolidated in the Ecolaboration programme. Launched in 2009, it focuses on all areas across the entire value chain: coffee sourcing, capsule recycling, and carbon reduction. The ultimate goal of Ecolaboration is 'creating more shared value for farmers, business partners and consumers', thus achieving sustainable business success.

Coffee sourcing

In order to organize the coffee procurement process more sustainably, in 2003 Nespresso announced its AAA Sustainable Quality Programme which is conducted in collaboration with the Rainforest Alliance, a non-governmental organization (NGO) which aims 'to conserve biodiversity and ensure sustainable livelihoods' for the local population. Since Nespresso only processes green coffee beans of the highest quality, only 1–2 per cent of the worldwide coffee harvest is suitable. Therefore, the main reason to engage in the AAA programme was originally to achieving economic sustainability, i.e. 'to help protect the future of the highest quality coffees required by Nespresso for its consumers'. The three As represent the different areas in which Nespresso is involved.

The first A is about coffee quality and means that agronomists teach farmers well-established methods of coffee cultivation and other best practices. The second A, sustainability, is the complement to economic sustainability and deals with the concept's remaining pillars which are people and the environment. In order for farmers to become more socially responsible and environmentally friendly, Nespresso applies a methodology called Tool for the Assessment of Sustainable Quality (TASQ) which is based on the social and environmental standards of the Rainforest Alliance and its umbrella organization Sustainable Agriculture Network (SAN). To remain in the AAA programme farmers have to implement these standards and stick to several rules and regulations. The last component of the AAA programme is productivity and aims at increasing famers' incomes via an initiative named Real Farmer Income. The aim is to increase productivity by offering coffee farmers training and technical assistance as well as organizing production methods more efficiently. It is assumed that if farmers in a community earn enough from their work, they will in turn spend the money and thus contribute to rural development. Moreover, if sustainability and quality criteria are met, Nespresso pays its farmers a premium which exceeds the prices paid for similar high quality coffee beans by 10–15 per cent.

The measures in the AAA programme imply a commitment by Nespresso to engage with its farmers in long-term relationships and give them security. Hence, in 2010 Nespresso already sourced 60 per cent of its coffee demand from farms which were members of the AAA programme and aimed at 80 per cent in 2013. Finally, AAA programme farmers' incomes were 27 per cent higher than those of conventional farmers.

Unfortunately, not all stakeholders were happy with the progress of the AAA programme. Mr Winkler was especially troubled by harsh criticism from non-governmental organizations. Solidar Suisse even created a video parodying one of the commercials from the Heaven campaign with the objective of inducing Nespresso to use Fairtrade coffee instead, implying that the company's current AAA programme is nothing more than greenwashing.

Capsule recycling

Nespresso capsules are made from aluminium because the company considers it to be the best material available to protect coffee quality from external influences such as light, oxygen, and humidity. Nespresso further states that the aluminium capsules can be recycled indefinitely. Nevertheless, Mr Winkler had to admit that the original extraction of aluminium is highly energy intensive and considered by experts to be very harmful to the environment. In order to produce 1 kg of primary aluminium from the parent material bauxite, 14 kilowatt hours of energy is consumed and about 8 kg of carbon dioxide are released. Additionally, the extraction of the ore bauxite involves clearing rain forests and landscapes are destroyed by surface mining. For all these reasons it is imperative to recycle aluminium and to avoid dumping it. Furthermore, recycling aluminium is more ecofriendly than extraction as it consumes only around 5 per cent of the original energy needed.

Therefore, Nespresso launched AluCycle, a programme which aims at increasing recycling capacity by encouraging Club members to collect their used capsules. The company was committed to increasing global collection capacity to 75 per cent in 2013. Yet Nespresso surpassed this goal by June 2012 when recycling capacity exceeded the target and reached 76.4 per cent. The company has capsule collection systems in place in 24 countries. Recycling units can be found in every Nespresso boutique or at machine retailers and disposal centres. Another way for customers to make their used capsules available for recycling is via doorstep collection, i.e. returning the used capsules to the courier when receiving the new Nespresso delivery. Furthermore, the company attempts to create awareness about the collection system and encourages its customers to make use of it. For instance, Club members can find information concerning the nearest collection point on the Internet and in the Nespresso iPhone app. Also leaflets and brochures dealing with capsule recycling are available in the boutiques. Finally, Nespresso created a dedicated TV commercial starring John Malkovich and brand ambassador George Clooney.

Additionally, Nespresso has established partnerships to further decrease its environmental impact and is engaged in innovative technological projects. For instance, Nespresso is a partner of the Club du Recyclage des Emballages Légers en Aluminium et Acier (CELAA), which 'has been testing an electromagnetic system that separates small-scale aluminium packaging from other waste', thus allowing aluminium recovery. Finally, together with other companies from the aluminium industry, Nespresso established the Aluminium Stewardship Initiative (ASI) which aims at making aluminium production more sustainable.

Carbon reduction

Nespresso's overall goal in this area is to decrease its potentially negative impact on the environment along the entire value chain from coffee growing to espresso consumption. In order to understand this effect, Nespresso employs a process called Life Cycle Assessment (LCA) to measure the effect of the business on the environment. Five indicators are used for measurement: Climate change (emissions of carbon dioxide and other greenhouse gases), water footprint (amount used), biodiversity (influence on ecosystem), energy (amount used), and human health (health and well-being). From this range, Nespresso has decided to focus its attention strongly on the carbon footprint area. It was found that the most negative impacts on the environment occur during coffee growing and machine use. Regarding emission reduction in coffee growing, several best practices related to sustainability were consequently incorporated in the AAA programme. Nespresso planned to decrease the carbon footprint of producing one cup of coffee by 20 per cent between 2009 and 2013.

Besides these initiatives, Nespresso seeks to ameliorate its entire environmental footprint as well. In the production and distribution centre in Avenches, a new roasting technique is employed which decreases energy consumption by up to 20 per cent compared with conventional methods. Another novelty is the internal use of collected rainwater. The handling of used capsules also contributes to the improvement of Nespresso's overall environmental footprint. Nespresso continuously reports on its progress regarding the Ecolaboration platform; the latest report dates back to June 2011 and assesses coffee sourcing, capsule recycling, and carbon dioxide reduction.

The coffee market

In 2011, coffee volume retail sales amounted to 41,118 tons and coffee value sales had grown to €565 million. Especially with single-serve systems, consumers appreciate the convenience and that they can brew exactly one cup of high quality coffee without any hassle. In 2012 35 per cent of Austrian coffee drinkers were already using a pad- or capsule-based single-serve system, 30 per cent used a fully-automatic coffee machine to prepare coffee, and the remaining 35 per cent a traditional drip coffee maker. The single-serve segment is expected to remain the one with the steepest growth curve, driving overall coffee volume and value sales. The reasons for this continuing growth are the importance of convenience to Austrian consumers, demographic trends, and the association of pods with high-quality coffee.

Besides some challenges, the portion segment is still highly attractive due to the growth rates and very good margins. Therefore, many companies have started operating in the market and others continue to join to get their share of the pie. Worldwide, Nespresso has around 50 competitors; in Austria there are approximately 20 of which Tassimo, Dolce Gusto, Cafissimo, and Cremesso are the largest.

A new competitor: the ethical coffee company

Another company has recently entered the group of capsule manufacturers. Ethical Coffee Company (ECC) offers biodegradable capsules which are compatible with almost all Nespresso machines and supposedly do not infringe any of Nespresso's patents. What is more, the company's CEO is a true Nespresso expert—the inventor of the ECC coffee capsule is no less than Jean-Paul Gaillard. This is intriguing since Gaillard worked for Nespresso for ten years and was the mastermind behind the Nespresso Club and the licensing approach which initiated Nespresso's commercial success.

Historical overview

During his time at Nestlé, Gaillard proposed launching a second capsule system which would generate growth by targeting the mass market and thus complement the existing Nespresso solution, but this idea was rejected by Nespresso managers. Therefore, Gaillard's idea was to develop his own proprietary system which would function with biodegradable capsules. Owing to his insights from Nespresso and thorough research, he discovered a loophole among the myriad registered patents and spotted an opportunity to market an environmentally friendly capsule that did not infringe any of the Nespresso patents. After confirmation from two law firms that his capsules were not violating any Nespresso patents, Gaillard officially founded ECC in April 2008 in Fribourg, Switzerland. Gaillard decided upon France for the very first launch of his new capsules, specifically the stores of the well-known supermarket chain Casino. The capsules became available in different retailers of the Rewe group across Germany in October 2011 and in Austria in November 2011. According to Gaillard, the capsules got off to a good start with nationwide sales amounting to six million capsules within the first four weeks and an immediate market share of 20 per cent.

A biodegradable capsule

ECC is clearly distinct from all its competitors because it offers a product that is not only environmentally friendly, but is also convenient. What stands out primarily is the ecological aspect: ECC's capsules are composed of plant-based material (plant fibre and starch) meaning that they are biodegradable and compostable within six months according to EU Standard 13432. They are also compatible with most Nespresso machines and can easily be disposed of in a residual or organic waste bin. An ECC capsule costs € 0.29 in Austria and is hence 20–34 per cent cheaper than Nespresso. Furthermore, they are widely available throughout Austria, since the company sells them more conveniently for consumers via a large retailer network consisting of around 1,000 Billa and 117 Merkur supermarkets.

Another important point on which ECC differs strongly from Nespresso is marketing. In accordance with its ecofriendly business model ECC does not really engage in any. The company spends little money on marketing as ECC does not have an expensive testimonial, does not publish a glossy magazine, and does not have the expense of supporting luxurious sales outlets. Gaillard firmly believes that most customers are not looking for ostentatious add-ons, but simply want high quality coffee at a reasonable price. The company's mission is thus to provide 'what is today considered [a] "luxury" product . . . to as wide an audience as possible'. ECC is doing so by selling high quality espresso ground coffee in an environmentally friendly manner. Not only did these new compatible capsules offset the benefits of Nespresso's lock-in system, but Mr Winkler was also aware that ECC's new business model, especially the components related to sustainability, distribution, and price, could constitute a real threat to the company's operations if consumers responded positively to the ECC capsules.

For ECC, the year following the market entries in several strategically important countries proved successful so that the company produced 280 million capsules in 2012. For 2013, Gaillard anticipates the production of 500 million capsules to serve the 24 countries in which the ECC capsules are available, either via retailers or e-commerce. Likewise experts from the German Coffee Association acknowledge the potential of Gaillard's innovative product forecasting that 'biodegradable capsules are interesting for consumers'.

Nespresso's uncertain future

Mr Winkler noted with pleasure that the success of the Nespresso system had continued unabated until today. In 2011 the company revenue exceeded 3.5 billion Swiss francs and had a growth rate of approximately 9 per cent compared with 2010. Nespresso was present in 50 countries worldwide and operated 270 boutiques in 168 cities. But at the end of 2012 he also had to conclude that business had become tougher for Nespresso. Not only had competitors entered the market with their own systems, but also competition had emerged that produced compatible capsules for the Nespresso system and were thus increasing the competitive pressure. Unfortunately, a majority of Nespresso customers were willing to give the ecofriendly capsules a trial. This development was worrying considering the expiry of important patents in 2012, leaving Nespresso more vulnerable. Unfortunately these developments were also reflected in declining growth rates. Mr Winkler wondered if Nespresso had put too much emphasis on organic growth during recent years and thereby maybe lost its claim to exclusivity. The poor results of the sustainability study gave him a headache as well. Despite Nespresso's attempts to establish awareness among its customers on aluminium recycling and induce them to return the used capsules, many consumers were either not aware of the multitude of recycling opportunities or simply did not make use of them. Mr Winkler was worried about this development, as the importance of sustainability was increasing and consumer society was strongly concerned about how companies are responding to this challenge. Therefore the accusations of greenwashing, made by several NGOs, came at an adverse point of time. Mr Winkler was wondering how the company should be steered to remain successful and how to tackle the looming issues.

Discussion questions

1. How should Nespresso react to the new competitor ECC? Develop a conclusive outline of Nespresso's strategic alternatives.

2. Are there any areas of improvement concerning Nespresso's sustainability orientation?

3. Put yourself into the shoes of Mr Gaillard. What are your success pillars and what would be your next steps?

4. Are there any product categories other than coffee in which sustainability is of increasing importance? Can you think of categories in which sustainability is not a big deal at all? Why are there such differences?

5. What do you think about company internal sustainability labels? Do they constitute a trustworthy and genuine effort of a company to contribute to a sustainable development? Or are they often just a marketing ploy? Can you think of any concrete examples?

This case was prepared by Professor Verena Gruber, Vienna University of Economics and Business, Vienna, Austria

Part V

Did we get there?

I. Introduction

1 Overview and strategy blueprint
2 Marketing strategy: analysis and perspectives

II. Where are we now?

3 Environmental and internal analysis: market information and intelligence

III. Where do we want to be?

4 Strategic marketing decisions, choices, and mistakes
5 Segmentation, targeting, and positioning strategies
6 Branding strategies
7 Relational and sustainability strategies

V. Did we get there?

14 Strategy implementation, control, and metrics

IV. How will we get there?

8 Product innovation and development strategies
9 Service marketing strategies
10 Pricing and distribution strategies
11 Marketing communications strategies
12 International marketing strategies
13 Social and ethical strategies

14 Strategy implementation, control, and metrics

I. Introduction

1 Overview and strategy blueprint
2 Marketing strategy: analysis and perspectives

II. Where are we now?

3 Environmental and internal analysis: market information and intelligence

III. Where do we want to be?

4 Strategic marketing decisions, choices, and mistakes
5 Segmentation, targeting, and positioning strategies
6 Branding strategies
7 Relational and sustainability strategies

V. Did we get there?

14 Strategy implementation, control, and metrics

IV. How will we get there?

8 Product innovation and development strategies
9 Service marketing strategies
10 Pricing and distribution strategies
11 Marketing communications strategies
12 International marketing strategies
13 Social and ethical strategies

 Case study: The problems of implementing, controlling, and measuring marketing strategy

The term 'strategy', like 'brand', is one of those overused and frequently misused words in marketing, imbuing anything to which it is appended with a sometimes undeserved veneer of professionalism and competence.

So what exactly is a marketing strategy? At its simplest it is a plan that sets out how an organization will achieve its marketing objectives, usually described in terms like sales, margin, or market share. It should reflect the overall business objectives of the business; in fact some people would argue that in a truly marketing-led organization, the marketing strategy should be *the* business strategy, and vice versa, but that is a debate for another day.

What makes a good marketing strategy

A good marketing strategy should have a number of key elements. It should describe current and prospective customers, perhaps including some form of segmentation and description of them beyond mere numbers and demographics. It should say something about how the product or service is relevant to these customers and how this relevance will be maintained, and it will set out, ideally in quantified terms, clear objectives and methods by which these objectives will be attained.

Again, some would argue that the most important feature of a marketing strategy is how precise and decisive it is in terms of setting out and describing the target audience and a differentiated customer 'proposition'. For many, it is the strength and appeal of this differentiation that should be at the heart of a good marketing strategy, although, as we shall see later, this might not always be as important as some think.

The marketing strategy should also set out the role and expectations for all the elements of the marketing 'mix' using the old, but simple, 5Ps model; for example, this would cover Product, Price, Promotion, Place, and People, and I will assume that most are familiar with what these terms refer to.

There are a number of other important features of a good strategy.

Decisiveness and rigour

I mentioned the importance of decisiveness and rigour, and it is these qualities that will mark out the best strategies. Marketing is a lot to do with analysis and choices; it is hard to please all of the people all of the time, as the saying goes, and most marketing involves a degree of focus on key audiences, features, and channels. Some reference to classical marketing theories (Porter, Ansoff, Andrews, et al.) can be a useful (although not essential) mark of a good plan.

Alignment and integration

All the elements of the marketing mix need to be aligned in the best marketing strategy. The functions in a modern business are increasingly specialized and fast moving, and it is vital that all are 'singing from the same hymn sheet'. For example, there is no point in promoting 'a no quibble guarantee' if that isn't recognized at point of sale.

Effectively communicated

Leading on from this, it is essential that the marketing strategy is effectively communicated. This means more than just 'marketing communications' ('MARCOMS') and external communications, and in fact for too many people there is mistaken belief that marketing is essentially just MARCOMS. These activities are important, but just as important are such things as the communication of the marketing strategy throughout the business. This is particularly important in service businesses where the ultimate delivery of the 'brand promise' to customers is heavily dependent upon the performance of staff in the business. We can all think of countless examples where it feels like the marketing is being done by a series of 'silos'.

'Show me the money'

This isn't an accountancy book. But money will be a key measure of success and unit of operation in most organizations. So a proper understanding of how and where the money is made—and how it is applied and measured in the pursuit of marketing objective—is another vital element in any integrated marketing strategy. A criticism frequently levelled at marketers is that they don't always understand the realities of business finance and that as a result marketing plans are not always properly grounded in the financial basics.

The Manifesto of the UK's Marketing Society proposes that one of the most important things that marketers can do to mobilize the organization towards achieving sustainable growth is to 'Quantify the cost and value of your work', and it is vital that any marketing strategy has a realistic and credible financial component.

This financial discipline should have two levels of focus: one strategic, where the emphasis will be on understanding how money is made and the role of marketing, and the rate and type of return on marketing activity, and the other more tactical, where the marketer will look to evaluate and control marketing activity such as advertising and promotion.

Measurement and accountability

Finally, you need to have systems and metrics in place to measure your marketing efforts. Reviewing the various approaches to marketing evaluation is worthy of a separate chapter in itself, but the most important task is to choose metrics that best track the chosen objectives and marketing tactics. Having a long-term as well as a short-term focus is important too. It is also helpful to think creatively and laterally about measurement, and many businesses are finding things like customer complaints and social media an increasingly valuable source of market feedback.

Putting it all together

So what are the issues that arise in implementing, controlling, and measuring marketing strategy? Not surprisingly, there are challenges at every stage in the process and I will review here just a few of the most common and important.

Where's the plan?

The first question is whether the organization even has a marketing strategy in the first place. Many don't or they do bits of the work but don't pull it together into a cohesive whole, understood by the whole business. I have already outlined what a proper marketing strategy needs to cover, and without a coherent plan a business is doomed to mediocrity.

Lack of differentiation or relevance

As discussed, marketing strategy is about making choices about such things as audience, price, and distribution channels. Having a strongly differentiated and clearly positioned offering is also vital. However, sometimes the quest for differentiation can be overdone (we've all heard about marketers constantly being urged to 'think outside the box'). But it can be argued that effective marketing is as much about consistent execution across a range of customer needs than out and out differentiation.

Overcomplication

Hard on the heels of an absence of strategy comes the strategy that is overcomplicated, over-analysed, and undeliverable. We've all heard of the 'elevator pitch', and the core of the marketing strategy needs that element of brevity and pithiness —particularly if you have to explain it to a few thousand employees.

Lack of integration

The most effective marketing strategies and plans are properly integrated; that is, all the elements of the marketing mix are aligned to the same objectives (and are measured in appropriate ways—see next section). There is an increasing recognition that effective marketing is about the total customer experience, not just about creative advertising for example. Staff and stakeholders also need to quickly understand their roles in delivering an appropriate product or service

Measuring the wrong thing (or not measuring them at all)

There's an old saying in business that what gets measured, gets done, and of course this can cut two ways. If the correct metrics have been identified this can lead to positive performance, but if the wrong metrics have been prioritized the efforts and resources of the business can be incorrectly focused. A frequent example is a salesforce measured on short-term sales performance and a marketing team focused on long-term brand metrics.

Another old marketing cliché, variously attributed, is that '50 per cent of my advertising is wasted, I just don't know which half'. I'm never sure whether this is meant to convey that advertising is a blunt instrument or to be a constant spur to measure as accurately as possible. In the end I think it means that however rigorous you are, some things will always be down to judgement.

Chicken—or egg?

Could you have the right strategy undermined by the wrong tactics—or the right tactics but the wrong strategy? We can all recall great ads where we can't remember the brand name. Or situations where an appealing product offer has been undermined by some aspect of the 'customer journey' such as poor service or late delivery.

A purist might argue that it is more important to have the right strategy and that tactics can be refined and improved, whilst good tactics can only paper over strategic weaknesses that will find you out in the end. An example is a strong brand positioning being undermined by repeated price promotion in search of market share.

The correct but somewhat glib answer of course is that in a properly integrated marketing strategy you need both—a solid strategic base and a tactical delivery or execution which is integrated and delivers the strategy in the most relevant ways.

The pursuit of excellence

So who does it well? It's relatively easy to round up the usual marketing success stories: Apple, Audi, Southwest Airlines, First Direct, Tesco.

Wait a minute—Tesco? This example highlights one of the challenges in controlling marketing—we can list the success stories as well as the problem children, but how do you identify the latter before they arise? Are the systems in place? Is the organization staying in touch with the market and its customers? And most importantly, does the organization have a management culture that, having identified issues, is prepared and able to act on them decisively, changing strategy if necessary?

This is perhaps the biggest challenge for any organization seeking to be truly great—to be able not only to identify the right things to do, but to act decisively to deliver them, instigating major change if necessary. And there is a limit to how much such an agile, flexible, and pragmatic approach can be built into any formal strategy.

As I stated at the outset, strategy is an overused term in marketing, and there are thousands of books and articles written on the subject of 'marketing strategy' alone. In the end it comes down to the basics: Who is our target audience? Why do they buy? How might we get more of them or get them to buy more or differently?—clearly analysed and quantified.

So in summary, effective marketing strategy is simply a function of decisive and rigorous planning combined with flawless execution at every stage of the marketing mix.

Sounds easy, doesn't it?

Christopher Macleod is responsible for a diverse portfolio of marketing and customer information programmes for Transport for London (TfL). His work ranges from promoting Oyster cards to Road Safety, Buses and Tubes to the Cycle Hire scheme. During his time at TfL it has won every major marketing and creative award including Campaign magazine's Advertiser of the Year, Cannes Gold Lions, and Marketing Society and IPA Effectivenesss Awards. Previously he worked at a number of leading agencies including Saatchi & Saatchi, McCann Erickson, and Collett Dickenson Pearce, where he was Chief Executive, and fast-moving consumer goods companies such as Papa John's. He is a regular on the Bakerloo Underground line in London.

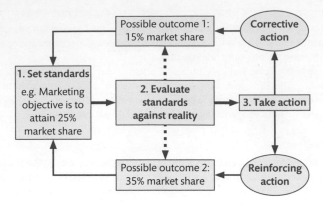

14.1 Steps in the Implementation and Control Process

Introduction

There is every indication that in the future a firm's marketing success will hinge not so much on having a good strategy, as on how well this strategy is implemented and controlled. The managerial act of control involves four steps.

1. Set targets of performance (these are typically in the form of goals or objectives).

2. Evaluate the reality of what occurs against these steps, i.e. failure or success.

3. Take corrective or reinforcing action where required.

4. Establish new targets in light of the situation at step 3.

These steps are illustrated in the marketing example in Figure 14.1.

Assume that a firm in Thailand sets a market share objective of 25 per cent, which is step 1 in the control process. At the next step, the manager compares reality against the standard and either fails to achieve 25 per cent or achieves/overachieves 25 per cent. At the third step, the manager takes either corrective or reinforcing action. If the market share achieved was only 15 per cent, then the manager would attempt to correct whatever aspects of marketing strategy caused this to happen. On the other hand, if the market share really achieved in Thailand was 25 per cent or more, the manager would seek to reinforce whatever actions caused this to happen. Note, though, that overachievement can often present its own problems. For example, owing to supply logistics, it may be extremely difficult to meet increased demand, which might lead to some kind of rationing or price increases (consider how demand rapidly outstripped the supply of the PlayStation 4 when it was first launched and the product achieved a higher than retail price on eBay in Europe in 2013). The final step is to establish the next set of targets in light of the outcomes of actions in step 2.

Having made these points, it must be emphasized that control is a process rather than a linear and sequential series of steps—the corrective and reinforcing step in turn becomes the source of information for the setting of subsequent standards. **Time** is a critical dimension. In reality, outcomes may be either higher or lower than the target figure set, or the objective set established, so most astute managers usually assign a time frame to an objective. For example, 'Our firm sets a market share objective of 25 per cent to be achieved within a year.'

Managers will then monitor achievement against this standard on a monthly, quarterly, or annual (or whatever is deemed appropriate) basis and it is at this time that the control process and related actions will be undertaken. Quite often the time frame for objectives can be longer term. For example, Coca-Cola's Chief Executive Officer (CEO) Muhtar Kent, who took the helm of the company in 2008, has reportedly set an ambitious goal of doubling its business by 2020, which is known internally as the '2020 Vision' (HBR Interview, 2011 b).

The act of implementation is the accomplishment or carrying into effect; it is the executing of a plan or strategy. Marketing strategy implementation consists of 'doing' the strategy. When strategic marketing failures occur, it is usually strategy formulation that is blamed; managers say things like, 'Our strategy was wrong'. Too often, they overlook the fact that there may have been nothing wrong with the strategy, but that the execution was flawed. As one executive ruefully put it, 'Our thinking was right. But we did it wrong!' For example, when Tesco entered the US market (Arizona, California, and Nevada) with its Fresh & Easy chain in late 2007, it had high hopes. Being a savvy marketer, Tesco undertook extensive qualitative research, rigged up a mock store in California, and developed clear and concise behavioural segmentations and positioning. Unfortunately, its mid-price point positioning proved a mistake. Not a great strategy when American consumers were tightening their belts and looking for deals. Hindsight is a wonderful thing!

The implementation of marketing strategy

The problem with poor implementation of strategy is that it is difficult to diagnose. This dilemma was recognized some years ago by Harvard Business School Marketing Professor Tom Bonoma (1984), who argued that **marketing managers trying to put marketing strategies into practice often confront structural and personnel problems**. The structural problems of marketing involve marketing functions, programmes, systems, and policy directives. Marketing functions often fail because of faulty management assumptions or inattention to marketing basics, while programmes are often contradicted by a lack of functional capabilities or insufficient management attention. Systems are limited by errors of ritual and politicization, and marketing policies regularly suffer from the lack of a marketing theme and culture. For example, an offer of half-price clothing via Groupon can backfire for a company if overworked or sceptical employees lead to a negative customer experience (Dholakia, 2011). However, good interaction, allocation, monitoring, and organization skills can overcome poor marketing practices; see, for example, the positive practices at General Electric (GE) in relation to marketing principles and ensuring appropriate roles and processes (Comstock et al., 2010). Bonoma suggests that marketers consider two aspects of their strategy when diagnosing (or indeed controlling for) its success or failure, which are mapped out in the grid in Figure 14.2.

The two dimensions on the grid consider **strategy formulation and strategy implementation**, which can range from poor to adequate. Bonoma's suggestion is that managers should use the grid to map the formulation of their own marketing strategy and its implementation. When strategy is well formulated and implemented, it is likely that **success** will follow. Similarly, when strategy is poorly formulated and implemented, not surprisingly it generally results in **failure**. It is when one of the other two situations on the diagonal in the grid occurs that marketing managers are faced with a dilemma.

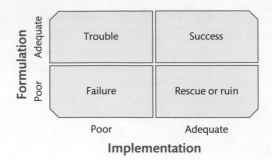

14.2 Strategy Formulation Implementation Grid

Strategy that is adequately formulated but poorly implemented leads to **trouble**. This is because, very often, poor results will be blamed on the strategy, not on its implementation. 'Our strategy was wrong', managers will say, and 'We shouldn't have done that'. However, what they might be saying after some introspection would be something like 'We had the right strategy, but we implemented it poorly'.

For example, a major consumer goods marketer in Brazil recognized that, although poor, the consumers in Rio de Janeiro's favelas (hillside slums) represented an attractive market segment for the products the firm made. The marketing team formulated a strategy that involved designing innovative new products targeted at this market, paying particular attention to issues like packaging (products needed to be portable, durable, and storable). They were also able to price the product range affordably. An innovative approach to promotion involved a tie-up with a popular local soccer team which produced good results in market research. In order to distribute the products, the firm would rely on the many informal neighbourhood shops (many of which were run from people's homes) that served the slum areas, rather than on large supermarkets that were often far from the consumers. However, six months after the implementation, the results in the target market were most disappointing. Rather than simply blame the strategy, the marketing director and his team undertook an in-depth analysis of implementation. It was discovered that the small informal shops frequently did not carry the products, and those that did were often out of stock. Further analysis revealed that the sales team seldom visited the stores concerned, either because they believed that individually the small stores didn't matter, or because they were in areas salespeople preferred not to enter. Second, deliveries to the stores were unpredictable and intermittent. Many of the favelas are situated on steep hillsides, and truck drivers simply chose not to deliver to them because it was difficult. So, a good marketing strategy failed because of implementation issues.

Returning to the grid in Figure 14.2, Bonoma suggests that strategy that is poorly formulated but well implemented leads to **rescue or ruin**. This is a particularly complex situation, because the consequences can frequently be dramatic and unpredictable. On the one hand, this situation can rescue a firm's poor marketing strategy because a well-implemented strategy can overcome weaknesses in formulation. On the other hand, effective implementation of a bad strategy can hasten a firm's downfall. In simple terms, if an idea is really stupid, and you do it really well, it shouldn't be surprising that disasters occur!

Deighton's (2002) article on the birth, demise, and resurrection of the soft drink brand Snapple provides a good example of a 'rescue or ruin' (in this case, ruin) situation. In 1994 Quaker purchased the Snapple brand from its founders for $1.7 billion. The thinking behind this strategy (its formulation) was that Snapple would be a good complement to Quaker's Gatorade brand of sports drinks. Whereas Snapple was strong in convenience stores, delis, and lunch restaurants, Gatorade was strong in supermarkets. If Quaker's marketers had formulated their strategy more carefully, they would have realized that Snapple's success was built on certain key issues.

1. **The theme of being 'natural':** while not a health drink, Snapple contained few additives and was seen as an alternative to cola drinks. The natural theme was enhanced through quirky advertising and the use of unconventional spokespersons for the brand, including 'shock jock' radio DJ Howard Stern.

2. **Snapple's range included dozens of different flavours,** some with rather bizarre mixes. While not all of these were successful in terms of sales, product development costs were very low, and the range of flavours made the product interesting in the eyes of the market as customers always wondered what the next new Snapple flavour would be. The product was also packaged in heavy chunky glass bottles, not cans.

3. **Snapple was sold at a premium price,** which consumers typically didn't perceive, as the drink was usually purchased as part of lunch. So, rather than notice that they were paying $2 or $3 for a soft drink, consumers spent $8 on lunch, which would typically include a sandwich and a Snapple.

When it was sold through supermarkets, Snapple's new marketing strategy quickly unravelled. In order to cut costs, Quaker ceased the natural and quirky promotional theme, including dropping Howard Stern who, as a consequence, called the drink 'Crapple' on his radio programme. As supermarkets do not tolerate lots of different product variations, the Snapple range had to be ruthlessly pruned, which caused the brand to lose its consumer interest factor. Consumers who considered purchasing Snapple in a supermarket quickly realized that a six-pack of bulky glass bottles was heavy and difficult to carry. Furthermore, when they were buying Snapple in isolation and in comparison to other soft drinks, they also recognized it was expensive—something they had overlooked when they had purchased it as a component of lunch. Gatorade also didn't sell well in the convenience/deli channel, as consumers did not want to drink a sports drink with their sandwiches.

Quaker had implemented its Snapple strategy ruthlessly and well. **The problem was that the strategy's formulation had been exceptionally poor**. So poor in fact, that the Snapple brand was sold off for $400 million (a brand equity write-off of $1.3 billion). Not a rescue situation in this case, but very much a ruin. (TriArc turned the Snapple brand around and subsequently sold it to Cadbury Schweppes. It achieved the turnaround by returning to the original Snapple strategy and implementing it well.) Thus, a poor implementation often obscures the effectiveness or ineffectiveness of the marketing strategy; therefore marketing practices should be examined before adjustments are made to strategy.

Why are marketing strategies not always implemented well? The reality is that it is often easier to develop a new strategy than to implement it. In too many organizations, marketing strategy is implicit and resides only in the minds of senior marketers. These individuals may have trouble explaining their strategy, so most of the other people in the marketing function are forced to guess what the strategy is, and they may guess wrongly. Marketing executives often develop their strategy in isolation, leaving people without ownership and with no understanding of the rationale behind it. As many members of the marketing function as possible should be involved in developing a strategy in order to achieve accurate understanding and proper execution. A good strategic marketing process will help management identify and proactively manage the implications of the strategy for the organization's products, markets, customers, and structure. According to Robert (1991), there are a number of barriers to the implementation of strategy that deserve brief consideration.

- **The marketing strategy is implicit, not explicit, and people cannot implement what they do not know:** when strategy resides in the head of the senior marketing executive others in the marketing department are forced to guess what it is—and they may guess wrong. This can be referred to as 'strategy by groping' because the strategy only becomes clear over a long period of time as people test what it might be by trial and error. **Implication:** make the marketing strategy explicit!

- **The marketing strategy is developed in isolation—and people cannot implement what they do not understand:** marketing strategy is often developed by a senior marketer or a few senior marketing executives, usually at a retreat at some exclusive resort. Others in the organization, and especially the marketing function, feel divorced from the marketing strategy, and also do not understand it. **Implication:** involve as many people as possible in the formulation of marketing strategy in order to achieve accurate understanding and proper execution. Also, consider appointing a CSO (Chief Strategic Officer) to work alongside the CEO. CSOs act as 'mini CEOs' and have the mandate to walk into any office and say: 'What we've been doing isn't in line with the company's strategy—and we need to fix that' (Breene et al., 2007).

- **Not everyone is a good strategic marketing thinker:** many individuals within the marketing function are involved in day-to-day marketing activities, so they don't spend much time thinking strategically and have difficulty coping with strategic issues, especially when these are sprung on them. If they are encouraged to understand the differences between strategic processes and everyday operational marketing issues, they will be better able and more willing to implement the formulated marketing strategy. **Implication:** encourage the participation of key marketing subordinates in strategy formulation, even if only for its educational value.

- **The marketing strategy is developed by an external consultant:** many firms employ consultants to formulate their marketing strategy for them. While there are roles for consultants in organizations, including conducting marketing audits, conducting research, and other specialist advice, formulating marketing strategy probably should not be one of them, and certainly not in isolation. The problem caused by having an external consultant/s formulate marketing strategy is that most members of the marketing function are not committed to this strategy because it is not their strategy. It may also send out the message that 'our own staff aren't up to it'. By engaging external consultants, organizations lose out on the commitment that comes from participation. At worst, this will often lead to so-called 'white-anting' (an Australian term for the process of internal erosion of a foundation—to subvert or undermine from within), whereby people actively work against and sabotage a strategy that they perceive to be someone else's. **Implication:** do not normally use external consultants to formulate marketing strategy—people will not implement a strategy they are not committed to.

- **The marketing strategy has unanticipated consequences:** when formulating strategy, many marketers do not think it through carefully enough to be able to foresee all the implications the strategy might have. When the strategy is then implemented, people who initially supported it often begin to say things like 'If we'd known that would happen, we wouldn't have supported it'. A good strategic marketing planning process will anticipate, identify, and proactively manage the implications of a marketing strategy on the organization's products and services, markets, customers, organizational structure, and personnel. **Implication:** identify strategic implications beforehand so that people don't give up on a strategy whose repercussions have not been foreseen.

Marketing budget

Having made these points, sometimes the issue is simply that the allocated budget is inappropriate. Setting an appropriate budget is crucial for two reasons: if too much is spent, short-term finances are stretched (West et al., 2014). However, if the budget is too small, longer-term opportunities may be lost and competitiveness eroded. A variety of methods are used to set budgets and most firms use multiple methods (on average around two or three). Here is a snapshot of the leading methods being used.

Judgemental methods

- *Arbitrary:* solely determined on the basis of what is 'felt' to be necessary to implement the strategy.
- *Affordable:* the organization determines what it can spend on other areas, such as production and operations, and then decides how much it can afford for marketing.

Objective and task

- Spending is in accordance with what is required to meet the marketing strategy objective(s). Ranked by importance, objectives are set, tasks agreed upon to meet these objectives, and then costs estimated. If the strategy cannot be afforded, lower-importance objective(s) are eliminated until the budget can be afforded.

Measurement

- *ROI:* marketing is considered an investment and money is spent to the point where the ROI is diminishing
- *Incremental:* the budget is allocated in an incremental series of tests. Spending is increased or decreased in line with the results achieved
- *Quantitative models:* computer simulation models are used involving statistical techniques such as multiple regression analysis.

Percentage of sales

- *Percentage of last year's sales:* set percentage of previous financial year's sales.
- *Percentage of anticipated sales:* set percentage of the firm's anticipated sales.
- *Unit sales:* the organization allocates a fixed percentage of unit price for marketing and then multiplies this amount by projected sales volume (e.g. 5% unit price × 200,000 cars sales forecast).

Competitive

- *Competitive absolute:* the budget is set in line with the closest rival
- *Competitive relative:* all the competitors in the market spend in line with their market share.

In terms of the methods used, indications for the US and UK broadly show that:

- about 35 per cent of budgets are set by judgemental methods
- about 30 per cent of budgets use objective and task
- about 25 per cent use measurement
- about 15 per cent use percentage of sales
- about 6 per cent use competitive methods
- on average, around two to three methods are combined.

Controlling marketing strategy

It is useful to distinguish three kinds of **control** with regard to managing marketing strategy.

1. **Annual plan control:** the objectives set in the annual marketing plan are evaluated against the results achieved. Corrective or reinforcing action is taken when necessary (see Figure 14.1).

2. **Financial or expense control:** considers the financial parameters and objectives set by a firm in its annual marketing plan, and the corrective or reinforcing actions needed to attain these. So, for example, a firm with a lower than budgeted return on sales may find there was excessive discounting by the salesforce. Management would need to take steps to ensure less discretion by sales staff with regard to pricing. In another example, a firm may have budgeted £100,000 for a trade exhibition, but only spent £80,000 and still achieved the planned results. A review of how the exhibition was managed might reveal that the reduction in spending was due to the judicious management of free samples and brochures through careful targeting. Management then ensures that the procedures adopted are reinforced throughout the marketing department for implementation at future exhibitions.

3. **Strategic control:** the purpose of strategic control is to ensure that the organization maximizes the opportunities in its environment. Strategic control often takes the form of a marketing audit. A marketing audit is a structured and in-depth examination of all the firm's marketing activities undertaken to identify those areas of marketing in which the firm is not performing to full potential, as well as those in which the firm is doing well. In order to ensure objectivity, many firms will choose to employ outside consultants to conduct a marketing audit.

Organization

Every organization has its own unique culture or set of values, whether it has consciously tried to create this or not. Usually, the culture of the organization is created unconsciously, based on the values of the top management or the organization's founders, and it forms a major factor in control. As already noted, writers such as Bonoma (1984) have noted that one of the most important reasons for the failure of marketing strategy is an inadequate **corporate culture**. Often, members of an organization will be heard to say things like 'In order to implement that strategy, we would have to change our culture', as if culture can be changed easily and quickly, like bed linen. The reality of organizational culture is that it is usually very deep-rooted. For example, eBay has cultivated a risk-taking culture to accompany its phenomenal growth. According to eBay's CEO John Donahoe: 'You're better off moving and, if you don't get it exactly right, making an adjustment. That's the only way to compete on the Internet today, because it's moving so fast' (HBR Interview, 2011a, p.96). Sometimes, it may be easier and better to try to understand the organization's culture, and to work with it, rather than change it—and this has wide and significant implications for the implementation of marketing strategy.

Culture

Marketing academics have long been interested in the effects that an organization's culture has on its ability to formulate and, more importantly, to implement marketing strategy. Badovick and Beatty (1987) found that shared organizational values (one aspect of culture) significantly impacted on strategic marketing implementation. Tse et al. (1988) investigated the relationship between national culture and marketing decision-making, finding that an executive's home (national) culture had a significant and predictable effect on decision-making. Qualls and Puto (1989) found that the cultural climate affects choice behaviours by influencing the decision-maker's reference points and decision frames. Webster (1991) investigated cultural consistency within service firms, and found that an employee's position influenced their attitudes towards their firm's actual and ideal marketing culture. Narver and Slater (1990) and Slater and Narver (1992) found that market orientation (a construct comprised of three elements: customer orientation, competitor orientation, and inter-functional coordination) was linked to business performance, and the authors use the concept of organizational culture to explain the relationship (see Mini Case 14.1). Bungay (2011) has emphasized the importance the contribution of military planning to business strategy.

It has been found that there is a direct link between organizational culture and business performance, while arguing that market orientation is a sub-component of culture (Webster, 1994; Deshpandé et al., 1993; Kumar et al., 2011). Companies with cultures that stress competitiveness (market cultures) and entrepreneurship (adhocracy cultures) outperform those with cultures that stress internal cohesiveness or rules. The influence of organizational culture and memory development on managers' perceptions of role-related problems has also been investigated (Berthon et al., 2001). Findings suggest that both organizational culture and memory influence managers' perceptions, with externally focused cultures emphasizing strategic problems, and organic process cultures emphasizing unstructured problems (see also Handy, 1978; Quinn, 1988; Campbell and Freeman, 1991; Goffee and Jones, 1996). The overall suggestion is that managers need to consider the existing organizational culture context and match this to their ability to take active steps to change cultural conditions before selecting strategy (Yarbrough et al., 2011).

Structure

Organizational structure plays a key role in control. There has been a great deal of interest over the years in the ways organizations maintain their internal and external viability in the light of market competiveness. If organizational culture is akin to an individual's sense of self, then organizational structure is akin to the biological functioning of the body to make a viable human being.

 Mini Case 14.1 Implementation, control, and metrics: the role of a marketing manager

One of the best ways to appreciate the importance of **implementation**, control, and metrics for marketing managers is to look at related job ads. Here is a listing of the responsibilities posted in a job ad for a marketing manager by a finance company in Mumbai, India. The listing has been modified, but the core requirements are real.

ROLE

To design and execute relevant measurable marketing strategies for our agents and end users/consumers across South Asia. The aim is to increase face values, transaction volumes, and profitability.

KEY ASPECTS OF THE JOB:

- Coordinate market research and gather secondary data.
- Analyse the relevant competitor strategies in terms of price, product, and service offerings.
- Work with the Marketing Director to develop and implement marketing, communication, and product enhancement/development plans to maximize transaction volumes and opportunities for countries within Asia.
- Implement ongoing tactical campaigns to drive market share and increases in volume.
- Closely monitor various aspects of the plan to ensure plan performance is in line with business objectives.
- Communicate with central and global marketing teams as necessary to ensure consistency of style and approach.
- Implement, report, and measure all initiatives on a monthly basis.
- Establish and implement a marketing control process to ensure that budgets, brand consistency, and integrity are maintained.
- Ensure the continued effectiveness of the control processes through regular communications with users.
- Manage post-marketing efforts and proactively provide feedback to the regional and Southeast Asia marketing team.
- Continually adapt marketing activity in line with competitive actions to ensure transaction volume targets continue to be met.
- Manage the marketing budget and gain pre-approval from the Marketing Director on all expenses and campaign expenditure.
- Organize the production and distribution of various marketing materials in appropriate languages, including promotional products/gifts at the right times.
- Conduct 'mystery shopper' campaigns with rivals to gain deeper understanding of their activities.
- Provide support and assistance to regional marketing resources in Mumbai and Bangalore to meet their regional marketing goals.
- Ad hoc duties as required by the office or team as they arise.

This is of course quite an extensive list of activities, but hopefully demonstrates the nature and scope of marketing management and the central role of implementation, control, and metrics.

14.3 Functional Organization

Organizations can take on a number of different marketing structures.

Figure 14.3 illustrates a basic **functional** organization which offers specialization in task activities to develop skills, with marketing tasks and responsibilities clearly defined. The **disadvantage** is that excess levels of hierarchy may reduce unity of control and direct lines of communication may be ignored, giving rise to conflicts and leaving integration a major problem for the chief marketing executive (CME). As such, functional structures are best suited to simple marketing operations where there is a single primary product or market.

Figures 14.4 and 14.5 illustrate specialization in **brand organization and services/ products**, respectively. Such an organization enables greater management attention to the specific marketing requirements of different brands/services/products and a faster reaction to brand/services/products related changes. The key disadvantages are the need for dual reporting, potentially too much product rather than market emphasis, and more management levels and costs. It fits best where there are wide product lines sold to homogeneous groups of customers, and where there are shared production/marketing systems.

A **market** organization, as in Figure 14.6, provides a fast reaction to market-related changes. However, as with brands and product structures, the **disadvantage** is the duplication of functions, the need for greater coordination, and more management levels. It is perhaps best suited where there is a limited standardized homogeneous product line sold to customers in different markets.

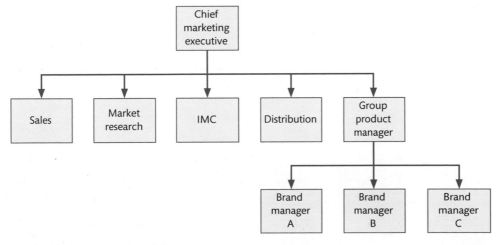

14.4 Brand Management Organization

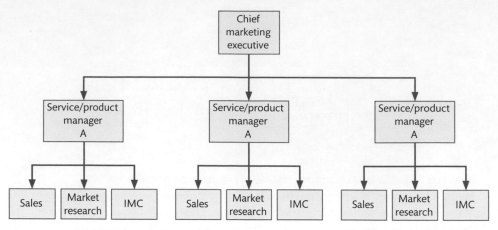

14.5 Service/Product Group Organization

Finally, Figure 14.7 shows a **combined service/product/market** organization which offers the advantage of functional services/products and market specialization integration. The **disadvantages** are that allocations of responsibilities are difficult and there will inevitably be some inefficient duplication. However, it is probably the best structure for a company with multiple products and multiple markets.

The traditional analysis of organizational control along the lines of function, brand, service, product, or market lines often misses the reality that organizations control their actions along a series of interconnected activity systems, and that rules and procedures are needed to coordinate the use of scarce resources while maintaining standards of quality (Bruning and Lockshin, 1994). Cybernetics, the science of communication and control in organisms

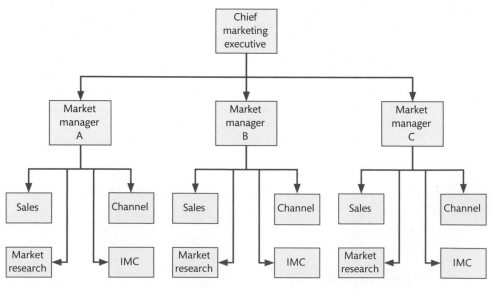

14.6 Market Organization

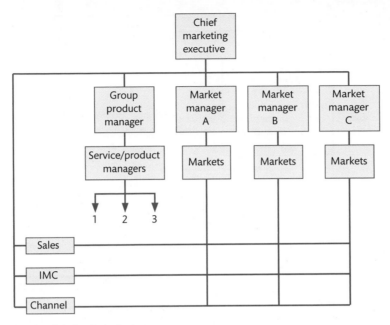

14.7 Service/Product/Market Organization

and machines, has made a particular contribution here with the concepts of **variety** and **requisite variety** (Jackson, 1988). Variety is the number of events or scenarios in an environment. In order to be viable, every organization must develop requisite variety with its environment; that is, an organization must have the capacity to match changes in its operating environment which will enable it to exert some control.

The founding father of cybernetics was W. Ross Ashby (see Brocklesby and Cummings, 1996), who worked for the US military during the Second World War. Ashby was particularly concerned with anti-aircraft and anti-missile systems. He argued that for a system to be viable, it had to go as low, and as high, and as fast, and as slow, as the objects in its environment in order to 'match' or 'destroy'.

Ashby's ideas were further developed by Stafford Beer (1979, 1981, 1985) who argued that any organism would only remain viable if it matched all the life-threatening varieties in its environment. For example, to use an analogy, the worm goes underground to escape the bird, the bird goes into the air to escape the cat, and the cat jumps up a tree to escape the dog (Brocklesby and Cummings, 1996). Thus, organizations have to match variety with variety, and this is the essence of successful control. Figure 14.8 depicts Beer's viable system model (VSM) with its five major systems.

- **System 1:** basic work unit(s) where the services/products/brand coordination is undertaken
- **System 2:** main regulatory centre
- **System 3:** operating management control centre
- **System 4:** intelligence and information-gathering centre
- **System 5:** overall strategic direction

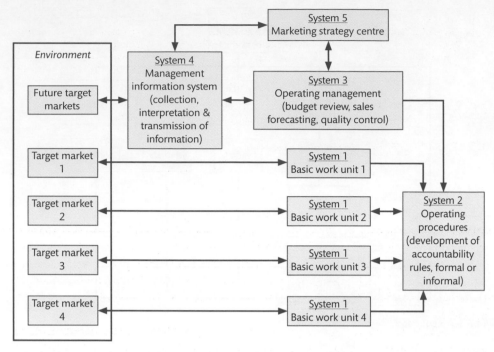

14.8 Modified Version of Stafford Beer's Viable System Model

The environment includes all the suppliers, regulatory bodies, customers, media, legislators, etc. that have an impact on the organization.

Beer's VSM certainly has its critics, particularly those who say that it gives little, if any, role to culture or power in organizations. However, from a marketing strategy perspective, it enables individuals to define their purpose with respect to their relevant unit and to those units with which they are connected. Beer also pointed out that the whole system could be placed within a business unit so that each unit could have its own subset of the operating procedures, operating management, information gathering, and strategy. His model has been used by governments in Chile and the UK (the Scottish Parliament, Welsh Assembly, and Northern Ireland Assembly can all be seen as 'work units' within the framework of the UK government), and companies such as Shell. For a specific example of its application, see the discussion by Brocklesby and Cummings (1996) of Telecom (New Zealand). It might also be argued that the root cause of failure of such companies as Comet (UK) has been an inability to develop the requisite variety needed to survive in the environment. Kesa Electronics had owned Comet when it was viable during the good years, but its market weaknesses and lack of focused position were exposed during the recession and shortly after it was sold to OpCapita, who took on the firm's pension deficit in 2012, it went bust. It simply had not made sufficient inroads into the all-important Internet market for electronic and household goods.

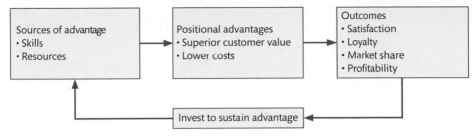

14.9 Day and Wensley's Model of Competitive Advantage (Modified)

Metrics

It has been found that the use of marketing metrics (performance measures related to the allocation of marketing resources such as awareness, satisfaction, and market share) by managers is positively associated with marketing performance (Mintz and Currim, 2013). Metrics underscore the ability to control marketing activities by setting specific measurement goals and also by helping organizations to understand their sources of competitive advantage by highlighting what is and what is not working amongst their marketing activities.

In the context of marketing metrics, Day and Wensley (1988) have alerted us to the management of competitive advantage as a process and hinted that the aspiration to a competitive advantage that was 'sustainable' was probably unrealistic for most firms. A slightly modified version of Day and Wensley's model of the process of competitive advantage can be seen in Figure 14.9.

Sources of competitive advantage

According to Day and Wensley (1988), there are only two sources of competitive advantage for a firm: it has either superior skills or superior resources, and, hopefully, both. 'Superior skills' is an all-embracing phrase for greater resources with regard to human talent, know-how, abilities, or competences. 'Superior resources' implies greater stocks of financial and other capital, better productive capacity, better location, access to supply, and the like.

Positional advantage

These sources of competitive advantage are used to achieve one of two positional advantages or ways of competing. Two generic competitive strategies can be identified: low relative cost or superior customer value (Porter, 1985). Supposedly, the low-cost competitor is able to produce and deliver the product or service at the lowest cost, with the advantages of margin and pricing flexibility that this confers. For those competitors who are unable to achieve the low-cost position, the only other course of action is to offer superior customer value. That is to say, these competitors must, for example, make the product or service bigger, smaller, faster, more colourful, better quality, or in a wider range. In short, they must differentiate their offerings in ways that will bestow superior customer values that people are prepared to pay a premium for. Porter (1985) implied that the two strategies are mutually exclusive and that to attempt to be a low-cost differentiator is to court the disaster of being stuck in the middle—increased costs without real differentiation. While that might have been true in the late 1970s and early 1980s, more recent developments such as flexible manufacturing technologies have made these choices less clear cut. Indeed, recent examples of firms such as Dell and Amazon.com might mean that it may not only be desirable to strive after both positions, but in many situations it may be the key to survival and success.

Performance outcomes

According to Day and Wensley (1988), when a firm exploits either of the two generic strategies of lower relative cost and/or providing superior customer value with some success, the outcomes will be evident in a number of variables and these variables form the foundations of marketing control; they are measurable.

Financial measures

Performance will manifest itself in financial productivity, measured by return on investment (ROI)—or for that matter, any of a number of financial acronyms. Indeed, the development of a marketing strategy would not be complete without an overview of the business's finances. It is important to note at the outset that the analysis is always sterile without comparative data (see, for example, Rosenzweig, 2007). Moreover, the financial analysis will prompt questions about the business rather than give answers. Wherever possible, comparisons should be made with other companies in the sector to gauge 'best in class', and, amongst other things, to ask:

- What do we need to do to improve our position?
- How can we maintain our current position in the face of strong competition?

Key issues

There are three interrelated issues which need to be considered in the context of a marketing strategy:

- profits and long-term profitability
- cash and long-term sustainable cash flows
- the value of the business and how the business creates value.

The initial financial analysis will show how these issues stand currently, and one key objective of the marketing strategy will be, inter alia, to optimize and improve all three in order to create shareholder value. Figure 14.10 illustrates the connections between the principal financial statements. It shows that shareholder return rests upon the ability of any business to generate cash to pay dividends and long-term profits and cash flows to grow investment in the business and subsequently the value of the business.

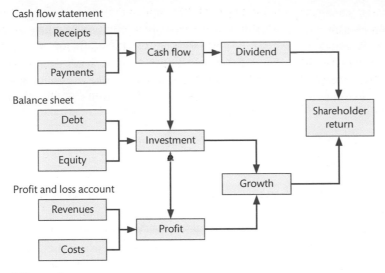

14.10 Financial Interactions

An example

There are a myriad of measures and analyses which could be used to understand a business's finances; however, a few key measures and techniques will give an initial picture of the business. Assume that the contents of Table 14.1 are extracts from the accounts of Oxtma plc (a fictitious company), which will be used to illustrate the analysis.

Table 14.1 The Accounts of Oxtma plc

	£million
Revenues: the total value of all goods and services sold to third parties in the normal course of trade	25.00
EBITDA: earnings before interest, taxation depreciation, and amortization	3.10
Operating profit: the profit after the deduction of all expenses (business overheads) other than interest and taxation (also known as profit before interest and tax)	2.50
Operating cash flow: the cash effects of transactions and other events relating to operating or trading activities	3.00
Total assets: the sum of all the assets, i.e. fixed and current	15.00
Total liabilities: the total financial claims of lenders and others who supply money, goods, and services	7.00
Shareholders' equity: the sum of share capital and **reserves** less any issued preference shares. Equity represents the ordinary shareholders' interest in the company	6.00
Trade debtors: people or businesses who owe money to the business; also referred to as **receivables**	5.00

The operating margin

The margin measures the profitability of sales revenues, as it reflects the combination of the cost and pricing structures of the business. Margins differ between sectors: for example, a supermarket might achieve between 2 and 5 per cent, whereas a pharmaceutical company might make between 20 and 30 per cent. Where the information is available, other margins can also be calculated as a ratio of sales revenues. Taking the example of Oxtma plc:

$$\frac{\text{Operation profit\%}}{\text{Revenues}} \frac{2.50}{25.00} = 10.00\%.$$

Revenues to total assets

Revenues to total assets (or asset turnover), which is a prime measure of efficiency, shows the intensity with which the total assets are employed in the business. The level of margin often depends upon the efficiency of investment in the business and the scale of revenues. The higher the ratio, the more efficient the business is in utilizing its assets. Highly capital-intensive businesses (e.g. power generation) will have relatively low ratios (i.e. below 1:1); on the other hand, low capital-intensive businesses (e.g. supermarkets) could have ratios of above 2:1. In the case of Oxtma plc, it is:

$$\frac{\text{Revenues}}{\text{Total assets}} \frac{25.00}{15.00} = 1.67{:}1.$$

Return on total assets (ROTA)

The third key measure is return on investment (ROI). Return on total assets (ROTA) gives a good indication of profitability and the efficiency of management by highlighting the relationship between the assets employed in the business and the profits the business has generated by using those assets. ROTA is closely connected to the return to shareholders (after taking account of debt and other liabilities); therefore, a key strategic objective is to optimize this figure through improved margins and efficiencies. Comparison with other companies and with previous years is essential, but a return in the region of 10—20 per cent should be expected, depending upon the riskiness of the business. Companies with high operating margins often have low revenues to total assets and vice versa. Oxtma's ROTA is:

$$\frac{\text{Operating profit}}{\text{Total assets}} \frac{2.50}{15.00} = 16.67\%.$$

Cash conversion

The ability to generate cash (cash flow) or to convert profits into cash (cash conversion) is key to the survival of the business. Cash conversion is important because businesses more often fail primarily through lack of cash rather than poor profitability. Operating cash flow to EBITDA measures the relationship between cash flow and profit. A strong indicator of possible cash-flow problems is when operating cash flow is less than EBITDA. A ratio of less than 90 per cent might give rise to concern, especially when there is a trend over a number of years. Using the example of Oxtma plc, cash conversion is:

$$\frac{\text{Operating cash flow}}{\text{EBITDA}} \frac{3.00}{3.10} = 96.77\%.$$

Days' sales outstanding (DSO)

Poor cash conversion might result from rapid revenue growth, poor receivables collection, or a number of other factors. Days' sales outstanding (DSO) is a crude calculation which often highlights the cause of cash conversion issues. A difficulty with this measure, as with others which associate an annual 'flow' figure with a year-end 'temperature' figure, is that the latter may not be typical of the level experienced throughout the year. This is especially true when a business is expanding or contracting rapidly. Oxtma's DSO looks like this:

$$\frac{\text{Trade debtors}}{\text{Revenues}} \frac{5.00 \times 365}{25.00} = 72\,\text{days}.$$

Gearing or leverage

Where a company has borrowed funds to finance the business, the drain on cash resources through interest payments and debt repayments can be an important issue. The level of debt can be assessed by comparing debt and equity. Debt to equity (gearing or leverage) measures the proportion of a business funded from borrowing or other non-equity sources of finance. If there is a high proportion of 'prior charges' (i.e. capital other than equity), then the gearing is high. There are no hard and fast rules, but levels of debt above 40—50 per cent might be a cause for concern, especially where there are cash flow problems. Oxtma plc's gearing is:

$$\frac{\text{Debit}}{\text{Equity}} \frac{2.00}{6.00} = 33.33\%.$$

Shareholder value

The final part is to understand the impact of the marketing strategy on the current value of the business (see Koller et al., 2005; Doyle, 2008). Shareholder value can be created by growing the value of the business and destroyed by shrinking it (see Figure 14.11).

Value can be measured in different ways, but in each case the principle of value creation remains the same. Some alternatives are:

- the value of the shareholders' equity in the business
- the total assets of the company
- or, for listed companies, the market value or market capitalization.

In summary, value ultimately depends upon the ability of the business to generate long-term sustainable cash flows and profits.

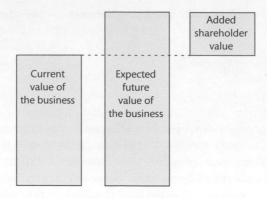

14.11 Shareholder value

Market share

Aside from financial measures, the successful competitor's performance will also be manifested in the form of increased market share or, at the very least, maintenance of it. There are two other outcomes of achieving a position of competitive advantage. One is customer satisfaction: a firm that offers customers the benefits of a differentiated offering, or passes on some of the rents achieved by lower cost, will satisfy customers, all things being equal. The other is loyalty: satisfied customers tend to remain loyal to the firm that really fulfils their expectations, and, given the choice, refrain from patronizing competitors.

Most managers give more attention to the outcomes of market share and financial productivity for two obvious reasons: these outcomes tend to be easier to measure, and managers are typically rewarded directly for improvements in them. Managers are also inclined to agree that customer satisfaction and loyalty are important and that they lead to market share and ROI (or other measures). However, they will likewise contend that these concepts are vague and less easy to measure.

To a large extent, they are right. While the attempts by consumer psychologists and marketing researchers to improve the measurement of customer satisfaction (Anderson et al., 1994) and service quality (Parasuraman et al., 1985, 1988) have been most laudable, it should not be forgotten that what they are trying to achieve is daunting indeed. Getting 'inside the heads' of customers and assessing complex human cognitive processes such as satisfaction using tools like five- and seven-point scales is not easy.

What makes market share and financial productivity measures appealing as outcomes of a position of competitive advantage is the fact that they are 'hard'—expressed in numbers that can easily be calculated, compared, and tracked. The main problem, however, is that they are historical—a good way of tracking the past, but not necessarily an indication of the future. They are not good diagnostics of strategic health. While customers may be capricious at times, all things being equal, they are not so fickle as to be satisfied today and dissatisfied with the same good offering tomorrow, or change the loyalty horse in midstream. Indeed, most customers are probably more tolerant of marketers' shortcomings than the latter would give them credit for, and only downgrade ratings or shift allegiances as the result of gross dereliction. Again, the problem with most measures of customer satisfaction and loyalty is that they are soft and impression-based. They are, however, about the future.

The logic of the process model presented in Figure 14.9 is that the astute firm will reinvest the financial outcomes of competitive advantage in the sources of competitive advantage itself. What kind of things? There is a considerable range to be considered such as tacit knowledge, money, personnel, information, technology, plant, and equipment, along with capabilities like consumer insights, package design, marketing communications support, R&D (e.g. innovation and support), and legal skills and knowledge (e.g. maintaining trademark and patent protection), and also including external suppliers (e.g. advertising and media agencies), and maybe a salesforce, plant management (production planning and scheduling), and the skills and ability to schedule and distribute (Morgan, 2012).

Reinvestment closes the loop in the model, and suggests that managing for competitive advantage is a process that is continually renewed, revived, and refreshed. Certainly, a marketing strategist's skills may well be distinguished by their knowledge of what sources of competitive advantage to invest in, what position(s) to adopt, and the ability to determine the outcome of the process effectively—what was referred to earlier in this chapter as 'control'. The variables which can be measured and controlled in the outcomes in the model in Figure 14.9 are illustrated in Table 14.2.

Customer equity

While the two sets of outcomes in the Day and Wensley model presented in Figure 14.9 each have their own particular strengths, each set also has its limitations (Pitt et al., 2000). The outcomes of ROI and market share are hard, but historical, and the outcomes of customer satisfaction and loyalty are future-oriented but soft. The ideal marketing control variable would be an outcome that is both hard (a number that can be expressed financially) and future (customer-oriented). **Customer lifetime value** (CLTV), which in turn leads to **customer equity**, is arguably that single appropriate outcome. Traditional accounting systems have viewed customers as sources of revenue. Increasingly, firms are beginning to use their accounting systems to view customers as assets, especially if they have access to web analytics (see Mini Case 14.2), and are basing their decisions on customers much as they would base their decisions on investments.

Customer lifetime value

Customer lifetime value (CLTV) is the net present value (NPV) of the profit that a firm stands to realize on the average new customer during a given number of years. This is illustrated in the calculations shown in the spreadsheet in Table 14.3. It can be calculated using the formula

$$\text{CLTV} \frac{n}{i=1} \sum (1+d)^{-i} \pi_i$$

where π_i is sales profit from this customer in period i plus any non-sales benefits (e.g. referrals) minus cost of maintaining the relationship in period i, d is the discount rate, and n is the final period, estimated to be lifetime horizon for customer.

Table 14.2 Metric Variables

Outcome	Operationalization	Typical Measure
Customer satisfaction/ dissatisfaction	Customers' overall satisfaction with an organization's products or services	Customer satisfaction survey, requiring customers to rate satisfaction, or various aspects of it, on an interval scale Focus groups, user-group forums, blogs, observational studies
	Difference between customer's expectations of the quality of a product or service and their perceptions of a particular product or service (also known as 'disconfirmation')	Service quality studies using instruments such as SERVQUAL (Parasuraman et al., 1988)
Customer experience	Customers' internal and subjective response to any direct or indirect contact with an organization	Surveys, targeted studies, observational studies, 'voice of customer' research (Meyer and Schwager, 2007)
Customer loyalty	The extent to which customers would be willing to choose an alternative over the organization's offering, given availability	Surveys of loyalty
	Customer churn (also known as customer retention rates or, conversely, customer defection rates)	How many customers who are in an organization's customer base at the beginning of a period (usually a year) are still in it at the end of a period? An indication of **retention**? How many customers who are in a firm's customer base at the beginning of a period (usually a year) will not be in it at the end of a period? An indication of **defection**? (See Reichheld and Sasser, 1990; Reichheld, 1993; Page et al., 1996; McGovern and Moon, 2007)
Market share	The percentage or proportion of the total available market or market segment that is being serviced by a company Increasing market share is one of the most common objectives used in business. The main advantage of using market share is that it abstracts from industry-wide macro-environmental variables such as the state of the economy, or changes in tax policy	Can be expressed as: a company's sales revenue (from that market) divided by the total sales revenue available in that market or a company's unit sales volume (in a market) divided by the total volume of units sold in that market
Measures of financial productivity	All of the measures below assess the ability of the organization to make a profit	
	Sales growth Analysis: look for a steady increase in sales If overall costs and inflation are on the rise, then you should watch for a related increase in your sales—if not, then this is an indicator that your prices are not keeping up with your costs	Percentage increase (or decrease) in sales between two time periods Formula: Current year's sales – Last year's sales/Last year's sales

(continued)

Table 14.2 (*continued*)

Outcome	Operationalization	Typical Measure
	COGS to sales Analysis: look for a stable ratio as an indicator that the company is controlling its gross margins	Percentage of sales used to pay for expenses that vary directly with sales Formula: Cost of goods sold/Sales
	Gross profit margin Analysis: compare with other businesses in the same industry to see if your business is operating as profitably as it should be. Look at the trend from month to month. Is it staying the same? Improving? Deteriorating? Is there enough gross profit in the business to cover your operating costs? Is there a positive gross margin on all your products?	Indicator of how much profit is earned on your products without consideration of selling and administration costs Formula: Gross profit/Total sales where Gross profit = Sales − Cost of goods sold
	SG&A to sales Analysis: look for a steady or decreasing percentage, indicating that the company is controlling its overhead expenses	Percentage of selling, general, and administrative costs to sales Formula: Selling, general, and administrative expenses/Sales
	Net profit margin Analysis: compare with other businesses in the same industry to see if your business is operating as profitably as it should be. Look at the trend from month to month. Is it staying the same? Improving? Deteriorating? Are you generating enough sales to leave an acceptable profit? Trend from month to month can show how well you are managing your operating or overhead costs	Shows how much profit comes from every pound of sales Formula: Net profit/Total sales
	Return on equity (ROE) Analysis: compare the return on equity with other investment alternatives, such as a savings accounts, stocks, or bonds Compare your ratio with other businesses in the same or similar industry	Determines the rate of return on your investment in the business. As an owner or shareholder this is one of the most important ratios as it shows the hard fact about the business. Are you making enough of a profit to compensate you for the risk of being in business? Formula: Net profit/Equity
	Return on assets (ROA) Analysis: ROA shows the amount of income for every pound tied up in assets Year-to-year trends may be an indicator—, but watch out for changes in the total asset figure as you depreciate your assets (a decrease or increase in the denominator can affect the ratio and doesn't necessarily mean the business is improving or declining)	Considered a measure of how effectively assets are used to generate a return (this ratio is not very useful for most businesses) Formula: Net profit/Total assets

Mini Case 14.2   Using web analytics

The ability to measure ROI (return on investment) has been one of the key features in the success of the web. Finance directors have long dreamt of being able to measure the impact of marketing investments and the web has certainly enabled that. Marketers can trace, track, and monitor every move beyond what was possible with traditional direct response marketing such as direct mail. That's the theory. Unfortunately, the reality of wading through masses of web analytics data showing where customers are coming from and tracking their behaviour when they arrive at your site can be daunting. The evidence is sketchy, but the indications are that only about a fifth of organizations are linking web analytics to their marketing strategy.

Site and external analytics are critical to improving acquisition, retention, and cross-selling.

The base level of approach to web analytics is to ask: how well are we selling products and services online? Firstly, look at your own main website microsite, which is a cluster of pages within the main site around a theme, and the landing page, which is where a visitor arrives when they click on an ad or a search engine. With PPC/CPC (pay per click/cost per click) or CPA (cost per action, be it a sale or registration), the landing page can be customized to measure the effectiveness of relative clickthroughs—the software can be crunched to show the best inward routes or key touch points such as online display, affiliate schemes (content-rich sites that provide hyperlinks to brands such as: <http://www.epinions.com>), and search. Search engine optimization (SEO) is a black art that attempts to manage the routes to landing pages organically so that key phrases and words are used that best lead to specific landing pages. Thus, the marketing spend can be optimized by focusing on the routes providing the best return.

Such web analytics can provide an organization with a good understanding of what appears to be working and, accordingly, what to do more of and what to do less of. But what does it have to do with marketing strategy?

Incorporating web analytics into marketing strategy takes a more holistic perspective of ROI, with a different set of questions and a wider range of ROI analytics. Standing back from the web component, marketers need to develop strategies based upon the synergies with wider marketing activities. Take the case of the T-Mobile TV 'flash mobbing' commercial, which featured hidden filming of 350 undercover dancers dancing to Lulu's 1965 hit 'Shout'. The dancers were surreptitiously positioned amongst surprised commuters at Liverpool Street Station. The dance routine was carefully choreographed and the result of intensive training. Strategically, the commercial provided a concise personification of the brand's positioning of 'Life is for sharing'. The ad reached the crucial and media-fragmented 18–24 audience and, at the time of writing, has attracted nearly 16 million views on YouTube.

Yes, it is possible to measure the Liverpool Street Station commercial with the effect on the T-Mobile website in terms of clickthroughs, PPAs, and CPAs. Other useful measures would be email sign-ups and social media interaction during the campaign and after it has ended, the amount of dwell time on the site, page depth, and the number of times the commercial was passed on (viral). However, web analytics only go so far in providing insight into the lasting effect of the campaign on the engagement with the brand. To gain a better strategic picture, qualitative research can be useful, for example monitoring media interest, discussions on social networks, word-of-mouth, and blogs. What is more, that old-fashioned technique of the focus group may also prove its worth.

Table 14.3 might be typical of a firm marketing a specialist academic journal subscription. If it is assumed that the firm sells 1,000 new subscriptions in Year 1 at £150 each, then the calculation of net revenue and also of net costs at 50 per cent of revenue are both simple procedures. A further important issue is retention: in simple terms, how many of the

Table 14.3 Example of the Calculation of CLTV

			Year 1	Year 2	Year 3	Year 4	Year 5
Revenue							
Customers	(A × B/100) t−1	A	1000	400	180	90	50
Retention rate (%)		B	40	45	50	55	60
Customer spend		C	£150	£150	£150	£150	£150
Total revenue	(A × C)	D	£150,000	£60,000	£27,000	£13,500	£7,500
Costs							
Cost (%)		E	50	50	50	50	50
Total costs	(D x E)/100	F	£75,000	£30,000	£13,500	£6,750	£3,750
Profits							
Gross profit	(D−F)	G	£75,000	£30,000	£13,500	£6,750	£3,750
Discount rate* (4%)		H	1.00	1.04	1.08	1.12	1.17
Net present value profit	(G/H)	I	£75,000	£28,846	£12,482	£6,001	£3,206
Cumulative profit (NPV)	(I) t1−5	J	£75,000	£103,846	£116,328	£122,328	£125,534
Lifetime value (NPV)	(J/1000)	K	£75	£104	£116	£122	£126

*$D = (1 + i)n$, where D = discount rate, i = interest rate, and n = number of years you have to wait for return.

customers at the beginning of a year are still subscribers at the end of the year? Table 14.3 assumes a retention rate of 40 per cent at the end of Year 1, and then increases this gradually over the five-year period. Thus, 400 customers are still subscribers at the beginning of Year 2 (0.4 × 1000), 180 at the beginning of Year 3 (0.45 × 400), and so forth.

The revenues and the costs for each year are functions of the number of customers at the beginning of that year. Calculation of gross profit is a subtraction procedure and what follows is perhaps the only, albeit slightly, complex calculation in the entire process. As in all investments, the returns for a customer five years from now are not worth what they are today. Therefore, there is a need to discount gross profits. The discount rate chosen in Table 14.3 is 4 per cent. This figure is discretionary, and its choice will vary from firm to firm; some may choose a premium bank rate, others an internal rate of return, and still others some minimum rate of investment acceptability. This is not critical to our discussion, for the principles remain the same. This discount rate is used to calculate the net present value (NPV) of the cumulative gross profit over the years. The final calculation is a simple one—what is the CLTV of a customer who was put on the books in Year 1? The answer is the NPV of the cumulative gross profit for the year divided by the number of customers (in this case 1,000) in Year 1. Thus, the CLTV of one of these customers in Year 4 would be £122, and in Year 5 £126, and so on.

An obvious application of this type of spreadsheet is its use in the calculation of 'What happens if we increase CLTV by x per cent?' The decision-maker can change variables such

Table 14.4 Example of the Calculation of CLTV + 5% Increase in Retention

			Year 1	Year 2	Year 3	Year 4	Year 5
Revenue							
Customers	(A × B/100) t−1	A	1000	420	197	105	50
Retention rate (%)		B	42	47	53	58	63
Customer spend		C	£150	£150	£150	£150	£150
Total revenue	(A × C)	D	£150,000	£63,000	£29,610	£15,693	£7,500
Costs							
Cost (%)		E	50	50	50	50	50
Total costs	(D × E)/100	F	£75,000	£31,000	£14,805	£7,847	£3,750
Profits							
Gross profit	(D−F)	G	£75,000	£31,500	£14,805	£7,847	£3,750
Discount rate* (4%)		H	1.00	1.04	1.08	1.12	1.17
Net present value profit	(G/H)	I	£75,000	£30,288	£13,688	£6,976	£3,206
Cumulative profit (NPV)	(I) t1−5	J	£75,000	£105,288	£118,977	£125,952	£129,158
Lifetime value (NPV)	(J/1000)	K	£75	£105	£119	£126	£129

$*D = (1 + i)n$, where D = discount rate, i = interest rate, and n = number of years you have to wait for return.

as price, costs, the discount rate, the number of years an individual will be a customer, and of course the retention rate, to determine the effects these will have on CLTV. For example, Table 14.4 uses the same data as in Table 14.3 with a hypothetical 5 per cent increase in retention. It can be seen in Table 14.4 that the final NPV increases from £126 to £129.

In more general terms, however, it is worth considering what can be done from a marketing strategy perspective to **maximize** CLTV—what marketing strategies need to be formulated? **Control** is another issue to consider—CLTV is a very powerful control variable that can be used to assess the success or otherwise of a marketing strategy and its implementation. Not only is the overall number a useful metric, but it can be broken down into its components and calculated not only by customer group or target market, but right down to the level of the individual customer.

In summary, CLTV can be increased by:

(1) increasing lifetime either by increasing retention rate, or increasing customer life (i.e. the number of years a customer can remain a customer)

(2) increasing sales to, or as a result of, a customer, either by increasing the firm's share of the customer's purchases, or by increasing the customer's referral rate (the number of times they refer others to the firm's products and services)

(3) cutting the costs of serving a customer.

Pitt et al. (2000) use a number of cases from well-known firms to illustrate these principles.

- **Increasing retention rates:** loyalty programmes operate in industries, ranging from airlines to restaurants and supermarkets to hotel chains. Their objective is to raise switching barriers for customers, thereby encouraging their loyalty. Tesco's Club Card in the UK, FlyBuys in Australia, and the Click's Card in South Africa are some excellent international examples of this strategy.

- **Increasing customer lifetime value:** Huggies disposable nappies developed a product extension branded 'Pullups' or 'Trainer Pants' in various international markets. The disposable pants were targeted at infants who were almost potty-trained, but whose parents still required the certainty that accidents could be avoided. The product added about six months to the life of a Huggies customer. While this may not seem like much, six months on a life of two years adds 25 per cent to CLTV!

- **Increasing sales of the same product:** Tia Maria is a liqueur usually consumed in small shot glasses after a meal, which limits its sales. The brand has since published recipe booklets encouraging the use of the product in cocktails, as a sauce over ice cream, and as an ingredient in desserts.

- **Increasing the sales of other products to the same customer:** while Amazon.com began its life in book sales, it quickly moved on to sales of music and DVDs and then to clothing, DIY and tools, jewellery, etc. as it understood its customers more effectively.

- **Exploiting customer referral rates:** Apple's iPod has been one of the most successful digital products in history. Yet Apple spends relatively little on promotion. The product is sold almost entirely on WOM (word-of-mouth) as owners enthusiastically advocate it to their friends.

- **Cutting the costs of serving customers:** the Internet has provided marketers with a wide range of applications to reduce the costs of serving customers without lowering service levels. For example, many customers do their banking online, purchase their airline tickets online, and check in and check the status of their frequent-flyer miles online. Most customers welcome the control this gives them over the purchasing situation, yet for the institutions involved, being able to rely on technology and the customer to 'do the work' means very significant cost savings. Furthermore, in future customers may control their personal profiles and be able to announce to the whole marketplace what their purchasing intentions are and what they are looking for. According to Searls (2012, p. 58):

In this 'intention economy', customers will determine the . . . permissions and restrictions regarding the use of their data. As a result, market conversations will be far more personal, substantive, and manipulation-free than the coupons, traffic-building promotions, and annoying 'personalised' messages consumers get now, based on readings of the data trails they leave behind.

From CLTV to customer equity

It is important to note that the simple spreadsheets presented in Tables 14.3 and 14.4 represent the CLTVs of 'average customers'. Yet, all customers have their own CLTVs. In different markets each day, there are attempts by marketers to capture the data to enable them to get closer to calculating the CLTV of an individual customer, for example customer databases, databases of loyalty cards and warranty registration schemes, and the like. If these CLTVs were then summed, the total value of the firm's customer base might be calculated—a process Blattberg and Deighton (1996) call **customer equity**.

Potentially, customer equity could be the ultimate marketing control measure; every marketing decision would be evaluated by whether or not it increased customer equity. For example, when thinking about customer acquisition and retention, the decision should be based on where the next marketing pound (euro, dollar, yen, or whatever) would be better spent: on getting new customers or keeping the existing ones? The answer: whichever one of the two strategies has the greatest effect on customer equity. Some companies have used customer equity analyses as the basis for decisions either to migrate their customers to a new provider, normally a partner, but who may also be a competitor, or to terminate the relationship with the customer altogether (Mittal et al., 2008). This is normally because the company no longer views the customer as profitable (e.g. insuring homes in a flood zone).

Rather than merely allocate marketing and advertising budgets according to such variables as media selection and spend, or territories, or even customer markets, in the future managers may wish to consciously split the budget between customer acquisition and customer retention activities. Customer equity becomes the basis upon which this decision can be made. Firms may even wish to consider organizing themselves along the lines of acquisition and retention, and to evaluate the performance of these divisions on their ability to contribute towards customer equity (Blattberg and Deighton, 1996).

Wachovia, a financial subsidiary of Wells Fargo, is a leading example of a company that has done this (Hanssens et al., 2008). In the absence of readily available tools to link marketing budgets to customer equity goals, the company set about building a model of customer equity based upon the three key elements of:

(1) customer acquisition

(2) customer retention

(3) cross-selling to existing customers.

The company built a market-response model with the aim of working out how marketing inputs affected the customer equity output and included a variety of variables such as historic advertising expenditures, changes in the branch network, and levels of customer satisfaction, and linked it up to acquisition, retention, and cross-selling amongst its customers grouped by household. The analysis showed that the inputs indicated in Table 14.5 have the greatest impact on Wachovia's customer equity.

Their model is not simple, for it has to calculate the impacts of thousands of different combinations of marketing allocations by media, market, and segment, and with a variety

Table 14.5 Primary Inputs on Wachovia's Customer Equity

Directly Controlled by Marketing	Indirectly Controlled by Marketing	External
● Media advertising	● News coverage	● Leading economic indicators
● Internet advertising	● Customer satisfaction	● Seasonality
● Direct mail	● Brand equity	● Identified shocks (e.g. economic or social)
● Sales employees per branch		
● Rate ratios		
● Sponsorships		

of constraints on budgets and outcomes. What they have found, though, is that there are no uniform effects on customer equity. For example, a marketing mix designed to maximize acquisitions in the short term would differ significantly from a mix designed to maximize long-term customer equity. Wachovia appreciate that the model is not infallible and so it is used as just one contribution to the overall discussion about the strategy.

Conclusion

Most firms spend an inordinate amount of time and effort on the formulation of marketing strategy, and it is likely that the reason for many strategic marketing failures and problems lies in implementation rather than in formulation. The problem with the implementation of marketing strategy is that it can easily mask formulation. When a well-formulated marketing strategy fails, the blame is frequently given to poor formulation, whereas poor implementation might have been the cause. Likewise, when marketing strategy is poorly formulated, good implementation can have two very different possible outcomes. On the one hand, good implementation can disguise a poorly formulated strategy and make it look good by leading to short-term success. On the other hand, when a poorly formulated strategy is well implemented, it can simply hasten the downfall by accelerating the impact of the weakness.

The managerial task of control lies at the heart of successful strategic implementation. If marketing objectives and goals are carefully and skilfully articulated and then regularly and systematically compared with performance, corrective action can be taken in time to bring strategy back on track.

The successful implementation of marketing strategy involves many behavioural issues within the organization. It has been demonstrated empirically that successful implementation of marketing strategy is influenced by the culture of the firm. Managers should, therefore, strive to understand the cultures of their organizations and the impact this will have on the successful implementation of marketing strategy.

Summary

This chapter defined control as a managerial task that sets targets, evaluates performance against those targets, and then takes corrective or reinforcing action where necessary. Control generally takes three forms: annual plan control, profitability control, or strategic control. Implementation is the act of execution of an endeavour and in the future it is likely that organizations will become as good at strategy implementation as they are at formulation. A number of causes of the inadequate implementation of marketing strategy within organizations were identified.

The implementation of marketing strategy in organizations was viewed through the lens of managing a process of competitive advantage. This process consists of identifying superior skills and superior resources and turning them into positions of competitive advantage, either a low-cost position or superior value. If a firm enjoys a position of competitive advantage, this will result in measurable and consequently controllable outcomes, principally customer satisfaction, loyalty, market share, and measures of financial productivity. The logic of the process of competitive advantage is that the superior returns enjoyed will be reinvested in the sources of competitive advantage. A significant change in marketing has been a shift from these four measures to the single yardstick of customer lifetime value (CLTV), which has become a critical measure to use to evaluate and control the successful implementation of an organization's marketing strategy. The summation of an organization's CLTVs is known as customer equity.

The successful implementation of a firm's marketing strategy is also partly a result of an organization's corporate culture, defined simply as 'the way we do things around here'. Three approaches were considered in this respect, looking at corporate culture (Handy, 1978; Deshpandé et al., 1993; Goffee and Jones, 1996).

Key terms

- **Control:** the managerial task of setting standards, evaluating these standards against reality, and the taking of corrective or reinforcing action where necessary.
- **Corporate culture:** the moral, social, and behavioural norms of an organization based on the beliefs, attitudes, and priorities of its members.
- **Customer equity:** the sum of all of the CLTVs of the customers estimated from an organization's customer database.
- **Customer lifetime value (CLTV):** the net present value of all future cash flows from a customer over their lifetime.
- **Financial analysis:** the assessment of the effectiveness with which funds (investment and debt) are employed in a firm.
- **Implementation:** executing an activity, or putting a plan into action.
- **Marketing budget:** the financial statement and programme put before top management for approval for spending on marketing in order to meet set objectives.

- **Process model of competitive advantage:** an approach to competitive advantage and the implementation of marketing strategy which views competitive advantage not as something static, but as an ongoing process which has to be formulated and controlled.
- **Strategy formulation–implementation grid:** a tool for the diagnosis of the successful or otherwise formulation and implementation of marketing strategy.
- **Viable system model (VSM):** a tool for anticipating, planning for, and implementing strategy.

Discussion questions

1. Briefly outline and describe the steps a marketing manager could take to ensure control of marketing activities at different levels.

2. What are the possible consequences for marketing strategy when a poor strategy is well implemented? Can you think of examples of this occurring, other than those mentioned in the text? What are the consequences for marketing strategy when a good strategy is poorly implemented? Can you think of examples of this occurring, other than those mentioned in the text?

3. List some of the reasons why marketing strategy is often not implemented successfully, and think of practical examples of this in organizations with which you are familiar.

4. Choose an organization with which you are familiar, and set up a process model of competitive advantage for it. What are the sources of its competitive advantage? How does it compete? What are the outcomes of this process for the organization? What skills or resources will it have to invest in the future if it is to survive and prosper?

5. Set up a simple spreadsheet and use it to estimate the lifetime values of:
   - an infant wearing nappies for two years
   - the credit card customer of a bank who takes a card at the age of 20 and is projected to live to the age of 75 (assuming that this is a middle-income customer).

6. Now, use your spreadsheet to predict what might happen if:
   - the above organizations could extend the lifetimes of their customers either by starting them earlier or ending them later. How might this be achieved?
   - the above organizations could get the customer to use more of their products
   - the above organizations could get customers to use their other products or services.

7. To what extent do you agree with the premise that the measurement of marketing success or failure is always sterile without comparative data?

Online resource centre

 Visit the Online Resource Centre for this book for lots of interesting additional material at: <**www.oxfordtextbooks.co.uk/orc/west3e/**>

References and further reading

Anderson, Erin, Claes Fornell, and Donald R. Lehmann (1994), 'Customer Satisfaction, Market Share, and Profitability', *Journal of Marketing*, 58, July, pp. 53–66.

Badovick, G. J. and Sharon E. Beatty (1987), 'Shared Organizational Values: Measurement and Impact upon Strategic Marketing Implementation', *Journal of the Academy of Marketing Science*, 15 (1), pp. 19–26.

Beer, Stafford (1979), *The Heart of Enterprise* (Chichester: John Wiley).

Beer, Stafford (1981), *Brain of the Firm*, 2nd edn (Chichester: John Wiley).

Beer, Stafford (1985), *Diagnosing the System for Organizations* (Chichester: John Wiley).

Berthon, Pierre R., James M. Hulbert, and Leyland F. Pitt (1997), 'Brands, Brand Managers, and the Management of Brands: Where to Next?' *Commentary Report*, pp. 97–122 (November) (Cambridge, MA: Marketing Science Institute).

Berthon, Pierre R., Leyland F. Pitt, and Michael T. Ewing (2001), 'Corollaries of the Collective: Effects of Corporate Culture and Organizational Memory on Decision-making Context', *Journal of the Academy of Marketing Science*, 29 (2), pp. 135–50.

Blattberg, Robert C. and John Deighton (1996), 'Manage Marketing by the Customer Equity Test', *Harvard Business Review*, July–August, pp. 136–45.

Bonoma, Thomas V. (1984), 'Making your Marketing Strategy Work', *Harvard Business Review*, March–April, pp. 69–77.

Breene, R. Timothy S., Paul F. Nunes, and Walter E. Shill (2007), 'The Chief Strategy Officer', *Harvard Business Review*, October, pp. 84–93.

Brocklesby, John and Stephen Cummings (1996), 'Designing a Viable Organisation Structure', *Long Range Planning*, 29 (1), pp. 49–57.

Bruning, Edward R. and Lawrence S. Lockshin (1994), 'Marketing's Role in Generating Organizational Competitiveness', *Journal of Strategic Marketing*, 2, pp. 163–87.

Bungay, Stephen (2011), 'How to Make the Most of Your Company's Strategy', *Harvard Business Review*, January–February, pp. 132–40.

Campbell, J. P. and Sarah J. Freeman (1991), 'Cultural Congruence, Strength, and Type: Relationships to Effectiveness', in Woodman, R.W. and Pasmore, W.(eds), *Research in Organizational Change and Development*, Vol. 5 (Greenwich, CT: JAI Press).

Comstock, Beth, Ranjay Gulati, and Stephen Liguori (2010), 'Unleashing the Power of Marketing: When GE Realised That Its Products Would No Longer Sell Themselves, It Had to Invent a Formidable Marketing function from Scratch', *Harvard Business Review*, October, pp. 90–8.

Day, George. S. and Robin Wensley (1988), 'Assessing Advantage: A Framework for Diagnosing Competitive Superiority', *Journal of Marketing*, 52' April, pp. 1–20.

Deighton, John (2002), 'How Snapple Got its Juice Back', *Harvard Business Review*, January), p. 47.

Deshpandé, Rohit, John U. Farley, and Frederick E. Webster (1993), 'Corporate Culture, Customer Orientation, and Innovativeness in Japanese Firms: A Quadrad Analysis', *Journal of Marketing*, 57, pp. 23–7.

Dholakia, Utpal M. (2011), 'Why Employees Can Wreck Promotional Offers', *Harvard Business Review*, January–February, p. 28.

Doyle, Peter (2008), *Value-based Marketing*, 2nd edn (Chichester: John Wiley).

Goffee, Rob and Gareth Jones (1996), 'What Holds the Modern Company Together?' *Harvard Business Review*, November–December, pp. 133–49.

Handy, Charles (1978), *The Gods of Management* (London: Pan).

Hanssens, Dominique M., Daniel Thorpe, and Carl Finkbeiner (2008), 'Marketing when Customer Equity Matters', *Harvard Business Review*, May, pp. 117–23.

HBR Interview (2011a), 'How eBay Developed a Culture of Experimentation,' *Harvard Business Review*, March, pp. 93–7.

HBR Interview (2011b), 'Shaking Things up at Coca-Cola,' *Harvard Business Review*, October, pp. 94–9.

Jackson, M. C. (1988), 'An Appreciation of Stafford Beer's 'Viable System' Viewpoint on Managerial Practice', *Journal of Management Studies*, 25 (6), pp. 557–73.

Koller Tim, Marc Goedhart, and David Wessels (2005), *Valuation, Measuring and Managing the Value of Companies*, 4th edn (New York: John Wiley).

Kumar, V., Eli Jones, Rajkumar Venkatesan, and Robert P. Leone (2011), 'Is Market Orientation a Source of Sustainable Competitive Advantage or Simply the Cost of Competing?', *Journal of Marketing*, 75, pp. 16–30.

McGovern, Gail, and Youngme Moon (2007), 'Companies and the Customers Who Hate Them', *Harvard Business Review*, June, pp. 78–84.

Meyer, Christopher and Andre Schwager (2007), 'Understanding Customer Experience', *Harvard Business Review*, February, pp. 117–26.

Mintz, Ofer and Imran S. Currim (2013), 'What Drives Managerial Use of Marketing and Financial Metrics and Does Metric Use Affect Performance of Marketing Mix Activities?', *Journal of Marketing*, 77, pp. 17–40.

Mittal, Vikas, Matthew Sarkees, and Feisal Murshed (2008), 'The Right Way to Manage Unprofitable Customers', *Harvard Business Review*, April, pp. 94–102.

Morgan, Neil A. (2012), 'Marketing and Business Performance', *Journal of the Academy of Marketing Science*, 40, pp. 102–19.

Narver, John C. and Stanley F. Slater (1990), 'The Effect of a Market Orientation on Business Profitability', *Journal of Marketing*, 54, October, pp. 20–35.

Page, Michael J., Leyland F. Pitt, and Pierre R. Berthon (1996), 'Analysing Customer Defections: Predicting the Effects on Corporate Performance', *Long Range Planning*, 29 (6), pp. 821–34.

Parasuraman, A., Valarie A. Zeithaml, and Leonard L. Berry (1985), 'A Conceptual Model of Service Quality and its Implications for Future Research', *Journal of Marketing*, 49, April, pp. 41–50.

Parasuraman, A., Valarie A. Zeithaml, and Leonard L. Berry (1988), 'SERVQUAL: A Multiple-item Scale for Measuring Customer Perceptions of Service Quality', *Journal of Retailing*, 64, Spring, pp. 12–40.

Pitt, Leyland F., Michael T. Ewing, and Pierre R. Berthon (2000), 'Turning Competitive Advantage into Customer Equity', *Business Horizons*, September–October, pp. 11–18.

Porter, Michael E. (1985), *Competitive Advantage: Creating and Sustaining Superior Performance* (New York: Free Press).

Qualls, William J. and Christopher P. Puto (1989), 'Organizational Climate and Decision Framing: An Integrated Approach to Analyzing Industrial Buying Decisions', *Journal of Marketing Research*, 26, May, pp. 179–92.

Quinn, Robert E. (1988), *Beyond Rational Management* (San Francisco, CA: Jossey-Bass).

Reichheld, Frederick F. (1993), 'Loyalty-based Management', *Harvard Business Review*, March–April, pp. 64–72.

Reichheld, Frederick F. and W. Earl Sasser (1990), 'Zero Defections: Quality Comes to Services', *Harvard Business Review*, September–October, pp. 301–7.

Robert, Michel M. (1991), 'Why CEOs have Difficulty Implementing their Strategies', *Journal of Business Strategy*, 12 (2), pp. 58–60.

Rosenzweig, Phil (2007), 'Misunderstanding the Nature of Company Performance: The Halo Effect and Other Business Delusions', *California Management Review*, 49 (4), pp. 6–20.

Searls, Doc (2012), 'Stop Collecting Customer Data: Let Consumers Control Their Personal Profiles', *Harvard Business Review*, January-February, pp. 57–8.

Slater, Stanley F. and John C. Narver (1992), 'Superior Customer Value and Business Performance: The Strong Evidence for a Market-driven Culture', *Marketing Science Institute Report* No. 92–125 (Cambridge, MA: Marketing Science Institute).

Tse, David K., K.-H. Lee, Ilan Vertinsky, and D. A. Wehrung (1988), 'Does Culture Matter? A Cross-cultural Study of Executives' Choice, Decisiveness, and Risk Adjustment in International Marketing', *Journal of Marketing*, 52, October, pp. 81–95.

Webster, Cynthia (1991), 'A Note on Cultural Consistency Within the Service Firm: The Effects of Employee Position on Attitudes Towards the Marketing Culture', *Journal of the Academy of Marketing Science*, 19 (4), pp. 341–6.

Webster, Frederick E. (1994), *Market-Driven Management: Using the New Marketing Concept to Create a Customer-Oriented Company* (New York: Wiley).

West, Douglas, John Ford, and Paul Farris (2014), 'How Corporate Culture Drives Advertising and Promotion Budgets: Best Practices Combine Heuristics and Algorithmic Tools', *Journal of Advertising Research*, 54 (2), pp. 149–62.

Yarbrough, Larry and, Neil A. Morgan and Douglas W. Vorhies (2011), 'The Impact of Product Market Strategy–Organizational Culture Fit on Business Performance', *Journal of the Academy of Marketing Science*, 39, pp. 555–73.

Key article abstracts

Hult, G. Tomas M. (2011), **'Toward a Theory of the Boundary-Spanning Marketing Organization and Insights from 31 Organization Theories'**, *Journal of the Academy of Marketing Science*, 39, pp. 509–36.

This paper provides an extensive literature integration of 31 organization theories. It's a valuable resource, particularly for students undertaking dissertations within the area of control, implementation, and metrics, by identifying and describing the scope and insights of leading organizational theories and the provision of a typology within which to frame them.

Abstract: Now more than ever, marketing is assuming a key boundary-spanning role—a role that has also redefined the composition of the marketing organization. In this paper, the marketing organization's integrative and mutually reinforcing components of marketing activities, customer value-creating processes, networks, and stakeholders are delineated within their boundary-spanning roles as a particular emphasis (labelled MOR theory). Thematic marketing insights from a collection of 31 organization theories are used to advance knowledge on the boundary-spanning marketing organization within four areas—strategic marketing resources, marketing leadership and decision making, network alliances and collaborations, and the domestic and global marketplace.

Dickinson, Sonia J. and B. Ramaseshan (2008), '**Maximising Performance Gains from Cooperative Marketing: Understanding the Role of Environmental Contexts**', *Journal of Marketing Management*, 24 (5/6), pp. 541–66.

Co-marketing strategic implementation has been largely neglected. This paper plugs the gap and examines the issue of cooperative marketing in particular and its impact on performance.

Abstract: Understanding the situational relevance of strategy is vital, given that strategies have varying utilities under different environmental settings which result in performance variations. Research remains silent regarding the situational relevance of cooperative marketing strategy implementation whereby performance outcomes are maximized. Through quantitative survey results, we explore the relationship between cooperative marketing and performance outcomes across varying environmental contexts (internal and external environments). While past studies acknowledge the importance of an open system's perspective and the influence of the environment on strategic outcomes, they fall prey to key shortcomings such as a reductionist perspective and inadequate measurement. The authors provide an insight into the environment–strategy–performance relationship by using a holistic environmental approach and detail the environments conducive to co-marketing strategy implementation. Managerial implications and future directions for research are also provided in the paper.

Lane, Nikala (2005), '**Strategy Implementation: The Implications of a Gender Perspective for Change Management**', *Journal of Strategic Marketing*, 13 (2), pp. 117–31.

This is a very interesting article, which examines how the managerial style of strategy implementation varies between male and female sales managers.

Abstract: The implementation of strategic marketing plans remains an elusive goal for many organizations, with many managers knowing what to do but not how to do it. A relevant question relating to the implementation capabilities of managers regards the characteristics of successful implementors. This question highlights several interesting issues, including the impact of manager gender. The current paper reveals the role of female managers in implementing new management techniques in sales organizations, namely the introduction of behaviour-based management control strategies as an indicator of a possible gender dimension in more general implementation capabilities. The author summarizes the findings from single-company and multi-company studies where the implementation capabilities of male and female field sales managers are examined. The provocative conclusion is that superior implementation capabilities are shown by female sales managers in the implementation of behaviour-based control strategies. The author suggests this finding may provide insight into implementation capabilities in strategic marketing and more generally.

Raps, Andreas (2004), '**Implementing Strategy**', *Strategic Finance*, 85 (12), pp. 48–53.

This paper highlights the low rate of success when it comes to strategy implementation. It encourages business organizations to pay more attention and invest more resources to develop and improve strategy implementation skills as they have done before for developing strategic planning skills.

Abstract: If your company has successfully implemented a strategic plan, then you're definitely in the minority. The real success rate is only 10 to 30 per cent. This low rate is discouraging, especially since a growing number of companies in recent years have invested considerable resources to develop strategic planning skills. Companies obviously need to improve strategy implementation activities but the pace of these activities and the implementation itself have many problems. Traditional strategy implementation concepts overemphasize structural aspects, reducing the whole effort to an organizational exercise. Ideally, an implementation effort is a 'no boundaries' set of activities that doesn't concentrate on implications of only one component, such as the organizational structure. You should concentrate on four key success factors: (1) culture; (2) organization; (3) people; and (4) control systems and instruments. It's worth the effort. An efficient strategy implementation has an enormous impact on a company's success.

Piest, Bert, and Henk Ritsema (1993), 'Corporate Strategy: Implementation and Control', *European Management Journal*, 11 (1), pp. 122–31.

This is an interesting article, which suggests incorporating the implementation process of corporate strategy into the control system in order for organizations to achieve their strategic objectives more effectively in the dynamic environment.

Abstract: Implementing and controlling corporate strategy is not an easy matter. What is called for is flexible control, combining individual creativity and direction without turning into rigidity. In a dynamic environment, change is the only constant factor. Therefore, possibilities of changing the corporate strategy should be incorporated into the control system. This sets specific demands concerning the process of controlling a strategy. Some of the basic issues with regard to implementation and control are discussed. These issues are: (1) using the business mission as a management instrument; (2) developing a control system that is directed towards the future; (3) discovering the limited value of financial figures; (4) finding information that is really meaningful; and (5) making 'What if?' analyses. Regarding the implementation of these management instruments, the control system should be kept simple and the company should be segmented into various entities.

 End of Chapter 14 case study: Social media impact on a brand launch at PepsiCo

Melissa Jones is a brand development manager at PepsiCo. During her 15 year career, she has worked her way up from a local marketing coordinator to now having responsibility for many of the new packages and brands the company launches. PepsiCo has a broad portfolio of beverages and foods and Melissa is responsible for the energy drink category.

As reported in *Convenience Store Decisions*, the energy drink category has seen a 16 per cent increase in 2011 and is expected to grow by 64 per cent by 2016. PepsiCo understands the importance of this category to future growth and has challenged Melissa to increase AMP's share of market against rival brands Monster and Red Bull. PepsiCo believes that a successful launch of the new lime flavour extension will help grow the brand.

The most recent launch of AMP Juice was not a success and marketing research results showed that the product and promotion did not reach the 18–35 male demographic. Melissa knows she needs to present an improved communications strategy to the executive team. She is constantly hearing from colleagues and trade journals that social media is an innovative approach to interaction with customers and has replaced or supplemented traditional marketing methods for competitors. Melissa does not know much about social media, but thinks it may be a new tactic for her to reach target consumers. Before her presentation to executives next week, she must figure out how social media will be a part of her marketing campaign.

Social media

Social media continues to grow at an extraordinary pace with new players entering the market and additional users accessing social networks. ComScore demonstrates that starting with just a few players in the early 2000s, social media now has many companies that reach 80 per cent of Internet users worldwide and account for 1.2 billion users. As both the number of social media users and the amount of time spent on social media content rise substantially, new players continue to enter this market, which Facebook continues to dominate.

Other trends in the evolution of social media include global penetration, mobile device usage, and adoption by males. The growth in social media is not solely in the United States; rather it is becoming a global trend. Despite various factors such as availability of Internet access and cultural practices, social networking is growing in every single country. In a study of ten major global markets, social networks and blogs are the top destination in each country and account for the majority of time spent online, while reaching at least 60 per cent of active Internet users. ComScore also found that more than half of local online populations in North and South America, Europe, the Middle East, Africa, and Asia Pacific engage in social media.

As the adoption of mobile devices rises, more users are accessing blogs and social networks every month. According to the Nielsen study 'The State of Social Media', nearly two in every five social media users access this tool from their phone. As a greater proportion of the population begins using smartphone mobile devices, that trend is likely to continue.

Finally, while females still tend to be the most frequent users of social media, the gender gap is starting to close. In a report by Eli Goodman, males were among the fastest growing segment of social networking users from July 2010 to October 2011. While women also spend more time on social networks than men, that gap is also starting to narrow, creating a larger audience of men, especially in the younger demographic.

Social media versus traditional media

As the use of and access to social media continues to grow, marketers must consider how to balance the use of traditional media, such as television, radio, and outdoor advertising, with social media marketing. There are several benefits that can be directly associated with social media. First, social media is much less expensive than traditional marketing. The CPM model is used to show how much you will pay for an advertisement to reach 1,000 people during the duration of its campaign. The cost of reaching 1,000 people with social media is nearly one-tenth of the cost of television ads and nearly one-sixtieth of the cost of direct mail.

Additionally, social media is much more engaging and interactive with customers than traditional media, which tends to be a one-way message. Customers have the ability to communicate back with a brand and have their voices and feelings heard. Finally, the success of social media is measurable. Marketers can look at metrics such as 'Likes' and 'Posts' on Facebook and 'Re-tweets' on Twitter, as well as clickthrough rates and impressions from advertising done through social media outlets. Marketers can test different techniques and messages, and are then able to easily see which are more effective and thus adapt to optimize those messages.

Issues and drawbacks

Although social media has many positive attributes, marketers must be aware of certain issues that may arise when using this approach to speak to consumers. Since social media provides an 'interaction' between the brand and the customer, the brand should listen to what is being said. Consumers may use social media as a forum to post negative or incorrect feedback, which might be seen by countless others.

Companies must also be aware of the negative impact that social media can have on image. For example, in a recent social media gaffe, Southwest Airlines ran into unexpected problems with a promotion. To celebrate their three millionth follower, on 3 August 2012 they offered a one-day promotion with 50 per cent off certain flights. The response to the sale overwhelmed the Southwest Airlines website. Customers who were lucky enough to purchase a deal were charged anywhere from a few times to more than a dozen additional times for the same flight, resulting in many furious customers. This technical glitch directly affected customer bank accounts for those using debit cards; for others, credit cards were maxed out due to the multiple charges. Unable to get through to the airline by phone, people began to express their complaints on Facebook. Although Southwest was trying to reward consumers, they may have lost some trust along the way.

Companies also need to consider aligning their social media strategy with other communication vehicles and employees, using social media to speak about the organization or its products.

Evaluating social media

Although companies know that social media is a great way to reach their customers, it is important to be able to evaluate their success and display their value to business stakeholders. In particular, companies need to recognize how they are reaching consumers, reacting to their feedback, and growing the brand and sales.

Airports have been able to utilize social media to communicate to passengers before and during their travel experience in order to maximize their non-aeronautical revenues. London's Gatwick Airport is a leader in this respect, having a screen displaying its Twitter mentions in full public view, allowing 'social customers' to tweet any issues that need attention. The airport needs to deploy a customer-centric social media strategy with the end goal being increased customer spending at airport retailers. According to the *Journal of Airport Management*, for an airport to have commercial success using social media for customer engagement, the programme must include three discrete steps.

- *Customer insight strategy:* develop customer knowledge—attract and recognize.
- *Customer value creation:* segmentation analysis to create one-to-one retail offers.
- *Customer retention:* capture all offer redemption data, such as services used at the airport, for marketing similar services again.

Companies can see the benefits of social media marketing across the customer life cycle, in acquisition, retention, value development, and managing cost to serve. The knowledge gained on customer attitudes will help drive benefits throughout the value chain. To achieve this knowledge, companies can forecast and plan better by listening to consumers. The firm Virtue has worked out that, on average, 'a fan base of 1 million translates to at least $3.6 million in equivalent media over a year, or $3.60 per fan. Virtue arrived at its $3.6 million figure by working off a $5 CPM, meaning a brand's 1 million fans generate about $300,000 in media value each month'.

Ultimately, companies need to be able to quantify and recognize how social media drives sales and customer retention in order to justify the investment that it takes to establish a successful social media programme (salaries, computers, etc.). Social media do not always directly cause a sale and are sometimes difficult to track. However, social media can be a large part of the customer shopping process. There are many ROI metrics that companies can use to determine if their social media marketing is effective, including social presence, traffic on the website, and social mentions across platforms. It is important to note that 'sales' ranks low on the list, showing that social media is aimed at enhancing other metrics that may ultimately lead to sales.

The decision

Melissa must use her knowledge of social media and its trends to develop the communications strategy for the launch of the new AMP line extension. She must be able to weigh the benefits and costs to determine the ideal blend of traditional and social media to reach consumers and grow the brand.

Discussion questions

1. What are the primary elements of control that Melissa should consider when presenting her brand launch strategy to the PepsiCo executives?

2. What methods or combination of methods would you advise Melissa to use to best set the energy drinks budget?

3. How might the concept of customer lifetime value influence her marketing plan?

4. Identify appropriate metrics for the launch and provide reasons for their choice.

5. Should the launch prove to be a failure, have you any advice on how Melissa might disentangle whether it was the wrong strategy with the right tactics or the right strategy with the wrong tactics?

Source: This case was prepared by Andrew Hoon and Scott Cruff, evening MBA students at Loyola College Maryland, under the supervision of Professor Hope Corrigan as the basis for analysis and class discussion and not to illustrate effective or ineffective handling of an administrative situation.

CASE 1:

Sustaining competitive advantage—Turk Telekom

This case was prepared by Selcen Ozturkcan and Burcu Gumus, Istanbul Bilgi University, Turkey

Overview

This case covers 'market scan/scenarios', 'internal analysis', and 'strategic fit' from phase 1 of the marketing strategy blueprint (see Chapter 1, Figure 1.8). It primarily focuses on the question: 'Where are we now?'

Turkish Telecommunications Market

Turk Telekom operates in the Turkish telecoms market, which is undergoing rapid changes. In recent years, new voice operators have entered the market as a result of new legislative regulations and licensing agreements. Adjustments made to agreements with GSM operators in 1998 resulted in a substantial steady growth in the number of mobile subscribers and in the penetration rate (see Table I.1). At the end of 2014 there were an estimated 70.1 million mobile subscribers, and the total number of fixed and mobile phone subscribers is expected to exceed 83 million. This suggests a highly penetrated market, since the population of Turkey in 2013 was reported to be 76.5 million. In addition, technological improvements present additional challenges to the telecoms market. Investment in fibre and 3G technology resulted in an increase in broadband subscribers from 6 million in 2008 to 35 million in 2013.

Competitors

Turk Telekom is well known as a landline phone operator, but it has also extended its operator services to mobile phone voice and data transfer. The operators in the mobile phone sector are the 'big three', namely Turkcell, Vodafone, and Avea which have market shares of 51.9 per cent, 28.17 per cent, and 19.93 per cent, respectively (see Exhibit I.1).

Turkcell has been operating in the mobile communication industry in Turkey since 1994. It was the first Turkish company to be listed on the New York Stock Exchange, and its stocks have been traded on the Istanbul and New York stock markets since 2000. Turkcell provides services in nine countries (Germany, Georgia, Moldova, Belarus, Ukraine, Turkey, Azerbaijan, and Kazakhstan) and it had 69.2 million subscribers at end of 2013.

In 2005, Vodafone bought Telsim, which was established by the Uzan Group, and changed the brand name to Vodafone Turkey.

Consumers

The national census results for 2013 report the population of Turkey as 76.5 million, half of whom are under 30 years of age. The median ages of the male and female population were 29.8 and 31,

Table I.1 Mobile and Internet Subscribers in Turkey

No. of Fixed and Mobile Telephone Subscribers			No. of Internet Subscribers		
Year	No. of Fixed Telephone Subscribers	No. of Mobile Telephone Subscribers	Total	Mobile Broadband Tariffs Less Than One Month Excluded[1]	Mobile Broadband Tariffs Less Than One Month[2]
2000	18,395,171	14,970,745	1,629,156	1,629,156	–
2001	18,904,486	19,502,897	1,619,270	1 619 270	–
2002	18,914,857	23,323,118	1 309 770	1,309,770	–
2003	18,916,721	27,887,535	906,650	906,650	–
2004	19,125,163	34,707,549	1,474,590	1,474,590	–
2005	18,978,223	43,608,965	2,248,105	2,248,105	–
2006	18,831,616	52,662,709	3,180,580	3,180,580	–
2007	18,201 006	61,975,807	4,842,798	4,842,798	–
2008	17,502,205	65,824,110	5,804,923	5,804,923	–
2009	16,534,356	62,779,554	8,849,779	6,782,657	2,067.122
2010	16 201 466	61,769,635	14,443,644	8,672,376	5,771,268
2011	15,210 846	65,321,745	22,371,441	14,117,815	8,253,626
2012	13,859 672	67,680,547	27,649,055	20,090,614	7,558,441
2013	13,551 705	69,661,108	32,613,930	22,916,052	9,697,878

[1]Includes dial-up and all other subscription packages (xDSL, mobile, cable, fibre, etc.) except mobile broadband tariffs less than one month.
[2]Mobile broadband tariffs less than one month include daily, weekly, or other broadband data usage with mobile phones, computers, etc.

Source: TurkStat, Ministry of Transport, Maritime Affairs and Communications, Information and Communication Technologies Authority.

- Nearly 78% of fixed broadband subscribers in Turkey prefer offers providing up to 8 MBps download speeds.

- The market share of alternative operators for local calls is 10.94%, while Türk Telekom has a market share of 89.06%. The market share for alternative operators for national calls is 20.86%, whereas Türk Telekom has a market share of 79.14%.

- The number of 3G subscribers has reached 43.9 million.

The communication sector in Turkey is growing rapidly.

- The number of broadband subscribers, which had been 6 million in 2008, is now over 20 million as of March 2013.

- The cable broadcasting services provider Türksat has 1,236,016 cable television subscribers and 542,908 digital cable television subscribers.

- The total number of employees in the sector in the second quarter of 2012 is 36,865.

Exhibit I.1 Overview of the Turkish Communications Sector
Source: Information and Communications Technology Report, 2014.

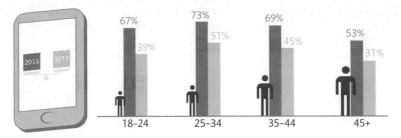

Exhibit I.2 Distribution of Smartphone Users in Turkey
Source: Deloitte Turkish Mobile Consumer Survey, 2013.

respectively. This young population provides a large source of labour, with a workforce of 27 million, which is the fourth largest workforce in Western Europe. The educational level of the population has increased with more than 3.8 million students enrolled in tertiary education, and some 600,000 students graduating from universities every year.

The average annual disposable income per Turkish household and the average annual equivalized household disposable income are 26.577 TL and 11.859 TL, respectively. Income is mostly in the form wages and salaries, which constitute 46.5 per cent of total income. According to the poverty threshold defined as 50 per cent of equivalized household disposable median income, 16.3 per cent of the total population is at risk of poverty. However, when poverty thresholds for urban and rural areas are defined separately, 13.8 per cent of the urban population and 16.3 per cent of the rural population are at risk of poverty.

Turkish culture is characterized by close interpersonal relationships. People have a network of close affiliation with their family members, relatives, and neighbours. Closeness and loyalty to parents and friends are perceived as an important part of Turkish culture. For example, it is customary in Turkey to contact parents and elderly relatives on special days such as holidays and New Year's Eve.

Smartphone usage has been following an increasingly upward trend (Exhibit I.2). In 2013, 73 per cent of the age group 25–34 were reported as using smartphones. This high penetration level of smartphones presents opportunities for alternatives to landline services, including WhatsApp, Viber, Tango, etc.

Regulatory structure

Telecommunications have been regulated by the Turkish Electronic Communication Law since 2008. The main aim of the law is to support successful competition in electronic communications sector, to promote technological development and communication infrastructure, and to protect consumer rights through regulations. Other bodies which regulate the Turkish communication sector are as follows.

1. The Ministry of Transportation: one of the main duties of the Ministry of Transportation is to establish strategies and policies for electronic communication services.

2. The Information Technologies and the Communications Authority has an administrative and financial autonomy.

3. The Competition Authority: the main responsibility of the Competition Authority is to prevent any threats to the competitive process in the markets for goods and services through the use of powers granted by law.

4. The Radio and Television Supreme Council redefined the scope and coverage of the mass communications field in broader terms.

In 2013 important regulations governing wholesale and retail fees were implemented. For instance, SMS interconnection fees were decreased by 75 per cent, call termination fees for voicemail were reduced by 20 per cent, and the maximum fee tariff for retail service prices was increased by 5.7 per cent for all service items excluding local and international SMS and e-invoice services.

Market economics

The Turkish economy grew by 5.1 per cent on average between 2003 and 2012. The GDP growth rate in 2013 was 4.4 per cent. Appliocation of careful monetary policies resulted in a reduction of the inflation rate from from double digit to single digit in over a period of ten years. The inflation rate was 18.4 per cent in 2003 and by 2013 had fallen to 7.4 per cent.

The high percentage of young people in the population has been considered to be an important indicator of Turkey's potential employees. However, this is also a significant reason for the high unemployment rates.

Turkey is listed as the seventeenth largest economy in the world and the sixth largest economy in Europe. The GDP of Turkey in 2012 was approximately $786 billion.

Technological trends

The proliferation of smartphones has boosted Internet usage. This increase is attributed to the rise in social media engagement, the widespread practice of using online maps, dictionaries, and online encyclopedias such as Wikipedia for mobile information searching, and the expansion of watching YouTube, Vimeo, and Turkish national TV channels via apps on mobile devices. Therefore not only the ability to transfer large amounts of data but also access to high-speed mobile Internet has become a necessity. Hence, high-capacity fibre connection has become a crucial service offer, as it facilitates the infrastructure needed for heavy Internet usage and information sharing via cloud technologies.

Turk Telekom

Turk Telekom provided a wide range of telecommunications and technology services to its customers ranging from fixed line to broadband, GSM, data, and innovative convergence technologies with global standards (Exhibit I.3). The Turk Telekom Group, which is the dominant fixed-line operator, had investments in both mobile and broadband services in Turkey as a state-owned enterprise.

Before privatization Turk Telekom operated in a monopolistic market. However, even though it was the only landline phone operator, the emerging mobile phone market presented strong competition. There are three main mobile network operators Turkcell, Vodafone, and Avea (listed in order of market share). Avea is a subsidiary of Turk Telekom.

Following privatization legislation in 2005, Oger Telecom bought a 55 per cent share of Turk Telekom, 30 per cent of the capital structure remained in the ownership of the Turkish government, and 15 per cent was publicly traded. The public offering of 15 per cent was the seventh largest in the world and brought in revenue of $1.9 billion (TL2.4 billion) to the Turkish government. The value of the firms in 2014 was reported as $15.5 billion.

The telecommunications sector was regulated the Ministry of Transportation until 2000. Since then, the Turkish Telecommunications Authority (TA) has taken over regulatory responsibility. However, basic regulations related to infrastructure, competition, market definitions, and quality of service standards are still being developed. TA board members are proposed by the Ministry of Transportation, and approved by the cabinet of the Turkish government. The Ministry of Transportation retains the power of exercising approval rights over the TA's proposals for changes in license fees.

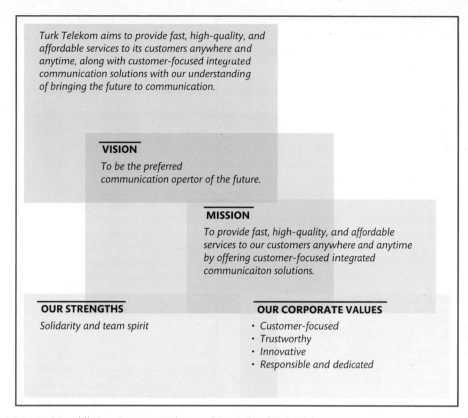

Turk Telekom aims to provide fast, high-quality, and affordable services to its customers anywhere and anytime, along with customer-focused integrated communication solutions with our understanding of bringing the future to communication.

VISION

To be the preferred communication opertor of the future.

MISSION

To provide fast, high-quality, and affordable services to our customers anywhere and anytime by offering customer-focused integrated communicaiton solutions.

OUR STRENGTHS

Solidarity and team spirit

OUR CORPORATE VALUES

- *Customer-focused*
- *Trustworthy*
- *Innovative*
- *Responsible and dedicated*

Exhibit I.3 Vision, Mission, Corporate Values, and Strengths of Turk Telekom

Source: Turk Telekom Annual Report 2013, p. 22.

Products and services

To achieve its aim of maximizing customer satisfaction. Turk Telekom has a wide range of products and services including the following:

- Cloud technology which provides access to various shared IT sources
- Wirofon—an app which can be loaded onto computers or mobile phones and enables customers to utilize lower phone charges for calling Turkish land or mobile phones when they are abroad
- TT SMS which allows customers to send SMS from both home and office phones, or over the Internet to mobile, home, or office phone numbers
- voicemail which provides an answering service for customers when they are absent or busy.

Subsidiaries

Turk Telekom is the owner of broadband provider TTNet, the convergence technologies company Argela, the IT solutions provider Innova, the online education company Sebit, the call centre company AssisTT, and the wholesale data and capacity service provider Turk Telekom International and its subsidiaries (Table I.2). In addition, Turk Telekom has a 90 per cent share in the mobile phone

Table I.2 Turk Telekom Group Companies

Company	Year Established	Core Business	Percentage Owned by Turk Telekom	No. of Employees	Website
Turk Telekom	1995	Telecommunications	90%	21,849	<www.turktelecom.com.tr>
Avea	2004	Mobile communication	100%	1,981	<www.avea.com.tr>
TTNet	2006	Internet service provider	100%	675	<www.ttnet.com.tr>
Turk Telekom International	2010	Wholesale voice, data, and infrastructure carrier	100%	319	<www.turktelecomint.com.tr>
Innova	1999	Information solutions and technology	100%	868	<www.innova.com.tr>
AssisTT	2007	Customer services and call centre	100%	8,292	<www.assistt.com.tr>
Argela	2004	Telecommunication solutions	100%	178	<www.argela.com>
Sebit	1988	Online education, content developer, and service provider	100%	279	<www.vitaminegitim.com> <www.adaptivecurriculum.com> <www.sebit.com.tr>

Source: Turk Telekom Annual Report 2013, p. 18.

operator Aves. At the end of 2013, Turk Telekom's fixed-line, broadband, and mobile subscribers totalled 13.7 million, 7.3 million, and 14.5 million, respectively.

Marketing

The marketing activities of Turk Telekom range from campaigns introducing new services to social projects and sponsorships. Some examples are as follows.

- Free calls to GSM between 7 p.m. and 7 a.m.: in this campaign Turk Telekom subscribers have free calling minutes from their home phones to mobile phones and they can use these free minutes from 7 p.m. to 7 a.m.
- In support of Turkish sport, Turk Telekom has a long-term business partnership with four major football clubs.
- Cooperation between Marvel Entertainment and Turk Telekom initiated a co-promotion marketing campaign based on Marvel Entertainment's film *Iron Man 2* using TV, banners, and mobile advertisements in order to reach Turkey's young population.
- A health campaign aimed at cancer prevention, smoking cessation, and obesity screening, coupled with a preventive medicine campaign offering vaccination and inoculation against several major diseases.

Discussion questions

1. Conduct a PEST analysis for market scanning.
2. Apply Porter's five forces model to the case for market scanning.
3. Define strengths and weaknesses for Turk Telekom (internal analysis).
4. Define market opportunities and threats (external analysis).
5. Analyse the strategic fit between the market opportunities and Turk Telekom's strengths.
6. Analyse the strategic fit between the market threats and Turk Telekom's weaknesses.
7. What is your overall evaluation of Turk Telekom given this analysis?

Ranbaxy's market entry strategy: an Indian pharmaceutical industry in the United Arab Emirates

Sushmera Manikanadan and Balan Sundarakani, University of Wollongong in Dubai, United Arab Emirates

Overview

This case covers 'market scan/scenarios', 'internal analysis' and 'strategic fit' from Phase 1 of the marketing strategy blueprint, and 'objectives and future directions', 'segment', 'target' and 'position' from Phase 2 (see Chapter 1, Figure 1.8). The case focuses on the question: 'Where do we want to be?'

Introduction

The pharmaceutical industry plays a vital role and is one of the most research intensive and rapidly growing global industries in the United Arab Emirates (UAE). It is also a major source of employment generation and foreign exchange earnings for many countries around the globe. Globalization in this sector has occurred with respect to both distribution of medicines in new markets and shifting of R&D and manufacturing to lower cost markets, with a resultant growth in pharmaceutical manufacturing centres in countries such as India, China, Korea, Brazil, the Middle East, and Russia. The pharmaceutical industry in the Middle East is of medium size, but is an emerging market which is growing at an average rate of 15 per cent. Currently it depends largely on imports of pharmaceuticals except for a few countries such as Egypt and Jordan which are over 80 per cent self-sufficient. Because of its direct link with the welfare and well-being of humans the pharmaceutical industry is of strategic importance for the development of a healthy and productive nation. Ranbaxy's mission is 'inspiring lives globally, with quality and affordable pharmaceuticals' with a strong presence in developed markets.

The pharmaceutical industry in India

The Indian pharmaceutical industry is one of the largest and most advanced among the developing countries. It provides employment to millions of people and ensures that essential drugs at affordable prices are available to the vast population of India. About 70 per cent of the country's demand for bulk drugs, drug intermediates, pharmaceutical formulations, chemicals, tablets, oral capsules, and vaccines is met by the Indian pharmaceutical industry. Many Indian pharmaceutical companies have adopted a strategy of inorganic growth though mergers and acquisitions. A well-developed manufacturing base, low cost R&D, and a large skilled workforce are some of the factors underlying the success of the Indian pharmaceutical industry in these segments of international business.

The pharmaceutical industry in the UAE

The UAE is one of the most fully developed pharmaceutical markets with high per capita expenditure on medical products and a strong health-care infrastructure. It also benefits from re-export markets

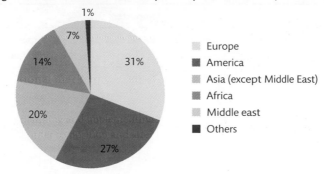

Exhibit II.1 India's Exports of Pharmaceutical Products Across the World (2006–2010)

Source: Directorate General of Commercial Intelligence and Statistics, 2012.

Exhibit II.2 Pharmaceutical Trade in the UAE

Source: Dubai Chamber of Commerce and Industry, 2012

such as Iran, Pakistan, Yemen, and Somalia, which are the major purchasers of re-exported pharmaceuticals from the UAE. In the UAE, and in the Gulf Cooperation Council (GCC) countries generally, growth prospects for the sector are enhanced, partly because of the emergence of a dynamic and rapidly growing middle class.

The UAE pharmaceutical sector faces several challenges as the local manufacturing sector is relatively small and focuses on basic medicines. Figure II.2 indicates that UAE has experienced a strong growth in pharmaceutical trade. Imports of pharmaceutical products have risen from AED 800 million in 2003 to AED 3 billion in 2010, while exports have risen from AED 100 million to AED 400 million over the same period.

Table II.1 shows that, in 2010, the top ten importers accounted for more than 80 per cent of pharmaceutical imports in the Organization of Islamic Cooperation (OIC) countries. Turkey was the top pharmaceutical importer with imports of $4778 million which constituted 30 per cent of total OIC pharmaceutical imports. The top five importers (Turkey, Algeria, the UAE, Egypt, and Malaysia) accounted for more than 60 per cent of OIC pharmaceutical imports. During the period 2005–2010, pharmaceutical imports in the OIC countries exceeded exports. This indicates that, as a group, the OIC countries are net pharmaceutical importers, with the majority still strongly reliant on imported medicines and vaccines to meet their increasing domestic demand.

Table II.1 Top Ten Pharmaceutical Exporters and Importers in the OIC, 2010

Exporters				Importers			
Rank	Country	Exports (million $)	Share of OIC Total (%)	Rank	Country	Imports (million $)	Share of OIC Total (%)
1	Jordan	688	26	1	Turkey	4778	30
2	Turkey	611	23	2	Algeria	1719	11
3	Indonesia	333	13	3	UAE	1259	8
4	Malaysia	308	12	4	Egypt	1246	8
5	Egypt	250	9	5	Malaysia	1133	7
6	UAE	162	6	6	Kazakhstan	940	6
7	Pakistan	136	5	7	Indonesia	736	5
8	Morocco	82	3	8	Pakistan	650	4
9	Oman	24	1	9	Morocco	548	3
10	Kazakhstan	17	1	10	Jordan	483	3

Source: UN Comtrade online database.

Pharmaceutical manufacturers in the UAE

The manufacture of pharmaceutical drugs in the UAE is at an early stage of development and is driven by either government pressure and/or joint ventures with global players. In this section three major UAE-based pharmaceutical manufacturers are described.

Julphar

Julphar was the first UAE drug company to become a multinational company. It has grown rapidly and has expanded its operations to more than 51 countries. Julphar is increasingly focused on exports, given the limited size of the domestic market. About 65 per cent of production in the Middle East and North Africa (MENA countries) consists of contract manufacturing licensed manufacturing, and generic manufacturing. The last of these is the most lucrative because generic drugs have the highest margins. Julphar is the largest domestic manufacturer of medicines and has an 8 per cent share of the UAE market.

Neopharma

Neopharma was set up by the New Medical Centre Group of the UAE in collaboration with Ranbaxy Global of India and Pfizer of the USA in 2004. Other partners now include Parke-Davis (USA), Dr Reddy's (India), Biocon (India), Apotex (Canada), Jamieson (Canada), SM Pharmaceuticals (Malaysia), and Lapgap (Switzerland). The total investment in the first phase of the plant is AED 70 million ($25 million). The plant has an annual production capacity under single-shift operation of 280 million tablets, 160 million capsules, 44 million bottles, and 22 million dry syrups.

Global Pharma

Global Pharma is a subsidiary of Dubai Investment, which holds a 65 per cent stake (AED 70 million) in the firm. Global Pharma provides various pharmaceutical services, including sales and marketing, contract manufacturing, licensing-in, and distribution. The company currently manufactures and markets its products in more than 20 countries in the GCC, the Middle East, Africa, and Asia.

Modern Pharmaceutical Company (MPC)

MPC is engaged in the import, supply, and retail of pharmaceuticals, cosmetics, toiletries, and medical equipment.It is privately owned, with 100 per cent of the shares held by the Al Batha Group. The company has fully owned subsidiaries and number of distribution agreements with leading international players, including Bristol Myer Squibb, Baxter, Altana, Sankyo, UCB, Pfizer, Merck, and GSK.

Ranbaxy in the UAEA

Ranbaxy is the largest generic pharmaceutical company in India by sales and a top ten generic company globally by sales. In 2008, a majority stake in the company was acquired by the Japanese pharmaceutical company Daiichi-Sankyo, the third largest pharmaceutical company in Japan, to create an innovative and generic pharmaceutical powerhouse. Ranbaxy operates as an integrated international pharmaceutical organization with businesses encompassing the value chain in the marketing, production, and distribution of pharmaceutical products. It operates in two sectors: pharmaceuticals and other business. Pharmaceuticals comprises the manufacture and trading of formulations, active pharmaceuticals ingredients (API), and intermediate, generics, drug discovery, and consumer health care products.. Other business comprises provision of financial services. In 2011, the company recorded global Sales of $2.1 billion.

Ranbaxy was ranked as the number one generic company in the UAE in the private sector and was ranked thirteenth of the pharmaceutical companies. It is growing at a rate of 27 per cent. The company market its products through a distributor with a dedicated sales team of approximately 15 front-line staff. Ranbaxy Histac became the leading brand in this category in the UAE, and Ranbaxy has two brands in the top fifty list, each valued at more than $1 million.

Ranbaxy has a global operation, producing its pharmaceutical preparations in manufacturing facilities in eight countries, supported by a global footprint of sales and marketing subsidiaries in 44 countries, reaching customers in more than 100 countries (Exhibit II.3). In 2011, sales in North America, the company's largest market, contributed $791 million, sales in Europe contributed $297 million, and sales in Asia contributed $503 million.

The UAE: a competitive landscape

Ranbaxy has strengthened its competitive position by setting up sophisticated laboratories, hiring hundreds of world-class chemists, and investing heavily in state-of-the-art factories which can scale up the manufacture of a drug quickly. Most of Ranbaxy's competitors are global players who have had a presence in UAE for more than decade. However, as shown in Table II.2, Ranbaxy has an eqivalent market share.

Ranbaxy's strategy

It is UAE national policy that any foreign company entering the UAE market has to have a local partner through a joint venture.

Manufacturing strategy

Ranbaxy entered the UAE market via a joint venture with the local firm Neopharma which would supply certain products already made and finished Ranbaxy products locally in India. Each had a 50 per cent stake with an initial investment of roughly $10 million. Ranbaxy has an agreement

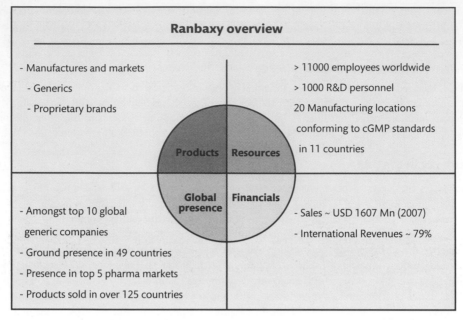

Exhibit II.3 Ranbaxy Worldwide

Table II.2 Ranbaxy's Competitors in the UAE

Company	Country	Product	Market Share	Applications	Entry Strategy
Ranbaxy	India	Generic drugs	10.25%	Mostly in lead molecules and therapeutic segments	Manufacturing, distribution, and sales through joint venture with UAE-based Neopharma
GlaxoSmithKline	UK	Drugs	13%	Mass communication campaigns	Dubai Healthcare City
Pfizer	USA	Drugs	10%	Regional medical and marketing headquarters	Licensing agreement with UAE-based Neopharma
Novartis	Switzerland	Drugs	10%	Consumer health care products	Joint venture with Dubai Healthcare City
Johnson & Johnson's	USA	Pharmaceuticals and consumer packaged goods	12%	Local diabetes market through its LifeScan blood test products	Strategic alliance with Dubai Healthcare City
Sanofi-Aventis	France	Pharmaceuticals	5.13%	Metabolic therapies.	Merger
Abbott Laboratories	USA	Diversified pharmaceuticals and health care goods	11%	Therapeutic assistance to regional anti-obesity campaign; paediatric diagnostics and drugs	Local manufacturing centre

with Neopharma to allow the manufacture of two cephalosporins at a custom-built module for the manufacture of cephalosporins and other beta-lactam products. The antibiotics unit conforms to all FDA and European standards. The plant will not only produce active pharmaceutical ingredients but will also carry out the full range of formulation, finishing, and packaging for a large portfolio of drugs and medicines. Substantial investment in the health-care sector such as the Dubai Healthcare City and Du Biotech projects will also encourage foreign direct investment in health care in the long term. To expand product lines with minimum investment, Ranbaxy provides turnkey manufacturing services, including API and dosage form development, to allow companies to focus on marketing and selling the product. This is an efficient way of diversifying product lines and increasing profit margins, taking advantage of Ranbaxy's manufacturing capabilities and expertise.

Distribution channel

Ranbaxy's distribution channel is the path that products follow on their way from the manufacturers to the consumer or industrial user. In addition, Ranbaxy also manufactures medicines from Julphar which are mainly focused on exports. Ranbaxy consists of at least one intermediary situated between the manufacturer and the consumer (medical practitioner). However, medical practitioners are not considered as part of distribution channel as they only influence patients. The pharmacist in the distribution channel should be a retail or hospital pharmacist.

Marketing strategy

One of the key tasks for Ranbaxy is to identify opportunities in various markets and distribution channels and pursue those to develop and establish new relationships in the marketplace. Innovation is the key to success of international business in the marketplace. Ranbaxy has trustworthy sales and marketing operations which are located in Dubai and Abu Dhabi. Each branch has a dedicated business centre to provide the daily secretarial needs of all the medical representatives.

Corporate social responsibility

Corporate social commitment and public service are deeply embedded in the cultural fabric of Ranbaxy. In the UAE, Ranbaxy promotes good health, social development, and better environment through various societal programmes that contribute to sustainable all-round growth. Ranbaxy's strategy is to go beyond business to community initiatives, and its core values is to be a good corporate citizen and to support the community through various social development programmes and health awareness initiatives as its investment in society. The UAE has a multicultural university which could make a significant contribution to education on good practice for healthy living. There has been enormous growth in the pharmaceutical industry in the UAE in the past few years which has focused on an 'innovation, sustainability and bringing real benefits to those most in need'. Drug donations, differential pricing strategies, building local health capacity, public–private partnerships, benefit sharing, and charitable foundations are six mechanisms used by Ranbaxy to contribute to alleviating global health problems.

Human resource policies

Ranbaxy face challenges due to very low pricing in the market and stringent regulatory requirements. Ranbaxy employees should innovate new ideas to work upon, as well as increasing their contribution to corporate success.

1. Ranbaxy's motto is 'Putting people first'. In order to sustain its success and renew its products, Ranbaxy should be focused on the people behind its products and not on the products.

2. Ranbaxy's strength should be people, i.e. both employees and customers. The strategy has been to recruit locally in host countries and to create multicultural portfolio of human resource skills.

3. Pharmaceutical production requires skilled human resources such as scientists, pharmacists, biologists, and laboratory technicians. Therefore the UAE health authorities should encourage and develop their education system to provide quality knowledge in academic disciplines such as chemistry, biology, medicine, and other natural sciences.

4. Ranbaxy should also pay attention to converting the 'brain drain' of highly skilled people into 'brain gain' by facilitating return of the national diaspora to their countries of origin.

5. The importance of human resource management as a catalytic agent of growth has been increasingly recognized by Ranbaxy, and the following factors have been identified:

   - a healthy climate, characterized by the values of openness, enthusiasm, trust, mutuality, and collaboration which are essential for developing human resources
   - human resource management should be planned and managed in ways that are beneficial both to the individual and organization
   - the company should offer challenging assignments, a world-class working environment, professional management, competitive salaries, stock options, and exceptional rewards.

Conclusion

The pharmaceutical industry has remained highly concentrated in the Middle East, which dominates global pharmaceutical production, consumption, and trade. The pharmaceutical industry relies heavily on R&D activities to develop an innovative pharmaceutical industry with the necessary financial resources. However, the UAE should collaborate with international agencies, such as the World Health Organization and the World Bank, to benefit from their expertise and financial support to develop its domestic pharmaceutical industry. Ranbaxy in the UAE benefits from a low cost of production, efficient technologies for a large number of generics, a large workforce with technical skills, and liberalization of government policies. Moreover, Ranbaxy has a number of foreign competitors in UAE and analysis using PESTEL and Porter's five forces model suggests that it can expand its business with the aim of providing customers with affordable quality health care through innovation in medicine. In addition, India has efficient foreign direct investments with the UAE, and the two nations have a long-term mutually beneficial trade relationship.

Discussion questions

1. What competitive advantages does the UAE offer Ranbaxy compared with the other countries in the MENA region?

2. What are the key factors to be considered when deciding the market entry strategy into a new country that will be useful for Ranbaxy?

3. Use Porter's five forces model to analyse Ranbaxy's situation in the UAE.

4. What is the target market for Ranbaxy in the UAE?

5. Does this make sense for Ranbaxy?

Heaven Kigali—knocking on heaven's door?

Nnamdi O. Madichie, Canadian University of Dubai, United Arab Emirates

Overview

This case covers 'objectives and future directions', 'segment', 'target', and 'position' from Phase 2 of the marketing strategy blueprint and 'action plan', marketing mix' and 'contingency' from Phase 3 (see Chapter 1, Figure 1.8). The major question that this case deals with is: 'How will we get there?'

Synopsis

Located in Kigali, the capital city of Rwanda in southern Africa, the Heaven Restaurant & Bar (Exhibits III.1 and III.2) is owned and managed by Alissa Ruxin, an American who moved to that country with her husband and young children in 2006. The launch of Heaven was borne out of the challenge of securing a job, even as a graduate, but perhaps more importantly as the result of the additional dual challenges of being a woman and being an expatriate without an aptitude in the widely spoken language—French. After starting up, however, the management of Heaven realized that there were other marketing and environmental challenges that required urgent action planning, as well as other challenges, primarily skills development and funding. Overall, the case highlights where Heaven planned/plans to be, despite these challenges, and especially on how it will eventually get there. According to Alissa, Heaven's Founder and CEO, 'I am always trying to think about the

Exhibit III.1 The Staff at Heaven

Source: Dr Nnamdi O. Madichie.

Exhibit III.2 The Entrance to Heaven

Source: Dr Nnamdi O Madichie)

sustainability of Heaven. I would love for Heaven to be both a restaurant and a school though I don't have the time or resources'. Overall, while Alissa may have a 'set course' of action for a long-term marketing strategy, for now it seems she's still knocking on heaven's door.

Introduction

The story of Heaven Restaurant & Bar (henceforth Heaven)[1] is similar to that of a guest house offering bed and breakfast accommodation in the Melville suburb of Johannesburg, South Africa. Both were small businesses, run and/or managed by women, and were based in the southern part of Sub-Saharan Africa (SSA) (Madichie, 2010) The case of Heaven was inspired by an article in *The Economist* entitled 'Business in Rwanda: Africa's Singapore' (Anon., 2012), albeit only as a passing commentary on the resurgence of Rwanda which had been ravaged by war in the mid-1990s (World Bank, 2013). However, before considering the case in detail, it is appropriate to highlight some of the forces (political, economic, social, and technological) at play in the macroeconomic environment of Rwanda.

The macroeconomic environment of Rwanda

Although the article on the achievements of Rwanda was acknowledged as a success story from SSA, the opening line of the article in *The Economist*, which is rather politically charged, highlighted that force is one of the key challenges that lies ahead (Anon., 2012). Indeed, the article described Rwanda in somewhat contradictory terms—first as a 'country with a bloody history' and, secondly, as a country on the verge of 'prosperity by becoming business friendly'. This comes as no surprise, as Rwanda

---

[1] This introduction is based on interview questions with the CEO based on her background, which includes her nationality, education, ethnicity, family, etc., as well as her motivation for opening Heaven, Kigali.

experienced SSA's worst genocide in modern times, with the country's recovery efforts having been repeatedly stalled by its intervention in the conflict in the neighbouring Democratic Republic of Congo (Anon., 2012). The country has been beset by ethnic tension associated with the traditionally unequal coexistence of the dominant ethnic groups in the country, notably the Tutsi minority and the Hutu majority. Although the 'ethnic' relationship was reversed in the late 1950s, when civil war prompted 200,000 Tutsis to flee to neighbouring Burundi, lingering resentment remained as there were periodic massacres of Tutsis by the Hutu majority. The most notorious of these began in April 1994, in the aftermath of the shooting down of the plane with both President Juvenal Habyarimana and his Burundian counterpart on board near the capital city of Kigali—an event that triggered the supposedly coordinated attempts by some Hutu leaders to eliminate the Tutsi population. In response, the Tutsi-led Rwandan Patriotic Front launched a military campaign to control the country at the cost of the lives of nearly a million Tutsis and moderate Hutus. However, although the political climate is a sour reminder of a bitter ethnic conflict in that country, some progress has been made on both the economic and social fronts.

From the economic perspective, Rwanda was named top performer in the *Doing Business* 2010 report (published by the World Bank), and was ranked among the ten most improved economies in 2011. In 2012, Rwanda was ranked as the third easiest place to do business in SSA (World Bank, 2014). Rwanda's growth performance has been remarkably strong over the past few years. Real growth accelerated to about 7.2 per cent in 2010 and 8.6 per cent in 2011 from 4.1 per cent in 2009. In the sociocultural environment, the issues of gender, age, and health-related matters feature prominently. Indeed, in its Economic Empowerment of Adolescent Girls and Young Women Project, the Ministry of Gender and Family Promotion (MIGEPROF) sought to provide assistance to adolescent girls and young women to establish businesses or resume their formal education (see the Ministry's official website at <http://www.migeprof.gov.rw/>).

However, the picture remains gloomy when it comes to the issue of women in the country, even with the Adolescent Girls Initiative (AGI) in place charged with financing and promoting the transition of adolescent girls from school to productive employment. The objectives of the AGI project are to improve employment, income, and empowerment of disadvantaged adolescent girls and young women in four districts in Rwanda. The project has three components: vocational skills and support for entrepreneurship, scholarships to resume formal education, and capacity building for MIGEPROF. A grant of $2.7 million was created to allow 2,700 women and girls to be trained in vocational skills under the supervision of the Workforce Development Authority. The grant also supports 120 girls through scholarships implemented by the Imbuto Foundation.[2]

The World Bank country manager at the time that the AGI was established highlighted reasons why the Bretton Woods Institution, and its development partners, chose to focus on young people and adolescent girls. According to the manager, 'Despite Rwanda's remarkable economic progress in the last few years, poverty remains widespread—with about 44.9 per cent of households still living below the poverty line and a significant proportion of these households (33 per cent) headed by females, and in some cases by young girls'. In addition to this gender imbalance, young people in Rwanda, as is the case across SSA, have been highlighted as being of critical importance in any tangible efforts at tackling socioeconomic problems, of which the population crisis, unemployment, and ultimately poverty are most pressing.

It has been reported that the level of unemployment among young people is a ticking time-bomb, with about 54 per cent of the population aged under 19 years. Added to this is the gender skew, with

---

[2] The Imbuto Foundation provides a package of services including fees, a daily stipend, child care, psychosocial counselling, and mentoring. Continuous monitoring and an impact evaluation at the end of the project will assist the government and its partners to answer questions such as what skills are needed to support female entrepreneurs and what financial products banks and private entities are able to offer young women.

about 18 per cent of women still classed as unpaid labourers and only 23 per cent of working women in non-farm-based employment. Indeed, social and institutional barriers have tended to impair the performance of the 'girl child' in schools in Rwanda. Only 11.9 per cent of girls have any secondary school education compared with 14.5 per cent of boys, and only 2.8 per cent actually go on to complete secondary education (<http://www.migeprof.gov.rw/?Adolescent-Girls-Initiative-Pilot>). Some of the reasons for the lower participation of girls in secondary education are the limited number of places in secondary school, social practices such as early marriage, and negative attitudes regarding educating girls. However, it is well known that educating girls beyond primary school empowers them in ways that primary school alone cannot provide. Girls who have received secondary education live longer, plan and raise healthy families, and in the process help to strengthen the economy (<http://www.migeprof.gov.rw/?Adolescent-Girls-Initiative-Pilot>).

Another cancer in the social fabric of most SSA countries is corruption (Madichie, 2005). However, despite Rwanda's president, Paul Kagame, being labelled a technocrat, his government seems to have made major strides in ridding the country of corruption. According to *The Economist* (Anon., 2012), 'No African country has done more to curb corruption'. Transparency International, a Berlin-based watchdog and publisher of the Corruption Perception Index, described efforts at tackling corruption in the country as follows: 'Rwanda is less graft-ridden than Greece or Italy (though companies owned by the ruling party play an outsized role in the economy)' (see Madichie, 2005). This achievement was confirmed in the course of this study when Josh Ruxin, co-owner of Heaven, pointed out, 'I have never paid a bribe and I don't know anyone who has had to pay a bribe'. Rwanda ranks 45th in the World Bank's index of 'ease of doing business', above all African nations except South Africa and Mauritius. Registering a firm takes three days and is 'dirt cheap'. Property rights are also strengthening—the government is giving peasants formal title to their land.

When it comes to the technological environment, Rwanda is one of only six SSA countries in the top 100 of the 148 countries listed in the World Economic Forum's Networked Readiness Index 2014, as reported in the 13th edition of the *Global Technology* Report,[3] which provides a comprehensive assessment of networked readiness, or how prepared an economy is to apply the benefits of information and communications technology (ICT) to promote economic growth and well-being. With a rank of 85, Rwanda is third in the SSA rankings behind Mauritius at 48 and South Africa at 70, but well ahead of its SSA peers Cape Verde (89), Kenya (92), Ghana (96), Botswana (103), Namibia (105), The Gambia (107), Nigeria (112), and Senegal (114). The Networked Readiness Index measures, on a scale from 1 (worst) to 7 (best), the performance of 148 economies in leveraging information and communications technologies to boost competitiveness and well-being. The rankings also show how far some countries have progressed in bridging the digital divide— in terms not only of developing ICT infrastructure, but also of economic and social impact—and highlight the main strengths and weaknesses countries are facing. Interestingly, the most recent edition of the report analyses in detail the rewards and risks associated with big data and what public and private organizations must do to benefit from it. The question then is: how, and where, does Heaven fit in?

Case background

The story of Heaven has been developed from an in-depth interview with Alissa Ruxin, the founder and CEO, over a six-month period between June and December 2012 via numerous email exchanges and telephone conversations. Heaven was first highlighted in a CNN documentary focusing on

---

[3] Using up-to-date methodology that was introduced in 2012, the *Global Information Technology Report* ranks the progress of 148 economies in leveraging ICT to increase productivity, economic growth and the number of quality jobs. The *Report* is the most comprehensive and authoritative international assessment of its kind. Retrieved from: <http://www3.weforum.org/docs/GITR/2014/GITR_OverallRanking_2014.pdf>.

developments in Africa. It is typically framed around a qualitative discourse reliant upon unpacking the marketing strategies adopted by a small business from the sourcing of start-up capital to coping with sometimes unfavourable government regulations and both monetary and fiscal policies, as well as plans for the survivability of the business—all through narrative of the founder.

Heaven is owned and managed by Alissa Ruxin, an American citizen who resides in a French-speaking country, Rwanda, with her husband and three young children. Alissa carried out her under-graduate studies at Wellesley College in Massachusetts, USA, before completing her master's degree at the Harvard School of Public Health. She moved to Rwanda in 2006 with her husband whose work necessitated the move. He is the Director of the Millennium Village in Rwanda, Director of the ACCESS project, and founder of Rwanda Works —all focused on improving public health and creat-ing prosperity.

Alissa spent the first few months of her residence in Rwanda volunteering with Orphans of Rwanda (now Generation Rwanda), a non-profit organization dedicated to providing scholarships for orphans to complete university education—her husband is on the Board of this organization. She found it extremely challenging to find work in 2006 because of three key constraints: all public health jobs were already taken, local non-governmental organizations (NGOs) were only hiring flu-ent French speakers, and employers were only interested in people who had already lived and worked in Africa.

These challenges motivated Alissa to build on her prior experience in the voluntary sector. Furthermore, given Rwanda's tourism plan under the presidency of Paul Kagame and his Vision 2020 commitment to improving hospitality and supporting tourism, Alissa believed that a restaurant would be an ideal contribution and therefore saw an opportunity to start up her own business in that sector. As she put it:

> I was competing with international applicants for positions in Rwanda. … Through my volunteer work with young people, mostly orphans, and learning of the extremely high unemployment rates (70 per cent unem-ployed) in Rwanda, I decided to start a business to create employment and skills training for young Rwandans.

Having set up Heaven, 'The rest', as the saying goes, 'is history'. While this may well be the norm, there are other key considerations beyond starting up. The task of running a business, whether small or large, requires some long-term planning, especially with regard to funding and marketing. This raises the usual questions revolving around: What? Where? How? Put simply, what was the key driver for starting-up Heaven? Where did Heaven plan to be? How would it get there?

Marketing strategy: what, where, and how?[4]

Although it was constructed between January and June 2007, Heaven did not open its doors for busi-ness until May 2008 (because its CEO was back home in the USA having her first baby). With 18 full-time employees, and an average of three interns from the Akilah Institute for Women (which in 2010 launched a new hospitality programme in Kigali, only for women), Heaven seemed to be reasonably well staffed. Furthermore, as part of its marketing strategy, Heaven partnered with the Akilah Insti-tute in a bid to improve its service levels. According to Alissa:

> The ladies we are providing internships for, have received more formal coursework and training than some of our older staff—the 'new women' I have been hiring through this partnership are going to be future leaders in Rwanda's hospitality sector.

---

[4] The contents of this section are based on three questions posed to the CEO. How do you stand within your community? What sort of neighbourhood is Heaven located in? Do you have lodging on site? Do you have staff training? Can you say a bit more on this?

Heaven has always been proud of its 100 per cent Rwandan cooks, which is a clear indication of serving the community within which it is located and operates. The firm also identifies its market segments based on demographic, psychographic, and/ or behavioural variables—notably professionals, business travellers, and the expatriate community.

Interestingly, Heaven reaches out to local market segments whose key attractions seem to be based on the initiatives undertaken by the business in its service to the local community. These include offering courses that will improve the skills of the local community, such as a course in entrepreneurship which commenced in September 2012 (<http://www.akilahinstitute.org/about/>). When it comes to its targeting strategy, Heaven has its sights set on international tourists, the expatriate community, business travellers, and Rwandan professionals. Although its core product is food, this needs to be augmented with quality service as its slogan suggests—'great food and drinks' which typically include 'great cocktails/tapas [...] mojitos with mint grown in our own garden, passion fruit margaritas, etc.'. In terms of its positioning strategy, Heaven's reputation seems to be a key focus. According to Alissa:

> Our reputation is positive. Some of the local expats consider Heaven to be a 'high-end' restaurant and may only come on special occasions due to their perception that our prices are higher than other local restaurants

In terms of its pricing strategy, after a careful analysis of its key competitors, Heaven considers itself to be 'in the middle', thus making it a mid-range business. It is also very well positioned on the 'place' element, as it is located only three streets away from the famous Mille Collines, a four-star hotel featured in the Hollywood blockbuster *Hotel Rwanda*, at the intersection of Avenue de l'Armée and Avenue de la République in Kiyovu, Kigali. Not surprisingly, this residential neighbourhood is 'quickly transitioning into more commercial properties'. However, its promotions strategy seems rather low key, despite being well regarded by tour operators and drawing in large group bookings.

Knocking on heaven's door?

Despite having set its priorities reasonably in terms of 'where' the business currently is located and 'where it needs to be', 'how to get there' remains fraught with challenges.[5] The most obvious of these is associated with the government's policies on enterprise development in the country. Any persuasive claims about the economic growth story of Rwanda as a preferred business destination are marred by high taxes and a lack of professional hospitality training programmes—one of the key value propositions of Heaven on its way to where it aspires to be. How Heaven will get there obviously depends on a range of factors on both the micro and macro levels—at the wider and/ or national level, and especially in the light of doing business in that country.

Although Rwanda has been lauded as a business-friendly destination in SSA, registering a company does not always translate to the requisite nurturing of the company. In the case of Heaven, registering the company and constructing the premises were relatively easy, but the fiscal policies in the institutional arrangement were not consistent with an enabling environment for starting up. Anecdotal evidence shows that, in Rwanda, there is extremely high taxation on both income and salaries with very few tax benefits, especially in the private sector, which has been at the heart of building a self-sustaining economy across the world. Bank loans charge interest of over 16 per cent and a business must demonstrate that it has invested over $250,000 in order to simply qualify for the right to import equipment and supplies tax free (Madichie and Hinson, 2014).

---

[5] Interview excerpts in this section are based on answers to the question: 'Please highlight the most pressing and memorable challenge, and perhaps how it was overcome?'

The talent search

Unlike neighbouring Eastern African countries, such as Kenya and Uganda which both have fledgling hospitality schools, Rwanda has only a few schools focusing on training Rwandans in culinary and hospitality skills, and they are mostly managed by Rwandan staff churning out graduates with little or no practical experience. Therefore it is not surprising that most of Heaven's staff had no prior work experience, so that the business had to spend the first few months of its launch training the staff (including basics such as how to smile and interact with customers), thus 'substituting for the state'. As Alissa put it, 'many of our [staff] had never dined in a restaurant before working at Heaven and our mission was to train staff to provide international standards of service'. In addition to development of these front-of-house skills, some back-office on-the-job training was also being undertaken:

> My husband and I introduce recipes on a regular basis which we teach our cooks—the international fusion cuisine we serve is palatable for international tourists but incorporates local ingredients … we have had to bring in American chefs and managers to help us run Heaven for the past four years.

These challenges indicate where Heaven needs to be in the short to medium term. As Alissa pointed out, 'I would love Heaven to be both a restaurant and a school though I don't have the time or resources to invest in a school (which is another business!)'.

So how can Heaven double as a bar and restaurant business and a training school at the same time? Although the business is open seven nights a week, it is closed during the day, and therefore would be an ideal practical training facility where coursework and culinary training could take place during the day and students could then have the opportunity to work in the restaurant at night as interns in order to develop their practical experience. With this innovative and altruistic approach to business, it would not be audacious to seek and attract investors in the business. As Alissa pointed out, 'I would love to find an investor interested in being co-owner of Heaven and building/renovating the space to professionalize the kitchen and run a school'. Indeed Heaven's greatest challenge is arguably that of management skills and development, which remain the key 'cogs in the wheel' of progress for the business. As a consequence, Heaven is 'still bringing in foreign managers' to fill the void due to the shortage of a skilled domestic workforce:

> It has been extremely difficult for me to find a Rwandan who can both oversee the administrative (operations, purchasing, marketing, HR) and customer service experience (interacting with customers, reservations management) and kitchen staff (ensuring freshness, consistency in the menu, etc.).

This has spurred Alissa, with the assistance and experience of her husband, into action. Since 2008, they have personally invested in training Heaven's staff in areas ranging from customer service to culinary skills (Madichie and Hinson, 2014). Alissa also hired two American chefs and three American managers over a four-year period in an effort to improve the original menu and to provide training in culinary skills such as hygiene, proper food storage, preparing sauces, grilling, following recipes, and pasta and bread making. As she pointed out repeatedly:

> Because of Heaven's existence, there is enormous social and economic benefit not only for our staff who are now gainfully employed (can pay for food, rent, healthcare and education for their families, etc.) but also for the maintenance workers, farmers, suppliers we work with and purchase from … hundreds of lives have been positively impacted because of our restaurant.

In describing Heaven's achievements and plans for the future, Alissa stated that 'being open, cash flow positive, and successful four years into a restaurant business is a great achievement anywhere in the world, so we are proud of what we've built'. She also highlights how Heaven's enhanced reputation has been internationally leveraged via customer review websites such as tripadvisor.com. As a result of these positive reviews, many tourists make special visits to Heaven. Likewise, both local businesses and NGOs reportedly know that the 'food and customer service' are excellent, thus prompting regular group bookings.

Conclusions

However, a lingering challenge remains. Has Heaven set its eyes on how to get to where it needs to be? By all indications, Heaven wants to be counted among the giants in the hospitality industry, not just in Rwanda but across SSA and beyond. Alissa was clear about where she would like to be in the next few years: '… my dream is to be bought out by an international hotel chain, like Marriott or Starwood—they could ensure professional training and management into the future for Heaven…'. How does she get there?

Considering that Alissa is a foreigner (an Anglo-Saxon for that matter) residing and doing business in Rwanda (a Francophone country), because of the attendant 'baggage of foreignness' there is only so much she can do. Nonetheless she remains upbeat on leaving a legacy for Heaven—her pet project. As she pointed out, 'I may not be in Rwanda for ever but would love to start thinking now about the long-term sustainability of the business'. For the time being, however, Alissa is still 'knocking on heaven's door'.

References

Anon. (2012), 'Business in Rwanda: Africa's Singapore'. *The Economist*, available online at: <http://www.economist.com/node/21548263>.

Madichie, N. (2005), 'Corruption in Nigeria: How Effective Is the Corruption Perception Index in Highlighting the Economic Malaise?', *World Review of Science, Technology and Sustainable Development,* 2 (3/4), pp. 320–35.

Madichie, N. (2010), 'Putting Melville on the World Stage—Let's Hear from Lize Krueger', CEO of Life on 3rd', in *Enterprising Matters* (Institute for Small Business and Entrepreneurship), available online at <http://www.isbe.org.uk/lifeonthird>.

Madichie, N. and Hinson, R. (2014), 'Women Entrepreneurship in Sub-Saharan Africa: A Case Approach', in Nwankwo, S. and Ibeh, K.I.N.(eds), *The Routledge Companion to Business in Africa* (New York: Routledge) Chapter 11.

World Bank (2013), *Doing Business 2014: Rwanda* (Washington, DC: World Bank).

Discussion questions

1. How would you describe the marketing strategy of Heaven? Is it sustainable?

2. Identify the top three macroenvironmental challenges facing Heaven. Can you identify any other challenges in Heaven's microenvironment?

3. How has Heaven managed these challenges? Could it do more than it has?

4. Heaven has long-term plans to be a training school as well as a bar and a restaurant business. Evaluate the possibilities. Does this make sense?

Marketing strategy of India's most successful e-tailer: Flipkart.com

Ramendra Singh, Indian Institute of Management Calcutta, India, and Anurag Beniwal, National Institute of Technology, India

Overview

This case covers 'action plan', 'marketing mix', and 'contingency' from Phase 3 of the marketing strategy blueprint, and 'monitor' and 'possible corrective action' from Phase 4. This case deals with the final question: 'Did we get there?'

Introduction

Coming out of the conference hall, Mr Nishant seems to be very tense. Why shouldn't he be? The Indian e-commerce industry is growing extremely quickly (Exhibit IV.1). There was a time when Flipkart, the harbinger of the Indian e-commerce era, had a monopoly position in online book shopping, but now a number competitors that are sometimes cheaper than Flipkart have entered the sector. Flipkart.com has been hailed as India's answer to Amazon. The ease of shopping, rapid delivery, low prices, and a wide range of books helps Flipkart to be the market leader in this segment. 'People in India are buying books like never before thanks to Flipkart and the spread of broadband to every nook and corner of the country', says Nishant, the Regional Channel Manager of Flipkart, Delhi. Pointing at a pile of complaints on his desk, Nishant says 'It's high time now that we should

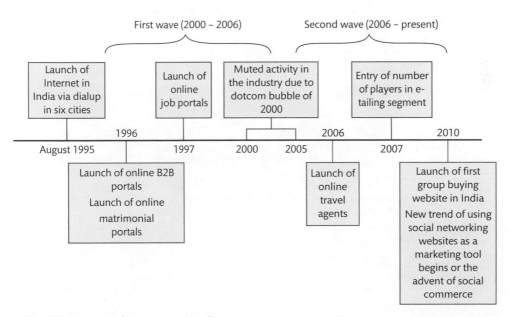

Exhibit IV.1 Evolution of E-commerce in India

have our own logistics. Flipkart is renowned for its excellent service and hence we need to keep our logistics intact'.

This case discusses various issues faced by an e-commerce company in India and how Flipkart was able to lead the way in this industry.

About Flipkart

Flipkart was co-founded by Sachin Bansal and Binny Bansal in October 2007. Since e-commerce had almost no penetration in India at that time, these two experienced coders decided to create their own e-commerce venture—Flipkart.com.

They started the company with an initial investment of 5 lakh rupees (500,000 rupees) using their own personal savings. It was never going to be easy, since Indian experience with e-commerce had been poor and many people were unwilling to spend money on something which they had not seen and handled for themselves. There was a lack of trust, and so Flipkart had to instil trust and confidence in their customers.

India's initial experience with e-commerce was in the areas of job search and matrimony. Indians were comfortable with these types of website because they were not selling products which would require handling. There were some e-tailers at the time, but they faced an uphill battle with consumers (Exhibit IV.2).

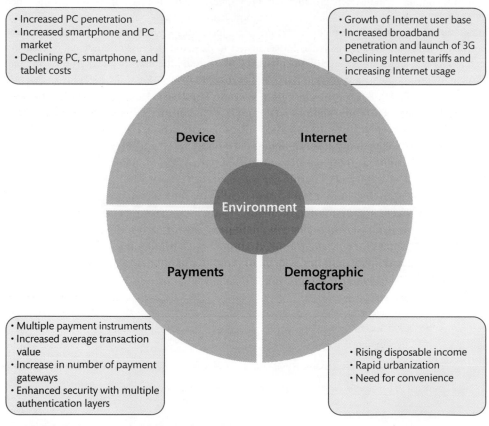

Exhibit IV.2 Environments that Supported E-commerce in India

Flipkart started with a consignment model (procurement based on demand). They had ties with only two distributors in Bangalore, and whenever a customer ordered a book, they personally collected it from the dealer, packed it in their office, and then couriered it to the customer.

Flipkart's successful strategies in the Indian economy

Location of warehouses and offices

Flipkart's offices and warehouses are located in the heart of the B2B supplier cluster: 'Our strong relationship with our distribution partners helped us to survive even under the consignment model', says Nishant. Flipkart had set up its sales office in the midst of the publishing houses in Daryaganj, which facilitated good communication with publishers and distributors. This enabled them to procure books quickly and efficiently, which in turn led to customer satisfaction. As Nishant says:

> Being situated in the midst of all the publishing houses gives us a strategic advantage as we can personally track and mend the irregularities in the supply chain, and easily upgrade our inventory. It is a *dhanda* (traditional business) and we are really traditional, in that we need to get down to the level of distributors in order to make long-lasting relationships, and our two-storey hut surrounded by distributors produces more business than any big glossy building of any corporate empire.

Transforming the confidence of publishers

In the USA, if you want to cover about 80 per cent of all the books that are published, you just have to tie up with three or four distributors, but in India you have to tie up with hundreds. But the company found the distributors far from enthusiastic. 'When we first approached a book distributor, we thought they would be enthusiastic—after all, we were offering to sell their products. But people like us were approaching them every day, and they were not too impressed', says Nishant. Besides, dealing with an online bookstore is not the same as dealing with a bricks and mortar bookstore—the catalogue had to be updated more often, and deliveries had to take place daily based on customer orders. However, they persisted, often altering their procedures to fit the suppliers' way of doing things. When they started the company they had ten suppliers, but this has now increased to 500. Mr Tarun, from Oxford University Press, says:

> Initially we didn't trust these online book portals and hence we dealt with them in the same way as we deal with our other book retailers (that is, through our book distributors as we had quite a mature relationship with our distributors and we could not afford to lose them by directly dealing with any of the online portals), but now, since they have established themselves in the market, we can think of dealing with them directly.

From no credit to long-term credit

The reason why most online book portals don't provide a large variety of products is that there is no guarantee that their products will be sold. If the product is not sold, the loss has to be incurred by the company. This is because most of the suppliers are sceptical about giving credit. The strong relationship between Flipkart and its distributors resulted in trust and willingness to offer long-term credit. Nishant says:

> Initially we had to pay the distributors for each individual purchase, but now, due to our strong relationship with the distributors, we manage to get credit lines of up to 3 months. We can return the unsold books in our inventory to the publisher over a period of 1–3 months depending on our relationship with the distributor.

Competitive prices: impact on the offline book retail industry

As well as delivering an excellent service, Flipkart was also successful in providing competitive prices. With Flipkart providing discounts of up to 60 per cent, customers preferred to buy a new book rather than a used copy or previous edition since they could pay as little as 50 per cent of the maximum retail price

The competitive prices offered by Flipkart have led to a decline in the offline book retail industry. 'Our sales have declined considerably during the past two years. Our market was famous all over India for providing all varieties of second-hand books at cheap rates, but now we have hardly any customers coming to us except for school students' says one of the retailers in the Daryaganj market.

Flipkart logistics system: an indirect way of gaining confidence!

The major factor responsible for the upsurge of e-commerce in India is the change in logistics systems. Previously, companies had tie-ups with courier companies which shipped their packages at a very low price but gave a poor service. However, companies have now realized that saving costs on logistics will not help in saving their companies, so major online portals like Flipkart now have partnerships with reliable best logistics service providers, which ensures timely delivery of goods to the customer.

The initial logistics of Flipkart

Placing an order

As soon as the customer presses the order button, Flipkart sends them a confirmation of their order with a tracking ID, so that the customer can track their order on the Blue Dart website. But is the process so rapid that the order is sent within a few seconds? 'Not exactly', says Vinod, the operations manager at Blue Dart Calicut:

> Since Flipkart gives us a lot of business, we give them tracking IDs even before the customer places any orders and hence Flipkart can send a tracking ID to the customer immediately. The product is actually packed and given to Blue Dart the day after the customer places the order.

Processing an order, shipping, and delivery

Once Flipkart receives an order, it is immediately communicated to the warehouse where the product is procured from inventory, packed, and sent to Blue Dart. The information regarding the product and mode of payment is conveyed to the local Blue Dart office from the central office in Delhi (see Exhibit IV.3). If the mode of payment is cash on delivery (COD), it is the responsibility of the vendor to collect cash from the customer. If the customer refuses to accept the product for any reason, the product is returned to Flipkart.com. The extra logistics charges are borne by Flipkart.com. However, according to Nishant:

> Even after considering the fact that they are the best in logistics, they have not been able to meet the efficiency level we expect, which is what we are known for. Because of the growing number of orders, the efficiency of the logistics system is decreasing as we are expanding but the courier services are not, and the number of goods is increasing while the transport capacity of the courier service providers is not improving. The biggest problem which Flipkart faces right now is the restriction of our areas of service because of the absence of courier service providers in remote areas which hinders our ability to expand.

The courier services aren't expanding at the same pace as Flipkart, which prevents Flipkart from reaching remote areas. What can be done by Flipkart in order to overcome this problem? How does Flipkart build this into its monitoring and control mechanisms to identify that it has a problem and that corrective action is needed? How do we know whether we are on track or not?

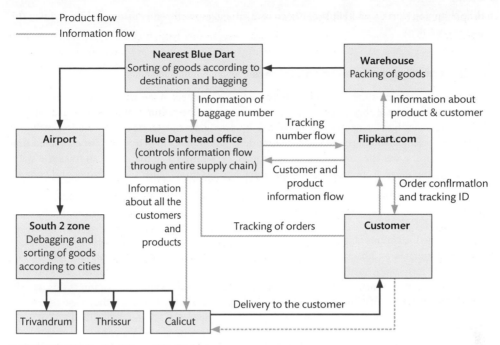

Exhibit IV.3 Distribution Channel for Flipkart

Flipkart logistics: building its own in-house logistics

Flipkart now has its own logistics operation which has improved efficiency in customer service as the delivery personnel work exclusively for Flipkart, which facilitates better customer experience and feedback. In-house logistics is economically feasible only when the volumes and return rates are high, so this a model cannot be implemented everywhere. Therefore Flipkart is adopting a hybrid last-mile delivery model consisting of both in-house and outsourced logistics.

Benefits of in-house logistics: gaining the trust of customers!

Delivering the product on time

The major customer concern when shopping online is delay in delivery because of poor logistics and delivery of the product to the wrong address. The strong logistics system of Flipkart has made customers trust online buying. The best thing is that Flipkart is now really able to 'Keep the promises they make', which is a key factor in the success of any business.

Efficient packing and replacement policy

The efficient packing of Flipkart products ensures that the product the customer receives is in perfect condition. It is difficult to transmit trusted warranties from an online shop to its customers because of the space and time discrepancies between the online shop and the customers. However, Flipkart. com has successfully offered a 'No-Questions-Return policy and replacement guarantee in a 30 day period', thus building credibility and the trust of the customer. The major issue for the customer previously had been that if they received the product on time but it was damaged, the company refused to take responsibility. This is a major drawback for Indian customers considering using online shopping portals, and Flipkart has created strong goodwill with customers by providing this type of guarantee.

Features of Flipkart's online experience

In an offline shopping store it is quite easy to assure customers about the quality of the product as they can examine it, but in the case of online portals, they cannot directly interact with the product. Flipkart has overcome this drawback by providing full product information including images, unbiased customer reviews, a complete description of the logistics, and the estimated time of delivery on the website, and giving the customer a tracking ID so that they can track the status of delivery. The idea was to provide as many safeguards as possible for the customer and enhance quality control.

Easy mode of payment

Because of the limitations of normal e-commerce in India, many individuals do not have confidence in shopping portals, and many are wary of online monetary transactions because cash transactions are preferred in India. Also, the number of credit card holders in India is fairly small. This problem has led to the failure of many e-commerce portals, but Flipkart has managed to address this issue by introducing an option of cash on delivery, in which customers only pay when they have receive the product in good condition and at the promised time. This approach has not only alleviated customer concern but also helped Flipkart to achieve exceptional sales growth. Nishant says:

> We were successful in understanding the pain of the Indian customer which the previous e-commerce start-ups failed to realize, which helped us in revamping the Indian e-commerce industry. As a result of cash on delivery we have been successful in gaining the faith of the Indian customer, and once this faith is developed, then we have money pouring in through credit and debit cards too.

Drawbacks of cash on delivery as a mode of payment

Additional cost to the company

Courier companies such as Blue Dart and First Flight make an additional charge of 1–2 per cent of the product cost for COD. Customers are generally unwilling to pay extra for the COD convenience that the company offers. Online payment channels make a similar charge, but the cash flow is much faster than withCOD, where it takes a long time for the cash to reach the company.

Excessive rates of return

According to the latest data from Blue Dart, the return rate for all e-commerce companies using COD is 40 per cent, although the channel manager at Flipkart disagrees with this figure. The rate actually varies from 15 per cent for some companies to 60 per cent for others depending on the bond they share with customers and the trust that the customer has in their products. The courier company also applies charges. If a company carries out 1,000 transactions daily, and for a company like Flipkart almost 60 per cent of these are via cash on delivery, it incurs a daily loss of about 30,000 rupees.

Reasons for such high return rates

- By clicking on the COD button, the customer does not confirm the purchase but rather just indicates an intention to purchase the product.
- After placing the order, the customer may change their mind about the product.

- The customer might be able to get a better deal with some other online portal.
- The customer may not be at home or may not have the required amount of cash when the order arrives.

In many cases the customer is not available to accept delivery and hence the cost of delivery is increased. This can be minimized by checking beforehand with the customer about their availability at their home address at the expected delivery time. Previous information on problem customers can be used to check the legitimacy of the order and the delivery. This can significantly reduce default rates and reduce costs.

Poor returns management due to outsourced logistics

Another problem with COD is the delay in receiving payment which directly affects the working capital of the company. This becomes a serious problem as the money is paid to the logistics partner and the revenue is not received by Flipkart until a significant amount of time later. On the one hand the introduction of COD has produced an exponential increase in the average number of orders, but on the other hand it has resulted in high return rates. What can be done to minimize return rates? This is a serious issue when the company has included expected revenue in their strategic planning, so how does the company improve this situation in their monitoring and controlling mechanisms?

Segmentation according to price

Owing to the changing preferences of the Indian customer with respect to cost and service, a product can be quoted at different prices depending on the services involved—for example, the quicker the delivery, the higher the price charged, but if the customer can wait a few days for the order, the price will be reduced. Such a structure should help Flipkart capture more customers. The premium or express facility of the logistics provider can be used for customers who prefer rapid delivery and can afford to pay for this service, whereas India Post or the economy service of the logistics provider can be used for the customer who is willing to accept slower delivery in order to obtain the product at a lower price. A number of e-commerce websites with average or below average inventories, primarily following the consignment model, that are able to offer large discounts on their products have recently appeared and are attracting a number of customers, but they do not offer the service levels provided by Flipkart. The main thing that they offer the customer is low prices. One of these companies is BookAdda.com which ships products via India Post, reducing the cost of the product but resulting in a delivery time of at least 6 or 7 days.

Who are these customers? They are the customers whose buying decisions are mostly governed by the price of the product. In most cases, customers can often wait for delivery of products such as books and laptop accessories rather than paying a high price for them. What is important for companies like Flipkart is that there are still many customers who expect good service and may be willing to compromise on low prices. This is an important issue for companies handling sales online.

Is customer segmentation becoming more important in e-commerce when there are a variety of priorities among customers relating to price and service? Can Flipkart introduce a mix of services focused on both the price-sensitive customer and the service-conscious customer on the same portal, or are different portals necessary? How would this segmentation be done? This again relates to the planning process in that the company may have to review its strategic expectations after monitoring changes in the marketplace. How would Flipkart approach this situation in terms of matching up ongoing performance to expected performance? What can they do at this point to take corrective action?

The concept of momentary customer value

The issue of customer segmentation is important as there are customers who value high service levels sometimes but prefer low cost at other times. The present e-commerce value chain is not flexible and hence loses a lot of revenue because of this. On one side we have Flipkart which must keep up its commitment to high service levels and therefore has introduced its own courier service company to end its reliance on outside courier services. This has led Flipkart to increase its prices, therefore positioning it on service and not on low price. Thus, customers who are not concerned about the time of delivery, but want low prices, will probably switch to online companies like BookAdda and Tradus which offer cheaper deals but may not guarantee rapid delivery. Indian e-customers seem to want to switch preferences between service quality and low prices, which means that companies are dependent on the feelings of the e-customer at the time they decide to make a purchase.

If Flipkart sticks to its commitment of providing excellent customer service and commensurate higher prices, it satisfies the inequality of customer value, and the customer value generated amounts to more than the resources expended. For example, most e-commerce companies offer customized gift offerings such that the gift/flowers reach the recipient on Valentine's Day, but this comes at a premium cost which the customer never regrets as the value produced by the gift arriving on the correct day is much higher than the costs incurred in making it possible. Alternatively, if a customer wants to buy an external hard drive and price is the most important consideration, immediate delivery is not their main concern. In such a case the present business model of Flipkart fails to generate a positive customer value (see Exhibit IV.4).

Why only books?

When most of the Indian e-commerce companies, such as Indiaplaza and Tradus, were dealing in a variety of retail offerings, why did Flipkart restrict its business to an online bookstore? Book retailing has the largest customer base of all products in India. It was the best place for Flipkart to start, as books require less investment than other businesses and less probability of damage during transportation. Nishant says:

> Starting with books, we tried to gain customer faith and to a great extent we were successful in doing that, and now since we enjoy customer faith we have started venturing into selling other products. Now we have people buying expensive gadgets like laptops and iPods from us. In short we have initiated an e-commerce revolution in India.

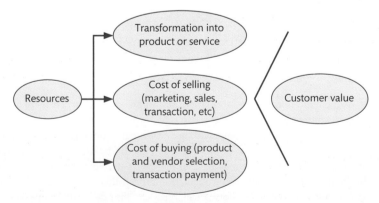

Exhibit IV.4 Customer Value İnequality for the Success of an E-commerce Business

Competition

Amazon has recently ventured into India[1] and presents a major threat to Flipkart. A new way of capturing the market share, which both companies are adopting, to is to obtain exclusive rights to products in order to increase traffic to their website. To counter the threat by Amazon, Flipkart acquired Myntra, the largest selling e-commerce website for fashion.

Amazon has launched a marketplace model in India. Given the large number of distributors in India, the commitment to superior customer service is important. In order to make sure that it keeps its promise of superior customer service within the heterogeneous market in India, Amazon has launched Fulfilment by Amazon (FBA). With this service, all a seller has to do is to ship the product to Amazon's warehouses and Amazon will take care of everything from shipment and delivery to managing returns. This ensures that Amazon maintains its high service standards.

Last-mile delivery is a crucial problem faced by all the e-commerce players in India, and in order to deal with this Amazon has started associating with local stores to serve as delivery points, thus enabling customers to collect their orders on time while reducing the costs associated with customer unavailability.

The e-commerce war in India is definitely favourable for customers and will trigger innovative methods of reducing costs and allowing companies to remain competitive in the market.

Big Bazaar Direct: an innovative model of e-commerce inclusion in semi-urban markets in India[2]

There was a time when people were apprehensive about e-commerce as a feasible business model in a country like India where consumer behaviour is as hard to predict as a financial crisis. A strange concoction of multiple cultures, castes, income distribution, and last but not the least the large variation in the tech-savviness of people creates a volatile marketplace.

Although e-commerce has been successful in the major cities, it has not been popular in medium-sized cities and small towns. Would the present model allow access to the bottom of pyramid markets in urban and semi-urban areas? This would be quite difficult.

Why the existing models of e-commerce cannot penetrate semi-urban and rural areas

- Poor ICT infrastructure
- Fewer literate people (or in that case fewer tech-savvy people)
- Few people own computers
- People do not have credit cards and are not used to online transactions
- In India (especially in rural areas) people will not buy a product unless they can handle it.

Most Indians buy either through word-of- mouth marketing or because they have a long relationship with the vendor and buy products on their recommendations. An interesting new development in marketing is the concept of Big Bazaar Direct.

Big Bazaar Direct

Each franchisee is provided with a tablet containing the complete product portfolio. Customers can select products from the tablet, and the franchisee helps them to place the order online. The

---

[1] See <http://businesstoday.intoday.in/story/amazon.in-to-open-second-warehouse-in-india/1/202488.html>

[2] See <http://www.nextbigwhat.com/big-bazaar-direct-franchise-future-group-297/>

franchisee receives cash from the customer and the product is directly dispatched to the customer's address from the nearest Big Bazaar warehouse. One of the greatest advantages of this model is that franchisee receives commission on each order without having to keep an inventory. This system can evolve much better with a tie-in with a microfinance organization, or new credit models can be introduced.

This is an example of a multichannel system (see Exhibit IV.5).

- The transaction method used is based on the day-to-day *kirana* (small stores) model.
- The e-commerce part ensures a large product portfolio with superior quality.
- The incentive for the franchisee owner is to use his relationship with the community and his sales skill to sell products without the responsibility of delivery, logistics, and inventory management.
- The credit models can emerge at the local level or the corporate level, or be a combination of both.
- Given that the COD return rate is high in urban areas, it is likely to be even higher in rural areas because of seasonal incomes, the fickle nature of the customers, and uncertainty about buying the product.
- This e-commerce model can facilitate the provision of larger product portfolios in rural areas where a smaller range of products are available because of logistics constraints.

The major innovation required to make this model successful and scalable is logistics. The major logistical challenges are the poor road infrastructure and the low population density in semi-urban and rural areas.

Conclusions

How will Flipkart develop the changes that will be required to effectively move its strategic planning process forward? What adjustments will need to be made for future planning given the changes noted during the current period?

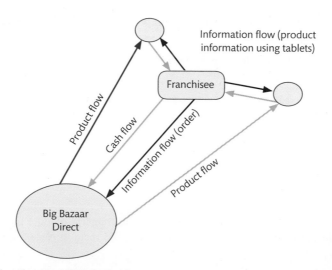

Exhibit IV.5 Product Flow in a Multi-channel System

Discussion questions

1. What can Flipkart do to overcome the problem of the slow pace of expansion for courier services in their plan to reach remote areas?

2. With the introduction of COD, the number of orders has grown rapidly, but Flipkart is struggling to handle the high rate of returns with this payment method. How can they minimize return rates?

3. Is customer segmentation becoming more important over time in e-commerce when there are varying types of priorities among customers relating to price and service?

4. Can Flipkart introduce a mix of services focused on both the price-sensitive customer and the service-conscious customer on the same or a different portal? How would this segmentation be done?

5. Has Flipkart set its strategic expectations correctly? Have they matched ongoing performance to expected performance? What can they do to take corrective action?

Index